T0183755

Lecture Notes in Computer Science 11256

Commenced Publication in 1973
Founding and Former Series Editors:
Gerhard Goos, Juris Hartmanis, and Jan van Leeuwen

More information about this series at http://www.springer.com/series/7412

Jian-Huang Lai · Cheng-Lin Liu
Xilin Chen · Jie Zhou · Tieniu Tan
Nanning Zheng · Hongbin Zha (Eds.)

Pattern Recognition and Computer Vision

First Chinese Conference, PRCV 2018
Guangzhou, China, November 23–26, 2018
Proceedings, Part I

Springer

Editors
Jian-Huang Lai
Sun Yat-sen University
Guangzhou, China

Cheng-Lin Liu
Institute of Automation
Chinese Academy of Sciences
Beijing, China

Xilin Chen
Institute of Computing Technology
Chinese Academy of Sciences
Beijing, China

Jie Zhou
Tsinghua University
Beijing, China

Tieniu Tan
Institute of Automation
Chinese Academy of Sciences
Beijing, China

Nanning Zheng
Xi'an Jiaotong University
Xi'an, China

Hongbin Zha
Peking University
Beijing, China

ISSN 0302-9743 ISSN 1611-3349 (electronic)
Lecture Notes in Computer Science
ISBN 978-3-030-03397-2 ISBN 978-3-030-03398-9 (eBook)
https://doi.org/10.1007/978-3-030-03398-9

Library of Congress Control Number: 2018959435

LNCS Sublibrary: SL6 – Image Processing, Computer Vision, Pattern Recognition, and Graphics

This Springer imprint is published by the registered company Springer Nature Switzerland AG
The registered company address is: Gewerbestrasse 11, 6330 Cham, Switzerland

Preface

Welcome to the proceedings of the First Chinese Conference on Pattern Recognition and Computer Vision (PRCV 2018) held in Guangzhou, China!

PRCV emerged from CCPR (Chinese Conference on Pattern Recognition) and CCCV (Chinese Conference on Computer Vision), which are both the most influential Chinese conferences on pattern recognition and computer vision, respectively. Pattern recognition and computer vision are closely inter-related and the two communities are largely overlapping. The goal of merging CCPR and CCCV into PRCV is to further boost the impact of the Chinese community in these two core areas of artificial intelligence and further improve the quality of academic communication. Accordingly, PRCV is co-sponsored by four major academic societies of China: the Chinese Association for Artificial Intelligence (CAAI), the China Computer Federation (CCF), the Chinese Association of Automation (CAA), and the China Society of Image and Graphics (CSIG).

PRCV aims at providing an interactive communication platform for researchers from academia and from industry. It promotes not only academic exchange, but also communication between academia and industry. In order to keep track of the frontier of academic trends and share the latest research achievements, innovative ideas, and scientific methods in the fields of pattern recognition and computer vision, international and local leading experts and professors are invited to deliver keynote speeches, introducing the latest advances in theories and methods in the fields of pattern recognition and computer vision.

PRCV 2018 was hosted by Sun Yat-sen University. We received 397 full submissions. Each submission was reviewed by at least two reviewers selected from the Program Committee and other qualified researchers. Based on the reviewers' reports, 178 papers were finally accepted for presentation at the conference, including 24 oral and 154 posters. The acceptance rate is 45%. The proceedings of the PRCV 2018 are published by Springer.

We are grateful to the keynote speakers, Prof. David Forsyth from University of Illinois at Urbana-Champaign, Dr. Zhengyou Zhang from Tencent, Prof. Tamara Berg from University of North Carolina Chapel Hill, and Prof. Michael S. Brown from York University.

We give sincere thanks to the authors of all submitted papers, the Program Committee members and the reviewers, and the Organizing Committee. Without their contributions, this conference would not be a success. Special thanks also go to all of the sponsors and the organizers of the special forums; their support made the conference a success. We are also grateful to Springer for publishing the proceedings and especially to Ms. Celine (Lanlan) Chang of Springer Asia for her efforts in coordinating the publication.

We hope you find the proceedings enjoyable and fruitful reading.

September 2018

Tieniu Tan
Nanning Zheng
Hongbin Zha
Jian-Huang Lai
Cheng-Lin Liu
Xilin Chen
Jie Zhou

Organization

Steering Chairs

Tieniu Tan	Institute of Automation, Chinese Academy of Sciences, China
Hongbin Zha	Peking University, China
Jie Zhou	Tsinghua University, China
Xilin Chen	Institute of Computing Technology, Chinese Academy of Sciences, China
Cheng-Lin Liu	Institute of Automation, Chinese Academy of Sciences, China
Long Quan	Hong Kong University of Science and Technology, SAR China
Yong Rui	Lenovo Group

General Chairs

Tieniu Tan	Institute of Automation, Chinese Academy of Sciences, China
Nanning Zheng	Xi'an Jiaotong University, China
Hongbin Zha	Peking University, China

Program Chairs

Jian-Huang Lai	Sun Yat sen University, China
Cheng-Lin Liu	Institute of Automation, Chinese Academy of Sciences, China
Xilin Chen	Institute of Computing Technology, Chinese Academy of Sciences, China
Jie Zhou	Tsinghua University, China

Organizing Chairs

Liang Wang	Institute of Automation, Chinese Academy of Sciences, China
Wei-Shi Zheng	Sun Yat-sen University, China

Publicity Chairs

Huimin Ma	Tsinghua University, China
Jian Yu	Beijing Jiaotong University, China
Xin Geng	Southeast University, China

International Liaison Chairs

Jingyi Yu	ShanghaiTech University, China
Pong C. Yuen	Hong Kong Baptist University, SAR China

Publication Chairs

Zhouchen Lin   Peking University, China
Zhenhua Guo   Tsinghua University, China

Tutorial Chairs

Huchuan Lu   Dalian University of Technology, China
Zhaoxiang Zhang   Institute of Automation, Chinese Academy of Sciences, China

Workshop Chairs

Yao Zhao   Beijing Jiaotong University, China
Yanning Zhang   Northwestern Polytechnical University, China

Sponsorship Chairs

Tao Wang   iQIYI Company, China
Jinfeng Yang   Civil Aviation University of China, China
Liang Lin   Sun Yat-sen University, China

Demo Chairs

Yunhong Wang   Beihang University, China
Junyong Zhu   Sun Yat-sen University, China

Competition Chairs

Xiaohua Xie   Sun Yat-sen University, China
Jiwen Lu   Tsinghua University, China

Website Chairs

Ming-Ming Cheng   Nankai University, China
Changdong Wang   Sun Yat-sen University, China

Finance Chairs

Huicheng Zheng   Sun Yat-sen University, China
Ruiping Wang   Institute of Computing Technology, Chinese Academy
                     of Sciences, China

Program Committee

Haizhou Ai   Tsinghua University, China
Xiang Bai   Huazhong University of Science and Technology, China

Xiaochun Cao	Institute of Information Engineering, Chinese Academy of Sciences, China
Hong Chang	Institute of Computing Technology, China
Songcan Chen	Chinese Academy of Sciences, China
Xilin Chen	Institute of Computing Technology, China
Hong Cheng	University of Electronic Science and Technology of China, China
Jian Cheng	Chinese Academy of Sciences, China
Ming-Ming Cheng	Nankai University, China
Yang Cong	Chinese Academy of Science, China
Dao-Qing Dai	Sun Yat-sen University, China
Junyu Dong	Ocean University of China, China
Yuchun Fang	Shanghai University, China
Jianjiang Feng	Tsinghua University, China
Shenghua Gao	ShanghaiTech University, China
Xinbo Gao	Xidian University, China
Xin Geng	Southeast University, China
Ping Guo	Beijing Normal University, China
Zhenhua Guo	Tsinghua University, China
Huiguang He	Institute of Automation, Chinese Academy of Sciences, China
Ran He	National Laboratory of Pattern Recognition, China
Richang Hong	Hefei University of Technology, China
Baogang Hu	Institute of Automation, Chinese Academy of Sciences, China
Hua Huang	Beijing Institute of Technology, China
Kaizhu Huang	Xi'an Jiaotong-Liverpool University, China
Rongrong Ji	Xiamen University, China
Wei Jia	Hefei University of Technology, China
Yunde Jia	Beijing Institute of Technology, China
Feng Jiang	Harbin Institute of Technology, China
Zhiguo Jiang	Beihang University, China
Lianwen Jin	South China University of Technology, China
Xiao-Yuan Jing	Wuhan University, China
Xiangwei Kong	Dalian University of Technology, China
Jian-Huang Lai	Sun Yat-sen University, China
Hua Li	Institute of Computing Technology, Chinese Academy of Sciences, China
Peihua Li	Dalian University of Technology, China
Shutao Li	Hunan University, China
Wu-Jun Li	Nanjing University, China
Xiu Li	Tsinghua University, China
Xuelong Li	Xi'an Institute of Optics and Precision Mechanics, Chinese Academy of Sciences, China
Yongjie Li	University of Electronic Science and Technology of China, China
Ronghua Liang	Zhejiang University of Technology, China
Zhouchen Lin	Peking University, China

Tao Wang	iQIYI Company, China
Yuanquan Wang	Hebei University of Technology, China
Zengfu Wang	University of Science and Technology of China, China
Shikui Wei	Beijing Jiaotong University, China
Wei Wei	Northwestern Polytechnical University, China
Jianxin Wu	Nanjing University, China
Yihong Wu	Institute of Automation, Chinese Academy of Sciences, China
Gui-Song Xia	Wuhan University, China
Shiming Xiang	Institute of Automation, Chinese Academy of Sciences, China
Xiaohua Xie	Sun Yat-sen University, China
Yong Xu	South China University of Technology, China
Zenglin Xu	University of Electronic and Technology of China, China
Jianru Xue	Xi'an Jiaotong University, China
Xiangyang Xue	Fudan University, China
Gongping Yang	Shandong University, China
Jie Yang	ShangHai JiaoTong University, China
Jinfeng Yang	Civil Aviation University of China, China
Jufeng Yang	Nankai University, China
Qixiang Ye	Chinese Academy of Sciences, China
Xinge You	Huazhong University of Science and Technology, China
Jian Yin	Sun Yat-sen University, China
Xu-Cheng Yin	University of Science and Technology Beijing, China
Xianghua Ying	Peking University, China
Jian Yu	Beijing Jiaotong University, China
Shiqi Yu	Shenzhen University, China
Bo Yuan	Tsinghua University, China
Pong C. Yuen	Hong Kong Baptist University, SAR China
Zheng-Jun Zha	University of Science and Technology of China, China
Daoqiang Zhang	Nanjing University of Aeronautics and Astronautics, China
Guofeng Zhang	Zhejiang University, China
Junping Zhang	Fudan University, China
Min-Ling Zhang	Southeast University, China
Wei Zhang	Shandong University, China
Yanning Zhang	Northwestern Polytechnical University, China
Zhaoxiang Zhang	Institute of Automation, Chinese Academy of Sciences, China
Qijun Zhao	Sichuan University, China
Huicheng Zheng	Sun Yat-sen University, China
Wei-Shi Zheng	Sun Yat-sen University, China
Wenming Zheng	Southeast University, China
Jie Zhou	Tsinghua University, China
Wangmeng Zuo	Harbin Institute of Technology, China

Contents – Part I

Computer Vision Application

Biometrics

Re-ranking Person Re-identification
with Adaptive Hard Sample Mining

Chuchu Han, Kezhou Chen, Jin Wang, Changxin Gao, and Nong Sang[✉]

Key Laboratory of Ministry of Education for Image Processing and Intelligent
Control, School of Automation, Huazhong University of Science and Technology,
Wuhan 430074, China
{hcc,kzchen,jinw,cgao,nsang}@hust.edu.cn

Abstract. Person re-identification (re-ID) aims at searching a specific
person among non-overlapping cameras, which can be considered as a
retrieval process, and the result is presented as a ranking list. There
always exists the phenomenon that true matches are not the first rank,
mainly owing to that they are more similar to other persons. In this
paper, we use an adaptive hard sample mining method to re-train the
selected samples in order to distinguish similar persons, which is applied
for re-ranking the re-ID results. Specifically, in re-training stage, we
divide the negative samples into three levels according to their ranking information. Meanwhile, we propose a coarse-fine tuning mechanism, which adaptively inflicts different punishment on the negative samples with the ranking information. Therefore, we can obtain a more
valid metric, which is suitable for the re-ranking task to distinguish
the easily-confused samples. Experimental results on VIPeR, PRID450S
and CUHK03 datasets demonstrate the effectiveness of our proposed
algorithm.

Keywords: Re-ranking · Hard sample mining · Metric learning
Adaptive

1 Introduction

In the last few years, person re-identification [6,15,23,29] has attracted increasing attention due to its wide application in computer vision. Actually, re-ID can
be viewed as a retrieval problem. Given a probe pedestrian image, the model
ranks all the person pictures in the gallery, according to their similarities with
the probe. What we want is the true matches in the top rankings. Nevertheless,
on account of the body partial occlusion, background noise, different viewpoints
and illumination conditions, great changes may happen to the appearance of
the same individual, making the initial ranking list less than satisfactory. Therefore, adding re-ranking step is a meaningful practice to improve the ranking of
relevant images.

Re-ranking [8,11,21,23,30] for Re-ID has made great achievement recently.
Quite a few methods [11,21,30] utilize the k-nearest neighbors information of the

© Springer Nature Switzerland AG 2018
J.-H. Lai et al. (Eds.): PRCV 2018, LNCS 11256, pp. 3–14, 2018.
https://doi.org/10.1007/978-3-030-03398-9_1

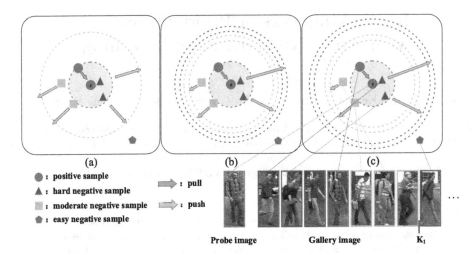

(a)

● : positive sample

▲ : hard negative sample

■ : moderate negative sample

⬟ : easy negative sample

⟹ : pull

⟹ : push

(b)

(c)

Probe image　　　　Gallery image　　　K₁

Fig. 1. Schematic illustration of adaptive margins. (a) shows the negative samples are treated equally with a fixed margin. (b) shows different margins are assigned according to the distance between negative samples with probe. (c) shows that negative samples are divided into three levels, and only the hard and moderate samples are re-trained, making it more suitable for re-ranking task. Based on (b), we also take the ranking information into account. Moreover, we inflict additional punishment on the wrong ranked samples, making the metric more discriminative for confusable individuals.

top-ranked images in the initial ranking list. Another manner is to re-train the samples, for instance, Discriminant Context Information Analysis (DCIA) [8] removes the visual ambiguities to obtain a discriminant feature space, which is finally exploited to compute the new ranking. Unlike the previous methods, we choose to improve the metric method in re-training stage, in order to obtain a specific metric, which can easily distinguish the easily-confused samples for re-ranking.

In general, existing algorithms calculate metrics mainly through two ways, pairwise constraint [17,24] and triplet constraint [5,19]. However, the two methods have a common potential weakness, which treat negative samples equally. As the Fig. 1(a) shows, all negative samples are pushed from probe with a fixed margin, which is defective. In order to obtain an optimal result, the hard samples should be paid more attention than others. Therefore the AMNN algorithm [27] pushes the nearer negative samples farther according to the distance. As shown in the Fig. 1(b), it can achieve better performance. Nevertheless, consider an extreme case where the distances are not much different, it is similar to the situation of fixed margin. Therefore, we take the ranking information into account, which is more flexible than distance. Moreover, we can inflict additional punishment on the wrong ranked samples. Specifically, when the training ranking is obtained, the negative samples are divided into three levels. As the Fig. 1 shows, for each probe, the images arranged before the positive sample are defined as the hard samples, and those between the positive sample and the set threshold

K_1 are the moderate samples, after K_1 are the easy ones. Then we propose a coarse-fine tuning mechanism in the re-training stage. First, we abnegate the easy samples, alleviating the imbalance of positive and negative sample pairs. Second, we assign larger margin to the nearer negative sample according to the rank. Third, based on the second condition, we inflict additional punishment on the wrong ranked samples, namely the defined hard negative samples. Therefore we can obtain a metric contraposing the confusable samples for re-ranking.

Combine the aforementioned introduction, this paper presents an adaptive hard sample mining metric learning method for re-ID re-ranking, which is composed of three steps. First, we use cross-validation on the training set, obtaining the training ranking. According to this, the hard and moderate samples are selected for each probe. Second, in the re-training stage, a more effective metric is learned by these selected samples. Meanwhile, under the coarse-fine tuning mechanism, the applied thrust is associated with the difficulty level and ranking of the sample, which can be deemed as an adaptive procedure. Finally, we use the new metric to calculate similarity scores, only top-m samples in the initial ranking are selected to be re-ranked.

We organize the rest of the paper as follows. In Sect. 2, we discuss previous work on metric learning and re-ranking methods. In Sect. 3 we describe our method in more detail. In Sect. 4, an extensive comparison with state-of-the-art algorithms is presented, as well as the analysis of our method. Finally, we make an conclusion of this paper in Sect. 5.

2   Related Work

Metric Learning. The metric learning approaches can be roughly splited into three groups according to the optimization criterions. The first class, including Keep It Simple and Straightforward Metric Learning (KISSME) [13] and Cross-view Quadratic Discriminant Analysis (XQDA) [16], which build the Gaussian model to formulate the distribution of the two classes. The Mahalanobis distance is derived from the log-likelihood ratio of two Gaussian distributions. The second class aims to learn a discriminative subspace, by means of decomposing the learned metric [2,4,20,28]. The third class focuses on learning a PSD Mahalanobis metric with several distance constraint, including pairwise constraints [12,17,24] and triplet constraints [5,19,25].

In consideration of the number of images in each individual constraint, the proposed method can be seen as a special kind of pairwise constraint. Our method forces inter-class distance to be a changeable value according to the difficult degree, aiming to punish the hardest negative samples. We encode each separate constraint with squared loss function.

Re-ranking. Re-ranking technique has caused more and more attention recent years. Earliest works utilize ranking SVMs [7] or boosting method [10] for feature selection. Liu et al. [18] proposed a one-shot Post-rank Optimisation (POP) method, which has quick convergence rate, but it needs select a single strong negative sample artificially as feedback. After that there comes a lot of unsupervised methods. Garcia et al. [8] exploited content and context set to remove the visual ambiguities, thus obtain the discriminant feature space. Meanwhile there are quite a few researchers have paid attention to the k-nearest neighbor methods. Jegou et al. [11] proposed a contextual dissimilarity measure (CDM) using the reciprocal neighbors. Qin et al. [21] formally employed the k-reciprocal neighbors to compute ranking lists. Zhong et al. [30] introduced a k-reciprocal encoding method, which aggregates the re-ranked Jaccard distance with the initial distance to amend the original result.

In contrast to use reciprocal or k-nearest neighbors methods to revise the rank, we propose to use metric learning to re-train the data, which can compensate the performance on small databases.

3   Proposed Approach

3.1   Problem Definition

For ease of presentation, our method is present in the single-shot scene, where each person only has one picture in each camera view. Similarly, it can be extended to multi-shot scenario easily. Suppose that we have a cross-view training set $\{\mathbf{X}_{tr}, \mathbf{Z}_{tr}\}$, where the probe set is denoted as $\mathbf{X}_{tr} = \{\mathbf{x}_1, \mathbf{x}_2, \cdots, \mathbf{x}_n\} \in \mathbb{R}^{d \times n}$, and the gallery set is denoted as $\mathbf{Z}_{tr} = \{\mathbf{z}_1, \mathbf{z}_2, \cdots, \mathbf{z}_n\} \in \mathbb{R}^{d \times n}$. We use $ID \in \mathbb{R}^{n \times n}$ to denote the matching label between $\mathbf{X}_{tr}$ and $\mathbf{Z}_{tr}$, with $id_{ij} = 1$ signifying that $\mathbf{x}_i$ and $\mathbf{z}_j$ are from the same class, $id_{ij} = -1$ indicating different class. Therefore, the similar set is defined as $\mathcal{S} = \{(\mathbf{x}_i, \mathbf{z}_j) | \ id_{ij} = 1\}$, and dissimilar set is $\mathcal{D} = \{(\mathbf{x}_i, \mathbf{z}_j) | \ id_{ij} = -1\}$.

After applying cross-validation on the training set, we obtain the training ranking $\mathbf{R}_{tr}$, as the Fig. 2 shows, as well as the hard and moderate negative samples for each probe $\mathbf{x}_i$:

$$\begin{aligned} \mathbf{L}_{hard}(\mathbf{x}_i) &= \{\mathbf{z}_j | \pi(\mathbf{z_j}) < \pi(\mathbf{z_i})\} \\ \mathbf{L}_{moderate}(\mathbf{x}_i) &= \{\mathbf{z}_j | \pi(\mathbf{z_i}) < \pi(\mathbf{z_j}) < K_1\}, \end{aligned} \tag{1}$$

for the probe $\mathbf{x}_i$, $\pi(\mathbf{z_j})$ denotes the rank of the negative sample $\mathbf{z}_j$ in $\mathbf{R}_{tr}$ while $\pi(\mathbf{z_i})$ denotes the rank of positive sample $\mathbf{z}_i$. We use $\tilde{\mathcal{S}}$ and $\tilde{\mathcal{D}}$ to denote the similar and dissimilar set in re-training stage.

3.2   Metric Learning

In the re-training stage, given the selected training set, our task is to learn a Mahalanobis distance function [26], measuring the similarity of two cross-view pictures:

$$D_{\mathbf{M}}^2(\mathbf{x}_i, \mathbf{z}_j) = ||\mathbf{x}_i - \mathbf{z}_j||_{\mathbf{M}}^2 = (\mathbf{x}_i - \mathbf{z}_j)^T \mathbf{M}(\mathbf{x}_i - \mathbf{z}_j), \tag{2}$$

where $\mathbf{M}$ is a positive semi-define matrix, insuring that $D_{\mathbf{M}}^2$ satisfies both the nonnegativity and the triangle inequality.

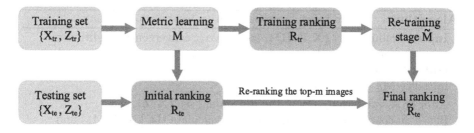

Fig. 2. A simple framework of our proposed re-identification method.

Based on the pairwise constraints, we propose to learn the metric by setting an adaptive variable for the distance of different hard sample pairs:

$$
\begin{cases}
D_{\mathbf{M}}^2(\mathbf{x}_i, \mathbf{z}_j) \leq \tau, (\mathbf{x}_i, \mathbf{z}_j) \in \tilde{\mathcal{S}} \\
D_{\mathbf{M}}^2(\mathbf{x}_i, \mathbf{z}_j) \geq \mu_j^i, (\mathbf{x}_i, \mathbf{z}_j) \in \tilde{\mathcal{D}}
\end{cases}, \tag{3}
$$

where τ and μ_j^i are two thresholds with $\tau < \mu_j^i$, which are specified in advance. The first inequality controls the compactness of the positive pairs. Our main contribution lies in the second constraint, in which distance is alterable with the difficulty of hard sample:

$$
\mu_j^i =
\begin{cases}
d + \beta_1 - \frac{\pi(z_j)-1}{\beta_2(n-1)}, z_j \in \mathbf{L}_{hard}(x_i) \\
d - \beta_1 - \frac{\pi(z_j)-1}{\beta_2(n-1)}, z_j \in \mathbf{L}_{moderate}(x_i)
\end{cases}, \tag{4}
$$

where d is the average Euclidean distance between negative sample pairs:

$$
d = \frac{1}{N(N-1)} \sum_{i \neq j} ||\mathbf{x}_i - \mathbf{z}_j||_2^2, \tag{5}
$$

and β_1 is the coarse tuning parameter, which roughly determines the distances between probe and hard samples are larger than those with moderate samples. β_2 is the fine tuning parameter, which precisely controls the margin between the ranking adjacent samples. Under this coarse-fine tuning mechanism, larger margin are assigned to the negative sample closer to probe, which is more flexible than AMNN [27]. Moreover, we inflict additional punishment on the wrong ranked samples, making the metric more discriminative for confusable persons.

In order to learn such an effective metric, we introduce the squared loss function to punish the violation of both constraints, which can be converted to an optimization problem in this way. So the overall loss function is formulated as:

$$
\begin{aligned}
L(\mathbf{M}) = &\frac{\alpha}{|\tilde{\mathcal{S}}|} \sum_{(\mathbf{x}_i, \mathbf{z}_j) \in \tilde{\mathcal{S}}} (D_{\mathbf{M}}^2(\mathbf{x}_i, \mathbf{z}_j) - \tau)^2 \\
&+ \frac{1-\alpha}{|\tilde{\mathcal{D}}|} \sum_{(\mathbf{x}_i, \mathbf{z}_j) \in \tilde{\mathcal{D}}} (D_{\mathbf{M}}^2(\mathbf{x}_i, \mathbf{z}_j) - \mu_j^i)^2 + \frac{\lambda}{2} ||\mathbf{M} - \mathbf{I}||_F^2,
\end{aligned} \tag{6}
$$

Algorithm 1. Metric Learning with adaptive hard sample mining

---

Input: Training set: $\{\mathbf{X}, \mathbf{Z}, \mathbf{ID}\}$, stepsize α_k, convergence condition ε,
　　　parameters α, λ, β_1 and β_2
Output: The metric $\tilde{\mathbf{M}}$
Initialize $\mathbf{M}_0 = \mathbf{I}$, $k = 0$;
After cross-validation, obtain the re-training set $\{\tilde{\mathbf{X}}, \tilde{\mathbf{Z}}\}$;
Based on coarse-fine tuning mechanism, calculate the loss $L(\mathbf{M}_k)$ and $L(\mathbf{M}_{k+1})$;
while $|\frac{L(\mathbf{M}_{k+1})-L(\mathbf{M}_k)}{L(\mathbf{M}_k)}| > \varepsilon$ **do**
　　Calculate the gradient $\nabla L(\mathbf{M}_k)$;
　　According to $\mathbf{M}_{k+1} = \mathbf{U}_k \mathbf{\Sigma}_k^+ \mathbf{U}_k^T$, project $\tilde{\mathbf{M}}_{k+1}$ onto the PSD cone ,
　　obtaining $\mathbf{M}_{k+1}$;
　　Update $\tilde{\mathbf{M}}_{k+1}$ according to $\tilde{\mathbf{M}}_{k+1} = \mathbf{M}_k - \alpha_k \nabla L(\mathbf{M}_k)$;
end

---

where $|\tilde{\mathcal{S}}|$ and $|\tilde{\mathcal{D}}|$ are the numbers of positive and negative samples respectively, and α controls the weight of two forces: one minimizing the distance of intra-class, the other increasing the distance. λ is a regularization parameter to prevent overfitting. The final optimization problem is formulated as:

$$\min L(\mathbf{M}), \ s.t. \ \mathbf{M} \succeq 0. \tag{7}$$

In consideration of the problem is a convex function constrained over a closed convex cone, so it has a unique global minimum solution. This kind of problem can be easily solved by projected gradient method [3]. The overall metric learning method is presented in Algorithm 1.

3.3   Selection of Re-ranking Samples

Generally, it has high probability that the true match is ranked at top positions. Therefore, it is unwise to select all the testing gallery samples into re-ranking step. In addition, our re-trained model is more appropriate for easily-confused images, thus we decided to select the top-m samples to re-rank. Following [8], for the first K_2 gallery features of the initial ranking, $\delta_i = d(\mathbf{x}, \mathbf{z}_{i+1}) - d(\mathbf{x}, \mathbf{z}_i)$ is calculated to explore the distance distribution. δ_m is the maximum value among all results, where $1 \leq m \leq K_2 - 1$.

$$\delta_m = max\{\delta_1, \delta_2 \cdots \delta_{k_2-1}\}. \tag{8}$$

As shown in Fig. 3, we have observed similarity distances between the samples before the largest gap and after this gap are different. Thus we can make a assumption that, the true match is supposed to locate among the first m images with high probability before this gap. Then, the rest images after the largest gap are removed, reducing the computational complexity of subsequent stages. In Fig. 3(a), $m = 1$ signifies that the similarity between probe and rank-1 gallery image is much higher than others. Then the initial rank-1 image is regarded as the true match, so the re-ranking step is skipped. Nevertheless, in Fig. 3(b), the first three gallery images all share similar distances with the probe under the original metric. Thus, the re-trained model should be used to find the true match from these m images.

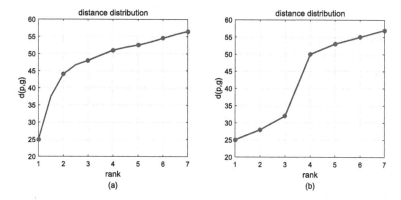

Fig. 3. Distance distribution between the probe and the top-K_2 gallery images of the initial ranking. (a) shows the largest gap is between the rank-1 and rank-2, so the re-ranking step is skipped. (b) shows the largest gap is between the rank-3 and rank-4, so the first three gallery images are selected to enter the re-ranking step.

4   Experiments

In this section, we evaluate the proposed re-ranking method on popular benchmarks, including VIPeR, PRID450S and CUHK03.

4.1   Datasets and Settings

VIPeR is a challenging person re-identification dataset [9]. It contains 1264 outdoor images of 632 persons captured by two disjoint cameras. Each person has two images from different views. There are severe lighting variations, different viewpoints and cluttered background in the VIPeR dataset. The experimental protocol is to split the data set into half randomly, 316 persons for training and 316 for testing. The entire evaluation procedure is repeated 10 times, then the average performance is reported.

PRID450S dataset [22] contains 450 single-shot pairs captured by two spatially disjoint cameras, which has significant and constant lighting variations. For the evaluation, we randomly divide this dataset into training and testing sets containing half of the available individuals. This procedure is repeated 10 times to obtain the average result.

CUHK03 dataset [14] includes 14,096 images of 1,467 identities, each identity is observed by two disjoint camera views, and has 4.8 images per identity on average in each camera. The dataset provides both manually labeled pedestrian bounding boxes and DPM-detected bounding boxes. In the following text, we denote the two manner as CUHK03D and CUHK03L respectively. The single shot setting protocol is adopted in the testing stage.

Parameter Setting. In our experiments, the stepsize α_k is set to be 1, the regularization parameter λ is set to be 10^{-5} for CUHK03 and 10^{-4} for others. We set the weighting parameter $\alpha = 0.5$ for VIPeR and PRID450S, $\alpha = 0.8$ for CUHK03. In addition, we set $\tau = 0$, expecting the intra-class distances to be as small as possible. There arc two vitally important parameters, including the coarse tuning parameter β_1 and fine tuning parameter β_2, which are specifically analyzed in the following text.

4.2   Re-ranking Performance Comparison

Result on VIPeR. In this dataset, we use LOMO and GoG as feature representation. In addition to using KISSME and XQDA methods, MLAPG is also chosen for global metric. We set $K_1 = 15, K_2 = 5, \beta_1 = 0.3, \beta_2 = 10$. Notice that $K_2 = 5$ means at most five pictures are selected for the re-ranking step, so our method mainly focuses on improving the value of rank-1. The performance comparisons of various methods with our method are shown in Table 1. There are some fluctuations when using KISSME algorithm, because it takes a strategy of randomly sampling negative samples. From the table we can observe that, our method invariably improves the rank-1 accuracy, especially over LOMO+KISSME, we achieve 7.98% improvement, which shows effectiveness of the proposed method.

Table 1. Comparison among various methods with our re-ranking approach on the VIPeR dataset.

Method	Rank 1	Rank 2	Rank 3	Rank 4	Rank 5
LOMO+XQDA	40.00	51.49	58.83	64.30	68.13
LOMO+XQDA+ours	**41.06**	51.87	58.99	64.37	68.13
LOMO+KISSME	29.11	40.57	47.97	52.89	57.01
LOMO+KISSME+ours	**37.09**	44.08	48.86	53.01	57.06
LOMO+MLAPG	40.73	53.32	60.73	65.92	69.94
LOMO+MLAPG+ours	**41.49**	53.68	60.94	65.98	69.94
GOG+XQDA	46.20	59.62	67.41	72.03	75.66
GOG+XQDA+ours	**47.97**	59.84	67.47	72.09	75.70
GOG+KISSME	38.64	51.11	58.69	63.91	67.82
GOG+KISSME+ours	**44.84**	53.51	59.59	64.02	67.82

Result on PRID450S. In this dataset, we remain original implementations, only change the parameters to $\beta_1 = 0.1, \beta_2 = 12$. The results of various methods with re-ranking are shown in Table 2. Our proposed method exceeds the performance of GOG+KISSME 9.57% at rank-1, indicating the advantages of our re-ranking method.

Table 2. Comparison among various methods with our re-ranking approach on the PRID450S dataset.

Method	Rank 1	Rank 2	Rank 3	Rank 4	Rank 5
LOMO+XQDA	59.05	70.58	76.56	80.15	82.37
LOMO+XQDA+ours	**59.56**	70.73	76.59	80.15	82.37
LOMO+KISSME	46.93	59.08	65.91	70.79	74.37
LOMO+KISSME+ours	**54.13**	60.89	66.01	70.99	74.46
GOG+XQDA	64.89	76.04	81.16	84.53	86.44
GOG+XQDA+ours	**67.02**	76.40	81.16	84.53	86.44
GOG+KISSME	52.36	65.67	72.36	76.38	79.59
GOG+KISSME+ours	**61.93**	68.42	72.80	76.40	79.69

Result on CUHK03. Table 3 shows the comparison results on CUHK03 labeled and detected datasets. We set K_1 to 40, β_1 to 0.7 and β_2 to 15. As we can see, when employ a single LOMO feature, the performance with our re-ranking strategy exceeds MLAPG 3.01% and 3.76% at rank-1 respectively. Moreover, our method gain about 4% improvement at XQDA, which works better than k-reciprocal re-ranking method.

Table 3. Comparison among various methods with our re-ranking method, and with another re-ranking approach on the CUHK03 dataset.

Dataset	CUHK03 Labeled			CUHK03 Detected		
Rank	Rank 1	Rank 5	Rank 10	Rank 1	Rank 5	Rank 10
LMNN [25]	7.29	19.23	30.77	6.25	17.69	28.46
KISSME [13]	14.17	37.50	52.31	11.70	33.46	48.46
IDLA [1]	54.75	86.15	94.23	44.96	75.77	83.46
XQDA [16]	49.70	-	-	44.6	-	-
XQDA+k-reciprocal [30]	**50.00**	-	-	**45.90**	-	-
XQDA+ours	**54.28**	-	-	**48.32**	-	-
MLAPG [17]	57.96	87.09	94.74	51.15	83.55	92.05
MLAPG+ours	**60.97**	87.09	94.74	**54.91**	83.55	92.05

4.3 Parameters Analysis

In this subsection the parameters of our method are analyzed. We first evaluate the influence of the β_1 and β_2, which adjust the distance of different negative pairs, next is α, which controls the balance of two forces. We choose LOMO+XQDA as baseline and the parameters are evaluated on the VIPeR dataset.

To evaluate the influence of β_1, we first fix $\beta_2 = 10$ and $\alpha = 0.5$. Figure 4(a) shows the result of matching rate at rank-1, the model gets the best result when β_1 is around 0.3. The figure also suggests that when β_1 is small, it lacks the extra thrust on hard samples, making the performance reduce. However, the β_1 is not the bigger the better. Pushing hard sample too far may cause the overfitting. Then we analyze the influence of β_2 by fixing $\beta_1 = 0.3$ and $\alpha = 0.5$. As Fig. 4(b) illustrated, when β_2 is around 10, the best result is achieved. As it increase to large enough, the result is no longer changed. Finally we fix $\beta_1 = 0.3$ and $\beta_2 = 10$ to analyze the influence of α. As Fig. 4(c) shows, when α is in the range of $[0.5, 0.7]$ the method performs best.

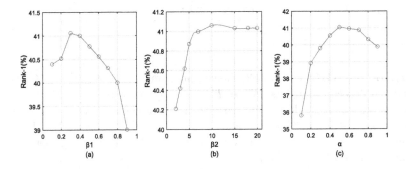

Fig. 4. Parameter sensitivity of β_1, β_2 and α on the VIPeR dataset.

5 Conclusion

In this paper, we use a re-trained manner to address the re-ranking problem in person re-identification (re-ID). In order to distinguish some similar samples, we propose a coarse-fine tuning mechanism, motivated by hard sample mining method, which can adaptively assign the margins of different negative sample pairs. Under this constraint an effective metric model is obtained, we calculate the similarity score for re-ranking. Meanwhile, the strategy of selecting re-ranking samples can alleviate computational complexity. The proposed method achieve effective improvement on the VIPeR, PRID450S and CUHK03 datasets.

Acknowledgements. This work was supported by the Project of the National Natural Science Foundation of China (No. 61876210), and the Fundamental Research Funds for the Central Universities (No. 2017KFYXJJ179).

References

1. Ahmed, E., Jones, M., Marks, T.K.: An improved deep learning architecture for person re-identification. In: Computer Vision and Pattern Recognition, pp. 3908–3916 (2015)
2. An, L., Kafai, M., Yang, S., Bhanu, B.: Person reidentification with reference descriptor. IEEE Trans. Circuits Syst. Video Technol. **26**(4), 776–787 (2016)
3. Bertsekas, D.P.: Nonlinear programming. J. Oper. Res. Soc. **48**(3), 334 (1997)
4. Chen, Y.C., Zheng, W.S., Lai, J.: Mirror representation for modeling view-specific transform in person re-identification. In: International Conference on Artificial Intelligence, pp. 3402–3408 (2015)
5. Cheng, D., Gong, Y., Zhou, S., Wang, J., Zheng, N.: Person re-identification by multi-channel parts-based CNN with improved triplet loss function. In: IEEE Conference on Computer Vision and Pattern Recognition, pp. 1335–1344 (2016)
6. Deng, W., Zheng, L., Kang, G., Yang, Y., Ye, Q., Jiao, J.: Image-image domain adaptation with preserved self-similarity and domain-dissimilarity for person re-identification. In: IEEE Conference on Computer Vision and Pattern Recognition (2017)
7. Engel, C., Baumgartner, P., Holzmann, M, Nutzel, J.F.: Person re-identification by support vector ranking. In: Proceedings of British Machine Vision Conference, BMVC 2010, Aberystwyth, 31 August–3 September 2010, pp. 1–11 (2010)
8. Garcia, J., Martinel, N., Gardel, A., Bravo, I., Foresti, G.L., Micheloni, C.: Discriminant context information analysis for post-ranking person re-identification. IEEE Trans. Image Process. **26**(4), 1650–1665 (2017)
9. Gray, D., Tao, H.: Viewpoint invariant pedestrian recognition with an ensemble of localized features. In: Forsyth, D., Torr, P., Zisserman, A. (eds.) ECCV 2008. LNCS, vol. 5302, pp. 262–275. Springer, Heidelberg (2008). https://doi.org/10.1007/978-3-540-88682-2_21
10. Hirzer, M., Beleznai, C., Roth, P.M., Bischof, H.: Person re-identification by descriptive and discriminative classification. In: Heyden, A., Kahl, F. (eds.) SCIA 2011. LNCS, vol. 6688, pp. 91–102. Springer, Heidelberg (2011). https://doi.org/10.1007/978-3-642-21227-7_9
11. Jegou, H., Harzallah, H., Schmid, C.: A contextual dissimilarity measure for accurate and efficient image search. In: IEEE Conference on Computer Vision and Pattern Recognition, CVPR 2007, pp. 1–8 (2007)
12. Jurie, F., Mignon, A.: PCCA: a new approach for distance learning from sparse pairwise constraints. In: Computer Vision and Pattern Recognition, pp. 2666–2672 (2012)
13. Köstinger, M., Hirzer, M., Wohlhart, P., Roth, P.M., Bischof, H.: Large scale metric learning from equivalence constraints. In: IEEE Conference on Computer Vision and Pattern Recognition, pp. 2288–2295 (2012)
14. Li, W., Zhao, R., Xiao, T., Wang, X.: DeepReID: deep filter pairing neural network for person re-identification. In: IEEE Conference on Computer Vision and Pattern Recognition, pp. 152–159 (2014)

15. Li, W., Zhu, X., Gong, S.: Harmonious attention network for person re-identification. In: IEEE Conference on Computer Vision and Pattern Recognition (2018)
16. Liao, S., Hu, Y., Zhu, X., Li, S.Z.: Person re-identification by local maximal occurrence representation and metric learning. In: Computer Vision and Pattern Recognition, pp. 2197–2206 (2015)
17. Liao, S., Li, S.Z.: Efficient PSD constrained asymmetric metric learning for person re-identification. In: IEEE International Conference on Computer Vision, pp. 3685–3693 (2015)
18. Liu, C., Chen, C.L., Gong, S., Wang, G.: POP: person re-identification post-rank optimisation. In: IEEE International Conference on Computer Vision, pp. 441–448 (2014)
19. Liu, H., Feng, J., Qi, M., Jiang, J., Yan, S.: End-to-end comparative attention networks for person re-identification. IEEE Trans. Image Process. **26**(7), 3492–3506 (2017)
20. Pedagadi, S., Orwell, J., Velastin, S., Boghossian, B.: Local fisher discriminant analysis for pedestrian re-identification. In: IEEE Conference on Computer Vision and Pattern Recognition, pp. 3318–3325 (2013)
21. Qin, D., Gammeter, S., Bossard, L., Quack, T., Van Gool, L.: Hello neighbor: accurate object retrieval with k-reciprocal nearest neighbors. In: Computer Vision and Pattern Recognition, pp. 777–784 (2011)
22. Roth, P.M., Hirzer, M., Köstinger, M., Beleznai, C., Bischof, H.: Mahalanobis distance learning for person re-identification. In: Gong, S., Cristani, M., Yan, S., Loy, C. (eds.) Person Re-identification. Springer, London (2014). https://doi.org/10.1007/978-1-4471-6296-4_12
23. Sarfraz, M.S., Schumann, A., Eberle, A., Stiefelhagen, R.: A pose-sensitive embedding for person re-identification with expanded cross neighborhood re-ranking. In: IEEE Conference on Computer Vision and Pattern Recognition (2017)
24. Varior, R.R., Haloi, M., Wang, G.: Gated Siamese convolutional neural network architecture for human re-identification. In: Leibe, B., Matas, J., Sebe, N., Welling, M. (eds.) ECCV 2016. LNCS, vol. 9912, pp. 791–808. Springer, Cham (2016). https://doi.org/10.1007/978-3-319-46484-8_48
25. Weinberger, K.Q., Saul, L.K.: Distance metric learning for large margin nearest neighbor classification. J. Mach. Learn. Res. **10**(1), 207–244 (2009)
26. Xing, E.P., Ng, A.Y., Jordan, M.I., Russell, S.: Distance metric learning, with application to clustering with side-information. In: International Conference on Neural Information Processing Systems, pp. 521–528 (2002)
27. Yao, L., et al.: Adaptive margin nearest neighbor for person re-identification. In: Ho, Y.-S., Sang, J., Ro, Y.M., Kim, J., Wu, F. (eds.) PCM 2015. LNCS, vol. 9314, pp. 75–84. Springer, Cham (2015). https://doi.org/10.1007/978-3-319-24075-6_8
28. Zhang, L., Xiang, T., Gong, S.: Learning a discriminative null space for person re-identification. In: Computer Vision and Pattern Recognition, pp. 1239–1248 (2016)
29. Zhang, Y., Xiang, T., Hospedales, T.M., Lu, H.: Deep mutual learning. In: IEEE Conference on Computer Vision and Pattern Recognition (2017)
30. Zhong, Z., Zheng, L., Cao, D., Li, S.: Re-ranking person re-identification with k-reciprocal encoding. In: IEEE Conference on Computer Vision and Pattern Recognition, pp. 3652–3661 (2017)

Global Feature Learning with Human Body Region Guided for Person Re-identification

Zhiqiang Li, Nong Sang$^{(\boxtimes)}$, Kezhou Chen, Chuchu Han, and Changxin Gao

Key Laboratory of Ministry of Education for Image Processing and Intelligent Control, School of Automation, Huazhong University of Science and Technology, Wuhan 430074, China
{zqli,nsang,kzchen,hcc,cgao}@hust.edu.cn

Abstract. Person reidentification (re-id) is a very challenging task in video surveillance due to background clutters, variations in occlusion, and the human body misalignment in the detected images. To tackle these problems, we utilize a multi-channel convolutional neural network (CNN) with a novel embedding training strategy. First, some parts of the body were detected with existing methods of human pose estimation and then different parts were feed into different network branches to learn local and global representations. But for the global network branch, we proposed a embedding strategy for training, which uses local features to guide learning more robust global features. The promising experimental results on the large-scale Market-1501 and CUHK03 datasets demonstrate the effectiveness of our proposed embedding training strategy for features.

Keywords: Person reidentification (re-id) · Fusion strategy Sub-regions

1 Introduction

Person re-identification (re-id) aims to match a specific person in a nonoverlapping camera network or across time within a single camera [3,13,27,29], which has attracted more and more attention in recent years due to the great prospect in video surveillance. But the person ReID task is still challenging because of the parameter setting and shooting angle of the camera, background clutter and occlusions, variations in human pose. In order to solve these problems, much of the previous research has focused on hand-craft feature design and metric learning [8,12,23], even Jing et al. [6] tried to get more robust features by learning to map low-resolution images to high-resolution images. Traditional works on feature design is trying to construct discriminative and robust descriptors as representation of the whole detected image, while the metric learning aims to learning a better similarity metric for feature comparison. But the effect of

© Springer Nature Switzerland AG 2018
J.-H. Lai et al. (Eds.): PRCV 2018, LNCS 11256, pp. 15–25, 2018.
https://doi.org/10.1007/978-3-030-03398-9_2

previous studies is still limited. Recently, Inspired by the successful application in other fields with Convolutional Neural Networks (CNN), deep learning method is gradually popular in re-id. Many researchers have designed different network frameworks to extract more robust features to cope with the complex problems that re-id is facing at the moment, and have achieved very effective improvements.

Fig. 1. Some common misaligned images in Market1501 (first row) and CUHK03 (second row).

In most of the existing methods, the features are usually extracted from the entire image as global representation [7,22]. However, the feature extracted in this way contains a lot of background information and contains too few details of the pedestrian, therefore such features are not robust. There are other studies [2,18,30] that divide the whole picture into a fixed number of blocks and send them into the different networks respectively, intend to learn the global representation and the local features. The effect of this approach is indeed superior to the method of extracting only global features, because more local details are obtained. However, as show in Fig. 1, it is difficult for the above methods to capture the discriminating descriptors from the image of misaligned person body caused by the shooting distance or angle. Some researchs take advantage of the results of the pedestrian pose estimation [5,20] and separate pedestrian limbs by key points for the purpose of alignment. Zhao et al. [26] proposed to use RPN to divide pedestrians into seven sub-regions and feed them into CNN, finally, all the features were merged by the tree structured fusion strategy, However, it is very common for pedestrians to be sideways or obscured in the picture. In these cases, CNN can not extract the information of so many sub-regions. Forcibly extracting so many sub-region features will have many misdetections, which leads to incorrect matching. Wei1 et al. [19] divided the pedestrian into three sub-regions and used the CNN of shared parameters to extract the features of each sub-region, finally, the features were directly connected in series as the final representation. This feature fusion strategy does not consider the relationship between the various sub-regions, making the final feature discriminant not strong enough. Lin et al. [10] designed Bilinear CNNs to blend different features, but did not consider spatial location when final pooling.

To better address these issues, we propose a new framework that includes four sub-regional branch networks for various sub-regions like [10]. However, the distribution of data in each sub-region varies greatly, so the parameters of each of our networks are not shared. Instead of training separately from each sub-region, we consider that the local feature is a subset of the global feature space to a certain extent, and the global feature contains more comprehensive information. Therefore, we use local features to guide global feature learning, which will make global branch learning more robust and discriminative features. In this paper, We propose a new way of feature fusion which is based on the idea of bilinear convolutional networks [10], because we note that the large-scale person re-identification can be seen as a category of fine-grained visual recognition. However, it is not like BCNN completely discarding spatial information in the process of bilinear convergence. We have adopted a special approach that allows local features to guide global feature learning while preserving the original spatial information of global features.

Contribution: The main contributions of this paper can be summarized as follows:

- We propose a new framework that adds local features to global network branch training to improve the robustness of global features.
- We propose a fusion method that uses local features to guide global feature learning, which not only preserves the original global feature space information, but also integrates the information of the local features to make the features more discriminant.

2   Related Work

This work involves deep learning methods for person re-id and bilinear-like feature fusion method. So we briefly review some methods in these two aspects.

2.1   Deep Learning in Person Reidentification

Deep learning approaches are becoming increasingly popular in person re-id because of their superior performance. Li et al. [7] propose a patch matching layer and a max-out grouping layer to mitigate the impact of pedestrian mis-alignment. Yi et al. [24] utilized the siamese architecture to learn more robust deep representations. Lin et al. [11] impose stronger constraints on the network that the pedestrian attributes and identity were joined the training at the same time. Pedagadi et al. [12] designed a multi-channel parts based network Cheng et al. [2] propose a multi-channel parts based network to learn global feature and sub-regions features simultaneously. More than this, an improved triplet loss is applied to further expand inter class distance which allows the network to learn more discriminating features. Wei et al. [19] divided the pedestrians into three precise parts (head, upper body, lower body) through the pedestrian key detec-tion method, which made the local features learned more accurate. However, [19] lacks consideration in the fusion of local and global features. Zhao et al. [26] proposed a Spindle Net which divides the pedestrian more precisely into seven parts and uses a tree structure to blend the features of the local sub-regions. But we usually get less than fine seven parts due to some occlusion in the real surveillance video. Therefore, in this paper, we also used pedestrian pose esti-mation [1] to detect pedestrians in three sections as [19] but with a new training strategy to better integrate global features and local features.

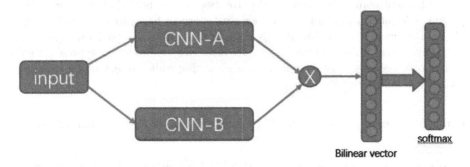

Fig. 2. Bilinear CNNs take an image into two CNNs, respectively, to learn different features, and then combine the two features in each position by matrix multiplication and average pooling as the last representation.

2.2   Bilinear CNNs

Recently, Bilinear convolutional networks (Bilinear CNNs) [10], as show in Fig. 2 has achieved state-of-the-art performance for a number of fine-grained classifica-tion tasks. Bilinear CNNs is composed of one input and two network branches. The two branches learn different features respectively, and then get the fused features from the bilinear pooling. Bilinear pooling is the form of multiplying two sets of features by a matrix and then using sum pool over all locations and normalization for each spatial dim, which not only requires a very large amount of computation, but also ignores the spatial location of feature maps when pooling. Ustinova et al. [16] proposed a new Bilinear pooling methods based Bilinear CNNS for person reid which transforms the two branches features into one dimension before matrix multiplication, and then pooling the feature map of each patch according to a predefined set of image regions, instead of sum pooling on the whole feature map. However, the features of these two branches are only the features of one region without considering the potential guiding relationship between different regions. The framework proposed in this article takes into account the possible guidance of the local features to the global features.

3   Proposed Method

In this section, we first introduce the framework we use to add local features to global branch training. Second, we present the changing bilinear pooling approach based on the BCNN to fusion features of both branches in details.

3.1   Network Architecture

Our network framework consists of four branches, as illustrated in Fig. 3, each training full image, head, upper body, lower body respectively. Each branch can be built by a network with better performance in computer vision recently, such as GoogLeNet [15], VGGNet [14], and ResNet [4]. And the loss generated by the local network branches of each sub-region only updates the parameters of its own network branch when it is back propagating. Here, for the three subnets of the body parts section, we change the stride and the number of final convolution output channels based on ResNet-50. The input image for head branch is resized to 56×56, and the output is a 1024-dimensional feature vector. For upper body and lower body sub-networks, the input image is resized to 112×112, and the output is also a 1024-dimensional feature vector.

However, for the global branch learning, the input image is resized to 224×224. We extract the sub-network features of all the parts of the body in series, and then merge the features of the global network branches built by ResNet-50 into the changed bilinear pooling layer to get the final characteristics of the global network.

3.2   Fusion and Pooling

The purpose of Bilinear CNNs is to mine the correlation between different features, but its pooling approach ignores the relationship between different spatial locations. Here, two inputs, f_a and f_b, are one-dimensional vectors, where f_a is the feature extracted by global network branch and f_b is the feature concatenated by the output of three body parts sub-network. Similarly to [10], the proposed fusion and pooling methods are an follows:

$$B = (I, f_A, f_B, F, P, D). \tag{1}$$

where f_A and f_B are feature extraction functions specifically refer to ResNet-50 in this paper, F is the fusion function, P is the pooling function after fusion, here we use the horizontal pooling, and D is a distance function. When an image I is entered into the function f, the function f will output a d-dimensional vector. It can be simply expressed as:

$$f : I \rightarrow R^d. \tag{2}$$

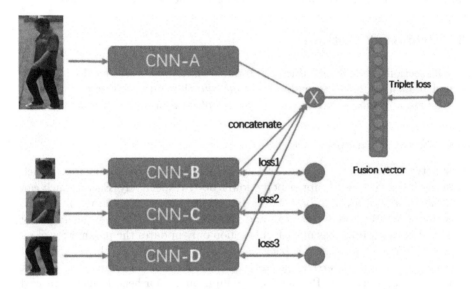

Fig. 3. The framework proposed in this paper is which, which contains four-stream CNN to train full-image, head, upper body and lower body respectively. But when training global branch, the other three parts of the pooling output cascade as one of the fusion structure input.

Here we assume that the output of f_A and f_B is n and m dimensions, respectively. Then, for two feature vector, We use the following feature fusion method:

$$F(im, f_A, f_B) = f_A(im)^T f_B(im). \tag{3}$$

where $im \in I$. After operating the above formula, we get a matrix of $n \times m$, which is used as the input to the pooling function. Then, we get an n dim vector, each of which references the information of another. Here we use the horizontal average pooling. Therefore, the function P can be expressed as:

$$P : M^{n \times m} \rightarrow R^n. \tag{4}$$

Finally, the distance function D is used to learn the features, here we use the triplet loss function which makes the intra-class feature distances to be less than inter-class ones and learn more discriminative feature. When testing, we can use the global branch pooling features or concatenate the four branches pooling features as the representations of the input picture, and then we use the features to calculate the cosine distance to get the final results.

4 Experiment

In order to evaluate the effectiveness of our proposed method, we conducted experiments on two challenging databases, Market-1501 [28] and CUHK03 [7]. To be fair, our assessment strategy is consistent with [28] on the two datasets.

4.1 Datasets

Market1501 [28] is a large-scale dataset in the person re-id field which contains 32,668 images of 1,501 identities captured from 6 different cameras. The training set for this database contains 12936 images of 751 identities, and the test set contains 19732 images of 750 identities. In the test, 3368 images with 750 identities were used as a query set to find the correct identities on the test set. In the whole experiment of this database, the loss function of each branch is triplet loss function, batch size is set to 32, 60 epochs are iterated, and the learning rate is 0.001.

The **CUHK03** [7] dataset includes 13164 images of 1467 identities, captured from 3 pairs of cameras. On average, each identity has 4.8 images in each view. This database provides the version of the bounding box detected by the detection algorithm and the manual labelled version. CUHK provides 20 split sets, each set contains a random selection of 1367 identities for training and 100 identities

Table 1. Comparison on Market-1501 dataset with some state-of-the-art methods. The baseline is a single-branched network whose input is the entire image constructed by ResNet-50. Here, **only 3 parts** refers to the direct connection of three local features, and the **baseline + 3 parts** refers to the direct connection of baseline's global features and three local features.

Methods	Rank 1	Rank 5	Rank 10	Rank 20
PersonNet [21]	48.2	-	-	-
NFST [25]	55.4	-	-	-
S-CNN[17]	65.9	-	-	-
Spindle[26]	76.9	91.5	94.6	96.7
baseline	76.07	89.63	93.14	96.02
Only 3 parts	39.01	64.81	74.34	82.36
Baseline + 3 parts	78.32	91.18	94.23	96.64
our Global	**78.62**	90.79	94.27	96.32
Global + 3 parts	**79.66**	91.86	94.89	96.94

for testing. We report the results on manual labelled versions of the data. In the whole experiment of this database, the loss function of each branch is triplet loss function, batch size is set to 32, 60 epochs are iterated, and the learning rate is 0.001.

4.2 Experimental Results

We use resnet-50 pre-trained on imagenet as the basic network framework, and We take the result of a single network of ResNet-50 trained on the whole image as a baseline. The comparison of the proposed method with some state-of-the-art works in recent years are listed in Tables 1 and 2. As can be seen, due to the inconsistent distribution among different datasets, directly using the trained pose estimation model on other datasets to obtain the components on the Market-1501 dataset, the effect of identifying only with the component images is not good. Despite this, we can use this local feature to assist global feature learning and still achieve certain effect. As shown in the table, the proposed feature fusion method, which concatenate the global features after fusing local features with the local features, is better than concatenate the local features with global features directly. The performance with the proposed method is better than baseline 3.59% at rank 1 in Market-1501 dataset while 2.34% in CUHK03 dataset. And our result of the global single branch network is also higher than the baseline 2.55% in Market1501 dataset, which shows the effectiveness of the method we proposed.

Table 2. Comparison on CUHK03 labeled dataset with some state-of-the-art methods. The baseline is a single-branched network whose input is the entire image constructed by ResNet-50. Here, **only 3 parts** refers to the direct connection of three local features, and the **baseline + 3 parts** refers to the direct connection of baseline's global features and three local features.

Methods	Rank 1	Rank 5	Rank 10	Rank 20
LOMO+XQDA [9]	52.2	82.2	94.1	96.3
PersonNet [21]	64.8	89.4	94.9	98.2
NFST [25]	62.6	90.1	94.8	98.1
S-CNN [17]	61.8	80.9	88.3	-
baseline	70.06	87.47	92.99	96.60
Only 3 parts	69.21	88.11	92.99	96.39
Baseline + 3 parts	71.93	87.54	93.81	96.92
our Global	**70.86**	87.51	93.26	96.78
Global + 3 parts	**72.40**	87.68	94.47	97.03

5   Conclusion

In this paper, we mainly employ the features of local network branches to guide global network branch learning features for improving the efficiency and accuracy of large-scale person re-id. And better performance will be obtained by a new feature fusion method presented in this article. However, the training process is a little troublesome, and in the future we will consider to integrate all of the parts and global part into a network to train together.

Acknowledgements. This work was supported by the Project of the National Natural Science Foundation of China (No. 61876210), and the Fundamental Research Funds for the Central Universities (No. 2017KFYXJJ179).

References

1. Cao, Z., Simon, T., Wei, S.-E., Sheikh, Y.: Realtime multi-person 2D pose estimation using part affinity fields. In: Proceedings of the IEEE Conference on Computer Vision and Pattern Recognition, pp. 1302–1310 (2017)
2. Cheng, D., Gong, Y., Zhou, S., Wang, J., Zheng, N.: Person re-identification by multi-channel parts-based CNN with improved triplet loss function. In: Proceedings of the IEEE Conference on Computer Vision and Pattern Recognition, pp. 1335–1344 (2016)
3. Gheissari, N., Sebastian, T.B., Hartley, R.: Person reidentification using spatiotemporal appearance. In: IEEE Computer Society Conference on Computer Vision and Pattern Recognition, vol. 2, pp. 1528–1535. IEEE (2006)
4. He, K., Zhang, X., Ren, S., Sun, J.: Deep residual learning for image recognition. In: Proceedings of the IEEE Conference on Computer Vision and Pattern Recognition, pp. 770–778 (2016)
5. Insafutdinov, E., Pishchulin, L., Andres, B., Andriluka, M., Schiele, B.: DeeperCut: a deeper, stronger, and faster multi-person pose estimation model. In: Leibe, B., Matas, J., Sebe, N., Welling, M. (eds.) ECCV 2016. LNCS, vol. 9910, pp. 34–50. Springer, Cham (2016). https://doi.org/10.1007/978-3-319-46466-4_3
6. Jing, X.Y., et al.: Super-resolution person re-identification with semi-coupled low-rank discriminant dictionary learning. IEEE Trans. Image Process. **26**(3), 1363–1378 (2017)
7. Li, W., Zhao, R., Xiao, T., Wang, X.: DeepReID: deep filter pairing neural network for person re-identification. In: Proceedings of the IEEE Conference on Computer Vision and Pattern Recognition, pp. 152–159 (2014)
8. Li, Z., Chang, S., Liang, F., Huang, T.S., Cao, L., Smith, J.R.: Learning locally-adaptive decision functions for person verification. In: IEEE Conference on Computer Vision and Pattern Recognition (CVPR), pp. 3610–3617. IEEE (2013)
9. Liao, S., Hu, Y., Zhu, X., Li, S.Z.: Person re-identification by local maximal occurrence representation and metric learning. In: Computer Vision and Pattern Recognition, pp. 2197–2206 (2015)
10. Lin, T.-Y., RoyChowdhury, A., Maji, S.: Bilinear CNN models for fine-grained visual recognition. In: Proceedings of the IEEE International Conference on Computer Vision, pp. 1449–1457 (2015)
11. Lin, Y., Zheng, L., Zheng, Z., Wu, Y., Yang, Y.: Improving person re-identification by attribute and identity learning. arXiv preprint arXiv:1703.07220 (2017)

12. Pedagadi, S., Orwell, J., Velastin, S., Boghossian, B.: Local fisher discriminant analysis for pedestrian re-identification. In: IEEE Conference on Computer Vision and Pattern Recognition (CVPR), pp. 3318–3325. IEEE (2013)
13. Roth, P.M., Hirzer, M., Köstinger, M., Beleznai, C., Bischof, H.: Mahalanobis distance learning for person re-identification. In: Gong, S., Cristani, M., Yan, S., Loy, C.C. (eds.) Person Re-Identification. ACVPR, pp. 247–267. Springer, London (2014). https://doi.org/10.1007/978-1-4471-6296-4_12
14. Simonyan, K., Zisserman, A.: Very deep convolutional networks for large-scale image recognition. Computer Science (2014)
15. Szegedy, C., et al.: Going deeper with convolutions. In: Computer Vision and Pattern Recognition, pp. 1–9 (2015)
16. Ustinova, E., Ganin, Y., Lempitsky, V.: Multi-region bilinear convolutional neural networks for person re-identification. In: IEEE International Conference on Advanced Video and Signal Based Surveillance, pp. 2993–3003 (2017)
17. Varior, R.R., Haloi, M., Wang, G.: Gated siamese convolutional neural network architecture for human re-identification. In: Leibe, B., Matas, J., Sebe, N., Welling, M. (eds.) ECCV 2016. LNCS, vol. 9912, pp. 791–808. Springer, Cham (2016). https://doi.org/10.1007/978-3-319-46484-8_48
18. Wang, J., Wang, Z., Gao, C., Sang, N., Huang, R.: DeepList: learning deep features with adaptive listwise constraint for person reidentification. IEEE Trans. Circuits Syst. Video Technol. **27**(3), 513–524 (2017)
19. Wei, L., Zhang, S., Yao, H., Gao, W., Tian, Q.: Glad: global-local-alignment descriptor for pedestrian retrieval. In: Proceedings of the 2017 ACM on Multimedia Conference, pp. 420–428. ACM (2017)
20. Wei, S.-E., Ramakrishna, V., Kanade, T., Sheikh, Y.: Convolutional pose machines. In: Proceedings of the IEEE Conference on Computer Vision and Pattern Recognition, pp. 4724–4732 (2016)
21. Wu, L., Shen, C., van den Hengel, A.: PersonNet: person re-identification with deep convolutional neural networks. arXiv preprint arXiv:1601.07255 (2016)
22. Xiao, T., Li, H., Ouyang, W., Wang, X.: Learning deep feature representations with domain guided dropout for person re-identification. In: IEEE Conference on Computer Vision and Pattern Recognition (CVPR), pp. 1249–1258. IEEE (2016)
23. Xiong, F., Gou, M., Camps, O., Sznaier, M.: Peron re-identification using kernel-based metric learning methods. In: Fleet, D., Pajdla, T., Schiele, B., Tuytelaars, T. (eds.) ECCV 2014. LNCS, vol. 8695, pp. 1–16. Springer, Cham (2014). https://doi.org/10.1007/978-3-319-10584-0_1
24. Yi, D., Lei, Z., Liao, S., Li, S.Z.: Deep metric learning for person re-identification. In: 22nd International Conference on Pattern Recognition (ICPR), pp. 34–39. IEEE (2014)
25. Zhang, L., Xiang, T., Gong, S.: Learning a discriminative null space for person re-identification. In: Computer Vision and Pattern Recognition, pp. 1239–1248 (2016)
26. Zhao, H., et al.: Spindle net: person re-identification with human body region guided feature decomposition and fusion. In: Proceedings of the IEEE Conference on Computer Vision and Pattern Recognition, pp. 1077–1085 (2017)
27. Zhao, R., Ouyang, W., Wang, X.: Learning mid-level filters for person re-identification. In: Proceedings of the IEEE Conference on Computer Vision and Pattern Recognition, pp. 144–151 (2014)
28. Zheng, L., Shen, L., Tian, L., Wang, S., Wang, J., Tian, Q.: Scalable person re-identification: a benchmark. In: Proceedings of the IEEE International Conference on Computer Vision, pp. 1116–1124 (2016)

29. Zheng, W.-S., Gong, S., Xiang, T.: Person re-identification by probabilistic relative distance comparison. In: IEEE Conference on Computer Vision and Pattern Recognition (CVPR), pp. 649–656. IEEE (2011)
30. Zhu, F., Kong, X., Zheng, L., Fu, H., Tian, Q.: Part-based deep hashing for large-scale person re-identification. IEEE Trans. Image Process. **26**(10), 4806–4817 (2017)

Hand Dorsal Vein Recognition Based on Deep Hash Network

Dexing Zhong$^{(\boxtimes)}$, Huikai Shao, and Yu Liu

School of Electronic and Information Engineering, Xi'an Jiaotong University,
Xi'an 710049, Shaanxi, People's Republic of China
bell@xjtu.edu.cn

Abstract. As a unique biometric technology that has emerged in recent decades, hand dorsal vein recognition has received increasing attention due to its higher safety and convenience. In order to further improve the recognition accuracy, in this paper we propose an end-to-end method for recognizing Hand dorsal vein Based on Deep hash network (DHN), called HBD. The hand dorsal vein image is input into the simplified Convolutional Neural Networks-Fast (SCNN-F) to obtain convolution features. At the last fully connected layer, for the outputs of 128 neurons, *sgn* function is used to encode each image as 128-bit code. By comparing the distances between images after coding, it can be judged whether they are from the same person. Using a special loss function and training strategy, we verify the effectiveness of HBD on the NCUT, GPDS, and NCUT+GPDS database, respectively. The experimental results show that the HBD method can achieve comparable accuracy to the state-of-the-arts. In NCUT database, when the ratio of training and test set is 7:3, the Equal Error Rate (EER) of the test set is 0.08%, which is an order of magnitude lower than other algorithms. More importantly, due to the adoption of a simpler network structure and hash coding, HBD operates more efficiently and has superior performance gains over other deep learning methods while ensuring the accuracy.

Keywords: Biometrics · Hand dorsal vein recognition · Deep hash network

1 Introduction

As one of the most convenient and safest identification technologies at present, biometric identification has received more and more attention from the academic community and industry [1–3]. Recently, as a new emerging biometric trait for identity authentication, the hand dorsal vein has been proved to possess considerable potential and practical significance, whether as a primary or auxiliary means of identification [4]. The characteristics of hand dorsal vein are considered to be unique and comparable to the retina. Compared with other popular biometric traits, hand dorsal vein recognition as a unique non-invasive biometric authentication has four characteristics: high security, easy-to-use, rapid identification, and highly accurate [5].

© Springer Nature Switzerland AG 2018
J.-H. Lai et al. (Eds.): PRCV 2018, LNCS 11256, pp. 26–37, 2018.
https://doi.org/10.1007/978-3-030-03398-9_3

The traditional hand dorsal vein recognition is mainly based on the characteristics of the veins, such as the width and direction of the vein. The main processes include image acquisition, preprocessing, feature extraction, and feature matching. Firstly, a hand dorsal vein image is collected by a CCD camera under an infrared beam of 700–1000 nm [6]. Then, a series of preprocessing operations such as filtering are performed to obtain a vein pattern. Finally, Scale Invariant Feature Transform (SIFT), Gabor, Support Vector Machine (SVM), hash coding, and other algorithms are used for feature extraction and matching to obtain recognition results. However, traditional methods are easily affected by the type of database and the external environment so as to not be able to obtain the ideal recognition results. In recent years, deep learning has developed rapidly. Because of its powerful identification capabilities, many researchers have applied deep learning networks to biometrics, especially Convolutional Neural Networks (CNN) [7]. Based on neural networks, the CNN is a feedforward neural network designed for image classification and recognition, which has been successfully used in biometrics such as palmprint recognition [8] and face recognition [9]. Here, CNN is used to identify the hand dorsal veins.

In this paper, a method for recognizing Hand dorsal vein Based on Deep hash network (DHN) [10] is proposed, called HBD. DHN is a deep supervised hashing method integrating deep convolutional neural networks and hash coding. Due to its high precision and high efficiency, DHN is mainly used for large-scale graphic search [11, 12]. In [13], DHN has also been used for palmprint recognition with great success, but the proposed method is a non-end-to-end recognition network. However, HBD is an end-to-end recognition network, which inputs an image and outputs a hash code. First, the hand dorsal vein image after preprocessing is input into the simplified Convolutional Neural Networks-Fast (SCNN-F) [14] to obtain the convolution features. SCNN-F is simpler than CNN-Medium and CNN-Slow architectures, so it is more efficient. At the final fully connected layer, a *sgn* function is used to convert the output of each neuron to −1 or 1, so that each image is edited as a K-bit hash code. In theory, the more likely the two images are from the same person, the more similar the features are, and the more similar the hash code is. Hence, by comparing the Hamming distance of the hash code between every image pair, it can be judged whether they belong to the same category. The overview of HBD is shown in Fig. 1.

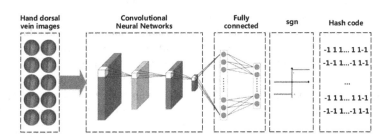

Fig. 1. Overview of our proposed hand dorsal vein identification based on HBD.

The objective of this paper is to further improve the accuracy of hand dorsal vein recognition through deep learning. Experiments are performed on the NCUT (North China University of Technology) [15], GPDS (Digital Signal Processing Group at the University of Las Palmas de Gran Canaria) [16], and NCUT+GPDS databases to evaluate the method. Experimental results show that the performance of HBD can reach the same level as the state-of-the-arts. When the ratio of training and test set is 7:3, the accuracy is higher and the Equal Error Rate (EER) is reduced to 0.08%. The specific contributions of our work are as following:

(a) Based on DHN, we proposed HBD for hand dorsal vein recognition. With proper loss and training strategies, HBD can achieve effective results on NCUT, GPDS, and NCUT+GPDS hand dorsal vein databases collected from different devices.

(b) The SCNN-F is applied to HBD. The structure of SCNN-F is simpler, with only four convolutional layers. When ensuring the accuracy, HBD has lower storage cost and faster query speed than the other methods based on VGG-Net.

The rest of the paper is organized as follows: Sect. 2 mainly introduces the related work. Section 3 presents the HBD method in detail. The detailed experiments and result analysis are presented in Sect. 4. Section 5 concludes the paper.

2 Related Work

Hand dorsal vein recognition is a new type of biometric technology developed in recent years and has received extensive attention. In terms of theoretical research, currently-used methods for identifying the hand dorsal veins include vein image template matching methods and vein character recognition-based methods. Tang et al. [17] used SIFT to realize vein recognition. In order to simplify the complexity of identifying characteristic matrices, Khan et al. [18] used the Principal Component Analysis (PCA) algorithm to ensure that information was not lost. Lajevardi et al. [19] used a novel algorithm called biometric graph matching (BGM), which extracted the global features of vein images and achieved relatively high accuracy in small and concise templates. Li et al. [20] proposed a modification Pyramid Local Binary Pattern (PLBP) by adding feature weighting, which combined multi-scale PLBP with structure information partition. Li et al. [21] built Width Skeleton Model, taking both the topology of the vein network and the width of the vessel into account.

In recent years, with the development of neural network technology, a large number of methods based on deep learning have also appeared in the field of hand dorsal vein recognition. J. Wang and G. Wang [22] imported the regularized Radical Basis Function (RBF) network into the CNN to realize the recognition task. Li et al. [23] investigated deep learning-based methods on hand dorsal vein recognition, and implemented AlexNet, VGG-Net, and GoogLeNet. Wan et al. [24] trained Reference-CaffeNet, AlexNet, and VGG depth CNN to extract vein image features, and the final recognition accuracy was over 99%.

As to DHN, it is mainly used for large-scale graphic search. Peng and Li [11] proposed a learning method of binary hashing based on DHN to accomplish large scale image retrieval. Song and Tan [12] presented a method to generate multi-level hashing codes for image retrieval based on DHN, and verified the effectiveness over several datasets. Using CNN and supervised Hashing, Cheng *et al.* [13] proposed a novel learnable palmprint coding representation and achieved satisfactory accuracy.

3 The Structure of HBD

DHN is an end-to-end framework of deep feature learning and binary hash encoding, combining CNN with hashing algorithm [25]. Based on DHN, HBD is also an end-to-end network for hand dorsal vein recognition. In HBD, first, every hand dorsal vein image is input into the neural network. After convolution and pooling operating, the convolution features are extracted and output at the last fully connected layer. Then the output of each neuron at output layer is converted to a code by a certain method. Ultimately, each hand dorsal vein image is converted into a K-bit hash code. The images from the same person are similar in hash codes and the distance between them is short; while the codes from dissimilar people have a big difference. The focus of HBD method is to set the structure of CNN and loss function reasonably.

3.1 The Structure of CNN

For the proposed HBD, the neural network structure has a great influence on the final recognition results. In fact, the efficiency of deep learning has always been a key factor restricting its wider application. For the same sample data, the complex network structure can obtain higher accuracy, but at the same time it will cause a lot of operational burden. In this paper, the Convolutional Neural Networks-Fast (CNN-F) is used as a neural network to obtain convolutional features. CNN-F is simpler than other popular network structures such as VGG-Net, and has been successfully used for palmprint recognition [13]. Due to the limited sample data size, the CNN-F network is simplified to avoid overfitting. The SCNN-F is shown in Table 1. SCNN-F consists of four layers of convolutions and three layers of full connectivity. The last layer has 128 neurons. The activation functions in the first few layers are Rectified Linear Unit (ReLU). In order to achieve coding, *tanh* function is used as activation function in the last full-connection layer, which ensures the output of neuron is limited to between -1 and 1. Then by using *sgn* function, the output value is set to -1 or 1. Therefore, every image can be ultimately encoded as a 128-bit hash code.

Table 1. Structures of simplified CNN-F and original CNN-F.

	Simplified CNN-F (SCNN-F)	Original CNN-F (OCNN-F)
Conv1	$9 \times 9 \times 32$, stride 4, ReLU, pad 0	$11 \times 11 \times 64$, stride 4, ReLU, pad 0
Pool1	2×2, Max, stride 1	2×2, Max, stride 1
Conv2	$5 \times 5 \times 128$, stride 1, ReLU, pad 2	$5 \times 5 \times 256$, stride 1, ReLU, pad 2
Pool2	2×2, Max, stride 1	2×2, Max, stride 1
Conv3	$3 \times 3 \times 128$, stride 1, ReLU, pad 1	$3 \times 3 \times 256$, stride 1, ReLU, pad 1
Conv4	$3 \times 3 \times 128$, stride 1, ReLU, pad 1	$3 \times 3 \times 256$, stride 1, ReLU, pad 1
Conv5	—	$3 \times 3 \times 256$, stride 1, ReLU, pad 1
Pool3	2×2, Max, stride 1	2×2, Max, stride 1
Full6/Full7/Full8	2048/2048/128tanh	4096/4096/1000softmax

3.2   Definition of Loss Function

In neural networks, the effects and optimization goals of the model are defined by the loss function. On the one hand, in DHN, quantization errors are inevitably generated when *sgn* function is used for encoding. It is necessary to consider the quantization loss in the loss function. The form of quantization loss can be defined as Eq. (1) [26].

$$L_d = \sum_{i=1}^{N} \frac{1}{2} (\|\,|h_i| - 1\,\|_2) \tag{1}$$

Where h_i is the encoding result of image g_i, $|\bullet|$ denotes absolute value operation, 1 is a vector of all ones, and $\|\bullet\|$ denotes $L_d - norm$ of vector.

On the other hand, the goal of optimization is that the codes of hand dorsal vein images from the same category are as similar as possible, while those from different classes are far away. Based on this goal, another loss, hash loss, is defined. Referring to the method in [26], for two images, g_i and g_j, the corresponding hash codes are h_i and h_j, and the hash loss between them is defined as Eq. (2).

$$L_h(h_i, h_j, r_{ij}) = \frac{1}{2} r_{ij} D_h(h_i, h_j) + \frac{1}{2} (1 - r_{ij}) max(T - D_h(h_i, h_j), 0) \tag{2}$$

Where $D_h(h_i, h_j)$ indicates the distance between h_i and h_j, and r_{ij} denotes the correlation between image g_i and g_j. If two images come from the same class, they will have a strong correlation, so $r_{ij} = 1$, otherwise $r_{ij} = 0$. Eq. (2) can be divided into two parts. The former assures that the distance between images of the same type is as small as possible, and the latter assures that the distance between dissimilarities is as large as possible [27]. In order to balance the two-part loss, a threshold T is set to limit the distance between two images. When $D_h(h_i, h_j) > T$, it means that the two images come from different categories, and the loss can be ignored directly. In training, assuming there are a total of N images, the total hash loss is:

$$L_h = \sum_{i=1}^{N-1} \sum_{j=i+1}^{N} L_h(h_i, h_j, r_{ij}) \tag{3}$$

Therefore, the total loss function contains two parts, quantization loss and hash loss. Two parts of the loss are combined by a weight W, as shown in Eq. (4).

$$L = wL_d + L_h \tag{4}$$

4   Experiments and Results

In order to evaluate the performance of HBD algorithm, we conducted experiments in the NCUT [15] and GPDS [16] hand dorsal vein databases. The NCUT is established by the North China University of Technology, and GPDS database is collected by GPDS group from University of Las Palmas de Gran Canaria, Spain.

4.1 Databases and Preprocessing

- **NCUT database** contains three sections, part A, B, and C. Most widely used by researchers, part A contains hand dorsal vein images from 102 individuals, including 50 males and 52 females. Each of them was collected 10 pictures from the right and left hands, respectively. The image in NCUT is a Near-Infrared (NIR) image of 640 × 480 pixels, which contains a complete back of the hand.
- **GPDS database** has 1030 hand dorsal vein images collected from 103 people. During the acquisition process, the hand was illuminated by two arrays of 64 LEDs with a wavelength around 850 nm. A cylindrical handle with two pegs for positional reference was used to fix the hand so that the rotation angle was not too big. By a CCD camera with an attached Infrared Radiation (IR) filter, a 1600 × 1200 pixel 8-bit greyscale image of the hand dorsum was acquired [16].

Due to the influence of hand placement angle and noise during acquisition, preprocessing was first performed, mainly including noise reduction and region of interest (ROI) extraction. In this study, the mean and median filters were used to perform noise reduction, and then the maximum inscribed circle of hand region was extracted as the ROI. In the end, each image was uniformly set to 128 × 128 and input into the neural network. As shown in Fig. 2.

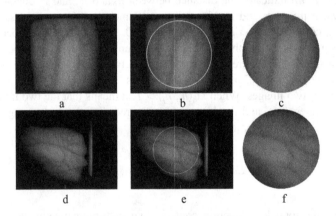

Fig. 2. Original image (a), ROI region (b), and extracted ROI (c) in NCUT database; original image (d), ROI region (e), and extracted ROI (f) in GPDS database.

4.2 Experiments and Result Analysis

In the experiments, data samples were divided into two parts: training set (G) and test set (P). The training and test sample size had a great influence on the experiments. Here, the ratio of the number of training and test sets was set to 5:5 and 7:3. In addition, the databases were combined into three forms, including NCUT, GPDS, and NCUT +GPDS, which contain 204, 103, and 307 categories, respectively. During training, the exponential decay learning rate was used, the parameter T was set to 180, and the weight w was set to 0.5. The pre-processed hand dorsal vein image was input into the network described in Chapter 3. After many iterations, the network parameters can be trained to the best.

During testing, each image in the test set was matched with the image of the same class in the training set as a genuine match and with the image of different class as an imposter match. Therefore, for NCUT database, a total of 5100 ($5 \times 5 \times 204$) genuine matches and 1035300 ($5 \times 203 \times 5 \times 204$) imposter matches were generated when G: P = 5:5, and 4284 ($3 \times 7 \times 204$) genuine matches and 869652 ($3 \times 203 \times 7 \times 204$) imposter matches when 7:3. For the GPDS database, there are a total of 2575 ($5 \times 5 \times 103$) genuine matches and 262650 ($5 \times 102 \times 5 \times 103$) imposter matches when 5:5, and 2163 ($3 \times 7 \times 103$) genuine matches and 220626 ($3 \times 102 \times 7 \times 103$) imposter matches when 7:3. And for NCUT+GPDS database, a total of 7675 ($5 \times 5 \times 307$) genuine matches and 2348550 ($5 \times 306 \times 5 \times 307$) imposter matches were generated when 5:5, and 6447 ($3 \times 7 \times 307$) genuine matches and 1972782 ($3 \times 306 \times 7 \times 307$) imposter matches when 7:3. The settings of test set are shown in Table 2.

Table 2. Settings of test set on different databases.

Database	G:P	Genuine matches	Imposter matches
NCUT	5:5	5100	1035300
NCUT	7:3	4284	869652
GPDS	5:5	2575	262650
GPDS	7:3	2163	220626
NCUT+GPDS	5:5	7675	2348550
NCUT+GPDS	7:3	6447	1972782

After obtaining the encoded data sets, Hamming distance between the genuine and imposter match was calculated respectively. By setting a threshold, they could be distinguished and the identification was completed. Then, combining the prior knowledge, we tested whether the output results were correct. Finally, the Receiver Operating Characteristics (ROCs) of the test sets were drawn, as shown in Fig. 3. The results of HBD algorithm on different databases are as shown in Table 3. The EERs of the test sets were 0.50% and 0.08% in NCUT, 1.11% and 0.43% in GPDS, and 1.20% and 0.60% in NCUT+GPDS, which proved that the HBD algorithm obtained satisfactory accuracy in the hand dorsal vein recognition. In NCUT, when G:P = 7:3, the accuracy rate reached the highest, and the EER dropped to almost 0. In addition, it can be seen that the accuracy of the GPDS is lower than that of the NCUT. This is because the number of samples in the GPDS is limited and the quality of image is low. At the same time, the performance is also better in the NCUT+GPDS, indicating that HBD can excellently identify the images captured in different devices.

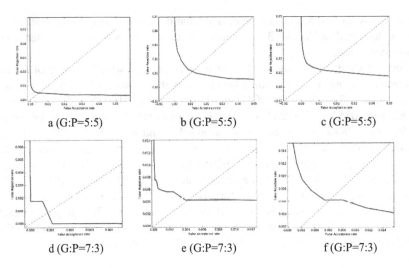

Fig. 3. ROCs of the test set in different databases. a and d in NCUT; b and e in GPDS; c and f in NCUT+GPDS.

Table 3. Results of HBD algorithm on different databases.

Database	Categories	G:P	Recognition rate
NCUT	204	5:5	99.50%
NCUT	204	7:3	99.92%
GPDS	103	5:5	98.89%
GPDS	103	7:3	99.57%
NCUT+GPDS	307	5:5	98.80%
NCUT+GPDS	307	7:3	99.40%

Comparing with the State-of-the-Art Methods. For comparison, we used traditional methods, Iterative Closest Point (ICP) and BGM algorithms, to conduct comparative tests on NCUT database. After the preprocessing of filtering, vein segmentation, refinement, and vein structure extraction, feature vectors were obtained by using ICP and BGM algorithms, respectively. Based on the feature vectors, final recognition was performed by using Kernel Density Estimation (KDE) and SVM. The recognition results are shown in Table 4. Furthermore, we refer to the methods using deep learning to identify hand dorsal veins, which are also performed on NCUT database in recent years, as shown in Table 4.

Table 4. Results of hand dorsal vein recognition on NCUT database in recent years.

Methods	G:P	Recognition rate
ICP	7:3	90.00%
BGM	7:3	80.00%
BC+Graph [28]	5:5	97.82%
Multi-source Keypoint+SIFT [29]	5:5	99.31%
WSM [21]	5:5	99.31%
VGG-16 [23]	5:5	99.31%
VGG-16 [24]	5:5	99.61%
VGG-19 [24]	5:5	99.70%
HBD (ours)	5:5	**99.50%**
HBD (ours)	7:3	**99.92%**

Compared with the non-deep learning methods, HBD can obtain better recognition results, which reflects the high reliability of deep learning for biometric identification. Compared with other deep learning methods, HBD can get comparable accuracy. When G:P = 7:3, the recognition rate is much higher than them. However, the models proposed in [23] and [24], such as VGG-16 and VGG-19, are so complex that the requirements for training time and hardware platform are particularly stringent. The structure of HBD we proposed is relatively simple, with only four convolution layers. Under the same level of accuracy, the operating conditions are much lower. At the same time, the use of hash coding further speeds up the operation and improves the recognition efficiency.

5   Conclusion

This paper applies DHN to the recognition of hand dorsal vein and proposes HBD method. After preprocessing, the hand dorsal vein image is input into SCNN-F. Then the *sgn* function is used to encode the output of the last network layer as −1 or +1. Finally, each image is encoded as a 128-bit code. By comparing the distances between hash codes, it can be judged whether they belong to the same class, so as to complete the identification. The advantage of hash coding is that by calculating the distance between codes, the similarity of two images can be easily obtained. Experiments on NCUT, GPDS, and NCUT+GPDS databases were performed to evaluate the proposed method. In order to make comparisons, traditional identification algorithms, ICP and BGM, were used for comparison tests on NCUT database. The experimental results show that the proposed algorithm can achieve higher accuracy compared with traditional non-deep learning methods. Besides, compared with other deep learning methods performed on NCUT database in recently years, our method can obtain the same level of accuracy and reduce the EER by an order of magnitude when G:P = 7:3. More importantly, since the structure of HBD is much simpler than the others such as VGG-Net, it can operate faster and efficiently while maintaining the same accuracy.

References

1. Meraoumia, A., Chitroub, S., Bouridane, A.: Robust human identity identification system by using hand biometric traits. In: 26th International Conference on Microelectronics (ICM), pp. 17–20. IEEE, Doha (2014)
2. Miura, N., Nagasaka, A., Miyatake, T.: Feature extraction of finger vein patterns based on iterative line tracking and its application to personal identification. Syst. Comput. Jpn. (USA) **35**(7), 61–71 (2004)
3. Zhong, D., Du, X., Zhong, K.: Decade progress of palmprint recognition: a brief survey. Neurocomputing (2018). https://doi.org/10.1016/j.neucom.2018.03.081
4. Wang, Y., Xie, W., Yu, X., Shark, L.-K.: An automatic physical access control system based on hand vein biometric Identification. IEEE Trans. Consum. Electron. **61**(3), 320–327 (2015)
5. Wang, J., Wang, G.Q.: Quality-specific hand vein recognition system. IEEE Trans. Inf. Forensics Secur. **12**(11), 2599–2610 (2017)
6. Sang-Kyun, I., Hyung-Man, P., Soo-Won, K., Chang-Kyung, C., Hwan-Soo, C.: Improved vein pattern extracting algorithm and its implementation. In: 2000 IEEE International Conference on Consumer Electronics (ICCE), pp. 2–3. IEEE, Los Angeles (2000)
7. Ahmad Radzi, S., Khalil-Hani, M., Bakhteri, R.: Finger-vein biometric identification using convolutional neural network. Turk. J. Electr. Eng. Comput. Sci. **24**(3), 1863–1878 (2016)
8. Yang, A., Zhang, J., Sun, Q., Zhang, Q.: Palmprint recognition based on CNN and local coding features. In: 2017 6th International Conference on Computer Science and Network Technology (ICCSNT), pp. 482–487. IEEE, Dalian (2017)
9. Bong, K., Choi, S., Kim, C., Yoo, H.-J.: Low-Power convolutional neural network processor for a face-recognition system. IEEE Micro **37**(6), 30–38 (2017)
10. Venkateswara, H., Eusebio, J., Chakraborty, S., Panchanathan, S.: Deep hashing network for unsupervised domain adaptation. In: 30th IEEE Conference on Computer Vision and Pattern Recognition, pp. 5385–5394. IEEE, Honolulu (2017)
11. Peng, T., Li, F.: Image retrieval based on deep convolutional neural networks and binary hashing learning. In: IEEE International Conference on Acoustics, Speech, and Signal Processing (ICASSP), pp. 1742–1746. IEEE, New Orleans (2017)
12. Song, G., Tan, X.Y.: Hierarchical deep hashing for image retrieval. Front. Comput. Sci. **11**(2), 253–265 (2017)
13. Jingdong, C., Qiule, S., Jianxin, Z., Qiang, Z.: Supervised hashing with deep convolutional features for palmprint recognition. In: Biometric Recognition. 12th Chinese Conference, CCBR 2017, pp. 259–268. Springer, Shenzhen (2017)
14. Chatfield, K., Simonyan, K., Vedaldi, A., Zisserman, A.: Return of the devil in the details: delving deep into convolutional nets. Comput. Sci. 1–6 (2014)
15. Wang, Y.D., Zhang, K., Shark, L.K.: Personal identification based on multiple keypoint sets of dorsal hand vein images. IET Biom. **3**(4), 234–245 (2014)
16. Ferrer, M.A., Morales, A., Ortega, L.: Infrared hand dorsum images for identification. Electron. Lett. **45**(6), 306–307 (2009)
17. Tang, Y.H., Huang, D., Wang, Y.H.: Hand-dorsa vein recognition based on multi-level keypoint detection and local feature matching. In: 21st International Conference on Pattern Recognition (ICPR), pp. 2837–2840. IEEE, University of Tsukuba, Tsukuba (2012)
18. Khan, M.H.-M., Subramanian, R.K., Khan, N.A.M.: Representation of hand dorsal vein features using a low dimensional representation integrating Cholesky decomposition. In: 2009 2nd International Congress on Image and Signal Processing, pp. 1–6. IEEE, Tianjin (2009)

19. Lajevardi, S.M., Arakala, A., Davis, S., Horadam, K.J.: Hand vein authentication using biometric graph matching. IET Biometrics **3**(4), 302–313 (2014)
20. Li, K., Zhang, G., Wang, Y., Wang, P., Ni, C.: Hand-dorsa vein recognition based on improved partition local binary patterns. Biometric Recognition. LNCS, vol. 9428, pp. 312–320. Springer, Cham (2015). https://doi.org/10.1007/978-3-319-25417-3_37
21. Li, X., Huang, D., Zhang, R., Wang, Y., Xie, X.: Hand dorsal vein recognition by matching Width skeleton models. In: 23rd IEEE International Conference on Image Processing (ICIP), pp. 3146–3150. IEEE, Phoenix (2016)
22. Wang, J., Wang, G.Q.: Hand-dorsa vein recognition with structure growing guided CNN. Optik **149**, 469–477 (2017)
23. Li, X., Huang, D., Wang, Y.: Comparative study of deep learning methods on dorsal hand vein recognition. In: You, Z., et al. (eds.) CCBR 2016. LNCS, vol. 9967, pp. 296–306. Springer, Cham (2016). https://doi.org/10.1007/978-3-319-46654-5_33
24. Wan, H.P., Chen, L., Song, H., Yang, J.: Dorsal hand vein recognition based on convolutional neural networks. In: IEEE International Conference on Bioinformatics and Biomedicine (IEEE BIBM), pp. 1215–1221. IEEE, Kansas City (2017)
25. Cao, Z.J., Long, M.S., Wang, J.M., Yu, P.S.: HashNet: deep learning to hash by continuation. In: 16th IEEE International Conference on Computer Vision (ICCV), pp. 5609–5618. IEEE, Venice (2017)
26. Liu, H.M., Wang, R.P., Shan, S.G., Chen, X.L.: Deep supervised hashing for fast image retrieval. In: 2016 IEEE Conference on Computer Vision and Pattern Recognition (CVPR), pp. 2064–2072. IEEE, Seattle (2016)
27. Zhong, D.X., Li, M.H., Shao, H.K., Liu, S.M.: Palmprint and dorsal hand vein dualmodal biometrics. In: 2018 IEEE International Conference on Multimedia and Expo, pp. 1–6. IEEE, San Diego (2018)
28. Zhu, X., Huang, D., Wang, Y.: Hand dorsal vein recognition based on shape representation of the venous network. In: Huet, B., Ngo, C.-W., Tang, J., Zhou, Z.-H., Hauptmann, Alexander G., Yan, S. (eds.) PCM 2013. LNCS, vol. 8294, pp. 158–169. Springer, Cham (2013). https://doi.org/10.1007/978-3-319-03731-8_15
29. Huang, D., Tang, Y.H., Wang, Y.D., Chen, L.M., Wang, Y.H.: Hand-dorsa vein recognition by matching local features of multisource keypoints. IEEE T. Cybern. **45**(9), 1823–1837 (2015)

Palm Vein Recognition with Deep Hashing Network

Dexing Zhong[✉], Shuming Liu, Wenting Wang, and Xuefeng Du

School of Electronic and Information Engineering, Xi'an Jiaotong University,
Xi'an 710049, Shaanxi, People's Republic of China
bell@xjtu.edu.cn

Abstract. Human biometrics has strong potential of robustness, safety and high authentication accuracy. As a new biometric trait, palm vein recognition attracts spacious attention nowadays. To further improve the recognition accuracy, we propose an end-to-end Deep Hashing Palm vein Network (DHPN) in this paper. Modified CNN-F architecture is employed to extract vein features and we use hashing code method to represent the image features with a fixed length binary code. By measuring the Hamming distances of two binary codes of different palm vein images, we can determine whether they belong to the same category. The experimental results show that our network can reach a remarkable EER = 0.0222% in PolyU database. Several comparative experiments are also conducted to discuss the impact of network structure, code bits, training test ratio and databases. The best performance of DHPN can reach EER = 0% with 256-bit code in PolyU database, which is better than the other state-of-art methods.

Keywords: Biometrics · Palm vein recognition · Neural network
Hashing code

1 Introduction

Human biometric recognition has been researched extensively in recent years, due to its great reliability and safety. Many occasions in our daily life require biometric recognition to confirm the individual's identity based on their physiological and behavioral characteristics [1]. As a new biometric technology, palm vein has considerable potential in terms of robustness, uniqueness, and high authentication accuracy. In addition, since the palm veins are only present in the living human body and exist inside the skin, the intruders are difficult to read, copy and forge [2]. Therefore, palm vein recognition has great prospects for human identification.

Nowadays, most traditional methods for palm vein recognition is based on the palm vein skeleton structure. Lajevardi et al. [3] used the Maximum Curvature Algorithm (MCA) to extract the skeleton of veins and performed matching by Biometric Graph Matching (BGM) algorithm. Chen et al. [4] used Gaussian Matched Filter (GMF) to extract the blood vessel and then Iterative Closest Point (ICP) algorithm was exerted on matching. Some other methods also focus on structural features to identify and classify [5–7]. In that these methods mentioned above rely too much on manually designed features, the generalization ability and recognition accuracy is not quite good, which

© Springer Nature Switzerland AG 2018
J.-H. Lai et al. (Eds.): PRCV 2018, LNCS 11256, pp. 38–49, 2018.
https://doi.org/10.1007/978-3-030-03398-9_4

means there are still some difficulties in palm vein recognition for practical applications.

Over the past few years, deep learning, especially Convolutional Neural Network (CNN), attracts more and more researchers' attention due to its powerful learning ability, parallel processing capacity, and strong capability for feature extraction [8], especially on computer vision and multimedia tasks. Recently, CNN with hashing method becomes much more prominent and has successfully been applied in the field of biometrics such as face and palmprint recognition [9]. While, palm vein with hash coding has not been studied yet. Accordingly, in this paper we propose Deep Hashing Palm vein Network (DHPN) based on previous works, which is an end-to-end neural network for palm vein recognition tasks.

In our work, modified CNN-F architecture is employed on DHPN, which can automatically obtain a 128-bit binary code of each palm vein image to conduct matching and recognition. The framework of the proposed DHPN method is illustrated in Fig. 1. First, resized palm vein images are sent into CNN to extract image features. Then through fully connected networks, a fixed-length palm vein code is obtained by using *tanh* function and *sgn* function. In neural network, the loss function is designed to generate similar codes for the image samples of the same person, while the codes of different person vary significantly. In matching part, Hamming distance of fixed-length codes of different pictures is calculated as their similarity. If the distance is smaller than the threshold, we can give a conclusion that these images are from the same person. Our experiment results show that DHPN can reach a remarkable EER of 0.0222% in PolyU database with 128-bit and 50% training test rate. Several comparative experiments are also conducted to discuss the leverage of network structure, code bits, training test ratio and databases. The best performance of DHPN can reach the lowest EER = 0% with 256-bit and 50% training test rate, which is better than the other state-of-art methods.

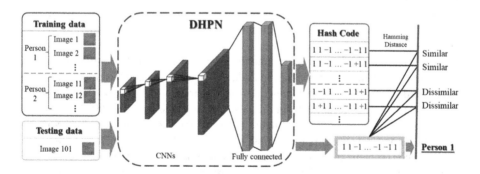

Fig. 1. The framework of the proposed DHPN method

The contributions of this paper can be summarized as follows.

1. To our best knowledge, we firstly use end-to-end CNN with hashing code method in the palm vein recognition successfully.

2. The proposed DHPN can extract the image features using a fixed-length binary code and the identification result can reach a lower EER than the other state-of-art algorithms.
3. Abundant comparative experiments are conducted in palm vein recognition to validate the comprehensive performance of our DHPN method.

The paper consists of 5 sections. Section 2 introduces the related works of palm vein recognition. Section 3 mainly describes the proposed DHPN, including hashing code method, network structure and the definition of the loss function. Many detailed comparative experiment results are presented in Sect. 4. Section 5 gives the conclusion.

2 Related Work

As a promising new biometrics, palm vein recognition gained comprehensive research interests in a recent decade. To get a high recognition performance, feature extraction is one of the most crucial processes. Traditional algorithms of palm vein recognition used physical patterns including minutiae points, ridges and texture to extract features for matching. For instance, multi-spectral adaptive method [10], 3D ultrasound method [11] and adaptive contrast enhancement method [12] are applied for improving image quality. Ma et al. [13] proposed a palm vein recognition scheme based on an adaptive 2D Gabor filter to optimize parameter selection. Yazdani et al. [14] presented a new method based on the estimate of wavelet coefficient with autoregressive model to extract texture feature for verification. Some novel methods were also presented to overcome the drawbacks, including image rotation, shadows, obscure and deformation [15, 16]. However, as the database grows larger, traditional techniques of palm vein recognition are prone to have higher time complexity, which has an adverse effect on the practical applications.

Recently, deep learning, as one of the most promising technologies, overturned traditional cognition and has also been introduced into the field of palm vein recognition. Fronitasari et al. [17] presented a palm vein extraction method which is a modified version of the Local Binary Pattern (LBP) and combined it with Probabilistic Neural Network (PNN) for matching. In addition, supervised deep hashing technology has attracted more attention on large-scale image retrieval due to its higher accuracy, stability and less time complexity in the last several years. Lu et al. [18] proposed a new Deep Hashing approach for scalable image search by a deep neural network to exploit linear and non-linear relationships. Liu et al. [19] proposed a Deep Supervised Hashing (DSH) scheme for fast image retrieval combined with a CNN architecture. The superior performance of deep hashing approaches for image retrieval inspires researchers to enlarge the applications of deep hashing from image searching to biometrics.

3   The Proposed DHPN Method

In computer vision, convolutional neural network is one of the most effective tools as deep learning has developed rapidly in recent years. However, with the expansion of Internet, the amount of image data has boosted significantly. In order to settle the issue of the storage space and retrieval time for pictures, hashing, as the representative method of nearest neighbor search, has received extensive attention and hash coding has been successfully applied to convolutional neural networks [20–22]. However, in biometrics, especially in palm vein recognition, CNN with hashing coding method has not been reported yet.

Thus, we propose a Deep Hashing Palm vein Network (DHPN), which can automatically obtain the codes of palm vein images to achieve matching. Being different from the prior image coding method [9], DHPN is an end-to-end network, which reduces artificial-designed features and can encode palm vein images directly.

3.1   Hashing Code Method

The intention of the hashing algorithm is to represent the sample as a fixed-length binary code, such as 0/1 or −1/1, so that the original information-rich sample is compressed into a short code string and thus, similar samples have similar codes and vice versa. For example, the Hamming distance of the hashing codes of two similar samples should be as small as possible, while the distance of dissimilar samples should be quite large. By measuring the difference between two hash codes of two images, it can be judged whether they belong to the same category. In practice, the speed of calculation can be increased by XOR operations.

Traditional hashing methods require manually designed features to further obtain binary encoding. In deep learning, the convolutional neural network can effectively extract the representative features of the image. Therefore, just inputting the palm vein image to the training network and quantizing the network output, we can directly obtain the binary code of the corresponding image. This end-to-end training method eliminates manual design steps, reduces feature extraction time, and significantly improves the accuracy of palm vein recognition.

3.2   Structure of DHPN

To find the most suitable neural network for palm vein recognition, we attempted the network structure in two different ways. As we known, fine-tuning trick can be used to obtain image features for small dataset tasks to learn binary encoding [23]. Firstly, we employed the first 5 layers of pre-trained VGG-16 [24] on the Image-Net dataset as the convolution feature. Hence, we inserted 3 fully connected layers and adjusted the fully connected parameters when training. The last layer is comprised of 128 neurons. To obtain a binary code, *tanh* is selected as the output layer activation function, which can output the value between −1 and 1. Then we used the sign function *sgn* to quantify the continuous 128-bit code to get a discrete binary code as formula (1).

$$sgn(x) = \begin{cases} -1, x < 0 \\ 1, x \geq 0 \end{cases} \tag{1}$$

However, in actual experiments, we find that due to too many network parameters of VGG-16, there is often an overfitting phenomenon in the palm vein test set with the inferior matching accuracy and long training time. Therefore, considering above drawbacks and small-data character for palm vein recognition, we chose a lighter-weight network as CNN-F.

The structure of CNN-F similar to AlexNet consists of 5 convolution layers and 3 fully connected layers [25]. To achieve higher accuracy and better coding performance in palm vein identification, we proposed DHPN based on the CNN-F structure. The detailed configuration is shown in Table 1. The parameters indicate the convolution stride ("st."), spatial padding ("pad"), Local Response Normalization (LRN), Batch Normalization (BN) and the max-pooling down sampling factor ("pool").

Table 1. The detailed configuration of DHPN.

Layer	CNN-F	DHPN (Modified CNN-F)
conv1	$64 \times 11 \times 11$, st.4, pad 0, LRN, $\times 2$ pool	$16 \times 3 \times 3$, st.4, pad 0, BN, $\times 2$ pool
conv2	$256 \times 5 \times 5$, st.1, pad 2, LRN, $\times 2$ pool	$32 \times 5 \times 5$, st.1, pad 2, BN, $\times 2$ pool
conv3	$256 \times 3 \times 3$, st.1, pad 1, -	$64 \times 3 \times 3$, st.1, pad 1
conv4	$256 \times 3 \times 3$, st.1, pad 1, -	–
conv5	$256 \times 3 \times 3$, st.1, pad 1, $\times 2$ pool	$128 \times 3 \times 3$, st.1, pad 1, $\times 2$ pool
full6	4096 dropout	2048 dropout
full7	4096 dropout	2048 dropout
full8	1000 softmax	128 *tanh* and *sgn*

3.3 Loss Function

It is important to design an appropriate loss function for DHPN. The literature [26] points out that controlling the quantization error and cross-entropy loss can effectively promote the network performance. Hence, the presented loss function for palm vein recognition task is based on two components, hash loss and quantization loss.

Hash Loss. In order to achieve the experimental outcome that similar pictures have similar codes, we designed a hash loss based on the pairwise similarity. Define pairwise similarity matrix as $P^{N \times N}$ and P_{ij} represents the relevance of the ith and jth pictures. When P_{ij} equals to 1, it means two pictures belong to the same class; otherwise P_{ij} is 0, indicating that the two pictures belong to different classes. So the hashing loss of the two pictures can be expressed as follows.

$$J\left(U_i, U_j, P_{ij}\right) = \frac{1}{2}P_{ij}D_h\left(U_i, U_j\right) + \frac{1}{2}\left(1 - P_{ij}\right)\max\left(M - D_h\left(U_i, U_j\right), 0\right) \qquad (2)$$

U_i and U_j denote the DHPN output of the ith image and the jth image respectively. $D_h(U_i, U_j)$ represents the Hamming distance of two encoded outputs. In formula (2), M is the distance threshold, that is, when ith image and the jth image are not from the same category and $D_h(U_i, U_j)$ is greater than M, the Hamming distance between two images reaches quite big and no further expansion is needed. In the experiment, M is set to 180.

If the training set size of vein images is N, the total hash loss can be declared as

$$J_H = \sum_{i=1}^{N} \sum_{j=1}^{N} J\left(U_i, U_j, P_{ij}\right) \qquad (3)$$

Quantization Loss. In the output of the neural network, if the last layer's output is randomly distributed, through *tanh* and *sgn* function for binarization, it will inevitably lead to large quantization error [26]. In order to reduce the quantization error, we define the following quantization loss J_Q, making each output closer to 1 or -1.

$$J_Q = \sum_{i=1}^{N} \frac{1}{2}\left(\|1 - |U_i|\|_2\right) \qquad (4)$$

Where $|U_i|$ denotes the absolute value of U_i and $\|\cdot\|_2$ stands for L2-norm of vector.

Thus, we can obtain the following optimization formula, where α indicates the scale factor.

$$\min J = \alpha J_H + J_Q \qquad (5)$$

4 Experiments and Results

In this section, we briefly introduce the palm vein databases and relevant comparison experiments. The databases include the Hong Kong Polytechnic University (PolyU) public palm vein database and our self-built database as Xi'an Jiaotong University (XJTU) palm vein database. In comparative experiment, we also adjusted the network structures, training ratios, code bits and different databases to discuss how these variables affect the performance of DHPN.

4.1 Experimental Database and Setting

At present, the PolyU palm vein database is a representative database for palm vein recognition [27], which consists of 6000 near-infrared palm vein images with 128×128 pixel from 500 individuals. In the PolyU database, the palm vein images of each hand are collected in two different time periods, each time they collected 6 images and 12 palm vein images per person in total. The samples are shown in Fig. 2.

Fig. 2. Typical palm vein ROI images of three people in PolyU database

In the experiment, we used the DHPN structure mentioned in Sect. 3.2 with exponential decaying learning rate. The parameter M was set to 180 and the balance factor α was set to 2. During the training, we chose training ratio to be 50%, which means 3000 images were used as the training set and the other 3000 images were used as the testing set. By optimizing the loss function J, we obtained the network parameters after training 8000 steps. Then, by inputting all 6000 original palm images into DHPN, we can get their 128-bit binary codes. Finally, the Hamming distance of binary codes between the genuine matches and imposter matches is calculated and a similarity threshold is then being given for judging the recognition result. By changing the threshold, we can get the Receiver Operator Characteristic (ROC) Curve shown in Fig. 3. As we can see, the EER = 0.0222%.

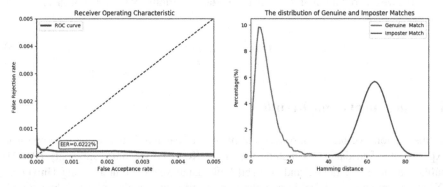

Fig. 3. ROC curve and distribution of genuine and imposter matches (Color figure online)

In PolyU dataset, we used the test images to match all the training pictures. By 50% training test ratio, genuine matches are total 18000 groups and imposter matches are 8,982,000 groups. The distribution of Hamming distances of all matches is shown in Fig. 3. Red curve and blue curve represent the distribution of genuine matches and imposter matches respectively. As what can be seen from the figure, genuine matches and imposter matches can be clearly distinguished by a reasonable threshold.

4.2   Experimental Results

Comparison of Network Structure. In Sect. 3.2, we have explained that the network structure has a great impact on the accuracy of matching. In this section, we tried three different network structures on PolyU database respectively, and evaluated their performance by measuring EER as shown in Table 2.

Table 2. Comparison of different networks

Network structure	EER
VGG-16 (fine-tuning)	1.3999%
CNN-F	2.6731%
CNN-F modified (Ours, 128 bit, 6:6,)	0.0222%

The results show that the pre-trained VGG-16 with fine-tuning trick cannot achieve good accuracy, which does not demonstrate the advantage of deep learning. Then we experimented the matching with the original CNN-F network and modified CNN-F network called DHPN, and results prove that our DHPN perform outstandingly on PolyU database. It can be seen that our proposed DHPN network achieves the lowest EER in different networks.

Training Ratio and Code Bits. Next, we naturally considered that the number of encoding bits and training ratio would also affect the accuracy of the DHPN. Because each people in PolyU database has 12 images, the training test ratios are set to 3:9, 6:6, 9:3, respectively. The comparative experiment results of different training ratio and code bits are shown in Table 3.

From Table 3, we can observe that the larger training test ratio, the lower the EER, and the best performance of EER can reach 0% in 128 bits. Due to supervised learning of DHPN, the network can learn image features better with larger training dataset, which explains the greater training test ratios have lower EER. At the same time, as the number of encoding bits grow bigger, the more image information will be learned, leading to the lower EER simultaneously.

Table 3. Comparison of different training ratio and code bits

Code bits	3:9	6:6	9:3
256 bits	0.04444%	0%	0%
128 bits	1.9259%	0.0222%	0%
64 bits	2.3860%	0.3132%	0.1582%

Experiment on Different Databases. Because of the representative of the PolyU database and the convenience of comparison, the previous experiments were all conducted on PolyU. In order to measure the generalization performance, we also test the proposed DHPN in our database (XJTU), which is our self-built palm vein database containing 600 images of 60 people. The detailed introduction and experiment results of two databases are as follows in Table 4.

Table 4. Comparison of different palm vein database

Database	PolyU	XJTU
Device	CCD camera	CMOS camera
Additional Light Source	An NIR LED round array	6 LEDs
Hand position	Palm close to desktop	Distance between palm and desktop
Brightness	Dark	Natural indoor sunlight
EER of DHPN	0.0222%	1.3333%
Example		

It can be seen from Table 4 that the collection environment of PolyU database is still an ideal laboratory environment and cannot represent the situation in the real world. Therefore, we established our own database to simulate a more practical environment to acquire palm vein images, but also as a cost, leading to a higher EER compared with PolyU database. While the DHPN also performs a good result of EER = 1.333%, which substantiates the effectiveness of our database and the promising generalization power of DHPN in palm vein recognition.

Contrast with the State-of-Art Methods. Finally, for palm vein recognition, we compared our DHPN method with the other state-of-art methods, as shown in Table 5.

Table 5. Comparison of the state-of-art methods on PolyU database

Methods	EER
SIFT [28]	3.6893%
2D Gabor [29]	3.6981%
PCA + LPP [30]	2.1218%
LBP [31]	0.13%
GRT [32]	0.09%
DHPN (Ours, 128-bit)	**0.0222%**
DHPN (Ours, 256-bit)	**0%**

It can be seen that the proposed DHPN method achieves the lowest EER compared to the other state-of-art methods. Therefore, we can conclude that the supervised deep learning structure of DHPN leads to a stronger feature learning ability for palm vein recognition, and its hash feature leads to higher recognition accuracy, which makes palm vein recognition have a good advantage of robustness, security and wider application scenarios. Therefore, DHPN can be considered as a effective and promising palm vein recognition method.

5   Conclusion

For the palm vein recognition task, this paper presents an end-to-end deep hashing palm vein network method named as DHPN. The modified CNN-F architecture was used to extract vein features, and a fixed-length binary hash code was obtained by the neural network output with *sgn* function. By measuring the Hamming distances of two binary codes, we can determine if two input palm vein images are from the same person. The experimental results show that in the PolyU database, our network can reach a significant EER = 0% in best performance. We also did several comparative experiments to discuss the effects of network structure, code bits, training test rates, and databases. In conclusion, DHPN not only has the advantage of strong image feature learning ability, spacious recognition scenario applications and high recognition accuracy, but also this end-to-end deep hashing code method can eliminate manual design steps and reduces feature extraction time. In the future work, we will further study the deep hashing method to improve the accuracy of palm vein recognition, especially on the basis of image retrieval knowledge, and test our algorithm in a larger database.

References

1. Jain, A.K., Ross, A., Prabhakar, S.: An introduction to biometric recognition. IEEE Trans. Circuits Syst. Video Technol. **14**(1), 4–20 (2004)
2. Liu, J., Xue, D.-Y., Cui, J.-J., Jia, X.: Palm-dorsa vein recognition based on kernel principal component analysis and locality preserving projection methods. J. Northeastern Univ. Nat. Sci. (China) **33**, 613–617 (2012)
3. Lajevardi, S.M., Arakala, A., Davis, S., Horadam, K.J.: Hand vein authentication using biometric graph matching. IET Biom. **3**, 302–313 (2014)
4. Chen, H., Lu, G., Wang, R.: A new palm vein matching method based on ICP algorithm. In: Proceedings of the 2nd International Conference on Interaction Sciences: Information Technology, Culture and Human, Seoul, pp. 1207–1211. ACM (2009)
5. Bhattacharyya, D., Das, P., Kim, T.H., Bandyopadhyay, S.K.: Vascular pattern analysis towards pervasive palm vein authentication. J. Univers. Comput. Sci. **15**, 1081–1089 (2009)
6. Xu, X., Yao, P.: Palm vein recognition algorithm based on HOG and improved SVM. Comput. Eng. Appl. (China) **52**, 175–214 (2016)
7. Elsayed, M.A., Hassaballah, M., Abdellatif, M.A.: Palm vein verification using Gabor filter. J. Sig. Inf. Process. **7**, 49–59 (2016)
8. Rawat, W., Wang, Z.H.: Deep convolutional neural networks for image classification: a comprehensive review. Neural Comput. **29**, 2352–2449 (2017)
9. Cheng, J., Sun, Q., Zhang, J., Zhang, Q.: Supervised hashing with deep convolutional features for palmprint recognition. In: Zhou, J., et al. (eds.) CCBR 2017. LNCS, vol. 10568, pp. 259–268. Springer, Cham (2017). https://doi.org/10.1007/978-3-319-69923-3_28

10. Dong, W.G., et al.: Research on multi-spectral adaptive method for palm vein capturing based on image quality. In: 32nd Youth Academic Annual Conference of Chinese Association of Automation, pp. 1154–1157. IEEE, New York (2017)

11. De Santis, M., Agnelli, S., Nardiello, D., Iula, A.: 3D ultrasound palm vein recognition through the centroid method for biometric purposes. In: 2017 IEEE International Ultrasonics Symposium. IEEE, New York (2017)

12. Sun, X., Ma, X., Wang, C., Zu, Z., Zheng, S., Zeng, X.: An adaptive contrast enhancement method for palm vein image. In: Zhou, J., et al. (eds.) CCBR 2017. LNCS, vol. 10568, pp. 240–249. Springer, Cham (2017). https://doi.org/10.1007/978-3-319-69923-3_26

13. Ma, X., Jing, X.J., Huang, H., Cui, Y.H., Mu, J.S.: Palm vein recognition scheme based on an adaptive Gabor filter. IET Biom. 6, 325–333 (2017)

14. Yazdani, F., Andani, M.E.: Verification based on palm vein by estimating wavelet coefficient with autoregressive model. In: 2nd Conference on Swarm Intelligence and Evolutionary Computation, pp. 118–122. IEEE, New York (2017)

15. Noh, Z.M., Ramli, A.R., Hanafi, M., Saripan, M.I., Khmag, A.: Method for correcting palm vein pattern image rotation by middle finger orientation checking. J. Comput. 12, 571–578 (2017)

16. Soh, S.C., Ibrahim, M.Z., Yakno, M.B., Mulvaney, D.J.: Palm vein recognition using scale invariant feature transform with RANSAC mismatching removal. In: Kim, K.J., Kim, H., Baek, N. (eds.) ICITS 2017. LNEE, vol. 449, pp. 202–209. Springer, Singapore (2018). https://doi.org/10.1007/978-981-10-6451-7_25

17. Fronitasari, D., Gunawan, D.: Palm vein recognition by using modified of local binary pattern (LBP) for extraction feature. In: 15th International Conference on Quality in Research, pp. 18–22. IEEE, New York (2017)

18. Lu, J.W., Liong, V.E., Zhou, J.: Deep hashing for scalable image search. IEEE Trans. Image Process. 26, 2352–2367 (2017)

19. Liu, H.M., Wang, R.P., Shan, S.G., Chen, X.L.: Deep supervised hashing for fast image retrieval. In: 2016 IEEE Conference on Computer Vision and Pattern Recognition, pp. 2064–2072. IEEE, New York (2016)

20. Lai, H., Pan, Y., Liu, Y., Yan, S.: Simultaneous feature learning and hash coding with deep neural networks. In: Proceedings of the IEEE Conference on Computer Vision and Pattern Recognition, pp. 3270–3278 (2015)

21. Li, W.J., Wang, S., Kang, W.C.: Feature learning based deep supervised hashing with pairwise labels. In: International Joint Conference on Artificial Intelligence, pp. 1711–1717 (2016)

22. Zhong, D.X., Li, M.H., Shao, H.K., Liu, S.M.: Palmprint and dorsal hand vein dualmodal biometrics. In: 2018 IEEE International Conference on Multimedia and Expo, San Diego, pp. 1–6. IEEE (2018)

23. Lin, K., Huei-Fang, Y., Jen-Hao, H., Chu-Song, C.: Deep learning of binary hash codes for fast image retrieval. In: 2015 IEEE Conference on Computer Vision and Pattern Recognition Workshops (CVPRW), pp. 27–35 (2015)

24. Simonyan, K., Zisserman, A.: Very deep convolutional networks for large-scale image recognition. arXiv preprint arXiv:1409.1556 (2014)

25. Chatfield, K., Simonyan, K., Vedaldi, A., Zisserman, A.: Return of the devil in the details: delving deep into convolutional nets. arXiv preprint arXiv:1405.3531 (2014)

26. Zhu, H., Long, M., Wang, J., Cao, Y.: Deep hashing network for efficient similarity retrieval. In: 13th AAAI Conference on Artificial Intelligence, pp. 2415–2421 (2016)

27. Zhang, D., Guo, Z.H., Lu, G.M., Zhang, L., Zuo, W.M.: An online system of multispectral palmprint verification. IEEE Trans. Instrum. Meas. 59, 480–490 (2010)

28. Ladoux, P.-O., Rosenberger, C., Dorizzi, B.: Palm vein verification system based on SIFT matching. In: Tistarelli, M., Nixon, M.S. (eds.) ICB 2009. LNCS, vol. 5558, pp. 1290–1298. Springer, Heidelberg (2009). https://doi.org/10.1007/978-3-642-01793-3_130
29. Lee, J.C.: A novel biometric system based on palm vein image. Pattern Recogn. Lett. **33**, 1520–1528 (2012)
30. Wang, H.G., Yau, W.Y., Suwandy, A., Sung, E.: Person recognition by fusing palmprint and palm vein images based on "Laplacianpalm" representation. Pattern Recogn. **41**, 1514–1527 (2008)
31. Ojala, T., Pietikainen, M., Maenpaa, T.: Multiresolution gray-scale and rotation invariant texture classification with local binary patterns. IEEE Trans. Pattern Anal. Mach. Intell. **24**, 971–987 (2002)
32. Zhou, Y.J., Liu, Y.Q., Feng, Q.J., Yang, F., Huang, J., Nie, Y.X.: Palm-vein classification based on principal orientation features. PLoS ONE **9**, 12 (2014)

Feature Fusion and Ellipse Segmentation for Person Re-identification

Meibin Qi[ID], Junxian Zeng[✉][ID], Jianguo Jiang[ID], and Cuiqun Chen[ID]

School of Computer and Information, Hefei University of Technology,
Hefei 230009, Anhui, China
qimeibin@163.com, junxian@mail.hfut.edu.cn, jgjiang@hfut.edu.cn,
chencuiqun@163.com

Abstract. Person re-identification refers a task of associating the same person in different camera views. Due to the variance of camera angles, pedestrian posture and lighting conditions, the appearance of the same pedestrian in different surveillance videos might change greatly, which becomes a major challenge for person re-identification. To solve the above problems, this paper proposes a feature fusion and ellipse segmentation algorithm for person re-identification. First of all, in order to reduce the impact of changes in light illumination, an image enhancement algorithm is used to process pedestrian images. Then the ellipse segmentation algorithm is applied to reduce the influence of background clutter in the image. After that, we extract features which contain more abundant information and merge them together. Finally, bilinear similarity metric is combined with Mahalanobis distance as a distance metric function, and the final metric matrix is obtained by using optimization algorithm. Experiments are performed on three public benchmark datasets including VIPeR, PRID450s, CUHK01, and the results clearly show the significant and consistent improvements over the state-of-the-art methods.

Keywords: Person re-identification · Feature fusion
Ellipse segmentation

1 Introduction

Person re-identification matches persons across non-overlapping camera views at different time. It is applied to criminal investigation, pedestrian search, and multi-camera pedestrian tracking, etc. And person re-identification plays a crucial role in the field of video surveillance. Actually, the pedestrian images come from different cameras, and the appearance of pedestrians will change greatly when the lighting, background and visual angle vary. In order to solve the above

Supported by organization National Natural Science Foundation of China Grant 61632007 and Key Research and Development Project of Anhui Province, China 1704d0802183.

J.-H. Lai et al. (Eds.): PRCV 2018, LNCS 11256, pp. 50–61, 2018.
https://doi.org/10.1007/978-3-030-03398-9_5

problems, many of the previous works mainly focus on two aspects: extracting features [11,15,16,19] from images and measuring the similarity [3,11,20] between images. The former is to extract the robust feature to solve the change of the pedestrian appearance. The latter is to make the similarity of different pedestrians smaller and the similarity of the same pedestrian greater.

At present, most features use color and texture information. The SCSP (Spatially Constrained Similarity function on Polynomial feature map) [3] uses color and texture features, and combines global and local features. However, its features are relatively simple, and the information contained is not comprehensive enough. To solve these problems, based on SCSP, this paper adopts more informative LOMO (Local Maximal Occurrence) [11] feature and GOG (Gaussian of Gaussians Descriptor) [15] feature. The LOMO feature contains color and texture information and the GOG feature contains position coordinates and gradient that the LOMO feature does not have. So LOMO and GOG can achieve complementarity, we use the two fused features to replace the global features of SCSP which has better performance than the SCSP. In addition, in order to reduce background noise, this paper proposes ellipse segmentation which has the advantages of effectiveness and simplicity.

Our contributions can be summarized as follows:

(1) We propose an effective feature representation that uses the fusion of LOMO and GOG features as the global feature and then combine the global and local features to form the final feature.
(2) We present a new and simple segmentation method called ellipse segmentation, which can effectively reduce the impact of background interference.
(3) We operate in-depth experiments to analyze various aspects of our approach, and the final results outperform the state-of-the-art over three benchmarks.

The rest of this paper is organized as followed. Section 2 reviews related works. Section 3 describes the details of the proposed method, include: how to extract the feature; the details of the image partition. The experiments and results are in Sect. 4. We finally make a conclusion and discuss possible future works in Sect. 5.

2   Related Works

Currently, person re-identification is mainly divided into two major research directions: deep learning methods [4,9,13,22,26] and traditional methods [2,7, 11,16,19].

Deep Learning Methods. The deep learning model is a data-driven model that learns high-level features by constructing models to discover complex structures and implicit information in large amount of data. In other words, the key point of deep learning technology is how to efficiently learn the high-level semantic expression of features from a large amount of data. In [26], the recognition rate of Rank1 on the small dataset VIPeR is only 45.9% using the deep learning method, while using the traditional method [3] is 53.54%. Therefore, traditional methods perform better on small datasets. In addition, the deep learning method cannot be used in the environment where the computing capacity of device is insufficient.

Traditional Methods. The traditional methods of person re-identification consist of two main steps: feature representation and metric learning.

The purpose of feature representation is to extract robust feature, thus solving pedestrian appearance changes. Liao et al. [11] propose an efficient feature representation called Local Maximal Occurrence (LOMO), which consists of color and SILTP (Scale Invariant Local Ternary Pattern) [12] histograms to represent person appearance. It uses sliding windows to describe local details. In each sub-window, SILTP histogram and HSV histogram are respectively counted, and the maximum probability value is taken as the final histogram value in the same horizontal sliding window. [16] divides the image into 6 non-overlapping horizontal regions and extracts four color features for each region and fuse them with LBP (Local Binary Pattern) texture features. [19] that is improved on the basis of [16] uses non-uniform image segmentation and extracts the feature which is the combination of four color features and SILTP texture features. The GOG (Gaussian of Gaussians Descriptor) feature is proposed in [15], which is based on a hierarchical Gaussian distribution of pixel features. In [11], it focuses on the global features. [15,16,19] divide the image horizontally, which obtain local features. Different from their work, we use the LOMO and GOG features and fuse them together. Furthermore, we use a combination of global and local features, which guarantees the integrity of the information as well as includes more detailed information.

Metric learning is also called similarity learning, which makes the similarity of different types of pictures as small as possible and the same type as large as possible. Most of the metric learning algorithms have the problems of time consuming and high complexity. To solve this problem, the KISSME (Keep It Simple and Straightforward Metric) method [20] learns metric matrix in Mahalanobis distance by considers the problem from the perspective of statistics. Based on KISSME, XQDA (Cross-view Quadratic Discriminant Analysis) [11] learns a discriminate low dimensional subspace by cross-view quadratic discriminate analysis and gets a QDA metric learned on the derived subspace at the same time. In [3], SCSP uses the combination of Mahalanobis distance and a bilinear similarity metric. The Mahalanobis distance compares the similarity of the same location. Bilinear similarity metric can be used to compare the similarity of different locations. This combined metric function is very robust. Therefore, we adopt this metric in this paper.

3   Our Approach

In this section, we describe our method in detail. This paper improves on the basis of SCSP [3], uses the ellipse segmentation and extracts the LOMO and GOG features from the segmented images, then fuses them to replace the global feature in SCSP, then combines the local features proposed in SCSP to form the final feature. In terms of metric learning, when the number of training samples is too small in practical applications, it is easy to overfit. In order to solve this problem, this paper uses the metric function combining the bilinear similarity metric and the Mahalanobis distance, and finally adopts the ADMM (Alternating Direction Method of Multipliers) [3] optimization algorithm to obtain the optimal metric matrix.

3.1   Ellipse Segmentation

Due to the particularity of pedestrian images, most person re-identification datasets are manually cropped using rectangular frames. This leads to the fact that most pedestrian images contain redundant background information. Because pedestrians are generally in the center of the rectangular box, and the four right-angled areas of the rectangular box are basically background information. In order to tackle this problem, this paper proposes a new segmentation method called ellipse segmentation. It can preserve the effective information of pedestrians and reduce the impact of background interference. The specific segmentation method is shown in Fig. 1.

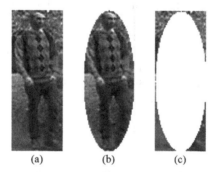

(a)   (b)   (c)

Fig. 1. Ellipse segmentation of image. (a) Original image: contains all the information for the entire image. (b) Ellipse area: retains valid pedestrian information after ellipse splitting and contains a small amount of background information. (c) Background area: contains background information and a small amount of pedestrian information.

3.2   Feature Extraction and Fusion

This paper combines global and local features. At the beginning, we use the image enhancement algorithm [19] to preprocess person images which can reduce the impact of the change of illumination. Then, we fuse the LOMO and GOG features as the global feature. Considering the LOMO feature contains the HSV color and SILTP texture information and the GOG feature contains four colors, position coordinates, gradient and other information, we combine LOMO with GOG to achieve their complementary power, which makes the features more expressive and robust. According to SCSP, we can know that its local features have good complementarity and recognition effects. Therefore, we use its local features in our method.

Extracting LOMO Feature. First, we perform the ellipse segmentation operation on the image and then extract the LOMO feature, and denote it as LOMO(b), as shown in Fig. 2. Like the literature [11], we use a subwindow whose size is 10×10 and overlapping step is 5 pixels to locate local patches in 128×48 images. Within each subwindow, we extract two scales of SILTP histograms, and an $8 \times 8 \times 8$-bin joint HSV histogram. To further consider the multi-scale information, we build a three-scale pyramid representation, which downsamples the original 128×48 image by two 2×2 local average pooling operations, and repeats the above feature extraction procedure. By concatenating all the computed local maximal occurrences, our LOMO(b) has ($8 \times 8 \times 8$ color bins $+ 3^4 \times 2$ SILTP bins) $* (24 + 11 + 5$ horizontal groups) $= 26960$ dimensions.

The elliptical region we selected has less background noise and more pedestrian information. However, it cannot completely accurately segment pedestrians. So, it may lost some useful information. The background noise in the elliptical region will correspondingly increase when the pedestrian's posture and camera angle change. Therefore, we also extract the LOMO feature from the original image to supplement the information, denote it as LOMO(a), as well as the improved mean LOMO (LOMO_mean) [6] to reduce the background noise in the elliptical region, which is denoted as LOMO(c). The mean value can increase the anti-interference of noise and improve the robustness, and reduce the randomness that brought by the maximum. Thus, we combine three LOMO features as LOMO(a+b+c).

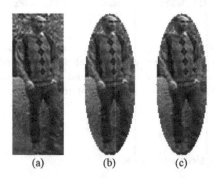

(a)   (b)   (c)

Fig. 2. LOMO feature composition: LOMO(a+b+c). (a) We extract the LOMO(a) feature from the whole picture. (b) We extract the LOMO(b) feature from the elliptical area. (c) We extract the LOMO(c) feature from the elliptical area.

Extracting GOG Feature. According to [15], the dimensionality of GOG descriptor is 27622 = 3 × ((45² + 3 × 45)/2 + 1) × G + 1 × ((36² + 3 × 36)/2 + 1) × G, G represents the number of overlapping horizontal strips we divide the image. We extract the GOG feature from the whole image as GOG(a) to ensure the integrity of the information. Simultaneously, we also extract the GOG feature from the ellipse region as GOG(b). we combine two features as GOG(a+b).

In summary, for the global feature, the dimensions of LOMO(a), LOMO(b) and LOMO(c) are all reduced from 26960 to 300 dimensions by PCA [8]. GOG(a) and GOG(b) features are reduced from 27622 to 300 dimensions, and then the above five features are concatenated to form the global feature. For local features, we also reduce them to 300 dimensions and then concatenate them in series to form local features. In the end, we concatenate global and local features to form the final feature.

4 Experiments

4.1 Datasets and Settings

Datasets. Three widely used datasets are selected for experiments, including VIPeR [7], PRID450s [21] and CUHK01 [10]. Each dataset is separated into the training set and test set. The test set is further divided into probe set and gallery set, and the two sets contains the different images of the same person. Finally, we take the average results of the 10 experiments.

VIPeR. The VIPeR dataset is one of most challenging datasets for person re-identification task that has been widely used for benchmark evaluation. It contains 632 persons. For each person, there are two 48 × 128 images taken from camera A and B under different viewpoints, poses and illumination conditions. We randomly select 316 persons for training, and the rest persons for testing.

PRID450s. The PRID450s dataset captures a total of 450 pedestrian image pairs from two disjoint surveillance cameras. Pedestrian detection rectangular box is manually marked and the original image resolution is 168 × 80 pixels. Each pedestrian contains two images with strong lighting changes. This paper normalizes the image size to 48 × 128. The dataset is randomly divided into two equal parts, one for training and the other for testing.

CUHK01. The CUHK01 dataset is captured by two cameras A and B in a campus environment. Each camera captures two pedestrian images. Namely, each pedestrian has four pedestrian images with a total of 971 pedestrians and 3884 pedestrian images. Camera A captures the front and back of the pedestrian, and camera B captures the side of the pedestrian. In the experiment, the persons are split to 485 for training and 486 for test.

Evaluation Metrics. We match each probe image with every image in gallery set, and rank the gallery images according to the similarity score. The results are evaluated by Cumulated Matching Characteristics (CMC) curves. In order to compare with the published results more easily, we report the cumulated matching result at selected rank-i (i ∈ 1, 5, 10, 20) in following tables.

4.2 Comparison to State-of-the-Art Approaches

Results on VIPeR. The training set and the testing set contain 316 persons respectively. The algorithm of this paper is compared with the existing algorithms on the VIPeR dataset. From the results in Table 1, we can conclude that our algorithm, based on SCSP, has significantly improved the matching rates in comparison with other algorithms. The recognition rate is 9% higher than SCSP on Rank1. At the same time, Rank5, Rank10 and Rank20 have been improved. The Table 1 shows that our method has stronger expression ability and better recognition effect.

Table 1. Matching rates (%) of different methods on VIPeR.

Methods	Rank-1	Rank-5	Rank-10	Rank-20
LOMO+XQDA [11]	40.00	68.13	80.51	91.08
S-SVM [32]	42.66	-	84.27	91.93
literature[19]	42.7	74.5	85.4	92.8
SSDAL [24]	43.50	71.80	81.50	89.00
ME [18]	45.89	77.40	88.87	95.84
Quadruplet+MargOHNM [5]	49.05	73.10	81.96	-
LRP [6]	49.05	74.08	84.43	93.10
Multi-Level Similarity [30]	50.10	73.10	84.35	-
NFST [31]	51.17	82.09	90.51	95.92
SCSP [3]	53.54	82.59	91.49	96.65
Fusion+SSM [1]	53.73	-	91.49	96.08
TLSTP [14]	59.17	73.49	78.62	-
Ours	**62.56**	**87.53**	**93.89**	**97.97**

Results on PRID450s. From the experimental data in Table 2, we can see that the algorithm in the PRID450s dataset has the highest recognition rate over the state-of-the-art methods. The best Rank1 identification rate of comparison methods is 68.47% [15], while we has achieved 73.29%, with an improvement by nearly 5%.

Results on CUHK01. In previous experiments, the VIPeR and PRID450s datasets are based on single image pair, that is single-shot. But such matching results are easily affected by the quality of single image, and the dataset is generally small. In order to fully embody the performance of the algorithm, a larger dataset CUHK01 is used under multi-shot. Table 3 shows the recognition

Table 2. Matching rates (%) of different methods on PRID450s.

Methods	Rank-1	Rank-5	Rank-10	Rank-20
KISSME [20]	33.0	59.8	71.0	79.0
SCNCD [28]	41.6	68.9	79.4	87.8
DRML [29]	56.4	-	82.2	90.2
LSSCDL [32]	60.5	-	88.6	93.6
LOMO+XQDA [11]	62.60	85.60	92.00	96.60
FFN [25]	66.6	86.8	92.8	96.9
GOG [15]	68.47	88.80	94.50	97.80
Fusion+SSM [1]	72.98	-	96.76	99.11
Ours	**73.29**	**91.78**	**95.11**	**97.73**

rates of the proposed algorithm and the existing algorithm on the CUHK01 dataset.

Table 3. Matching rates (%) of different methods on CUHK01.

Methods	Rank-1	Rank-5	Rank-10	Rank-20
PCCA [17]	17.8	42.4	55.9	69.1
KISSME [20]	17.9	38.1	48.0	58.8
kLFDA [27]	29.1	55.2	66.4	77.3
Semantic [23]	31.5	52.5	65.8	77.6
FFN [25]	55.5	78.4	83.7	92.6
Quadruplet+MargOHNM [5]	62.55	83.44	89.71	-
LOMO+XQDA [11]	63.2	-	90.8	94.9
GOG [15]	67.3	86.9	91.8	95.9
NFST [31]	69.09	86.87	91.77	95.39
LRP [6]	70.45	87.92	92.67	96.34
Ours	**76.19**	**92.24**	**95.58**	**98.09**

It can be seen that the algorithm still has significant improvements in the recognition rates in comparison with the existing algorithms on large datasets. Compared with LRP (Local Region Partition) [6], the algorithm of this paper improves about 6% on Rank1. Moreover, our method is 9% higher than the GOG. The improvement of our method is particularly significant on CUHK01.

4.3   Contribution of Major Components

In order to verify the effectiveness of the proposed method, we analyze the algorithm of this paper in detail on the VIPeR dataset. The two sets of Probe and Gallery both have 316 persons.

The Fusion of GOG and LOMO Features. To compare the combination of LOMO and GOG features and the global feature (SCSP-G) [3], Table 4 lists the comparison results of the algorithm in this paper when no segmentation is performed.

Table 4. Matching rates (%) of using LOMO+GOG features and SCSP-G.

Feature	Recognition rate of VIPeR (%)			
	Rank-1	Rank-5	Rank-10	Rank-20
LOMO(a)	40.16	71.33	83.67	92.50
GOG(a)	46.90	78.89	88.61	94.94
SCSP-G [3]	48.10	79.30	89.78	95.76
LOMO(a)+GOG(a)	**53.92**	**83.70**	**92.06**	**96.65**

It can be seen from the experimental data in Table 4. The LOMO(a)+GOG(a) features has a significant improvement over the SCSP-G [3]. In particular, there is an increase of 5.82% in Rank1, which is 13% and 7% higher than the LOMO(a) and GOG(a) features on Rank1 respectively. It shows that LOMO and GOG can complement each other. Therefore, the features selected in this paper contain more complete pedestrian information and have stronger robustness.

Ellipse Segmentation. To verify the validity of the ellipse segmentation, Table 5 lists the recognition results that the algorithm only uses the ellipse-segmented feature and the original feature without local features.

Table 5. Matching rates (%) of original image and ellipse segmentation.

Feature	Recognition rate of VIPeR (%)			
	Rank-1	Rank-5	Rank-10	Rank-20
GOG(a)	46.90	78.89	88.61	94.94
GOG(b)	47.85	77.31	88.01	94.11
GOG(a+b)	**49.46**	**79.94**	**89.78**	**95.00**
LOMO(a)	40.16	71.33	83.67	92.50
LOMO(b)	41.60	73.29	85.38	92.18
LOMO(a+b+c)	**45.60**	**76.52**	**88.01**	**95.03**

From the experimental data in Table 5, it can be seen that the GOG(b) can achieve 47.85% Rank1 matching rate, which outperforms the rate of the GOG(a), and the LOMO(b) increases by nearly 1.5% on Rank1 over the LOMO(a). It shows that the ellipse segmentation feature is more effective than the original. However, Rank5 and Rank10 have decreased. It is because that the segmentation causes the loss of part of the information. After the addition of original feature as supplemental information, the combined feature GOG(a+b) has significantly improved on the Rank1, Rank5, etc. Especially, our method has achieved 49.46%, with an improvement of 2.5%. Moreover, LOMO (a+b+c) increases by 5.5% on Rank1. Therefore, we can conclude that the combined feature with the ellipse segmentation performs better and has a better recognition effect.

5   Conclusions

In this paper, the proposed method fuses LOMO(a+b+c) and GOG(a+b) features as the global feature, and combines them with local features, thus forming more robust feature for the changes of illumination and visual angle. Meanwhile, the algorithm of ellipse segmentation reduces background noise. Furthermore, it can increase the proportion of effective area for pedestrians and enhance the robustness of final joint features. Experimental results show that the proposed algorithm significantly improves the recognition rate of pedestrian re-identification. The recognition rate on Rank10 in the VIPeR, PRID450s, and CUHK01 datasets all reach over 90%, which has practical application of great value.

References

1. Bai, S., Bai, X., Tian, Q.: Scalable person re-identification on supervised smoothed manifold, pp. 3356–3365 (2017)
2. Braz, J., Mestetskiy, L.: Proceedings of the International Conference on Computer Vision Theory and Application: Foreword (2011)
3. Chen, D., Yuan, Z., Chen, B., Zheng, N.: Similarity learning with spatial constraints for person re-identification. In: IEEE Conference on Computer Vision and Pattern Recognition, pp. 1268–1277 (2016)
4. Chen, W., Chen, X., Zhang, J., Huang, K.: Beyond triplet loss: a deep quadruplet network for person re-identification, pp. 1320–1329 (2017)
5. Chen, W., Chen, X., Zhang, J., Huang, K.: Beyond triplet loss: a deep quadruplet network for person re-identification. In: IEEE Conference on Computer Vision and Pattern Recognition, pp. 1320–1329 (2017)
6. Chu, H., Qi, M., Liu, H., Jiang, J.: Local region partition for person re-identification. Multimed. Tools Appl. **7**, 1–17 (2017)
7. Gray, D., Brennan, S., Tao, H.: Evaluating appearance models for recognition, reacquisition, and tracking (2007)
8. Jégou, H., Chum, O.: Negative evidences and co-occurences in image retrieval: the benefit of PCA and whitening. In: Fitzgibbon, A., Lazebnik, S., Perona, P., Sato, Y., Schmid, C. (eds.) ECCV 2012. LNCS, pp. 774–787. Springer, Heidelberg (2012). https://doi.org/10.1007/978-3-642-33709-3_55

9. Li, D., Chen, X., Zhang, Z., Huang, K.: Learning deep context-aware features over body and latent parts for person re-identification. In: IEEE Conference on Computer Vision and Pattern Recognition (2017)
10. Li, W., Wang, X.: Locally aligned feature transforms across views. In: IEEE Conference on Computer Vision and Pattern Recognition, pp. 3594–3601 (2013)
11. Liao, S., Hu, Y., Zhu, X., Li, S.Z.: Person re-identification by local maximal occurrence representation and metric learning. In: Computer Vision and Pattern Recognition, pp. 2197–2206 (2015)
12. Liao, S., Zhao, G., Kellokumpu, V., Pietikäinen, M., Li, S.Z.: Modeling pixel process with scale invariant local patterns for background subtraction in complex scenes. In: Computer Vision and Pattern Recognition, pp. 1301–1306 (2010)
13. Lin, J., Ren, L., Lu, J., Feng, J., Zhou, J.: Consistent-aware deep learning for person re-identification in a camera network. In: Computer Vision and Pattern Recognition, pp. 3396–3405 (2017)
14. Lv, J., Chen, W., Li, Q., Yang, C.: Unsupervised cross-dataset person re-identification by transfer learning of spatial-temporal patterns. CoRR abs/1803.07293 (2018). http://arxiv.org/abs/1803.07293
15. Matsukawa, T., Okabe, T., Suzuki, E., Sato, Y.: Hierarchical Gaussian descriptor for person re-identification. In: Computer Vision and Pattern Recognition, pp. 1363–1372 (2016)
16. Mei-Bin, Q.I., Tan, S.S., Wang, Y.X., Liu, H., Jiang, J.G.: Multi-feature subspace and kernel learning for person re-identification. Acta Automatica Sinica **42**(2), 299–308 (2016)
17. Mignon, A.: PCCA: a new approach for distance learning from sparse pairwise constraints. In: Computer Vision and Pattern Recognition, pp. 2666–2672 (2012)
18. Paisitkriangkrai, S., Shen, C., Hengel, A.V.D.: Learning to rank in person re-identification with metric ensembles, vol. 1, pp. 1846–1855 (2015)
19. Qi, M., Hu, L., Jiang, J., Gao, C.: Person re-identification based on multi-features fusion and independent metric learning. J. Image Graph. (2016)
20. Roth, P.M., Wohlhart, P., Hirzer, M., Kostinger, M., Bischof, H.: Large scale metric learning from equivalence constraints. In: IEEE Conference on Computer Vision and Pattern Recognition, pp. 2288–2295 (2012)
21. Roth, P.M., Hirzer, M., Kostinger, M., Beleznai, C., Bischof, H.: Mahalanobis distance learning for person re-identification, pp. 247–267 (2014)
22. Schroff, F., Kalenichenko, D., Philbin, J.: FaceNet: a unified embedding for face recognition and clustering. In: IEEE Conference on Computer Vision and Pattern Recognition, pp. 815–823 (2015)
23. Shi, Z., Hospedales, T.M., Xiang, T.: Transferring a semantic representation for person re-identification and search. In: Computer Vision and Pattern Recognition, pp. 4184–4193 (2015)
24. Su, C., Zhang, S., Xing, J., Gao, W., Tian, Q.: Deep attributes driven multi-camera person re-identification. In: Leibe, B., Matas, J., Sebe, N., Welling, M. (eds.) ECCV 2016. LNCS, vol. 9906, pp. 475–491. Springer, Cham (2016). https://doi.org/10.1007/978-3-319-46475-6_30
25. Wu, S., Chen, Y.C., Li, X., Wu, A.C., You, J.J., Zheng, W.S.: An enhanced deep feature representation for person re-identification. In: Applications of Computer Vision, pp. 1–8 (2016)
26. Xiao, T., Li, H., Ouyang, W., Wang, X.: Learning deep feature representations with domain guided dropout for person re-identification, pp. 1249–1258 (2016)

27. Xiong, F., Gou, M., Camps, O., Sznaier, M.: Person re-identification using kernel-based metric learning methods. In: Fleet, D., Pajdla, T., Schiele, B., Tuytelaars, T. (eds.) ECCV 2014. LNCS, vol. 8695, pp. 1–16. Springer, Cham (2014). https://doi.org/10.1007/978-3-319-10584-0_1

28. Yang, Y., Yang, J., Yan, J., Liao, S., Yi, D., Li, S.Z.: Salient color names for person re-identification. In: Fleet, D., Pajdla, T., Schiele, B., Tuytelaars, T. (eds.) ECCV 2014. LNCS, vol. 8689, pp. 536–551. Springer, Cham (2014). https://doi.org/10.1007/978-3-319-10590-1_35

29. Yao, W., Weng, Z., Zhu, Y.: Diversity regularized metric learning for person re-identification. In: IEEE International Conference on Image Processing, pp. 4264–4268 (2016)

30. Guo, Y., Ngai-Man, C.: Efficient and deep person re-identification using multi-level similarity. In: Computer Vision and Pattern Recognition, pp. 2335–2344 (2018)

31. Zhang, L., Xiang, T., Gong, S.: Learning a discriminative null space for person re-identification. In: Computer Vision and Pattern Recognition, pp. 1239–1248 (2016)

32. Zhang, Y., Li, B., Lu, H., Irie, A., Xiang, R.: Sample-specific SVM learning for person re-identification. In: Computer Vision and Pattern Recognition, pp. 1278–1287 (2016)

Online Signature Verification Based on Shape Context and Function Features

Yu Jia and Linlin Huang(✉)

Beijing Jiaotong University, No. 3 Shangyuancun, Beijing, China
{16120010, huangll}@bjtu.edu.cn

Abstract. Online signature verification is becoming quite attractive due to its potential applications. In this paper, we present a method using shape context and function features as well as cascade structure for accurate online signature verification. Specifically, in the first stage features of shape context are extracted and classification is made based on distance metric. Only the input passing by the first stage will be further verified using a set of function features and Dynamic Time Warping (DTW). We also incorporate shape context into DTW get a more accurate matching. The proposed method is tested on SVC2004 database comprising a total of 80 individuals and 3,200 signatures. Experiment result achieves an Equal Error Rate of 2.45% demonstrating the effectiveness of the proposed method.

Keywords: Online signature verification · Shape context · Function features
Cascade structure

1 Introduction

Verifying personal identity through the inherent characteristics of individuals, biometric verification technology is attracting great attention as a more trustable alternative to token/knowledge-based security system. Some physiological biometric attributes like fingerprint or face are already familiar to the public. There is another biometric type called behavioral biometric attributes which are related to the pattern of behavior of a person, such as voice or signature [1]. Compared to physiological ones, they are more accessible and less intrusive. Among them, signature remains the most widespread and recognized socially and legally individual verification approach. Moreover, signing is a rapid movement driven by long-term writing habit, which will lead to the differences in both the signing process and the appearance of a signature. Therefore, it's not possible that a forgery is exactly the same as the genuine signatures. That is, verification based on signature is feasible theoretically. Practically, affected by either environment condition or mental state variations among the signatures from a user occur inevitably, making it a challenging task.

Signature verification technique may be split into two categories: offline and online [20]. Offline signature verification works on the static digital signature images acquired after the signing process. The input of online signature verification is temporal signals captured by electronic devices like tablets, smart phones during the signing process. Usually, online signature verification system ensures a higher accuracy and security

© Springer Nature Switzerland AG 2018
J.-H. Lai et al. (Eds.): PRCV 2018, LNCS 11256, pp. 62–73, 2018.
https://doi.org/10.1007/978-3-030-03398-9_6

owing to dynamic information collected in the writing process. It makes the signature more unique and more difficult to forge.

Based on employed features, online signature verification techniques can broadly be divided into two groups: global features based and function features based approaches. In the framework of global features based methods, a signature is characterized as a vector of elements, each one representative of the value of a feature [1]. Examples of such attributes include width, height, etc. As for function features based methods, a signature is described in terms of a set of time function whose values constitute the feature set. Examples are position trajectory, velocity, pressure, etc. With regards to the classifiers, approaches like neural network (NN), support vector machine (SVM), dynamic time warping (DTW), hidden Markov Model (HMM) are adopted. Among them, DTW is considered as the most common technique. Sharma and Sundaram [3] explore the utility of information derived from DTW cost matrix and devise a novel score that describes the characteristic of the warping paths. Then they incorporate the derived warping path score with DTW score to make decision. Yanikoglu and Kholmatov [4] present a novel system based on the fusion of the Fast Fourier Transform and DTW. Kholmatov and Yanikoglu [8] match the test signatures against a set of reference signatures using DTW. Then, using the alignment scores, the test signatures are classified by standard pattern classification techniques.

Regardless of the method mentioned, the focus of them is mainly the dynamics of the signatures instead of shape. In online system, the shape of a signature is represented by its x-y coordinate. Gupta and Joyce [6] capture the shape using the position extrema points of a signature and propose the edit-distance-based string matching algorithm for comparing the sequence of two signatures. Shape context proposed by Belogie and Malik [16] offers a globally characterization to shape, making it a robust, compact and highly discriminative descriptor. That inspires us to exploit shape context based signature characterization. Besides, more distinguish characteristics usually exist in the signing process. In order to improve the accuracy further, function features based approach is utilized subsequently to form a cascade framework.

The rest of this paper is organized as follows: Sect. 2 gives our proposed method in detail. Section 3 shows the database used in our experiment and experimental results. Section 4 offers the conclusion.

2 Proposed Method

The proposed method for online signature verification is detailed in the following subsections. Figure 1 shows the diagram representation of the proposed system. The input signature is first passed through preprocessing model. After that, we use shape context to capture its shape feature and the calculated shape distance is fed into a classifier. Only after passing the first stage test will it enter the second stage. In this stage, its function features are extracted and SC-DTW is employed to get a distance. Then the distance is used to verify the authenticity of the signature.

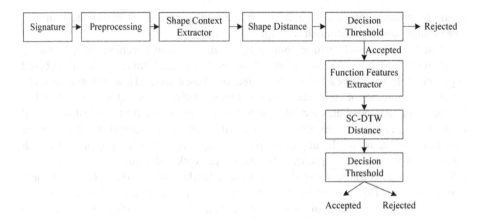

Fig. 1. Diagram of proposed verification system

2.1   Signature Preprocessing

Because signatures are captured by electronic devices, noises and fluctuations are interrupted unavoidably. And there's no guarantee that signatures acquired at different time or places of one individual will always be the same. Those variations will decrease the similarities between test and reference signatures. In order to address those issues, preprocessing comprising of smoothing and normalization is adopted as the first step.

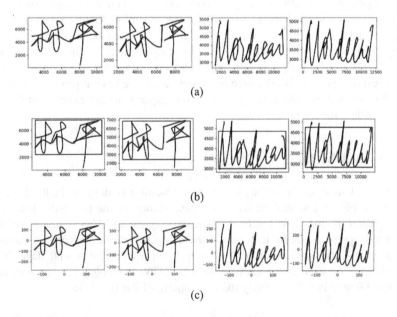

Fig. 2. Examples for signature preprocessing. (a) Original signatures in SVC 2004. (b) Window calculated by moment of corresponding signatures. (c) Corresponding preprocessed signatures.

Gaussian smoothing can be employed to reduce those artifacts. The normalization step standardizes the size and location of signature at different inputs. The commonly used method of size normalization is the utilization of maxi-min normalization. The size depends on the maximum and minimum in the horizontal and vertical directions. Despite relative simplicity, it cannot represent the exact size as is attested by Fig. 2. Figure 2(a) shows the genuine signatures and skilled forgery from two user. As we can see, some people tend to write longer strokes at times, for example, some downward and upward strokes. Our solution is the introduction of moment-based normalization [9]. The size of a signature depends on the width and height of the window calculated by its moment, and Fig. 2(b) shows the window. Some research shows that y coordinate provides more distinctive information. Therefore, the height of the signature is normalized to a predefined value and the width is adjusted accordingly in order to keep the aspect ratio. For location normalization, the signature is centered at (0, 0). Figure 2 shows the original signatures and corresponding preprocessed signature. After preprocessing, the signatures have the same size and location.

2.2 Shape Context Based Signature Characterization

The shape context captures the distribution over relative positions of other shape points and thus summarizes global shape in a rich, local descriptor. The shape is represented by a set of points sampled from the shape contours which in this work is (x_i, y_i), $i = 1, 2,..., N$, N is the number of points. Different people writes at different speed and the data acquisition equipment samples the signature at fixed interval, which means the number and the distribution of sample points acquired varies with person. The speed information that is proved to be one of the most discriminative feature is implicit in the (x_i, y_i). Shape Context is capable of extract those differences.

As we can see from Fig. 3(a–c), the number and the distribution of the sample points from two genuine signatures are more similar. Taking one point as the origin of polar coordinate, the shape context of this point is calculated as illustrated. Log-polar histogram bins are used to represent the shape contexts and we choose five bins for log r and twelve bins for θ. The number of neighboring points that fall into the very bin is just the histogram value.

Consider a point p_i on the first shape and a point q_j on the second shape. Denote $C_{ij} = C(p_i, q_j)$ as the matching cost of these two points, given by

$$C_{ij} = C(p_i, q_j) = \frac{1}{2} \sum_{k=1}^{K} \frac{\left[h_i[k] - h_j[k]\right]^2}{h_i[k] + h_j[k]} \tag{1}$$

where $h_i[k]$ and $h_j[k]$ denote the K-bin histogram at p_i and q_j respectively.

Given the set of costs C_{ij} between all pairs of points p_i on the first shape and q_j on the second shape, the Hungarian method is implemented to find the optimal alignment. The cost between shape contexts is based on the chi-square test statistic, so thin plate spline (TPS) model is adopted for transformation. After that, the distance between two shapes can be measured generally.

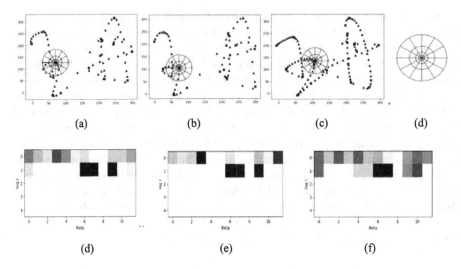

Fig. 3. Shape contexts computation and matching. (a–b) Two genuine signatures. (c) A skilled forgery. They are all from the same person. Note that the square marker points represents trend-transition-points (TTPs) extracted. (d) Diagram of log-polar histogram bins used in computing the shape contexts. (e-g) Example shape contexts histograms for certain trend-transition-point marked in (a–c).

2.3   Trend-Transition-Point (TTP) Extraction

The presentation for signature shape should not only captures the essentials of the shape but allows considerable variation. Besides, the more points, the greater the computational load. There's no need to use all points to represent the shape, and just a few selected points could do it. Based on the above, we propose a trend-transition-point (TTP) extraction method and note that the shape context is calculated on every point, but only extracted points are involved in computing the shape distance.

TTPs include local extrema points and corner points. The trends before and after the TTPs are completely different while between two successive TTPs, its shape approximates to a straight line. So TTPs keep its shape thus the signature could be reconstructed with these selected points. The method of corner point detection we adopted is proposed in [7], which makes use of eigenvalues of covariance matrices of different support regions.

Let $S_k(s_i)$ denotes the region of support (ROS) of point s_i, which contains itself and k points in its left and right neighborhoods. That is $S_k(s_i) = \{s_j \mid j = i - k, i - k + 1, ..., i + k - 1, i + k\}$, $s_j = \{x_j, y_j\}$. λ_L and λ_S are the eigenvalues obtained from the covariance matrix of $S_k(s_i)$. Sharper the corner is, larger λ_S is. When the shape in an ROS is close to a straight line, its λ_S will approaches to zero. So corners can be determined according to λ_S exceeding a threshold.

As a summary, the algorithm is implemented as follows. The start and end points as extrema points are chosen. As to the others, if its corresponding x or y coordinate value is higher or lower than both the left and right one, it is an extreme point. If not, its λ_S

would be calculated. In order to avoid the determination of threshold, whether the point is a TTP is decided by its neighborhood. That is, unless the λ_S of this point is greater than the left and right points, it can be categorized as a TTP. After the rough extraction mentioned, one of the two successive points whose distance is lower than a threshold will be deleted depending on its λ_S.

2.4 Function Features Based Signature Characterization

The signature is considered as a ballistic movement. The dissimilarity of shape can be helpful to tell the genuine signature from random and minor skilled forgeries while not that discriminative to well-skilled forgeries. A set of function features are shown in Table 1.

Table 1. Function features of online signature verification

No.	Symbols	Description
1	Change of x coordinate	$\Delta x(n) = x(n+4) - x(n)$
2	Change of y coordinate	$\Delta y(n) = y(n+4) - y(n)$
3	Pressure	$p(n)$
4	Change of pressure	$\Delta p(n) = p(n+4) - p(n)$
5	Change of displacement	$\Delta S(n) = \sqrt{(\Delta x(n))^2 + (\Delta y(n))^2}$
6	x velocity	$V_x(n) = [x(n+1) - x(n-1)]/2$
7	y velocity	$V_y(n) = [y(n+1) - y(n-1)]/2$
8	Total velocity	$V(n) = \sqrt{V_x^2(n) + V_y^2(n)}$
9	x acceleration	$a_x(n) = [V_x(n+1) - V_x(n-1)]/2$
10	y acceleration	$a_y(n) = [V_y(n+1) - V_y(n-1)]/2$
11	Total acceleration	$a(n) = \sqrt{a_x^2(n) + a_y^2(n)}$
12	Cosine of the angle between x-axis and signature curve	$\cos \alpha = \dfrac{x(n+1)-x(n)}{\sqrt{[x(n+1)-x(n)]^2 + [y(n+1)-y(n)]^2}}$
13	Sine of the angle between x-axis and signature curve	$\sin \alpha = \dfrac{y(n+1)-y(n)}{\sqrt{[x(n+1)-x(n)]^2 + [y(n+1)-y(n)]^2}}$
14	Cosine of the angle between x velocity and total velocity	$\cos = V_x(n)/V(n)$
15	Sine of the angle between y velocity and total velocity	$\sin = V_y(n)/V(n)$
16	Angle between x-axis and signature curve	$\theta(n) = \tan^{-1} \dfrac{y(n+1)-y(n)}{x(n+1)-x(n)}$

2.5 DTW Based Matching

In general, dynamic time warping or DTW is a method that calculate an optimal match between two given sequences based on the dynamic programming (DP) algorithm such that the overall distance between them is minimized.

Classical DTW. For the past a few years, DTW has become a major technique in signature verification. It is employed extensively along with function features, since it enables the time axis of two temporal functions to be compressed or expanded locally, in order to obtain the minimum of a given distance measure [3].

More specifically, denote $T = \{t_1, t_2, \ldots, t_N\}$ and $S = \{s_1, s_2, \ldots, s_M\}$ as two time series of different length N and M respectively. A matrix termed "cost matrix" denoted by $d(n, m)$ is constructed whose $(n, m)th$ cell represents the dissimilarity between the nth point of T and the mth point of S. The cost matrix is defined as:

$$d(n, m) = \|t_n - s_m\| \tag{2}$$

The overall distance is calculated as shown in the following equation:

$$D(n, m) = d(n, m) + min \begin{cases} C(n, m-1) \\ C(n-1, m-1) \\ C(n-1, m) \end{cases} \tag{3}$$

where $D(n, m)$ is the cumulative distance up-to the current element.

SC-DTW. DTW has been an effective method of finding the alignment between two signatures with different length. However, DTW usually warps time series according to their numerical characteristics as Eq. (2) but ignores their shape nature, and can lead to abnormal alignment sometimes. Inspired by Zhang and Tang's idea [5], we apply shape context to DTW in order to obtain a more feature to feature alignment. In this method, time series is considered as a 1-D array and a 2-D shape.

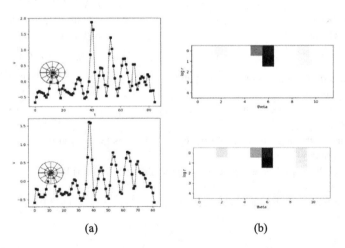

(a)   (b)

Fig. 4. SC-DTW. (a) The time series of total velocity v from two signature and a pair of corresponding points found by shape context. (b) The shape context histograms of the points marked in (a).

When finding the alignment between two time series, the cost matrix is replaced by the cost between shape contexts, which means

$$d(n, m) = C_{ij} \tag{4}$$

where C_{ij} is defined in Eq. (1).

It is worth noting that shape context is merely used to find the alignment between two time series and the cumulative distance is still obtained by the original cost matrix. The SC-DTW is computed on each signature segments divided by TTPs. The final dissimilarity of two signatures is the average of distances computed on each function features (Fig. 4).

2.6   Verification

Due to a limited number of genuine signatures and rare well-skilled forgeries available in practical applications, we, in this paper, propose a cascade verification system. In the first stage, the test signature is verified on account of the dissimilarity in shape. Random forgeries and minor skilled forgeries can be distinguished easily while well skilled forgeries not. That promotes a second stage for further verification. Dynamic features symbolize the information during the signing process, even though an adept forger couldn't imitate them completely. Hence, they could be helpful when verifying skilled forgeries.

During enrolment, the user supplies several signatures as reference signatures. They are pairwise coupled to get the distances between shape context and function features. When verifying a test signature, the signature is compared with all the reference signatures belonging to the claimed ID in terms of shape context firstly. After normalized by the corresponding averages of the reference signatures, the shape distances' average is used in classification. Unless classified as a genuine signature, this test signature steps into next stage. At the second stage, the difference is that test signature is compared with regards to function features distances through SC-DTW and others are alike. The average DTW distances is the basis of classification.

3   Experiments and Evaluation

In this section, we present the database we used and then analyze the experimental results we get. The performance is evaluated with Equal Error Rate (EER), which is calculated as the point at which the False Rejection Rate (FRR) of genuine signatures equals the False Acceptance Rate (FAR) of forgery signatures. We average the EERs obtained across all users enrolled.

And the writing pressure has been recognized as one of the most effective and discriminative feature and is quite helpful to make decision. However, some small pen-based input devices such as personal digital assistants (PDA) cannot collect the pressure information, and in the mobile scenario where finger is used as writing-tool, pressure is hard to obtain. The study of interoperability between devices and the effects of mobile conditions has been a hot topic in the field of online signature verification. So we test our proposed method in the case of with and without pressure information being used.

3.1 Database

The database we use is publicly available SVC 2004, which contains two tasks—task1 and task2. The signature data for task1 contain coordinate information only, but the signature data for task2 also contain additional information including pressure. Every task has 40 users respectively and for each user, 20 genuine and 20 skilled forgeries were collected using a graphic tablet (WACOM Intuos). And the genuine signatures are collected in two sessions, spaced apart by at least one week. The signatures are mostly in either English or Chinese.

3.2 Verification Results

In our experiment, we randomly select 5 genuine signatures for enrolment as reference signatures from each user. The resting 15 genuine signatures and 20 skilled forgeries of the users are employed for testing. For the random forgeries scenario, 20 signatures from other users are randomly selected. The trial is conducted for ten times for each user and the average EER is computed as the measure of performance. And we evaluate the method on the condition of common threshold and user-dependent threshold. In the common threshold set-up, the matching scores from all users are compared with a predefined threshold. While in user-dependent threshold case, the threshold is taken from 1.0 to 2.0 with a step size 0.1. We also test the system both with and without pressure information. Task1 and task2 are all usable in the absence of pressure information, while in the case of considering pressure information, only task2 is used.

In the first stage, shape distance is fed into a distance-based classifier. It is not a discriminative enough feature to tell the skilled signatures. However, it is good at distinguishing the random forgeries from genuine signatures. As we can see from Table 2, the EER between genuine signature and random forgeries is lower and approaches to zero in the user threshold set-up. It can classify the signatures roughly in this stage. Because the damage brought by rejecting a genuine signature is higher than by accepting a forgery, the test signature judged as a genuine one will be fed into next stage. In the second stage, the test signature is classified on the ground of DTW distance which is more reliable. In Table 3, we compare the results from classical DTW and our proposed SC-DTW, showing that SC-DTW could get lower EER. The test signature is classified again and it is a determinate genuine signature unless it is accepted. The final EER we get is 2.85% when the threshold is user-dependent. In Table 4, we list the SC-DTW and cascade structure verification results in the presence and absence of pressure information in the condition of user threshold. The pressure is an enough effective dynamic feature and the EER could be significantly decreased. Given the circumstances of user threshold and cascade structure, the EER is 2.45%.

Table 2. Verification results (%) based on shape distance for SVC2004

Method	Common threshold		User threshold	
Shape distance	EER(SF)[1]	EER(RF)[2]	EER(SF)[1]	EER(RF)[2]
	17.4	4.5	10.45	0.05

[1]Skilled forgeries
[2]Random forgeries

Table 3. Verification results (%) of different stages with common threshold and user threshold for SVC2004

Method	Common threshold	User threshold
Shape distance	17.4	10.45
Classical DTW	12.0	5.37
SC-DTW	10.27	4.28
Cascade structure	8.4	2.85

Table 4. Verification results (%) in the presence and absence of pressure information with user threshold for SVC2004

Method	Without pressure	With pressure
SC-DTW	4.28	3.63
Cascade structure	2.85	2.45

3.3 Comparisons

In this subsection, we give the results of prior works tested on SVC2004 as is showed in Table 5. The number of reference signatures is all five in the listed works. And their results are obtained based on SVC2004 task2. With pressure information help, the EER of our proposed method is slightly lower than the state-of-the-art, demonstrating its effectiveness and competitiveness. But without pressure information, the result is not the best but still can be acceptable.

Table 5. Comparisons between proposed and prior works on the SVC 2004

Works	Method	EER (%)
Sharma et al. [3]	DTW + VQ	2.53
Rashidi et al. [10]	DTW	3.37
Song et al. [12]	DTW with SCC	2.89
Liu et al. [13]	Spare representation	3.98
Xia et al. [20]	GMM + DTW with SCC	2.63
Proposed method	**Shape context + SC-DTW**	**2.45**

4 Conclusion

In this paper, we present a novel online signature verification technique based on shape context and function features. When only x and y coordinates are considered, shape context is a robust descriptor to capture the shape of signature. The shape distance is computed accordingly. In order to reduce the computational complexity, we propose a trend-transition-point (TTP) extraction algorithm and only these point is participated in the calculation of shape distance. In order to improve the performance further, a set of dynamic function features are derived and we use SC-DTW to get the similarity. We incorporate shape context into DTW to measure the dissimilarity between two points, thus getting a more feature-to-feature alignment. And the process takes place in the segments divided by TTPs. Then we talk about the effect of pressure information. The results we get is competitive given the absence of pressure and pen inclination and the like which are not available in certain scenario. It provide a possibility of the usability of shape in online system and a prospect for the study of interoperability between devices and the effects of mobile conditions, which will be our future work.

References

1. Impedovo, D., Pirlo, G.: Automatic signature verification: the state of the art. IEEE Trans. Syst. Man Cybern. Part C **38**(5), 609–635 (2008)
2. Kar, B., Mukherjee, A., Dutta, P.K.: Stroke point warping-based reference selection and verification of online signature. IEEE Trans. Instrum. Measur. **67**(1), 2–11 (2017)
3. Sharma, A., Sundaram, S.: On the exploration of information from the DTW cost matrix for online signature verification. IEEE Trans. Cybern. **48**(2), 611–624 (2018)
4. Yanikoglu, B., Kholmatov, A.: Online signature verification using Fourier descriptors. Eurasip J. Adv. Signal Process. **2009**(1), 1–13 (2009)
5. Zhang, Z., Tang, P., Duan, R.: Dynamic time warping under pointwise shape context. Inf. Sci. **315**, 88–101 (2015)
6. Gupta, G.K., Joyce, R.C.: Using position extrema points to capture shape in on-line handwritten signature verification. Elsevier Science Inc. (2007)
7. Tsai, D.M., Hou, H.T., Su, H.J.: Boundary-based corner detection using eigenvalues of covariance matrices. Elsevier Science Inc. (1999)
8. Kholmatov, A., Yanikoglu, B.: Identity authentication using improved online signature verification method. Pattern Recogn. Lett. **26**(15), 2400–2408 (2005)
9. Liu, C.L., Nakashima, K., Sako, H., Fujisawa, H.: Handwritten digit recognition: investigation of normalization and feature extraction techniques. Pattern Recogn. **37**(2), 265–279 (2004)
10. Rashidi, S., Fallah, A., Towhidkhah, F.: Feature extraction based DCT on dynamic signature verification. Scientia Iranica **19**(6), 1810–1819 (2012)
11. Yang, L., Jin, X., Jiang, Q.: Online handwritten signature verification based on the most stable feature and partition. Cluster Comput. **6**, 1–11 (2018)
12. Song, X., Xia, X., Luan, F.: Online signature verification based on stable features extracted dynamically. IEEE Trans. Syst. Man Cybern. Syst. **47**(10), 1–14 (2016)
13. Liu, Y., Yang, Z., Yang, L.: Online signature verification based on DCT and sparse representation. IEEE Trans. Cybern. **45**(11), 2498–2511 (2017)

14. Arora, M., Singh, H., Kaur, A.: Distance based verification techniques for online signature verification system. In: International Conference on Recent Advances in Engineering & Computational Sciences (2016)
15. Fierrez, J., Ortega-Garcia, J., Ramos, D., Gonzalez-Rodriguez, J.: HMM-based on-line signature verification: feature extraction and signature modeling. Pattern Recogn. Lett. **28** (16), 2325–2334 (2007)
16. Belongie, S., Malik, J., Puzicha, J.: Shape context: a new descriptor for shape matching and object recognition, pp. 831–837 (2000)
17. Cpałka, K., Zalasiński, M., Rutkowski, L.: New method for the on-line signature verification based on horizontal partitioning. Pattern Recogn. **47**(8), 2652–2661 (2014)
18. Sharma, A., Sundaram, S.: An enhanced contextual DTW based system for online signature verification using vector quantization. Pattern Recogn. Lett. **84**, 22–28 (2016)
19. Mohammed, R.A., Nabi, R.M., Mahmood, S.M., Nabi, R.M.: State-of-the-art in handwritten signature verification system. In: International Conference on Computational Science and Computational Intelligence, pp. 519–525 (2016)
20. Xia, X., et al.: Discriminative feature selection for on-line signature verification. Pattern Recogn. **74**, 422–433 (2017)
21. Swanepoel, J., Coetzer, J.: Feature weighted support vector machines for writer-independent on-line signature verification. In: International Conference on Frontiers in Handwriting Recognition, pp. 434–439 (2014)

Off-Line Signature Verification Using a Region Based Metric Learning Network

Li Liu[1], Linlin Huang[1(✉)], Fei Yin[2(✉)], and Youbin Chen[3]

[1] Beijing Jiaotong University, Beijing, Haidian, China
{16120014,huangll}@bjtu.edu.cn
[2] Institute of Automation Chinese Academy of Sciences, Beijing, Haidian, China
fyin@nlpr.ia.ac.cn
[3] MicroPattern Co. Ltd., Dongguan, Guangdong, China
Youbin.chen@micropattern.com

Abstract. Handwritten signature verification is a challenging problem due to the high similarity between genuine signatures and skilled forgeries. In this paper, we propose a novel framework for off-line signature verification using a Deep Convolutional Siamese Network for metric learning. For improving the discrimination ability, we extract features from local regions instead of the whole signature image and fuse the similarity measures of multiple regions for verification. Feature extractors of different regions share the convolutional layers in the convolutional network, which is trained with signature image pairs. In experiments on the benchmark datasets CEDAR and GPDS, the proposed method achieved 4.55% EER and 8.89% EER, respectively, which are competitive to state-of-the-art approaches.

Keywords: Signature verification · Siamese Network
Metric learning · Region fusion

1 Introduction

Handwritten signature verification is important for person identification and document authentication. It is increasingly being adopted in many civilian applications for enhanced security and privacy [14]. Among various biometrics, signature is a kind of behavioral characteristics, which are related to the pattern of behavior of a person [9]. Compared with physiological characteristics and other behavioral characteristics, handwritten signature has advantages in terms of accessibility and privacy protection. The use of handwritten signature for person verification has a long history, and so, occupies a special place in the variety of biometric traits due to the tradition. However, signature verification is difficult due to the variation of personal writing behavior and the high similarity between genuine signatures and forgeries.

In the past decades, many methods of signature verification have been proposed. The methods can be divided into on-line signature verification [1,4,26]

© Springer Nature Switzerland AG 2018
J.-H. Lai et al. (Eds.): PRCV 2018, LNCS 11256, pp. 74–86, 2018.
https://doi.org/10.1007/978-3-030-03398-9_7

and off-line signature verification [9,12,19] depending on the manner of data acquisition and recording. On-line signature verification is achieved through the acquisition of temporal stroke trajectory information using special electronic devices. Off-line signature verification is done by using signature images obtained by scanning or camera capturing. Off-line signature verification is more challenging because the temporal information of strokes is not available. However, due to the popularity of handwritten documents, off-line signature verification is needed in many applications.

Most works of signature verification have focused on the techniques of feature representation and similarity/distance metric evaluation, similarly in face verification and person re-identification etc. [27]. For feature extraction, different descriptors had been presented. Gilperez et al. encoded directional properties of signature contours and the length of regions enclosed inside letters [8]. Guerbai et al. used the energy of the curvelet coefficient computed from signature image [9]. And Kumar et al. designed surroundedness feature containing both shape and texture property of signature image [19]. Some methods learn feature representation using convolutional neural network [10,27,28]. According to the strategy used in metric learning stage, the methods can be grouped as writer-dependent and writer-independent methods. In writer-dependent case, a specialized metric model is learned for each individual writer during training phase, and then the learned metric model is used to classify the signature as particular writer, genuine or forgery one. In writer-independent case, there is only one metric model for all writers (tested in a separate set of users). Several types of classifiers have been proposed for metric learning, such as neural networks [19], Hidden Markov Model [21], Support Vector Machines [9,19] and ensemble of these classifiers [12].

For off-line signature verification, most existing methods extract features from the whole signature image. However, the distinguishable characteristics of writing style are usually contained in writing details, such as the strokes, which are very difficult to be forged even for the skilled writers. On the other hand, some parts of signature can be relatively easier to be copied. Therefore, extracting features from whole images cannot suffice the verification accuracy.

In this paper, we propose a novel framework for off-line signature verification of writer-independent scenario. We use a Deep Convolutional Siamese Network for feature extraction and metric learning, and to improve the verification performance, we extract features from local regions instead of the whole signature image. The similarity measures of multiple regions are fused for final decision. The convolutional network is trained end-to-end on signature image pairs. We evaluated the verification performance of the proposed method on two benchmark datasets CEDAR and GPDS, and achieved 4.55% EER and 8.89% EER, respectively. These results are competitive to the state-of-the-art approaches.

The rest of this paper is organized as follows: Sect. 2 gives a detailed introduction of the proposed method; Sect. 3 presents experimental results, and Sect. 4 offers concluding remarks.

2   Proposed Method

The diagram of the proposed method is given in Fig. 1. The system consists of preprocessing, local region segmentation, feature extraction and metric model. The signature image pairs undergone preprocessing procedure are firstly segmented into a series of overlapping regions. Then, the local region images are fed into a Deep Convolutional Siamese Networks to learn the features and the feature differences between the corresponding local regions of input signature image pairs are used to build the metric model. The similarity measures of multiple regions are finally fused for verification. In training, the parameters are adjusted in the mode that similarity between matched pairs should be larger than those between mismatched pairs.

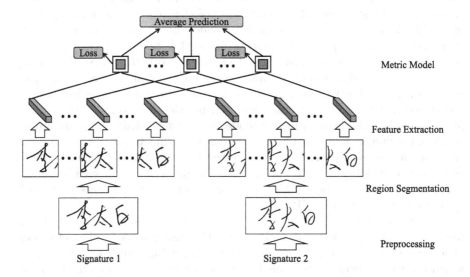

Fig. 1. The framework of presented method. It consists of four parts: preprocessing, a region segmentation layer, a feature extractor and a metric model.

2.1   Preprocessing

Preprocessing plays an important role in off-line signature verification as with most pattern recognition problems. In real applications, signature images may present variations in terms of background, pen thickness, scale, rotation, etc., even among authentic signatures of the same user, as shown in Fig. 2.

As Fig. 3 shows, we convert the input signature image as grayscale image firstly. Many samples in CEDAR database are rotated, so we need one more step of preprocessing for CEDAR database. The tilt correction method introduced by Kalera et al. [15] is employed to rectify the image. And the samples in CEDAR and ChnSig database are not clean in background. Therefore, we

Fig. 2. Some signature samples in CEDAR (column 1), GPDS (column 2) and ChnSig (column 3) database. And the first two rows show genuine samples, the third row shows the skilled forgeries.

employ Otsu's method [22] to binarize the signature image to get mask of foreground and background. Then we reset the pixels of background as 255 according to the mask of background to remove the background. For the foreground, we employ normalization method to normalize the distribution of grayscale in the foreground according to the mask of foreground, in order to remove the influence of illumination and various types of pen used by writers as follows:

$$g'_f = \frac{(g_f - E(g_f)) \cdot 10}{\delta(g_f)} + 30 \tag{1}$$

where g_f and g'_f denote original and normalized grayscale respectively, $E(g_f)$ and $\delta(g_f)$ denote the mean and variance of the original grayscale in foreground. In this way, the mean and variance of grayscale in foreground are normalized as 30 and 10 in experiments.

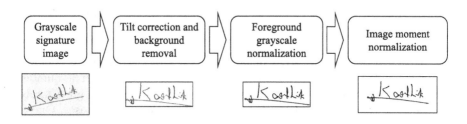

Fig. 3. The preprocessing strategy of the proposed method.

The signature images may have different resolutions or sizes, and the locations of signature strokes may present variation in different images. In order to match the locations of signature strokes to some extent from different images, we employ moment normalization [20] method to normalize the sizes and locations of signatures. Let $f(x, y)$ means the pixel of original image in the location (x, y), and $f'(x', y')$ means the pixel of normalized image in the location (x', y'). Then we can map $f(x, y)$ to $f'(x', y')$ as follows:

$$x = (x' - x'_c)/\alpha + x_c \tag{2}$$

$$y = (y' - y'_c)/\alpha + y_c \tag{3}$$

where x'_c and y'_c denote the center of normalized signature, x_c and y_c denote the center of original signature, and α is the ratio of the normalized signature size to the original signature size that can be estimated by the center moments of inverted image (signature strokes are in gray and background is black) as follows:

$$\alpha = 0.6 \cdot min(\frac{H_{norm}\sqrt{\mu_{00}}}{2\sqrt{2\mu_{02}}}, \frac{W_{norm}\sqrt{\mu_{00}}}{2\sqrt{2\mu_{20}}}) \tag{4}$$

where H_{norm} and W_{norm} denote height and width of normalized image, and μ_{pq} denotes the center moments:

$$\mu_{pq} = \sum_x \sum_y (x - x_c)^p (y - y_c)^q [255 - f(x, y)] \tag{5}$$

We set H_{norm} and W_{norm} as 224 and 512 in experiments, which means that we normalized the size of signature images as 512×224 for the following feature extraction.

2.2   Feature Extraction

We used the Deep Convolutional Siamese Network which is composed of two convolutional neural network (CNN) branches sharing the same parameters to learn the feature representation of local regions of signature images. There are many popular CNN architectures such as AlexNet [17], VGG [23], ResNet [11] and DenseNet [13]. Through the experimental comparison, we choose a DenseNet-36 to constitute the Deep Convolutional Siamese Network for feature extraction. The structure of the DenseNet-36 is shown in Table 1.

In particular, we feed inverted image into DenseNet-36, and we do not set dropout but add batch normalization for each convolution layers. The number of channels of the first convolution layer is set to be $N_{init} = 64$, and growth rate set to be $k = 32$ as described by Huang et al. [13]. We test two cases. One is that the input is the whole signature image, denoting as 'whole'. The other case is that the input is the local region of the signature image, denoting as 'region'. Therefore, we have different output sizes as described in Table 1. In all two cases, we flatten the feature maps of the last DenseBlock as feature vector, which is in $244 \times 16 \times 7 = 27328$ dimensions for 'whole' or in $244 \times 7 \times 7 = 11956$ dimensions for 'region'.

Table 1. The structure of DenseNet-36

Layers	Output size (whole/region)	Kernel size
Convolution	$256 \times 112/112 \times 112$	7×7 conv, stride 2
Pooling	$128 \times 56/56 \times 56$	3×3 max pool, stride 2
DenseBlock(1)	$128 \times 56/56 \times 56$	$\begin{bmatrix} 1 \times 1 \text{ conv} \\ 3 \times 3 \text{ conv} \end{bmatrix} \times 3$
Transition Layer(1)	$128 \times 56/56 \times 56$	1×1 conv
	$64 \times 28/28 \times 28$	2×2 average pool, stride 2
DenseBlock(2)	$64 \times 28/28 \times 28$	$\begin{bmatrix} 1 \times 1 \text{ conv} \\ 3 \times 3 \text{ conv} \end{bmatrix} \times 4$
Transition Layer(2)	$64 \times 28/28 \times 28$	1×1 conv
	$32 \times 14/14 \times 14$	2×2 average pool, stride 2
DenseBlock(3)	$32 \times 14/14 \times 14$	$\begin{bmatrix} 1 \times 1 \text{ conv} \\ 3 \times 3 \text{ conv} \end{bmatrix} \times 6$
Transition Layer(3)	$32 \times 14/14 \times 14$	1×1 conv
	$16 \times 7/7 \times 7$	2×2 average pool, stride 2
DenseBlock(4)	$16 \times 7/7 \times 7$	$\begin{bmatrix} 1 \times 1 \text{ conv} \\ 3 \times 3 \text{ conv} \end{bmatrix} \times 3$

2.3 Metric Model

After feeding two signature images or the local region of the signature images into the Deep Convolutional Siamese Network, we can get feature vector in pairs, represented by $F_1, F_2 \in \Re^d$, where d is the dimension of feature vector. The difference between these corresponding feature vector pairs is applied to be the similarity measure. We have tried Cosine, Euclidean distance, and absolute value of feature vector pairs as the difference measure and found that the "absolute value", denoted as $F = |F_1 - F_2|$, performs the best. Then, a linear layer is added to project the feature vector F to a 2-dimensional space with base vectors of $(\hat{p}_1, \hat{p}_2)^T$, where $\hat{p}_1$ represents the predicted probability that the two signature belong to the same user, and $\hat{p}_2$ represents the predicted probability of the opposite situation $(\hat{p}_2 + \hat{p}_1 = 1)$. In this way, the signature verification can be treated as binary-class classification problem and use cross-entropy loss as object function to optimize our model as follows:

$$Loss(p, \hat{p}) = -[p \cdot ln(\hat{p}_1) + (1 - p) \cdot ln(\hat{p}_2)] = \sum_{i=1}^{2} -p_i \cdot ln(\hat{p}_i) \qquad (6)$$

where p is the target class (same or different) and $\hat{p}$ is the predicted probability. If the two signatures are written by the same user $p_1 = 1$ and $p_2 = 0$, otherwise $p_1 = 0$ and $p_2 = 1$. Then we can use $\hat{p}_1$ to approximate similarity measure of the two signatures.

2.4   Region Based Metric Learning

As described before, in order to improve the verification accuracy, we extract the features from local regions instead of the whole signature image. The local regions are obtained by a sliding window of size 224 × 224, scanning across the input signature image with a step of 36 pixels. Among the resulted 9 overlapping local regions from 512 × 224 signature images, the first and last regions are abandoned since they do not contain much useful information for verification. The remained 7 regions are applied to the Deep Convolutional Siamese Network for feature extraction and metric learning. Specifically, the difference between the corresponding regions obtained from the input signature image pairs are employed to be similarity measure and are finally fused by averaging for final decision. All the 7 regions are used to optimize the metric model learning in training stage while differences between several regions are chosen in testing stage for verification.

3   Experiments

There are three metrics for evaluating the off-line signature verification system: False Rejection Rate (FRR), False Acceptance Rate for skilled forgeries (FAR$_{skilled}$, in this paper we only consider about skilled forgeries, so we use FAR for convenience) and the Equal Error Rate (EER). The first one is the rate of false rejections of genuine signatures, the second one is the rate of false acceptance of forged signatures, and the last one can be determined by ROC analysis [5] where FAR is same as FRR.

3.1   Datasets and Implementation Details

Three databases are used for evaluation. There are two popular benchmarks: CEDAR [15] and GPDS [7] database, the third one is established by us consisting of Chinese handwritten signature database named ChnSig.

CEDAR database is an off-line signature database created with data from 55 users. At random, users were asked to create forgeries for signatures from other writers. Each user has 24 genuine signatures and 24 skilled forgeries. So we can get $C_{24}^2 = 276$ genuine-genuine pairs of signatures as positive samples and $C_{24}^1 \times C_{24}^1 = 576$ genuine-forged pairs of signatures as negative samples for each user. We randomly selected 50 user as training set and the remaining 5 users are testing set. Totally, we get 42600 samples for training and 4260 samples for testing.

GPDS database is an off-line signature database created with data from 4000 users. Each user has 24 genuine signatures and 30 skilled forgeries. So we can get $C_{24}^2 = 276$ positive samples and $C_{24}^1 \times C_{30}^1 = 720$ negative samples for each user. We randomly selected 2000 user as training set and the remaining 2000 users are testing set. Totally, we get 1992000 samples for training and 1992000 samples for testing.

ChnSig database is an Chinese off-line signature database created by ourself with data from 1243 users. At random, users were asked to create forgeries for signatures from other writers. Each user has 10 genuine signatures and 16 skilled forgeries. So we can get $C_{10}^2 = 45$ positive samples and $C_{10}^1 \times C_{16}^1 = 160$ negative samples for each user. We randomly selected 1000 user as training set and the remaining 243 users are testing set. Totally, we get 205000 samples for training and 49815 samples for testing.

We implemented our model on the platform of PyTorch, and trained our model using Adam [16] with the learning rate of 0.001. We used mini-batches of 64 pairs of signature regions (32 for whole images). Meanwhile, the dropout was set to be 0.3 on linear layer. For CEDAR and ChnSig database, we used the model trained in GPDS database for fine-tuning. Experiments were performed on a workstation with the Intel(R) Xeon(R) E5-2680 CPU, 256 GB RAM and a NVIDIA GeForce GTX TITAN X GPUs. The system takes only 10 ms to verify a pair of signatures on average.

3.2 CNN Architectures for Feature Extraction

We fed the whole of signature images into different CNN architectures for feature extraction, then measure the similarity of two signatures on GPDS database, in order to determine the architectures of feature extractor.

Table 2. Effects of different CNN architectures on performance (%) on GPDS database

Architectures	Accuracy	FRR	FAR	EER	Model size
AlexNet	87.23	29.52	6.35	14.13	9.9 MB
ResNet-18	88.67	30.38	**4.03**	11.74	11.4 MB
VGG-16	90.01	22.79	5.09	10.95	14.8 MB
DenseNet-36	**90.10**	**17.23**	7.10	**10.93**	**4.2** MB

Table 3. Effects of hyperparameter selection of DenseNet on performance (%) on GPDS database

DenseBlocks	N_{init}	k	Feature map size	EER
(3, 4, 3)	16	4	32×14	13.31
(3, 4, 6, 3)	16	4	16×7	11.98
	64	32	16×7	**10.93**
	72	48	16×7	11.52
(3, 4, 6, 6, 3)	16	4	8×3	12.63

As Table 2 shows, the DenseNet-36 architecture achieves the best performance and the model size is also smallest. So we determined DenseNet-36 architecture to be the feature extractor. To achieve better performance, we designed experiments for hyperparameter selection of DenseNet. We set different Dense-Blocks and changed N_{init} and growth rate k, which are proposed by Huang et al. [13]. As Table 3 shows, the performance is better when the DenseBlocks are set as (3, 4, 6, 3) with $N_{init} = 64$ and $k = 32$.

3.3 Region Fusion

After determining the structure of feature extractor, we trained our model by regions of signature images described in Sect. 2.4. Firstly, we mark the regions from left to right as 1 to 7 and then test our model of system in them, and the results are shown in Table 4, where {i} means that we test our model on the i-th region. We can note that our model achieves the best performance in 4-th region. The reason is that the location of signature is normalized on the center of image by preprocessing, while 4-th region is just on the center of signature image, so that there is more information about signature strokes in the regions around center of image. Therefore, we choose regions around 4-th region to test the model in region fusion case.

Table 4. Performance of system in different regions (EER %)

Database	{1}	{2}	{3}	{4}	{5}	{6}	{7}
GPDS	12.37	10.80	10.32	**10.28**	10.41	11.04	12.66
CEDAR	11.32	11.32	8.75	**8.51**	8.92	9.41	11.39
ChnSig	12.19	11.53	**11.50**	11.72	12.18	12.52	13.02

In the region fusion case, we take different groups of regions that are symmetrical about the center of the signature image, then fuse the similarity measures of these regions. In Table 5, 'Whole' means that we feed the whole of signature image into our model, and {i, j, ...} means that we fuse the similarity measures of i-th, j-th, etc. regions. As Table 5 shows, we can note that feeding 4-th region achieves better performance than feeding the whole of signature images into the model. The reason is that it is difficult to extract good features in details from

Table 5. Performance of system in different region fusion cases (EER %)

Database	Whole	{4}	{1, 4, 7}	{2, 3, 4, 5, 6}	{1, 2, 3, 4, 5, 6, 7}
GPDS	10.93	10.28	8.89	9.15	**8.81**
CEDAR	11.53	8.51	**4.55**	6.22	5.38
ChnSig	11.82	11.72	**9.91**	10.44	9.97

the whole of signature image, so that the metric model is easy to be effected by the areas where the signature strokes are similar. And the system achieves better performance when we fuse the similarity measures of 1-st, 4-th and 7-th regions comparing to other cases. In addition, the proposed method also performs well in Chinese corpus, that our system achieves 9.91% EER on ChnSig database.

3.4 Comparative Evaluation

We choose the combination of the parameters that achieve the best performance in the above discussion, and evaluate our model on two public benchmarks of off-line signature verification. The results are listed in Tables 6 and 7 with comparison to state-of-the-art methods. It should be mentioned that some methods presented the Average Error Rate (AER) instead of EER, which is the average of FAR and FRR. The difference between EER and AER is not great, so we consider them equivalent.

Table 6. Comparison between proposed and other published methods on CEDAR database (%)

System	#User	Accuracy	EER (or ARE)
Chen et al. [2]	55	83.60	16.40
Chen et al. [3]	55	92.10	7.90
Kumar et al. [18]	55	88.41	11.59
Kumar et al. [19]	55	91.67	8.33
Xing et al. [27]	55	91.50	8.50
Ours	55	**95.45**	**4.55**

Table 7. Comparison between proposed and other published methods on GPDS database (%)

System	#User	Accuracy	EER (or AER)
Ferrer et al. [6]	160	86.65	13.35
Vargas et al. [25]	160	87.67	12.23
Kumar et al. [19]	300	86.24	13.76
Hu et al. [12]	300	90.06	9.94
Guerbai et al. [9]	300	84.05	15.95
Soleimani et al. [24]	4000	86.70	13.30
Xing et al. [27]	4000	89.63	10.37
Ours	4000	**91.11**	**8.89**

From Tables 6 and 7 we can see that the proposed system outperforms all the compared methods on CEDAR and GPDS database. And the system of Chen et al. [2] and Chen et al. [3] reported in Table 6 are writer-dependent, which have to be updated if a new writer is added. On the other hand, the proposed system can be used for any newly added writer without re-training the system. The other systems reported in Table 7 (except Soleimani et al. [24] and Xing et al. [27]) are tested on GPDS database with different numbers of user. It is more persuasive that our system is tested on the biggest database and achieves state-of-the-art comparing with the other systems.

4 Conclusion and Future Work

In this paper, we propose a novel framework for off-line signature verification using a Deep Convolutional Siamese Network for metric learning. For improving the discrimination ability, we extract features from local regions instead of the whole signature image and fuse the similarity measures of multiple regions for verification. Feature extractors of different regions share the convolutional layers in the convolutional network, which is trained with signature image pairs. In experiments on the benchmark datasets CEDAR and GPDS, the proposed method achieved 4.55% EER and 8.89% EER, respectively, which are competitive to state-of-the-art approaches. The method can be further improved by polishing metric model and using more challenging datasets.

References

1. Bromley, J., Guyon, I., LeCun, Y., Säckinger, E., Shah, R.: Signature verification using a "siamese" time delay neural network. In: Advances in Neural Information Processing Systems, pp. 737–744 (1994)
2. Chen, S.Y., Srihari, S.: Use of exterior contours and shape features in off-line signature verification. In: Proceedings of the Eighth International Conference on Document Analysis and Recognition, pp. 1280–1284. IEEE (2005)
3. Chen, S.Y., Srihari, S.: A new off-line signature verification method based on graph. In: 18th International Conference on Pattern Recognition, ICPR 2006, vol. 2, pp. 869–872. IEEE (2006)
4. Cpałka, K., Zalasiński, M., Rutkowski, L.: New method for the on-line signature verification based on horizontal partitioning. Pattern Recognit. **47**(8), 2652–2661 (2014)
5. Fawcett, T.: An introduction to ROC analysis. Pattern Recognit. Lett. **27**(8), 861–874 (2006)
6. Ferrer, M.A., Alonso, J.B., Travieso, C.M.: Offline geometric parameters for automatic signature verification using fixed-point arithmetic. IEEE Trans. Pattern Anal. Mach. Intell. **27**(6), 993–997 (2005)
7. Ferrer, M.A., Diaz-Cabrera, M., Morales, A.: Static signature synthesis: a neuromotor inspired approach for biometrics. IEEE Trans. Pattern Anal. Mach. Intell. **37**(3), 667–680 (2015)

8. Gilperez, A., Alonso-Fernandez, F., Pecharroman, S., Fierrez, J., Ortega-Garcia, J.: Off-line signature verification using contour features. In: 11th International Conference on Frontiers in Handwriting Recognition, Montreal, 19–21 August 2008. CENPARMI, Concordia University (2008)
9. Guerbai, Y., Chibani, Y., Hadjadji, B.: The effective use of the one-class SVM classifier for handwritten signature verification based on writer-independent parameters. Pattern Recognit. **48**(1), 103–113 (2015)
10. Hafemann, L.G., Sabourin, R., Oliveira, L.S.: Writer-independent feature learning for offline signature verification using deep convolutional neural networks. In: International Joint Conference on Neural Networks (IJCNN), pp. 2576–2583. IEEE (2016)
11. He, K.M., Zhang, X.Y., Ren, S.Q., Sun, J.: Deep residual learning for image recognition. In: Proceedings of the IEEE Conference on Computer Vision and Pattern Recognition, pp. 770–778 (2016)
12. Hu, J., Chen, Y.B.: Offline signature verification using real adaboost classifier combination of pseudo-dynamic features. In: 12th International Conference on Document Analysis and Recognition (ICDAR), pp. 1345–1349. IEEE (2013)
13. Huang, G., Liu, Z., Weinberger, K.Q., Maaten, L.V.D.: Densely connected convolutional networks. In: Proceedings of the IEEE conference on Computer Vision and Pattern Recognition, vol. 1, p. 3 (2017)
14. Jain, A.K., Ross, A., Prabhakar, S.: An introduction to biometric recognition. IEEE Trans. Circuits Syst. Video Technol. **14**(1), 4–20 (2004)
15. Kalera, M.K., Srihari, S., Xu, A.H.: Offline signature verification and identification using distance statistics. Int. J. Pattern Recognit. Artif. Intell. **18**(07), 1339–1360 (2004)
16. Kingma, D.P., Ba, J.: Adam: a method for stochastic optimization. arXiv preprint arXiv:1412.6980 (2014)
17. Krizhevsky, A., Sutskever, I., Hinton, G.E.: ImageNet classification with deep convolutional neural networks. In: Advances in Neural Information Processing Systems, pp. 1097–1105 (2012)
18. Kumar, R., Kundu, L., Chanda, B., Sharma, J.: A writer-independent off-line signature verification system based on signature morphology. In: Proceedings of the First International Conference on Intelligent Interactive Technologies and Multimedia, pp. 261–265. ACM (2010)
19. Kumar, R., Sharma, J., Chanda, B.: Writer-independent off-line signature verification using surroundedness feature. Pattern Recognit. Lett. **33**(3), 301–308 (2012)
20. Liu, C.L., Nakashima, K., Sako, H., Fujisawa, H.: Handwritten digit recognition: investigation of normalization and feature extraction techniques. Pattern Recognit. **37**(2), 265–279 (2004)
21. Oliveira, L.S., Justino, E., Freitas, C., Sabourin, R.: The graphology applied to signature verification. In: 12th Conference of the International Graphonomics Society, pp. 286–290 (2005)
22. Otsu, N.: A threshold selection method from gray-level histograms. IEEE Trans. Syst. Man Cybern. **9**(1), 62–66 (1979)
23. Simonyan, K., Zisserman, A.: Very deep convolutional networks for large-scale image recognition. arXiv preprint arXiv:1409.1556 (2014)
24. Soleimani, A., Araabi, B.N., Fouladi, K.: Deep multitask metric learning for offline signature verification. Pattern Recognit. Lett. **80**, 84–90 (2016)

25. Vargas, J.F., Ferrer, M.A., Travieso, C.M., Alonso, J.B.: Off-line signature verification based on high pressure polar distribution. In: Proceedings of the 11th International Conference on Frontiers in Handwriting Recognition, ICFHR 2008, pp. 373–378 (2008)
26. Xia, X.H., Song, X.Y., Luan, F.G., Zheng, J.G., Chen, Z.L., Ma, X.F.: Discriminative feature selection for on-line signature verification. Pattern Recognit. **74**, 422–433 (2018)
27. Xing, Z.J., Yin, F., Wu, Y.C., Liu, C.L.: Offline signature verification using convolution siamese network. In: Ninth International Conference on Graphic and Image Processing (ICGIP 2017), vol. 10615, p. 106151I. International Society for Optics and Photonics (2018)
28. Zhang, Z.H., Liu, X.Q., Cui, Y.: Multi-phase offline signature verification system using deep convolutional generative adversarial networks. In: 9th International Symposium on Computational Intelligence and Design (ISCID), vol. 2, pp. 103–107. IEEE (2016)

Finger-Vein Image Inpainting Based on an Encoder-Decoder Generative Network

Dan Li[1,2(✉)], Xiaojing Guo[2], Haigang Zhang[1,2], Guimin Jia[1,2], and Jinfeng Yang[1,2]

[1] Tianjin Key Lab for Advanced Signal Processing, Tianjin, China
iamhappy0713@163.com
[2] Civil Aviation University of China, Tianjin, China

Abstract. Finger-vein patterns are usually used for biometric recognition. There may be spots or stains on fingers when capturing finger-vein images. Therefore, the obtained finger-vein images may have irregular incompleteness. In addition, due to light attenuation in biological tissue, the collected finger-vein images are often seriously degraded. It is essential to establish an image inpainting and enhancement model for the finger-vein recognition scheme. In this paper, we proposed a novel image restoration mechanism for finger vein image including three main steps. First, the finger-vein images are enhanced by the combination of Gabor filter and Weber's low. Second, an encoder-decoder generative network is employed to make image inpainting. Finally, different loss functions are taken into consideration for the model optimization. In the simulation part, we carry out some comparative experiments, which demonstrates the effectiveness and practicality of the proposed finger-vein image restoration mechanism.

Keywords: Finger-vein images · Image inpainting
Encoder-decoder generative network

1 Introduction

Finger-vein recognition technology uses the texture of the finger-vein to perform identity verification, which is harmless and difficult to be forged. It is relatively easy for the acquisition of finger-vein image, and the recognition process is user-friendly. Therefore, the finger-vein recognition technology can be widely applied to the access control system in the fields of banking finance and government agencies.

Finger-vein is distributed below the skin with complex shape. The morphology of finger-vein is the result of the interaction of human DNA and finger development. Different fingers in the same person have different morphologies. These biological properties guarantee the uniqueness of the finger-vein. It also laid a solid biological foundation for the development of finger-vein biometrics.

Typically, finger-vein images are captured by near-infrared (NIR) light in a transillumination manner [1]. During the process of transmission, the NIR light

© Springer Nature Switzerland AG 2018
J.-H. Lai et al. (Eds.): PRCV 2018, LNCS 11256, pp. 87–97, 2018.
https://doi.org/10.1007/978-3-030-03398-9_8

is absorbed by hemoglobin flowing in the venous blood [2]. Then the finger-vein image with light and dark vascular lines is formed. The quality of the finger-vein images is very poor due to the attenuation of light in tissues [3]. Therefore, it is often difficult to extract reliable finger-vein features directly from original finger-vein images [4].

In some cases, finger-vein images may have irregular incompleteness due to external factors, like spots or stains on fingers, when capturing finger-vein images, as shown in Fig. 1. Hence, it is a common phenomenon that vascular networks are incomplete in the finger-vein images.

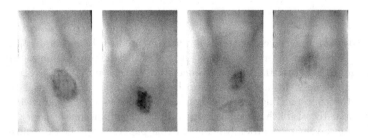

Fig. 1. Finger-vein images with spots or stains.

For the accurate feature extraction, it is an important topic to generate a realistic finger-vein vascular network based on the obtained finger-vein image. As far as we know, there is a few works to deal with the incomplete finger-vein collection, which motivates our work.

Recently, Convolutional Neural Networks (CNNs) have been widely applied in computer vision, especially in the field of image classification and image generation [5]. They also could be used to solve the problem of image inpainting and reconstruction. The finger-vein images with spots or stains belongs to the problem of image inpainting. Therefore, CNNs-based can also use in the finger-vein images inpainting and reconstruction. In [6], a multi-scale neural patch synthesis method is proposed, which achieves better performance for high-resolution image inpainting on the ImageNet dataset. In general, to achieve reasonable inpainting results, a lot of images are needed to train models. In [7], an image inpainting method based on contextual attention is proposed, which is very effective on large datasets such as the CelebA faces dataset. However, our dataset does not have so many images for training models. In addition, low-resolution grayscale images can affect the inpainting result. [8] proposes a context encoder approach for image inpainting using the combination of the reconstruction (L2) loss and adversarial loss [9]. Nevertheless, for the inpainting of the finger-vein image, blurred without smooth edges of vein is generated.

In this paper, inspired by these methods, we propose an inpainting scheme for finger-vein image with spots or stains. The detailed presentation of the proposed scheme as follows. First, the combination of Gabor filter and Weber's low are used for image enhancement by removing illumination variation in finger-vein images. Second, we design a novel finger-vein image inpainting frame based on an encoder-decoder network. Finally, different loss functions are used to optimize the inpainting frame. Experimental results show that the proposed method can achieve better performance in finger-vein image inpainting of irregular incompleteness.

2 Finger-Vein Image Acquisition

Finger is the most flexible part of the human body. Finger-vein images can be captured by placing the finger into imaging device. To obtain finger-vein images, we have designed a homemade finger-vein image acquisition device [10], as shown in Fig. 2(a). The device uses a NIR light to illuminate a finger. A vascular network of finger-vein is acquired by image sensor.

Extraction of ROI regions is essential for improving the accuracy of finger-vein recognition. We employ the effective method proposed in [11] to locate the ROIs from finger-vein images, as shown in Fig. 2(b). Some finger-vein ROIs of the same collector are listed in Fig. 2(c).

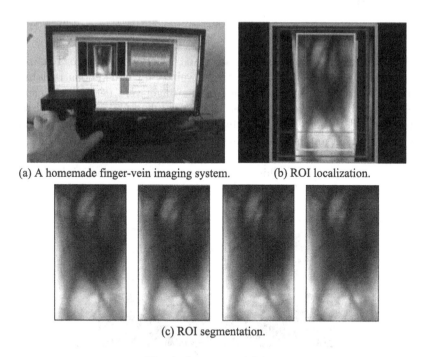

(a) A homemade finger-vein imaging system.   (b) ROI localization.

(c) ROI segmentation.

Fig. 2. Image acquisition.

The homemade dataset is included 5,850 grayscale images of finger-vein, which are commonly used for biometric recognition. The ROIs of captured finger-vein images are resized to 91 × 200 pixel. We enhance the grayscale images and resize them to 96 × 192 pixel. Most of the finger-vein images are complete, and only a few are incomplete during the acquisition process. The imbalanced class distribution can destroy the training of the model. Therefore, we have manually added some samples of finger-vein images with spots or stains, as shown in Fig. 3. They are incomplete images of finger-vein with square-region, single irregular-region and multiple irregular-region. These incomplete situations need to be reconstructed in the experiments. The encoder-decoder network is trained to regress the corrupting pixel values and reconstruct them as complete images.

Fig. 3. Finger-vein image with spots or stains.

3   Method

3.1   Image Enhancement

In NIR imaging, finger-vein images are often severely degraded. This results in a particularly poor separation between veins and non-venous regions (see Fig. 4(a)). In order to reliably strengthen the finger-vein networks, finger-vein images need to be effectively enhanced. Here, a bank of Gabor filters [12] with 8 orientations and Weber's Law Descriptor (WLD) [13] are combined for venous region enhancement and light attenuation elimination (see Fig. 4(b)). The Gabor filter is a linear filter for edge extraction, which is very suitable for texture expression and separation. This paper uses 8 orientations of Gabor filter to extract features. The WLD is used to improve the robustness of illumination.

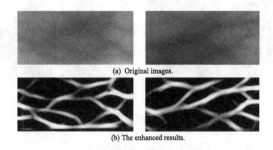

(a) Original images.

(b) The enhanced results.

Fig. 4. The results of image enhancement.

3.2   Image Inpainting Scheme

The finger-vein images inpainting scheme of the incomplete information can be achieved by four steps. First, finger-vein images with spots or stains are fed into the encoder as input images. The region of spots or stains are represented by larger pixel values in order to appear more apparent. And latent features are learned from the input images. Second, the learned features are propagated to decoder through a channel-wise fully-connected layer. Third, the decoder uses these features representation to obtain the image content of spots or stains. The output images of the encoder-decoder network are generated with the same size as the input images. Finally, the inpainting images are optimized by comparing with the ground-truth images. Figure 5 presents the overall architecture for the proposed image inpainting scheme.

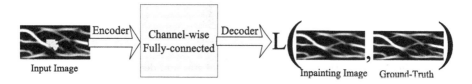

Fig. 5. The overall process of finger-vein image inpainting.

Encoder-Decoder Generative Network. Figure 6 shows an overview of our encoder-decoder generative network architecture. The encoder-decoder genera-tive network consists of three blocks: encoder, channel-wise fully-connected layer and decoder. The encoder is derived from AlexNet architecture [14]. The effect of encoder is to compress high dimensional input data into low dimensional repre-sentation. The encoder block has five convolutional layers using 4×4 kernels. The first convolution layer uses a stride of $[2, 4]$ to reduce the spatial dimension. And a square feature of 48×48 is obtained. The following four convolutional layers use a stride of $[2, 2]$. Given an input image of size 96×192, we use the first five con-volutional layers to compress the image into feature representation of $3 \times 3 \times 768$ dimension. The channel-wise fully-connected layer is a bridge between encoder features and decoder features propagated information (see Fig. 7). The decoder is the final function of training encoder-decoder. It reconstructs the input image using five convolutional layers. The feature representation of $3 \times 3 \times 768$ dimen-sion abstracted by the encoder use five up-sampling layers to generate an image of size 96×192.

3.3   Loss Function

There are usually multiple ways to fill an image content with spots or stains. Different loss functions result in different inpainting results. Optimizer minimizes the loss between the inpainting images and the ground-truth images. Proper loss

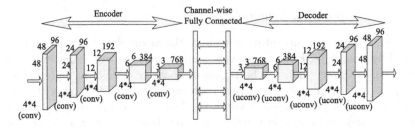

Fig. 6. Overview of our basic encoder-decoder generative network architecture.

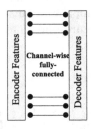

Fig. 7. Connection between encoder features and decoder features.

function makes the inpainting images very realistic and maintain the consistence with the given context. In this paper, we employ L1 loss to train the proposed finger-vein image inpainting model. In [6], L2+adv loss function has achieved better performance in the field of image inpainting. The comparative experiments use L2 loss function, joint L2 loss with adversarial loss, and joint L1 loss with adversarial loss the same way as the Context Encoder [7]. For each training image, the L1 and L2 loss is defined as:

$$L_{L1}(G) = E_{x,x_g}[||x - G(x_g)||], \tag{1}$$

$$L_{L2}(G) = E_{x,x_g}[||x - G(x_g)||^2], \tag{2}$$

where x, represents the ground-truth image, x_g denotes a finger-vein image with spots or stains, G denotes encoder-decoder generative network, $G(x_g)$ represents the generated inpainting image.

The adversarial loss is defined as:

$$L_{adv}(G) = E_{x_g}[-\log[D(G(x_g)) + \sigma]], \tag{3}$$

where D is an adversarial discriminator, which predicts the probability that the input image is a real image rather than a generated one, and σ is set to a small value in case the logarithm of the true number is equal to zero.

The joint L2 loss with adversarial loss is defined as:

$$L = \mu L_{L2}(G) + 1 - \mu L_{adv}(G), \tag{4}$$

The joint L1 loss with adversarial loss is defined as:

$$L = \mu L_{L1}(G) + 1 - \mu L_{adv}(G), \tag{5}$$

where μ is the weight of the two losses, which is used to balance the magnitude of the two losses in our experiments.

3.4 Evaluation

Peak Signal to Noise Ratio (PSNR), a full reference image quality evaluation index, which is used to calculate the peak signal-to-noise ratio between the ground-truth image and the inpainting image.

$$MSE = \frac{1}{H * W} \sum_{1}^{H} \sum_{1}^{W} (X(i,j) - Y(i,j))^2, \tag{6}$$

$$PSNR = 10 \lg \frac{(2^n - 1)^2}{MSE}, \tag{7}$$

where X presents the ground-truth image, Y presents the inpainting image; H and W respectively are the height and width of the image; n is the number of bits per pixel, which is generally taken as 8, that is, the pixel grayscale number is 256.

We report our evaluation in terms of mean L1 loss, mean L2 loss and PSNR on test set. Our method performs better in terms of L1 loss, L2 loss and PSNR during the experiment.

4   Experiments

We evaluate the proposed inpainting model on homemade dataset. This dataset includes 5850 finger-vein images, 5616 for training, 117 for validation, and 117 for testing. Our encoder-decoder generative network is trained using four different loss functions respectively to compare their performance. For these loss functions, the parameters of encoder-decoder are set in the same way. The four loss functions are: (a) L2+adv loss, (b) L1+adv loss, (c) L2 loss, (d) L1 loss. From top to bottom, we input three images with arbitrary incompleteness as the first row. And we use (a)-(d) to refer to these loss functions. The ground-truth images correspond to the input images are placed in the last row. In the experiment, incomplete information is randomly generated. In the following, the effectiveness of our method is illustrated by images and specific data. In 4.3, the practicality of the proposed method is verified by the finger-vein images with square-region incomplete.

4.1   Single Irregular-Region Incomplete

We use the four methods discussed above to reconstruct finger-vein images with a spot or stain, that is, an irregular incompleteness needs to be reconstructed. The encoder-decoder generative network is trained with a constant learning rate of 0.0001.The inpainting results for single irregular-region incomplete using the four loss functions are shown in Fig. 8. High-quality inpainting results are not only clear on the finger-vein vascular networks but also consistent with surrounding regions, where the finger-vein images are spots or stains at different shapes. In practice, L2+adv and L1+adv loss produce blurred images without smooth edges of veins. The pixel values of vein region are obviously lost based on L2 loss. Compared with other methods, a smooth and complete finger-vein network is generated based on the method proposed in this paper. Table 1 shows qualitative results from these experiments. As shown in Table 1, our method achieves the lowest mean L1 loss and the highest PSNR.

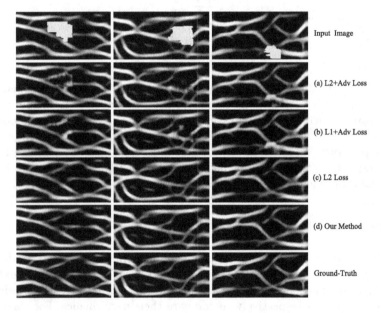

Fig. 8. Performance comparisons use four methods to inpainting single irregular-region incomplete.

Table 1. Numerical comparison on single irregular-region incomplete with four methods.

Method	Mean L1 Loss	Mean L2 Loss	PSNR
L2+Adv Loss	8.01%	4.31%	20.22 dB
L1+Adv Loss	6.45%	4.32%	20.27 dB
L2 Loss	9.58%	2.49%	22.43 dB
Our method	8.42%	2.32%	22.86 dB

4.2 Multiple Irregular-Region Incomplete

Similarly, we use the four loss functions to reconstruct finger-vein images with spots or stains, that is, multiple regions need to be reconstructed. The inpainting results for multiple irregular-region incomplete using the four methods are shown in Fig. 9. In practice, methods based on L2+adv and L1+adv loss produce blurred images without smooth edges of veins and pixels gathered together without any rules. Also, L2 loss makes the original pixel value loss more obvious. However, the inpainting images based on the L1 loss function are close to the ground truth images than the other methods. As Table 2 shows, the PSNR value is higher than the other methods. These results mean that the proposed method can achieve higher similarity with the ground-truth images than the other methods.

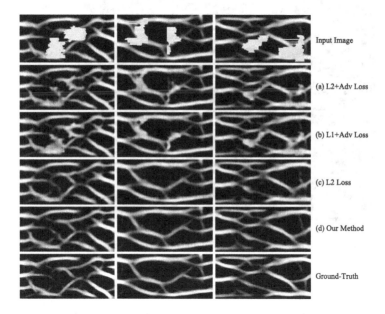

Fig. 9. Performance comparisons use four methods to inpainting multiple irregular-region incomplete.

4.3 Square-Region Incomplete

The practicality and effectiveness of the proposed method is verified by the finger-vein images with square-region incomplete. Here, we also use the four methods to reconstruct finger-vein images with square-region incomplete. The inpainting results for square-region incomplete using the four loss functions are shown in Fig. 10. We can see that the results of using our proposed method

Table 2. Numerical comparison on multiple irregular-region incomplete with four methods.

Method	Mean L1 Loss	Mean L2 Loss	PSNR
L2+Adv Loss	12.23%	7.79%	17.55 dB
L1+Adv Loss	8.99%	6.85%	18.13 dB
L2 Loss	10.53%	3.08%	21.48 dB
Our method	9.67%	3.03%	21.65 dB

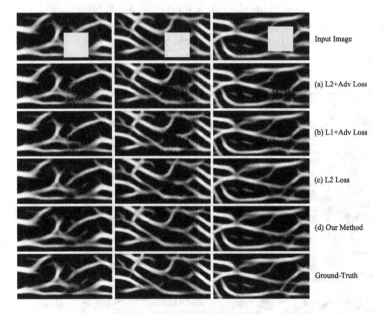

Fig. 10. Performance comparisons use four methods to inpainting square-region incomplete.

Table 3. Numerical comparison on square-region incomplete with four methods.

Method	Mean L1 Loss	Mean L1 Loss	PSNR
L2+Adv Loss	12.51%	3.33%	20.96 dB
L1+Adv Loss	5.28%	3.25%	21.53 dB
L2 Loss	8.51%	1.82%	23.92 dB
Our method	7.56%	1.80%	24.01 dB

are closer to the ground-truth images. Blurred images are generated based on L2+adv loss and L1+adv loss. In addition, the pixel values are seriously lost in the masked vein regions. Both visual images and specific data can show that our proposed method is effective (Table 3).

5   Conclusion

In this paper, a method for inpainting finger-vein grayscale images with spots or stains based on L1 loss function is proposed. A series of experiments are performed using four methods, and the proposed method is proved to be effective. As a future work, we plan to extend the method to ensure that all indicators are optimal.

Acknowledgements. This work is supported by National Natural Science Foundation of Chi-na (No.6150050657, No.61806208) and the Fundamental Research Funds for the Central Universities (NO.3122017001).

References

1. Kono, M., Ueki, H., Umemura, S.: Near-infrared finger vein patterns for personal identification. Appl. Opt. **41**(35), 7429–7436 (2002)
2. Zharov, V.P., Ferguson, S.: Infrared imaging of subcutaneous veins. Lasers Surg. Med. **34**(1), 56–61 (2010)
3. Sprawls, P.: Physical principles of medical imaging. Med. Phys. **22**(12), 2123–2123 (1995)
4. Yang, J.F., Shi, Y.H., Jia, G.M.: Finger-vein image matching based on adaptive curve transformation. Pattern Recogn. **66**, 34–43 (2017)
5. Denton, E., Chintala, S., Szlam, A., Fergus, R.: Deep generative image models using a Laplacian pyramid of adversarial networks. In: International Conference on Neural Information Processing Systems, pp. 1486–1494 (2015)
6. Yang, C., Lu, X., et al.: High-resolution image inpainting using multi-scale neural patch synthesis, pp. 4076–4084 (2017)
7. Pathak, D., Krahenbuhl, P., Donahue, J., Darrell, T.: Context encoders: feature learning by inpainting. In: Proceedings of the IEEE Conference on Computer Vision and Pattern Recognition, pp. 2536–2544 (2016)
8. Zhao, H., Gallo, O., Frosio, I., Kautz, J.: Loss functions for image restoration with neural networks. In: IEEE Transactions on Computational Imaging, pp. 47–57 (2017)
9. Yu, J., Lin, Z., Yang, J., et al.: Generative image inpainting with contextual attention (2018)
10. Yang, J.F., Shi, Y.H.: Towards finger-vein image restoration and enhancement for finger-vein recognition. Inf. Sci. **268**(6), 33–52 (2014)
11. Yang, J., Li, X.: Efficient finger-vein localization and recognition. In: International Conference on Pattern Recognition, pp. 1148–1151 (2010)
12. Yang, J., Shi, Y.: Finger-vein ROI localization and vein ridge enhancement. Elsevier Sci. **33**(12), 1569–1579 (2012)
13. Chen, J., Shan, S., He, C., et al.: WLD: a robust local image descriptor. IEEE Trans. Pattern Anal. Mach. Intell. **32**(9), 1705–1720 (2010)
14. Krizhevsky, A., Sutskever, I. and Hinton, G.E.: ImageNet classification with deep convolutional neural networks. In: International Conference on Neural Information Processing Systems, pp. 1097–1105 (2012)

Center-Level Verification Model for Person Re-identification

Ruochen Zheng, Yang Chen, Changqian Yu, Chuchu Han, Changxin Gao[(✉)], and Nong Sang

Key Laboratory of Ministry of Education for Image Processing and Intelligent Control, School of Automation, Huazhong University of Science and Technology, Wuhan 430074, China
{m201772447,cgao}@hust.edu.cn

Abstract. In past years, convolutional neural network is increasingly used in person re-identification due to its promising performance. Especially, the siamese network has been widely used with the combination of verification loss and identification loss. However, the loss functions are based on the individual samples, which cannot represent the distribution of the identity in the scenario of deep learning. In this paper, we introduce a novel center-level verification (CLEVER) model for the siamese network, which simply represents the distribution as a center and calculates the loss based on the center. To simultaneously consider both intra-class and inter-class variation, we propose an intra-center submodel and an inter-center submodel respectively. The loss of CLEVER model, combined with identification loss and verification loss, is used to train the deep network, which gets state-of-the-art results on CUHK03, CUHK01 and VIPeR datasets.

Keywords: Center-level · Intra-class variation · Inter-class distance

1 Introduction

Person re-identification (re-id), which aims at identifying persons at non-overlapping camera views, is an active task in computer vision for its wide range of applications. Because of the interference caused by different camera views, lighting conditions and body poses, many traditional approaches are proposed to solve these problems from two categories: feature extracting [10,12,14,21] and metric learning [8,12,16,20]. With the development of deep learning and the emergence of large datasets, deep neural network shows impressive performance in re-id [1,6,15,17,23]. The verification loss and triplet loss are widely used in deep learning. The verification loss [1,6,15,17,23] can be divided into two forms according to loss function differences: contrastive loss and cross-entropy loss. Both of them punish the dissimilarity of the same person and the similarity of the different persons. And the triplet loss [3–5,13,16] embeds space to make data points with the same label closer than the data points with different labels.

© Springer Nature Switzerland AG 2018
J.-H. Lai et al. (Eds.): PRCV 2018, LNCS 11256, pp. 98–107, 2018.
https://doi.org/10.1007/978-3-030-03398-9_9

Note that, both verification loss and triplet loss only take sample-level loss as consideration. However, the sample-level loss is not quite appropriate to deep leaning based method. Because mini batch is the common strategy adopted in both verification loss and triplet loss, in the training stage of deep learning. In a batch, only one image or several images are randomly selected in a camera for one identity, which cannot represent the real distribution of the image sets of the identity.

Recurrent neural network (RNN) [15, 17] provide a possible solutions for this problem by establishing a link between frames. However, temporal sequences are needed for RNN model in re-id task, so RNN can only work in video sequence. For the image set, center loss [18], which models a class as a center, may provide a simple yet effective way to address this problem. It is effective to punish intra-class variation by center loss. For each class, the center loss is calculated with the samples and the center, the center will be recorded and updated during training stage. Therefore, to some extent, the center can be considered as a representation of the distribution of the corresponding class. [9] has applied center loss on person re-identification. However, it only pays attention to reducing the intra-class variation, ignoring the inter-class distance. We argue that an effective constraint for inter-class distance will further boost the performance.

Motivated by center loss [18], this paper introduces a new architecture named Center-LEvel VERification (CLEVER) model for the siamese network, to overcome the shortcoming of sample-level loss. For each person identity, we take its center as the simple representation of its distribution. Based on the centers, we propose to simultaneously reduce intra-class variation and enlarge inter-class distance, by using *intra-center loss* and *inter-center loss* respectively, as shown in Fig. 1. Similar with the contrastive loss, a margin for the distances of different centers is set to limit the minimum inter-class distance, the distance less than the margin will be punished as inter-center loss. Moreover, by taking center-level as consideration, the combination of CLEVER model, identification loss and verification loss performs better than only combining identification loss and verification loss.

In summary, our contributions are two-fold: (1) We propose a center-level verification (CLEVER) model based on siamese network, which can both reduce intra-class variation and enlarge inter-class distance. (2) We show competitive results on CUHK03 [11], CUHK01 [10] and VIPeR [7], proving the effectiveness of our method.

2   Related Work

In this section, we describe previous works relevant to our method, including methods based on loss function models on person re-identification and methods trying to reduce the intra-class variation and enlarging inter-class distance.

Many works adopt the combination of identification loss and verification loss to train a network. Verification loss can be divided into cross-entropy form and contrastive loss according to differences of loss function. Cross-entropy form

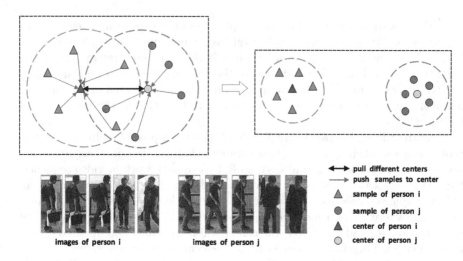

Fig. 1. Illustration of our motivation. Our CLEVER model makes a discriminate separation between two similar persons, by pushing images to their corresponding center and pulling their centers away.

adopts softmax layer to measure the similarity and dissimilarity of image pairs. [6,23] adopts the form of cross-entropy loss, combining with identification loss in their network. Different from cross-entropy loss, contrastive loss [15,17] form owns a margin to get a definite separation between positive pairs and negative pairs. However, both cross-entropy form and contrastive loss pay attention on sample-level, ignoring the real distribution of the whole image set.

Another loss function associated with our model is center loss. [18] adopts combination of center loss and softmax loss on face recognition task. And [9] applies center loss on the person re-id task to reduce intra-class variation. However, the neglect of constraint on inter-class distance limits the performance of these tasks.

The approach closest to our CLEVER model in motivation is the method [24,25]. Both of the methods concentrate on reducing the intra-class variation and enlarging inter-class distance. However, the two methods and area of concern are different from our CLEVER model. [24] pays attention on "image to video retrieval" problem with dictionary learning method, [25] tries to solve video based ReID with metric learning method. Our CLEVER model bases on 'image to image' ReID with deep learning method.

3   Our Approach

In this section, we present the architecture of our CLEVER model, as shown in overview. The CLEVER model has two main components: intra-center submodel and inter-center submodel. Intra-center submodel pushes samples to its corresponding center, while inter-center pulling different centers away. Specially, we take the form of image pairs as input to the siamese network. The images from two cameras with same identity, termed as positive pairs, are taken as input to intra-center submodel. In contrast, inter-center submodel adopts negative pairs, which represent images of different identities. In this section, we first introduce intra-center submodel and then inter-center submodel. The combination of sample-level will be presented at last.

3.1 Intra-center Model

In intra-center submodel, positive pairs are taken as the input of network. The distances between center and positive pairs will be punished by intra-center loss as follows:

$$L_{intra} = \frac{1}{2m} \sum_{i=1}^{m} (\|x_{i1} - c_{y_i}\|_2^2 + \|x_{i2} - c_{y_i}\|_2^2) \tag{1}$$

where x_{i1} and x_{i2} are the features extracting from images of identity y_i. And c_{y_i} is the center y_i corresponding. Specially, the center is updated as:

$$\frac{\partial L_c}{x_{i1}} = x_{i1} - c_{y_i} \tag{2}$$

$$\frac{\partial L_c}{x_{i2}} = x_{i2} - c_{y_i} \tag{3}$$

$$\triangle c_j = \frac{\sum_{i=1}^{m} \delta(y_i = k) \cdot (2 \cdot c_k - x_{i1} - x_{i2})}{1 + \sum_{i=1}^{m} \delta(y_i = k)} \tag{4}$$

$$c_k^{t+1} = c_k^t - \alpha \cdot \triangle c_k^t \tag{5}$$

where $\sum_{i=1}^{m} \delta(y_i = k)$ counts the number of pairs that belong to class k in a batch. The value of α, which ranges from 0 to 1, could be seen as learning rate of centers. The main difference of our inter-center submodel and center loss is that we adopt positive-image pair as input. Our method benefits from taking positive image pairs to update center simultaneously, so that we can learn a center closer to real center of image set. We conduct experiments to prove the effectiveness of this strategy.

However, intra-center model only cares about reducing the intra-class variation, the combination of identification loss still shows a weak ability to distinguish similar but different identities, which often occur in person re-identification task. Therefore, we propose inter-center loss to enlarge the distances of different classes in Sect. 3.2.

3.2 Inter-center Model

In the case of small intra-class variation based on intra-center submodel, we propose an inter-center submodel, which limits the minimum distances between different centers to pull different classes away. The inter-center distances less than margin will be punished by inter-center loss as follows:

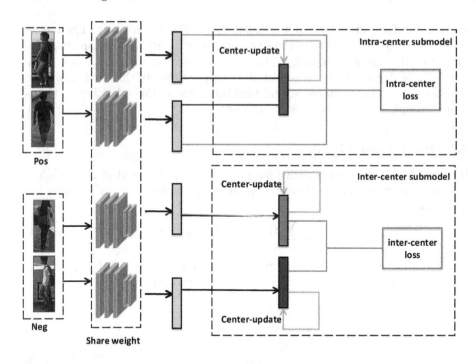

Fig. 2. An overview of the proposed CLEVER architecture. It contains intra-center submodel and inter-center submodel.

$$L_{inter} = \frac{1}{m} \sum_{j=1}^{m} \max(0, d - \|c_{y_{j1}} - c_{y_{j2}}\|_2^2) \tag{6}$$

$$y_{j1} \neq y_{j2}$$

where $\|c_{y_{j1}} - c_{y_{j2}}\|_2^2$ is the squared Euclidean distance between the center of c_{j1} and c_{j2}. And d plays a role as margin of the distances, m is the number of pairs in a batch. Negative pairs will be taken as input for inter-center submodel. They will also participate in the update of their corresponding centers.

3.3 Joint Optimization of Center-Level and Sample-Level

By setting the weight of center loss and inter-center loss. The center-level loss function can be formulated as follows:

$$L_{CLEVER} = \beta \cdot L_{intra} + \gamma \cdot L_{inter} \tag{7}$$

where β and γ control the balance of two terms. Our center-level loss function has the similar form to contrastive loss of image-level, thus it can be seen as the verification loss of center level.

The architecture of our center-level model is showed in Fig. 2. For the intra-center submodel, images of same identity coming from two cameras will be randomly selected as a positive pair for input. The two images of different camera will jointly update the corresponding center, which makes the operation more efficient and accuracy. Negative pairs will also update their corresponding centers in inter-center submodel. The architecture of center-level is also capable with image-level, which makes it possible for combining verification loss based on sample-level with our center-level model. Therefore, the final loss function could be formulated as follows:

$$L = L_I + L_V + L_{CLEVER} \tag{8}$$

where L_I is the identification loss coming from siamese network of two cameras, L_V is the verification loss, which adopts the cross-entropy loss form for it is more concise. The verification loss plays a role as dividing hard samples, which is very helpful for training the network.

Table 1. Results on CUHK03 using the single-shot setting. The results of several different combinations of components are listed. [9] offers code of * "IV", we adopt the code and get a slightly different result. Here we report the result we get.

Method	rank1	rank5	rank10
baseline IC [9]	80.20	96.10	97.90
CLEVER(intra only)+I	81.45	96.25	98.00
baseline IV*	81.90	95.30	97.75
CLEVER(intra only)+IV	83.10	96.35	98.40
CLEVER(inter only)+IV	81.45	95.30	97.80
CLEVER+I	82.00	96.45	98.45
CLEVER+IV	84.85	97.15	98.25

4 Experiment

4.1 Datasets

We conduct our experiments on CUHK03, CUHK01 and VIPeR datasets. CUHK03 contains 13164 images of 1360 identities. It provides two settings, one is annotated by human and the other one is annotated from deformable part models (DPM). We will evaluate our model on the bounding boxes detected by DPM, which is closer to practical scenarios. Following the conventional experimental setting, 1160 persons will be used for training and 100 persons for testing. The results of single shot will be reported. CUHK01 contains 971 identities with two camera views, and each identity owns two images. VIPeR contains 632 identities with two camera views, each identity owns one image. For the CUHK01 and VIPeR datasets, we randomly divide the individuals into two equal parts, with one used for training and the other for testing. Both CUHK01 and VIPeR adopt single-shot setting.

4.2   Implementation Details

We set [9] as our baseline. A CNN that contains only nine convolutional layers and four max pooling layers is proposed in [9], for more detail about structure can be found in [9]. Each image is resized to 128×48 to adjust to convolution network. Note that, smaller inputs make feature maps smaller, and shallower networks have fewer parameters, which makes the depth network easier to apply to real-world scenarios. Before training, the mean of training images will be subtracted from all the images.

For the hyper parameters setting, the batch size is set to 200, 100 images for positive pairs and the other for negative pairs. α is set as 0.5, β and γ are set as 0.01 and 0.008, respectively. The value of d is set as 250. The number of training iterations is 25k, the initial learning rate is 0.001, decayed by 0.1 after 22k iterations. For the value of centers, we uniformly initialize them with zero vector with the same size as features.

For the experiment on CUHK03, we follow the protocol in [11], all experiments are repeated 20 times with different splitting of training and testing sets, the results will be averaged to ensure stable results. For the CUHK01 and VIPeR datasets, we conduct experiment following the set of [6]. The model will be pretrained on CUHK03 [11] and Market1501 [22] at first. Then we fine-tune it on CUHK01 and VIPeR. The experiment will be repeated with 10 random splits. To evaluate the performance of our methods, the Cumulative Matching Characteristic curve (CMC) will be used. The CMC curves represents the number of true matching in first k ranks.

4.3   Effectiveness of Each Component

We evaluate the effectiveness of the components of the CLEVER model on CUHK03 dataset. The results are shown in Table 1. For the abbreviations for different combinations, the combination of identification loss and verification loss is called "IV". "IC" means the combination of identification loss and center loss. Taking identification loss only is called "I". From Table 1, we can see the combination of our "CLEVER" model and "IV" gets best performance, it achieves 84.85% rank-1 accuracy, obtaining 2.95% improvement on "IV", which proves the effectiveness of our CLEVER model. The strategy of pair image input gets proved on the comparison between "IC" and "CLEVER(intra only)+I". The accuracy of rank-1 obtains 1.25% improvement.

Another interesting result comes from the contrast experiment of verification loss. We replace "CLEVER+IV" by "CLEVER+I", the accuracy drops 2% in rank-1 accuracy, which prove the importance of verification loss. We analyzes that verification loss can serve as verifying the hard samples, which is helpful for training. The validity of the inter-center submodel can be verified from the comparative experiments of "CLEVER+IV" and "CLEVER(intra only)+IV". By setting a minimum distances among different centers, the model obtain 1.75% improvement.

4.4   Comparison with the State of the Arts

Table 2 summarizes the comparison of our method with the state-of-the-art methods. It is obvious that our method performs better than most of approaches above, which proves competitiveness of our method. It should be noted that "CNN Embedding" [23] and "Deep Transfer" [6] uses ImageNet data for pre-training, but we get higher rank-1 accuracy than them on CUHK03 datasets without ImageNet pretraining. In CUHK01 and VIPeR datasets, "Deep Transfer" gets best performance for its advantage of taking ImageNet data, and our method still show competitive results.

Table 2. Comparison with state-of-the-art methods on CUHK03 (detected), CUHK01 and VIPeR datasets using the single-shot setting.

Dataset	CUHK03			CUHK01			VIPeR		
Method	rank1	rank5	rank10	rank1	rank5	rank10	rank1	rank5	rank10
Siamese LSTM [17]	57.30	80.10	88.30	-	-	-	42.40	68.70	79.40
CNN Embedding [23]	83.40	97.10	98.70	-	-	-	-	-	-
GOG [14]	67.30	91.00	96.00	57.80	79.10	86.20	49.70	**79.70**	88.70
MCP-CNN [4]	-	-	-	53.70	84.30	91.00	47.80	74.70	84.80
Ensembles [16]	62.10	89.10	94.30	53.40	76.30	84.40	45.90	77.50	**88.90**
CNN-FRW-IC [9]	82.10	96.20	98.20	70.50	90.00	94.80	50.40	77.60	85.80
IDLA [1]	54.74	86.50	94.00	47.53	71.50	80.00	34.81	63.32	74.79
Deep Transfer [6]	84.10	-	-	**77.00**	-	-	**56.30**	-	-
DGD [19]	80.50	94.90	97.10	71.70	88.60	92.60	35.40	62.30	69.30
Quadruplet+MargOHNM [2]	75.53	95.15	**99.16**	62.55	83.44	89.71	49.05	73.10	81.96
CLEVER+iv	**84.85**	**97.15**	98.25	70.90	**90.86**	**94.92**	52.33	79.41	88.53

4.5   Discussions on CLEVER Model

The sample-based approaches in past years pay attention to optimizing the network by controlling the distance between individuals. However, such a strategy cannot effectively use the information of the global distribution in each comparison, because only two or three images are utilized in the comparison process. Our method records the center information based on sample level, and the center information can be seen as the representation of the global information. The significance of the existence of the center is not only to control the intra-class variation, but also to limit the distance between different classes. Our approach proves the effectiveness of this strategy in person re-identification.

5   Conclusion

In this paper, we have proposed a center-level verification model named CLEVER model for person re-identification, to handle the weakness of the sample-level models. The loss function of the CLEVER model is calculated by the samples and their centers, which to some extent represent the corresponding distributions. Finally, we combine the proposed center-level loss and the sample-level loss, to simultaneously control the intra-class variation and inter-class distance. The control of center improves the generation ability of network, which has outperformed most of the state-of-the-art methods on CUHK03, CUHK01 and VIPeR.

Acknowledgements. This work was supported by National Key R&D Program of China (No. 2018YFB1004600), the Project of the National Natural Science Foundation of China (No. 61876210), and Natural Science Foundation of Hubei Province (No. 2018CFB426).

References

1. Ahmed, E., Jones, M., Marks, T.K.: An improved deep learning architecture for person re-identification. In: Proceedings of the IEEE Conference on Computer Vision and Pattern Recognition, pp. 3908–3916 (2015)
2. Chen, W., Chen, X., Zhang, J., Huang, K.: Beyond triplet loss: a deep quadruplet network for person re-identification. In: Proceedings of the CVPR, vol. 2 (2017)
3. Chen, W., Chen, X., Zhang, J., Huang, K.: A multi-task deep network for person re-identification. In: AAAI, vol. 1, p. 3 (2017)
4. Cheng, D., Gong, Y., Zhou, S., Wang, J., Zheng, N.: Person re-identification by multi-channel parts-based CNN with improved triplet loss function. In: Proceedings of the IEEE Conference on Computer Vision and Pattern Recognition, pp. 1335–1344 (2016)
5. Ding, S., Lin, L., Wang, G., Chao, H.: Deep feature learning with relative distance comparison for person re-identification. Pattern Recognit. **48**(10), 2993–3003 (2015)
6. Geng, M., Wang, Y., Xiang, T., Tian, Y.: Deep transfer learning for person re-identification. arXiv preprint arXiv:1611.05244 (2016)
7. Gray, D., Brennan, S., Tao, H.: Evaluating appearance models for recognition, reacquisition, and tracking. In: Proceedings of the IEEE International Workshop on Performance Evaluation for Tracking and Surveillance (PETS), vol. 3, pp. 1–7. Citeseer (2007)
8. Hirzer, M.: Large scale metric learning from equivalence constraints. In: Proceedings of the 2012 IEEE Conference on Computer Vision and Pattern Recognition (CVPR), pp. 2288–2295. IEEE Computer Society (2012)
9. Jin, H., Wang, X., Liao, S., Li, S.Z.: Deep person re-identification with improved embedding. arXiv preprint arXiv:1705.03332 (2017)
10. Li, W., Wang, X.: Locally aligned feature transforms across views. In: 2013 IEEE Conference on Computer Vision and Pattern Recognition (CVPR), pp. 3594–3601. IEEE (2013)

11. Li, W., Zhao, R., Xiao, T., Wang, X.: Deepreid: deep filter pairing neural network for person re-identification. In: Proceedings of the IEEE Conference on Computer Vision and Pattern Recognition, pp. 152–159 (2014)

12. Liao, S., Hu, Y., Zhu, X., Li, S.Z.: Person re-identification by local maximal occurrence representation and metric learning. In: Proceedings of the IEEE Conference on Computer Vision and Pattern Recognition, pp. 2197–2206 (2015)

13. Liu, J., et al.: Multi-scale triplet CNN for person re-identification. In: Proceedings of the 2016 ACM on Multimedia Conference, pp. 192–196. ACM (2016)

14. Matsukawa, T., Okabe, T., Suzuki, E., Sato, Y.: Hierarchical Gaussian descriptor for person re-identification. In: Proceedings of the IEEE Conference on Computer Vision and Pattern Recognition, pp. 1363–1372 (2016)

15. McLaughlin, N., del Rincon, J.M., Miller, P.: Recurrent convolutional network for video-based person re-identification. In: 2016 IEEE Conference on Computer Vision and Pattern Recognition (CVPR), pp. 1325–1334. IEEE (2016)

16. Paisitkriangkrai, S., Shen, C., van den Hengel, A.: Learning to rank in person re-identification with metric ensembles. In: Proceedings of the IEEE Conference on Computer Vision and Pattern Recognition, pp. 1846–1855 (2015)

17. Varior, R.R., Shuai, B., Lu, J., Xu, D., Wang, G.: A siamese long short-term memory architecture for human re-identification. In: Leibe, B., Matas, J., Sebe, N., Welling, M. (eds.) ECCV 2016. LNCS, vol. 9911, pp. 135–153. Springer, Cham (2016). https://doi.org/10.1007/978-3-319-46478-7_9

18. Wen, Y., Zhang, K., Li, Z., Qiao, Y.: A discriminative feature learning approach for deep face recognition. In: Leibe, B., Matas, J., Sebe, N., Welling, M. (eds.) ECCV 2016. LNCS, vol. 9911, pp. 499–515. Springer, Cham (2016). https://doi.org/10.1007/978-3-319-46478-7_31

19. Xiao, T., Li, H., Ouyang, W., Wang, X.: Learning deep feature representations with domain guided dropout for person re-identification. In: 2016 IEEE Conference on Computer Vision and Pattern Recognition (CVPR), pp. 1249–1258. IEEE (2016)

20. Zhang, L., Xiang, T., Gong, S.: Learning a discriminative null space for person re-identification. In: Proceedings of the IEEE Conference on Computer Vision and Pattern Recognition, pp. 1239–1248 (2016)

21. Zhao, R., Ouyang, W., Wang, X.: Learning mid-level filters for person re-identification. In: Proceedings of the IEEE Conference on Computer Vision and Pattern Recognition, pp. 144–151 (2014)

22. Zheng, L., Shen, L., Tian, L., Wang, S., Wang, J., Tian, Q.: Scalable person re-identification: a benchmark. In: Proceedings of the IEEE International Conference on Computer Vision, pp. 1116–1124 (2015)

23. Zheng, Z., Zheng, L., Yang, Y.: A discriminatively learned CNN embedding for person reidentification. ACM Trans. Multimed. Comput. Commun. Appl. (TOMM) **14**(1), 13 (2017)

24. Zhu, X., Jing, X.-Y., Wu, F., Wang, Y., Zuo, W., Zheng, W.-S.: Learning heterogeneous dictionary pair with feature projection matrix for pedestrian video retrieval via single query image. In: AAAI, pp. 4341–4348 (2017)

25. Zhu, X., Jing, X.-Y., You, X., Zhang, X., Zhang, T.: Video-based person re-identification by simultaneously learning intra-video and inter-video distance metrics. IEEE Trans. Image Process. **27**(11), 5683–5695 (2018)

Non-negative Dual Graph Regularized Sparse Ranking for Multi-shot Person Re-identification

Aihua Zheng, Hongchao Li, Bo Jiang$^{(\boxtimes)}$, Chenglong Li, Jin Tang, and Bin Luo

School of Computer Science and Technology, Anhui University, Hefei, China
{ahzheng214,tj,luobin}@ahu.edu.cn, {lhc950304,lcl1314}@foxmail.com,
zeyiabc@163.com

Abstract. Person re-identification (Re-ID) has recently attracted enthusiastic attention due to its potential applications in social security and smart city surveillance. The promising achievement of sparse coding in image based recognition gives rise to a number of development on Re-ID especially with limited samples. However, most of existing sparse ranking based Re-ID methods lack of considering the geometric structure on the data. In this paper, we design a non-negative dual graph regularized sparse ranking method for multi-shot person Re-ID. First, we enforce a global graph regularizer into the sparse ranking model to encourage the probe images from the same person generating similar coefficients. Second, we enforce additional local graph regularizer to encourage the gallery images of the same person making similar contributions to the reconstruction. At last, we impose the non-negative constraint to ensure the meaningful interpretation of the coefficients. Based on these three cues, we design a unified sparse ranking framework for multi-shot Re-ID, which aims to simultaneously capture the meaningful geometric structures within both probe and gallery images. Finally, we provide an iterative optimization algorithm by Accelerated Proximal Gradient (APG) to learn the reconstruction coefficients. The ranking results of a certain probe against given gallery are obtained by accumulating the redistributed reconstruction coefficients. Extensive experiments on three benchmark datasets, i-LIDS, CAVIARA4REID and MARS with both hand-crafted and deep features yield impressive performance in multi-shot Re-ID.

Keywords: Person re-identification · Sparse ranking
Dual graph regularization · Non-negativity

1 Introduction

Person re-identification (Re-ID), which aims to identify person images from the gallery that shares the same identity as the given probe, is an active task driven by the applications of visual surveillance and social security. Despite of years of

© Springer Nature Switzerland AG 2018
J.-H. Lai et al. (Eds.): PRCV 2018, LNCS 11256, pp. 108–120, 2018.
https://doi.org/10.1007/978-3-030-03398-9_10

extensive efforts [2,5,30–32], it still faces various challenges due to the changes of illumination, pose, camera view and occlusions.

From the data point of view, Re-ID task fails into two categories: (1) Single-shot Re-ID, where only a single image is recorded for each person under each camera view. Despite of extensive studied in recent years [16,21,29], the performance is restrained by the limited information in a single person image. (2) Multi-shot Re-ID, where multiple frames are recorded for each person, is more realistic in real-life applications with more visual aspects. We focus on multi-shot Re-ID in this paper. The main stream of solving Re-ID problem devote to two aspects or both: (1) Appearance modeling [2,3,29,30], which develops a robust feature descriptor to leverage the various changes and occlusions between cameras. (2) Learning-based methods [16,18,21,31], which learns a metric distance to mitigate the appearance gaps between the low-level features and the high-level semantics. Recently, deep neural networks have made a remarkable progress on feature learning for Re-ID [14,17,24,28,34]. However, most of existing methods require large labor of training procedure.

Sparse ranking [22], as a powerful subspace learning and representation technique, has been successfully applied to extensive image based applications which gives rise to a number of development on Re-ID. The basic idea is to characterize the probe image as a linear combination of few items/images from an over-complete dictionary gallery. Liu et al. [19] proposed to learn two coupled dictionaries for both probe and gallery from both labeled and unlabeled images to transfer the features of the same person from different cameras. Karanam et al. [12] learnt a single dictionary for both gallery and probe images to overcome the viewpoint and associated appearance changes and then discriminatively trained the dictionary by enforcing explicit constraints on the associated sparse representations. Zheng et al. [33] proposed a weight-based sparse coding approach to reduce the influence of abnormal residuals caused by occlusion and body variation. Lisanti et al. [18] proposed to learn a discriminative sparse basis expansions of targets in terms of a labeled gallery of known individuals followed by a soft- and hard- re-weighting to redistribute energy among the most relevant contributing elements. Jing et al. [11] proposed a semi-coupled low-rank discriminant dictionary learning with discriminant term and a low-rank regularization term to characterize intrinsic feature space with different resolution for Re-ID.

However, most of existing sparse ranking based Re-ID methods encoded the probe images from the same person independently therefore failed to take advantage of their intrinsic geometric structure information, especially in multi-shot Re-ID. As we observed that, the same person under the same camera are generally with similar appearance. Therefore, we argue to preserve this geometrical structure embedded in both probe and gallery images. Inspired by the great superiority of graph regularized sparse coding in image based applications [9,25,26], we propose to explore the intrinsic geometry in multi-shot Re-ID via a non-negative dual graph regularized sparse ranking approach in this paper. After rendering the Re-ID task as sparse coding based multi-class classification problem, we first explore the global geometrical structure by enforcing the smoothness between the coefficients referring the images from the same person in probe. Then, we explore the local geometrical structure by encouraging the images from the same person in the gallery making similar contributions while reconstructing a certain probe image. The optimized coefficients considering both global and local information are obtained via iterative optimization by Accelerated Proximal Gradient (APG) [20]. The final rankings of the certain probe against given gallery are achieved by accumulating the reconstruction coefficients.

2   Problem Statement

Given $\mathbf{X} = [\mathbf{x}_1, \mathbf{x}_2, \ldots, \mathbf{x}_n] \in R^{d \times n}$, where n denotes the number of images of a person in probe, where $\mathbf{x}_j \in R^{d \times 1}, j = \{1, \ldots, n\}$ denotes the corresponding d-dimensional feature. While $\mathbf{D} = [\mathbf{D}^1, \mathbf{D}^2, \ldots, \mathbf{D}^G] \in R^{d \times M}$ denotes the total M images of G persons in gallery, where $\mathbf{D}^p = [\mathbf{d}_1^p, \mathbf{d}_2^p, \ldots, \mathbf{d}_{g_p}^p] \in R^{d \times g_p}, p = \{1, \ldots, G\}$ represents the matrix of g_p basis feature vectors for the p-th person, g_p denotes the number of images of the p-th person in gallery. Obviously, $M = \sum_{p=1}^{G} g_p$. The basic idea of sparse ranking based Re-ID is to reconstruct a testing probe image $\mathbf{x}_j$ with linear spanned training gallery images of G persons:

$$\mathbf{x}_j \approx \sum_{p=1}^{G} \mathbf{D}^p \mathbf{c}_j^p$$
$$= \mathbf{D} \mathbf{c}_j \tag{1}$$

where $\mathbf{c}_j^p = [\mathbf{c}_{j,1}^p, \mathbf{c}_{j,2}^p, \ldots, \mathbf{c}_{j,g_p}^p]^T \in R^{g_p \times 1}$ represents the coding coefficients of the p-th person against the probe instance $\mathbf{x}_j$. The dictionary $\mathbf{D}$ can be highly overcomplete. In order to concentratively reconstruct the probe via relatively few dictionary atoms from the gallery, we can impose the sparsity constraint into above formulation as an ℓ_1-norm regularized least squares problem:

$$\min_{\mathbf{c}_j} \|\mathbf{x}_j - \mathbf{D} \mathbf{c}_j\|_2^2, \ s.t. \ \|\mathbf{c}_j\|_1 \le \epsilon, \ \epsilon > 0 \tag{2}$$

where ϵ is error bound of the sparsity. It is equivalent to the LASSO problem [7], which could be formulated as

$$\min_{\mathbf{c}_j} \|\mathbf{x}_j - \mathbf{D} \mathbf{c}_j\|_2^2 + \lambda \|\mathbf{c}_j\|_1 \tag{3}$$

where λ controls the tradeoff between minimization of the ℓ_2 reconstruction error and the ℓ_1-norm of the sparsity used to reconstruct $\mathbf{x}_j$.

It worth noting that Eq. (3) reconstructs each probe image independently while ignoring the intrinsic geometry within the probe images. Moreover, it lacks of considering the dependency of the dictionary atoms in gallery when reconstructing a certain probe.

3   Non-negative Dual Graph Regularized Sparse Ranking

Based on above discussion, we design a non-negative dual graph regularized sparse ranking (NNDGSR) to simultaneously exploit the global and local geometric structures in both probe and gallery for multi-shot Re-ID.

3.1   Dual Graph Regularized Sparse Ranking

Global Graph Regularization. On the one hand, we argue that the feature vectors derived from the multiple images of the same person tend to have similar geometric distribution. To exploit the intrinsic geometric distribution among the probe images, we first enforce a global graph regularizer over the reconstruction coefficients:

$$\min_{\mathbf{c}_j} \sum_{j=1}^{n} \|\mathbf{x}_j - \mathbf{D}\mathbf{c}_j\|_2^2 + \lambda\|\mathbf{c}_j\|_1 + \frac{1}{2}\beta \sum_{i,j\in\{1,\dots,n\}} \|\mathbf{c}_i - \mathbf{c}_j\|_2^2 \mathbf{S}_{i,j}, \qquad (4)$$

$\{\mathbf{c}_i, \mathbf{c}_j\} \in R^{M\times1}$ is the reconstruction coefficients of images $\mathbf{x}_i$ and $\mathbf{x}_j$ from the same person over gallery dictionary $\mathbf{D}$ respectively. β is a balance parameter controlling the contribution of the regularizer. The similarity matrix $\mathbf{S} \in R^{n\times n}$ is defined as:

$$\mathbf{S}_{i,j} = exp(\frac{-\|\mathbf{x}_i - \mathbf{x}_j\|_2^2}{2\sigma_1^2}), \qquad (5)$$

where σ_1 is a parameter fixed as 0.2 in this paper. The global regularizer in Eq. (4) encourages the probe images from the same person with higher similarity to generate closer coefficients during reconstruction.

Local Graph Regularization On the other hand, we further argue that the multiple images of the same person in gallery fail into similar geometry. To exploit the intrinsic geometry among the gallery images, we further enforce a local graph regularizer over the reconstruction coefficients:

$$\min_{\mathbf{c}_j} \sum_{j=1}^{n} \|\mathbf{x}_j - \mathbf{D}\mathbf{c}_j\|_2^2 + \lambda\|\mathbf{c}_j\|_1 + \frac{1}{2}\beta \sum_{i,j\in\{1,\dots,n\}} \|\mathbf{c}_i - \mathbf{c}_j\|_2^2 \mathbf{S}_{i,j}$$
$$+ \frac{1}{2}\gamma \sum_{p=1}^{G}\sum_{j=1}^{n} \sum_{k,l\in\{1,\dots,g_p\}} (\mathbf{c}_{j,k}^p - \mathbf{c}_{j,l}^p)^2 \mathbf{B}_{k,l}^p, \qquad (6)$$

where the $\mathbf{c}_j^p = [\mathbf{c}_{j,1}^p, \mathbf{c}_{j,2}^p, \dots, \mathbf{c}_{j,g_p}^p]^T \in R^{g_p\times1}$ represents the coefficients to reconstruct $\mathbf{x}_j$ for the p-th person. γ is a parameter to signify the local regularizer. The similarity matrix $\mathbf{B} = diag\{\mathbf{B}^1, \mathbf{B}^2, \dots, \mathbf{B}^G\} \in R^{M\times M}$, and each element $\mathbf{B}^p \in R^{g_p\times g_p}$ is defined as:

$$\mathbf{B}_{k,l}^p = exp(\frac{-\|\mathbf{d}_k^p - \mathbf{d}_l^p\|_2^2}{2\sigma_2^2}), \qquad (7)$$

where σ_2 is a parameter fixed as 0.2 in this paper. $\mathbf{D} = [\mathbf{D}^1, \mathbf{D}^2, \ldots, \mathbf{D}^G] \in R^{d \times M}$ denotes the total M images of G persons in gallery, where $\mathbf{D}^p = [\mathbf{d}_1^p, \mathbf{d}_2^p, \ldots, \mathbf{d}_{g_p}^p] \in R^{d \times g_p}, p = \{1, \ldots, G\}$ represents the matrix of g_p basis feature vectors for the p-th person. The local regularizer in Eq. (6) encourages the higher similarity between the gallery images from the same person, the closer contribution to the reconstruction. With simple algebra, Eq. (6) can be rewritten as:

$$\min_{\mathbf{C}} \|\mathbf{X} - \mathbf{DC}\|_F^2 + \lambda \|\mathbf{C}\|_1 + \beta tr(\mathbf{CL}_1\mathbf{C}^T) + \gamma tr(\mathbf{C}^T\mathbf{L}_2\mathbf{C}). \qquad (8)$$

where $\mathbf{C} = [\mathbf{c}_1, \mathbf{c}_2, \ldots, \mathbf{c}_n] \in R^{M \times n}$, $\mathbf{L}_1 = \mathbf{H} - \mathbf{S}$ is the graph Laplacian matrix, $\mathbf{H} = \text{diag}\{\sum_j \mathbf{S}_{1,j}, \sum_j \mathbf{S}_{2,j}, \cdots\}$ is the degree matrix of $\mathbf{S}$, and $\text{diag}\{\cdots\}$ indicates the diagonal operation, $tr\{\cdots\}$ indicates the trace of a matrix. Analogously, $\mathbf{L}_2 = \mathbf{T} - \mathbf{B}$ is the graph Laplacian matrix, and $\mathbf{T} = \text{diag}\{\sum_j \mathbf{B}_{1,j}, \sum_j \mathbf{B}_{2,j}, \cdots\}$ is the degree matrix of $\mathbf{B}$.

3.2   Non-negative Dual Graph Regularized Sparse Ranking

Thinking that the reconstruction coefficients are meaningless while representing similarity measures between probe and gallery, we further enforce the non-negative constraint on the reconstruction coefficients in the proposed model, and the final formulation is as follows:

$$\min_{\mathbf{C}} \|\mathbf{X} - \mathbf{DC}\|_F^2 + \lambda \|\mathbf{C}\|_1 + \beta tr(\mathbf{CL}_1\mathbf{C}^T) + \gamma tr(\mathbf{C}^T\mathbf{L}_2\mathbf{C}), \ s.t. \ \mathbf{C} \geq \mathbf{0}. \qquad (9)$$

which is named NNDGSR in this paper. The non-negative constraint ensures that the probe image should be represented by the gallery images in a non-subtractive way.

3.3   Model Optimization

Due to the non-negativeness of the elements in $\mathbf{C}$, Eq. (10) can be written as:

$$\min_{\mathbf{C}} \|\mathbf{X} - \mathbf{DC}\|_F^2 + \lambda \mathbf{1}^T\mathbf{C1} + \beta tr(\mathbf{CL}_1\mathbf{C}^T) + \gamma tr(\mathbf{C}^T\mathbf{L}_2\mathbf{C}), \ s.t. \ \mathbf{C} \geq \mathbf{0}, \qquad (10)$$

where $\mathbf{1}$ denotes the vector that its all elements are 1. To solve Eq. (10), we convert it to an unconstrained form as:

$$\min_{\mathbf{C}} \|\mathbf{X} - \mathbf{DC}\|_F^2 + \lambda \mathbf{1}^T\mathbf{C1} + \beta tr(\mathbf{CL}_1\mathbf{C}^T) + \gamma tr(\mathbf{C}^T\mathbf{L}_2\mathbf{C}) + \psi(\mathbf{C}), \qquad (11)$$

where

$$\psi(\mathbf{c}_{j,k}^p) = \begin{cases} 0, & if \ \mathbf{c}_{j,k}^p \geq 0, \\ \infty, & otherwise. \end{cases} \qquad (12)$$

In this paper, we utilize the accelerated proximal gradient (APG) [20] approach to optimize efficiently. We denote:

$$F(\mathbf{C}) = \min_{\mathbf{C}} \|\mathbf{X} - \mathbf{DC}\|_F^2 + \lambda \mathbf{1}^T\mathbf{C1} + \beta tr(\mathbf{CL}_1\mathbf{C}^T) + \gamma tr(\mathbf{C}^T\mathbf{L}_2\mathbf{C})$$
$$Q(\mathbf{C}) = \psi(\mathbf{C}) \qquad (13)$$

Obviously, $F(\mathbf{C})$ and $Q(\mathbf{C})$ are a differentiable convex function and a non-smooth convex function, respectively. Therefore, according to the APG method, we obtain:

$$\mathbf{C}_{k+1} = \min_{\mathbf{C}} \frac{\xi}{2}\|\mathbf{C} - \mathbf{K}_{k+1} + \frac{\nabla F(\mathbf{K}_{k+1})}{\xi}\|_F^2 + Q(\mathbf{C}), \tag{14}$$

where k indicates the current iteration time, and ξ is the Lipschitz constant. $\mathbf{K}_{k+1} = \mathbf{C}_k + \frac{\rho_{k-1}-1}{\rho_k}(\mathbf{C}_k - \mathbf{C}_{k-1})$, where ρ_k is a positive sequence with $\rho_0 = \rho_1 = 1$. Equation (14) can be solved by:

$$\mathbf{C}_{k+1} = \max(0, \mathbf{K}_{k+1} - \frac{\nabla F(\mathbf{K}_{k+1})}{\xi}). \tag{15}$$

Algorithm 1 summarizes the whole optimization procedure.

Algorithm 1. Optimization Procedure to Eq. (13)

Input: query feature matrix $\mathbf{X}$, dictionary/gallery feature matrix $\mathbf{D}$, Laplacian matrix $\mathbf{L}_1$ and $\mathbf{L}_2$, parameters λ, β and γ;
Set $\mathbf{C}_0 = \mathbf{C}_1 = \mathbf{0}, \xi = 1.8 \times 10^3, \varepsilon = 10^{-4}, \rho_0 = \rho_1 = 1, maxIter = 150, k = 1$
Output: $\mathbf{C}$
1: While not converged **do**
2: Update $\mathbf{K}_{k+1}$ by $\mathbf{K}_{k+1} = \mathbf{C}_k + \frac{\rho_{k-1}-1}{\rho_k}(\mathbf{C}_k - \mathbf{C}_{k-1})$;
3: Update $\mathbf{C}_{k+1}$ by Eq. (15);
4: Update $\rho_{k+1} = \frac{1+\sqrt{1+4\rho_k^2}}{2}$;
5: Update k by $k = k + 1$;
6: The convergence condition: maximum number of iterations reaches $maxIter$ or the maximum element change of $\mathbf{C}$ between two consecutive iterations is less than ε.
7: **end While**

---

4   Ranking Implementation for Multi-shot Re-ID

Due to the sparsity of the reconstruction coefficients, the majority of which collapse to zero after few higher coefficients. Therefore, we can not support ranking for all the individuals in gallery. To cope this issue, we develop an error distribution technique. First, we can obtain the normalized reconstruction error for current probe $\mathbf{x}_j$ according to coefficients as:

$$e_j = \frac{\|\mathbf{x}_j - \mathbf{D}\mathbf{c}_j\|_2}{\|\mathbf{x}_j\|_2}. \tag{16}$$

Then, we re-distribute the reconstruction errors into the gallery individuals according to their similarity to the current probe image $\mathbf{x}_j$ as:

$$\mathbf{W}_{j,k}^p = \frac{1/dis(\mathbf{x}_j, \mathbf{d}_k^p)}{\sum_{p=1}^{G}\sum_{k=1}^{g_p}(1/dis(\mathbf{x}_j, \mathbf{d}_k^p))}, \quad k = \{1, \ldots, g_p\}, \tag{17}$$

where $\mathbf{d}_k^p$ represents the feature of the k-th image from the p-th person in gallery/dictionary $\mathbf{D}$, $dis(\mathbf{x}_j, \mathbf{d}_k^p)$ denotes the Euclidean distance between probe $\mathbf{x}_j$ and each element $\mathbf{d}_k^p$ in gallery. $\mathbf{W}_{j,k}^p$ indicates the similarity/weight of $\mathbf{d}_k^p$ relative to $\mathbf{x}_j$.

In this paper, we employ the reconstruction coefficients as the similarity measures, and define the accumulated all reconstruction coefficients from the p-th person as a part of the ranking value of the probe person with n images against the p-th person. Moreover, we use the reconstruction residues to make the p-th category whose reconstruction coefficients are all zeros has ranking value. Therefore, the final ranking value of the probe person with n images against the p-th person in gallery is defined as follows:

$$\mathbf{r}^p = \sum_{j=1}^{n} \sum_{k=1}^{g_p} \mathbf{c}_{j,k}^p + \mathbf{W}_{j,k}^p * e_j, \ p = \{1, ..., G\}. \tag{18}$$

The higher similarity of $\mathbf{d}_k^p$ relative to $\mathbf{x}_j$, the higher value distributed to $\mathbf{c}_{j,k}^p$. Since e_j is usually small, the value distributed to $\mathbf{c}_{j,k}^p$ is also very small, which will not change the ranks of the non-zero coefficients but will reorder the zero coefficients according to Euclidean distance.

Our final decision rule is :

$$class(\mathbf{X}) = \arg \max_p \mathbf{r}^p. \tag{19}$$

5   Experimental Results

We evaluate our method on three benchmark datasets including i-LIDS [30], CAVIAR4REID [6] and MARS [28] comparing to the state-of-the-art algorithms for multi-shot Re-ID. We use the standard measurement named Cumulated Match Characteristic (CMC) curve to figure out the matching results, where the matching rate at rank-n indicates the percentage of correct matchings in top n candidates according to the learnt ranking function Eq. (18).

5.1   Datasets and Settings

i-LIDS [30] is composed by 479 images of 119 people, which was captured at an airport arrival hall under two non-overlapping camera views with almost two images each person per camera views. This dataset consists challenging scenarios with heavy occlusions and pose variance.

CAVIAR4REID [6] contains 72 unique individuals with averagely 11.2 images per person extracted from two non-overlapping cameras in a shopping center: 50 of which with both the camera views and the remaining 22 with only one camera view. The images for each camera view have variations with respect to resolution changes, light conditions, occlusions and pose changes.

MARS [28] is the largest and newly collected dataset for video based Re-ID. It is collected from six near-synchronized cameras in the campus of Tsinghua

University. MARS consists of 1261 pedestrians each of which appears at least two cameras. It contains 625 identities with 8298 tracklets for training and 636 identities with 12180 tracklets for testing. Different from the other datasets, it also consists of 23380 junk bounding boxes and 147743 distractors bounding boxes in the testing samples.

Parameters. There are three important parameters in our model: λ controls the tradeoff between minimization of the ℓ_2 reconstruction error and the ℓ_1 sparsity of the coefficients. β controls the global regularizer in queries. γ controls the local regularizer in gallery. We empirically set: $\{\lambda, \beta, \gamma\} = \{0.2, 0.5, 0.5\}$.

5.2   Evaluation on Benchmarks

The performance of the proposed approach on the three benchmark datasets comparing with the state-of-the-art algorithms is reported in this section. We evaluate the proposed NNDGSR on both hand-crafted features and deep features. Followed by the protocol in [18], we use WHOS feature [18] as hand-crafted features. As for deep features, we generate APR [17] features based on ResNet-50, which is pre-trained on large Re-ID dataset Market-1501 [29] for i-LIDS [30] and CAVIAR4REID [6], while utilize IDE feature [28] for MARS [28] as provided.

Comparison on i-LIDS. Evaluation results on i-LIDS dataset are shown in Table 1 and Fig. 1 (a). From which we can see, Our approach significantly outperforms the state-of-the-arts. The rank-1 accuracies of our approach achieve 84.3% and 78.4% on hand-crafted and deep features respectively, which improve 21.4% and 1.2% than the second best method ISR [18]. It is worth noting that: (1) The limited number of samples in i-LIDS compromises the performance of deep learning. (2) Our NNDGSR significantly improves the ranking results on both hand-crafted and deep features.

Comparison on CAVIAR4REID. Evaluation results on CAVIAR4REID [6] are shown in Table 1 and Fig. 1 (b). We evaluate our method with APR [17] deep features in the same manner as on i-LIDS and adopt the same experimental protocols as ISR [18] by 50 random trials. Clearly, our approach significantly outperforms the state-of-the-art algorithms on both hand-crafted and deep features. Specifically, the Rank-1 accuracies with $N = 5$ achieve 93.2% and 89.0% on hand-crafted features and deep features respectively. Together with the results on i-LIDS, it suggests that the proposed method achieves impressive performance on small size datasets.

Comparison on MARS. In this dataset, the query tracklets are automatically generated from the testing samples. For each query tracklet, we construct two feature vectors via max pooling and average pooling respectively on the provide deep features, IDE [28]. For the remaining testing tracklets, since there are multiple tracklets for each person under a certain camera, we conduct the max pooling for each tracklet to construct the multiple feature vectors followed by the state-of-the-art methods on MARS [28]. Note that, our method

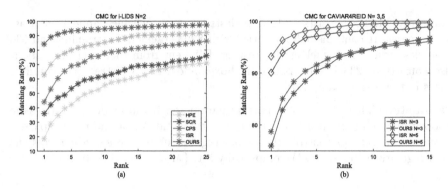

Fig. 1. The cumulative match characteristic curves on i-LIDS and CAVIRA4REID with hand-crafted feature comparing with the state-of-the-arts.

Table 1. Comparison results at Rank-1 on i-LIDS and CAVIAR4REID (in %)

Features	Methods:	i-LIDS	CAVIAR4REID		References:
		N = 2	N = 3	N = 5	
Hand-craft features	HPE [2]	18.5	-	-	ICPR2010
	AHPE [3]	32	7.5	7.5	PRL2012
	SCR [4]	36	-	-	ICAVSS2010
	MRCG [1]	46	-	-	ICAVSS2011
	SDALF [8]	39	8.5	8.3	CVPR2010
	CPS [6]	44	13	17.5	BMVC2011
	COSMATI [5]	44	-	-	ECCV2012
	WHOS + ISR [18]	62.9	75.1	90.1	PAMI2015
	WHOS [18] **+NNDGSR**	**84.3**	**78.7**	**93.2**	-
Deep features	APR [17] + EU [17]	67.7	44.3	53.8	Arxiv2017
	APR [17] + ISR [18]	77.2	65.7	80.7	Arxiv2017+PAMI2015
	APR [17] + **NNDGSR**	**78.4**	**70.4**	**89.0**	-

doesn't require any training therefore only the testing set containing with the query set is utilized. The performance of our method against different metrics is reported in Table 2. As we can see: (1) CNN based methods generally outperforms the traditional metric learning methods on hand-crafted features. (2) The sparse ranking based method outperforms on the powerful deep feature comparing with the traditional Euclidian distance. (3) By introducing the nonnegative dual graph regularized into the sparse ranking framework, our method can significantly boost the performance by increasing 9.5% at Rank-1 accuracy.

Table 2. Comparison with baseline on MARS dataset (in %)

Features	Methods:	Rank-1	Rank-5	Rank-20	References:
Hand-craft Features	HOG3D [13]+ KISSME [21]	2.6	6.4	12.4	BMVC2010+CVPR2012
	GEI[10]+ KISSME[21]	1.2	2.8	7.4	PAMI2005+CVPR2012
	HistLBP[23]+ XQDA[16]	18.6	33.0	45.9	ECCV2014+CVPR2015
	BoW[29]+ kissme[21]	30.6	46.2	59.2	ICCV2015+CVPR2012
	LOMO+ XQDA[16]	30.7	46.6	60.9	CVPR2015
Deep features	ASTPN [24]	44	70	81	ICCV2017
	LCAR [27]	55.5	70.2	80.2	Arxiv2017
	SATPP [15]	69.7	84.7	92.8	Arxiv2017
	SFT [34]	70.6	90	97.6	CVPR2017
	MSCAN [14]	71.8	86.6	93.1	CVPR2017
	IDE+EU [28]	58.7	77.1	86.8	ECCV2016
	IDE [28] + ISR [18]	63	77.1	85.6	ECCV2016+PAMI2015
	IDE[28] + NNDGSR	**72.50**	**88.0**	**93.30**	-

Table 3. Evaluation on individual component on CAVIAR4REID dataset with N =5 on APR deep features (in %)

Components:	Rank-1	Rank-5	Rank-10	Rank-20
ISR	80.7	95.8	97.9	**99.4**
SR+NN	84.3	94.9	97.3	98.6
SR+NN+GG	87.8	96.7	**98.2**	**99.4**
SR+NN+GG+LG (NNDGSR)	**89.0**	**96.8**	98.2	99.3

5.3 Component Analysis

To verify the contribution of the proposed non-negative dual graph regularized sparse ranking for multi-shot Re-ID, we further evaluate the components of our method on CAVIAR4REID [6] with APR features [17] and report the results in Table 3, where: SR indicates the original sparse ranking without any non-negative or regularization as Eq. (3). NN, GG and LG denotes introducing the Non-negative constraint, global graph regularizer and local graph regularizer respectively. From which we can see: (1) Both non-negative constraint and the dual graph regularizers play important roles. (2) By enforcing the non-negative constraint on the coefficients, it can improve 3.6% at rank-1 accuracy. (3) Global and local graph regularizers can further improve the performance by 3.5% and 1.2% respectively in Rank-1, which demonstrates the contribution of the components of non-negative dual graph regularized sparse ranking.

6 Conclusion

In this paper, we have proposed a novel sparse ranking based multi-shot person Re-ID approach. In order to simultaneously capture the intrinsic geometric structures in both probe and gallery, we design a non-negative dual graph regularized sparse ranking method for multi-shot Re-ID. Then we provide a fast optimization for the proposed unified sparse ranking framework. Experiments on three challenging multi-shot person Re-ID datasets demonstrate the promising performance of the proposed method especially on small size datasets where the performance of deep learning is compromised. In the future, we will investigate the effective way of fusing key-feature information from video-based Re-ID.

Acknowledgement. This study was funded by the National Nature Science Foundation of China (61502006, 61602001, 61702002, 61872005, 61860206004) and the Natural Science Foundation of Anhui Higher Education Institutions of China (KJ2017A017).

References

1. Bak, S., Corvee, E., Bremond, F., Thonnat, M.: Multiple-shot human re-identification by mean riemannian covariance grid. In: IEEE International Conference on Advanced Video and Signal-Based Surveillance, pp. 179–184 (2011)
2. Bazzani, L., Cristani, M., Perina, A., Farenzena, M., Murino, V.: Multiple-shot person re-identification by HPE signature. In: International Conference on Pattern Recognition, pp. 1413–1416 (2010)
3. Bazzani, L., Cristani, M., Perina, A., Murino, V.: Multiple-shot person re-identification by chromatic and epitomic analyses. Pattern Recogn. Lett. **33**(7), 898–903 (2012)
4. Bk, S., Corvee, E., Bremond, F., Thonnat, M.: Person re-identification using spatial covariance regions of human body parts. In: IEEE International Conference on Advanced Video and Signal Based Surveillance, pp. 435–440 (2010)
5. Charpiat, G., Thonnat, M.: Learning to match appearances by correlations in a covariance metric space. In: European Conference on Computer Vision, pp. 806–820 (2012)
6. Dong, S.C., Cristani, M., Stoppa, M., Bazzani, L., Murino, V.: Custom pictorial structures for re-identification. In: British Machine Vision Conference, pp. 68.1–68.11 (2011)
7. Efron, B., Hastie, T., Johnstone, I., Tibshirani, R.: Least angle regression. Ann. Stat. **32**(2), 407–451 (2004)
8. Farenzena, M., Bazzani, L., Perina, A., Murino, V., Cristani, M.: Person re-identification by symmetry-driven accumulation of local features. In: Computer Vision and Pattern Recognition, pp. 2360–2367 (2010)
9. Feng, X., Wu, S., Tang, Z., Li, Z.: Sparse latent model with dual graph regularization for collaborative filtering. Neurocomputing (2018)
10. Han, J., Bhanu, B.: Individual recognition using gait energy image. IEEE Trans. Pattern Anal. Mach. Intell. **28**(2), 316–322 (2005)
11. Jing, X.Y., et al.: Super-resolution person re-identification with semi-coupled low-rank discriminant dictionary learning. IEEE Trans. Image Process. **26**(3), 1363–1378 (2017)

12. Karanam, S., Li, Y., Radke, R.J.: Person re-identification with discriminatively trained viewpoint invariant dictionaries. In: IEEE International Conference on Computer Vision, pp. 4516–4524 (2015)

13. Klaser, A.: A spatiotemporal descriptor based on 3D-gradients. In: British Machine Vision Conference, September 2010

14. Li, D., Chen, X., Zhang, Z., Huang, K.: Learning deep context-aware features over body and latent parts for person re-identification. In: IEEE Conference on Computer Vision and Pattern Recognition (2017)

15. Li, J., Zhang, S., Wang, J., Gao, W., Tian, Q.: LVreID: person re-identification with long sequence videos. arXiv preprint arXiv:1712.07286 (2017)

16. Liao, S., Hu, Y., Zhu, X., Li, S.Z.: Person re-identification by local maximal occurrence representation and metric learning. In: Computer Vision and Pattern Recognition, pp. 2197–2206 (2015)

17. Lin, Y., Zheng, L., Zheng, Z., Wu, Y., Yang, Y.: Improving person re-identification by attribute and identity learning. arXiv preprint arXiv:1703.07220 (2017)

18. Lisanti, G., Masi, I., Bagdanov, A.D., Bimbo, A.D.: Person re-identification by iterative re-weighted sparse ranking. IEEE Trans. Pattern Anal. Mach. Intell. **37**(8), 1629–1642 (2015)

19. Liu, X., Song, M., Tao, D., Zhou, X., Chen, C., Bu, J.: Semi-supervised coupled dictionary learning for person re-identification. In: Computer Vision and Pattern Recognition, pp. 3550–3557 (2014)

20. Parikh, N., Boyd, S.: Proximal algorithms. Found. Trends Optim. **1**(3), 127–239 (2014)

21. Roth, P.M., Wohlhart, P., Hirzer, M., Kostinger, M., Bischof, H.: Large scale metric learning from equivalence constraints. In: IEEE Conference on Computer Vision and Pattern Recognition, pp. 2288–2295 (2012)

22. Wright, J., Ganesh, A., Zhou, Z., Wagner, A., Ma, Y.: Demo: robust face recognition via sparse representation. In: IEEE International Conference on Automatic Face Gesture Recognition, pp. 1–2 (2009)

23. Xiong, F., Gou, M., Camps, O., Sznaier, M.: Person re-identification using kernel-based metric learning methods. In: European Conference on Computer Vision, pp. 1–16 (2014)

24. Xu, S., Cheng, Y., Gu, K., Yang, Y., Chang, S., Zhou, P.: Jointly attentive spatial-temporal pooling networks for video-based person re-identification. arXiv preprint arXiv:1708.02286 (2017)

25. Yankelevsky, Y., Elad, M.: Dual graph regularized dictionary learning. IEEE Trans. Signal Inf. Process. Netw. **2**(4), 611–624 (2017)

26. Yin, M., Gao, J., Lin, Z., Shi, Q., Guo, Y.: Dual graph regularized latent low-rank representation for subspace clustering. IEEE Trans. Image Process. Publ. IEEE Signal Process. Soc. **24**(12), 4918–4933 (2015)

27. Zhang, W., Hu, S., Liu, K.: Learning compact appearance representation for video-based person re-identification. arXiv preprint arXiv:1702.06294 (2017)

28. Zheng, L., et al.: MARS: a video benchmark for large-scale person re-identification. In: European Conference on Computer Vision, pp. 868–884 (2016)

29. Zheng, L., Shen, L., Tian, L., Wang, S., Wang, J., Tian, Q.: Scalable person re-identification: a benchmark. In: IEEE International Conference on Computer Vision, pp. 1116–1124 (2015)

30. Zheng, W.S., Gong, S., Xiang, T.: Associating groups of people. Active Range Imaging Dataset for Indoor Surveillance (2009)

31. Zheng, W.S., Gong, S., Xiang, T.: Reidentification by Relative Distance Comparison. IEEE Computer Society (2013)

32. Zheng, W., Gong, S., Xiang, T.: Towards open-world person re-identification by one-shot group-based verification. IEEE Trans. Pattern Anal. Mach. Intell. **38**(3), 591–606 (2016)
33. Zheng, Y.W., Hao, S., Zhang, B.C., Zhang, J., Zhang, X.: Weight-based sparse coding for multi-shot person re-identification. Sci. China Inf. Sci. **58**(10), 100104–100104 (2015)
34. Zhou, Z., Huang, Y., Wang, W., Wang, L., Tan, T.: See the forest for the trees: joint spatial and temporal recurrent neural networks for video-based person re-identification. In: IEEE Conference on Computer Vision and Pattern Recognition, pp. 6776–6785 (2017)

Computer Vision Application

Nonuniformity Correction Method of Thermal Radiation Effects in Infrared Images

Hanyu Hong[1,2], Yu Shi[1,2(✉)], Tianxu Zhang[1,2,3], and Zhao Liu[1,2]

[1] Princeton University, Princeton, NJ 08544, USA
shiyu0125@163.com
[2] Hubei Engineering Research Center of Video Image and HD Projection,
School of Electrical and Information Engineering,
Wuhan Institute of Technology,
Wuhan 430074, Hubei, People's Republic of China
[3] National Key Laboratory of Science and Technology on Multi-Spectral
Information Processing, School of Automation, Huazhong University of Science
and Technology, Wuhan 430074, People's Republic of China

Abstract. This paper proposes a correction method based on dark channel prior. The method takes full advantage of the sparseness of dark channels of latent images. It applies an L0 norm constraint of dark channels to the latent images, and an L2 norm constraint with smoothing gradient to the intensity bias field caused by the aero-optic thermal radiation effects. And finally it adopts split Bregman method to solve the nonconvex and nonlinear optimization problem. The experimental results show that compared with the existing methods, this method greatly reduces aero-optic thermal radiation effects in infrared imaging detection system.

Keywords: Nonuniformity · Correction · Thermal radiation effects

1 Introduction

When aircraft with optical imaging detection system flies at high speed, the air density around its cap has changed drastically because of the intense interaction between the cap and the air flow. Meanwhile, the gradient of atmospheric refractive index in the mixing layer has also changed. The fluctuation of atmospheric refractive index and high temperature will cause distortion and heat of the optical window, and make the target image produce the phenomena such as pixel bias, phase jitter, shake and blur, a phenomenon known as aero-optical effects [1, 2]. Because of the strong thermal radiation effect, the details of the over-saturated image become unintelligible and the detection performance is seriously affected. There are several measures that could be taken to reduce the aero-optic thermal radiation effects: (1) selecting appropriate detector angle, spectral bandwidth, detector integration time and other detector parameters [3], (2) limiting the window temperature to a lower range [4]. All these measures can physically reduce the aero-optic thermal radiation effects. However, these correction and processing measures are only partial and insufficient, since, on the one hand, they are complex in construction, expensive in cost, and inconvenient in maintenance; and, on the other hand, they can only

© Springer Nature Switzerland AG 2018
J.-H. Lai et al. (Eds.): PRCV 2018, LNCS 11256, pp. 123–131, 2018.
https://doi.org/10.1007/978-3-030-03398-9_11

be applied to the correction of thermal radiation effects under limited conditions. Therefore, due to the urgent need of economy, applicability and detection, it is necessary to further correct the degraded image with thermal radiation effects. In this paper, a post correction method is proposed to improve the infrared image quality against the aero-optic thermal radiation effects.

A few researchers have studied the principles and methods of correcting aero-optic thermal radiation effects. In literature [5], the authors analyzed and modeled the aero-optic thermal radiation in air according to the experimental data. Cao and Tisse construct a correction model by fitting the derivatives of bivariate polynomial to the gradient information of infrared image, and correct the aero-optic thermal radiation effects of an uncooled long wave infrared image acquisition camera from a single image [6]. Liu modeled the low-frequency intensity bias field as a representation of the bivariate polynomial representation and estimated it by using an isotropic total variation model [7]. In literature [8], the authors noted that infrared images usually have smaller targets, and proposed a variational model based on L_0 regularization, using prior knowledge, to complete the nonuniformity correction depending on optical temperature. And yet, for these correction methods, intensity bias field is considered to be the representation of K degree bivariate polynomials, which makes their calculation more than necessarily complex. In addition, the correction of aero-optic thermal radiation effects is not significant enough, so there is still much room for improvement.

In this paper, by comparing clear image and infrared image with aero-optic thermal radiation effects, it is found that the dark channel of infrared images with thermal radiation effects is globally bright, while the dark channel of clear images is generally dark. This means that value zero is in the majority of the dark channel of the infrared image without aero-optic thermal radiation effects.

2 Intensity Nonuniformity Correction Method Based on Dark Channel Prior

Dark channel was first introduced by He in image dehazing. He concluded that in most local non-sky areas, some pixels always have at least one color channel with lower values based on statistics of a large number of hazy images and haze-free images [9]. In this section, dark channel prior is introduced into the correction model of aero-optic thermal radiation effects for the first time, and then split Bregman method [10] is used to solve the nonconvex nonlinear minimization problem and the intensity bias field estimation is obtained. The intensity bias field is substracted from the degraded image to eliminate the aero-optic thermal radiation effects.

Since the intensity bias field caused by aero-optic thermal radiation effects is additive and varies smoothly, the general model of aero-optic thermal radiation effects degradation can be expressed as:

$$z = f + b + n \tag{1}$$

Where z denotes an observed infrared image with aero-optic thermal radiation effects, f denotes a latent clear image (without aero-optic thermal radiation effects),

b denotes intensity bias field induced by aero-optic thermal radiation effects, and n denotes the system noise.

For a color image f, the dark channel is defined as follow

$$D(f)(x) = \min_{y \in N(x)} \left(\min_{c \in \{r,g,b\}} f^c(y) \right) \tag{2}$$

Where x and y denote the position of pixels, $N(x)$ denotes an image block centered on pixel x, f^c denotes c color channels, and the dark channel is the minimum pixel value of the three channels. The clear image and degraded image with aero-optic thermal radiation effects both are gray-scale images, we have $\min_{c \in \{r,g,b\}} f^c(y) = f(y)$. The dark channel prior is used to describe the minimum values in neighbourhood. It is found that dark channel of degraded image with aero-optic thermal radiation effects is less sparse. The elements of dark channel for clear image are almost zero and dark channel for degraded image with aero-optic thermal radiation effects has fewer zero elements.

2.1 Intensity Nonuniformity Corrected Model

Adding dark channels prior, we present a correction model of aero-optic thermal radiation effects:

$$\min_{f,b} \|z - f - b\|_2^2 + \alpha \|\nabla f\|_0 + \beta \|D(f)\|_0 + \gamma \|\nabla b\|_2^2 \tag{3}$$

where regularization parameters α, β, γ are positive values. The degraded images are often contaminated by Gaussian noise. Suppose that n is Gaussian noise, then we can fit the aero-optic thermal radiation effects correction model by an L2 norm shown in the first term of functional (3). We use the second term to constrain the gradient of latent clear image, where $\nabla f = (f_x, f_y)'$. The nonzero values of ∇f in real infrared aero-optic thermal radiation effects images are denser than in clear images. Therefore, the gradient of a clear image and a degraded image can be differentiated by an L_0 norm $\|\nabla f\|_0$ which counts the number of nonzero values of ∇f. We use the fourth term to constrain the gradient of the intensity bias field, where $\nabla b = (b_x, b_y)'$ is the first-order spatial derivative, and we use the gradient prior to penalize high-frequency components of b. Since parameter γ controls the gradient regularization strength, the noise will be not well suppressed if γ is too small; however, if γ is too large, the edge and detailed information will be covered by aero-optic thermal radiation effects. The third term we use in this model is the dark channel prior term with the L_0 norm representation. Because the infrared image is a gray image, and the three color channels of the image are the same, the dark channel representation can be obtained just by calculating the minimum value of a single channel. The dark channel corresponding to clear images without aero-optic thermal radiation effects is usually dark, with almost no information, and 0 values are the majority. The dark channel corresponding to images with aero-optic thermal radiation effects is usually bright and the non-zero values are the majority. Therefore, the dark channel corresponding to the clear image without aero-optic thermal radiation effects is sparse, and the norm L_0 is used to represent its sparsity.

2.2   Intensity Bias Field Estimation

We use the split Bregman method to facilitate the solution. The variables d_1, d_2 and the auxiliary variables b_1, b_2 are introduced to rewrite problem (3) as an unconstrained optimization problem:

$$\min_{f,b,d_1,d_2,b_1,b_2} \|z - f - b\|_2^2 + \alpha\|d_1\|_0 + \beta\|d_2\|_0 + \gamma\|\nabla b\|_2^2 + \gamma_1\|d_1 - \nabla f - b_1\|_2^2 + \gamma_2\|d_2 - D(f) - b_2\|_2^2 \quad (4)$$

where regularization parameters γ_1, γ_2 are positive values. Since $D(f)$ is a nonlinear operator, it is difficult to solve the minimization of f in formula (4). We therefore use a linear operator M to transform it [11]. Let $y = \arg\min_{q \in N(x)} f(q)$, then the linear operator M is defined as:

$$M(x, q) = \begin{cases} 1, & q = y, \\ 0, & \text{otherwise} \end{cases} \quad (5)$$

For a true clear image, $Mf = D(f)$ strictly holds. The approximation of M is computed using the intermediate clear image at each iteration. As the intermediate clear image becomes closer to the true clear image, the linear operator M approximates to the desired nonlinear operator D. Given the linear operator M, the minimization problem in regard to variable f can be rewritten as:

$$\min_f \|z - f - b\|_2^2 + \gamma_1\|d_1 - \nabla f - b_1\|_2^2 + \gamma_2\|d_2 - Mf - b_2\|_2^2 \quad (6)$$

Problem (6) is an $L_2 - L_2$ norm form minimization problem. It is a quadratic function. Let the partial derivative of the energy function f equal to 0, and we get a closed form solution of problem (6). Then, according to the Parseval's theorem, the solution of f can be easily obtained in frequency domain:

$$f = \frac{F^{-1}(F(z-b) + \gamma_1 F(\nabla^T(d_1 - b_1)) + \gamma_2 F(M^T(d_2 - b_2)))}{1 + \gamma_1 \nabla^T \nabla + \gamma_2 M^T M} \quad (7)$$

where $F(\cdot)$ and $F^{-1}(\cdot)$ denote FFT and inverse FFT respectively. Given f, the minimization problem of variable d_1 becomes:

$$\min_{d_1} \alpha\|d_1\|_0 + \gamma_1\|d_1 - \nabla f - b_1\|_2^2 \quad (8)$$

The solution of the variable d_1 is obtained based on [12].

Similarly, given f, the minimization problem of variable d_2 becomes:

$$\min_{d_2} \beta\|d_2\|_0 + \gamma_2\|d_2 - D(f) - b_2\|_2^2 \tag{9}$$

The auxiliary variables b_1 and b_2 are updated to be:

$$b_1 = b_1 + \nabla f - d_1$$
$$b_2 = b_2 + D(f) - d_2 \tag{10}$$

Given f, intensity bias field b is updated as follows:

$$\min_b \|z - f - b\|_2^2 + \gamma\|\nabla b\|_2^2 \tag{11}$$

This is an $L_2 - L_2$ norm form minimization problem. Intensity bias field b can be obtained by Euler-Lagrange linear equation:

$$b = \frac{z - f}{1 + \gamma\nabla^T\nabla} \tag{12}$$

In the previous section, the intermediate latent sharp image f is estimated, which is in turn used to estimate exactly the intensity bias field b. And the final clear image after correction is $z - b$.

3 Experimental Results and Analysis

To illustrate the efficiency of the proposed method for the correction of simulating aero-optic thermal radiation effects, the proposed method is compared with the current state-of-art correction methods, Cao's method [6] and Liu's method [7]. We take the simulated degraded images with aero-optic thermal radiation effects from the Liu's reference. The three images in the first row at the top of Fig. 1 are the aero-optic thermal radiation effects images obtained during flight. Images in the second, third, and fourth rows in Fig. 1 are the corresponding images obtained with Cao's method and Liu's method, and our correction methods for the aero-optic thermal radiation effects respectively. By comparison, although Cao's method and Liu's method can reduce aero-optic thermal radiation effects and both of them have a good correction effect, whereas theirs still have residual aero-optic thermal radiation effects. The results of our method seem to be more homogeneous and better, because our method completely eliminates the aero-optic thermal radiation effects and has better image details.

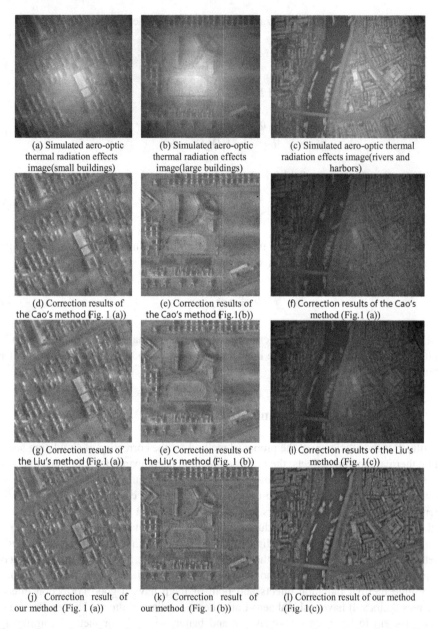

(a) Simulated aero-optic thermal radiation effects image(small buildings)

(b) Simulated aero-optic thermal radiation effects image(large buildings)

(c) Simulated aero-optic thermal radiation effects image(rivers and harbors)

(d) Correction results of the Cao's method (Fig. 1 (a))

(e) Correction results of the Cao's method (Fig.1(b))

(f) Correction results of the Cao's method (Fig.1 (a))

(g) Correction results of the Liu's method (Fig.1 (a))

(e) Correction results of the Liu's method (Fig. 1 (b))

(i) Correction results of the Liu's method (Fig. 1(c))

(j) Correction result of our method (Fig. 1 (a))

(k) Correction result of our method (Fig. 1 (b))

(l) Correction result of our method (Fig. 1(c))

Fig. 1. Comparison of simulation methods for correction of aero-optic thermal radiation effects.

The first line in Fig. 2 is the intensity bias field map obtained by our proposed method. The second line in Fig. 2 is 3D display. It can be seen that it is a good indication of the aero-optic thermal radiation effects. In addition, variance coefficient [13] (cv(f) = variance(f)/mean(f)) is used to evaluate the correction performance of three methods quantitatively, where variance(f) is the variance of image f, and mean(f) is the mean of image f. The lower the variance coefficient value, the better the image quality. As shown in Table 1, our method has a lower variance coefficient.

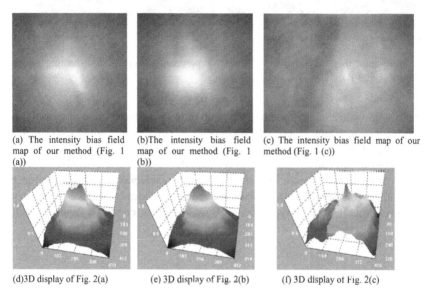

(a) The intensity bias field map of our method (Fig. 1 (a))

(b)The intensity bias field map of our method (Fig. 1 (b))

(c) The intensity bias field map of our method (Fig. 1 (c))

(d)3D display of Fig. 2(a)

(e) 3D display of Fig. 2(b)

(f) 3D display of Fig. 2(c)

Fig. 2. Intensity bias field map and 3D display.

Table 1. Comparison of CV values of three correction methods.

Image	Degraded image	Cao's method	Liu's method	Our method
Large buildings	0.4068	0.1794	0.1747	**0.1225**
Small buildings	0.4016	0.2085	0.2062	**0.1234**
Rivers and harbors	0.3141	0.3161	0.3484	**0.2110**

Figure 3(a) is a real infrared aero-optic thermal radiation effects images obtained by infrared window heating test, wherein the experimental temperature of Fig. 3(a) is 599 K, Fig. 3(b) is the correction result of the Cao's method, Fig. 3(c) is the correction result of Liu's method, and Fig. 3(d) is the correction result of our proposed method. By contrast, the background of our method's corrected image is smoother and the target area is more clearly visible.

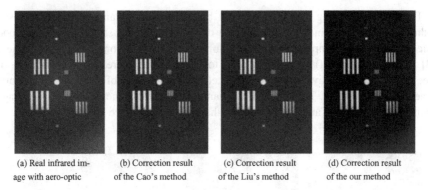

| (a) Real infrared im-age with aero-optic | (b) Correction result of the Cao's method | (c) Correction result of the Liu's method | (d) Correction result of the our method |

Fig. 3. Aero-optic thermal radiation correction experiment under window heating (window temperature is 599 K).

In the window heating experiment, the pixel gray value distribution of the real aero-optic image with aero-optic thermal radiation effects, correction result of Cao's method, correction result of Liu's method, correction result of our proposed method are shown in Fig. 4. Figure 4(a) and (c) are pixel gray value distribution of the 160th column and 200th row from Fig. 3. Figure 4(a) shows that the pixel gray value distribution has three peaks, the regions with larger pixel gray values are located at three target points, and the background pixel gray values are low, which is consistent with the actual situation.

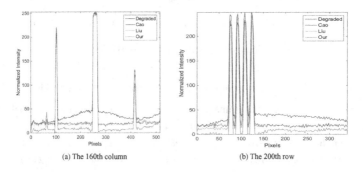

| (a) The 160th column | (b) The 200th row |

Fig. 4. Pixel gray value distribution (Fig. 3).

4   Conclusion

In this paper, a correction method based on the dark channel prior is proposed to reduce the aero-optic thermal radiation effects. By comparing the degraded images with aero-optic thermal effects and clear images, the dark channel prior constraints of latent images is added to the additive correction model, the L_2 norm constraint is applied to the gradient of the intensity bias field, and a correction model of aero-optic thermal radiation effects based on dark channel is established. In order to solve the nonconvex and nonlinear optimization problem, the split Bregman method is introduced into the proposed model. The minimum problem of multi-variables is split into a series of single variable minimum problems, which accelerates the iterative convergence. The experimental results show that, compared with the state-of-art methods, this method can obtain better aero-optic thermal radiation correction results.

FundingThis work was supported by the key project of National Science Foundation of China (No. 61433007), National Science Foundation of China (No. 61671337) and the National Science Foundation of China (No. 61701353).

References

1. Yin, X.: Aero-Optical Principle. Chinese Aerospace Press, Beijing (2003)
2. Zhang, T., Hong, H., Zhang, X.: Aero-optical effect correction: principles methods and applications. University of Science and Technology, China Press, Hefei (2014)
3. Fei, J.: Preliminary analysis of aero-optics effects correction technology. Infrared Laser Eng. **28**(5), 10–16 (1999)
4. Au, R.H.: Optical window materials for hypersonic flow. In: Proceeding of SPIE, vol. 1112, pp. 330–339 (1989)
5. Liu, L., Meng, W., Li, Y., et al.: Analysis and modeling of aerothermal radiation based on experimental data. Infrared Phys. Technol. **62**(1), 18–28 (2014)
6. Cao, Y., Tisse, C.: Single-image-based solution for optics temperature dependent nonuniformity correction in an uncooled long-wave infrared camera. Opt. Lett. **39**(3), 646–648 (2014)
7. Liu, L., Yan, L., Zhao, H., et al.: Correction of aeroheating-induced intensity nonuniformity in infrared images. Infrared Phys. Technol. **76**, 235–241 (2016)
8. Liu, L., Zhang, T.: Optics temperature-dependent nonuniformity correction via l_0-regularized prior for airborne infrared imaging systems. IEEE Photonics J. **8**(5), 1–10 (2016)
9. He, K., Sun, J., Tang, X.: Single image haze removal using dark channel prior. IEEE Trans. Pattern Anal. Mach. Intell. **33**(12), 2341–2353 (2011)
10. Goldstein, T., Osher, S.: The split Bregman method for l_1-regularized problems. SIAM J. Imaging Sci. **2**(2), 323–343 (2009)
11. Pan, J., Sun, D., Pfister, H., et al.: Blind image deblurring using dark channel prior. In: Conference on Computer Vision and Pattern Recognition, pp. 1628–1636 (2016)
12. Xu, L., Lu, C., Xu, Y., et al.: Image smoothing via l0 gradient minimization. ACM Trans. Graph. **30**(6), 1–12 (2011)
13. Aja-Fernández, S., Alberola-López, C.: On the estimation of the coefficient of variation for anisotropic diffusion speckle filtering. IEEE Trans. Image Process. **15**(9), 2694–2701 (2006)

Co-saliency Detection for RGBD Images Based on Multi-constraint Superpixels Matching and Co-cellular Automata

Zhengyi Liu[1(✉)] and Feng Xie[2]

[1] Key Laboratory of Intelligent Computing and Signal Processing,
Ministry of Education, Anhui University, Hefei, China
22927463@qq.com
[2] Co-Innovation Center for Information Supply and Assurance Technology,
Hefei, China
811173098@qq.com

Abstract. Co-saliency detection aims at extracting the common salient regions from an image group containing two or more relevant images. It is a newly emerging topic in computer vision community. Different from the existing co-saliency methods focusing on RGB images, this paper proposes a novel co-saliency detection model for RGBD images, which utilizes the depth information to enhance identification of co-saliency. First, we utilize the existing single saliency maps as the initialization, then we use multiple cues to compute combination inter-images similarity to match inter-neighbors for each super-pixel. Especially, we extract high dimensional features for each image region with a deep convolutional neural network as semantic cue. Finally, we introduce a modified 2-layer Co-cellular Automata to exploit depth information and the intrinsic relevance of similar regions through interactions with neighbors in multi-scene. The experiments on two RGBD co-saliency datasets demonstrate the effectiveness of our proposed framework.

Keywords: RGBD · Co-saliency · Cellular automata · Semantic feature
Multi-constraint

1 Introduction

In recent years, co-saliency detection has become an emerging issue in saliency detection, which detects the common salient regions among multiple images [1–4]. Different from the traditional single saliency detection model, co-saliency detection model aims at discovering the common salient objects from an image group containing two or more relevant images, while the categories, intrinsic characteristics, and locations of the salient objects are entirely unknown [5]. The co-salient objects simultaneously exhibit two properties, i.e. (1) The co-salient regions should be salient with respect to the background in each image, and (2) All these co-salient regions should be similar in appearance among multiple images. Due to its superior expansibility, co-saliency detection has been widely used in many computer vision tasks, such as foreground co-segmentation [6], object co-localization and detection [7], and image matching [8].

© Springer Nature Switzerland AG 2018
J.-H. Lai et al. (Eds.): PRCV 2018, LNCS 11256, pp. 132–143, 2018.
https://doi.org/10.1007/978-3-030-03398-9_12

Most existing co-saliency detection models are focused on RGB images and have achieved satisfactory performances [9–16]. Recently, Co-saliency detection for RGBD images has become one of the popular and challenging problem. RGBD co-saliency detection in [17] is firstly discussed. They proposed a RGBD co-saliency model using bagging-based clustering. Then, Cong et al. [18] proposed an iterative RGBD co-saliency framework, which utilized the existing single saliency maps as the initialization, and generated the final RGBD co-saliency map by using a refinement-cycle model. In their another paper [19], they proposed a co-saliency model based on multi-constraint feature matching and cross label propagation. In this paper, for combining depth and repeatability, we firstly propose a matching algorithm based on neighboring superpixel sets of Multi-Constraint distance to calculate the similarity between images and to depict the occurrence of area repetition. Secondly, inspired by Ref. [23], we propose a 2-Layer co-cellular automata model to calculate the saliency spread of intra-images and inter-images, in order to ensure complete saliency of targeted area. Besides, the depth information and high dimensional features are considered in our method to achieve better result. The major contributions of the proposed co-saliency detection method are summarized as follows.

(1) We extract high dimensional features for each image region with a deep convolutional neural network as semantic cue and combine it with color cue, depth cue, and saliency cue to calculate the similarity between two superpixels for the first time.

(2) A modified 2-layer co-cellular automata model is used to calculate the saliency spread of intra-images and inter-images, in order to ensure complete saliency of targeted area.

(3) Both semantic information and depth information are considered in cellular automata to optimize this co-saliency model in our method.

The rest of this paper is organized as follows. Section 2 introduces the proposed method in detail. The experimental results with qualitative and quantitative evaluations are presented in Sect. 3. Finally, the conclusion is drawn in Sect. 4.

2   Proposed Method

The proposed RGBD co-saliency framework is introduced in this section. Figure 1 shows the framework of the proposed method. Our method is initialized by the existing single saliency maps, and then we propose a matching algorithm based on neighboring superpixel sets of Multi-Constraint distance to calculate the similarity between images and to depict the occurrence of area repetition. Finally, inspired by Ref. [23], we propose a 2-Layer co-cellular automata model to calculate the saliency spread of intra-images and inter-images, in order to ensure complete saliency of targeted area.

Notations: Given N input images $\{I^i\}_{i=1}^N$, and the corresponding depth maps are denoted as $\{D^i\}_{i=1}^N$. The M_i single saliency maps for image I^i produced by existing single image saliency models are represented as $S^i = \left\{S_j^i\right\}_{j=1}^{M_i}$. In our method, the superpixel-level region is regarded as the basic unit for processing. Thus, each RGB image I^i is abstracted into superpixels $R^i = \left\{r_m^i\right\}_{m=1}^{N_i}$ using SLIC algorithm [24] firstly, where N_i is the number of superpixels for image I^i.

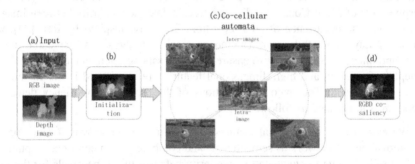

Fig. 1. The framework of our algorithm. (a) Input RGB image and the corresponding depth map. (b) Initialization. (c) Superpixel matching and parallel evolution via co-cellular automata. (d) The final saliency result.

2.1   Initialization

The proposed co-saliency framework aims at discovering the co-salient objects from multiple images in a group with the assistance of existing single saliency maps. Therefore, some existing saliency maps produced by single saliency models are used to initialize the framework. It is well known that different saliency methods own different superiority in detecting salient regions. In a way, these saliency maps are complementary in some regions, thus, the fused result can inherit the merits of the multiple saliency maps, and produce more robust and superior detection baseline. In our method, the simple average function is used to achieve a more generalized initialization result. The initialized saliency map for image I^i is denoted as:

$$S_f^i\left(r_m^i\right) = \frac{1}{M}\sum_{j=1}^{M_i} S_j^i\left(r_m^i\right) \tag{1}$$

Where $S_j^i\left(r_m^i\right)$ denotes the saliency value of superpixel r_m^i produced by j^{th} saliency method for image I^i. In our experiments, four saliency methods including RC [20], DCLC [21], RRWR [22], and BSCA [23], are used to produce the initialized saliency map.

2.2   Superpixel Matching via Multi-constraint Cues

For convenience of calculations and intrinsic structural information, the image is firstly segmented into a set of superpixels by simple linear iterative clustering (SLIC) algorithm [24]. The core of detecting the common salient object is the superpixel matching in different images. In this paper, superpixel matching means, for any superpixel r_m^i in image I^i, finding a set of superpixels with high similarity in another image I^j. Note that not all superpixels can be matched and one superpixel can have several matching superpixels in other images. In this paper, high-dimensional semantic cue and low-dimensional cue are both utilizing to compute the similarity between images.

High-Dimensional Cue. We extract high-dimensional features for each image region with a deep convolutional neural network originally trained over the ImageNet dataset using Caffe, an open source framework for CNN training and testing. The architecture of this CNN has eight layers including five convolutional layers and three fully-connected layers. Features are extracted from the output of the second last fully connected layer, which has 4096 neurons. Although this CNN was originally trained on a dataset for visual recognition, automatically extracted CNN features turn out to be highly versatile and can be more effective than traditional handcrafted features on other visual computing tasks.

Since an image region may have an irregular shape while CNN features have to be extracted from a rectangular region, to make the CNN features only relevant to the pixels inside the region, we define the rectangular region for CNN feature extraction to be the bounding box of the image region and fill the pixels outside the region but still inside its bounding box with the mean pixel values at the same locations across all ImageNet training images. These pixel values become zero after mean subtraction and do not have any impact on subsequent results. We warp the region in the bounding box to a square with 227×227 pixels to make it compatible with the deep CNN trained for ImageNet. The warped RGB image region is then fed to the deep CNN and a 4096-dimensional feature vector is obtained by forward propagating a mean-subtracted input image region through all the convolutional layers and fully connected layers. We name this vector feature F.

Thus, the high-dimensional semantic similarity is defined as:

$$S_h\left(r_m^i, r_n^j\right) = \exp\left(-\frac{\left\|F_m^i - F_k^j\right\|_2}{\sigma^2}\right) \tag{2}$$

where F_m^i denotes 4096 high-dimensional features contrast of superpixel r_m^i, and σ^2 is a constant.

Low-Dimensional Cue. Three low-dimensional cues include color cue, depth cue, and saliency cue are used to gain a multi-constraint cue.

RGB Similarity. The color histogram [25] are used to represent the RGB feature on the superpixel level, which are denoted as HC_m^i. Then, the Chi-square measure is employed to compute the feature difference. Thus, the RGB similarity is defined as:

$$S_c\left(r_m^i, r_n^j\right) = 1 - \frac{1}{2}\chi^2\left(HC_m^i, HC_n^j\right) \tag{3}$$

where r_m^i and r_n^j are the superpixels in image I^i and I^j, respectively, and $\chi^2(\cdot)$ denotes the Chi-square distance function.

Depth Similarity. Two depth consistency measurements, namely depth value consistency and depth contrast consistency, are composed of the final depth similarity measurement, which is defined as:

$$S_d\left(r_m^i, r_n^j\right) = \exp\left(-\frac{W_d\left(r_m^i, r_n^j\right) + W_c\left(r_m^i, r_n^j\right)}{\sigma^2}\right) \tag{4}$$

where $W_d\left(r_m^i, r_n^j\right)$ is the depth value consistency measurement to evaluate the inter-image depth consistency, due to the fact that the common regions should appear similar depth values.

$$W_d\left(r_m^i, r_n^j\right) = \left|d_m^i - d_n^j\right| \tag{5}$$

$W_c\left(r_m^i, r_n^j\right)$ describes the depth contrast consistency, because the common regions should represent more similar characteristic in depth contrast measurement.

$$W_c\left(r_m^i, r_n^j\right) = \left|D_c\left(r_m^i\right) - D_c\left(r_n^j\right)\right| \tag{6}$$

with

$$D_c(r_m^i) = \sum_{k \neq m}\left|d_m^i - d_m^j\right|\exp\left(-\frac{\left\|p_m^i - p_k^i\right\|_2}{\sigma^2}\right) \tag{7}$$

where $D_c\left(r_m^i\right)$ denotes the depth contrast of superpixel r_m^i, p_m^i denotes the position of superpixel r_m^i, and σ^2 is a constant.

Saliency Similarity. Inspired by the prior that the common regions should appear more similar in single saliency map compared to other regions, the output saliency map from the addition scheme is used to define the saliency similarity measurement in our work:

$$S_s\left(r_m^i, r_n^j\right) = \exp\left(-\left|S_{sp}^i\left(r_m^i\right) - S_{sp}^j\left(r_n^j\right)\right|\right) \tag{8}$$

where $S_{sp}^i\left(r_m^i\right)$ is saliency score of superpixel r_m^i via initialization.

Based on these cues, the combination similarity measurement is defined as the average of the four similarity measurements.

$$S_M\left(r_m^i, r_n^j\right) = \frac{S_h\left(r_m^i, r_n^j\right) + S_c\left(r_m^i, r_n^j\right) + S_d\left(r_m^i, r_n^j\right) + S_s\left(r_m^i, r_n^j\right)}{4} \tag{9}$$

where $S_h\left(r_m^i, r_n^j\right)$, $S_c\left(r_m^i, r_n^j\right)$, $S_d\left(r_m^i, r_n^j\right)$, and $S_s\left(r_m^i, r_n^j\right)$ are the normalized semantic, RGB, depth, and saliency similarities between superpixel r_m^i and r_n^j, respectively. A larger $S_M\left(r_m^i, r_n^j\right)$ value corresponds to greater similarity between two superpixels.

2.3   Co-saliency Detection via 2-Layer Co-cellular Automata

In Ref. [23], Cellular Automata method was proposed to calculate the saliency of a single image. The core concept of this method is that the saliency of one superpixel is affected by itself and the adjacent superpixels. All of the superpixels will converge after several times of spread. However, for co-saliency detection, as shown in Fig. 2, the saliency of one superpixel is affected by its intra-neighbor (blue and yellow spots) and its inter-neighbor (purple spot) at the same time.

According to this theory, we propose 2-layer Co-cellular Automata via intra image and inter images spread:

$$S_{m+1}^i = (1 - \kappa_1 - \kappa_2)S_m^i + \kappa_1 F_{intra}^i S_m^i + \kappa_2 \sum_{j=1, j \neq i}^{n} F_{inter}^{i,j} S_m^j \tag{10}$$

where S_m^i is the saliency of all superpixels in I^i after m times of status updates, S_0^i is the initial saliency via Eq. (1), F_{intra}^i is the influence matrix of superpixels in I^i, $F_{inter}^{i,j}$ is the influence matrix from I_j to I_i, κ_1 and κ_2 are impact factors. In this model, we utilize the structural information of intra-image, also, the corresponding relationship is considered here.

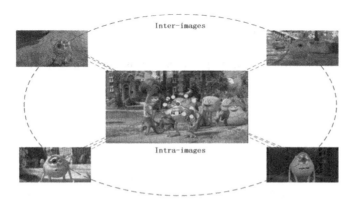

Fig. 2. Co-saliency detection model. The saliency of one superpixel (red spots) is not only affected by the adjacent superpixels (blue and yellow spots) but also affected by the matched superpixels in other images (purple spots). (Color figure online)

Intra-image Influence Matrix. In Ref. [23], the similarity of intra-image superpixels is calculated by color similarity in CIELab color space. Here, we also consider the affect of depth cue and semantic cue. We define the initial intra-image influence matrix as $F_{intra}^{\prime i} = \left[f_{s,t}^{i} \right]_{N^i \times N^i}$.

$$f_{s,t}^{i} = \begin{cases} \exp\left(-\frac{\|c_s^i - c_t^i\|^2 + \|d_s^i - d_t^i\| + \|F_s^i - F_t^i\|^2}{2\sigma_f^2} \right) & t \in N_s^i \\ 0 & t = s \text{ or others} \end{cases} \tag{11}$$

Where N_s^i is superpixels's 2-layer adjacent region (not only includes its neighbor, but also its neighbor's neighbor). In order to normalize impact factor matrix, a degree matrix $D_{intra}^i = diag\{d_1, d_2, \ldots, d_{N^i}\}$, where $d_i = \sum f_{s,t}^i$. Finally, a row-normalized impact factor matrix can be clearly calculated as follows:

$$F_{intra}^i = \left[D_{intra}^i \right]^{-1} \bullet F_{intra}^{\prime i} \tag{12}$$

Inter-Image Influence Matrix. To utilize the affect of other images in the same set, we use the method introduced in Sect. 2.2 to obtain $S_M\left(r_m^i, r_n^j \right)$, then the initial inter-image influence matrix is defined as $F_{inter}^{\prime i}\left[f_{s,t}^{i,j} \right]_{N^i * N^j}$ to capture the relationship of any two superpixels in different images.

$$f_{s,t}^{i,j} = \begin{cases} S_M\left(r_m^i, r_n^j \right) & S_M\left(r_m^i, r_n^j \right) > \delta \\ 0 & \text{others} \end{cases} \tag{13}$$

where δ is a threshold to match saliency. Here this parameter is set to be 0.9 according to our experience. Same as above, degree matrix $D_{inter}^i = diag\{d_1, d_2, \ldots d_{N^i}\}$, where $d_i = \sum f_{s,t}^{i,j}$. And the row-normalized impact factor matrix is indicated as:

$$F_{inter}^i = \frac{1}{N-1} \bullet \left[D_{inter}^i \right]^{-1} \bullet F_{inter}^{\prime i} \tag{14}$$

The overall framework of the proposed method is summarized in Table 1.

Table 1. The procedure of our method.

Alogrithm 1. The Overall Framework.
Input: The RGB images and depth maps in an image group.
Output: The co-saliency map for each image.
1: for each image in the group do
2: Obtain the initialized saliency map using Eq. (1) ;
3: end for
4: for each image in the group do
5: Calculate the intra-image impact factor matrix F^i_{intra} using Eq. (11-12);
6:   Calculate matching similarity $S_M\left(r^i_m, r^j_n\right)$ of any two superpixels in different images using Eq. (2-9);
7: Obtain the inter-image impact factor matrix F^i_{inter} using Eq. (13-14);
8: while m<M do
9: update saliency map using Eq. (10);
10: end while
11: end for

3   Experiment

In this section, we would evaluate the proposed RGBD co-saliency framework on two RGBD co-saliency datasets. The qualitative and quantitative comparison with other state-of-the-art methods are presented.

3.1   Experimental Settings

Two RGBD benchmarks: the RGBD Coseg183 dataset [27] and the RGBD Cosal150 dataset [18] are used to evaluate our method. The RGBD Coseg183 dataset is composed of 183 pictures, and these pictures are distributed in 16 groups. And the RGBD Cosal150 dataset contains 150 images that are distributed in 21 image sets.

We adopted two quantitative criteria to evaluate the co-saliency map, which is Precision-Recall(PR) curve and F-measure score. The precision and recall score are computed by ground truth. F-measure [28] is defined as the weighted mean of precision P and recall R, which is denoted as:

$$F - measure = \frac{\left(1 + \beta^2\right) \times P \times R}{\beta^2 \times P + R} \tag{15}$$

Where β^2 is set to 0.3, because the precision is more important than Recall.

In this method, the number of superpixels of each image is set to 200, the maximum number of iterations M is set to 20. And the parameter κ_1 and κ_2 in Eq. (9) is set to 0.3 and 0.5, respectively.

3.2 Comparison with State-of-the-Art Methods

In this section, we compare our method with 10 state-of-the-art methods, which are RC [20], DCLC [21], RRWR [22], BSCA [23], SE [33], FP [34], CCS [4], EMR [13], AIF [18] and MCLP [19]. The first four methods are single image saliency methods, also they are regarded as the input of this method. SE and FP are classic RGBD single saliency algorithms. CCS and EMR are co-saliency methods for RGB images. The last two method are the latest co-saliency methods for RGDB images.

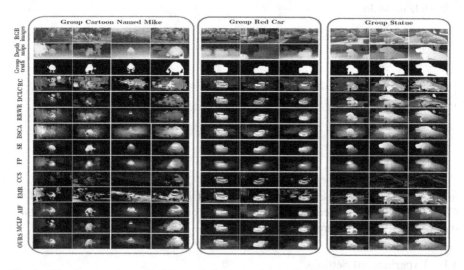

Fig. 3. Visual comparison of different saliency and co-saliency detection methods on two datasets.

Some visual examples on two datasets are shown in Fig. 3. The quantitative comparison results including the PR curves and F-measure scores are reported in Fig. 4. As can be seen, on the RGBD Cosal150 dataset, the proposed method's curve intersects with SE, FP, AIF and MCLP, but the F-measure score of the proposed method is only slightly lower than MCLP. In contrast, the RGBD Coseg183 dataset is more difficult and challenging for co-saliency detection, however, the proposed method's curve achieves the highest precision of the whole PR curves, and the F-measure is only slightly lower than MCLP, too.

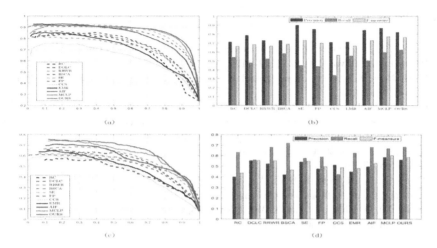

Fig. 4. Quantitative comparisons between the proposed method and the state-of-the-art methods on two datasets. "OURS" means the proposed method. (a) and (b) are PR curves and F-measure scores on RGBD Cosal150 dataset, respectively. (c) and (d) are PR curves and F-measure scores on RGBD Coseg183 dataset, respectively.

Table 2 shows the comparison of average run time to process one image between our proposed model and the other two RGBD co-saliency detection methods (AIF, MCLP). The measurement environment is Intel (R) Core (TM) i5-4570 CPU 3.20.GHz workstation with 8 GB RAM under Matlab R2012a platform. It can be seen from the table that our proposed algorithm is faster than AIF and MCLP.

Table 2. Comparison of average run time to process one image between different algorithm.

Method	Run time (s)
AIF	42.67
MCLP	41.03
OURS	13.07

4 Conclusion

In this paper, we present a co-saliency detection model for RGBD images, which utilize mutli-constraint cues to capture the relationship among multiple images for superpixels matching. Further on, impact factor matrix are constructed for intra-images and inter-images, and the depth cue and high-dimensional semantic cue are considered in intra-images impact factor matrix constructing. In the end, a modified 2-layer co-cellular automata model is using to update initial saliency maps. The comprehensive comparison and discussion on two RGBD co-saliency datasets have demonstrated that the proposed method outperforms other state-of-the-art saliency and co-saliency models.

References

1. Chen, H.T.: Preattentive co-saliency detection. In: IEEE International Conference on Image Processing 2010, vol. 119, pp. 1117–1120. IEEE (2010)
2. Li, H., Ngan, K.N.: A co-saliency model of image pairs. IEEE Trans. Image Process. **20**(12), 3365–3375 (2011)
3. Chang, K.Y., Liu, T.L., Lai, S.H.: From co-saliency to co-segmentation: an efficient and fully unsupervised energy minimization model. In: IEEE Conference on Computer Vision and Pattern Recognition 2011, vol. 42, pp. 2129–2136. IEEE Computer Society (2011)
4. Fu, H., Cao, X., Tu, Z.: Cluster-based co-saliency detection. IEEE Trans. Image Process. **22**(10), 3766–3778 (2013)
5. Zhang, D., Fu, H., Han, J., Borji, A., Li, X.: A review of co-saliency detection technique: fundamentals, applications, and challenges (2016)
6. Fu, H., Xu, D., Zhang, B., Lin, S., Ward, R.K.: Object-based multiple foreground video co-segmentation via multi-state selection graph. IEEE Trans. Image Process. **24**(11), 3415–3424 (2015)
7. Tang, K., Joulin, A., Li, L.J., Li, F.F.: Co-localization in real-world images. In: IEEE Computer Vision and Pattern Recognition 2014, pp. 1464–1471. IEEE (2014)
8. Toshev, A., Shi, J., Daniilidis, K.: Image matching via saliency region correspondences. In: IEEE Computer Vision and Pattern Recognition 2007, pp. 1–8. IEEE (2007)
9. Liu, Z., Zou, W., Li, L., Shen, L., Meur, O.L.: Co-saliency detection based on hierarchical segmentation. IEEE Sig. Process. Lett. **21**(1), 88–92 (2013)
10. Ge, C., Fu, K., Liu, F., Bai, L., Yang, J.: Co-saliency detection via inter and intra saliency propagation. Sig. Process. Image Commun. **44**(C), 69–83 (2016)
11. Cao, X., Tao, Z., Zhang, B., Fu, H., Li, X.: Saliency map fusion based on rank-one constraint. In: IEEE International Conference on Multimedia and Expo 2013, pp. 1–6 (2013)
12. Cao, X., Tao, Z., Zhang, B., Fu, H., Feng, W.: Self-adaptively weighted co-saliency detection via rank constraint. IEEE Trans. Image Process. Publ. IEEE Signal Process. Soc. **23**(9), 4175–4186 (2014)
13. Li, Y., Fu, K., Liu, Z., Yang, J.: Efficient saliency-model-guided visual co-saliency detection. IEEE Signal Process. Lett. **22**(5), 588–592 (2014)
14. Huang, R., Feng, W., Sun, J.: Saliency and co-saliency detection by low-rank multiscale fusion. In: IEEE International Conference on Multimedia and Expo 2015, pp. 1–6 (2015)
15. Zhang, D., Han, J., Li, C., Wang, J.: Co-saliency detection via looking deep and wide. In: IEEE Computer Vision and Pattern Recognition 2015, pp. 2994–3002 (2015)
16. Zhang, D., Meng, D., Li, C., Jiang, L.: A self-paced multiple-instance learning framework for co-saliency detection. In: IEEE International Conference on Computer Vision 2015, pp. 594–602 (2015)
17. Song, H., Liu, Z., Xie, Y., Wu, L., Huang, M.: RGBD co-saliency detection via bagging-based clustering. IEEE Sig. Process. Lett. **23**(12), 1722–1726 (2016)
18. Cong, R., Lei, J., Fu, H., Lin, W., Huang, Q., Cao, X., et al.: An iterative co-saliency framework for RGBD images. IEEE Trans. Cybern. **PP**(99), 1–14 (2017)
19. Cong, R., et al.: Co-saliency detection for RGBD images based on multi-constraint feature matching and cross label propagation. IEEE Trans. Image Process. **PP**(99), 1 (2018)

20. Cheng, M.M., Zhang, G.X., Mitra, N.J., Huang, X., Hu, S.M.: Global contrast based salient region detection. In: IEEE CVPR 2011, vol. 37, pp. 409–416 (2011)

21. Zhou, L., Yang, Z., Yuan, Q., Zhou, Z., Hu, D.: Salient region detection via integrating diffusion-based compactness and local contrast. IEEE Trans. Image Process. **24**(11), 3308–3320 (2015)

22. Li, C., Yuan, Y., Cai, W., Xia, Y.: Robust saliency detection via regularized random walks ranking, pp. 2710–2717 (2015)

23. Qin, Y., Lu, H., Xu, Y., Wang, H.: Saliency detection via cellular automata. In: IEEE Computer Vision and Pattern Recognition 2015, pp. 110–119 (2015)

24. Achanta, R., Shaji, A., Smith, K., Lucchi, A., Fua, P., Susstrunk, S.: Slic superpixels compared to state-of-the-art superpixel methods. IEEE Trans. Pattern Anal. Mach. Intell. **34**(11), 2274–2282 (2012)

25. Leung, T., Malik, J.: Recognizing surfaces using three-dimensional textons. In: IEEE International Conference on Computer Vision 1999, vol. 2, pp. 1010–1017 (1999)

26. Fu, H., Xu, D., Lin, S., Liu, J.: Object-based RGBD image co-segmentation with mutex constraint. In: IEEE Conference on Computer Vision and Pattern Recognition 2017, pp. 4428–4436 (2017)

27. Achanta, R., Hemami, S., Estrada, F., Susstrunk, S.: Frequency-tuned salient region detection. In: Proceedings of CVPR, June 2009, pp. 1597–1604 (2009)

28. Ju, R., Liu, Y., Ren, T., Ge, L., Wu, G.: Depth-aware salient object detection using anisotropic center-surround difference. Sig. Process. Image Commun. **38**(C), 115–126 (2015)

29. Peng, H., Li, B., Xiong, W., Hu, W., Ji, R.: RGBD salient object detection: a benchmark and algorithms. In: Fleet, D., Pajdla, T., Schiele, B., Tuytelaars, T. (eds.) ECCV 2014. LNCS, vol. 8691, pp. 92–109. Springer, Cham (2014). https://doi.org/10.1007/978-3-319-10578-9_7

30. Feng, D., Barnes, N., You, S., Mccarthy, C.: Local background enclosure for RGB-D salient object detection. In: IEEE Conference on Computer Vision and Pattern Recognition 2016, pp. 2343–2350. IEEE Computer Society (2016)

31. Cong, R., Lei, J., Zhang, C., Huang, Q., Cao, X., Hou, C.: Saliency detection for stereoscopic images based on depth confidence analysis and multiple cues fusion. IEEE Sig. Process. Lett. **23**(6), 819–823 (2016)

32. Quo, J., Ren, T., Bei, J.: Salient object detection for RGB-D image via saliency evolution. In: IEEE International Conference on Multimedia and Expo, pp. 1–6. IEEE (2016)

33. Guo, J., Ren, T., Bei, J.: Salient object detection in RGB-D image based on saliency fusion and propagation. In: 7th International Conference on Internet Multimedia Computing and Service, 59. ACM (2015)

34. Li, H., Lu, H., Lin, Z., Shen, X., Price, B.: Inner and inter label propagation: salient object detection in the wild. The first five years of the Communist International. New Park Pub., 3176–3186 (1973)

35. Chen, T., Lin, L., Liu, L., Luo, X., Li, X.: DISC: deep image saliency computing via progressive representation learning. IEEE Trans. Neural Netw. Learn. Syst. **27**(6), 1135 (2015)

36. He, S., Lau, R.W.H., Liu, W., Huang, Z., Yang, Q.: Supercnn: a superpixelwise convolutional neural network for salient object detection. Int. J. Comput. Vision **115**(3), 330–344 (2015)

37. Lee, G., Tai, Y.W., Kim, J.: Deep saliency with encoded low level distance map and high level features. In: Computer Vision and Pattern Recognition, pp. 660–668. IEEE (2016)

38. Li, G., Yu, Y.: Deep contrast learning for salient object detection. In: IEEE Conference on Computer Vision and Pattern Recognition, pp. 478–487. IEEE Computer Society (2016)

Double-Line Multi-scale Fusion Pedestrian Saliency Detection

Jiaxuan Zhuo[1,3] and Jianhuang Lai[1,2,3(✉)]

[1] The School of Data and Computer Science, Sun Yat-sen University,
Guangzhou 510006, China
{zhuojx5,stsljh}@mail.sysu.edu.cn
[2] The School of Information Science and Technology, XinHua College,
Sun Yat-sen University, Guangzhou, People's Republic of China
[3] The Guangdong Key Laboratory of Information Security Technology,
Guangzhou 510006, China

Abstract. Pedestrian salient detection aims at identifying person body parts in occluded person images, which is greatly significant in occluded person re-identification. To achieve pedestrian salient detection, we propose a double-line multi-scale fusion (DMF) network, which not only extracts double-line features and retains both high-level and low-level semantic information but also fuses high-level information and low-level information for better complement. CRF is then used to further improve its performance. Finally, our method is used to deal with occluded person images into partial person images to achieve partial person re-identification matching. Experiment results on five benchmark datasets show the superiority of our proposed method, and result on two occluded person re-identification datasets indicate the effectiveness of our proposal on pedestrian salient detection.

Keywords: Double-line multi-scale fusion network
Pedestrian salient detection · Occluded person re-identification

1 Introduction

Nowadays, video surveillance has been widely used in many security-sensitive places, such as hospital, school, bank, museum, etc and the areas of video surveillance are often non-overlapping. Therefore, person re-identification (re-id) [1–5] across non-overlapping cameras was proposed and widely studied. However, person re-id has encountered many challenges, the most serious one of which is occlusion.

As we know, in crowed public places, there are always some pedestrians occluded by some objects, e.g. cars, trees, garbage cans. So occluded person re-id is needed for actual pedestrian applications. In occluded person re-id, one of the hardest problems is how to deal with occluded person images because pedestrian images detected by most of pedestrian detectors always include occlusions.

© Springer Nature Switzerland AG 2018
J.-H. Lai et al. (Eds.): PRCV 2018, LNCS 11256, pp. 144–154, 2018.
https://doi.org/10.1007/978-3-030-03398-9_13

While the useful information what we need is only the person body parts. These occlusion areas cause interference for person re-id and bring more redundant information in matching process, which leads to the dropping performance of re-id. As shown in Fig. 1, among the works related with occluded person re-id [6,7], Zheng [7] used partial person images to match the full-body person images by the framework combining a local-to-local matching model with a global-to-local matching model and achieved effective results. However, in the practical situation, there are no suitable detectors to detect the occlusions for occlusions with diverse characteristics, such as colors, sizes, shapes, and positions. The partial person images are gained by manually cropping, which brings operational trouble and time waste (See Fig. 1). Differed from the idea of detecting occlusions, we consider detecting the useful information needed in occluded person images, that is, the person body parts.

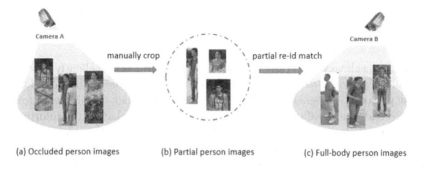

Fig. 1. Illustration of partial person re-id solving occlusions. (a): occluded person images detected by existing pedestrian detector; (b): partial person images after manually crop ping; (c): full-body person images which partial person re-id searches for.

Referring to other works on detecting human body parts, most of works aim to detect or cluster specific local part regions, such as head, shoulder, arm, leg and foot of persons. For occluded images, since either the occlusion or non-occluded body parts are always irregular, it is difficult to get a definite boundaries between body and occlusions using methods with detecting bounding boxes, which results in poor cutting. Differed from other works, we used a deep learning based saliency detection framework to detect person body parts and obtain partial person regions. There are two main reasons using saliency detection framework: Firstly, the saliency detection methods are able to separate the foreground and the background of an image in the pixel level, which leads to higher definition. It can better find the boundaries between the regions of person body parts and the regions of backgrounds or noise areas. Second, the deep learning based saliency detection network has ability to learn semantic information, which helps the framework distinguish the semantics of the parts that we need to acquire, namely the person body parts regions (Fig. 2).

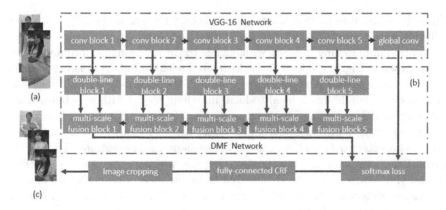

Fig. 2. Illustration of partial person re-id solving occlusions. (a): occluded person images detected by existing pedestrian detector; (b): partial person images after manually crop ping; (c): full-body person images which partial person re-id searches for.

Although saliency detection methods have been studied excellently, few works make initial attempts to solve occluded person re-id. Due to the poor quality of most person re-id benchmark datasets, there are higher requirements for the extracted features of saliency detection being proposed, that is, the information of images needs to be carefully preserved as far as possible. This paper proposes a double-line multi-scale fusion (DMF) network, which not only extracts richer features by double-line block and multi-scale fusion block but further improves the feature fusion process to make the high-level and low-level information better complemented. Besides, a fully-connected CRF [8] is used after DMF network for further improvement. After using the saliency detection network proposed in this paper to preprocess the occluded person images, we can obtain masks of occluded person images and crop the interesting regions in occluded person images into partial person images so as to achieve partial person re-id. In summary, this paper makes three main contributions.

- It is a new attempt that saliency detection is used in occluded person re-id problem, which is used to detect the person body parts on the pixel-level and then crop occluded person images into partial person images.
- To reach complementation of high-level and lower-level information, we propose a double-line multi-scale fusion (DMF) network consisting of the double-line feature extraction block and multi-scale feature fusion block. The former makes information diverse and the latter makes information from different scales fusing and complemented.
- Experiments on five heterogeneous benchmark datasets show high performance of our approach compared with other state-of-art methods. Besides, our approach is used in two banchmask occluded person re-id datasets to deal with occluded person images.

2   Proposed Method

We propose a double-line multi-scale fusion (DMF) network for saliency detection, which is based on the VGG-16 [9] network, as shown in Fig. 3. The DMF network includes two main components: the double-line feature extraction block and multi-scale feature fusion block. To make extracted features more diverse, the double-line block calculates the difference of the feature after average pooling and then we connect it with the original feature in order to get richer information. The multi-scale fusion block aims to combine high-level information with lower-level information to reduce the loss of details on the ground floor. Finally, features form the based network VGG-16 and double-line multi-scale fusion are connected and put into softmax loss to obtain predicted masks. We also use a fully-connected CRF [8] as a post-processing step. This saliency detection can be used in the process of dealing with occluded person images in occluded person re-id.

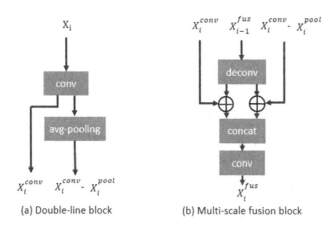

Fig. 3. Illustration of partial person re-id solving occlusions. (a): occluded person images detected by existing pedestrian detector; (b): partial person images after manually crop ping; (c): full-body person images which partial person re-id searches for.

2.1   Double-Line Feature Extraction

For saliency detection, it is greatly important that extracted features have ability to distinguish the foreground and the background, so we need to extract richer features to do determination. In this paper, we adopt a structure similar to feature pyramid [10]. Our network first used VGG-16 as basic network to extract features, in which all the convolution layers are divided into five convolution blocks and output features from each convolution block. This way aims to retain information from each floor and increase the diversity of features. In addition, the more important ways to increase the feature diversity is the double-line feature extraction part. As shown in Fig. 3(a), this structure of this part consists of a convolutional layer and an average pooling layer, which has two outputs. One output X_i^{conv} is the feature X_i through the convolutional layer, and the other $X_i^{conv} - X_i^{pool}$ is similar to pooling residual structure, which means the difference (D-value) between X_i and X_i after average pooling. Then the double-line output is connected in series as final output. In this process, the pooling residual structure can offer other abundant information because average pooling has the effect to smooth images and the difference between original images and smoothing images can embody some outstanding information, which we desire to grasp.

Let $X_i(i = 1, 2, 3, 4, 5)$ denote output features after each convolution block of VGG-16 network, and X_i^{conv} and X_i^{pool} are feature X_i through the convolutional layer and the average pooling layer, respectively. The result of double-line feature extraction block can be expressed as:

$$X_i^{out} = \{X_i^{conv}, X_i^{conv} - X_i^{pool}\} \tag{1}$$

After double-line feature extraction, features are merged with the deconvolution upsampling of the next block as the final double-line output, and then enter the multi-scale feature fusion block. The concrete fusion operation will be explained in the next section.

2.2 Multi-scale Feature Fusion

Actually, if we only grasp high-level features, the output would lose plenty of important details in low-level feature floor, leading to poor saliency detection. Considering the above condition, we use a multi-scale feature fusion structure to fuse high-level and low-level features until all the feature floors are fused together. In order to make unified fusion size between upper and lower layer, we do the deconvolution upsampling for high-level floor and then add to low-level double-line features, respectively. After fusing, we use a convolution layer to smooth the fusion results. In this way, our final output features greatly incorporate all high-level semantic information and low-level semantic information. The concrete structure is shown in Fig. 3(b). In the paper [11], the high-level low-level features are directly concated to lower level features, which only retains multiple levels of information. While our network further lets these information be merged to achieve a complementary effect so that the final output features both focus on large objects and details or small objects, achieving stronger saliency detection.

The operation of feature fusion is mathematically that sum the corresponding pixel points of deconvoluted high-level feature maps and the last double-line features, which is formulated as

$$X_i^{fus} = conv(\{X_i^{conv}, X_i^{conv} - X_i^{pool}\} + deconv(X_{i-1}^{fus})) \tag{2}$$

where X_i^{fus} is output features after one multi-scale feature fusion block corresponding to the i_{th} convolution block. Finally, features including information from five convolutional floors are connected with global futures form the based VGG-16 network, and then are used in the calculation of softmax loss and fully-connected CRF post-processing.

2.3 DMF in Occluded Person Re-id

DMF network can better combine high-level semantics information and low-level semantic information, and use VGG-16 network as basic network, which has ability to identify the different object categories. Therefore, DMF network can successfully achieve fine pedestrian salient detection and we use it to distinguish salient person body parts and backgrounds or noise information from occlusions. After DMF salient detection, occluded person images are cropped into partial person images according to predicted salient regions. The process is shown in Algorithm 1.

Algorithm 1. Occluded Person Images Cropping

Input: salient detection model DMF, occlude person images I^O (with N images)
Output: partial person images I^P
for i in range (N)
  1 : obtain mask Z_i of I_i^O by salient detection model DMF
  2 : do the corrosion and expansion for mask Z_i
  3 : calculate the maximum connectivity area of mask Z_i
  4 : calculate proportion R^W, R^H of the largest wrapping rectangle occupying I^O
  5 : if $R^W > R^H$ $I_i^P \leftarrow$ horizontal cropping operation
  6 : else $I_i^P \leftarrow$ vertical cropping operation
end

---

3   Experiment

3.1   Datasets

We evaluate the proposed method on five public benchmark datasets: MSRA-B [12], ECSSD [13], PASCAL-S [14], HKU-IS [15], DUT-OMRON [16]. Besides, we use our method on two occluded person re-id datasets Occluded REID dataset [17] and Partial REID dataset [7] to verify the effectiveness in occluded person re-id.

MSRA-B has been widely used for salient object detection, which contains 5000 images and corresponding pixel-wise ground truth.

ECSSD contains 1000 complex and natural images with complex structure acquired from the internet.

PASCAL-S contains 850 natural images with both pixel-wise saliency ground truth which are chosen from the validation set of the PASCAL VOC 2010 segmentation dataset.

HKU-IS is large-scale dataset containing 4447 images, which is split into 2500 training images, 500 validation images and the remaining test images.

DUT-OMRON includes 5168 challenging images, each of which has one or more salient objects.

Partial REID dataset is the first for partial person re-id [7], which includes 900 images of 60 people, with 5 full-body images, 5 partial images and 5 occluded images per person.

Occluded REID dataset consists of 2000 images of 200 persons. Each one has 5 full-body images and 5 occluded images with different types of severe occlusions. All of images with different viewpoints and backgrounds.

3.2 Experiment Setting

Methods for Comparison. To evaluate the superiority of our method, we compare our method with several recent state-of-the-art methods: Geodesic Saliency (GS) [18], Manifold Ranking (MR) [16], optimized WeightedContrast (wCtr*) [19], Background based Single-layer Cellular Automata (BSCA) [20], Local Estimation and Global Search (LEGS) [21], Multi-Context (MC) [22], Multiscale Deep Features (MDF) [15] and Deep Contrast Learning (DCL) [23]. Among these methods, LEGS, MC, MDF and DCL are the recent saliency detection methods based on deep learning.

Evaluation Metrics. Max F-measure (F_β) and mean absolute error (MAE) score are used to evaluate the performance. Max F_β is computed from the PR curve, which is defined as

$$F_\beta = \frac{(1+\beta^2) \times Precision \times Recall}{\beta^2 \times Precision + Recall}. \tag{3}$$

MAE score means the average pixel-wise absolute difference between predicted mask P and its corresponding ground truth L, which is computed as

$$MAE = \frac{1}{W \times H} \sum_{x=1}^{W} \sum_{y=1}^{H} |\hat{P}(x,y) - \hat{L}(x,y)|. \tag{4}$$

where $\hat{P}$ and $\hat{L}$ are the continuous saliency map and the ground truth that are normalized to $[0,1]$. W and H is the width and height of the input image.

Parameter Setting. Our method is easily implemented in Pytorch, which is initialized with the pretrained weights of VGG-16 [9]. We randomly take 2500 images of MSRA-B dataset as training data and select 2000 images of the remaining images as testing data. The other datasets are all regarded as testing data. All the input images are resized to 352×352 for training and test. The experiments are conducted with the initial learning rate of 10^{-6}, batch size $= 40$ and parameter of evaluation metrics β^2 is 0.3. Parameters of fully-connected CRF follow as [8].

Table 1. Comparison on five public benchmark datasets with state-of-the-art

Cat	Methods	Data									
		MSRA-B		ECSSD		PASCAL-S		HKU-IS		DUT-OMRON	
		max F_β	MAE	max F_β	MAE	max F_β	MAE	max F_β	MAE	max F_β	MAE
A	GS [18]	0.777	0.144	0.661	0.206	0.624	0.224	0.682	0.167	0.557	0.173
	MR [16]	0.824	0.127	0.736	0.189	0.666	0.223	0.715	0.174	0.610	0.187
	wCtr* [19]	0.820	0.110	0.716	0.171	0.659	0.201	0.726	0.141	0.630	0.144
	BSCA [20]	0.830	0.130	0.758	0.183	0.666	0.224	0.723	0.174	0.616	0.191
B	LEGS [21]	0.870	0.081	0.827	0.118	0.756	0.157	0.770	0.118	0.669	0.133
	MC [22]	0.894	0.054	0.822	0.106	0.740	0.145	0.798	0.102	0.703	0.088
	MDF [15]	0.885	0.066	0.832	0.105	0.764	0.145	0.861	**0.076**	0.694	0.092
	DCL [23]	0.905	0.052	**0.887**	**0.072**	**0.815**	**0.113**	**0.892**	0.054	**0.733**	0.084
C	DMF	**0.900**	**0.057**	0.900	0.065	0.822	0.109	0.899	0.054	0.750	**0.085**

Compared with State-of-the-Art. We compare our approach with several recent state-of-the-art methods in terms of max F_β and MAE score on five benchmark datasets, which is shown in Table 1. We collect eight methods including (A) non-deep learning ones and (B) deep learning ones. It can be seen that our method presents the best performance in the whole and largely outperforms non-deep learning methods because deep neural network has ability to learn and update the model automatically. Besides, our method surpasses the 2nd best method on ECSSD, PASCAL-S, HKU-IS and DUT-OMRON in almost max F_β and MAE score, which indicates our model can be directly applied in practical application due to good generalization.

Used on Occluded Person Re-identification. We do the visual comparison among our approach and the compared methods in Table 1 on two occluded person re-id datasets, Occluded REID dataset and Partial REID dataset, and process occluded person images into partial person images according to Algorithm 1, Sect. 2.3. Experimental result is shown in Fig. 4, which can be easily seen that our proposed method can not only highlight the most relevant regions, person body parts but also find the exact boundary to obtain better partial person images. Therefore, our proposed method is able to apply to pedestrian salient detection in occluded person re-id.

3.3 Experiment Results

3.4 Time Costing

We measure the speed of deep learning salient detection methods by computing the average time of obtaining a saliency map of one image. Table 2 shows the comparison between five deep leaning based methods: LEGS [21], MC [22], MDF [15], DCL [23] and our method, using a Titan GPU. Our method takes the least time to achieve salient detection and is 4 to 50 times faster than other methods, which illustrates the superiority of our method in terms of computing speed.

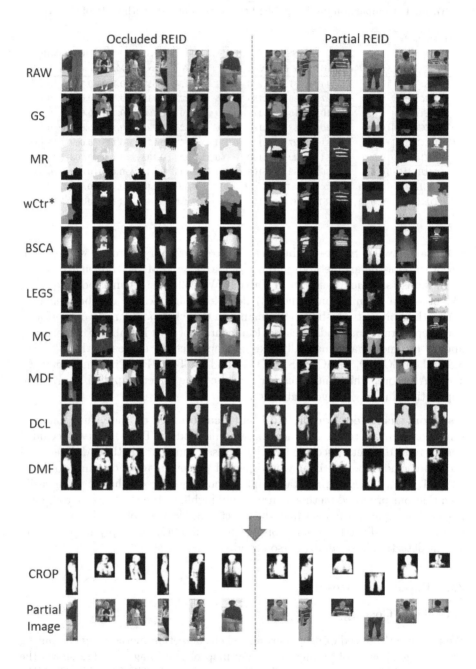

Fig. 4. Visual comparison with eight existing methods and examples of cropping mask to obtain partial person images. As can be seen, our proposal produces more accuracy and coherent salient maps than all other methods.

Table 2. Time costing of obtaining a salient map

Time	LEGS	MC	MDF	DCL	DMF
s/img	2	1.6	8	1.5	0.4

4   Conclusion

In this paper, we make the first attempt to deal with occluded person images in occluded person re-id by pedestrian salient detection. To fine detect person body parts, the double-line multi-scale fusion (DMF) network is proposed to get more semantic information by double-line feature extraction and multi-scale fusion by fusing high-level and low-level information from high floor to low floor. We finally used a full-connected CRF as post-processing step after DMF network. Experimental results on benchmarks about salient detection and on occluded person re-id datasets both show the effectiveness and superiority of our method.

This project is supported by the Natural Science Foundation of China (61573387) and Guangdong Project (2017B030306018).

References

1. Wang, G.C., Lai, J.H., Xie, X.H.: P2SNeT: can an image match a video for person re-identification in an end-to-end way? IEEE TCSVT (2017)
2. Chen, Y.C., Zhu, X.T., Zheng, W.S., Lai, J.H.: Person re-identification by camera correlation aware feature augmentation. IEEE Trans. Pattern Anal. Mach. Intell. **40**(2), 392–408 (2018)
3. Chen, S.Z., Guo, C.C., Lai, J.H.: Deep ranking for person re-identification via joint representation learning. IEEE Trans. Image Process. **25**(5), 2353–2367 (2016)
4. Shi, S.C., Guo, C.C., Lai, J.H., Chen, S.Z., Hu, X.J.: Person re-identification with multi-level adaptive correspondence models. Neurocomputing **168**, 550–559 (2015)
5. Guo, C.C., Chen, S.Z., Lai, J.H., Hu, X.J., Shi, S.C.: Multi-shot person re-identification with automatic ambiguity inference and removal. In: 22nd International Conference on Pattern Recognition, ICPR 2014, Stockholm, Sweden, 24–28 August 2014, pp. 3540–3545 (2014)
6. Zhuo, J.X., Chen, Z.Y., Lai, J.H., Wang, G.C.: Occluded person re-identification. arXiv preprint arXiv:1804.02792 (2018)
7. Zheng, W.S., Li, X., Xiang, T., Liao, S.C., Lai, J.H., Gong, S.G.: Partial person re-identification. In: Proceedings of the IEEE International Conference on Computer Vision, pp. 4678–4686 (2015)
8. Krähenbühl, P., Koltun, V.: Efficient inference in fully connected CRFs with Gaussian edge potentials. In: Advances in Neural Information Processing Systems 24: 25th Annual Conference on Neural Information Processing Systems 2011. Proceedings of a Meeting Held 12–14 December 2011, Granada, Spain, pp. 109–117 (2011)
9. Simonyan, K., Zisserman, A.: Very deep convolutional networks for large-scale image recognition. CoRR, vol. abs/1409.1556 (2014)
10. Lin, T.Y., Dollár, P., Girshick, R., He, K.M., Hariharan, B., Belongie, S.: Feature pyramid networks for object detection. In: 2017 IEEE Conference on Computer Vision and Pattern Recognition, CVPR 2017, Honolulu, HI, USA, 21–26 July 2017, pp. 936–944 (2017)

11. Ronneberger, O., Fischer, P., Brox, T.: U-Net: convolutional networks for biomedical image segmentation. In: Navab, N., Hornegger, J., Wells, W.M., Frangi, A.F. (eds.) MICCAI 2015, Part III. LNCS, vol. 9351, pp. 234–241. Springer, Cham (2015). https://doi.org/10.1007/978-3-319-24574-4_28

12. Liu, T., et al.: Learning to detect a salient object. IEEE Trans. Pattern Anal. Mach. Intell. **33**(2), 353–367 (2011)

13. Yan, Q., Xu, L., Shi, J.P., Jia, J.Y.: Hierarchical saliency detection. In: 2013 IEEE Conference on Computer Vision and Pattern Recognition, Portland, OR, USA, 23–28 June 2013, pp. 1155–1162 (2013)

14. Li, Y., Hou, X.D., Koch, C., Rehg, J.M., Yuille, A.L.: The secrets of salient object segmentation. In: 2014 IEEE Conference on Computer Vision and Pattern Recognition, CVPR 2014, Columbus, OH, USA, 23–28 June 2014, pp. 280–287 (2014)

15. Li, G.B., Yu, Y.Z.: Visual saliency based on multiscale deep features. In: IEEE Conference on Computer Vision and Pattern Recognition, CVPR 2015, Boston, MA, USA, 7–12 June 2015, pp. 5455–5463 (2015)

16. Yang, C., Zhang, L.H., Lu, H.C., Ruan, X., Yang, M.H.: Saliency detection via graph-based manifold ranking. In: 2013 IEEE Conference on Computer Vision and Pattern Recognition, Portland, OR, USA, 23–28 June 2013, pp. 3166–3173 (2013)

17. Luo, Z.M., Mishra, A., Achkar, A., Eichel, J., Li, S.Z., Jodoin, P.M.: Non-local deep features for salient object detection. In: 2017 IEEE Conference on Computer Vision and Pattern Recognition, CVPR 2017, Honolulu, HI, USA, July 21–26, 2017, pp. 6593–6601 (2017)

18. Wei, Y., Wen, F., Zhu, W., Sun, J.: Geodesic saliency using background priors. In: Fitzgibbon, A., Lazebnik, S., Perona, P., Sato, Y., Schmid, C. (eds.) ECCV 2012, Part III. LNCS, vol. 7574, pp. 29–42. Springer, Heidelberg (2012). https://doi.org/10.1007/978-3-642-33712-3_3

19. Zhu, W.J., Liang, S., Wei, Y.C., Sun, J.: Saliency optimization from robust background detection. In: 2014 IEEE Conference on Computer Vision and Pattern Recognition, CVPR 2014, Columbus, OH, USA, 23–28 June 2014, pp. 2814–2821 (2014)

20. Liu, H., Tao, S.N., Li, Z.Y.: Saliency detection via global-object-seed-guided cellular automata. In: 2016 IEEE International Conference on Image Processing, ICIP 2016, Phoenix, AZ, USA, 25–28 September 2016, pp. 2772–2776 (2016)

21. Wang, L.J., Lu, H.C., Ruan, X., Yang, M.H.: Deep networks for saliency detection via local estimation and global search. In: IEEE Conference on Computer Vision and Pattern Recognition, CVPR 2015, Boston, MA, USA, 7–12 June 2015, pp. 3183–3192 (2015)

22. Zhao, R., Ouyang, W.L., Li, H.H., Wang, X.G.: Saliency detection by multi-context deep learning. In: IEEE Conference on Computer Vision and Pattern Recognition, CVPR 2015, Boston, MA, USA, 7–12 June 2015, pp. 1265–1274 (2015)

23. Li, G.B., Yu, Y.Z.: Deep contrast learning for salient object detection. In: 2016 IEEE Conference on Computer Vision and Pattern Recognition, CVPR 2016, Las Vegas, NV, USA, 27–30 June 2016, pp. 478–487 (2016)

Multispectral Image Super-Resolution Using Structure-Guided RGB Image Fusion

Zhi-Wei Pan and Hui-Liang Shen[✉]

College of Information Science and Electronic Engineering, Zhejiang University,
Hangzhou 310027, China
{pankdda,shenhl}@zju.edu.cn

Abstract. Due to hardware limitation, multispectral imaging device usually cannot achieve high spatial resolution. To address the issue, this paper proposes a multispectral image super-resolution algorithm by fusing the low-resolution multispectral image and the high-resolution RGB image. The fusion is formulated as an optimization problem according to the linear image degradation models. Meanwhile, the fusion is guided by the edge structure of RGB image via the directional total variation regularizer. Then the fusion problem is solved by the alternating direction method of multipliers algorithm through iteration. The subproblems in each iterative step is simple and can be solved in closed-form. The effectiveness of the proposed algorithm is evaluated on both public datasets and our image set. Experimental results validate that the algorithm outperforms the state-of-the-arts in terms of both reconstruction accuracy and computational efficiency.

Keywords: Multispectral imaging · Super-resolution
Directional total variation · Image reconstruction · Image fusion

1 Introduction

Multispectral imaging has been widely applied in various application fields, including biomedicine [1], remote sensing [2], color reproduction [3], and etc. Multispectral imaging can achieve high spectral resolution, but lacks spatial information when compared with general RGB cameras. The objective of this work is to reconstruct a high-resolution (HR) multispectral image by fusing a low-resolution (LR) multispectral image and an HR RGB image of the same scene.

This work was supported by the National Natural Science Foundation of China under Grant 61371160, in part by the Zhejiang Provincial Key Research and Development Project under Grant 2017C01044, and in part by the Fundamental Research Funds for the Central Universities under Grant 2017XZZX009-01.
Student as first author.

© Springer Nature Switzerland AG 2018
J.-H. Lai et al. (Eds.): PRCV 2018, LNCS 11256, pp. 155–167, 2018.
https://doi.org/10.1007/978-3-030-03398-9_14

The fusion of multispectral and RGB image can be conveniently formulated in the Bayesian inference framework. The work [4] estimates the signal-dependent noise statistics to generate the conditional probability distribution of acquired images, and makes the reconstruction robust to noise corruption. Extracting auxiliary information in Bayesian framework requires additional calculations and influences the reconstruction efficiency to some degree.

Matrix factorization has been widely employed in image fusion. As spectral bands are highly correlated, principal component analysis (PCA) is used in [5] to decompose the image data. By adopting the coupled nonnegative matrix factorization criterion, the spectral unmixing principle is employed in [6] to unmix the hyperspectral and multispectral image in a coupled fashion. Meanwhile, tensor factorization has the potential to fully exploit the inherent spatial-spectral structures during image fusion. The work [7] incorporates the non-local spatial self-similarity into sparse tensor factorization and casts the image fusion problem as estimating sparse core tensor and dictionaries of three modes.

Regularization techniques can be employed to produce a reasonable approximate solution when the fusion problem is ill-posed. The HySure algorithm [8] uses vector total variation as an edge-preserving regularizer to promote a piecewise-smooth solution. The NSSR algorithm [9] uses a clustering-based regularizer to exploit the spatial correlations among local and nonlocal similar pixels. The regularization problem is usually solved though iteration. To decrease the computational complexity, the R-FUSE algorithm [10] derives a robust and efficient solution to the regularized image fusion problem based on a generalized Sylvester equation. In addition, the work [11] explores the properties of decimation matrix and derives an analytical solution for the $\ell 2$ norm regularized super-resolution problem.

Deep learning presents new solutions for the multispectral image super-resolution. The work [12] learns a mapping function between LR and HR images by training a deep neural network with the modified sparse denoising autoencoder. PanNet [13] has the ability to preserve both the spectral and spatial information during the learning process, as its network parameters are trained on the high-pass components of the PAN and upsampled LR multispectral images.

Inspired by the above works, this paper proposes a super-resolution algorithm to reconstruct the target HR multispectral data via structure-guided RGB image fusion. In the algorithm, the spatial and spectral degradation models are used to fit the acquired image data. An edge-preserving regularizer, which is in the form of directional total variation (dTV) [14], is used to guide the image reconstruction. It is based on the reasonable assumption that the spectral images and RGB image share not only the edge location but also the edge direction. To avoid the singularity induced by spectral dependence, the reconstruction is performed on a subspace of the LR multispectral image. The fusion problem is finally solved by the alternating direction method of multipliers (ADMM) algorithm [15] through iteration. The solutions of subproblems are in closed-form and can be accelerated in frequency domain.

The main contributions of this paper include: (1) The image fusion accuracy is improved by guiding the recovered edge structure in accordance to that of RGB image, and (2) The image fusion efficiency is improved by solving the subproblems in closed-form and accelerating the solutions in frequency domain. These makes the proposed algorithm more suitable for practical applications.

2   Problem Formulation

The acquired LR multispectral image is denoted as $\widetilde{\mathbf{Y}} \in \mathbb{R}^{m \times n \times L}$, where $m \times n$ is the spatial resolution and L is the number of spectral bands. The acquired HR RGB image $\widetilde{\mathbf{Z}} \in \mathbb{R}^{M \times N \times 3}$ has the spatial resolution $M \times N$. Denoting the scale factor of resolution improvement with d, the spatial dimensions are related by $M = m \times d$ and $N = n \times d$. The goal of super-resolution is to estimate the HR multispectral image $\widetilde{\mathbf{X}} \in \mathbb{R}^{M \times N \times L}$ by fusing $\widetilde{\mathbf{Y}}$ and $\widetilde{\mathbf{Z}}$.

2.1   Observation Model

By indexing pixels in lexicographic order, the image cubes $\widetilde{\mathbf{Y}}$, $\widetilde{\mathbf{Z}}$ and $\widetilde{\mathbf{X}}$ can be represented by matrices $\mathbf{Y} \in \mathbb{R}^{L \times mn}$, $\mathbf{Z} \in \mathbb{R}^{3 \times MN}$ and $\mathbf{X} \in \mathbb{R}^{L \times MN}$ respectively. The row vectors of these matrices are actually the vectorized band images. With this treatment, the spatial degradation model can be constructed as

$$\mathbf{Y} = \mathbf{XBS}, \tag{1}$$

where matrix $\mathbf{B} \in \mathbb{R}^{MN \times MN}$ is a spatial blurring matrix representing the point spread function (PSF) of multispectral sensor in the spatial domain of $\mathbf{X}$. It is assumed under circular boundary conditions. Matrix $\mathbf{S} \in \mathbb{R}^{MN \times mn}$ accounts for a uniform downsampling of image with scale factor d.

The spectral degradation model can be formulated as

$$\mathbf{Z} = \mathbf{RX}, \tag{2}$$

where matrix $\mathbf{R} \in \mathbb{R}^{3 \times L}$ denotes the spectral sensitivity function (SSF) and holds in its rows the spectral responses of RGB camera.

2.2   Edge-Preserving Regularizer

A regularizer, which is in the form of dTV [14], is used to preserve both the location and direction of image edges during the super-resolution procedure. It is based on a priori knowledge that the RGB image and spectral images are likely to show very similar edge structures.

The edge-preserving dTV regularizer is formulated as

$$\begin{aligned} \mathrm{dTV}(\mathbf{XD}_x, \mathbf{XD}_y) = &\|\mathbf{XD}_x - [\mathbf{G}_x \odot (\mathbf{XD}_x) + \mathbf{G}_y \odot (\mathbf{XD}_y)] \odot \mathbf{G}_x\|_1 \\ &+ \|\mathbf{XD}_y - [\mathbf{G}_x \odot (\mathbf{XD}_x) + \mathbf{G}_y \odot (\mathbf{XD}_y)] \odot \mathbf{G}_y\|_1, \end{aligned} \tag{3}$$

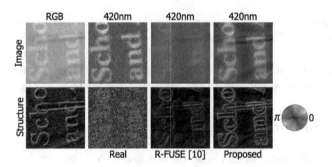

Fig. 1. Demonstration of edge structure preserving effect by the proposed algorithm. From left to right: An HR image region and its edge structure, real band image at band 420 nm, reconstructed band image using R-FUSE [10], reconstructed band image using the proposed algorithm. The spatial resolution is improved by 16×.

where $\odot$ and $\|\cdot\|_1$ denote the Hadamard product and element-wise ℓ_1 norm respectively. Matrices $\mathbf{D}_x$ and $\mathbf{D}_y \in \mathbb{R}^{MN \times MN}$ represent the first-order horizontal and vertical derivative matrices under circular boundary conditions. Matrix $\mathbf{G}_x$ and $\mathbf{G}_y$ denote the normalized horizontal and vertical gradient components of RGB image $\mathbf{Z}$, which can be computed in advance as

$$\mathbf{G}_* = \frac{\mathbf{f}(\mathbf{ZD}_*)}{\sqrt{\mathbf{f}(\mathbf{ZD}_x) \odot \mathbf{f}(\mathbf{ZD}_x) + \mathbf{f}(\mathbf{ZD}_y) \odot \mathbf{f}(\mathbf{ZD}_y) + \eta^2}}, \quad * := x, y$$

where $\cdot/\cdot$ and $\sqrt{\cdot}$ are element-wise division and square root operators. Grayscale conversion function $\mathbf{f}(\cdot)$ integrates image gradient information across the visible spectrum. Constant η adjusts the relative magnitude of edges and is set to 0.01 in this work. Through the regulating effect of Eq. (3), the component of reconstructed gradient that is orthogonal to the one from RGB image in the same edge location will be penalized. Thus the reconstructed image $\mathbf{X}$ tends to share the same edge direction with RGB image $\mathbf{Z}$. Meanwhile, the noise of the reconstructed image will be suppressed in flat area since Eq. (3) reduces to total variation there. Figure 1 shows that the proposed algorithm keeps the edge structure of reconstructed band image in consistent with the one of RGB image, and also suppresses the band image noise. In comparison, the R-FUSE [10] algorithm, which is based on dictionary learning and sparse representation, fails to recover the edge structure.

2.3 Optimization Problem

The target HR multispectral image $\mathbf{X}$ usually lives in a linear subspace, i.e.,

$$\mathbf{X} = \mathbf{\Psi}\mathbf{C}, \tag{4}$$

where matrix $\mathbf{\Psi} \in \mathbb{R}^{L \times K_\Psi}$ is the subspace basis that can be obtained in advance by applying PCA on the LR multispectral image $\mathbf{Y}$, and the dimension K_Ψ is set to 10 in this work. Matrix $\mathbf{C} \in \mathbb{R}^{K_{\Psi} \times MN}$ is the corresponding projection coefficients of $\mathbf{X}$.

In this case, based on degradation models with the proposed regularizer, the reconstruction problem can be converted to the problem of estimating the unknown coefficient matrix $\mathbf{C}$ from the following optimization equation

$$\mathbf{C} = \arg\min_{\mathbf{C}} \frac{1}{2}\|\mathbf{Y} - \mathbf{\Psi CBS}\|_F^2 + \frac{\beta}{2}\|\mathbf{Z} - \mathbf{R\Psi C}\|_F^2 + \gamma \mathrm{dTV}(\mathbf{\Psi CD}_x, \mathbf{\Psi CD}_y), \quad (5)$$

where β and λ are weighting and regularization parameters, respectively, and $\|.\|_F$ denotes the Forbenious norm.

3   Optimization Method

Due to the nature of dTV regularizer, which is nonquadratic and nonsmooth, the ADMM algorithm [15] is employed to solve problem (5) through the variable splitting technique. Each subproblem can be efficiently solved.

3.1   ADMM for Problem (5)

By introducing 5 auxiliary variables, the original problem (5) is reformulated as

$$\min \quad \frac{1}{2}\|\mathbf{Y} - \mathbf{\Psi CBS}\|_F^2 + \frac{\beta}{2}\|\mathbf{Z} - \mathbf{R\Psi V}_1\|_F^2 + \gamma\{\|\mathbf{V}_2\|_1 + \|\mathbf{V}_3\|_1\}_{\mathrm{dTV}}$$
$$\text{s.t.} \quad \mathbf{V}_1 = \mathbf{C}, \quad\quad\quad\quad\quad\quad\quad\quad\quad\quad\quad\quad\quad\quad\quad\quad (6)$$
$$\mathbf{V}_2 = \mathbf{V}_x - (\mathbf{G}_x \odot \mathbf{V}_x + \mathbf{G}_y \odot \mathbf{V}_y) \odot \mathbf{G}_x, \quad \mathbf{V}_x = \mathbf{\Psi CD}_x,$$
$$\mathbf{V}_3 = \mathbf{V}_y - (\mathbf{G}_x \odot \mathbf{V}_x + \mathbf{G}_y \odot \mathbf{V}_y) \odot \mathbf{G}_y, \quad \mathbf{V}_y = \mathbf{\Psi CD}_y.$$

The auxiliary variable $\mathbf{V}_1$ helps bypass singularity. The auxiliary variables $\mathbf{V}_2$ and $\mathbf{V}_3$ help generate closed-form solutions associated with the dTV regularizer. The auxiliary variables $\mathbf{V}_x$ and $\mathbf{V}_y$ help compute the coefficient matrix $\mathbf{C}$ in frequency domain. Problem (6) has the following augmented Lagrangian

$$\min \mathcal{L}_\rho(\mathbf{C}, \mathbf{V}_1, \mathbf{V}_2, \mathbf{V}_3, \mathbf{V}_x, \mathbf{V}_y, \mathbf{A}_1, \mathbf{A}_2, \mathbf{A}_3, \mathbf{A}_x, \mathbf{A}_y)$$
$$= \frac{1}{2}\|\mathbf{Y} - \mathbf{\Psi CBS}\|_F^2 + \frac{\beta}{2}\|\mathbf{Z} - \mathbf{R\Psi V}_1\|_F^2 + \frac{\rho}{2}\|\mathbf{C} - \mathbf{V}_1 - \mathbf{A}_1\|_F^2$$
$$+ \gamma\|\mathbf{V}_2\|_1 + \frac{\rho}{2}\|[\mathbf{V}_x - (\mathbf{G}_x \odot \mathbf{V}_x + \mathbf{G}_y \odot \mathbf{V}_y) \odot \mathbf{G}_x] - \mathbf{V}_2 - \mathbf{A}_2\|_F^2 \quad (7)$$
$$+ \gamma\|\mathbf{V}_3\|_1 + \frac{\rho}{2}\|[\mathbf{V}_y - (\mathbf{G}_x \odot \mathbf{V}_x + \mathbf{G}_y \odot \mathbf{V}_y) \odot \mathbf{G}_y] - \mathbf{V}_3 - \mathbf{A}_3\|_F^2$$
$$+ \frac{\rho}{2}\|\mathbf{\Psi CD}_x - \mathbf{V}_x - \mathbf{A}_x\|_F^2 + \frac{\rho}{2}\|\mathbf{\Psi CD}_y - \mathbf{V}_y - \mathbf{A}_y\|_F^2,$$

where matrices $\mathbf{A}_1, \mathbf{A}_2, \mathbf{A}_3, \mathbf{A}_x, \mathbf{A}_y$ represent five scaled dual variables, and ρ denotes the penalty parameter.

The variables in (7) are solved through iteration. The subproblem of coefficient matrix $\mathbf{C}^{j+1}$ can be fast minimized in frequency domain, which will be detailed in Subsect. 3.2.

The auxiliary variable $\mathbf{V}_1$ has the following closed-form solution of an unconstrained least squares problem

$$\mathbf{V}_1^{j+1} = \left(\beta(\mathbf{R}\boldsymbol{\Psi})^{\mathsf{H}}(\mathbf{R}\boldsymbol{\Psi}) + \rho\mathbf{I}\right)^{-1}\left(\beta(\mathbf{R}\boldsymbol{\Psi})^{\mathsf{H}}\mathbf{Z} + \rho(\mathbf{C}^{j+1} - \mathbf{A}_1^j)\right), \qquad (8)$$

where $(\cdot)^{\mathsf{H}}$ denotes matrix conjugate transpose and $\mathbf{I}$ represents the unit matrix with proper dimensions.

By using soft shrinkage operator, the minimization problems involving $\mathbf{V}_2$ and $\mathbf{V}_3$ have the analytical solutions

$$\begin{aligned}
\mathbf{V}_2^{j+1} &= \mathsf{shrink}\left\{\left[\mathbf{V}_x^j - \left(\mathbf{G}_x \odot \mathbf{V}_x^j + \mathbf{G}_y \odot \mathbf{V}_y^j\right) \odot \mathbf{G}_x\right] - \mathbf{A}_2^j, \; \gamma/\rho\right\}, \\
\mathbf{V}_3^{j+1} &= \mathsf{shrink}\left\{\left[\mathbf{V}_y^j - \left(\mathbf{G}_x \odot \mathbf{V}_x^j + \mathbf{G}_y \odot \mathbf{V}_y^j\right) \odot \mathbf{G}_y\right] - \mathbf{A}_3^j, \; \gamma/\rho\right\},
\end{aligned} \qquad (9)$$

where $\mathsf{shrink}\{y,\kappa\} := \mathsf{sgn}(y) \cdot \mathsf{max}(|y| - \kappa, 0)$, with the sign and maximum functions denoted by $\mathsf{sgn}(\cdot)$ and $\mathsf{max}(\cdot,\cdot)$ respectively.

Under the definitions of Hadamard product and Forbenious norm, every matrix element of $\mathbf{V}_x^{j+1}$ and $\mathbf{V}_y^{j+1}$ can be solved independently by minimizing a simple quadratic function. The solution details are omitted for the sake of simplicity.

Then the scaled dual variables are updated according to the ADMM iterative framework [15]. At the end of iteration, the target HR image $\mathbf{X}$ is recovered as $\mathbf{X} = \boldsymbol{\Psi}\mathbf{C}$. Algorithm 1 lists the procedure of this reconstruction. For any $\beta > 0$, $\gamma > 0$, and $\rho > 0$, Algorithm 1 will converge to a solution of (5) as its ADMM steps are all closed, proper, and convex [15]. Our study reveals that 20 iterations are enough to obtain a satisfactory HR image.

Algorithm 1. Reconstruct $\mathbf{X}$ using ADMM

Input: LR multispectral matrix $\mathbf{Y} \in \mathbb{R}^{L \times mn}$, HR RGB matrix $\mathbf{Z} \in \mathbb{R}^{3 \times MN}$,
      SSF $\mathbf{R} \in \mathbb{R}^{3 \times L}$.
Output: HR multispectral matrix $\mathbf{X}$.
Compute gradient matrices $\mathbf{G}_x$ and $\mathbf{G}_y$ from $\mathbf{Z}$;
Train the subspace basis $\boldsymbol{\Psi}$ from $\mathbf{Y}$;
for $j = 1$ **to** 20 **do**
    | Compute $\mathbf{C}^j$ according to Section 3.2;
    | Compute $\mathbf{V}_1^j$ using (8);
    | Compute $\mathbf{V}_2^j$ and $\mathbf{V}_3^j$ using (9);
    | Compute $\mathbf{V}_x^j$ and $\mathbf{V}_y^j$;
    | Update $\mathbf{A}_1^j$, $\mathbf{A}_2^j$, $\mathbf{A}_3^j$, $\mathbf{A}_4^j$, and $\mathbf{A}_5^j$;
end
Compute $\mathbf{X} = \boldsymbol{\Psi}\mathbf{C}$.

3.2 Solving Coefficient Matrix

By forcing the derivative of (5) w.r.t. $\mathbf{C}$ to be zero, an efficient analytical solution can be derived in terms of solving the following Sylvester function

$$\mathbf{C}^{j+1}\mathbf{W}_1 + \mathbf{W}_2\mathbf{C}^{j+1} = \mathbf{W}_3, \tag{10}$$

where

$$\mathbf{W}_1 = \mathbf{BSS}^{\mathsf{H}}\mathbf{B}^{\mathsf{H}} + \rho\mathbf{D}_x\mathbf{D}_x^{\mathsf{H}} + \rho\mathbf{D}_y\mathbf{D}_y^{\mathsf{H}},$$

$$\mathbf{W}_2 = \rho(\mathbf{\Psi}^{\mathsf{H}}\mathbf{\Psi})^{-1},$$

and

$$\mathbf{W}_3 = (\mathbf{\Psi}^{\mathsf{H}}\mathbf{\Psi})^{-1}[\mathbf{\Psi}^{\mathsf{H}}\mathbf{YS}^{\mathsf{H}}\mathbf{B}^{\mathsf{H}} + \rho(\mathbf{V}_1^j + \mathbf{A}_1^j) + \rho\mathbf{\Psi}^{\mathsf{H}}(\mathbf{V}_x^j + \mathbf{A}_x^j)\mathbf{D}_x^{\mathsf{H}}$$
$$+ \rho\mathbf{\Psi}^{\mathsf{H}}(\mathbf{V}_y^j + \mathbf{A}_y^j)\mathbf{D}_y^{\mathsf{H}}].$$

Using the decomposition $\mathbf{W}_2 = \mathbf{Q}\mathbf{\Lambda}\mathbf{Q}^{-1}$ and multiplying both sides of (10) by $\mathbf{Q}^{-1}$ leads to

$$\overline{\mathbf{C}}\mathbf{W}_1 + \mathbf{\Lambda}\overline{\mathbf{C}} = \overline{\mathbf{W}}_3,$$

where $\overline{\mathbf{C}} = \mathbf{Q}^{-1}\mathbf{C}^{j+1}$ and $\overline{\mathbf{W}}_3 = \mathbf{Q}^{-1}\mathbf{W}_3$. Thus each row of $\overline{\mathbf{C}}$ can be solved independently as

$$\overline{\mathbf{C}}_i = \overline{\mathbf{W}}_3(\mathbf{W}_1 + \lambda_i\mathbf{I})^{-1}, \ \ 1 \leq i \leq K_\Psi, \tag{11}$$

where i denotes the row index, and λ_i denotes the ith eigenvalue of $\mathbf{W}_2$.

Utilizing the properties of convolution and decimation matrices, the solution (11) can be accelerated in frequency domain. Convolution matrices $\mathbf{B}$, $\mathbf{D}_x$ and $\mathbf{D}_y$ can be diagonalized by Fourier matrix $\mathbf{F} \in \mathbb{R}^{MN \times MN}$, i.e., $\mathbf{B} = \mathbf{F}\mathbf{\Lambda}_B\mathbf{F}^{\mathsf{H}}$, $\mathbf{D}_x = \mathbf{F}\mathbf{\Lambda}_x\mathbf{F}^{\mathsf{H}}$ and $\mathbf{D}_y = \mathbf{F}\mathbf{\Lambda}_y\mathbf{F}^{\mathsf{H}}$. Then when computing $\overline{\mathbf{W}}_3$, right multiplying with these matrices can be achieved through fast Fourier transform (FFT) and entry-wise multiplication operations. Meanwhile, right multiplying with $\mathbf{S}^{\mathsf{H}}$ is equivalent to the simple upsampling operation.

For further simplification, the matrix inverse in (11) is represented as

$$\mathbf{F}\left(\mathbf{\Lambda}_B\mathbf{F}^{\mathsf{H}}\mathbf{SS}^{\mathsf{H}}\mathbf{F}\mathbf{\Lambda}_B^{\mathsf{H}} + \rho\mathbf{\Lambda}_x^2 + \rho\mathbf{\Lambda}_y^2 + \lambda_i\mathbf{I}\right)^{-1}\mathbf{F}^{\mathsf{H}} := \mathbf{F}\mathbf{K}^{-1}\mathbf{F}^{\mathsf{H}}.$$

By translating the frequency properties of decimation matrix [10] into

$$\mathbf{F}^{\mathsf{H}}\mathbf{SS}^{\mathsf{H}}\mathbf{F} = \mathbf{PP}^{\mathsf{H}}/d^2,$$

$\mathbf{K}$ can be consolidated as

$$\mathbf{K} = \frac{1}{d^2}\mathbf{\Lambda}_B\mathbf{PP}^{\mathsf{H}}\mathbf{\Lambda}_B^{\mathsf{H}} + \mathbf{\Lambda}_K,$$

where $\mathbf{\Lambda}_K = \rho\mathbf{\Lambda}_x^2 + \rho\mathbf{\Lambda}_y^2 + \lambda_i\mathbf{I}$ is a diagonal matrix, $\mathbf{P} \in \mathbb{R}^{MN \times mn}$ is a transform matrix with 0 and 1 elements. Right multiplying with $\mathbf{P}$ and $\mathbf{P}^{\mathsf{H}}$ can be achieved by performing sub-block accumulating and image copying operations to the corresponding image. As the inverse of large-scale matrix is difficult, the Woodbury inversion lemma [11] is used to decompose $\mathbf{K}^{-1}$ as

$$\mathbf{K}^{-1} = \boldsymbol{\Lambda}_K^{-1} - \boldsymbol{\Lambda}_K^{-1} \boldsymbol{\Lambda}_B \mathbf{P} \left(d^2 \mathbf{I} + \mathbf{P}^\mathsf{H} \boldsymbol{\Lambda}_B^\mathsf{H} \boldsymbol{\Lambda}_K^{-1} \boldsymbol{\Lambda}_B \mathbf{P} \right)^{-1} \mathbf{P}^\mathsf{H} \boldsymbol{\Lambda}_B^\mathsf{H} \boldsymbol{\Lambda}_K^{-1}, \quad (12)$$

where matrix $d^2 \mathbf{I} + \mathbf{P}^\mathsf{H} \boldsymbol{\Lambda}_B^\mathsf{H} \boldsymbol{\Lambda}_K^{-1} \boldsymbol{\Lambda}_B \mathbf{P}$ is diagonal.

Inserting (12) into (11) yields the final solution

$$\overline{\mathbf{C}}_i = \overline{\mathbf{W}}_3 \mathbf{F} \boldsymbol{\Lambda}_K^{-1} \mathbf{F}^\mathsf{H} - \overline{\mathbf{W}}_3 \mathbf{F} \boldsymbol{\Lambda}_K^{-1} \boldsymbol{\Lambda}_B \mathbf{P} \left(d^2 \mathbf{I} + \mathbf{P}^\mathsf{H} \boldsymbol{\Lambda}_B^\mathsf{H} \boldsymbol{\Lambda}_K^{-1} \boldsymbol{\Lambda}_B \mathbf{P} \right)^{-1}$$
$$\mathbf{P}^\mathsf{H} \boldsymbol{\Lambda}_B^\mathsf{H} \boldsymbol{\Lambda}_K^{-1} \mathbf{F}^\mathsf{H}, \quad 1 \le i \le K_\Psi, \tag{13}$$

and the coefficient matrix is computed as $\mathbf{C}^{j+1} = \mathbf{Q}\overline{\mathbf{C}}$. Noting that this solution procedure mainly contains the efficient FFT, entry-wise multiplication, sub-block accumulating, and image copying operations.

4   Experiments

Experiments are performed on both simulated and our acquired LR multispectral images. In the simulation, the LR multispectral images with 31 bands are generated by applying Gaussian blur and downsampling operations to the images in the Harvard scene dataset [16][1] and CAVE object dataset [17][2]. The HR RGB images are generated using the SSF of Canon 60D camera provided in the Cam-Spec database [18]. In our real image set, the LR multispectral images with 31 bands are acquired across the visible spectrum 400–720 nm by an imaging system consisting of a liquid crystal tunable filters and a CoolSnap monochrome camera. The HR RGB images are captured using a Canon 70D camera. The acquired multispectral and RGB images are aligned according to [19].

To evaluate the quality of reconstructed multispectral images, four objective quality metrics namely spectral angle mapper (SAM) [6], root mean squared error (RMSE) [6], relative dimensionless global error in synthesis (ERGAS) [6], and peak signal to noise ration (PSNR) [6] are used in our study. For comparison, three leading super-resolution methods namely HySure [8], R-FUSE [10], and NSSR [9] are also implemented under the same environment. Their source codes are publicly available online[3,4,5].

4.1   Parameter Setting

We evaluate the effect of three key parameters (weighting parameter β, regularization parameter γ, and penalty parameter ρ) on the reconstruction accuracy

---

[1] http://vision.seas.harvard.edu/hyperspec/download.html.

[2] http://www1.cs.columbia.edu/CAVE/databases/multispectral/.

[3] https://github.com/alfaiate/HySure.

[4] https://github.com/qw245/BlindFuse.

[5] http://see.xidian.edu.cn/faculty/wsdong/Code_release/NSSR_HSI_SR.rar.

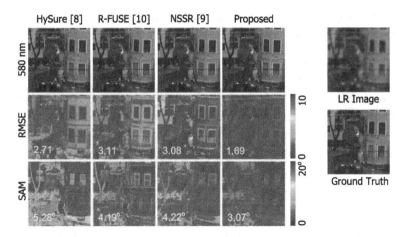

Fig. 2. Reconstruction results of *imgc4* with 16× spatial resolution improvement. The 1st row shows the reconstructed HR images at 580 nm using different algorithms. The LR image and ground truth image are listed on the right. The remaining rows illustrate the corresponding RMSE maps and SAM maps calculated across all the spectral bands.

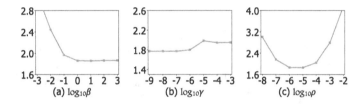

Fig. 3. The average RMSE values of all the reconstructed images with respect to parameters (a) $\log_{10}\beta$, (b) $\log_{10}\gamma$, and (c) $\log_{10}\rho$.

of proposed algorithm. Figure 3 plots the average RMSE values of all the reconstructed images with respect to these parameters. In this work, we set $\beta = 1$, $\gamma = 10^{-6}$, and $\rho = 10^{-5}$ that result in small RMSE value. We note that setting the β value too large will overemphasize the importance of RGB data term, and setting the γ value too small will decrease the role of RGB edge guidance.

4.2 Results on Simulated Images

Figure 2 shows the reconstruction results of *imgc4* with 16× spatial resolution improvement, as well as the detailed RMSE maps and SAM maps. The average RMSE and SAM values are also listed for quantitative comparison. It is observed that the HySure [8] algorithm exhibits large spectral errors, and the R-FUSE [10] and NSSR [9] algorithms do not handle the spatial details well. In comparison, the proposed algorithm produces relatively accurate HR images.

Table 1 shows the average SAM, RMSE, ERGAS, and PSNR values of all the reconstructed multispectral images in Harvard and CAVE datasets. The spatial

Table 1. Average SAM, RMSE, ERGAS, and PSNR values produced by different algorithms on two datasets. The resolution is improved with 16×

	Harvard dataset				CAVE dataset			
	SAM	RMSE	ERGAS	PSNR	SAM	RMSE	ERGAS	PSNR
HySure [8]	8.36	2.57	0.96	36.92	16.70	4.08	1.00	38.81
R-FUSE [10]	5.70	2.72	1.00	35.57	6.38	3.85	0.95	38.71
NSSR [9]	4.65	1.85	0.68	40.00	5.34	4.71	1.01	39.60
Proposed	**4.06**	**1.69**	**0.57**	**40.56**	**5.24**	**3.42**	**0.75**	**40.97**

resolution is improved by 16 times. It is observed that the proposed algorithm outperforms all the competitors when evaluated using these metrics. Furthermore, Fig. 4 shows the overall reconstruction accuracy on the 109 multispectral images of the two datasets in terms of RMSE and SAM. For clear demonstration, the image indexes are sorted in ascending order with respect to the metric values produced by the proposed algorithm. It is observed that in most cases the proposed algorithm performs better than the competing methods when evaluated using either spatial or spectral metrics.

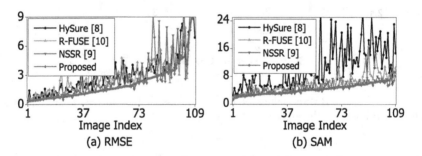

Fig. 4. (a) RMSE and (b) SAM values produced by different algorithms on all the stimulated data with scale factors $d = 16$.

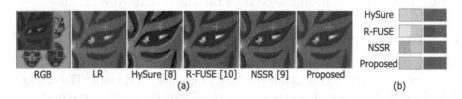

Fig. 5. (a) Reconstruction results on real data *Masks* at band 590 nm with 8× spatial resolution improvement. (b) Marked pixels in reconstructed images compared with the ones in original LR image.

4.3   Results on Real Images

We also evaluate the performance of the proposed algorithm on real images acquired in our laboratory. The RGB image is linearized beforehand with the inverse camera response function estimated by [20]. The SSF is computed through linear regression with existing image data. Figure 5(a) shows the original HR RGB image and LR band image at 590 nm of *Masks*, as well as the corresponding reconstructed results with 8× spatial resolution improvement. Figure 5(b) shows the marked pixels in smooth regions. Each marked pixel in the reconstructed HR image is compared with the one in the original LR image, and it is desired that the intensity of the two pixels should be close. It is observed that the face edges produced by HySure and NSSR are not clear, and the intensity of eye produced by R-FUSE is too high. In comparison, the proposed algorithm performs well in handling these details.

4.4   Computational Complexity

The complexity of the proposed algorithm is dominated by the FFTs when computing coefficient matrix $\mathbf{C}$, and is of order $\mathcal{O}(K_{\Psi}MN\log(MN))$ per ADMM iteration. Table 2 shows the running times of the HySure [8], R-FUSE [10], NSSR [9], and proposed algorithms for reconstructing an HR multispectral image with 31 spectral bands and 1392 × 1040 spatial resolution. These algorithms are all implemented using MATLAB R2016a on a personal computer with 2.60 GHz CPU (Intel Xeon E5-2630) and 64 GB RAM. The proposed algorithm gains improvement in computational efficiency.

Table 2. Running times (in seconds) of different algorithms for reconstructing an HR multispectral image with 31 bands and 1392 × 1040 spatial resolution. The numbers in parentheses are the speedup of the proposed algorithm over the corresponding competitors

HySure [8]	R-FUSE [10]	NSSR [9]	Proposed
1256.8 (7×)	6758.5 (36×)	998.8 (5×)	185.7

5   Conclusions

This paper has proposed a super-resolution algorithm to improve the spatial resolution of multispectral image with an HR RGB image. The HR multispectral image is efficiently reconstructed according to the linear image degradation models, and the dTV operator is used to keep the recovered edge locations and directions in accordance with those of the RGB image. Experimental results validate that the proposed algorithm performs better than the state-of-the-arts in terms of both reconstruction accuracy and computational efficiency.

References

1. Levenson, R.M., Mansfield, J.R.: Multispectral imaging in biology and medicine: slices of life. Cytom. Part A **69**(8), 748–758 (2006)
2. Shaw, G.A., Burke, H.H.K.: Spectral imaging for remote sensing. Linc. Lab. J. **14**(1), 3–28 (2003)
3. Berns, R.S.: Color-accurate image archives using spectral imaging. In: Scientific Examination of Art: Modern Techniques in Conservation and Analysis, pp. 105–119 (2005)
4. Pan, Z.W., Shen, H.L., Li, C., Chen, S.J., Xin, J.H.: Fast multispectral imaging by spatial pixel-binning and spectral unmixing. IEEE Trans. Image Process. **25**(8), 3612–3625 (2016)
5. Wei, Q., Bioucas-Dias, J., Dobigeon, N., Tourneret, J.Y.: Hyperspectral and multispectral image fusion based on a sparse representation. IEEE Trans. Geosci. Remote. Sens. **53**(7), 3658–3668 (2015)
6. Lin, C.H., Ma, F., Chi, C.Y., Hsieh, C.H.: A convex optimization-based coupled nonnegative matrix factorization algorithm for hyperspectral and multispectral data fusion. IEEE Trans. Geosci. Remote. Sens. **56**(3), 1652–1667 (2018)
7. Dian, R., Fang, L., Li, S.: Hyperspectral image super-resolution via non-local sparse tensor factorization. In: IEEE Conference on Computer Vision and Pattern Recognition, pp. 5344–5353. IEEE (2017)
8. Simões, M., Bioucas-Dias, J., Almeida, L.B., Chanussot, J.: A convex formulation for hyperspectral image superresolution via subspace-based regularization. IEEE Trans. Geosci. Remote. Sens. **53**(6), 3373–3388 (2015)
9. Dong, W., et al.: Hyperspectral image super-resolution via non-negative structured sparse representation. IEEE Trans. Image Process. **25**(5), 2337–2352 (2016)
10. Wei, Q., Dobigeon, N., Tourneret, J.Y., Bioucas-Dias, J., Godsill, S.: R-FUSE: robust fast fusion of multiband images based on solving a Sylvester equation. IEEE Signal Process. Lett. **23**(11), 1632–1636 (2016)
11. Zhao, N., Wei, Q., Basarab, A., Kouamé, D., Tourneret, J.Y.: Single image super-resolution of medical ultrasound images using a fast algorithm. In: IEEE 13th International Symposium on Biomedical Imaging, pp. 473–476. IEEE (2016)
12. Huang, W., Xiao, L., Wei, Z., Liu, H., Tang, S.: A new pan-sharpening method with deep neural networks. IEEE Geosci. Remote. Sens. Lett. **12**(5), 1037–1041 (2015)
13. Yang, J., Fu, X., Hu, Y., Huang, Y., Ding, X., Paisley, J.: PanNet: a deep network architecture for pan-sharpening. In: IEEE International Conference on Computer Vision, pp. 1753–1761. IEEE (2017)
14. Ehrhardt, M.J., Betcke, M.M.: Multicontrast MRI reconstruction with structure-guided total variation. SIAM J. Imaging Sci. **9**(3), 1084–1106 (2016)
15. Boyd, S., Parikh, N., Chu, E., Peleato, B., Eckstein, J.: Distributed optimization and statistical learning via the alternating direction method of multipliers. Found. Trends® Mach. Learn. **3**(1), 1–122 (2011)
16. Chakrabarti, A., Zickler, T.: Statistics of real-world hyperspectral images. In: IEEE Conference on Computer Vision and Pattern Recognition, pp. 193–200. IEEE (2011)
17. Yasuma, F., Mitsunaga, T., Iso, D., Nayar, S.K.: Generalized assorted pixel camera: postcapture control of resolution, dynamic range, and spectrum. IEEE Trans. Image Process. **19**(9), 2241–2253 (2010)

18. Jiang, J., Liu, D., Gu, J., Süsstrunk, S.: What is the space of spectral sensitivity functions for digital color cameras? In: IEEE Workshop on Applications of Computer Vision, pp. 168–179. IEEE (2013)

19. Chen, S.J., Shen, H.L., Li, C., Xin, J.H.: Normalized total gradient: a new measure for multispectral image registration. IEEE Trans. Image Process. **27**(3), 1297–1310 (2018)

20. Lee, J.Y., Matsushita, Y., Shi, B., Kweon, I.S., Ikeuchi, K.: Radiometric calibration by rank minimization. IEEE Trans. Pattern Anal. Mach. Intell. **35**(1), 144–156 (2013)

RGB-D Co-Segmentation on Indoor Scene with Geometric Prior and Hypothesis Filtering

Lingxiao Hang, Zhiguo Cao[✉], Yang Xiao, and Hao Lu

National Key Lab of Science and Technology of Multispectral Information
Processing, School of Automation, Huazhong University of Science and Technology,
Wuhan 430074, Hubei, China
{lxhang,zgcao,Yang_Xiao,poppinace}@hust.edu.cn

Abstract. Indoor scene parsing is crucial for applications like home surveillance systems. Although deep learning based models like FCNs [10] have achieved outstanding performance, they rely on huge amounts of hand-labeled training samples at pixel level, which are hard to obtain. To alleviate labeling burden and provide meaningful clues for indoor applications, it's promising to use unsupervised co-segmentation methods to segment out main furniture, such as bed and sofa. Following traditional bottom-up co-segmentation framework for RGB images, we focus on the task of co-segmenting main furniture of indoor scene and fully utilize the complementary information of RGB-D images. First, a simple but effective geometric prior is introduced, using bounding planes of indoor scene to better distinguish between foreground and background. A two-stage hypothesis filtering strategy is further integrated to refine both global and local object candidate generation. To evaluate our method, the *NYUD-COSEG* dataset is constructed, on which our method shows significantly higher accuracy compared with previous ones. We also prove and analyze the effectiveness of both bounding plane prior and hypothesis filtering strategy with extensive experiments.

Keywords: Indoor RGB-D co-segmentation
Geometric prior for indoor scene · Object hypothesis generation

1 Introduction

Indoor scene parsing has great significance for applications like home surveillance systems. Deep learning models such as Fully Convolutional Networks (FCNs) [10]

This work is jointly support by the National High-tech R&D Program of China (863 Program) (Grant No. 2015AA015904), the National Natural Science Foundation of China (Grant No. 61502187), the International Science & Technology Cooperation Program of Hubei Province, China (Grant No. 2017AHB051), the HUST Interdisciplinary Innovation Team Foundation (Grant No. 2016JCTD120).
The First Author of This Paper is a Student.

ⓒ Springer Nature Switzerland AG 2018
J.-H. Lai et al. (Eds.): PRCV 2018, LNCS 11256, pp. 168–179, 2018.
https://doi.org/10.1007/978-3-030-03398-9_15

has achieved great success. However, training these models heavily relies on labeling huge amounts of samples, which is time consuming and labor intensive. In contrast, the unsupervised co-segmentation methods can simultaneously partition multiple images that depict the same or similar object into foreground and background. It can considerably alleviate labeling burden by producing object masks without semantic labels, which can be used as ground truth for training of deep neural networks [17]. Besides, co-segmenting main indoor furniture (bed, table, etc.) can provide meaningful clues for room layout estimation and human action analysis.

Although RGB co-segmentation has been studied thoroughly, RGB-D indoor scene co-segmentation remains an untouched problem. We discover two challenges when directly applying previous RGB methods. First, foreground and background appearance models are initialized using intuitive priors such as assuming pixels around the image frame boundaries as background, which fails in complex indoor scene. Second, the cluttering and occlusion of indoor condition make it hard to generate high-quality object candidates depending on RGB only in the unsupervised manner of co-segmentation.

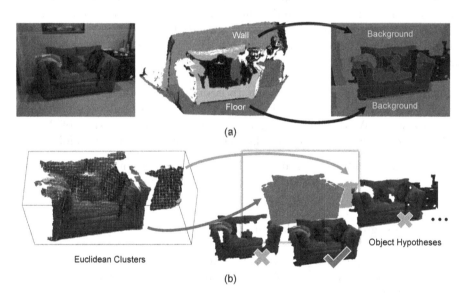

(a)

(b)

Fig. 1. Demonstration of our main contributions. (a) The geometric prior is used to reliably classify bounding planes of indoor scene, like wall and floor, as background. (b) The Euclidean clusters corresponding to foreground objects are leveraged to filter incomplete or overstretched object hypotheses.

To handle these challenges, we propose to integrate the geometric prior and hypothesis filtering strategy, shown in Fig. 1, into the traditional bottom-up co-segmentation pipeline. Our method fully utilizes the intrinsic properties of RGB-

D indoor scene to remedy the deficiencies of previous methods. The motivation of our method is detailed in the following two aspects.

First, our geometric prior addresses the problem of disentangling foreground from background. Existing unsupervised methods rely on boundary prior [1, 12], saliency prior [11,15] or even objectness prior [3,4] that requires training. All these priors are either ineffective or complicated in terms of indoor scene. On the one hand indoor objects commonly have intersection with image frame boundaries and show little contrast with background. On the other hand, the objectness methods are not specifically trained for indoor scene, which requires re-training on large labeled datasets. Instead, considering the abundant plane structures, shown in Fig. 1(a), our approach utilizes the unsupervised bounding plane prior that reliably specifies background regions. This simple but effective prior has no burden on manpower or computing resources.

Second, we improve object hypothesis generation for indoor images by going beyond simply combining connected segments in 2D RGB images. Since two neighboring segments that belong to different objects could be adjacent in 2D image plane but are spatially separated in 2.5D real world coordination. Inspired by this insight, our object hypothesis generation exploits a two-stage filtering strategy, using Euclidean clustering in 2.5D space to obtain separated point clusters. This improvement on hypothesis generation is able to increase the proportion of physically reasonable and high-quality proposals, which reduces the error during hypothesis clustering, especially for large objects.

To the best of our knowledge, this is the first paper addressing co-segmentation in RGB-D indoor scene. To evaluate our method, we re-organize the *NYUD v2* dataset [18] to establish a proper benchmark for co-segmentation of indoor scene. We demonstrate that our method can achieve state-of-the-art performance on our RGB-D indoor dataset. Our contributions are as follows:

- Our work provides the field of indoor RGB-D co-segmentation the first methodology focusing on large objects, which can help reduce the manual labeling effort for CNNs.
- A simple but effective bounding plane prior is first proposed to better distinguish foreground and background for RGB-D co-segmentation of complex indoor scene.
- A two-stage hypothesis generation filtering strategy is devised to overcome cluttering and occlusion problems of indoor scene, producing high-quality object proposals.

2   Related Work

Work Related to Unsupervised Co-Segmentation. Co-segmentation aims at jointly segmenting common foreground from a set of images. One setting is that only one common object is presented in each image. Color histogram was embedded as a global matching term into MRF-based segmentation model [14]. In [5] co-segmentation was formulated as a discriminative clustering problem with classifiers trained to separate foreground and background maximally. Yet another more challenging setting is to extract multiple objects from a set of images, which is called the MFC (Multiple Foreground Co-segmentation). It was first addressed in [6] by building appearance models for objects of interest, followed by beam search to generate proposals. Recently RGB-D co-segmenting small props was tackled using integer quadratic programming [3]. Different from previous works, our method features RGB-D indoor scene.

Work Related to Co-Segmentation of Indoor Point Cloud Data. Another similar line of work aims at co-segmenting a full 3D scene at multiple times after changes of objects' poses due to human actions. Different tree structures [9,16] were used to store relations between object patches and present semantical results. However, the depth images we use are single viewed in 2.5D space, which suffer from the occlusion and cluttering problem eluded by their full 3D counterparts. Our proposed method is able to overcome these challenges by exploiting rich information of RGB-D image, without resorting to full viewed 3D data.

3   Bottom-Up RGB-D Indoor Co-Segmentation Pipeline

3.1   The Overall Framework for Bottom-Up Co-Segmentation

Our co-segmentation of main furniture for indoor images can be categorized as the MFC (Multiple Foreground Co-segmentation) problem. Given the input images $\mathcal{I} = \{I_1, ..., I_M\}$ of the same indoor scene, the goal is to jointly segment K different foreground objects $\mathcal{F} = \{F_1, ..., F_K\}$ from $\mathcal{I}$. As a result, each I_i is divided into non-overlapping regions with labels containing a subset of K foregrounds plus a background G_{I_i}. According to scenario knowledge, we define common foreground as major indoor furniture with certain functionality.

Traditional bottom-up pipeline for MFC co-segmentation [1] consists of three main steps, namely superpixel clustering, region matching and hypothesis generation. The first step merges locally consistent superpixels into compact segments. The second step refines segments in each image by imposing global consistency constraints, with the result that similar segments across images have the same label. The third step goes to a higher level that object candidates are generated by combining segments, which are later clustered to form final segmentation result.

With the motivation in Sect. 1, we made improvements to the first and the third step of the bottom-up pipeline, utilizing 2.5D depth information as a companion to RGB space so as to reduce ambiguity resulted from relying 2D color image only.

The pipeline of our method is shown in Fig. 2. For simplicity and clarity, we only show the co-segmentation pipeline of a single RGB-D image. Also, the second step in the traditional MFC of imposing consistency constraints across images is not shown, which directly follows [1].

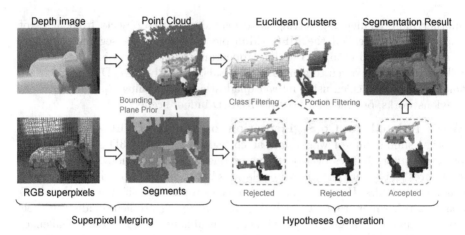

Fig. 2. The main technical pipeline of our RGB-D co-segmentation using the bounding plane prior and the two-stage hypothesis filtering. For simplicity, we exemplify the bottom-up segmentation with only one RGB-D image sample in M input images.

3.2   Superpixel Merging with Bounding Plane Prior

Given a depth image, we can use the pin-hole camera model to transform it into the 2.5D space, where each pixel p_i in 2D image has a 3D real-world coordinate $p_s(x, y, z)$.

For indoor scene, there are rich geometric structures and space relationships that can be very useful as guidance for unsupervised CV task, such as large planes, affordance of objects, etc. As can be apparently observed, the bounding planes, which correspond to walls, floors and ceilings in a real indoor scene, can be taken as a reliable prior for background regions. These bounding planes have two features to define the background. One feature is that these planes are the outer-most planes within the 2.5D space, whose only functionality is to enclose foreground objects within the room inside. The other feature is that dominant foreground objects in the scene always take up a certain amount of cubic space, whose consisting points will not lie on a sole plane.

Following [2], we first perform plane segmentation using 2.5D point cloud data. Iteratively using RANSAC to estimate plane parameters and Euclidean distances to assign points to planes and all planes in a image can be found, denoted by $\mathcal{P}_{I_i}$. Suppose the normal vector of each plane points towards the camera, the set of bounding planes $\mathcal{BP}_{I_i}$ for I_i is selected by its first feature, defined as:

$$\mathcal{BP}_{I_i} = \left\{ P_k \middle| P_k \in \mathcal{P}_{I_i}, \frac{1}{N} \sum_{s=1}^{N} \mathbb{1}\left\{D(p_s, P_k) < 0\right\} < \tau \right\}, i = \{1, ..., M\} \quad (1)$$

where $D(p_s, P_k)$ is the Euclidean distance of point p_s to plane P_k and $\mathbb{1}\{\cdot\}$ is the indicator function. Referring to the first feature of bounding plane, the ratio of points on the outer side of the plane should be lower than a given threshold τ.

As the first main step in our bottom-up co-segmentation framework, merging locally similar superpixels into segments begins with the method of [8] to produce superpixels for each image respectively (the number of superpixels for each images is set to $N = 1200$). For superpixel merging, each superpixel S in $\mathcal{S}_{I_i}$ excluded by $\mathcal{BP}_{I_i}$ is assigned to an initial foreground segment R_c with probability given by a set of parametric functions v^c, $c = \{1, ..., C\}$. The parametric function $v^c : \mathcal{S}_{I_i} \rightarrow \mathbb{R}$ can be defined by the c-th foreground model, which in this paper is GMM (Gaussian Mixture Model). We use GMM with 32 Gaussian components to determine the color histogram $\mathbf{h}_S$ for each superpixel S. Thus, the probability of S belonging to the set of c-th foreground segments R_c is measured by the normalized χ^2 distance between $\mathbf{h}_S$ and $\mathbf{h}_{R_c}$. In terms of S included by $\mathcal{BP}_{I_i}$, we use $C + 1$ to denote background segment label and the probability is assumed to win over other segment label. The overall segment label probability for every superpixel is given by

$$P(R_c|S) = \begin{cases} \chi^2(\mathbf{h}_S, \mathbf{h}_{R_c}) & \text{if } S \notin \mathcal{BP}_{I_i} \\ 1 - \epsilon & \text{if } S \in \mathcal{BP}_{I_i}, c = C + 1 \\ \epsilon/C & \text{otherwise} \end{cases} \tag{2}$$

where ϵ is a quantity close to 0. After initializing the probability of assigning each superpixel S to segment R_c, we refine this merging result by GrabCut [13] using $P(R_c|S)$. Thus we can get the refined set of segments for each image, denoted as $\mathcal{R}_{I_i}$.

3.3   Two-Stage Hypothesis Filtering with Point Cloud Clustering

As the third main step of our bottom-up pipeline, hypothesis generation step combines arbitrary numbers of connected segments to form a pool of object candidates, which is crucial for the final foreground segmentation. Sensible hypotheses can accurately be clustered into K objects contained in the input images. We make the observation that final segmenting of objects is determined by two properties of object hypotheses, diversity and reliability. Diversity means that the hypothesis pool should involve all possible objects in the image without missing any. Reliability is the probability that a candidate belongs to a whole foreground object. Our goal is to find a pool with suffice diversity wherein each candidate is of maximal reliability.

Naively combining all possible connected segments in $\mathcal{R}_{I_i}$ to form object candidate reaches the maximum of pool diversity but the minimum of reliability. To make a trade-off, we propose a two-stage hypothesis filtering strategy to enlarge the proportion of reliable candidates while still retain the diversity.

Before filtering, we first provide a measurement tool for reliable candidate or in other words, *objectness*. While it is challenging for general purposed objectness prediction, in the case of RGB-D indoor scene it can be reduced to Euclidean clustering. In 2.5D point cloud, ignoring the bounding planes found in Sect. 3.2, we can find dominant clusters using Euclidean distance within a neighborhood tolerance and map them back to 2D image frame. These clusters, denoted as

$Q_k \in \mathcal{E}_{I_i}$ of image I_i, represent occupancy of dominant objects in the image, hence candidates who coincide with them are reliable.

Class Filtering. Spatially isolated point cloud clusters Q_k represent different objects respectively. We use class filtering to rid off hypotheses with coverage over two or more clusters. Let $\mathcal{H}_0$ denote hypothesis pool without filtering, $\mathcal{H}_1$ with class filtering, then the first selection step of candidates h can be expressed as

$$\mathcal{H}_1 = \left\{ h \,\middle|\, \sum_{k=1}^{\|\mathcal{E}_{I_i}\|} \mathbb{1}\left\{h \cap Q_k \neq \emptyset\right\} = 1, h \in \mathcal{H}_0 \right\} \tag{3}$$

The class filtering can refine the global segmentation result of foreground objects, largely alleviating the problem of segmenting out two or more objects that are in close proximity to each other as a single object.

Portion Filtering. Due to the inconsistent texture or piled clutter on the main furniture, it is likely to divide a whole object into locally consistent subsegments. To further improve the segmentation accuracy for main objects of indoor scene, we additionally impose portion filtering. Hypotheses that are overlapping with Q_k under a given threshold are discarded, leaving the most reliable candidate pool $\mathcal{H}_2$, which can be expressed as

$$\mathcal{H}_2 = \left\{ h \,\middle|\, \frac{area(h \cap Q_k)}{area(Q_k)} > \theta, h \in \mathcal{H}_1 \right\} \tag{4}$$

The portion filtering refines the segmentation for single main object, which in particular reduce the case where large objects are partially segmented.

4   Results and Discussion

4.1   *NYUD-COSEG* Dataset and Experimental Setup

Previous work on RGB-D co-segmentation such as [3] used the dataset of images captured under controlled lab environment or estimated depth images from general RGB image. No dataset of indoor scene suited for co-segmentation has been put forward. Based on the widely used RGB-D indoor dataset *NYUD v2* [18] for supervised learning algorithms, we propose a new dataset, *NYUD-COSEG*, with modification to the original *NYUD v2* dataset to extensively test our method and compare with other state of the art co-segmentation methods.

Since large furniture plays a more important role in scene layout estimation or applications involving daily human actions, we take classes like floor, wall and ceiling as background while furniture like bed, table and sofa as foreground. With this definition of object class of interest, we construct the *NYUD-COSEG* dataset by firstly grouping images captured in the same scene with aforementioned foreground classes. Each group contains 2 to 4 images and can be taken as input for any co-segmentation algorithm. Next, the original ground truths are re-labeled. Trivial classes such as small props are removed. Small objects overlapped with large furniture are merged as the latter, exemplified by taking the pillow class as the bed class. The class-simplified ground truth is more sensible for evaluation of unsupervised methods.

After the organizing, the *NYUD-COSEG* dataset can be divided into of 3 main classes as Bed, Table and Sofa, each containing 104, 31 and 21 images respectively. It contains 62 classes in total (we consider all classes during evaluation).

We randomly choose 20% of images in the *NYUD-COSEG* dataset as validation set and apply grid search to find the optimal value for parameters. In our implementation, we set $C = 8$ in Eq. (2) and $\theta = 0.8$ in Eq. (4) as default.

4.2 Evaluation Metric and Comparison Study on NYUD-COSEG

The evaluation metric we adopt for co-segmentation algorithm on indoor scene is frequency weighted IOU (f.w.IOU). This choice takes into consideration that for room layout estimation and its applications, dominant objects (bed, sofa, etc.) of an image has more significance than less obvious ones (cup, books, etc.). On the contrary, metrics such as pixel accuracy, mean accuracy and mean IOU make no different treat on large and small objects, which is not practical for unsupervised co-segmentation algorithm comparison on indoor dataset. Let n_{ij} be the number of pixels of class i classified as class j, $t_i = \sum_j n_{ij}$ be the total number of pixels belonging to class i, and $t = \sum_i t_i$ be the number of all pixels. The f.w.IOU can be defined as $\frac{1}{t} \sum_i t_i n_{ii} / \left(t_i + \sum_j n_{ji} - n_{ii} \right)$.

We first make self-comparison among our proposed method and its several variants to verify the effectiveness of bounding plane prior and hypothesis filtering. We show the result of our method with center prior instead of bounding plane prior (BP$^-$), with class filtering only (PF$^-$), with portion filtering only (CF$^-$), without any filtering (F^{2-}), and our full version (Our), respectively. We then compare our method with two recent RGB co-segmentation of multiple foreground objects [1,7], with code available on the Internet.

Table 1 lists the f.w.IOU scores of each method on our *NYUD-COSEG* dataset. Some of the visual results are shown in Fig. 3. From both quantitative and qualitative results, we can make the following observations: (i) Our method and its variants have significantly higher f.w.IOU than other methods, with our full version exceeding previous RGB methods by at least 16% on average. The result confirms that the depth information has great potential in unsupervised co-segmentation. (ii) The bounding plane prior is the most decisive part in performance boosting, of which the absence causes the lowest average score among all variants. Correctly distinguishing between foreground and background is essential for further clustering and segmentation. (iii) The two-stage hypothesis filtering is also effective. Class filtering has more effect than portion filtering. The former avoids merging of different objects in the global image and the latter adds more detailed refinement to single objects.

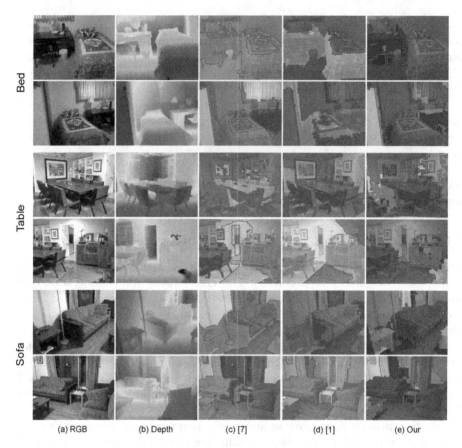

Bed

Table

Sofa

(a) RGB   (b) Depth   (c) [7]   (d) [1]   (e) Our

Fig. 3. Some qualitative co-segmentation results on our RGB-D indoor co-segmentation dataset *NYUD-COSEG*. From left to right: input RGB images, depth maps, results of [1,7], Our full version. (Common objects are shown in the same color with red separating boundaries.). (Color figure online)

4.3   Parameter Evaluation and Discussion

As mentioned in Sect. 4.1, our method contains two important parameters: cluster number C for superpixel merging and portion ratio θ for portion filtering. We fix one parameter to default and vary the other in a reasonable range to see how the f.w.IOU score will change accordingly, as shown in Fig. 4. The purple line indicating mean f.w.IOU score proves that our default values for the two parameters are optimal. Additionally, we find in Fig. 4(a) that too many clusters will not improve segmentation accuracy. Besides, in hypothesis generation step, the time costing is proportional to 2^C. As shown in Fig. 4(b) the accuracy varies mildly with respect to portion ratio θ, within 2.6%, although higher θ has the tendency to improve the result in view of mean f.w.IOU score.

Table 1. Comparison of f.w.IOU score of different methods (%) on *NYUD-COSEG* dataset. The highest is marked in bold.

Method	[7]	[1]	BP$^-$	CF$^-$	PF$^-$	F^{2-}	Our
Bed	43.56	46.37	53.08	62.59	65.85	61.18	**68.42**
Table	46.13	42.63	48.16	52.68	57.21	51.69	**58.31**
Sofa	46.66	53.82	59.96	54.69	62.40	56.69	**64.56**
Mean	45.45	47.61	53.73	56.65	61.82	56.52	**63.76**

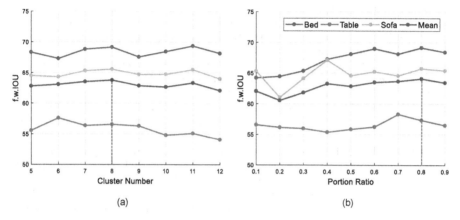

(a)   (b)

Fig. 4. The accuracy changing with respect to variation of two parameters of our co-segmentation method. (Color figure online)

5 Conclusion

In this paper the problem of RGB-D indoor co-segmentation of main furniture is considered. Previous methods use RGB images only. As indoor scene are typical of cluttering and occlusion, foreground merged with similar background and low quality object hypotheses are the two main factors that hinder the performance. We propose to handle these challenges using geometric and spatial information provided by depth channel. Bounding plane prior and a two-stage hypothesis filtering strategy are introduced and integrated into traditional bottom-up co-segmentation framework. To evaluate our method, the *NYUD-COSEG* dataset is constructed based on *NYUD v2*, with thorough experiments proving the effectiveness of our two improvements.

As the first work on the task of indoor co-segmentation, our method is limited in segmenting small objects like stuff on the table, which is most challenging in terms of unsupervised machine learning condition. In the future work we plane to extending our model by incorporating more supervising signals such as supporting relationship to discern small objects. Besides, the question of how to use probabilistic models to formulate our bounding plane prior and hypothesis filtering is worth studying. We believe it will reduce the number of parameters needed to be set manually and thus can elevate the robustness of our method.

References

1. Chang, H.S., Wang, Y.C.F.: Optimizing the decomposition for multiple foreground cosegmentation. Comput. Vis. Image Underst. **141**, 18–27 (2015)
2. Deng, Z., Todorovic, S., Latecki, L.J.: Unsupervised object region proposals for RGB-D indoor scenes. Comput. Vis. Image Underst. **154**, 127–136 (2017)
3. Fu, H., Xu, D., Lin, S., Liu, J.: Object-based RGBD image co-segmentation with mutex constraint (2015)
4. Fu, H., Xu, D., Zhang, B., Lin, S.: Object-based multiple foreground video co-segmentation. In: Proceedings of the IEEE Conference on Computer Vision and Pattern Recognition, pp. 3166–3173 (2014)
5. Joulin, A., Bach, F., Ponce, J.: Discriminative clustering for image co-segmentation. In: 2010 IEEE Conference on Computer Vision and Pattern Recognition (CVPR), pp. 1943–1950. IEEE (2010)
6. Kim, G., Xing, E.P.: On multiple foreground cosegmentation. In: 2012 IEEE Conference on Computer Vision and Pattern Recognition (CVPR), pp. 837–844. IEEE (2012)
7. Kim, G., Xing, E.P., Fei-Fei, L., Kanade, T.: Distributed cosegmentation via submodular optimization on anisotropic diffusion. In: 2011 IEEE International Conference on Computer Vision (ICCV), pp. 169–176. IEEE (2011)
8. Levinshtein, A., Stere, A., Kutulakos, K.N., Fleet, D.J., Dickinson, S.J., Siddiqi, K.: TurboPixels: fast superpixels using geometric flows. IEEE Trans. Pattern Anal. Mach. Intell. **31**(12), 2290–2297 (2009)
9. Lin, Y.: Hierarchical co-segmentation of 3D point clouds for indoor scene. In: 2017 International Conference on Systems, Signals and Image Processing (IWSSIP), pp. 1–5. IEEE (2017)
10. Long, J., Shelhamer, E., Darrell, T.: Fully convolutional networks for semantic segmentation. In: Proceedings of the IEEE Conference on Computer Vision and Pattern Recognition, pp. 3431–3440 (2015)
11. Meng, F., Li, H., Liu, G., Ngan, K.N.: Object co-segmentation based on shortest path algorithm and saliency model. IEEE Trans. Multimed. **14**(5), 1429–1441 (2012)
12. Quan, R., Han, J., Zhang, D., Nie, F.: Object co-segmentation via graph optimized-flexible manifold ranking. In: Proceedings of the IEEE Conference on Computer Vision and Pattern Recognition, pp. 687–695 (2016)
13. Rother, C., Kolmogorov, V., Blake, A.: GrabCut: interactive foreground extraction using iterated graph cuts. ACM Trans. Graph. (TOG) **23**, 309–314 (2004)
14. Rother, C., Minka, T., Blake, A., Kolmogorov, V.: Cosegmentation of image pairs by histogram matching-incorporating a global constraint into MRFs. In: 2006 IEEE Computer Society Conference on Computer Vision and Pattern Recognition, vol. 1, pp. 993–1000. IEEE (2006)
15. Rubinstein, M., Joulin, A., Kopf, J., Liu, C.: Unsupervised joint object discovery and segmentation in internet images. In: 2013 IEEE Conference on Computer Vision and Pattern Recognition (CVPR), pp. 1939–1946. IEEE (2013)
16. Sharf, A., Huang, H., Liang, C., Zhang, J., Chen, B., Gong, M.: Mobility-trees for indoor scenes manipulation. In: Computer Graphics Forum, vol. 33, pp. 2–14. Wiley Online Library (2014)

17. Shen, T., Lin, G., Liu, L., Shen, C., Reid, I.: Weakly supervised semantic segmentation based on co-segmentation. arXiv preprint arXiv:1705.09052 (2017)
18. Silberman, N., Hoiem, D., Kohli, P., Fergus, R.: Indoor segmentation and support inference from RGBD images. In: Fitzgibbon, A., Lazebnik, S., Perona, P., Sato, Y., Schmid, C. (eds.) ECCV 2012. LNCS, vol. 7576, pp. 746–760. Springer, Heidelberg (2012). https://doi.org/10.1007/978-3-642-33715-4_54

Violence Detection Based on Spatio-Temporal Feature and Fisher Vector

Huangkai Cai[1], He Jiang[1], Xiaolin Huang[1], Jie Yang[1(✉)], and Xiangjian He[2]

[1] Institution of Image Processing and Pattern Recognition, Shanghai Jiao Tong University, Shanghai, China
jieyang@sjtu.edu.cn
[2] School of Electrical and Data Engineering, University of Technology Sydney, Ultimo, Australia

Abstract. A novel framework based on local spatio-temporal features and a Bag-of-Words (BoW) model is proposed for violence detection. The framework utilizes Dense Trajectories (DT) and MPEG flow video descriptor (MF) as feature descriptors and employs Fisher Vector (FV) in feature coding. DT and MF algorithms are more descriptive and robust, because they are combinations of various feature descriptors, which describe trajectory shape, appearance, motion and motion boundary, respectively. FV is applied to transform low level features to high level features. FV method preserves much information, because not only the affiliations of descriptors are found in the codebook, but also the first and second order statistics are used to represent videos. Some tricks, that PCA, K-means++ and codebook size, are used to improve the final performance of video classification. In comprehensive consideration of accuracy, speed and application scenarios, the proposed method for violence detection is analysed. Experimental results show that the proposed approach outperforms the state-of-the-art approaches for violence detection in both crowd scenes and non-crowd scenes.

Keywords: Violence detection · Dense Trajectories
MPEG flow video descriptor · Fisher Vector
Linear support vector machine

1 Introduction

Violence detection is to determine whether a scene has an attribute of violence. Violence is artificially defined, and video clips are artificially labelled as 'normal' and 'violence'. Violence detection is considered as not only a branch of action recognition, but also an instance of video classification. Techniques of violence detection can be applied to real life in intelligent monitoring systems and for reviewing videos automatically on the Internet.

© Springer Nature Switzerland AG 2018
J.-H. Lai et al. (Eds.): PRCV 2018, LNCS 11256, pp. 180–190, 2018.
https://doi.org/10.1007/978-3-030-03398-9_16

Early approaches of action recognition are based on trajectories, which need to detect human bodies and track them for video analysis. They are complicated and indirect, because human detection and tracking have to be solved in advance. Recently, the methods based on local spatio-temporal features [16,17] have dominated the field of action recognition. These approaches use local spatio-temporal features to represent global features of videos directly. Moreover, their performance is excellent and robust under various conditions such as background variations, illumination changes and noise. In [11], a Bag-of-Words (BoW) model was used to effectively transform low level features to high level features.

Motivated by the performance of local spatio-temporal features and BoW models, a new framework using Dense Trajectories (DT) [16], MPEG flow video descriptor (MF) [7] and Fisher Vector (FV) [10] for violence detection is proposed as illustrated in Fig. 1. We provide the reasons for why DT and MF are chosen for feature extraction and why FV is chosen for feature coding as follows.

For feature extraction, a variety of feature descriptors based on local spatio-temporal features can be applied. These descriptors include Histogram of Oriented Gradients (HOG) and Histogram of Oriented Flow (HOF) [8], Motion SIFT (MoSIFT) [2], Motion Weber Local Descriptor (MoWLD) [21] and Motion Improved Weber Local Descriptor (MoIWLD) [20]. The applications of these feature descriptors to describe human appearance and motion for violence detection can be found in [11,18,20,21].

For the purpose of extracting more descriptive features to improve the performance of violence detection, DT and MF are utilized for the first time for violence detection in this paper. The interest points that are densely sampled by DT preserve more information than all other features mentioned above. DT is a combination of multiple features including trajectory shape, HOG, HOF and Motion Boundary Histogram (MBH), so it takes the advantages of these features. On the premise of ensuring prediction accuracy, MF improves the computational cost and time consumption compared to DT.

For feature coding, Vector Quantization (VQ) [14] and Sparse Coding (SC) [19] are two commonly used methods for encoding the final representations. VQ votes for a feature only when the feature 'word' is similar to a word in the codebook, so it may result in information loss. SC reconstructs the features by referring to the codebook, preserves the affiliations of descriptors and stores only the zeroth order statistics. The work using SC or its variants for violence detection can be found in [18,20,21].

Compared with VQ and SC, Fisher Vector generates a high dimensional vector that stores not only the zeroth order statistics, but also the first and second order statistics. Moreover, the running time of FV is much less than VQ and SC, hence it is used for feature coding in this paper.

The contributions of this paper are summarized as follows. A novel framework for violence detection is proposed. It uses DT and MF feature descriptors as local spatio-temporal features and utilizes FV for feature coding. Some tricks, that PCA, K-means++ and codebook size, are applied to improve the performance of violence detection. Our proposed framework of violence detection is analysed from various aspects including accuracy, speed and application scenarios. Experimental results demonstrate that the proposed approach outperforms the state-of-the-art techniques on both crowd and non-crowd datasets in terms of accuracies.

The rest of this paper is organized as follows. In Sect. 2, we will elaborate the proposed framework including Dense Trajectories, MPEG flow video descriptor and Fisher Vector. In Sect. 3, the experimental results in crowd scenes and non-crowd scenes will be showed and analysed. In Sect. 4, conclusions will be discussed.

2   Methodology

This article proposes a novel framework of violence detection using Dense Trajectories (DT), MPEG flow video descriptor (MF) and Fisher Vector (FV) as illustrated in Fig. 1. Firstly, from the violent video clips for training and testing, DT or MF feature vectors are extracted and they describe trajectory shape, appearance, motion and motion boundaries. Secondly, PCA is applied to eliminate redundant information after low level representations are generated. Thirdly, testing videos are encoded as high level representations by FV according to the codebook generated by Gaussian Mixture Models (GMM). Finally, linear SVM is employed to classify the videos into two categories of normal patterns and violence patterns. The algorithm for violence detection in videos based on this framework is detailed in the following subsections.

2.1   Dense Trajectories and MPEG Flow Video Descriptor

Dense Trajectories proposed in [16] is an excellent algorithm of feature extraction for action recognition. DT extracts four types of features that are trajectory shape, HOG, HOF and MBH. These features are combined to represent a local region in the visual aspects of trajectory shape, appearance, motion and motion boundaries.

MPEG flow video descriptor proposed in [7] is an efficient video descriptor which uses motion information in video compression. The computational cost of MF is much less than DT, because the spare MPEG flow is applied to replace the dense optical flow. Furthermore, there exists only minor reduction in the performance of video classification in contrast to DT. The design of MPEG flow video descriptor follows Dense Trajectories except features based on trajectory shape.

The feature descriptor of DT is a 426 dimensional feature vector, which contains a 30 dimensional trajectory shape descriptor, a 96 dimensional HOG descriptor, a 108 dimensional HOF descriptor and a 192 dimensional MBH descriptor. Compared to DT descriptor, MF is a 396 dimensional feature vector without a 30 dimensional trajectory shape descriptor. As types of feature descriptor, DT and MF are pretty descriptive and robust because of the combination of multiple descriptors.

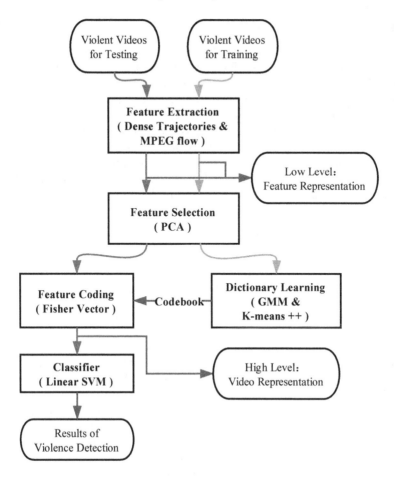

Fig. 1. The proposed framework of violence detection

2.2 Principal Component Analysis

Principal Component Analysis [9,15] is a statistical algorithm for dimensionality reduction. Due to the high dimension of DT (426 dimensional) and MF (396 dimensional), PCA is utilized to reduce the dimension of feature vectors in order to speed up the process of dictionary learning and improve the accuracy of classification. In addition, a whitening process usually follows the PCA, which ensures all features to have the same variance. The transform equation is illustrated as follows.

$$x_{PCA} = \Lambda U^T x_{Original} \tag{1}$$

where $x_{Original} \in R^M$ denotes an original feature, $x_{PCA} \in R^N$ denotes the PCA-Whiten result, $U \in R^{M \times N}$ is the transform matrix of the PCA algorithm, $\Lambda \in R^{N \times N}$ is the whitening diagonal matrix.

2.3 Fisher Vector

Fisher Vector [12,13] is an efficient algorithm for feature coding. It is derived from a fisher kernel [6]. Moreover, FV is usually employed to encode a high level representation of a high dimension for image classification [10]. Both of the first and second order statistics are encoded leading to a high separability of the final feature representations. The FV algorithm is described as follows.

GMM is employed to learn the codebook, which uses generative models to describe the probability distribution of feature vectors. Let $X = \{x_1, \dots, x_N\}$ be a set of D dimensional feature vectors processed through the DT and PCA algorithms, where N is the number of feature vectors. The density $p(x|\lambda)$ and the k-th Gaussian distribution $p_k(x|\mu_k, \Sigma_k)$ are defined as:

$$p(x|\lambda) = \sum_{k=1}^{K} \omega_k p_k(x|\mu_k, \Sigma_k), \tag{2}$$

and

$$p_k(x|\mu_k, \Sigma_k) = \frac{exp[-\frac{1}{2}(x - \mu_k)^T \Sigma_k^{-1}(x - \mu_k)]}{(2\pi)^{D/2}|\Sigma_k|^{1/2}}, \tag{3}$$

where K denotes the mixture number, $\lambda = (\omega_k, \mu_k, \Sigma_k : k = 1, \dots, K)$ are the GMM parameters that fit the distribution of the feature vectors, ω_k denotes the mixture weight, μ_k denotes the mean vector and Σ_k denotes the covariance matrix.

The optimal parameters forming λ of GMM are learned by the Expectation Maximization (EM) algorithm [3]. Furthermore, the initial values of these parameters have an important influence on the final codebook, so k-means++ [1] results are calculated as the initial values.

In the following equation, y_{ik} represents the occupancy probability, which is the soft assignment of the feature descriptor x_i to Gaussian k:

$$y_{ik} = \frac{exp[-\frac{1}{2}(x_i - \mu_k)^T \Sigma_k^{-1}(x_i - \mu_k)]}{\sum_{t=1}^{K} exp[-\frac{1}{2}(x_i - \mu_t)^T \Sigma_k^{-1}(x_i - \mu_t)]}. \tag{4}$$

Then, the gradient vector $g_{\mu,d,k}^X$ with respect to the mean μ_{dk} of Gaussian k and the gradient vector $g_{\sigma,d,k}^X$ with respect to the standard deviation σ_{dk} of Gaussian k could be calculated. Their mathematical expressions are:

$$g_{\mu,d,k}^X = \frac{1}{N\sqrt{\omega_k}} \sum_{i=1}^{N} y_{ik} \frac{x_{di} - \mu_{dk}}{\sigma_{dk}}, \tag{5}$$

and

$$g_{\sigma,d,k}^X = \frac{1}{N\sqrt{2\omega_k}} \sum_{i=1}^{N} y_{ik}[(\frac{x_{di} - \mu_{dk}}{\sigma_{dk}})^2 - 1], \tag{6}$$

where $d = 1, \ldots, D$ for D representing the dimension of the feature vectors.

Finally, the Fisher Vector is the concatenation of $g^X_{\mu,d,k}$ and $g^X_{\sigma,d,k}$ for $k = 1, \ldots K$ and $d = 1, \ldots, D$, and it is represented by

$$\Phi(X) = [g^X_{\mu,d,k}, \ g^X_{\sigma,d,k}]. \tag{7}$$

Therefore, the final representation of a video is $2 \times K \times D$ dimensional.

2.4   Linear Support Vector Machine

Before applying the video representations in the linear SVM, the power and ℓ_2 normalization are applied to the Fisher Vector $\Phi(X)$ as shown in [13]. Then, the linear SVM [4] is used for the violence classification of each video encoded by FV.

3   Experiments

3.1   Datasets

In our experiments, two public datasets are applied to detect whether a scene has a characteristic of violence. These datasets are Hockey Fight dataset (HF dataset) [11] and Crowd Violence dataset (CV dataset) [5]. HF dataset shows non-crowd scenes, while CV dataset shows crowd scenes. The validity of the proposed framework for violence detection will be verified in both crowd scenes and non-crowd scenes. Some frame samples taken from them are displayed in Fig. 2. The datasets are introduced briefly below.

Fig. 2. Frame samples from the Hockey Fight dataset (first row) and the Crowd Violence dataset (second row). The first row shows non-crowd scenes, while the second row shows crowd scenes. The left three columns show violent scenes, while the right three columns show non-violent scenes.

Hockey Fight Dataset. This dataset contains 1000 video clips from ice hockey games of the National Hockey League (NHL). There are 500 video clips labelled as violence, while other 500 video clips are manually labelled as non-violence. The resolution of each video clip is 360×288 pixels.

Crowd Violence Dataset. This dataset contains 246 video clips of crowd behaviours, and these clips are collected from YouTube. It consists of 123 violent clips and 123 non-violent clips with a resolution of 320×240 pixels.

Table 1. Violence detection results using Sparse Coding (SC) on Hockey Fight dataset

Visual words	MoSIFT + SC [18]		MoWLD + SC [21]	
	ACC	AUC	ACC	AUC
50 words	85.4	0.9211	89.1	0.9318
100 words	88.4	0.9345	90.5	0.9492
150 words	89.6	0.9407	**92.4**	0.9618
200 words	89.6	0.9469	93.1	0.9708
300 words	91.8	0.9575	93.5	0.9638
500 words	92.3	0.9655	93.3	0.9706
1000 words	93.0	0.9669	93.7	0.9781
Visual words	DT + SC		MF + SC	
	ACC	AUC	ACC	AUC
50 words	90.3	0.9542	**91.4**	**0.9564**
100 words	91.6	0.9662	**92.7**	**0.9700**
150 words	91.2	0.9621	92.1	**0.9744**
200 words	92.3	0.9718	**93.5**	**0.9766**
300 words	92.5	0.9759	**93.9**	**0.9792**
500 words	92.4	0.9776	**94.4**	**0.9823**
1000 words	94.4	0.9831	**94.9**	**0.9868**

3.2 Experimental Settings

In feature extraction, experiments are conducted based on three feature descriptors, which are MoSIFT [2] (256 dimensional), Dense Trajectories (DT) [16] (426 dimensional) and MPEG flow video descriptor (MF) [7] (396 dimensional).

For feature selection, PCA is utilized to reduce the abovementioned three types of features to the same dimension of $D = 200$.

For dictionary learning, $100,000$ features are randomly sampled from the training set. For GMM training, k-means++ [1] is used to initialize the covariance matrix of each mixture. It is an important trick for improving the final performance and making the results more stable. The mixture number of GMMs is set to be $K = 256$.

After the codebook is generated, the results using FV are compared with the results using SC in feature coding. The parameter settings of SC are according to those in [18]. The final feature vectors of videos are powered and ℓ_2-normalized.

Finally, the linear SVM [4] is employed for classification of the testing videos, and the penalty parameter is set to be $C = 100$.

5-fold cross validation is used for evaluating the accuracies of video classification. The experimental results are reported in terms of mean prediction accuracy (ACC) and the area under the ROC curve (AUC).

3.3   Experimental Results on Hockey Fight Dataset

We perform a series of experiments for testing the superiority of 4 types of feature descriptors. The 4 types of features are MoSIFT, MoWLD [21], DT and MF, and they are used together with SC on the Hockey Fight dataset. The results from DT + SC and MF + SC are compared with those using the methods recently developed in [18,21]. Furthermore, in order to assess the effect of the codebook size, we set 7 groups of experiments using SC, where the codebook sizes range from 50 words to 1000 words.

Table 2. Violence detection results using Fisher Vector (FV) on Hockey Fight dataset

Methods	ACC	AUC
MoSIFT + FV	93.8	0.9843
DT + FV	94.7	0.9830
MF + FV	95.8	0.9897
MoSIFT + PCA + FV	93.6	0.9859
DT + PCA + FV	95.2	0.9849
MF + PCA + FV	**95.8**	**0.9899**

As shown in Table 1, it is firmly convinced that the features of DT and MF are more effective and discriminative in contrast with the MoSIFT and MoWLD features. DT and MF features are introduced to violence detection for the first time, but they show strong adaptability to non-crowd scenes. In overall consideration of ACC and AUC values, the performance of MF features is the best in these experiments.

The experimental results also indicate that the performance of these algorithms improves with the increase of visual words, i.e., the codebook size contributes to the accuracy of violence detection. In practical application, time consumption will increase if the codebook size expands. So, we can utilize codebook size as a trick to trade off prediction accuracy and time consumption.

FV is applied as an algorithm for feature coding on the Hockey Fight dataset. The performance of FV demonstrated in Table 2 is superior to the performance of SC shown in Table 1. Furthermore, the employment of PCA contributes to the improvement of ACC and AUC, as particularly seen in the results using DT.

In summary, our proposed framework of violence detection, MF + PCA + FV, outperforms the state-of-the-art methods in non-crowd scenes.

3.4   Experimental Results on Crowd Violence Dataset

We compare our proposed algorithm with various state-of-the-art methods including ViF [5], MoSIFT + SC [18], MoWLD + SC [21] and MoIWLD +

Table 3. Violence detection results of various methods on Crowd Violence dataset

Methods	ACC	AUC
ViF [5]	81.30	0.8500
MoSIFT + SC [18]	80.47	0.9008
MoWLD + SC [21]	86.39	0.9018
MoIWLD + SRC [20]	93.19	0.9508
MF + SC	90.63	0.9630
DT + SC	91.45	0.9664
MF + FV	89.83	0.9672
DT + FV	93.50	**0.9889**
MF + PCA + FV	91.89	0.9789
DT + PCA + FV	**95.11**	0.9866

SRC [20] on the Crowd Violence dataset. The codebook size of the compared methods is set to be 500 visual words.

Obviously, our FV based method outperforms the state-of-the-art approaches as shown in Table 3. Moreover, the utilization of PCA effectively improves the accuracy of violence detection.

In crowd scenes, the performance of MF features is inferior to DT features. Because, the information which MF preserves is insufficient due to video compression.

3.5 Analysis of Violence Detection

Comparative analysis of accuracy and speed for violence detection is as shown in Table 4. Speed means that how many frame pictures can be processed per second by different algorithms of feature extraction. We mainly analyse our proposed framework that DT + PCA + FV and MF + PCA + FV in different scenes.

Table 4. Comparative analysis of accuracy and speed for violence detection

Methods	HF dataset		CV dataset		Speed (fps)
	ACC	AUC	ACC	AUC	
DT	95.20	0.9849	95.11	0.9866	1.2
MF	95.80	0.9899	91.89	0.9789	168.4

If time consumption becomes a primary consideration, the framework based on MF will be the optimal choice in both crowd scenes and non-crowd scenes.

Nevertheless, the diversity of application scenarios will result in different options if prediction accuracy is major concerned. The prediction accuracy of

MF is superior to DT in non-crowd scenes, while DT outperforms MF in crowd scenes.

4 Conclusion

This paper has proposed a novel framework of violence detection using Dense Trajectories, MPEG flow video descriptor and Fisher Vector. Firstly, the experimental results have shown that DT and MF as types of discriminative feature descriptors outperform other commonly used features for violence detection. Secondly, FV as an excellent feature coding algorithm has been proven to be superior to Sparse Coding. Thirdly, some tricks including PCA, K-means++ and codebook size have contributed to the improvement of accuracy and AUC values in violence detection. Fourthly, our proposed framework of violence detection was analysed in overall consideration of accuracy, speed and application scenarios. Fifthly, the performance of the proposed method was better than the state-of-the-art techniques for violence detection in both crowd scenes and non-crowd scenes. As our future work, whether DT, MF and FV are suitable for other tasks of video analysis will be further researched.

Acknowledgements. This research is partly supported by NSFC, China (No: 61572315, 6151101179) and 973 Plan, China (No. 2015CB856004).

References

1. Arthur, D., Vassilvitskii, S.: k-means++: the advantages of careful seeding. In: Eighteenth ACM-SIAM Symposium on Discrete Algorithms, pp. 1027–1035 (2007)
2. Chen, M.Y., Hauptmann, A.: MoSIFT: recognizing human actions in surveillance videos. Ann. Pharmacother. **39**(1), 150–152 (2009)
3. Dempster, A.P.: Maximum likelihood estimation from incomplete data via the EM algorithm. J. R. Stat. Soc. **39**(1), 1–38 (1977)
4. Fan, R.E., Chang, K.W., Hsieh, C.J., Wang, X.R., Lin, C.J.: Liblinear: a library for large linear classification. J. Mach. Learn. Res. **9**(9), 1871–1874 (2008)
5. Hassner, T., Itcher, Y., Kliper-Gross, O.: Violent flows: real-time detection of violent crowd behavior. In: IEEE Conference on Computer Vision and Pattern Recognition Workshops, pp. 1–6 (2012)
6. Jaakkola, T.S., Haussler, D.: Exploiting generative models in discriminative classifiers. In: International Conference on Neural Information Processing Systems, pp. 487–493 (1998)
7. Kantorov, V., Laptev, I.: Efficient feature extraction, encoding, and classification for action recognition. In: IEEE Conference on Computer Vision and Pattern Recognition, pp. 2593–2600 (2014)
8. Laptev, I., Marszalek, M., Schmid, C., Rozenfeld, B.: Learning realistic human actions from movies. In: IEEE Conference on Computer Vision and Pattern Recognition, pp. 1–8 (2008)
9. Martinsson, P.G., Rokhlin, V., Tygert, M.: A randomized algorithm for the decomposition of matrices. Appl. Comput. Harmon. Anal. **30**(1), 47–68 (2011)

10. Nchez, J., Perronnin, F., Mensink, T., Verbeek, J.: Image classification with the fisher vector: theory and practice. Int. J. Comput. Vis. **105**(3), 222–245 (2013)
11. Bermejo Nievas, E., Deniz Suarez, O., Bueno García, G., Sukthankar, R.: Violence detection in video using computer vision techniques. In: Real, P., Diaz-Pernil, D., Molina-Abril, H., Berciano, A., Kropatsch, W. (eds.) CAIP 2011. LNCS, vol. 6855, pp. 332–339. Springer, Heidelberg (2011). https://doi.org/10.1007/978-3-642-23678-5_39
12. Perronnin, F., Dance, C.: Fisher kernels on visual vocabularies for image categorization. In: IEEE Conference on Computer Vision and Pattern Recognition, pp. 1–8 (2007)
13. Perronnin, F., Sánchez, J., Mensink, T.: Improving the fisher kernel for large-scale image classification. In: Daniilidis, K., Maragos, P., Paragios, N. (eds.) ECCV 2010. LNCS, vol. 6314, pp. 143–156. Springer, Heidelberg (2010). https://doi.org/10.1007/978-3-642-15561-1_11
14. Sivic, J., Zisserman, A.: Video Google: a text retrieval approach to object matching in videos. In: IEEE International Conference on Computer Vision, p. 1470 (2003)
15. Tipping, M.E., Bishop, C.M.: Mixtures of probabilistic principal component analyzers. J. Neural Comput. **11**(2), 443–482 (1999)
16. Wang, H., Kläser, A., Schmid, C., Liu, C.L.: Dense trajectories and motion boundary descriptors for action recognition. Int. J. Comput. Vis. **103**(1), 60–79 (2013)
17. Wang, H., Schmid, C.: Action recognition with improved trajectories. In: IEEE International Conference on Computer Vision, pp. 3551–3558 (2014)
18. Xu, L., Gong, C., Yang, J., Wu, Q., Yao, L.: Violent video detection based on MoSIFT feature and sparse coding. In: IEEE Conference on Acoustics, Speech and Signal Processing, pp. 3538–3542 (2014)
19. Yang, J., Yu, K., Gong, Y., Huang, T.: Linear spatial pyramid matching using sparse coding for image classification. In: IEEE Conference on Computer Vision and Pattern Recognition, pp. 1794–1801 (2009)
20. Zhang, T., Jia, W., He, X., Yang, J.: Discriminative dictionary learning with motion weber local descriptor for violence detection. IEEE Trans. Circuits Syst. Video Technol. **27**(3), 696–709 (2017)
21. Zhang, T., Jia, W., Yang, B., Yang, J., He, X., Zheng, Z.: MoWLD: a robust motion image descriptor for violence detection. Multimed. Tools Appl. **76**(1), 1–20 (2017)

Speckle Noise Removal Based on Adaptive Total Variation Model

Bo Chen[1,2(✉)], Jinbin Zou[1], Wensheng Chen[1,2], Xiangjun Kong[3], Jianhua Ma[4], and Feng Li[5]

[1] Shenzhen Key Laboratory of Advanced Machine Learning and Applications,
College of Mathematics and Statistics,
Shenzhen University, Shenzhen 518060, China
chenbo@szu.edu.cn
[2] Shenzhen Key Laboratory of Media Security, Shenzhen University,
Shenzhen 518060, China
[3] School of Mathematical Sciences, Qufu Normal University,
Qufu 273165, China
[4] Department of Biomedical Engineering, Southern Medical University,
Guangzhou 510515, China
[5] China Ship Scientific Research Center, Wuxi 214082, China

Abstract. For removing the speckle noise in ultrasound images, researchers have proposed many models based on energy minimization methods. At the same time, traditional models have some disadvantages, such as, the low speed of energy diffusion which can not preserve the sharp edges. In order to overcome those disadvantages, we introduce an adaptive total variation model to deal with speckle noise in ultrasound image for retaining the fine detail effectively and enhancing the speed of energy diffusion. Firstly, a new convex function is employed as regularization term in the adaptive total variation model. Secondly, the diffusion properties of the new model are analyzed through the physical characteristics of local coordinates. The new energy model has different diffusion velocities in different gradient regions. Numerical experimental results show that the proposed model for speckle noise removal is superior to traditional models, not only in visual effect, but also in quantitative measures.

Keywords: Image denoising · Speckle noise · Total variation
Diffusion properties

1 Introduction

Image processing has been widely studied over the past decades and image denoising is very important in the field of image processing. It is well-known that speckle noise in medical ultrasonic images will bring a significant decline in the quality of ultrasonic images and cover up the lesions of some important tissues. Furthermore, speckle noise will bring great difficulties to the doctors diagnosis and certain specific diseases identification. As mentioned in article [1], the speckle noise in medical ultrasonic images can be written in the following form:

© Springer Nature Switzerland AG 2018
J.-H. Lai et al. (Eds.): PRCV 2018, LNCS 11256, pp. 191–202, 2018.
https://doi.org/10.1007/978-3-030-03398-9_17

$$f = u + \sqrt{u}n, \tag{1}$$

where $u : \Omega \to \mathbb{R}$ is an original image that is without noise, f is a noisy image and n represent the Gaussian random noise with mean zero and standard deviation σ.

Many methods have been proposed for image restoration, such as Lee filter [2], kuan filter [3], locally adaptive statistic filters [1, 4, 5], PDE-based and curvature-based methods [6, 7], Non-Local means filters [8, 9], wavelet transform based thresholding methods [10] and total variational [11, 12] and so on. Most procedures of them transform the model minimization problem into solving the Euler-Lagrange equation. Rudin et al. proposed a numerical algorithms [13] that use the finite difference method to solve the Euler-Lagrange equation directly.

Motivated by these works, we adopt the idea of variational model to restore image by minimizing the energy function. Compared with other restoration model, the Total Variation (TV) model has lower complexity and better restoration effect locally. But TV model causes stair casing effect when filling in large smooth domain [14]. In order to preserve the edges and avoid staircase effect, we present an image restoration model based on an energy function and it can work with different diffusion speeds in different domains adaptively.

The rest of this paper is as follows. In Sect. 2, we review some related denoising works. In Sect. 3, we propose a new model based on variation and meanwhile we analyze diffusion performance of the proposed model. The corresponding numerical algorithm is given in Sect. 4. Section 5 shows the experimental results. The conclusion is drawn in Sect. 6.

2   Some Related Works

In 1992, Rudin et al. [13] proposed a denoising model based on total variation:

$$E_\lambda(u) = \int_\Omega |Du|dx + \frac{\lambda}{2}\int_\Omega |u - u^0|^2 dx, \tag{2}$$

where $\int_\Omega |Du|dx = \sup\{\int_\Omega u\,div(\varphi)|\varphi \in C_c^1(\Omega, \mathbb{R}^n), ||\varphi||_\infty \leq 1\}$ represents the TV regularization term, $u^0 = u + n$ is noisy image and n represent the Gaussian random noise with mean zero and standard deviation σ. $\lambda > 0$ represents the regularization parameter which can balance fidelity terms and regularized terms in TV model, $|Du|$ represent the L^1 norm of the image gradient.

In order to deal with the degenerate model (see Eq. (1)). In article [15], Krissian and Kikinis et al. derived a convex fidelity term:

$$\int_\Omega \frac{(f - u)^2}{u}dx = \sigma^2, \tag{3}$$

where f is noise image.

2.1 JIN's Model

In [12], motivates by the classical ROF model [13], the authors proposed a convex variational model (JIN's model) for removing the speckle noise in ultrasound image. The convex variational model involving the TV regularization term and convex fidelity term (see Eq. (3)):

$$\min_u \left[\int_\Omega |Du|dx + \lambda \int_\Omega \frac{(f-u)^2}{u} dx \right],$$ (4)

where $\int_\Omega |\nabla u| dx$ and λ are similar to Eq. (2). The correspond Euler-Lagrange equation is as follow:

$$\nabla \left(\frac{\nabla u}{|\nabla u|} \right) + \lambda \left(\frac{f^2}{u^2} - 1 \right) = 0,$$ (5)

Using gradient descent method, we can get the model as follows:

$$\begin{cases} u_t = \nabla \left(\frac{\nabla u}{|\nabla u|} \right) + \lambda \left(\frac{f^2}{u^2} - 1 \right), & t > 0 \ x, y \ in \ \Omega \\ \frac{\partial u}{\partial \vec{n}} = 0 & on \ the \ boundar \ of \ \Omega, \\ u|_{t=0} = u_0 & in \ \bar{\Omega} \end{cases}$$ (6)

where $\vec{n}$ is the unit out normal vector of $\partial \Omega$. Finally, through the iterative method, the desired image can be obtain.

2.2 The Selection of TV Regularization Term

Although TV regularization is very effective in image restoration, but some scholars have used general variational methods to write models:

$$J_1(u) = \int_\Omega \varphi(|\nabla u|),$$ (7)

where $\varphi(x)$ represents a convex function, the case $\varphi(x) = x$ leads to the total variation regularization term. In the literature [16], the author Costanzino chooses $\varphi(x) = x^2$ that leads to the well-known harmonic model.

In order to carry out anisotropic diffusion on the edges and restoration domain and isotropic diffusion in regular regions, it is well known that the function $\varphi(x)$ should satisfy:

$$\begin{cases} \varphi'(0) = 0, \ \lim_{x \to 0^+} \varphi''(x) = \lim_{x \to 0^+} \frac{\varphi'(x)}{x} = c > 0 \\ \lim_{x \to \infty} \varphi''(x) = \lim_{x \to \infty} \frac{\varphi'(x)}{x} = 0, \ \lim_{x \to \infty} \frac{x\varphi''(x)}{\varphi'(x)} = 0 \end{cases},$$ (8)

In this paper, we will choose function $\varphi(x) = x \log(1 + x)$; Obviously this function satisfies the above conditions.

3   The Proposed Restoration Model

3.1   Selection of Regularization Term

In this section, we proposed our model as follows.

$$\min_u \left[\int_\Omega \varphi(|Du|)dx + \lambda \int_\Omega \frac{(f-u)^2}{u}dx \right], \tag{9}$$

where $\varphi(x) = x \log (1 + x)$. The corresponding Euler-Lagrange equation is:

$$\nabla \left[\left(\frac{\log(1+|\nabla u|)}{|\nabla u|} + \frac{1}{1+|\nabla u|} \right) \nabla u \right] + \lambda \left(\frac{f^2}{u^2} - 1 \right) = 0, \tag{10}$$

Using gradient descent method, Eq. (10) can be transformed to:

$$\begin{cases} u_t = \nabla \left[\left(\frac{\log(1+|\nabla u|)}{|\nabla u|} + \frac{1}{1+|\nabla u|} \right) \nabla u \right] + \lambda \left(\frac{f^2}{u^2} - 1 \right) & in\ \Omega \\ \frac{\partial u}{\partial \vec{n}} = 0 & on\ the\ boundar\ of\ \ \Omega, \\ u|_{t=0} = u_0 & in\ \bar{\Omega} \end{cases} \tag{11}$$

where $\vec{n}$ is the unit out normal vector of $\partial\Omega$.

3.2   Performance of Diffusion

In order to analyze the diffusion performance, local image coordinate system $\xi - \eta$ is established. As shown in the Fig. 1, the η-axis represents the direction parallel to the image gradient at the pixel level, and the ξ-axis is the corresponding vertical direction.

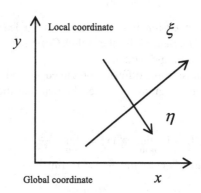

Fig. 1. Global and local coordinate schematic diagram

According to Fig. 1, we can know:

$$\begin{cases} \xi = \frac{1}{|\nabla u|}(-u_y, u_x) \\ \eta = \frac{1}{|\nabla u|}(u_x, u_y) \end{cases}, \tag{12}$$

So Eq. (11) can be rewritten as:

$$u_t = \varphi_1(|\nabla u|)u_{\xi\xi} + \varphi_2(|\nabla u|)u_{\eta\eta} + \lambda\left(\frac{f^2}{u^2} - 1\right), \tag{13}$$

where:

$$\begin{cases} \varphi_1(|\nabla u|) = \dfrac{\log(1 + |\nabla u|)}{|\nabla u|} + \dfrac{1}{1 + |\nabla u|} \\ \varphi_2(|\nabla u|) = \dfrac{1}{1 + |\nabla u|} + \dfrac{1}{(1 + |\nabla u|)^2} \end{cases}, \tag{14}$$

$$\begin{cases} u_{\xi\xi} = \dfrac{u_y^2 u_{xx} - 2u_x u_y u_{xy} + u_x^2 u_{yy}}{|\nabla u|^2} \\ u_{\eta\eta} = \dfrac{u_x^2 u_{xx} + 2u_x u_y u_{xy} + u_y^2 u_{yy}}{|\nabla u|^2} \end{cases}, \tag{15}$$

The $\varphi_1(|\nabla u|)$ and $\varphi_2(|\nabla u|)$ are control functions of the diffusion along the ξ direction and η direction respectively. Now we consider the diffusion of image restoration.

Smooth Area. When $|\nabla u| \to 0$, $\lim\limits_{|\nabla u| \to 0} \varphi_1(|\nabla u|) = 2$ and $\lim\limits_{|\nabla u| \to 0} \varphi_2(|\nabla u|) = 2$. So the Eq. (14) is essentially isotropic diffusion equation. That is to say, on the smooth region the diffusion along the ξ direction and η direction in the process of image restoration.

Sharp Area. When $|\nabla u| \to \infty$, we obtain $\lim\limits_{|\nabla u| \to 0} \frac{\varphi_2(|\nabla u|)}{\varphi_1(|\nabla u|)} = 0$. So the diffusion rate in ξ direction in Eq. (14) is much larger than that in the η direction in the sharp region.

Diffusion analysis. According to the analysis about the diffusion of image restoration, we can see that when the image region is smooth, energy can diffuse along ξ and η direction, and when the image area is sharp, the energy diffuse only along the ξ direction. In addition, for image denoising, our proposed model can avoid the staircase effect in smooth regions and preserve sharp edges effectively.

4   Numerical Implementation

We will describe the corresponding numerical algorithm in this section. The proposed model can be solve by discretization as follows.

$$u_{i,j}^{k+1} = u_{i,j}^k + \Delta t[\nabla(T(|\nabla u^k|)\nabla u^k)_{i,j} + \lambda^k(\frac{f^2}{(u^k)^2} - 1)_{i,j}], \qquad (16)$$

where $T(|\nabla u^k|) = \frac{\log(1+|\nabla u^k|)}{|\nabla u^k|} + \frac{1}{1+|\nabla u^k|}$, and Δt represents time step. Furthermore, the iterative formula can approximate as:

$$u_{i,j}^{k+1} = u_{i,j}^k + \Delta t[A(D_x^+ u^k)_{i,j} + \lambda^k(\frac{f^2}{(u^k)^2} - 1)_{i,j}], \qquad (17)$$

for $i = 1,\ldots,M; j = 1,\ldots,N$, and $M \times N$ represent the size of the image. Here:

$$A(D_x^+ u^k)_{i,j} = D_x^-(T(|D_x^+ u^k|)D_x^+ u^k)_{i,j} + D_y^-(T(|D_y^+ u^k|)D_y^+ u^k)_{i,j}, \qquad (18)$$

$$\begin{cases} D_x^\pm(u_{i,j}) = \pm(u_{i\pm1,j} - u_{i,j}) \\ D_y^\pm(u_{i,j}) = \pm(u_{i\pm1,j} - u_{i,j}) \\ |D_x(u_{i,j})| = \sqrt{(D_x^+(u_{i,j}))^2 + (m[D_y^+(u_{i,j}), D_y^-(u_{i,j})])^2 + \delta} \\ |D_y(u_{i,j})| = \sqrt{(D_y^+(u_{i,j}))^2 + (m[D_x^+(u_{i,j}), D_x^-(u_{i,j})])^2 + \delta} \end{cases}, \qquad (19)$$

where $m[a,b] = (\frac{sign\,a + sign\,b}{2}) \cdot \min([|a|,|b|])$ and $\delta > 0$ is a positive parameter that is close to zero. With boundary conditions:

$$\begin{cases} u_{0,j}^k = u_{1,j}^k; & u_{N,j}^k = u_{N-1,j}^k \\ u_{i,0}^k = u_{i,1}^k; & u_{i,N}^k = u_{i,N-1}^k \end{cases}, \qquad (20)$$

Now note the Eq. (11), the two sides are multiplied by $\frac{(f-u)u}{f+u}$, and then the integral on the domain Ω can be obtained:

$$\lambda \int_\Omega \frac{(f-u)^2}{u} = \int_\Omega \nabla \cdot \left[\left(\frac{\log(1+|\nabla u|)}{|\nabla u|} + \frac{1}{1+|\nabla u|}\right)\nabla u\right] \frac{(u-f)u}{u+f}, \qquad (21)$$

According to the assumption that the Gaussian noise n have mean 0 and variance σ^2, we can obtain:

$$\lambda^k = \frac{1}{\sigma^2|\Omega|} \sum_{i,j} \left(\left[D_x^-(T(|D_x^+ u^k|)D_x^+ u^k) + D_y^-(T(|D_y^+ u^k|)D_y^+ u^k)\right]\right) \frac{(u^k - f)}{u^k + f}, \qquad (22)$$

5 Experimental Results

In the numerical experiment, we will use the noise image as the initial value, that is $f = u_0$. Firstly, we display the denoising results about image 'map1' and 'map2' by the proposed model. Secondly, we compare the repair performance of the ROF model [13], ATV model [17], JIN's model [12] with proposed model for some images. Finally, we display the denoising results about ultrasound image 'ultra1', 'ultra2' and 'ultra3'by the proposed model.

To evaluate the quality of restored images, we use the peak signal-to-noise ratio (PSNR) value and the structure similarity (SSIM) index, which are defined as follows:

$$PSNR(u, \bar{u}) = 10 \log_{10} \left(\frac{255^2 mn}{\|u - \bar{u}\|_2^2} \right), \tag{23}$$

$$SSIM(u, \bar{u}) = \frac{(2\mu_{\bar{u}}\mu_u + c_1)(\sigma_{\bar{u}u} + c_2)}{(\mu_{\bar{u}}^2 + \mu_u^2 + c_1)(\sigma_{\bar{u}}^2 + \sigma_u^2 + c_2)}, \tag{24}$$

where $u \in \mathbb{R}^{m \times n}$ is the clean image, $\bar{u} \in \mathbb{R}^{m \times n}$ is the restored image. μ_a is the average of a, σ_a is the standard deviation of a, and c_1 and c_2 are some constants for stability.

Figures 2 and 3 display the restoration results for image ('map1' and 'map2') by our proposed model, where the noise level $\sigma = 2, 3$, respectively. Table 1 shows that the PSNR values for the different test images can be got by using the proposed model. It is obvious that the proposed model is fairly effective in reducing the speckle noise in some images (Fig. 5).

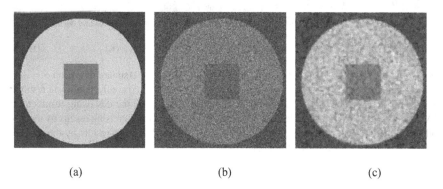

| (a) | (b) | (c) |

Fig. 2. Numerical result of the 'map1' image with noise standard deviation $\sigma = 3$. (a) Original image (map1); (b) Noisy image; (c) restored image by the proposed model

Figures 4 and 6 display the restoration results for images ('lena', 'house', 'peppers' and 'boat') through ROF model [13], ATV model [17], JIN's model [12] and the proposed model. Table 2 shows PSNR values for different test images by using the ROF model, ATV model, JIN's model and the proposed model. Compared with traditional models, the proposed model gets the higher PSNR value. This means that our proposed model is available in reducing the speckle noise in some images.

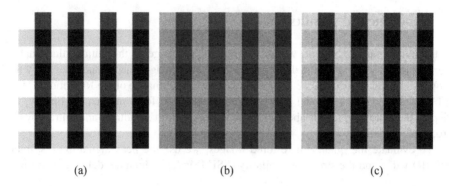

(a)   (b)   (c)

Fig. 3. Numerical result of the 'map2' image with noise standard deviation $\sigma = 2$. (a) Original image (map2); (b) Noisy image; (c) restored image by the proposed model

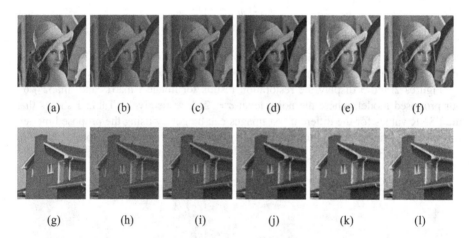

(a)   (b)   (c)   (d)   (e)   (f)

(g)   (h)   (i)   (j)   (k)   (l)

Fig. 4. Numerical result of the 'lena' and 'house' image with noise standard deviation $\sigma = 3$. (a), (g) are Original image; (b), (h) correspond to the noisy version; (c), (i) are the denoising results by the ROF model [13], PSNR = 23.20(lena)/22.48(house); (d), (j) are the denoising results by the ATV model [17], PSNR = 27.88(lena)/27.57(house); (e), (k) are the denoising results by the JIN's model [12], PSNR = 28.49(lena)/27.92(house); (f), (l) are the denoising results by the proposed model, PSNR = 29.07(lena)/28.09(house)

Table 1. Numerical result of the 'map1' and 'map2' image by the proposed model

Image	σ	PSNR	Iter
map1	2	35.12	35
map2	2	36.49	65
map1	3	33.84	65
map2	3	31.48	192

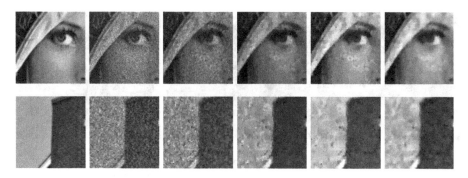

Fig. 5. The detailed image of Fig. 4

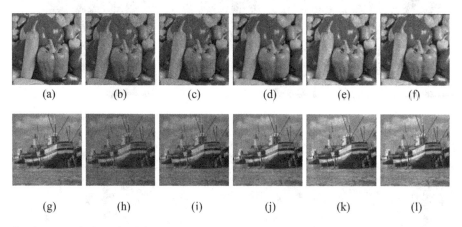

| (a) | (b) | (c) | (d) | (e) | (f) |

| (g) | (h) | (i) | (j) | (k) | (l) |

Fig. 6. Numerical result of the 'peppers' and 'boat' image with noise standard deviation $\sigma = 2$. (a), (g) are Original image; (b), (h) correspond to the noisy version; (c), (i) are the denoising results by the ROF model [13], PSNR = 27.63(peppers)/27.28(boat); (d), (j) are the denoising results by the ATV model [17], PSNR = 28.68(peppers)/27.93(boat); (e), (k) are the denoising results by the JIN's model [12], PSNR = 29.46(peppers)/28.54(boat); (f), (l) are the denoising results by the proposed model, PSNR = 29.57(peppers)/28.71(boat)

Table 2. The PSNR of the restored images by the different model

Image	σ	ROF (PSNR/SSIM)	ATV (PSNR/SSIM)	JIN's (PSNR/SSIM)	Proposed (PSNR/SSIM)
Lena	2	28.16/0.7981	29.96/0.8934	29.98/0.8665	**30.68/0.9035**
House	2	27.48/0.6200	28.96/0.8090	29.56/0.7380	**30.34/0.8097**
Peppers	2	27.63/0.7196	28.68/0.8379	29.46/0.8195	**29.57/0.8468**
Boat	2	27.28/0.8246	27.93/0.8548	28.54/0.8695	**28.71/0.8739**
Lena	3	23.20/0.6385	27.88/0.8098	28.49/0.8298	**29.07/0.8526**
House	3	22.48/0.3985	27.57/0.6771	27.92/0.7125	**28.09/0.7152**
Peppers	3	22.99/0.5122	26.71/0.7421	27.55/0.7841	**27.56/0.7846**
Boat	3	22.69/0.6745	26.48/0.7993	26.85/0.8172	**26.97/0.8181**

Best denoising performance are given in bold

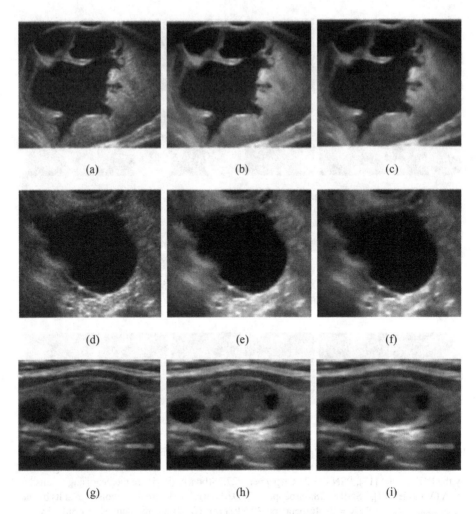

Fig. 7. Numerical result of the real ultrasound image (the real ultrasound image from [18]). (a), (d), (g) are noisy image; (b), (e), (h) are the denoising results by the JIN's model [12]; (c), (f), (1) are the denoising results by the proposed model

Table 3. The iteration of the restored ultrasound images by the different model

Image	JIN's (iter/time)	Proposed (iter/time)
Ultra1	81/0.46 s	**25/0.24 s**
Ultra2	76/0.49 s	**23/0.26 s**
Ultra3	88/0.45 s	**26/0.25 s**

Best denoising performance are given in bold

Figure 7 shows that the experimental results of real ultrasound images by applying JIN's model and the proposed model. Table 3 shows that the different iteration for the different test images by using the JIN's model and the Proposed model. We find that the proposed model is much effective than JIN's model in obtaining the satisfactory restored images.

6 Conclusion

In this paper, we propose a new speckle noise restoration model based on adaptive TV method. A new convex function is introduced as the TV regularization term. The physical characteristics of the local coordinate system are also be analyzed. Our model can avoid the step effect in the smooth region of the image and keep the sharp edge effectively. Numerical experiments results also show the high efficiency of proposed model in image restoration.

Acknowledgement. This paper is partially supported by the Natural Science Foundation of Guangdong Province (2018A030313364), the Science and Technology Planning Project of Shenzhen City (JCYJ20140828163633997), the Natural Science Foundation of Shenzhen (JCYJ20170818091621856) and the China Scholarship Council Project (201508440370).

References

1. Loupas, T., Mcdicken, W., Allan, P.L.: An adaptive weighted median filter for speckle suppression in medical ultrasonic images. IEEE Trans. Circ. Syst. **36**(1), 129–135 (1989)
2. Arsenault, H.: Speckle suppression and analysis for synthetic aperture radar images. Opt. Eng. **25**(5), 636–643 (1986)
3. Kuan, D., Sawchuk, A., Strand, T., et al.: Adaptive restoration of images with speckle. IEEE Trans. Acoust. Speech Sig. Process. **35**(3), 373–383 (1987)
4. Yu, Y., Acton, S.: Speckle reducing anisotropic diffusion. IEEE Trans. Image Process. **11**(11), 1260–1270 (2002)
5. Krissian, K., Westin, C., Kikinis, R., et al.: Oriented speckle reducing anisotropic diffusion. IEEE Trans. Image Process. **16**(5), 1412–1424 (2007)
6. Chan, T., Shen, J.: Mathematical models for local nontexture inpaintings. SIAM J. Appl. Math. **62**(3), 1019–1043 (2001)
7. Chan, T., Kang, S., Shen, J.: Euler's elastica and curvature-based inpainting. SIAM J. Appl. Math. **63**(2), 564–592 (2002)
8. Buades, A., Coll, B., Morel, J.: A review of image denoising algorithms, with a new one. SIAM J. Multiscale Model. Simul. **4**(2), 490–530 (2005)
9. Jin, Q., Grama, I., Kervrann, C., et al.: Nonlocal means and optimal weights for noise removal. SIAM J. Imaging Sci. **10**(4), 1878–1920 (2017)
10. Jin, J., Liu, Y., Wang, Q., et al.: Ultrasonic speckle reduction based on soft thresholding in quaternion wavelet domain. In: IEEE Instrumentation and Measurement Technology Conference, pp. 255–262 (2012)
11. Kang, M., Kang, M., Jung, M.: Total generalized variation based denoising models for ultrasound images. J. Sci. Comput. **72**(1), 172–197 (2017)

12. Jin, Z., Yang, X.: A variational model to remove the multiplicative noise in ultrasound images. J. Math. Imaging Vis. **39**(1), 62–74 (2011)
13. Rudin, L., Osher, S., Fatemi, E.: Nonlinear total variation based noise removal algorithms. Phys. D Nonlinear Phenom. **60**(1–4), 259–268 (2008)
14. Komodakis, N., Tziritas, G.: Image completion using efficient belief propagation via priority scheduling and dynamic pruning. IEEE Trans. Image Process. **16**(11), 2649–2661 (2007)
15. Krissian, K., Kikinis, R., Westin, C.F., et al.: Speckle-constrained filtering of ultrasound images. In: IEEE Computer Society Conference on Computer Vision and Pattern Recognition, pp. 547–552 (2005)
16. Costanzino, N.: Structure inpainting via variational methods. http://www.lems.brown.edu/nc (2002)
17. Fehrenbach, J., Mirebeau, J.: Sparse non-negative stencils for anisotropic diffusion. J. Math. Imaging Vis. **49**(1), 123–147 (2014)
18. Hacini, M., Hachouf, F., Djemal, K.: A new speckle filtering method for ultrasound images based on a weighted multiplicative total variation. Sig. Process. **103**(103), 214–229 (2014)

Frame Interpolation Algorithm Using Improved 3-D Recursive Search

HongGang Xie[1,2(✉)], Lei Wang[1], JinSheng Xiao[3], and Qian Jia[4]

[1] School of Electrical and Electronic Engineering,
Hubei University of Technology, Wuhan 430068, China
xiehg@hbut.edu.cn
[2] Collaborative Innovation Center of Industrial Bigdata,
Hubei University of Technology, Wuhan, China
[3] School of Electronic Information, Wuhan University, Wuhan 430072, China
[4] School of Physics and Information Engineering, Jianghan University,
Wuhan, China

Abstract. A low-complexity and high efficiency method for Motion-Compensated Frame Interpolation is developed in this paper. The 3-D recursive search technique is used together with bilateral motion estimation scheme to predict the block motion vector field without yielding the hole and overlapping problems. A stepwise multi-stage block-motion estimation scheme is designed to deal with the complex motion object in a block. To reduce the block artifact and keep the computational efficiency, a simplified median filter is developed to smooth the estimated motion vector field. Experimental results show that the proposed algorithm provides a better image quality than several broadly used methods both objectively and subjectively. The high computational efficiency makes this proposed algorithm a useful tool for real-time decoder of high-quality video sequences.

Keywords: Frame rate up conversion
Motion Compensated Interpolation (MCI) · Bilateral Motion Estimation (BME)
3-D Recursive Search (3-D RS) · Multi-stage block segmentation

1 Introduction

Video data is usually encoded to low bitrate when it is transmit through bandwidth-limited channels. To restore the original frame rate and improve the temporal quality, Frame rate up-conversion (FRUC) is necessary at the decoder side. People usually use frame interpolation technique to reconstruct the video. How to accurately reconstruct the skipped frames without introducing significant computational complexity is a key challenge in real-time video broadcast applications.

As most of the video including moving object, algorithms considering motion-compensated frame interpolation (MCFI) have been developed to reduce the motion jerkiness and blurring of moving objects in the interpolated frames caused by some simple approaches of frame reconstruction. The interpolation performance can be improved significantly in this way. The key point in MCFI algorithms to accurately

© Springer Nature Switzerland AG 2018
J.-H. Lai et al. (Eds.): PRCV 2018, LNCS 11256, pp. 203–212, 2018.
https://doi.org/10.1007/978-3-030-03398-9_18

obtain the motion vector field of the moving objects basing on which interpolating frames including true motion information could be reconstructed faithfully. Considering the lower computational complexity, block-matching algorithms (BMA) are usually used for motion estimation (ME) in most MCFI algorithms [1, 2]. Several approaches for accurate motion estimation have been proposed recently [3–5], among these, the 3-D recursive ME proposed by Hann et al. [6] have been applied to several MCFI scheme due to its fast convergence and the good performance on smoothness of velocity field.

When BMA is used for MCFI, hole and overlapping problems often occur which degrade the qualities of the interpolate frames significantly. Several methods have been proposed to handle the hole and overlapped regions [7–10], for example the median filter [7], and an improved sub-pixel blocking matching algorithm [9].However these methods are complicated. Bilateral ME (BME), which has been used by several MCFI schemes to estimate the motion vectors of an interpolating frame directly [11, 12], is a scheme preventing the hole and overlapping problems with high efficiency.

General BMAs are based on the assumption that the motion vector in a block is uniform. Block artifact will occur in the interpolated frame when the objects in a block have multiple motions. Block artifact can be reduced by using overlapped block MC (OBMC) technique [13]. However, the quality of the interpolated frame may be degraded due to over smoothing effect when OBMC is used to all blocks uniformly. Kim and Sunwoo [11] dealt well with the block artifact by employing adaptive OBMC and applying the variable-size block MC scheme. Though their algorithm is rather complex, they provide a proper way to reduce block artifact.

In this paper, we propose a low-complexity MCFI method with good performance. The 3DRS and BME are integrated to work for the motion estimation of the interpolated frame, which predict a smooth and accurate motion vector field with low complexity and prevent the occurrences of hole and overlapping regions. The block artifact is reduced by applying a simplified median filter without introducing much computing burden. Moreover, the proposed algorithm applies a motion segmentation scheme to divide a frame into several object regions and using a three-stage block MC (TSBMC) scheme to further reduce the blocking artifacts.

2   Proposed Algorithm

The proposed method comprises several steps, as shown in Fig. 1. First, the 3DRS is used together with BME to predict the motion vector field of the interpolated frame from the information in the former and the following frames. The initial block is set to be 16 × 16. Second, the up-to-three-stage motion segmentation will be performed to ensure that each motion vector in a complicate motion could be accurately estimated. Third, a simplified median filter is performed to further smooth the motion vectors of all the three-stage blocks. Finally, overlapped block motion compensation (OBMC) is employed to generate the interpolated frame.

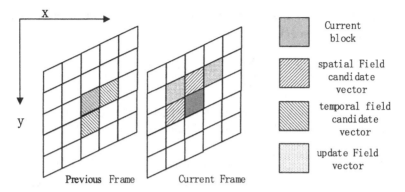

Fig. 1. 3-D RS temporal and spatial estimation candidate vector.

2.1   3-D Recursion Search and Bilateral Motion Estimation

We employ 3DRS [6] method to predict the motion vectors of the interpolated frame. The search of the block motion vector is in the order of raster scan. We get the first motion vector estimator $\vec{V}_a$ of each block in the interpolated frame by scanning the blocks forward from top left to bottom right, and then calculate the second estimator $\vec{V}_b$ by scanning the blocks backward from bottom right to top left. For a block $B(\bar{X})$ with N × N pixels in the interpolated frame, where $\bar{X} = (X, Y)$ is the position in the block grids, the $\vec{V}(\bar{X})$ is obtained by searching the candidate vector set CV_a:

$$CV_a = \left\{ \begin{array}{l} \vec{V}(\bar{X} - u_x, t), \vec{V}(\bar{X} - u_y, t), \\ \vec{V}(\bar{X} + u_x, t - T), \vec{V}(\bar{X}, t - T), \vec{V}(\bar{X} + u_y, t - T), \\ \vec{V}(\bar{X} - u_x - u_y, t) + U_{\vec{V}}, \vec{V}(\bar{X} + u_x - u_y, t) + U_{\vec{V}} \end{array} \right\} \qquad (1)$$

where u_x and u_y are horizontal and vertical unit grid in block grids, t is the time, T is the field period, $\vec{V}(\cdot, t)$ is spatial correlated candidate vector which has been estimated, $\vec{V}(\cdot, t - T)$ is temporal correlated candidate vector which has be obtained from the previously interpolated frame, $U_{\vec{V}}$ is the update vector which follows [6] as:

$$U_{\vec{V}} = \left\{ \begin{pmatrix} 0 \\ 0 \end{pmatrix}, \begin{pmatrix} 0 \\ 1 \end{pmatrix}, \begin{pmatrix} 0 \\ -1 \end{pmatrix}, \begin{pmatrix} 0 \\ 2 \end{pmatrix}, \begin{pmatrix} 0 \\ -2 \end{pmatrix}, \begin{pmatrix} 1 \\ 0 \end{pmatrix}, \begin{pmatrix} -1 \\ 0 \end{pmatrix}, \begin{pmatrix} 3 \\ 0 \end{pmatrix}, \begin{pmatrix} -3 \\ 0 \end{pmatrix} \right\} \qquad (2)$$

The candidate vectors are shown in Fig. 1. The resulting $\vec{V}(\bar{X})$ should equal to the candidate vector $\vec{V}$ in CV_a with the smallest match error $e(\vec{V}, \bar{X}, t)$.

To avoid the occurrence of hole or overlapping problems in the interpolated frame, we apply BME instead of unidirectional estimation (Fig. 2). Information in previous and the following frames are used to calculate the match error. Let x denote a pixel in the interpolated frame f_t, f_{t-1} and f_{t+1} denote consecutive frames in a video sequence. The match error function $e(\vec{V}, \bar{X}, t)$ is set to be:

$$e(\vec{V}, \bar{X}, t) = \sum_{x \in B(\bar{X})} \left| f_{t-1}(x - \vec{V}) - f_{t+1}(x + \vec{V}) \right| \tag{3}$$

Hann et al. [6] added penalties related to the length of the difference vector to the error function to distinguish the priority of different types of candidate vectors.

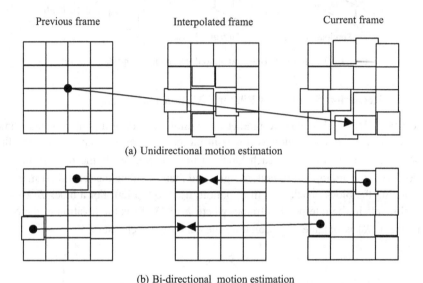

(a) Unidirectional motion estimation

(b) Bi-directional motion estimation

Fig. 2. Unidirectional motion estimation and bilateral motion estimation.

Here we simplify the added penalties α to three constants 0, 1, 2 for spatial candidate vector, temporal candidate vector, and update vector, respectively. Which assure the priority of the candidate vector being in the order of spatial estimation, temporal estimation and update vector estimation. The estimator $\vec{V}_a$ is obtained by the following formula:

$$\vec{V} = \arg \min_{\vec{V} \in CV_a} \{ e(\vec{V}, \bar{X}, t) + \alpha \} \tag{4}$$

We then search backward to get the second estimator $\vec{V}_b$ for each block $B(\bar{X})$. The candidate set of motion vector now is CV_b (as shown in Fig. 1):

$$CV_b = \left\{ \begin{array}{l} \vec{V}(\bar{X} + u_x, t), \vec{V}(\bar{X} + u_y, t), \\ \vec{V}(\bar{X} - u_x, t - T), \vec{V}(\bar{X}, t - T), \vec{V}(\bar{X} - u_y, t - T), \\ \vec{V}(\bar{X} - u_x + u_y, t) + U_{\vec{V}}, \vec{V}(\bar{X} + u_x + u_y, t) + U_{\vec{V}} \end{array} \right\} \tag{5}$$

$\vec{V}_b(\bar{X})$ is obtained from CV_b by the same way as obtaining $\vec{V}_a(\bar{X})$. The final estimated displacement vector $\vec{V}(\bar{X})$ for block $B(\bar{X})$ is set to be the estimator with the smaller match error. i.e.

$$\vec{V}(\bar{X}) = \begin{cases} \vec{V}_a(\bar{X}), & \text{if } e(\vec{V}_a, \bar{X}, t) < e(\vec{V}_b, \bar{X}, t) \\ \vec{V}_b(\bar{X}), & \text{if } e(\vec{V}_a, \bar{X}, t) > e(\vec{V}_b, \bar{X}, t) \end{cases} \tag{6}$$

$\vec{V}(\bar{X})$ is assigned to all the pixels in block $B(\bar{X})$.

2.2 Multi-stage Block Motion Estimation

After the 3DRS and BME, we get the estimated motion vector and the match error for each block $B(\bar{X})$ in the interpolated frame. The initial block size is set to be 16×16 pixels in this paper. For a block with multiple moving object, the estimated vector is not the actual vector for all the pixels in this block which will result in a quite big match error. Thus we can find these blocks out and search the proper motion vectors for different pixels in this block in a way described as follows.

Multi-stage Block Segmentation

1. *Perform the simplified median filter.* If the match error of a block is larger than a predefined threshold, the block is labeled to be processed further.
2. *Splite the labeled block with size of 16 × 16 pixels into four 8 × 8 sub-blocks; Estimate the motion vector of each sub-block by using the 3DRS and BME method.* Perform the simplified median filter; Assign the new estimated motion vector to pixels in the sub-block. If the match error of a sub-block is larger than $\tau/4$, the sub-block is labeled.
3. *Splite the labeled 8 × 8 sub-block into four 4 × 4 sub-blocks; Estimate the motion vector of each sub-block by using Hexagon search method.* Assign the new estimated motion vector to pixels in the corresponding 4 × 4 sub-blocks. Perform the simplified median filter. If the match error of a 4 × 4 sub-block is larger than, the motion vector of this sub-block is set to be the median of its neighbor blocks.

The simplified median filter method will be described in the following section.

Multi-stage Block Motion Vector Correction.

If the motion field estimated in some positions (usually at boundaries of some blocks) are discontinuous, motion compensation may introduce visible block structures in the interpolated picture. The size we adopted here will give rise to very visible artifacts. A post-filter on the vector is often used to overcome this problem [1].

It has to be pointed out that the classical 3×3 block median filter is rather complex for an on-time FRUC algorithm. Therefore we simplify the median filter to lower the computational complexity of proposed MCI algorithm.

For a block $B(\bar{X})$ of size N × N (N = 16, 8, or 4), the median filter is performed on a window of 3 × 3 blocks of the same size centered at $B(\bar{X})$. We label each of the nine blocks with a certain number between 1 and 9, and denote them as B_k, $k = 1, \cdots, 9$. We set penalties $P_x(k)$ and $P_y(k)$ to each of the x and y components of the estimated vector of block B_k.we sort the x and y of the estimated vector separately in descending order, and denote the respective ordered matrix of subscript as I_x and I_y. Let $AP = (4, 3, 2, 1, 0, 1, 2, 3, 4)$ and $BP = (20, 15, 10, 5, 0, 5, 10, 15, 20)$ be two constant matrixes. We also denote the estimated vector of the center block as $\vec{V} = (v_x, v_y)$. $P_x(k)$ and $P_y(k)$ are set as following:

$$if \quad v_x > v_y, \begin{cases} P_x(k) = BP(I_x(k)), \\ P_y(k) = AP(I_y(k)) \end{cases} k = 1, \cdots, 9$$

$$else, \begin{cases} P_x(k) = AP(I_x(k)), \\ P_y(k) = BP(I_y(k)) \end{cases} k = 1, \cdots, 9 \tag{7}$$

After that, we find out the block B_{k0} with the minimum sum of $P_x(k0)$ and $P_y(k0)$. The median vector $\vec{V}_m = (v_{mx}, v_{my})$ of this 3 × 3 window is set to be estimated vector of B_{k0}. The estimated vector $\vec{V} = (v_x, v_y)$ of the central block $B(\bar{X})$ is replaced according to the following rule:

$$\vec{V} = \begin{cases} \vec{V}, \text{ when } |v_x - v_{mx}| < T, \text{ and } |v_y - v_{my}| < T \\ \vec{V}_m, \quad otherwise \end{cases} \tag{8}$$

where $T = 8, 4$ and 2 for the blocks of size 16 × 16, 8 × 8, and 4 × 4 pixels, respectively. This simplified median filter method is effective in finding out the actual motion vector and lower the complexity of the post-filter significantly.

After the motion field of the interpolated frame is obtained, we reconstruct the interpolated frame by using the information in the previous and the following frames according to the following formula:

$$f(x, t) = \frac{1}{2} \left(f_{t-1}(x - \vec{V}) + f_{t+1}(x + \vec{V}) \right) \tag{9}$$

We perform this simplified median filter method and a classical median-filter method [1] to interpolate the even frames in akiyo video sequence for comparison. The interpolated 142th frames by these two methods are shown in Fig. 3. It shows that the proposed filter method is effective in reducing the block artifacts.

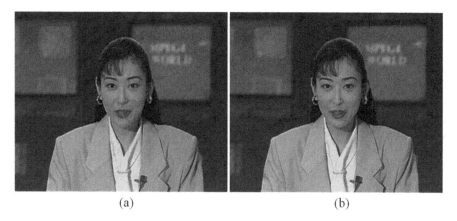

(a)   (b)

Fig. 3. The 142th interpolated frame in akiyo Sequence. (a) Interpolated Frame Obtained by MV Median Filter Method in [1]. (b) Interpolated Frame Obtained by improved MV Median Filter.

3   The Experiment Result and Analysis

Eight video sequences (YUV4:2:0) are used to demonstrate the performance of the proposed algorithm. Seven of them are in CIF standard format, which are Football, Bowing, Susan, Carphone, News, Silent, and Forman sequences; the Sunflower sequence is in HD standard format. These eight video sequences involve almost all kinds of motions except for rotating and zooming, therefore, the evaluation of the proposed algorithm is convincing.

In evaluating, the frame rate of each sequence is halved first by skipping the even frames. And then we interpolate the skipped frames to restore the original frame rate by applying the proposed MCFI algorithm.

3.1   Objective Evaluation

The quality of interpolated frame is measured by computing the PSNR between the interpolated frame and the corresponding original frame. We implemented two other methods and compare the PSNR with our proposed method. Method 1 is full search BME algorithm with traditional median filter for post-processing of estimated motion vector. The block size is set to be 16×16 pixels for BME step, and the search radius is 8 blocks. Method 2 is a MCI algorithm based on predictive motion vector field adaptive search technique described in [14]. We also cite the PSNR results of Method 3 [15], where only four video sequences in CFI standard format are involved. The PSNR results are shown in Table 1. The average PSNR values of the eight test sequences are 32.47, 33.14, and 33.22 for method 1, method 2 and the proposed method. The proposed method achieves higher PSNR performance in average than the other methods. The proposed method performs better than method 1 in 6 test sequences except for Carphone and Forman sequences, and better than method 2 in 7 test sequences except for the Sunflower sequence. In the Football sequence and Susan sequence, the PSNR of proposed method is increased more than 2 dB comparing to method 1.

Table 1. Average PSNR (dB) of different test sequences adopting

Sequence	Number of Interpolated Frames	Method 1	Method 2 [14]	Method 3 [15]	Proposed Method
Bowing	150	42.55	42.61	—	42.71
News	150	34.62	35.33	35.60	35.46
Silent	150	34.90	35.67	35.44	35.79
Forman	150	33.72	33.21	32.37	33.37
Susan	14	28.60	30.73	—	30.98
Football	130	20.37	22.60	21.32	22.70
Carphone	191	29.99	29.65	—	29.71
Sunflower	250	35.02	35.31	—	35.06

Table 2 compares the average processing time of three methods. For the seven test sequences in CFI standard format, the total average processing time are 178.76 ms, 44.95 ms, and 30.85 ms for method 1, method 2 and the proposed, respectively. The speed of proposed method is obviously faster than the other two methods. While for the Sunflower sequence in HD standard format, the advantage of the proposed method is more prominent. These indicate the computational complexity of the proposed method is greatly lower than the other two methods.

Table 2. Average times (ms) to interpolate frame for algorithms above

Sequence	Method 1	Method 2	Proposed Method
Carphone	24.95	7.57	4.01
An	25.64	8.92	8.92
Bowing	30.94	6.77	4.29
News	31.57	5.56	4.18
Football	31.60	9.20	4.84
Silent	34.06	6.93	4.61
Sunflower	590.07	174.46	56.80

3.2 Subjective Evaluation

As most of the video sequences are used for viewing, subject image quality is as important as the object quality. Figure 4 shows the 570 interpolated frame in Kristen And Sara 720P video sequence. It can be seen that the subject quality of the proposed method is better than method 1 in the parts of hand and necklace, and better than method 2 in the detail of hand.

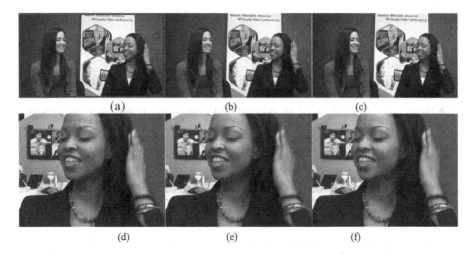

Fig. 4. Subjective Quality in the interpolated Frame of Kristen And Sara Sequence. (a) No. 1 Method. (b) No. 2 Method. (c) Method in this paper. (d) Enlarge Fig (a) partially. (e) Enlarge Fig (b) partially. (f) Enlarge Fig (c) partially.

4   Conclusion

This paper proposes a multi-stage block MCI FRUC algorithm. 3DRS and BME is adopted to estimate the motion vector of the interpolated frame. A simplified median filter method is designed to post process the motion field. The penalty in error function of classical 3DRS is improved. We compared the performance of the proposed algorithm with those of other two methods. Method 1 is the conventional full search motion estimation plus median filter, method 2 is an adaptive BME algorithm. Test results demonstrate that the proposed algorithm provides better image quality than the other two methods both objectively and subjectively. Specifically it is shown that the computational complexity of the proposed algorithm is rather low. For all the seven CFI test sequences, the proposed algorithm runs 5.7 times faster than method 1 in average, and 1.5 times faster than method 2; while for the HD test sequence, the proposed algorithm runs 10 times faster than method 1 and 3 times faster than method 2. The proposed algorithm is suitable for the application of real-time FRUC of HD videos.

Acknowledgment. This work was supported in part by the National Natural Science Foundation of China (Grant No. 61573002), and Hubei Provincial Natural Science Foundation of China (Grant No. 2016CFB499).

References

1. Zhai, J., et al.: A low complexity motion compensated frame interpolation method. In: IEEE International Symposium on Circuits and Systems, pp. 4927–4930. IEEE (2005)
2. Wu, C.M., Huang, J.Y.: A new block matching algorithm for motion estimation. In: Applied Mechanics and Materials, vol. 855, pp. 178–183. Trans Tech Publications (2017)
3. Konstantoudakis, K., et al.: High accuracy block-matching sub-pixel motion estimation through detection of error surface minima. Multimedia Tools Appl. 1–20 (2017)
4. Al-kadi, G., et al.: Meandering based parallel 3DRS algorithm for the multicore era. In: IEEE International Conference on Digest of Technical Papers, pp. 21–22 (2010)
5. Takami, K., et al.: Recursive Bayesian estimation of NFOV target using diffraction and reflection signals. In: IEEE International Conference on Information Fusion (FUSION), pp. 1923–1930 (2016)
6. De Haan, G., et al.: True-motion estimation with 3-D recursive search block matching. IEEE Trans. Circuits Syst. Video Technol. 3(5), 368–379 (1993)
7. Kuo, T.Y., Kuo, C.-C.J.: Motion-compensated interpolation for low-bit-rate video quality enhancement. In: Proceedings of SPIE Visual Communication Image Process, vol. 3460, pp. 277–288 (1998)
8. Yang, Y.-T., Tung, Y.-S., Wu, J.-L.: Quality enhancement of frame rate up-converted video by adaptive frame skip and reliable motion extraction. IEEE Trans. Circuits Syst. Video Technol. 17(12), 1700–1713 (2007)
9. Xiao, J., et al.: Detail enhancement of image super-resolution based on detail synthesis. Signal Process. Image Commun. 50, 21–33 (2017)
10. Jeon, B.-W., Lee, G.-I., Lee, S.-H., Park, R.-H.: Coarse-to-fine frame interpolation for frame rate up-conversion using pyramid structure. IEEE Trans. Consum. Electron. 49(3), 499–508 (2003)
11. Kim, U.S., Sunwoo, M.H.: New frame rate up-conversion algorithms with low computational complexity. IEEE Trans. Circuits Syst. Video Technol. 24(3), 384–393 (2014)
12. Kim, J.-H., et al.: Frame rate up-conversion method based on texture adaptive bilateral motion estimation. IEEE Trans. Consum. Electron. 60(3), 445–452 (2014)
13. Orchard, M.T., Sullivan, G.J.: Overlapped block motion compensation: an estimation-theoretic approach. IEEE Trans. Image Process. 3(5), 693–699 (1994)
14. Li, L., Hou, Z.-X.: Research on adaptive algorithm for frame rate up conversion. Appl. Res. Comput. 4(26), 1575–1577 (2009)
15. Choi, K.-S., Hwang, M.-C.: Motion-compensated frame interpolation using a parabolic motion model and adaptive motion vector selection. ETRI J. 33(2), 295–298 (2011)

Image Segmentation Based on Semantic Knowledge and Hierarchical Conditional Random Fields

Cao Qin[1], Yunzhou Zhang[1,2(⊠)], Meiyu Hu[1], Hao Chu[2], and Lei Wang[2]

[1] College of Information Science and Engineering, Northeastern University,
Shenyang, China
zhangyunzhou@mail.neu.edu.cn
[2] Faculty of Robot Science and Engineering, Northeastern University,
Shenyang, China

Abstract. Semantic segmentation is a fundamental and challenging task for semantic mapping. Most of the existing approaches focus on taking advantage of deep learning and conditional random fields (CRFs) based techniques to acquire pixel-level labeling. One major issue among these methods is the limited capacity of deep learning techniques on utilizing the obvious relationships among different objects which are specified as semantic knowledge. For CRFs, their basic low-order forms cannot bring substantial enhancement for labeling performance. To this end, we propose a novel approach that employs semantic knowledge to intensify the image segmentation capability. The semantic constraints are established by constructing an ontology-based knowledge network. In particular, hierarchical conditional random fields fused with semantic knowledge are used to infer and optimize the final segmentation. Experimental comparison with the state-of-the-art semantic segmentation methods has been carried out. Results reveal that our method improves the performance in terms of pixel and object-level.

Keywords: Image segmentation · Semantic knowledge · Ontology
Conditional random fields

1 Introduction

Mobile robots intended to perform in human environments need to access a world model that includes the representation of the surroundings. Since most people concentrate on the accurate geometry of the world, the semantic information arises and becomes a vital factor that assists the robot in executing tasks. Semantic segmentation can just provide this kind of information. Its purpose is

Research supported by National Natural Science Foundation of China (No. 61471110, 61733003), National Key R&D Program of China (No. 2017YFC0805000/5005), Fundamental Research Funds for the Central Universities (N172608005, N160413002).

© Springer Nature Switzerland AG 2018
J.-H. Lai et al. (Eds.): PRCV 2018, LNCS 11256, pp. 213–225, 2018.
https://doi.org/10.1007/978-3-030-03398-9_19

to divide the image into several groups of pixels with a certain meaning and to assign the corresponding label to each region. However, image semantic segmentation has become an intractable task due to the varieties of different objects, unconstrained layouts of indoor environments.

The seemingly complicated living environments for people possess a variety of repeated specific structures and spatial relations between different objects. For instance, a monitor is more likely found in a living room than in a kitchen. Also, a cup is more likely on the table than on the floor. Such kinds of specific objects and spatial relations can be defined as an alternative semantic knowledge which improves the quality of image segmentation and helps robots to recognize the interesting things.

Traditional image segmentation methods [5] take advantage of the low-level semantic information, including the color, texture, and shape of the image, to achieve the purpose of segmentation. But the result is not ideal enough in the case of complex scenes. In recent years, researchers have been committed to using convolution neural networks to enhance the segmentation of images. However, the method of deep learning to deal with the pixel tags only draws the outline of the objects coarsely. There also exists the problem that only local independent information is accessible and the deficiency of surrounding context constraints. [6] constructed the Conditional Random Fields model (CRF) [13] according to the pixel results produced by the neural network. This approach is designed to enhance the smoothness of the label, maintain the mask consistency of the adjacent pixels. Although the above-mentioned methods achieve remarkable pixel-level semantic segmentation, they only make use of the constrained relations among low-level features.

In this paper, we propose a semantic knowledge based hierarchical CRF approach to image semantic segmentation. Our method not only achieves better segmentation effect at pixel-level but also gets great improvements on the object-level. Figure 1 shows the overall framework of our method and the main contributions are summarized as follows:

- We construct an ontology-based knowledge network which is utilized to express the semantic constraints.
- We first propose an original hierarchical CRF model fused with semantic knowledge from the ontology.
- We make great progress in error classification at object-level by embedding the global observation of the image and using the high-level semantic concept correlation.

2 Related Works

2.1 Image Segmentation Based on CNNs and CRFs

Semantic image segmentation has been always a popular topic in the field of computer vision. In recent years, the methods of deep convolution neural network have made an unprecedented breakthrough in this field. [8] proposed an

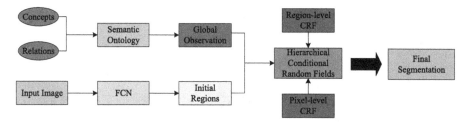

Fig. 1. Overall framework of our method. Concepts and relations are gathered from human's elicitation according to the image database. Global observation is derived from the semantic ontology network composed of the concepts and relations. FCN [15] accepts inputting image in any size and generates initial segmentation region which is utilized in both pixel-level CRF and region-level CRF. A hierarchical CRF model is constructed to combine two kinds of CRF models and produces the final segmentation.

R-CNN (regions with CNN features) method which combined region proposals with CNNs. It deals with the problem of object detection and semantic segmentation but needs a lot of storage and has limitation on efficiency. Prominent work FCN [15] designed a novel end to-end fully convolutional network which accepted inputting image for any size and achieved pixel classification. Based on FCN, Vijay et al. [3] replicated the maximum pooling index and constructed an original and practical deep fully CNN architecture called SegNet. Although these methods have made good progress through CNNs, they lack the spatial consistency because of the neglect of the relationship between pixels.

On the basis of [15], Zheng et al. [22] modeled the conditional random fields as a recurrent neural network. This network utilized the back propagation algorithm for end-to-end training directly without the offline training on CNN and CRF models respectively. Lin et al. [14] introduced the contextual information into the semantic segmentation, and improved the rough prediction by capturing the semantic relations of the adjacent image. In contrast to the above methods, our method pays more attention to improve the segmentation of the region and object layer, which also help to promote the segmentation accuracy at the pixel level in a subtle way.

2.2   Semantic Knowledge

Semantics, as the carrier of knowledge information, transform the whole image content into intuitive and understandable semantic expression. Ontology has become a standard expressive form of relations between semantic concepts.

Wang et al. [20] constructed ontology network using the OWL DL language. Ontology network captures the hidden relationships between features in the feature diagrams precisely and helps to solve the task of feature modeling. An ontology-based approach to object recognition was presented in [7]. It endowed the object semantic meaning through the relations between the objects and the concepts in the ontology. Ruiz et al. [17] utilized the expert knowledge established

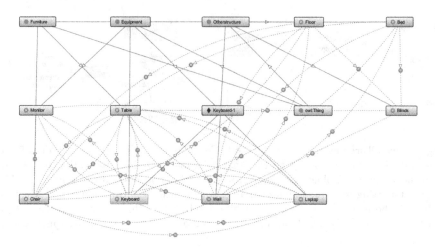

Fig. 2. A part of established ontology on the images of the NUY v2 dataset. The root concept is *Thing*. The blue, purple and brown lines represent the relation *has_subclass*, *has_individual* and *hasAppearedwith*, respectively. (Color figure online)

manually to extract semantic knowledge and trained probabilistic graph model. Subsequently, they proposed a hybrid system based on probabilistic graph model and semantic knowledge in [18]. The system makes full use of the context of the object in the image and shows excellent recognition effect even in complex or uncertain scenes. However, this method requires the laboriously manual design of the training data of the PGM model and only gets performance in the aspect of object recognition.

A related but very different work to our method is introduced in [21]. This work facilitated the semantic information to transform the low-level features of the image into the high-level feature space and assign the corresponding class labels to each object parts. In our work, we obtain the prediction directly from the FCN and utilize the combination of hierarchical CRFs and the ontology network to optimize the regional label. It has great advantages in efficiency because it does not need to train multiple CRF models.

2.3   Hierarchical CRFs

Primary CRF model only uses the local features of the images, such as pixel features and cannot utilize the high-level features, such as regional features and global features. [19] adopted the original potential energy function of CRF to define the constraint relation between the local feature and the high-level features and constructed the hierarchical CRF model. Huang et al. [10] established a hierarchical two-stage CRF model on the basis of the idea of parametric and nonparametric image labeling. Benjamin et al. [16] paid attention to both the pixel and object-level performance by merging region-based CRF model with dense pixel random fields in a hierarchical way. Compared with [16], our approach adds the global observation information from the ontology network into the hierarchical CRF which makes the system more robust in the global segmentation performance.

3   Approach

3.1   Semantic Knowledge Acquirement

3.1.1   Ontology Definition

Different semantic labels will appear in the same image. An image is usually labeled with a variety of semantic labels. The ontology is a clear and formal specification of shared concepts that is applied to define concepts and the relationships between concepts and concepts. In this work, we utilize the ontology as the carrier of semantic knowledge to form a reasoning engine for object labeling. Ontology is generated by human elicitation. For example, an indoor scene can be modeled by defining the types of objects that occur in the environment. E.g. Desk, Table, Bookshelf, etc.... In addition, the properties of the object and the contextual relations that exist between the objects should be formulated. As Fig. 2 illustrates, a multi-layer ontology-based structure is proposed to give the most understandable semantic representation of the image content. This graph is generated by using the software Protégé[11] based on the OWL DL language. The root concept is *Thing*, and its subordinate concept such as *furniture*, *equipment*, and *otherstructures* are easy to be found in a typical indoor environment. The ultimate goal of using ontology is to ensure that the labels of objects appearing in the image are consistent.

3.1.2   Semantic Constraints

The situation that objects contained in a specific scene owns certain probability of occurrence from the overall consideration. Therefore, each class that appears in the ontology should have a propriety which is defined as *has_Frequency* from the perspective of fuzzy description logics [2]. More importantly, what we should consider is how to generate the probability that two objects appear in one scene at the same time. We define the co-occurrence of the two objects by rule *hasAppearedwith* in the ontology.

As mentioned above, the context relations between objects are obtained by fuzzy description logics. The occurrence probability of a concept and the previous definition *has_Frequency* of each class are defined by the following formula:

$$has\_Frequency(C_i) = prob(C_i) = \frac{n_i}{N} \tag{1}$$

Where n_i refers to numbers of concept C_i appears in the image. N represents the number of images used in the dataset. Similarly, the probability of two objects appear in an image at the same time is formulated:

$$prob(C_i, C_j) = \frac{n_{i,j}}{N} \tag{2}$$

$n_{i,j}$ refers to the number of images in which concept C_i and C_j appear simultaneously in an image. On the basis of equation (2), we compute the Normalized Pointwise Mutual Information (NPMI) according to [4]:

$$p(C_i, C_j) = log\frac{prob(C_i, C_j)}{prob(C_i) * prob(C_j)} \tag{3}$$

If C_i and C_j are independent concepts mutually, it is easy to deduce that $prob(C_i, C_j) = 0$. In a word, $prob(C_i, C_j)$ measures the the degree of sharing information between concept C_i and C_j.

To normalize $prob(C_i, C_j)$ to the interval $[0, 1]$, we obtain the fuzzy representation of $hasAppearedwith$:

$$hasAppearedwith(C_i, C_j) = \frac{p(C_i, C_j)}{-log[max(prob(C_i), prob(C_j))]} \tag{4}$$

3.2 Hierarchical Conditional Random Fields

3.2.1 Pixel-Level CRFs

CRFs applied in semantic segmentation is a probabilistic model for the segmentation of class labels associated with given observation data. In CRF model, observation variable $Y = \{y_1, y_2, ..., y_N\}$ indicates the image pixel and the implicit random variable $X = \{x_1, x_2, ..., x_N\}$ refers to the labels of pixels. Given a graph $G = (V, E)$, $V = \{1, 2, ..., N\}$. $e_{ij} \in E$ means the collection of edges of adjacent variables x_i and x_j. Random variable x is defined over the set $L = \{l_1, l_2, ...l_K\}$. Under the premise of the given condition Y, the joint probability y distribution of the random variable X follows the Gibbs distribution:

$$P(X|y) = \frac{1}{Z}exp(-E(X|y)) \tag{5}$$

Energy function is defined by:

$$E(X|y) = \sum_{i \in V} E_i(x_i) + \alpha \sum_{\{i,j\} \in E} E_{ij}(x_i, x_j) \tag{6}$$

Where α is the weight coefficient, Z is the normalization factor. E_i is the unary potential, which includes the relationship between random variables and the observed values. Unary potential is usually deduced by some other classifiers that generate distributions over class labels. The unary potential used in this paper is produced by the FCN [15]. E_{ij} denotes the pairwise potentials, which represents the smoothness constraints on adjacent pixels for the same label and include the relationships between adjacent random variable nodes. According to [13], we model the pairwise potentials as follows:

$$E_{ij}(x_i, x_j) = u(x_i, x_j) \sum_{a=1}^{M} \omega^{(a)} k^{(a)}(f_i, f_j) \tag{7}$$

Where $k^{(a)}$ is a Gaussian kernel, $w^{(a)}$ is a weight parameter for kernel $k^{(a)}$ and f_i is a feature vector for pixel i. Function $u(.,.)$ is called the label compatibility function, which captures the compatibility between connected pairs of nodes that are assigned different labels. Since the above mentioned two kinds of energy items contain fewer hidden variables, they are also called low-order energy terms.

The main task of semantic segmentation is to select l_i from the set L and assign it to each random variable x_i. Thus, an energy expression is constructed to solve X which meets the maximum of a posteriori probability:

$$X^* = \arg\max_X \ P(X|y) = \arg\min_X \ E(X|y) \tag{8}$$

3.2.2   HCRF

As shown in Fig. 3, HCRF model consists of two layers: the pixel layer and the region layer. The pixel layer is composed of hidden random variable X, whose definition is consistent with the CRF model. The region layer is formed by the segmentation blocks obtained from FCN. $r = \{x_1, x_2, ...x_m\}$ represents a region block unit that is a set of the hidden random variables x. $R = \{r_1, r_2, ...r_p\}$ denotes a collection of all area blocks. According to the model described above, the energy expression for HCRF model is defined as follows:

$$\begin{aligned} E(X|y) = \sum_{i \in V} E_i(x_i) + \alpha \sum_{\{i,j\} \in E} E_{ij}(x_i, x_j) \\ + \beta \sum_{m \in R} E_m(r_m) + \gamma \sum_{\{m,n\} \in E'} E_{mn}(r_m, r_n) \end{aligned} \tag{9}$$

The pixel layer corresponds to the CRF model uses pixels as the basic processing unit, including the low-order energy terms described above. The energy term reflects the constraints of the local texture feature for the pixel class and smoothness constraint between pixels. E_m depicts the unary potential defined in the region layer, which is the key to associating the pixel layer and the segmentation layer. It also reflects the constraints of the descriptive feature to the categories of segmentation region. β and γ are the weights of the corresponding energy function of the region.

The unary potential is divided into two parts in the regional energy function model. The one is the local observation part, which relates to the observation of the image region. The other one is the global observation part, which denotes the observation of relevant semantic label on the entire image dataset. In order to combine the pixel layer and the region layer, the region unary potential is formulated:

$$E_m(r_m) = -ln(f_i^r(x_i)) * occur(x_i) \tag{10}$$

Where $f_i^r(.)$ is the normalized region probability distribution of the region i as the local observation. It is computed from the implicit FCN pixel distribution. $occur(x_i) = prob(x_i)$ is the probability that the label of region r_m occurs in the whole image dataset as the global observation, which is calculated by the

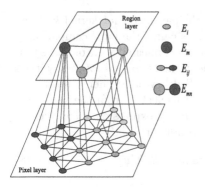

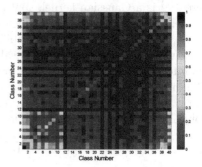

Fig. 3. Illustration of hierarchical conditional random fields. The smaller ellipses correspond to the unary potentials of the pixel, and the larger circles represent the unary potential defined in the region layer. Different colors mean different object labels.

Fig. 4. Visualization of the occurrence probabilities of different classes. Off-diagonal entries are the probabilities of simultaneous occurrence of two concepts, while diagonal entries are the occurrence probabilities of the individual concepts. The class numbers correspond to the 40 different classes in the image dataset. (Color figure online)

has_Frequency in the last section. The global observation of the image is introduced to the unary potential function so that the unary potential is enhanced by the knowledge in a higher level. This is an effective complement to the limitations and deficiencies of the local observations and promotes the modeling ability of the unary potential function.

To take advantage of the context information, we utilize the pairwise potentials between the regions. The pairwise energy term is defined:

$$E_{mn}(r_m, r_n) = \begin{cases} 0 & \text{if } hasAppearedwith(x_m, x_n) \geq \tau \\ T & \text{otherwise} \end{cases} \qquad (11)$$

Where $hasAppearedwith(x_m, x_n)$ implies the probability that the labels of region r_m and r_n appear simultaneously in a picture. τ is a given threshold. T means the given penalty. Pairwise energy term of region E_{mn} is quite different from the pairwise energy term of pixel E_{ij}. E_{ij} encourages adjacent pixels to obtain the same class label. E_{mn} makes the label of the adjacent region in the semantic layer constrained and gives the mark of the irrelevant object in the adjacent area great punishment. Owing to the setting of the above parameters, our method has achieved excellent results in the experiment of misclassification at the object-level, as discussed in Sect. 4.2. As for calculating the weight parameters in the HCRF, we use the method of layer by layer weight parameter learning proposed by AHCRF [19].

The final semantic segmentation results are obtained by minimizing the energy function $E(X|y)$ as described in the formula (8). Because we introduce the potential energy function based on global observation, the graph cut based method proposed by Kahlil et al. [12] is used to complete the model inference.

4 Experiments and Analysis

4.1 Experimental Setup

4.1.1 Dataset

The semantic segmentation method we propose is evaluated by the dataset NYU v2. It contains 1449 images collected from 28 different indoor scenes. The whole dataset is divided into 795 training images and 654 test images. We exploit the 40-classes version provided by Gupta et al. [9]. As shown in Fig. 5, we can see the various objects marked with different colors in the image.

4.1.2 Implementation Details

In our approach, the highly expressive OWL DL language is employed to design and form the ontology of the dataset. In order to build the ontology model and obtain the data we need, we use the Protégé as our ontology editor. The semantic rules are applied on the dataset to construct the ontology. Figure 2 represents the generated ontology for the semantic classes of the NYU v2 dataset. It can be clearly seen that the degree of correlation between the two concepts which is also defined as the fuzzy rule *hasAppearedwith*. It cannot be ignored that *has_Frequency* has become the underlying properties of each concept. Figure 4 visualizes the occurrence probabilities of the concepts as a matrix representation. Element (i, j) of this matrix relates to $prob(C_i, C_j)$ and element (i, i) corresponds to $prob(C_i)$. There are obvious red areas in the lower left corner and the upper right corner of the picture, which indicates that these classes are more likely to appear. In more detail, the class 1 and 2 represent *wall* and *floor* respectively and the class 40 means *otherprop*. These classes are extremely common and appear in almost every image of the dataset.

The semantic segmentation maps are generated by the up-to-date FCN network. In addition, the final result gets improvement by the optimization of back-end hierarchical conditional random fields. Thus, our method will be compared to the effect of FCN only and the FCN with dense CRF [13]. We utilize the TensorFlow [1] to construct the deep CNN in Linux operation system. Our approach runs at 14 Hz on the TITAN-X GPU. Image segmentation is the most computationally intense task, taking 170 ms to segment an image of 480 * 640 pixels.

4.1.3 Evaluation Metrics

The pixel accuracy (PA) is the ratio of correctly labeled pixels in an image to all pixels. It is specified by $\frac{\sum_i N_{ii}}{\sum_{i,j} N_{ij}}$, where N_{ij} represents the number of pixels of label i being labeled as j. Mean accuracy is defined as $\frac{1}{k} \frac{\sum_i N_{ii}}{\sum_j N_{ij} + \sum_j N_{ji} - \sum_i N_{ii}}$.

However, the mere use of the above three criteria at the pixel level is not sufficient to reflect the advantages of the method presented in this paper. Similar to [16], we calculate the number of object False Positives which represents the number of prediction regions that do not have any overlap with a ground truth instance of the same class. It is designed to evaluate the error-classification degree in order to reflect the excellent performance at the object-level.

4.2   Results and Analysis

For the sake of evaluating our method with existing approaches under the same circumstances, we conduct two series of experiments with NYU v2 dataset. First, we train our framework to distinguish between 40 semantic classes and compare our results to [15] directly. We can observe from the Table 1 that our method achieves the best results and outperforms the original FCN by more than 4% in pixel accuracy. Expectedly, we also get progress in Mean IU which achieves 33.4% and outperforms both of the compared methods.

Table 1. Quantitative results on NYU v2 dataset.

Algorithm	Performance			
	Pixel Acc.	Mean Acc.	Mean IU	False Positives
FCN [15]	60.0	42.2	29.2	43726
FCN + Dense CRF [13]	61.5	43.4	31.5	22350
Benjamin et al. [16]	63.4	-	32.5	17668
Ours	65.5	46.0	33.4	9813

In the aspect of object-level, the number of False Positives defined earlier is used to evaluate the performance. FCN results in 43726 False Positives which are much more than any other methods. This is because the initial result of the FCN is coarse, and it is full of false positive samples that have been misclassified as described in Fig. 5. Although Benjamin et al. [16] have made a great improvement on this value, our approach shows a strong dominance in this respect. In our experiments on the test set, we reduce the False Positives by almost 78% over FCN and nearly 50% over [16]. Apparently, it is beneficial to utilize the global observation and hierarchical random fields to optimize the results.

In Fig. 5, we further visually display the qualitative comparison with the other approaches. It shows that the contours of the objects in FCN results are not very clear. More importantly, there are more or less different classes with Ground Truth. From the result of FCN with Dense CRF, we can observe that the performance does not get significantly improved. In our case, our method considers the global observation jointly and leverages the benefit from the HCRF. Therefore, it can achieve more consistent performance with the Ground Truth.

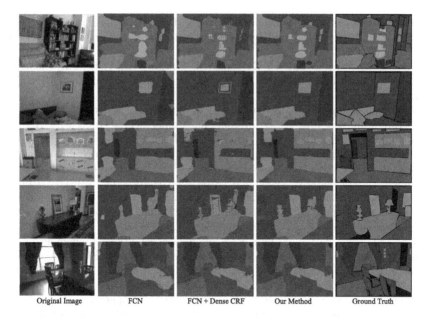

Fig. 5. Qualitative comparison with the other approaches. Left to right column: Original Image, FCN [15], FCN+ Dense CRF [13], Our Method and Ground Truth. Different colors indicate different classes.

5   Conclusion

We propose a novel approach that utilizes semantic knowledge to enhance the image segmentation performance. We formulate the problem in a hierarchical CRF integrated with the global observation. Our method achieves promising results in both pixel and object-level. However, the whole framework is not an end-to-end system and time-consuming. Future work includes replacing FCN with other approach which can achieve better performance on the initial segmentation. We will also improve the method by adding more semantic constrains rather than only using the pair-wise relation.

References

1. Abadi, M., et al.: TensorFlow: large-scale machine learning on heterogeneous distributed systems. arXiv preprint arXiv:1603.04467 (2016)
2. Baader, F.: The Description Logic Handbook: Theory, Implementation and Applications. Cambridge University Press, Cambridge (2003)
3. Badrinarayanan, V., Kendall, A., Cipolla, R.: SegNet: a deep convolutional encoder-decoder architecture for image segmentation. IEEE Trans. Pattern Anal. Mach. Intell. **39**(12), 2481–2495 (2017)
4. Bannour, H., Hudelot, C.: Building and using fuzzy multimedia ontologies for semantic image annotation. Multimed. Tools Appl. **72**, 2107–2141 (2014)

5. Belongie, S., Carson, C., Greenspan, H., Malik, J.: Color- and Texture-Based Image Segmentation Using EM and Its Application to Content-Based Image Retrieval (1998)
6. Chen, L.C., Papandreou, G., Kokkinos, I., Murphy, K., Yuille, A.L.: Semantic image segmentation with deep convolutional nets and fully connected CRFs. Comput. Sci. **4**, 357–361 (2014)
7. Durand, N., et al.: Ontology-based object recognition for remote sensing image interpretation. In: 19th IEEE International Conference on Tools with Artificial Intelligence, ICTAI 2007, vol. 1, pp. 472–479. IEEE (2007)
8. Girshick, R., Donahue, J., Darrell, T., Malik, J.: Rich feature hierarchies for accurate object detection and semantic segmentation. In: Proceedings of the IEEE Conference on Computer Vision and Pattern Recognition, pp. 580–587 (2014)
9. Gupta, S., Arbelaez, P., Malik, J.: Perceptual organization and recognition of indoor scenes from RGB-D images. In: 2013 IEEE Conference on Computer Vision and Pattern Recognition (CVPR), pp. 564–571. IEEE (2013)
10. Huang, Q., Han, M., Wu, B., Ioffe, S.: A hierarchical conditional random field model for labeling and segmenting images of street scenes. In: 2011 IEEE Conference on Computer Vision and Pattern Recognition (CVPR), pp. 1953–1960. IEEE (2011)
11. Knublauch, H., Fergerson, R.W., Noy, N.F., Musen, M.A.: The Protégé OWL plugin: an open development environment for semantic web applications. In: McIlraith, S.A., Plexousakis, D., van Harmelen, F. (eds.) ISWC 2004. LNCS, vol. 3298, pp. 229–243. Springer, Heidelberg (2004). https://doi.org/10.1007/978-3-540-30475-3_17
12. Kohli, P., Torr, P.H., et al.: Robust higher order potentials for enforcing label consistency. Int. J. Comput. Vis. **82**(3), 302–324 (2009)
13. Krähenbühl, P., Koltun, V.: Efficient inference in fully connected CRFs with Gaussian edge potentials. In: Advances in Neural Information Processing Systems, pp. 109–117 (2011)
14. Lin, G., Shen, C., Van Den Hengel, A., Reid, I.: Efficient piecewise training of deep structured models for semantic segmentation. In: Proceedings of the IEEE Conference on Computer Vision and Pattern Recognition, pp. 3194–3203 (2016)
15. Long, J., Shelhamer, E., Darrell, T.: Fully convolutional networks for semantic segmentation. In: Proceedings of the IEEE Conference on Computer Vision and Pattern Recognition, pp. 3431–3440 (2015)
16. Meyer, B.J., Drummond, T.: Improved semantic segmentation for robotic applications with hierarchical conditional random fields. In: 2017 IEEE International Conference on Robotics and Automation (ICRA), pp. 5258–5265. IEEE (2017)
17. Ruiz-Sarmiento, J.R., Galindo, C., Gonzalez-Jimenez, J.: Exploiting semantic knowledge for robot object recognition. Knowl. Based Syst. **86**, 131–142 (2015)
18. Ruiz-Sarmiento, J.R., Galindo, C., Gonzalez-Jimenez, J.: Scene object recognition for mobile robots through semantic knowledge and probabilistic graphical models. Expert. Syst. Appl. **42**(22), 8805–8816 (2015)
19. Russell, C., Kohli, P., Torr, P.H., et al.: Associative hierarchical CRFs for object class image segmentation. In: 2009 IEEE 12th International Conference on Computer Vision, pp. 739–746. IEEE (2009)
20. Wang, H.H., Li, Y.F., Sun, J., Zhang, H., Pan, J.: Verifying feature models using owl. Web Semant. Sci., Serv. Agents World Wide Web **5**(2), 117–129 (2007)

21. Zand, M., Doraisamy, S., Halin, A.A., Mustaffa, M.R.: Ontology-based semantic image segmentation using mixture models and multiple CRFs. IEEE Trans. Image Process. **25**(7), 3233–3248 (2016)
22. Zheng, S., et al.: Conditional random fields as recurrent neural networks. In: Proceedings of the IEEE International Conference on Computer Vision, pp. 1529–1537 (2015)

Fast Depth Intra Mode Decision Based on DCT in 3D-HEVC

Renbin Yang[1], Guojun Dai[1], Hua Zhang[1,2]([⊠]), Wenhui Zhou[1], Shifang Yu[1], and Jie Feng[3]

[1] School of Computer Science and Technology, Hangzhou Dianzi University, Hangzhou, China
zhangh@hdu.edu.cn
[2] Key Laboratory of Network Multimedia Technology of Zhejiang Province, Zhejiang University, Hangzhou, China
[3] Zhejiang SCI-Tech University, Hangzhou, China

Abstract. The state-of-the-art 3D High Efficiency Video Coding (3D-HEVC) is an extension of the High Efficiency Video Coding (HEVC) standard dealing with the multi-view texture videos plus depth map format. But current 3D-HEVC with all intra mode prediction leads to extremely high computational complexity. In this paper, we propose two techniques to speed up the encoding of depth video, including DCT decision and fast CU split decision. For DCT decision, early determination of Depth Modeling Modes (DMMs) is performed if the DCT coefficients in the lower right part of the current Coding Unit (CU) are completely zero. For fast CU split decision, current CU is split when the variance of CU is bigger than threshold. Experimental results demonstrate that the proposed decision can reduce 52.45% coding runtime on average while maintaining considerable rate-distortion (RD) performance as the original 3D-HEVC encoder.

Keywords: 3D-HEVC · Depth map · Mode decision · Intra mode Coding Unit

1 Introduction

With the rapid development of 3D video services, the efficient compression of 3D video data has become a popular research topic over the past few years. 3D-HEVC is an extension of the well-known video coding standard High Efficiency Video Coding (HEVC), and has a more complex and complete structure compared with HEVC and MV-HEVC. The MV-HEVC and 3D-HEVC both use the multi-viewpoint coding structure, while only 3D-HEVC encodes the depth sequences in term of corresponding viewpoints.

Conventional HEVC intra prediction modes were applied in almost smooth depth maps very well, but they will produce ringing effect in the sharp edge, resulting in that the intermediate synthesis view can not meet the expectations of

© Springer Nature Switzerland AG 2018
J.-H. Lai et al. (Eds.): PRCV 2018, LNCS 11256, pp. 226–236, 2018.
https://doi.org/10.1007/978-3-030-03398-9_20

the quality of the video. JCT-3V developed two kinds of intra partition modes for depth maps named DMM1 (Wedgelets) and DMM4 (Contour) [1]. In Wedgelets, the PB (prediction block) is divided into two SBP (sub-block partition) by a straight line. And in Contour, the separation line between the two regions cannot be easily described by a geometrical function.

However, DMMs in the 3D-HEVC mode decision process introduce a huge computational load. There has been many previous works in intra depth of 3D-HEVC [2–10]. Gu et al. [2,3] terminated the unnecessary prediction modes by full RD cost calculation in 3D-HEVC. Park et al. [4] omitted unnecessary DMMs in the mode decision process based on the edge classification results. Peng [5] proposed two techniques including fast intra mode decision and fast Coding Unit (CU) size decision to speed up the encoding of depth video. In [6], Sanchez et al. applied a filter to the borders of the encoded block and determined the best positions to evaluate the DMM 1, reducing the computational effort of DMM 1 process. Zhang et al. [7] simplified the intra mode decision in 3D-HEVC depth map coding based on the way of obtaining the picture texture from the mode with Sum of Absolute Transform Difference (SATD) in rough mode decision. Ruhan [8] put forward a novel early Skip/DIS mode decision for 3D-HEVC depth encoding which aims at reducing the complexity effort of this process. The proposed solution is based on an adaptive threshold model, which takes into consideration the occurrence rate of both Skip and DIS modes. Zhang [9] applied a method for early determination of segment-wise DC coding (SDC) decision based on the hierarchical coding structure. In [10], the proposed algorithm exploits the edge orientation of the depth blocks to reduce the number of modes to be evaluated in the intra mode decision. In addition, the correlation between the Planar mode choice and the most probable modes (MPMs) selected is also exploited, to accelerate the depth intra coding.

This paper proposes propose two techniques to speed up the encoding of depth video, including DCT decision and fast CU split decision. Based on the result of analysis that the CU blocks in the smooth region usually do not perform the DMM mode, we determine DMMs are not added into the candidate modes list if the DCT coefficients in the lower right part of the current CU are completely zero. The experimental results show that the proposed decision reduces 52.45% computational runtime on average while maintaining almost the same coding performance as the original 3D-HEVC encoder.

2 DCT in Depth

Depth maps contain the information of distance. Most depth maps are composed of large nearly constant areas or slowly varying sample values (which represent object areas) and sharp edges (which represent object borders). Thus, the depth map differs from the texture map is that the depth map is composed of large smooth areas and sharp edges. For depth map coding in each CU, there are 37 intra prediction modes, including 35 conventional intra prediction modes and 2 DMMs. And in the DMMs, there are two different types of partition patterns

Table 1. The optimal intra prediction modes of CUs

Sequence	Conventional modes	Contour	Wedgelets
Balloons	98.77%	0.52%	0.71%
Kendo	99.10%	0.37%	0.53%
UndoDancer	99.06%	0.44%	0.50%
GTFly	97.48%	2.07%	0.45%
Newspaper	97.41%	0.93%	1.66%
PoznanHall2	99.74%	0.12%	0.14%
PoznanStreet	99.16%	0.43%	0.41%
Shark	94.96%	4.20%	0.84%
Average	**98.21%**	**1.14%**	**0.65%**

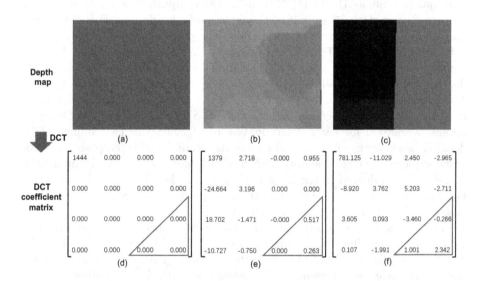

Fig. 1. DCT coefficient matrix in depth (Color figure online)

called Wedgelets and Contour. Table 1 represents that the optimal intra prediction modes of CUs. It contains 98.21% conventional modes and 1.79% DMMs on average. It means that most of DMMs are unnecessary for depth coding [1]. As we known, Wedgelets and Contour are always performed in sharp edges. If CUs contain edges can be identified in advance, the DMMs can be decided that whether to add into the candidate modes list. It will significantly reduce the computational time.

DCT is a transformation associated with Fast Fourier Transform (FFT). 2D DCT is usually used in signal and image processing, especially lossy compression, which has a strong concentration of energy distribution. And DCT is usually used to distinguish smooth region from maps.

As shown in Fig. 1, Fig. 1(a)–(c) is depth maps (4×4), and Fig. 1(d)–(f) is DCT coefficient matrixes. We use $DCT_{lowerright}$ to represent the numbers in the lower right part of the matrix which marked in red triangle. In Fig. 1(d), $DCT_{lowerright}$ are all zero while the depth map in Fig. 1(a) is smooth. The depth map in Fig. 1(b) changes slowly and $DCT_{lowerright}$ in Fig. 1(e) are nearly zero. And in Fig. 1(f), $DCT_{lowerright}$ are not zero because there is an obvious sharp edge in depth map Fig. 1(c). It can be analyzed that for CUs with a slow gray value variation, most energy after DCT is in the upper left part which called low-frequency region. Conversely, if the CUs contain more detail texture information, more energy is scattered in the lower right part, which called high frequency region.

Based on Table 1 and the analysis that only few CUs with edges in depth maps select the best modes as DMMs for intra mode prediction, we conjecture that the $DCT_{lowerright}$, which are all zero, can be used as the basis for judging smooth region. More than 34 hundred million CUs from eight depth sequences released by JCT-3V Group are statisticed, and the results is shown in Table 2. It presents the hit rate of that depth CU chooses conventional HEVC intra mode as the best prediction mode while $DCT_{lowerright}$ are completely zero. It means that about 99% CUs select conventional modes and only less than 1% select DMMs as best intra mode while $DCT_{lowerright}$ are all zero. Thus, DCT can be used to distinguish between smooth regions and sharp edges, which decides DMMs whether to add into the candidate modes list. The current CU only calculate conventional modes with SATD and don't add DMMs into the candidate modes list when $DCT_{lowerright}$ are all zero.

Table 2. Statistical analysis for conventional modes hit rate in 3D-HEVC intra coding

Sequence	Hit rate			
	QP34	QP39	QP42	QP45
Balloons	99.39%	99.75%	99.88%	99.84%
Kendo	99.54%	99.80%	99.89%	99.84%
UndoDancer	99.51%	99.72%	99.51%	98.79%
GTFly	99.31%	99.11%	98.15%	96.67%
Newspaper	98.29%	99.44%	99.78%	99.82%
PoznanHall2	99.78%	99.89%	99.91%	99.85%
PoznanStreet	99.57%	99.91%	99.94%	99.94%
Shark	99.32%	99.23%	99.07%	98.97%
Average	**99.33%**	**99.61%**	**99.52%**	**99.21%**

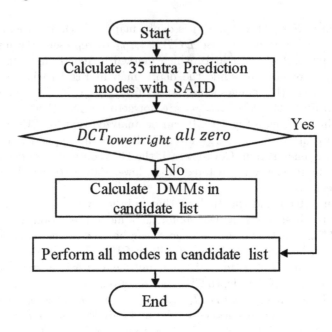

Fig. 2. The processing flow of DCT decision

3   Proposed Decision

Based on the observation in Sect. 2, we propose two fast coding techniques and describe them in detail in the following.

3.1   DCT Decision

We compute the DCT coefficient matrix of current CU and calculate the $DCT_{lowerright}$. If they are not zero, we believe that current CU has sharp edges and DMMs should be added into the candidate modes list for intra mode prediction.

The flowchart of the proposed DCT decision is shown in Fig. 2. If $DCT_{lowerright}$ are all zero, DMMs will not be added into the candidate modes list. Otherwise, all modes in the candidate modes list will be coded. Because of high computational complexity of traditional DCT, we use integer DCT technology of H.265/HEVC, which adopts a fast butterfly-shaped algorithm [11].

However, as shown in Table 3, with the size of CUs increasing, the proportion of the blocks whose $DCT_{lowerright}$ are all zero is decreased. Balloons and Kendo reach 69.76% and 75.44% on average. Big CUs (16×16, 32×32) of GTFly achieves to 30.97% and 17.33%, and PoznanStreet even only achieves up to 14.58% and 5.77%. Small CUs (4×4, 8×8) of GTFly achieves to 86.88% and 60.05%, and PoznanStreet achieves to 64.70% and 34.67%. And the number of small CUs whose $DCT_{lowerright}$ are all zero is greatly larger than big CUs.

Table 3. The proportion of all zero blocks (QP42)

Sequence	Size	Modes with $DCT_{lowerright}$ all zero	All modes	Ratio (%)
Balloons	4×4	40064567	44244224	**90.55**
	8×8	8588702	1106156	**78.52**
	16×16	1662757	2765264	**62.44**
	32×32	289611	691316	**47.53**
Kendo	4×4	41322887	44236800	**93.53**
	8×8	9241840	11059200	**84.27**
	16×16	1881912	2764800	**70.06**
	32×32	339686	691200	**53.88**
GTFly	4×4	84895998	979200	**86.88**
	8×8	14699841	24480000	**60.05**
	16×16	1895485	6120000	**30.97**
	32×32	265191	1530000	**17.33**
PoznanStreet	4×4	63355603	97920000	**64.70**
	8×8	8487299	24480000	**34.67**
	16×16	892209	6120000	**14.58**
	32×32	80580	1530000	**5.77**

Meanwhile, computational complexity of big CUs is higher than the small and it's wasteful to compute the DCT coefficient matrixes whose $DCT_{lowerright}$ are not all zero. Based on the analysis, we believe that it's expensive to compute DCT coefficient matrixes of big CUs.

3.2 Fast CU Split Decision

Depth maps have large smooth and uniform areas. Hence, in current CU split decisions, the runtime of RD-Cost computation can be reduced and the sharp areas should be divided more carefully. Since the DCT decision is not suitable for big CUs, an early CU splitting termination algorithm is proposed.

In 2014, the variance of CU and threshold was firstly used to describe whether the CU is smooth [3]. The algorithm of Park [4] and Peng [5] also use variance as a condition, but Park modified the threshold which determines whether DMMs should be added into the candidate modes list and performed better than Gu. Peng applied threshold and variance in CU split, which shows that the variance and threshold decision is a good method to judge whether the depth map is smooth.

Above all, we choose variance and threshold decision as our fast CU split decision, as is shown in Fig. 3, $Th_{CU} = \{(max(QP \gg 3 - 1, 3))^2 - 8\} \ll 2$. If Var_{CU} is bigger than Th_{CU}, current CU should be divided into four partition CUs. Otherwise, it shows that intra Prediction of current CU performs better than partition CUs.

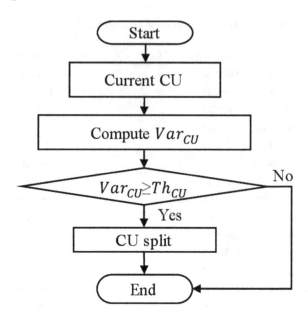

Fig. 3. The processing flow of Fast CU split decision

4   Experimental Results

In the experiments, we test eight sequences to verify the coding efficiency of the proposed decision and 300 frames are tested. All the experiments are implemented on the 3D-HEVC Test Model (HTM13.0) under all intra configuration. The encoder configuration is as follows: 3 view case, the coding treeblock has a fixed size of 64 × 64 pixels and depth range is from 0 to 3. The texture maps use the QPs at 25, 30, 35, 40 and the depth maps use 34, 39, 42, 45. The proposed algorithm is evaluated with Bjontegaard Delta bitrate (BD-rate) and Bjontegarrd Delta bitrate (BD-PSNR) [12] under all-intra configuration. BD-rate represents the total bitrates differences, BD-PSNR represents rendered PSNR change. We define Time Saving (TS) in Eq. (1), which represents reduction of total encoding time, including texture video coding and depth video coding under the all intra configuration.

$$Time\ Saving = 1 - \frac{runtime\ of\ proposed\ algorithm}{runtime\ of\ orignal\ encoder\ (HTM13.0)} \tag{1}$$

Performance of DCT decision compared with encoder (HTM 13.0) is shown in Table 4, four sequences are tested. DCT decision only reduce 5.9% computational complexity on average while achieving 1.0 BD-rate increasing in depth coding. Not surprising, it's a waste of time by computing DCT coefficient matrix of big CUs whose $DCT_{lowerright}$ are all zero.

Table 4. Performance of DCT decision

Sequence	BD-rate in video (%)	BD-rate in depth (%)	TS (%)
Balloons	0.0	0.8	9.2
Kendo	0.0	1.1	9.9
GTFly	0.0	1.9	10.2
PoznanStreet	0.0	0.0	−5.6
Average	**0.0**	**1.0**	**5.9**

Table 5 shows the performance of fast CU split decision under four video sequences. Up to 40.2% time saving is achieved. On average, the time saving is 29.9% at a cost of 0.5% bitrate increasing.

Table 5. Performance of fast CU split decision

Sequence	BD-rate in video (%)	BD-rate in depth (%)	TS (%)
Balloons	0.0	−0.1	24.4
Kendo	0.0	0.1	22.7
GTFly	0.0	0.2	40.2
PoznanStreet	0.0	0.8	32.4
Average	**0.0**	**0.5**	**29.9**

Table 6 presents the detail of time saving of proposed decision under different QPs for four sequences. The proposed decision combines DCT decision and Fast CU Split decision. It can be observed from Table 6 that time saving on average of proposed decision when QP is 25 are almost the same as fast CU split decision. As the QP increases, proposed decision achieves more complexity reduction of coding on average.

Table 6. The detail of Time Saving (%) of proposed decision under different QPs for four sequences

Sequence	QPs			
	25	30	35	40
Balloons	28.5%	32.1%	49.1%	53.3%
Kendo	33.8%	37.0%	52.0%	67.7%
GTFly	39.3%	40.6%	61.5%	66.0%
Poznanstreet	39.3%	40.6%	61.5%	65.9%
Average	**35.2%**	**37.6%**	**56.0%**	**63.2%**

Table 7 shows the experimental results of the coding performance and complexity reduction compared with HTM13.0. Compared with Table 5, although GTFly achieves up to 40.2% time saving in fast CU split decision and 57.0% time saving in proposed decision, it also save 16.8% runtime by DCT decision. It's satisfied that Kendo in proposed decision achieves 46.0% time reduction rather than 22.7% in fast CU split decision. Based on the above, DCT decision can save time by deciding whether to add DMMs into the candidate modes list. And it's obvious that DCT decision performs well in distinguish smooth maps between maps with sharp edges. And proposed decision leads to 0.03 BD-rate increasing for video and 2.71 decreasing for depth on average. It's observed that fast CU split decision only affects time reduction rather than video quality and DCT decision plays an important role in the quality of rebuilt videos. Our proposed decision achieves 52.45% complexity reduction of coding on average. And the proposed decision save time from 37.30% to 68.60% without significant performance loss.

Table 8 compares the proposed algorithm with the state-of-arts for intra coding. The BD-Rate is measured on the synthesized views. Most researches on intra prediction mode decision achieve 27.8%–37.65% time reduction with negligible loss. Our decision can save 52.45% coding runtime while maintaining almost the same RD performance as the original 3D-HEVC encoder.

Table 7. Experimental results compared with original encoder

Sequence		BD-rate (video%)	BD-rate (depth%)	TS (%)
1024 × 768	Balloons	0.00	−0.60	41.7
	Kendo	0.00	−0.10	46.0
	Newspaper	0.00	−4.17	37.3
1920 × 1088	GTFly	0.10	0.97	57.0
	PoznanHall2	0.10	−8.07	68.6
	Poznanstreet	0.00	−9.67	53.4
	UndoDancer	0.00	0.40	63.1
	Shark	0.10	−0.43	52.5
Average		**0.03**	**−2.71**	**52.45**

Table 8. Comparison result

Sequence	Platform	BD-Rate (%)	TS (%)
Gu [2]	HTM 5.1	0.31	27.80
Gu [3]	HTM 7.0	0.30	34.40
Park [4]	HTM 9.1	0.13	37.65
Peng [5]	HTM 13.0	0.80	37.60
Proposed	**HTM 13.0**	**1.10**	**52.45**

5 Conclusion

In this paper, we propose a fast intra mode decision algorithm based on DCT to reduce the computational complexity of 3D-HEVC encoder. Although DCT decision encodes better in small CUs, the ratio of big CUs whose $DCT_{lowerright}$ are all zero is extremely small, which leads to high complexity of DCT. We add existing fast CU split decision into the proposed decision to divide big CUs. The recent 3D-HEVC test model (HTM 13.0) is applied to evaluate the proposed decision. The experimental results show that the proposed decision can significantly save the encoding time while maintaining nearly the same RD performance as the original 3D-HEVC encoder. Meanwhile, it performs well in comparison with the state-of-art fast algorithm for 3D-HEVC.

Acknowledgements. This work is supported by the National Natural Science Foundation of China (No. 61471150, No. 61501402, No. U1509216), the Key Program of Zhejiang Provincial Natural Science Foundation of China (No. LZ14F020003). Thanks for support and assistance from Key Laboratory of Network Multimedia Technology of Zhejiang Province.

References

1. Chen, Y., Tech, G., Wegner, K., Yea, S.: Test model 11 of 3D-HEVC and MV-HEVC. JCT-3V Document, JCT3V-J1003, Geneva, CH (2015)
2. Gu, Z., Zheng, J., Ling, N., Zhang, P.: Fast depth modeling mode selection for 3D HEVC depth intra coding. In: IEEE International Conference on Multimedia and Expo Workshops, pp. 1–4 (2013)
3. Gu, Z., Zhong, J., Ling, N., Zhang, P.: Fast bi-partition mode selection for 3D HEVC depth intra coding. In: 2014 IEEE International Conference on Multimedia and Expo (ICME), pp. 1–6. IEEE (2014)
4. Park, C.-S.: Edge-based intramode selection for depth-map coding in 3D-HEVC. IEEE Trans. Image Process. **24**(1), 155–162 (2015)
5. Peng, K.K., Chiang, J.C., Lie, W.N.: Low complexity depth intra coding combining fast intra mode and fast CU size decision in 3D-HEVC. In: IEEE International Conference on Image Processing, pp. 1126–1130 (2016)
6. Sanchez, G., Saldanha, M., Balota, G., Zatt, B., Porto, M., Agostini, L.: A complexity reduction algorithm for depth maps intra prediction on the 3D-HEVC. In: Visual Communications and Image Processing Conference, pp. 49–57 (2015)
7. Zhang, M., Zhao, C., Xu, J., Bai, H.: A fast depth-map wedgelet partitioning scheme for intra prediction in 3D video coding. In: 2013 IEEE International Symposium on Circuits and Systems (ISCAS), pp. 2852–2855. IEEE (2013)
8. Conceição, R., Avila, G., Corrêa, G., Porto, M., Zatt, B., Agostini, L.: Complexity reduction for 3D-HEVC depth map coding based on early skip and early DIS scheme. In: IEEE International Conference on Image Processing, pp. 1116–1120 (2016)
9. Zhang, H.B., Tsang, S.H., Chan, Y.L., Fu, C.H.: Early determination of intra mode and segment-wise DC coding for depth map based on hierarchical coding structure in 3D-HEVC. In: Asia-Pacific Signal and Information Processing Association Summit and Conference, pp. 374–378 (2015)

10. Da Silva, T.L., Agostini, L.V., Da Silva Cruz, L.A.: Complexity reduction of depth intra coding for 3D video extension of HEVC. In: Visual Communications and Image Processing Conference, pp. 229–232 (2015)
11. Rao, K.R., Kim, D.N., Hwang, J.-J.: Fast Fourier Transform-Algorithms and Applications. Springer, 10.1007/978-1-4020-6629-0 (2011). https://doi.org/10.1007/978-1-4020-6629-0
12. Bjontegarrd, G.: Calculation of average PSNR differences between RD-curves. VCEG-M33 (2001)

Damage Online Inspection
in Large-Aperture Final Optics

Guodong Liu[1], Fupeng Wei[1,2(✉)] ⓘ, Fengdong Chen[1], Zhitao Peng[2],
and Jun Tang[2]

[1] Institute of Optical Measurement and Intellectualization,
Harbin Institute of Technology, Nangang District, Harbin 150001, China
weifupeng@yeah.net
[2] Research Center of Laser Fusion, China Academy of Engineering Physics,
Youxian District, Mianyang 621900, China

Abstract. Under the condition of inhomogeneous total internal reflection illumination, a novel approach based on machine learning is proposed to solve the problem of damage online inspection in large-aperture final optics. The damage online inspection mainly includes three problems: automatic classification of true and false laser-induced damage (LID), automatic classification of input and exit surface LID and size measurement of the LID. We first use the local area signal-to-noise ratio (LASNR) algorithm to segment all the candidate sites in the image, then use kernel-based extreme learning machine (K-ELM) to distinguish the true and false damage sites from the candidate sites, propose autoencoder-based extreme learning machine (A-ELM) to distinguish the input and exit surface damage sites from the true damage sites, and finally propose hierarchical kernel extreme learning machine (HK-ELM) to predict the damage size. The experimental results show that the method proposed in this paper has a better performance than traditional methods. The accuracy rate is 97.46% in the classification of true and false damage; the accuracy rate is 97.66% in the classification of input and exit surface damage; the mean relative error of the predicted size is within 10%. So the proposed method meets the technical requirements for the damage online inspection.

Keywords: Machine learning · Laser-induced damage
Damage online inspection · Classification · Size measurement

1 Introduction

High-power laser facilities for inertial confinement fusion (ICF), such as the National Ignition Facility (NIF) [1], the Laser Megajoule (LMJ) [2] and the Shenguang-III (SG-III) laser facility [3] are ultimately limited in operation by laser-induced damage (LID) of their final optics. The research results in recent years have shown that once the LID are initiated, the LID on the input surface

© Springer Nature Switzerland AG 2018
J.-H. Lai et al. (Eds.): PRCV 2018, LNCS 11256, pp. 237–248, 2018.
https://doi.org/10.1007/978-3-030-03398-9_21

tend to grow linearly with the number of laser shots [4]; while the LID on the exit surface tend to grow exponentially with the number of laser shots [5]. The LID need to be detected in time to avoid irreparable damage to the final optics. The most convenient approach is to set up an inspection instrument based on machine learning in the ICF target chamber center. In the time interval between two laser shots, the instrument needs to complete the damage online inspection for 432 final optics in 48 final optics assemblies (FOA), including image acquisition, image processing, damage analysis, and so on. The machine learning model used in the instrument is trained offline with LID image dataset. When applied to online inspection, only a single forward pass is computed. That is to say, with the help of the trained machine learning model, the instrument can simultaneously acquire images and detect LID in the acquired images online.

In recent years, machine learning has been widely used in ICF experiments, it is mainly focused on solving problems that are difficult to be solved by traditional solutions. Scientists in Lawrence Livermore National Laboratory (LLNL) have done a lot of valuable research [6]. Abdulla et al. conducted ensemble of decision trees (EDT) to identify HR-type false damage sites from candidate sites with 99.8% accuracy [7], which substantially reduces the interference of false damage on the inspection result. Carr et al. also used EDT to distinguish the input and exit surface true damage sites with 95% accuracy. Liao et al. used logistic regression to predict damage growth under different laser parameters (such as cumulative fluence, total growth factor, shot number, previous size, current size and local fluence) [8]. They found that using machine learning can obtain more accurate prediction results than Monte Carlo simulations. Kegelmeyer et al. developed the Avatar Machine Learning Suite of Tools to optimize Blockers, which are used to temporarily shadow identified damage sites from high-power laser exposure [9]. The above are the works conducted by LLNL scientists in the field of damage online inspection for NIF. However, at present, the damage online inspection based on machine learning for SG-III laser facility is still in its infancy stage. Since the imaging technology used in our inspection instrument is inhomogeneous internal reflection illumination, which is quite different from the homogeneous internal reflection illumination technology used in NIF. If the existing methods of NIF are directly used in our experiments, it is difficult to obtain the experimental results with the same accuracy. In addition, deep learning relies heavily on big data for labeled samples, which often requires tens of thousands to millions of labeled samples, and it is difficult to obtain such a huge samples for damage online inspection. In the field of damage online inspection, the current common practice is to use manually feature extraction from the damage sites instead of neural network's feature learning, thereby reducing the depth of the neural network and the number of training samples.

In this paper, we present the method of damage online inspection and its experimental system, which solves three problems: classification of true and false LID, classification of input and exit surface LID and size measurement of the LID. This fills the gap in the damage online inspection for large-aperture final optics in the SG-III laser facility. The method improves the inspection efficiency and accuracy, which has important practical significance for maintaining the load capacity of a high-power laser facility.

2 Theoretical Model

2.1 Classification Method

Machine learning is an effective method for managing complex classification problems. In this paper, we use the kernel-based extreme learning machine (K-ELM) to solve the automatic classification problem for true and false damage. The K-ELM classification model we used in this paper is as follows [10]:

$$
f(\mathbf{x}) = \begin{bmatrix} K(\mathbf{x}, \mathbf{x}_1) \\ \vdots \\ K(\mathbf{x}, \mathbf{x}_M) \end{bmatrix}^{\mathrm{T}} \left(\frac{\mathbf{I}}{C} + \mathbf{\Omega}_{train} \right)^{-1} \mathbf{T} \tag{1}
$$

where $K(\mathbf{x}, \mathbf{x}_i)$ is the kernel function, $\mathbf{x} = [x^{(1)}, ..., x^{(16)}]$ is the input sample to be classified, $\mathbf{x}_i = [x_i^{(1)}, ..., x_i^{(16)}]$ ($i = 1, ..., M$) is the training sample, M is the number of all training samples, $\mathbf{I}$ is the unit matrix, C is a constant, $\mathbf{\Omega}_{train}$ is a kernel matrix composed of training samples, $(\mathbf{\Omega}_{train})_{i,j} = K(\mathbf{x}_i, \mathbf{x}_j)$, ($i, j = 1, ..., M$), and $\mathbf{T} = [y_1, ..., y_M]^{\mathrm{T}}$ is a column vector composed of the class labels of the training samples. In our experiment, $K(\mathbf{x}, \mathbf{x}_i) = \exp(-\gamma \|\mathbf{x} - \mathbf{x}_i\|^2)$, and γ is a constant.

We propose autoencoder-based extreme learning machine (A-ELM) to solve the automatic classification problem for the input and exit surface damage sites. The A-ELM consists of two parts: unsupervised feature encoding (sparse autoencoder) and supervised feature classification (ELM). As shown in Fig. 1.

This is a neural network with 4 layers, n_i ($i = 0, 1, 2, 3$) is the number of neurons in the corresponding layer. $\mathbf{W}^{[i]}$ ($i = 1, 2, 3$) is the connection weight. $\mathbf{b}^{[i]}$ ($i = 0, 1, 2, 3$) is the bias factors. The bias factors in the input layer and the output layer are both zero, $\mathbf{b}^{[0]} = \mathbf{b}^{[3]} = \mathbf{0}$. For the damage site $\mathbf{X}$ in the image, we use n_0 operators $\mathbf{f} = [f_1, f_2, ..., f_{n_0}]$ to extract the n_0 features. $\mathbf{x} = [x^{(1)}, ..., x^{(n_0)}]^{\mathrm{T}}$, $x^{(i)} = f_i(\mathbf{X})$, $i = 1, 2, ..., n_0$. The network outputs only two results, so $n_3 = 2$. We use $\mathbf{x}^{[i]}$ and $\mathbf{h}^{[i]}$ ($i = 0, 1, 2, 3$) denote the input and output data of the corresponding layer, respectively; here $\mathbf{x} = \mathbf{x}^{[0]}$, $\mathbf{h}^{[3]} = \hat{\mathbf{t}} = [\hat{t}_1, \hat{t}_2]^{\mathrm{T}}$. The forward propagation process is as follows:

$$
\begin{cases}
\mathbf{h}^{[0]} = \mathbf{x} = \mathbf{f}(\mathbf{X}) \\
\mathbf{h}^{[1]} = f^{[1]}(\mathbf{W}^{[1]}\mathbf{h}^{[0]} + \mathbf{b}^{[1]}) \\
\mathbf{h}^{[2]} = f^{[2]}(\mathbf{W}^{[2]}\mathbf{h}^{[1]} + \mathbf{b}^{[2]}) \\
\hat{\mathbf{t}} = \mathbf{W}^{[3]}\mathbf{h}^{[2]}
\end{cases} \tag{2}
$$

where $f^{[k]}(\cdot)$ is the activation function in hidden layer k, ($k = 1, 2$). The activation functions could be, but not limited to the following: sigmoid function, tanh function and rectified linear units (ReLU) [10].

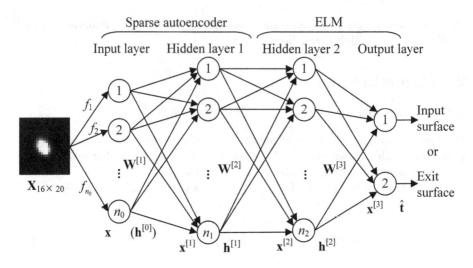

Fig. 1. The overall framework of A-ELM.

For sparse autoencoder, its decoding data $\hat{\mathbf{x}}$ is required to be able to restore the original data $\mathbf{x}$. The decoding data can be described as $\hat{\mathbf{x}} = g(\mathbf{W}^{[1]\mathrm{T}}\mathbf{h}^{[1]} + \mathbf{b}^{[1]})$, where $g(\cdot)$ is decoding function, it is also the activation function. To simplify the calculation, we can set $\mathbf{b}^{[1]} = \mathbf{1}$, so the encoding output from the hidden layer 1 can be described as $\mathbf{h}^{[1]} = f^{[1]}(\mathbf{W}^{[1]}\mathbf{x} + \mathbf{b}^{[1]})$. The loss function of the reconstruction error is defined as $L_{loss} = (1/M)\sum_{i=1}^{M} ||\mathbf{x}_i - \hat{\mathbf{x}}_i||^2$. We use L_2 norm regularization term to prevent overfitting: $\Omega_{weights} = (1/2)||\mathbf{W}^{[1]}||^2$. Since sparse autoencoders are typically used to learn features for classification [11], and in order to discover interesting structure in the input data, we impose a sparsity constraint (Sparsity regularization) on the hidden layer 1. We choose the Kullback-Leibler divergence as sparsity regularization term:

$$\Omega_{sparsity} = \sum_{i=1}^{n_1} \left[\rho\log\left(\frac{\rho}{\hat{\rho}_i}\right) + (1-\rho)\log\left(\frac{1-\rho}{1-\hat{\rho}_i}\right)\right] \tag{3}$$

where ρ is a sparsity parameter, typically a small value close to zero (such as $\rho = 0.05$). $\hat{\rho}_i$ is the average activation of hidden neuron i (averaged over the training set), it is defined as $\hat{\rho}_i = (1/M)\sum_{j=1}^{M} f(\mathbf{w}_i^{[1]\mathrm{T}}\mathbf{x}_j + b_i^{[1]})$. Now, we define the cost function for training a sparse autoencoder as follows:

$$J_{\mathrm{cost}} = L_{loss} + \alpha \cdot \Omega_{weights} + \beta \cdot \Omega_{sparsity} \tag{4}$$

where α is the coefficient for the L_2 regularization term and β is the coefficient for the sparsity regularization term, they are user-specified parameters. The hidden weight $\mathbf{W}^{[1]}$ can be solved according to the following optimization problem:

$$\mathbf{W}^{[1]*} = \arg\min_{\mathbf{W}^{[1]}} \{J_{\mathrm{cost}}\} \tag{5}$$

The Eq. (5) can be solved by the fast iterative shrinkage-thresholding algorithm (FISTA) or conjugate gradient algorithm [12,13].

The output of autoencoder is used as the input of ELM. According to the theory of Huang et al. the typical implementation of ELM is that the hidden neuron parameters $(\mathbf{W}^{[2]}, \mathbf{b}^{[2]})$ of ELM can be randomly generated [14,15]. So the weight $\mathbf{W}^{[2]}$ and bias $\mathbf{b}^{[2]}$ are given randomly:

$$\begin{cases} \mathbf{W}^{[2]} = rand(n_2, n_1), & \text{and } -1 \le w_{ij}^{[2]} \le 1 \\ \mathbf{b}^{[2]} = rand(n_2, 1), & \text{and } -1 \le b_i^{[2]} \le 1 \end{cases} \quad (6)$$

where $i = 1, 2, ..., n_2; j = 1, 2, ..., n_1$. We use $\mathbf{T} = [\mathbf{t}_1, ..., \mathbf{t}_M]$ to denote the target matrix of training data, where $\mathbf{t}_i = [t_{i,1}, t_{i,2}]^{\mathrm{T}}$. The output data from the hidden layer 2 is $\mathbf{H}^{[2]} = [\mathbf{h}_1^{[2]}, ..., \mathbf{h}_M^{[2]}]$. The hidden weight $\mathbf{W}^{[3]}$ can be solved according to the following optimization problem:

$$\mathbf{W}^{[3]*} = \underset{\mathbf{W}^{[3]}}{\arg\min} \left\{ \frac{1}{2} \left\| \mathbf{W}^{[3]} \right\|^2 + \frac{C}{2} \left\| \mathbf{W}^{[3]} \mathbf{H}^{[2]} - \mathbf{T} \right\| \right\} \quad (7)$$

where C is a user-specified parameter, it provides a tradeoff between the distance of the separating margin and the training error. Huang et al. have proved that the stable solutions of Eq. (7) is that [14–16]:

$$\mathbf{W}^{[3]*} = \left[\mathbf{H}^{[2]\mathrm{T}} \left(\frac{\mathbf{I}}{C} + \mathbf{H}^{[2]} \mathbf{H}^{[2]\mathrm{T}} \right)^{-1} \mathbf{T} \right]^{\mathrm{T}} \quad (8)$$

2.2 Regression Method

We propose hierarchical kernel extreme learning machine (HK-ELM) to solve the size measurement problem for the LID. HK-ELM is a novel method, which consists of two parts: unsupervised multilayer feature encoding (ELM sparse autoencoder) and supervised feature regression (K-ELM) [17–20]. As shown in Fig. 2.

For the LID $\mathbf{X}$, we use $\mathbf{f} = [f_1, f_2, ..., f_{25}]$ to extract the 25 features; thus, $\mathbf{x} = \mathbf{f}(\mathbf{X}) = [x^{(1)}, ..., x^{(25)}]$, $x^{(i)} = f_i(\mathbf{X})$, $i = 1, ..., 25$. $\mathbf{x}^{[i]}$ and $\mathbf{h}^{[i]}$ denote the input and output data of the i-th layer, respectively; n_i denotes the number of neurons in the i-th layer, $i = 0, 1, ..., N + 2$; $\mathbf{x} = \mathbf{x}^{[0]}$. The weight $\boldsymbol{\beta}^{[i]}$ can be solved according to the following optimization problem $(i = 0, 1, ..., N)$:

$$\boldsymbol{\beta}^{[i]*} = \underset{\boldsymbol{\beta}^{[i]}}{\arg\min} \left\{ \sum_{j=1}^{M} \left\| \hat{\mathbf{x}}_j^{[i]} - \mathbf{x}_j^{[i]} \right\|^2 + \lambda^{[i]} \left\| \boldsymbol{\beta}^{[i]} \right\| \right\} \quad (9)$$

where M is the number of training samples. $f^{[i]}(\cdot)$ is the activation function in the i-th layer $(i = 0, 1, ..., N)$, $\mathbf{h}_j^{[0]} = f^{[0]}(\mathbf{x}_j^{[0]})$, $\mathbf{x}_j^{[i]} = \mathbf{h}_j^{[i-1]} \boldsymbol{\beta}_j^{[i-1]}$, $\mathbf{h}_j^{[i]} = f^{[i]}(\mathbf{x}_j^{[i]})$, $\hat{\mathbf{x}}_j^{[i]} = g^{[i]}(\mathbf{h}^{[i]} \boldsymbol{\beta}^{[i]\mathrm{T}})$, $(i = 1, 2, ..., N; j = 1, 2, ..., M)$. $g^{[i]}(\cdot)$ is the decoding

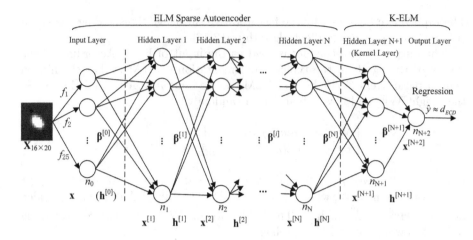

Fig. 2. The overall framework of HK-ELM.

function in the i-th layer, it is also an activation function. $\lambda^{[i]}$ $(i = 0, 1, ..., N)$ is the coefficient for the L_1 norm regularization, and it is a user-specified parameter. The Eq. (9) can be solved by the FISTA [12]. According to Eq. (1), the output of the kernel layer can be obtained as $\mathbf{h}^{[N+1]} = [K(\mathbf{z}, \mathbf{z}_1), ..., K(\mathbf{z}, \mathbf{z}_M)]$, where $\mathbf{z} = \mathbf{x}^{[N+1]} = \mathbf{h}^{[N]}\beta^{[N]}$ is the vector to be inputed to the K-ELM, $\mathbf{z}_i = \mathbf{x}_i^{[N+1]} = \mathbf{h}_i^{[N]}\beta_i^{[N]}$ is the output of the training sample $\mathbf{x}_i$ $(i = 1, 2, ..., M)$ after passing through the ELM sparse autoencoder. $K(\mathbf{z}, \mathbf{z}_i) = \exp(-\gamma \|\mathbf{z} - \mathbf{z}_i\|^2)$ is the kernel function in the neurons inside the kernel layer. The output weight $\beta^{[N+1]}$ is

$$\beta^{[N+1]} = \left(\frac{\mathbf{I}}{C} + \Omega_{train} \right)^{-1} \mathbf{T} \tag{10}$$

where $\mathbf{I}$ is a unit matrix, C is a constant. Ω_{train} is the kernel matrix, and the elements in the kernel matrix are $(\Omega_{train})_{i,j} = K(\mathbf{z}_i, \mathbf{z}_j)$, $(i, j = 1, 2, ..., M)$, M is the number of training samples. $\mathbf{T} = [y_1, y_2, ..., y_M]^T$ is a column vector composed of the regression labels of the training samples.

There is no activation function in the neurons inside the output layer. Finally, the output scalar $\hat{y} = \mathbf{x}^{[N+2]} \in \mathbf{R}^{1 \times 1}$ is

$$\hat{y} = \mathbf{h}^{[N+1]}\beta^{[N+1]} \tag{11}$$

3   Experiment

3.1   Final Optics Damage Inspection (FODI) for SG-III Facility

We developed the FODI system for damage online inspection. FODI system obtains online images in a vacuum target chamber. As shown in Fig. 3. The distance between the imaging and posture adjustment system (IPAS) and the final optics in FOA is 3.7–5.1 m. There is a FODI camera in the IPAS. Each FOA contains 9 large-aperture final optics. The aperture size of the final optics is 430 mm × 430 mm. The resolution of FODI camera is about 110 μm at 3.7 m working distance, 140 μm at 5.1 m working distance. The CCD image format is 4872 × 3248 pixels with 16 bits, and the pixel size is 7.4 μm. Since what we concerned about is those LID between 100 μm and 500 μm, the FODI online image is a low-resolution image for the LID. The vacuum target chamber is a sphere with a diameter of 6 m, which is connected with 48 FOA. The positioning system move IPAS to the target chamber center, the IPAS adjusts the posture of FODI camera to make it aiming at the inspected optic, only the light source of the inspected optic is turned on, after the online image of inspected optic is captured, data-processing system will use machine learning algorithm to analyze the damage sites in image, the results are stored in the database. Master control system controls the entire process to be executed automatically.

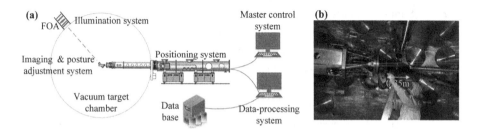

Fig. 3. (a) Structure diagram of FODI system (b) The IPAS in the SG-III laser facility

We mark all candidate sites in the FODI online image using the LASNR algorithm [19], and characterize these candidate sites with a feature vector $\mathbf{x} = [x^{(1)}, ..., x^{(m)}]$, the meaning of each attribute $x^{(i)}$ is shown in Table 1.

In the following experiments, the training LID samples and testing LID samples are taken from online images acquired by FODI system. After collecting these online images, these inspected optics are removed from the SG-III facility and placed under the microscope. We use the microscope to obtain the labels of these LID samples, such as the types of the LID and the size of the LID. After completing the learning on the training LID samples, if the FODI system still performs well on the testing LID samples, the FODI system can perform online inspection for other unlabeled LID on the final optics.

3.2   Classification of True and False LID

Due to the presence of stray light, a significant amount of noise is present in FODI images in addition to true damage sites, as shown in Fig. 4, which are referred to as false damage sites.

These candidate sites can generally be divided into these categories: damage site, hardware reflection (HR), damaged CCD pixels (DC), reflection of a damage site (RD), and attachments (Att) [20]. Damage sites are also called true damage

Table 1. The 25 attributes (Attrs) associated with each damage site.

Attrs	Meaning
$x^{(1)}$	Area in pixels of the measured site
$x^{(2)}$	Sum of all pixel intensity values of the measured site in signal image
$x^{(3)}$	Sum of all pixel intensity values of the measured site in noise image
$x^{(4)}$	Mean pixel intensity of the measured site in signal image
$x^{(5)}$	Standard deviation of the measured site in signal image
$x^{(6)}$	Mean pixel intensity of the measured site in noise image
$x^{(7)}$	Max pixel intensity of the measured site in signal image
$x^{(8)}$	Max pixel intensity of the measured site in noise image
$x^{(9)}$	Short axis of best fitting ellipse
$x^{(10)}$	Long axis of best fitting ellipse
$x^{(11)}$	Signal energy to noise energy ratio of the measured site
$x^{(12)}$	Sum of signal-to-noise ratio for the measured site in LASNR image
$x^{(13)}$	Saturation area ratio of the measured site
$x^{(14)}$	Saturation intensity ratio of the measured site
$x^{(15)}$	X location of the measured site
$x^{(16)}$	Y location of the measured site
$x^{(17)}$	Standard deviation of the measured site in noise image
$x^{(18)}$	Sum of the intensity values of the perimeter within the gradient image
$x^{(19)}$	Mean of the intensity values of the perimeter within the gradient image
$x^{(20)}$	Standard deviation of the gradient of the measured site boundary
$x^{(21)}$	The perimeter of the measured site boundary
$x^{(22)}$	Sum of all pixel intensity values of the measured site in FODI image
$x^{(23)}$	Mean pixel intensity of the measured site in FODI image
$x^{(24)}$	Standard deviation of the measured site in FODI image
$x^{(25)}$	Max pixel intensity of the measured site in FODI image

sites or true sites, the others are called false damage sites or false sites. We characterize each candidate site with a feature vector $\mathbf{x} = [x^{(1)}, ..., x^{(16)}]$, the meaning of $x^{(i)}$ is shown in Table 1. We use "$y_i = -1$" to denote the label of the false site and "$y_i = 1$" to denote the label of the true site. In our training and testing samples, which include true sites and all types of false sites, the damage size range is 50–200 μm. For comparison, we test the accuracy of the EDT with 12 features (denoted as EDT1) proposed in reference [7] and the EDT with 16 features (denoted as EDT2) proposed in this paper. Lastly, we also provide the classification results obtained using the error backpropagation neural network (BPNN) and support vector machine (SVM) methods in Table 2.

Table 2 shows that the testing accuracy rate of the K-ELM is the highest among these classifiers. The training speed of the K-ELM is the fastest of all.

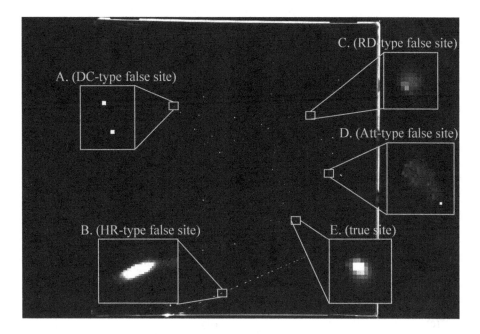

Fig. 4. True and false damage sites in an SG-III FODI online image

Table 2. Testing results of different classifiers (T: true sites, F: false sites).

Training data	Testing data	Classifiers				
368(T) 335(F)	368(T) 336(F)	EDT1	EDT2	BPNN	SVM	K-ELM
Testing accuracy rate		90.00%	94.29%	92.43%	96.91%	97.46%
Training time		1.17 s	1.30 s	0.73 s	72.35 ms	24.40 ms
Testing time		0.23 s	0.24 s	0.57 s	14.59 ms	16.38 ms

The testing speed of the K-ELM is only slightly lower than that of the SVM. Overall, K-ELM has the best performance in terms of practical application.

3.3   Classification of Input and Exit Surface LID

Each true site in FODI online image is characterized by a feature vector $\mathbf{x} = [x^{(1)}, ..., x^{(16)}]$. We use "$y_i = -1$" to denote the label of the input surface and "$y_i = 1$" to denote the label of the exit surface. The number of training and testing samples are 1527 and 1466, respectively. There are 635 input surface LID and 892 exit surface LID in the training set, there are 613 input surface LID and 853 exit surface LID in the testing set. The LID size range is 50–1200 μm. In experiments, the parameters of A-ELM are set as $\alpha = 0.001$, $\beta = 0.56$, $\rho = 0.05$ and $C = 4.75$. The performance evaluation between EDT2 and A-ELM are shown in Table 3. Where ACC_{train} is training accuracy, ACC_{test} is testing

Table 3. Performance evaluation between EDT2 and A-ELM.

Performance	EDT2	A-ELM
$ACC_{train} \pm std$	100% ± 0% ($n > 100$)	98.20% ± 0.42% ($n_1 > 100$, $n_2 > 1000$)
$ACC_{test} \pm std$	94.45% ± 0.27% ($n > 100$)	96.50% ± 0.31% ($n_1 > 100$, $n_2 > 1000$)
Max value of ACC_{test}	95.23% ($n = 198$)	97.66% ($n_1 = 260$, $n_2 = 1400$)

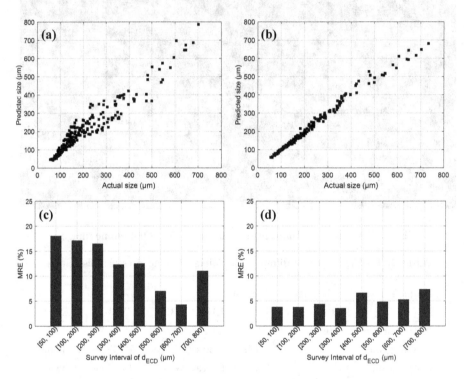

Fig. 5. The comparison between radiometric method and HK-ELM. (a) The predicted sizes are calculated by the radiometric method. (b) The predicted sizes are calculated by HK-ELM. (c) The MRE of the radiometric method. (d) The MRE of HK-ELM.

accuracy, std is standard deviation, n is the number of decision trees, n_1 and n_2 are the number of neurons in the hidden layer 1 and hidden layer 2 respectively.

The Table 3 shows that, from the point of view of the difference between ACC_{train} and ACC_{test}, the generalization ability of A-ELM is stronger than that of EDT2. From the point of view of the testing accuracy ($ACC_{test} \pm std$ and Max ACC_{test}), A-ELM is about 2% higher than EDT2.

3.4   Size Measurement of LID

In our experiment, a total of 450 samples were randomly selected on the inspected optics to form a data set $T = \{(\mathbf{x}_i, y_i) | \mathbf{x}_i \in \mathbf{R}^{25}, y_i \in R, i = 1, ..., P\}$, here, y_i is the actual size of the i-th LID, it is measured by the microscope, $P = 450$, the size range is 50–750 μm. We randomly divided the data set T into two parts: the training data set $T_{train} = \{(\mathbf{x}_i, y_i)|\mathbf{x}_i \in \mathbf{R}^{25}, y_i \in R, i = 1, ..., M\}$ and the testing data set $T_{test} = \{(\mathbf{x}_i, y_i)|\mathbf{x}_i \in \mathbf{R}^{25}, y_i \in R, i = 1, ..., N\}$, $M = N = P/2$. The numbers of neurons in the i-th layer are $n_0 = 25$, $n_1 = 240$, $n_2 = 240$, $n_3 = 500$, $n_4 = 445$, and $n_5 = 1$. We choose the tanh function as the activation function in the ELM sparse autoencoder, and we choose the Gaussian kernel function as the kernel function in the kernel layer. All the user-specified parameters are set as follows: $\lambda^{[i]} = 1 \times 10^{-3}$ ($i = 0, 1, 2, 3$), $C = 1$, and $\sigma = 1.49$. The performance evaluation between radiometric method and HK-ELM on the testing samples are shown in Fig. 5. Here, The radiometric method was proposed by LLNL scientists to calculate the size of LID in the FODI image [21].

Figures 5(a) and (b) shows that, compared with the predicted sizes calculated by HK-ELM, there are larger deviations between the predicted sizes calculated by the radiometric method and the actual sizes. Figures 5(c) and (d) shows that the radiometric method has larger MRE than that of HK-ELM. For the LID smaller than the FODI resolution, HK-ELM can achieve ultra-resolution measurement, which meets the technical requirements for precision measurement of LID size in large-aperture final optics with inhomogeneous illumination.

4 Conclusion

The method based on machine learning proposed in this paper solves the three problems of damage online inspection in large-aperture final optics. The three problems are: classification of true and false LID, classification of input and exit surface LID and size measurement of the LID. The method proposed in this paper is suitable for machine learning on small samples. Therefore, it has important practical significance. For damage online inspection in large-aperture final optics, it is difficult to collect a large number of labeled samples. The experimental results show that the method proposed in this paper has achieved satisfactory results on small samples.

References

1. Spaeth, M.L., Manes, K.R., Kalantar, D.H., et al.: Description of the NIF laser. Fusion Sci. Technol. **69**(1), 25–145 (2016)
2. Caillaud, T., Alozy, E., Briat, M., et al.: Recent advance in target diagnostics on the laser mégajoule (LMJ). In: Proceedings of SPIE, vol. 9966, p. 7 (2016)
3. Zheng, Y., Ding, L., Zhou, X., et al.: Preliminary study of the damage resistance of type I doubler KDP crystals at 532 nm. Chin. Opt. Lett. **14**(5), 051601 (2016)
4. Sozet, M., Neauport, J., Lavastre, E., Roquin, N., Gallais, L., Lamaignère, L.: Laser damage growth with picosecond pulses. Opt. Lett. **41**(10), 2342–2345 (2016)
5. Negres, R.A., Cross, D.A., Liao, Z.M., Matthews, M.J., Carr, C.W.: Growth model for laser-induced damage on the exit surface of fused silica under UV, ns laser irradiation. Opt. Express **22**(4), 3824–3844 (2014)

6. Kegelmeyer, L.M., Clark, R., Leach Jr., R.R., et al.: Automated optics inspection analysis for NIF. Fusion Eng. Des. **87**(12), 2120–2124 (2012)
7. Abdulla, G.M., Kegelmeyer, L.M., Liao, Z.M., Carr, W.: Effective and efficient optics inspection approach using machine learning algorithms. In: Proceedings of SPIE, vol. 7842, p. 78421D (2010). https://doi.org/10.1117/12.867648
8. Liao, Z.M., Abdulla, G.M., Negres, R.A., Cross, D.A., Carr, C.W.: Predictive modeling techniques for nanosecond-laser damage growth in fused silica optics. Opt. Express **20**(14), 15569–15579 (2012)
9. Kegelmeyer, L.M., Senecal, J.G., Conder, A.D., Lane, L.A., Nostrand, M.C., Whitman, P.K.: Optimizing blocker usage on NIF using image analysis and machine learning*. In: ICALEPCS 2013, Livermore, CA, USA, p. 5 (2013). http://www.osti.gov/scitech/servlets/purl/1097712
10. Huang, G.B., Zhou, H., Ding, X., Zhang, R.: Extreme learning machine for regression and multiclass classification. IEEE Trans. Syst. Man Cybern. B **42**(2), 513–529 (2012)
11. Goodfellow, I., Bengio, Y., Courville, A.: Deep Learning. MIT Press, Cambridge (2016). http://www.deeplearningbook.org
12. Beck, A., Teboulle, M.: A fast iterative shrinkage-thresholding algorithm for linear inverse problems. SIAM J. Imaging Sci. **2**(1), 183–202 (2009)
13. Livieris, I.E., Pintelas, P.: A new conjugate gradient algorithm for training neural networks based on a modified secant equation. Appl. Math. Comput. **221**(Suppl. C), 491–502 (2013)
14. Huang, G.B., Wang, D.H., Lan, Y.: Extreme learning machines: a survey. Int. J. Mach. Learn. Cybern. **2**(2), 107–122 (2011)
15. Huang, G.B.: What are extreme learning machines? Filling the gap between Frank Rosenblatt's dream and John von Neumann's puzzle. Cogn. Comput. **7**(3), 263–278 (2015)
16. Tang, J., Deng, C., Huang, G.B.: Extreme learning machine for multilayer perceptron. IEEE Trans. Neural Netw. Learn. **27**(4), 809–821 (2015)
17. He, B., Sun, T., Yan, T., Shen, Y., Nian, R.: A pruning ensemble model of extreme learning machine with L1/2 regularizer. Multidimens. Syst. Signal Process. **28**(3), 1051–1069 (2017)
18. Huang, G.B.: An insight into extreme learning machines: random neurons, random features and kernels. Cogn. Comput. **6**(3), 376–390 (2014)
19. Mascio Kegelmeyer, L., Fong, P.W., Glenn, S.M., Liebman, J.A.: Local area signal-to-noise ratio (LASNR) algorithm for image segmentation. In: Proceedings of SPIE, vol. 6696, p. 66962H (2007). https://doi.org/10.1117/12.732493
20. Wei, F., Chen, F., Liu, B., et al.: Automatic classification of true and false laser-induced damage in large aperture optics. Opt. Eng. **57**(5), 053112 (2018)
21. Conder, A., Chang, J., Kegelmeyer, L., Spaeth, M., Whitman, P.: Final optics damage inspection (FODI) for the national ignition facility. In: Proceedings of SPIE, vol. 7797, p. 77970P (2010). https://doi.org/10.1117/12.862596

Automated and Robust Geographic Atrophy Segmentation for Time Series SD-OCT Images

Yuchun Li[1], Sijie Niu[2], Zexuan Ji[1], and Qiang Chen[1,3(✉)]

[1] School of Computer Science and Engineering,
Nanjing University of Science and Technology, Nanjing, China
chen2qiang@njust.edu.cn
[2] School of Information Science and Engineering, University of Jinan, Jinan, China
[3] Fujian Provincial Key Laboratory of Information Processing and Intelligent
Control, Minjiang University, Fuzhou, China

Abstract. Geographic atrophy (GA), mainly characterized by atrophy of the retinal pigment epithelium (RPE), is an advanced form of age-related macular degeneration (AMD) which will lead to vision loss. Automated and robust GA segmentation in three-dimensional (3D) spectral-domain optical coherence tomography (SD-OCT) images is still an enormous challenge. This paper presents an automated and robust GA segmentation method based on object tracking strategy for time series SD-OCT volumetric images. Considering the sheer volume of data, it is unrealistic for experts to segment GA lesion region manually. However, in our proposed scenario, experts only need to manually calibrate GA lesion area for the first moment of each patient, and then the GA of the following moments will be automatically detected. In order to fully embody the outstanding features of GA, a new sample construction method is proposed for more effectively extracting histogram of oriented gradient (HOG) features to generate random forest models. The experiments on SD-OCT cubes from 10 eyes in 7 patients with GA demonstrate that our results have a high correlation with the manual segmentations. The average of correlation coefficients and overlap ratio for GA projection area are 0.9881 and 82.62%, respectively.

Keywords: Geographic atrophy · HOG features
Image segmentation · Spectral-domain optical coherence tomography

1 Introduction

Geographic atrophy (GA) is an advanced stage of non-exudative age-related macular degeneration (AMD) that is a leading cause of progressive and irreversible

This work was supported by the National Natural Science Foundation of China (61671242, 61701192, 61701222, 61473310), Suzhou Industrial Innovation Project (SS201759), and the Open Fund Project of Fujian Provincial Key Laboratory of Information Processing and Intelligent Control (Minjiang University) (No. MJUKF201706).

© Springer Nature Switzerland AG 2018
J.-H. Lai et al. (Eds.): PRCV 2018, LNCS 11256, pp. 249–261, 2018.
https://doi.org/10.1007/978-3-030-03398-9_22

vision loss among elderly individuals [1, 2]. Geographic atrophy, with loss of the retinal pigment epithelium (RPE) and choriocapillaris, is represented by the presence of sharply demarcated atrophic lesions, resulting in affecting the central vision field [3]. In most cases, GA lesions usually first appear in the surrounding macular, initially reserved for the concave center, and often expand and coalesce to include the fovea as time goes on [4]. Characterization of GA regions, helping clinicians to objectively monitor AMD progression, is essential step in the diagnosis of advanced AMD. However, this characterization is directly dependent on the precise segmentation and quantification of the areas affected by GA, as well as their properties [5]. Generally, manual segmentation of GA characterization is required, but it is time consuming and subject to user-variability. Thus, automatic and robust segmentation of GA-affected retinal regions is fundamental and important in the diagnosis of advanced AMD.

To the best of our knowledge, very few methods [7, 8] have been described for detection and segmentation of GA lesions in spectral-domain optical coherence tomography (SD-OCT) volumetric images. In previous works [6], clinicians just focus on qualitative evaluation of GA based on the thickness measurement of RPE Because of retinal thinning and loss of the retinal pigment epithelium (RPE) and photoreceptors in GA regions. But, that are not accurate in detecting GA. In order to identify the GA lesion directly through representing RPE, the early algorithms [8, 9] segment GA regions mainly based on the restricted projection image generated by the area between RPE and the choroid layers. Chen et al. [7] utilized a geometric active contour model to automatically detect and segment the extent of GA in the projection images. Level set approach was employed to segment GA regions in both SD-OCT and FAF images [8]. However, the result would be bad if the initialization was a bit incorrectly. Niu et al. [9] proposed an automated GA segmentation method for SD-OCT images by using a Chan-Vese model via local similarity factor to improve accuracy and stability. As mentioned above, these methods based on the restricted projection image have great limitations in the detection and segmentation of GA. Deep learning has achieved outstanding performance in many fields of computer vision application and medical image processing. Ji et al. [10] constructed a voting system with deep VGG16 convolutional neural networks to automatically detect GA in SD-OCT images. However, the deep neural network requires a large number of manually labeled training samples, and the voting system requires 10 training models, which is time-consuming.

This paper presents an automated and robust GA segmentation method based on the histogram of oriented gradient (HOG) [11] feature in time series SD-OCT volumetric images. Considering the sheer volume of data, it is unrealistic for experts to segment GA lesion region manually. In our proposed scheme, for time series, experts just need to manually calibrate GA lesion area for the first moment of each patient, then GA from the following moments will be automatically detected. Considering the characteristics of GA lesion in SD-OCT images, a new sample construction method is proposed for more effectively extracting HOG features to generate random forest models. According to GA segmentation results in OCT slices, quantitative evaluation of GA can be performed on OCT projection images.

2 Method

2.1 Method Overview

The whole framework of our method is shown in Fig. 1. For each patient, in the stage of image pre-processing, noise removal and layer segmentation are performed on each B-scan. We propose a new sample construction method which is conducive to the effective implementation of subsequent steps. Consequently, we divide sample-patches into positive and negative samples and extract HOG features. Finally, random forest is utilized to train a prediction model. In the testing phase, we first do the same processing on the testing data and obtain the GA segmentation result based on the random forest model trained by training phase.

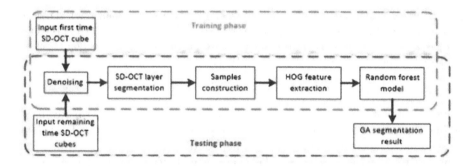

Fig. 1. Framework of the proposed method.

2.2 Preprocessing

Denoise. In the OCT imaging process, a mass of speckle noise is caused because of random interference of scattered light. These noise flood the valid information in the image, thus the accuracy of the algorithm is greatly reduced. According to the noise distribution characteristics of SD-OCT images, this paper uses the bilateral filter algorithm to reduce noise. Figure 2(b) is the original image and Fig. 2(c) is the denoised image using bilateral filter.

Layer Segmentation. We just focus on the information between internal limiting membrane (ILM) and Choroid, hence, layer segmentation is necessary. Gradual intensity distance method [12] is used to segment the Bruch's membrane (BM) layer and the ILM layer. As shown in the Fig. 2(d), the blue line is the ILM layer and the yellow line is the BM layer.

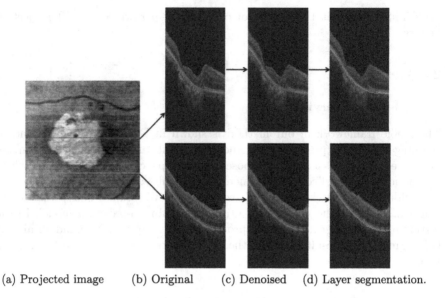

(a) Projected image   (b) Original   (c) Denoised   (d) Layer segmentation.

Fig. 2. Preprocessing for one GA (first row) and one normal (second row) SD-OCT images. The red line (a) corresponds to the cross section of retina visualized in the first row B-scan shown (b) and The green line (a) corresponds to the cross section of retina visualized in the second row B-scan shown (b). (Color figure online)

2.3 Samples Construction and Classification

Longitudinal data from 9 eyes in 7 patients, all the cases presented with advanced non-nonvascular AMD with extensive GA, were included in this paper. For a data set, two independent readers draw a manual outline by projecting the image in two repetitive separate sessions, and obtain ground truth segment outline from it by considering those areas that are outlined by two or more readers or sessions. In the preprocessing step, ILM layer and BM layer are depicted in B-scan, as shown in Fig. 3(a). In the GA region of the B-scan, there are bright pixels area under the RPE of the B-scan because RPE atrophies [7]. Regions of interest need to be restricted to the ILM and the lower areas of BM layers (100 pixels below the BM layer in this paper). As shown in Fig. 3(b), between the yellow line and the purple line, the GA regions increase the reflectivity compared to other regions. At the same time, there is a huge difference between the GA regions and other regions above the BM layer. The average distance between the blue line and the purple line (Fig. 3(b)) is calculated as the standard distance expressed by D. And then, the ILM layer be shifted down by D pixels as the lower boundary (Fig. 3(c)). Finally, we flatten the area between the top boundary and the lower boundary, which contains information about GA and other retina areas, and then a new image is obtained (Fig. 3(d)).

The new image of each B-scan are extracted to construct training and testing samples using sliding window method, and then we can extract HOG features from the samples. Experiment has proved 64×128 (width $\times$ height) is the best

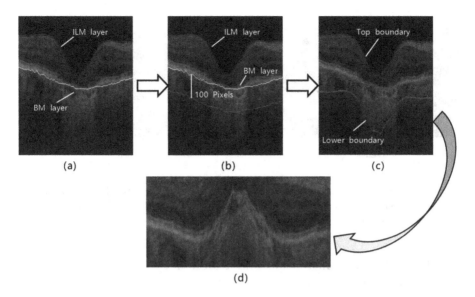

Fig. 3. Flowchart of constructing a region of interest. (a) is the layer segmentation image, the top boundary and the lower boundary of the projection sub-volume are marked with parallel blue line and red line in (c), flatten the area between the top boundary and the lower boundary, a new image is obtained in (d). (Color figure online)

image size for extracting HOG feature [11]. Therefore, we resize all the preprocessed images to 512×128. As shown in Fig. 4(a), the size of sample is 64×128. For the lateral direction, the optimum step size is (in this paper). Tiny step size will lead to high similarity between training samples, which will reduce the efficiency and increase time cost. On the contrary, it will affect the accuracy of segmentation. The red line (Fig. 4(b)) indicates GA area. If the training sample is within the red manual division line, we mark it as the positive sample (Area2 in Fig. 4(b)). In contrast, we mark it as the negative sample (Area1 in Fig. 4(b)). However, when the sliding window contains positive and negative samples (Area3 in Fig. 4(b)), we mark it as the positive sample if the number of columns containing GA exceeds the half width of the sliding window, the negative sample or not. The formula of training samples for each B-scan is as follows:

$$m = (W/l) - (w/l - 1) \tag{1}$$

where W is the width of B-scan, w is the width of sliding window, l is the step size of sliding window. Based on the above procedures and formula ($W = 512$, $w = 64$, $l = 8$) we will get 7296 training samples for each SD-OCT volumetric image (57 samples are obtained in each B-scan) with 128 B-scans.

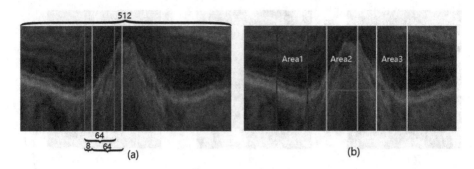

Fig. 4. Construct training samples. (a) Shows the step size and the size of sliding windows, (b) shows the categories of training samples, Area1 is the negative sample, Ares2 is the positive sample. (Color figure online)

2.4 HOG Feature Extraction and Random Forest Model Construction

HOG descriptors provide a dense overlapping description of image regions [11]. The main idea of HOG feature is that the appearance and shape of local objects can be well described by the directional density distribution of gradients or edges. The HOG feature is formed by calculating and counting the gradient direction histograms of the local area of the image.

In this paper, we extend the traditional HOG feature. We firstly normalize the input image with Gamma standardization (formula (2)) to adjust image contrast, reduce the influence of local shadows, and suppress the noise interference. Then the gradient magnitude is computed by formula (3). In two-dimensional (2D) images, we need to calculate the gradient direction in x-y plan. Then the gradient direction in the x-y are calculated as formula (4).

$$I(x, y, z) = I(x, y, z)^{Gamma} \tag{2}$$

$$\delta f(x, y) = \sqrt{f_x(x, y)^2 + f_y(x, y)^2} \tag{3}$$

$$\theta(x, y) = tan^{-1} \left(\frac{f_y(x, y)}{f_x(x, y)} \right) \tag{4}$$

where Gamma is set to 0.5 in formula (2), $f_x(x, y)$ and $f_y(x, y)$ represent the image gradients along the x, y directions in formulas (3) and (4), respectively.

Finally, the gradient direction of each cell will be divided into 9 directions in x-y plans. In this way, each pixel in the cell is graded in the histogram with a weighted projection (mapped to a fixed angular range) to obtain a gradient histogram, that is, an 9-dimensional eigenvector corresponding to the cell. The gradient magnitude is used as the weight of the projection. Then, the feature vectors of all cells in a block are concatenated to obtain the HOG feature. HOG features from all overlapping blocks are concatenated to the ultimate features for classification.

Random forest is an important ensemble learning method based on "Bagging", which can be used for classification, regression and other issues. In this paper, HOG feature is used for training random forest model to accomplish the GA segmentation.

3 Experiments

Our algorithm was implemented in Matlab and ran on a 4.0 GHz Pentium 4 PC with 16.0 GB memory. We obtained a lot of SD-OCT volumetric image datasets from 10 eyes in 7 patients with GA to quantitatively test our algorithm. The SD-OCT cubes are 512 (lateral) × 1024 (axial) × 128 (azimuthal) corresponding to a $6 \times 6 \times 2 \, mm^3$ volume centered at the retinal macular region generated with a Cirrus HD-OCT device. Several metrics [8] were used to assess the GA area differences: correlation coefficient (cc), the absolute area difference (ADD), overlap ratio (Overlap) evaluation.

The quantitative results in inter-observer and intra-observer agreement evaluation for this data set are summarized in Table 1, where A_i $(i = 1, 2)$ represents the segmentations of the first grader in the i-th session, and B_i $(i = 1, 2)$ represents the segmentations of the second grader in the i-th session. Inter-observer differences were computed by considering the union of both sessions for each grader: $A_{1\&2}$ and $B_{1\&2}$ represent the first and second grader, respectively. The intra-observer and inter-observer comparison showed very high correlations coefficients (cc) indicating very high linear correlation between different readers and for the same reader at different sessions. The overlap ratios (all > 90%) and the absolute GA area differences (all < 5%) indicate very high inter-observer and intra-observer agreement, highlighting that the measurement and quantification of GA regions in the generated projection images seem effective and feasible [9].

Table 1. Intra-observer and inter-observer correlation coefficients (cc), absolute GA area differences (AAD) and overlap ratio (OR) evaluation

Methods compared	cc (mean, std)	AAD [mm²] (mean, std)	ADD [%] (mean, std)	Overlap [%] (mean, std)
ExpertA$_1$-ExpertA$_2$	0.998	0.239 ± 0.210	3.70 ± 2.97	93.29 ± 3.02
ExpertB$_1$-ExpertB$_2$	0.996	0.243 ± 0.412	3.34 ± 5.37	93.06 ± 5.79
ExpertA$_{1\&2}$-ExpertB$_{1\&2}$	0.995	0.314 ± 0.466	4.68 ± 5.70	91.28 ± 6.04

3.1 Qualitative Analysis

Comparison with Average Gold Standard. Figure 5 shows the GA segmentation results in B-scan where the green transparent areas represent the manual segmentation and the red lines are our automated segmentation results.

Due to the characteristic of GA, it is difficult for the GA segmentation. However, our proposed method is effective to deal with many difficulties, such as (1) non-uniform reflectivity within GA ((b)(d)(e)(h)(i)), (2) influence of other retinal diseases ((b)(c)(e)(f)), and (3) the discontinuous of GA sizes ((c)(j)). Because our segmentation precision is high and robust in B-scan images, we can also obtain a relatively high segmentation precision in their projection images. Figure 6 shows the GA projection images collected at six patients. In Fig. 5, the red lines are the manual segmentation and the green lines are our segmentation in the projection images. It can be seen from Fig. 6 that our automated GA segmentation is similar with the manual segmentation.

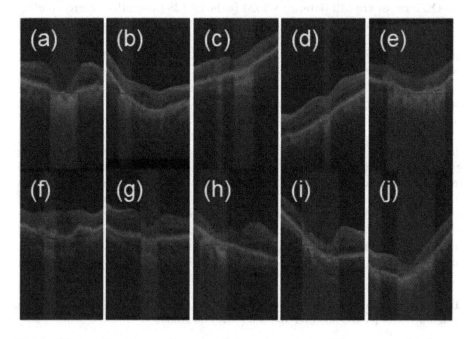

Fig. 5. GA segmentation results and each image represents different example of eyes, the green transparent areas represent the manual segmentation and the red lines are our automated segmentation results. (Color figure online)

Comparison with Traditional Methods. Figure 7 shows the comparison of GA segmentation results overlaid on projection images, where the outlines generated by average ground truth (red lines), Chen's method (blue lines), Niu's method (purple lines) and our method (green lines). In each subfigure, (a) and (c) shows the segmentation results overlaid on full projection images, (b) and (d) shows the enlarged view of the rectangles region marked by a white box. As shown in Fig. 7(b) and (d), both Chen's and Niu's methods failed to detect parts of the boundaries between GA lesions because of the impact of the low contrast. Comparatively, our method obtained higher consistency with the average ground truths.

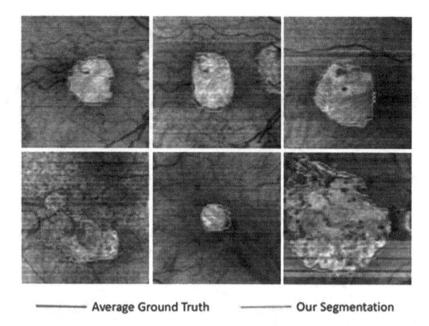

————— **Average Ground Truth** ————— **Our Segmentation**

Fig. 6. Segmentation results overlaid on full projection images for six example cases selected from six eyes. where the average ground truths are overlaid with a red line, and the segmentations obtained with our method are overlaid with blue line. (Color figure online)

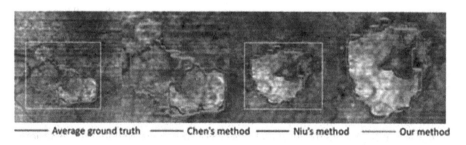

————— Average ground truth ————— Chen's method ————— Niu's method ————— Our method

Fig. 7. Comparison of segmentation results overlaid on full projection images for 2 example cases. (Color figure online)

Comparison with Deep Learning. Ji et al. [11] constructed a voting system with deep VGG16 convolutional neural networks to automatically detect GA in SD-OCT images. They trained ten deep network models, by randomly selecting training samples. Because the training samples are determined in our method, we only utilize one deep network to obtain GA segmentation results. Figure 8 shows the comparison of GA segmentation results in projection image, where the outlines generated by average ground truth (red lines), one deep network (yellow lines) and our method (green lines). In each subfigure, (a) and (c) shows

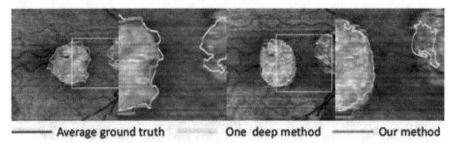

——— Average ground truth ——— One deep method ——— Our method

Fig. 8. Comparison of segmentation results overlaid on full projection images for 2 example cases. (Color figure online)

Table 2. The summarizations of the quantitative results (mean ± standard deviation) between the traditional segmentations and manual gold standards (individual reader segmentations and the average expert segmentations) on dataset.

Methods	Criterions	ExpertA$_1$	ExpertA$_2$	ExpertB$_1$	ExpertB$_2$	Avg.Expert
Chen's method	cc	0.967	0.964	0.968	0.977	0.970
	AAD [mm^2]	1.31 ± 1.28	1.40 ± 1.31	1.60 ± 1.33	1.47 ± 1.14	1.44 ± 1.26
	ADD [%]	25.2 ± 22.7	26.1 ± 21.4	29.2 ± 22.1	27.6 ± 20.5	27.1 ± 22.0
	OR [%]	73.2 ± 15.6	73.1 ± 15.1	71.1 ± 15.4	72.1 ± 14.8	72.6 ± 12.0
Niu's method	cc	0.975	0.976	0.976	0.975	0.979
	AAD [mm^2]	0.76 ± 0.99	0.85 ± 1.04	0.98 ± 1.08	0.90 ± 1.05	0.81 ± 0.94
	ADD [%]	12.6 ± 12.8	13.3 ± 12.7	14.9 ± 12.6	14.0 ± 11.7	12.9 ± 11.8
	OR [%]	81.4 ± 12.1	81.6 ± 12.2	80.0 ± 13.0	80.6 ± 12.5	81.8 ± 12.0
Our method	cc	**0.9884**	**0.9826**	**0.9885**	**0.9918**	**0.9881**
	ADD [mm^2]	**0.44 ± 0.68**	**0.48 ± 1.04**	**0.49 ± 1.21**	**0.44 ± 0.73**	**0.44 ± 0.65**
	ADD [%]	**8.94 ± 7.71**	**9.95 ± 9.12**	**9.72 ± 8.67**	**8.88 ± 7.54**	**9.37 ± 8.06**
	OR [%]	**82.4 ± 10.6**	**82.8 ± 10.3**	**82.3 ± 9.9**	**82.7 ± 10.5**	**82.6 ± 9.84**

the segmentation results overlaid on full projection images, (b) and (d) shows the enlarged view of the rectangles region marked by an white box. As shown in Fig. 8(b) and (d), one deep model misclassified normal regions as GA lesions. Moreover, our method not only obtained higher consistency with the average ground truths but also perform higher efficiency.

3.2   Quantitative Evaluation

Comparison with Traditional Methods. We quantitatively compared our automated results with tow traditional methods (Chen's and Niu's) and the manual segmentations drawn by 4 expert readers. Table 2 shows the agreement of GA projection area in the axial direction between each segmentation result and the ground truth (individual reader segmentations and the average expert segmentations). From Table 2, comparing each segmentation method to the manual outlines drawn in FAF images, we can observe that the correlation coefficient

Table 3. The summarizations of the quantitative results (mean ± standard deviation) between the deep learning segmentations and manual gold standards (individual reader segmentations and the average expert segmentations) on dataset.

Methods	Criterions	ExpertA$_1$	ExpertA$_2$	ExpertB$_1$	ExpertB$_2$	Avg.Expert
One deep model	cc	0.903	0.900	0.914	0.905	0.900
	AAD [mm^2]	1.43 ± 1.85	1.39 ± 1.85	1.33 ± 1.63	1.37 ± 1.78	1.41 ± 1.82
	ADD [%]	20.9 ± 24.6	20.8 ± 25.2	19.3 ± 23.5	19.8 ± 24.0	20.4 ± 24.6
	OR [%]	72.7 ± 16.3	73.1 ± 16.2	72.4 ± 15.5	72.6 ± 15.5	72.8 ± 15.9
Our method	cc	**0.9884**	**0.9826**	**0.9885**	**0.9918**	**0.9881**
	ADD [mm^2]	**0.44 ± 0.68**	**0.48 ± 1.04**	**0.49 ± 1.21**	**0.44 ± 0.73**	**0.44 ± 0.65**
	ADD [%]	**8.94 ± 7.71**	**9.95 ± 9.12**	**9.72 ± 8.67**	**8.88 ± 7.54**	**9.37 ± 8.06**
	OR [%]	**82.4 ± 10.6**	**82.8 ± 10.3**	**82.3 ± 9.9**	**82.7 ± 10.5**	**82.6 ± 9.84**

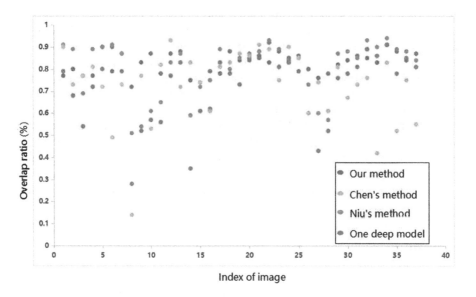

Fig. 9. The overlap ratio comparisons between the segmentations and average expert segmentations on all the cases.

(0.9881 vs 0.970 and 0.979) and overlap ratio (82.64% vs 72.6% and 81.86%) of our method are high for GA projection area. The absolute area difference of our method is low (0.44 vs 1.44 and 0.81) which indicating the areas estimated by our method are closer to those manual productions.

Comparison with Deep Learning. We quantitatively compared our automated results with deep VGG16 convolutional neural networks (one deep model) and the manual segmentations drawn by 4 expert readers. Table 3 shows the agreement of GA projection area in the axial direction between the segmentation result and the ground truth (individual reader segmentations and the average expert segmentations). From Table 3, comparing segmentation method based on one deep model to the manual outlines drawn in FAF images, we can observe that the correlation coefficient (0.9881 vs 0.900) and overlap ratio (82.64% vs 72.8%) of our method are high for GA projection area. The absolute area difference of our method is low (0.44 vs 1.41) which indicating the areas estimated by our method are closer to those manual productions. Moreover, it is time consuming that deep learning methods require extensive training samples and labels to construct training model.

From Fig. 9, Tables 2 and 3, comparatively, the variance of the overlap rate of our method is smaller than other methods, so our method is more robust.

4   Conclusions

In this paper, we presented an automated and robust GA segmentation method based on object tracking strategy for time series SD-OCT volumetric images. In our proposed scenario, experts only need to manually calibrate GA lesion area for the first moment of each patient, and then the GA of the following moments will be automatically, robustly and accurately detected. In order to fully embody the outstanding features of GA, a new sample construction method is proposed for more effectively extracting HOG features to generate random forest models. The experiments on several SD-OCT volumetric images with GA demonstrate that our method shows good agreement when compared to manual segmentation by different experts at different sessions. The comparative experiments with semi-automated method, region-based C-V model and deep VGG16 convolutional neural network obtain more accurate GA segmentations, better stability and higher effectiveness.

References

1. Klein, R., Klein, B.E., Knudtson, M.D., Meuer, S.M., Swift, M., Gangnon, R.E.: Fifteen-year cumulative incidence of age-related macular degeneration: the Beaver Dam Eye Study. Ophthalmology **114**(2), 253–262 (2007)
2. Schatz, H., McDonald, H.R.: Atrophic macular degeneration. Rate of spread of geographic atrophy and visual loss. Ophthalmology **96**(10), 1541–1551 (1989)
3. Bhutto, I., Lutty, G.: Understanding age-related macular degeneration (AMD): relationships between the photoreceptor/retinal pigment epithelium/Bruch's membrane/choriocapillaris complex. Mol. Aspects Med. **33**(4), 295–317 (2012)
4. Sunness, J.S., et al.: Enlargement of atrophy and visual acuity loss in the geographic atrophy form of age-related macular degeneration. Ophthalmology **106**(9), 1768–1779 (1999)
5. Chaikitmongkol, V., Tadarati, M., Bressler, N.M.: Recent approaches to evaluating and monitoring geographic atrophy. Curr. Opin. Ophthalmol. **27**, 217–223 (2016)
6. Folgar, F.A., Age Related Eye Disease Study 2 Ancillary Spectral-Domain Optical Coherence Tomography Study Group, et al.: Drusen volume and retinal pigment epithelium abnormal thinning volume predict 2-year progression of age-related macular degeneration. Ophthalmology **123**(1), 39–50 (2016)

7. Chen, Q., de Sisternes, L., Leng, T., Zheng, L., Kutzscher, L., Rubin, D.L.: Semi-automatic geographic atrophy segmentation for SD-OCT images. Biomed. Opt. Express **4**(12), 2729–2750 (2013)
8. Hu, Z., Medioni, G.G., Hernandez, M., Hariri, A., Wu, X., Sadda, S.R.: Segmentation of the geographic atrophy in spectral-domain optical coherence tomography and fundus autofluorescence images. Invest. Ophthalmol. Vis. Sci. **54**(13), 8375–8383 (2013)
9. Niu, S., de Sisternes, L., Chen, Q., Leng, T., Rubin, D.L.: Automated geographic atrophy segmentation for SD-OCT images using region-based CV model via local similarity factor. Biomed. Opt. Express **7**, 581–600 (2016)
10. Ji, Z., Chen, Q., Niu, S., Leng, T., Rubin, D.L.: Beyond retinal layers: a deep voting model for automated geographic atrophy segmentation in SD-OCT images. Transl. Vis. Sci. Technol. **7**(1), 2063 (2018)
11. Dalal, N., Triggs, B.: Histograms of oriented gradients for human detection. In: IEEE Computer Society Conference on Computer Vision and Pattern Recognition, pp. 1063–6919 (2005)
12. Chen, Q., Fan, W., Niu, S., Shi, J., Shen, H., Yuan, S.: Automated choroid segmentation based on gradual intensity distance in HD-OCT images. Opt. Express **23**(7), 8974–8994 (2015)

Human Trajectory Prediction with Social Information Encoding

Siqi Ren, Yue Zhou[✉], and Liming He

Institute of Image Processing and Pattern Recognition,
Shanghai Jiao Tong University, Shanghai, China
{rensiqi_stju,zhouyue,heliming}@sjtu.edu.cn

Abstract. Trajectory prediction is a particularly challenging problem which is of great significance with the rapid development of socially-aware robots and intelligent security systems. Recent works have focused on using deep recurrent neural networks (RNNs) to model objects trajectories with the target of learning time-dependent representations. However, problems urgently needing to be solved in how to model the object trajectory jointly in a scene, as we all know that objects couldn't move alone without his neighborhood's influence. Since the sequence to sequence architecture have been proven to be powerful in sequence prediction tasks, different from the traditional architecture, we propose a novel sequence to sequence architecture to model the interaction between objects and model every trajectory's moving pattern. We demonstrate that our approach can achieve state-of-the-art result on publicly available crowd datasets.

Keywords: Trajectory prediction · Seq2seq architecture
Social interaction

1 Introduction

Nowadays, with the popularization of intelligent security systems and socially-aware robots, understanding and predicting object behaviour in complex real world scenarios has a vast number of applications. Although significant effort has been made in prediction domains like human motion prediction, it is still an enormous challenge for researchers to model and predict object behaviour. Similarly, since human trajectory is the result of both intentions of themselves and intentions of people around them, it's a complex task to predict human trajectory. In this paper, we focus on how to model human trajectory from their previous positions and their neighbor's positions. More specifically, we are interested in trajectory prediction, we forecast the most likely future trajectory of a person given their past position.

Trajectory prediction is a tough work because of the complexity of the situation. As is shown in Fig. 1, they are the 7340th and the 7380th frame in dataset

© Springer Nature Switzerland AG 2018
J.-H. Lai et al. (Eds.): PRCV 2018, LNCS 11256, pp. 262–273, 2018.
https://doi.org/10.1007/978-3-030-03398-9_23

Fig. 1. Examples of pedestrians exhibiting cooperative behavior. (Color figure online)

[27]. To name a few, in the red box, some pedestrians are staying there without moving, and in the yellow box and green box, there are lots of pedestrians exhibiting cooperative behavior. In green box, two pedestrian walk along and in red box, many people are passing through a small region. Apparently their trajectories will be influenced by the others.

1.1 Related Work

Traditional approaches use hand-crafted functions to model interactions such as [2,3,10,21,22,27], they are proven to be effective on modeling simple interactions and might fail to model some complex interactions. They are not in a data-driven fashion.

Recently, Long-Short Term Memory networks (LSTM) [12] are of great success in sequences prediction such as machine translation [23], speech recognition [5,9,11], human dynamics [8], caption generation [14,25] and so on. RNNs are excellent at time-series modelling and some researchers have already extend LSTM for human trajectory prediction such as [1].

More recently, attention mechanism [4] is proven to be effective in domains like sentiment classification [20] and visual attention [17]. [7,24] have made some attempts in the domain. We suppose that attention mechanism is important for predicting trajectory since one object will be strongly influenced by his history moving pattern and attention will help the model learn it.

Furthermore, sequence to sequence model [19] has been proven to be powerful in some fields like neural machine translation, and is also powerful in human motion prediction like [13,16]. In some trajectory analysis domains like trajectory clustering, seq2seq architecture [26] is also proven to be effective.

Inspired by the recent success of RNN which benefit from large publicly available crowd dataset and with the success of seq2seq architecture and attention mechanism, we propose a change to the standard RNN models typically used for human trajectory prediction which can be illustrated in Fig. 2. Individual information and neighborhood information will gathered separately by individual encoder and social encoder. The decoder will predict the positions of the

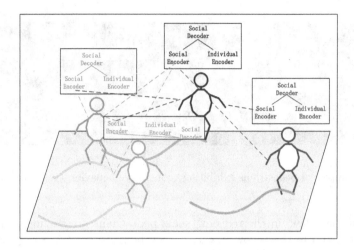

Fig. 2. A sample surveillance scene.

object in the next time period with a embedded feature extracted by a social encoder and an individual encoder.

Recent work has validated its performance via two different metrics. Similar to [18], typically measured a distance between predicted location and true location. Average displacement error calculate mean square error over all points of a trajectory, and Final displacement error calculate only the final destination of a trajectory.

2   Proposed Method

For trajectory prediction task, we note that there are a lot of work need to be done to improve the accuracy of the current model. In this section, we describe our crowd seq2seq model (Fig. 3) which can jointly predict all people's trajectories in a scene.

2.1   Problem Formulation

Consider a set of trajectories $S = \{s_1, s_2, ..., s_n\}$ in a scene, at time t, the ith trajectory s_i^t is represented by its coordinates $(x_t, y_t)_i$. $h_{t,i}$ represents the ith individual encoder's state at time t, the state during the observation period from time t to time $t + obs - 1$ will be embedded into a vector $H_{t,i}^C$ via attention. And $I_{t,i}$ represents the neighbor vector of the ith trajectory at time t. Then a social encoder will encode the neighbor vector into a vector $H_{t,i}^I$. After that, $H_{t,i}^C$ and $H_{t,i}^I$ will be concatenated into one vector and a social decoder will predict objects positions from time $t + obs$ to time $t + 2obs - 1$.

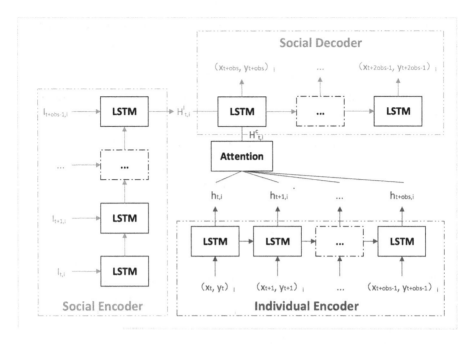

Fig. 3. Overview of the proposed model. A seperate sequence to sequence model is used for each object in the scene. We set an individual encoder with an attention mechanism to model the pattern of individual trajectory, and a social encoder to model the interaction between the object and his neighbor objectes. The states of these two encoder $H_{t,i}^C$ and $H_{t,i}^I$ will be concatenated and it will be used in a social decoder to predict the future trajectory.

2.2   Model Architecture

As shown in Fig. 3, we set each trajectory a seq2seq architecture to learn its specific motion properties. There are three parts in our model: individual encoder, social encoder and social decoder. We will explain them in the following sections.

Individual Encoder. We first convert a set of trajectory coordinates to a set of moving vectors $(x_i^t, y_i^t, v_i^t, r_i^t)$ at time t where (x_i^t, y_i^t) is the coordinates. Given a time gap between two records $\tau > 0$, the speed v_i^t can be calculated by:

$$v_i^t = \frac{\sqrt{(x_i^t - x_i^{t-1})^2 + (y_i^t - y_i^{t-1})^2}}{\tau} \tag{1}$$

And the angle r_i^t can be calculated by:

$$r_i^t = \arctan \frac{y_i^t - y_i^{t-1}}{x_i^t - x_i^{t-1}} \tag{2}$$

In each individual encoder, a set of moving vector of the trajectory will be encoded into a set of state vector $\{h_i^t, h_i^{t+1}, ..., h_i^{t+obs-1}\}$. The encoding function can be denoted by

$$h_{t,i} = LSTM(x_i^t, y_i^t, v_i^t, r_i^t, h_i^{t-1}) \tag{3}$$

We set a soft attention mechanism after the individual encoder encoding the interested trajectory moving pattern into one vector $H_{t,i}^C$. The function can be denoted by

$$u_i^k = \tanh(W_w \times (concat(hd_i^{t-1}, h_i^{t+k})) + b_w) \tag{4}$$

$$\alpha_i^k = \frac{\exp((u_i^k)^T u_w)}{\sum_k^{obs} \exp((u_i^k)^T u_w)} \tag{5}$$

$$H_{t,i}^C = \sum_k^{obs} (\alpha_i^{t+k} \times (h_i^{t+k})) \tag{6}$$

where hd_i^{t-1} is the hidden state of the decoder at time $t - 1$, k is the kth record during the current observation period $(t, t + obs - 1)$, W_w, b_w and u_w are the hyperparameters which will be learnt during the feed forward neural network of the model.

With the help of distinct embedded vectors we are able to focus on different degrees of attention towards different parts of the trajectory states.

Social Encoder. However, in real life trajectories interact with each other and can't be regarded as isolated, and not all trajectories' influence equally to the current trajectory. So we set a social encoder for it in order to jointly reason across multiple trajectories.

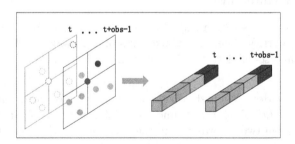

Fig. 4. Picture demonstrates how to calculate the neighbor vector. Red point represents the current trajectory of interest. Different color represents different relative position of a trajectory in a grid. (Color figure online)

Apparently, the one which is closer to the trajectory of interest has a greater impact on the modelled trajectory. So we set a neighbor vector similar to [1] before social encoder to model the social interaction between crowds and help the model predict the positions more accuracy. The neighbor grid we set can be seen in Fig. 4. The red point denotes the position of the ith object at time t, and the other points denotes the surrounding objects. Different colors represent that they are in the different cell of grid. We discretize the space around the current location of the trajectory into a $N \times N$ size grid. Then the ith trajectory's neighbor vector at time t can be denoted by

$$I_{t,i}(a + N(b - 1)) = \sum P_{a,b}(j)[x_j^t - x_i^t, y_j^t - y_i^t] \tag{7}$$

where $P_{a,b}(j) = 1$ is an indicator function to check if the jth object is in the (a, b) cell of the grid. After the function, we flatten the neighbor matrix and then we get the neighbor vector $I_{t,i}$ of the ith trajectory. Then the neighbor vector during observation time obs will be encoded into a cell state $H_{t,i}^I$ by social encoder, which can be denoted by

$$H_{t,i}^I = LSTM(I_{t,i}, h_{t-1}^I) \tag{8}$$

Then, we concatenate $H_{t,i}^I$ and $H_{t,i}^C$ into one vector $H_{t,i}$ as our final encoded vector. With the aid of the above equation we could encode the trajectory information comprehensively and help the decoder predict the position more accurately.

Social Decoder. In our case, let $hd_{t-1,i}$ be the social decoder's hidden state at time $t - 1$, $H_{t,i}$ be the encoded vector, the decoder output at time t is computed by

$$h_{di}^t = LSTM(H_{t,i}, hd_{t-1,i}) \tag{9}$$

Position Estimation. For position estimation, we follow the method mentioned in [1] which makes the model predicting the position as

$$(x_{i,t}^{pred}, y_{i,t}^{pred}) \sim N(\mu_i^t, \sigma_i^t, \rho_i^t) \tag{10}$$

the decoder's hidden state will be passed through a linear layer to get a predicted vector. Functions are as follows:

$$(\mu_i^t, \sigma_i^t, \rho_i^t) = W_p hd_i^t \tag{11}$$

In which μ_i^t represents the mean of predicted position, σ_i^t represents the standard deviation and ρ_i^t represents the correlation.

By minimizing the loss L which is shown as follows, we can train the entire model together.

$$L = - \sum_{t+obs}^{t+2obs-1} \log(P(x_{i,t}^{truth}, y_{i,t}^{truth} | \mu_i^t, \sigma_i^t, \rho_i^t)) \tag{12}$$

In which $(x_{i,t}^{truth}, y_{i,t}^{truth})$ is the ground truth coordinates of the ith trajectory of current time step t.

Implementation Details. We use an embedding dimension of 64 for the moving vectors of individual encoder and social vector of social encoder. We used a 4 × 4 sum neighborhood grid size without overlap for neighbor vector and a local neighborhood of size 128 px was considered. We used a fixed hidden state dimension of 128 for both social encoder, individual encoder and 256 for social decoder. We used a learning rate of 0.0005 and RMS-prop [6] for training the model. The model was trained on a CPU with a Tensorflow implementation.

3   Experiments

We have conducted two experiments to test our approach.

For the first one, we present experiments on two publicly available human-trajectory datasets: ETH [18] and UCY [15]. There are 5 sets of data with a total of 1536 non-linear trajectories in these two datasets, whose trajectories are with complex interaction such as pedestrian groups crossing each other, joint collision avoidance and walking together and so on during the pedestrian walking. In order to make full use of the datasets while training, we use a leave-one-out approach, similar with [1], we train and validate our model on 4 crowd sets and test it on the remaining crowd set. We set the observation length of our model to be 10 and we will forecast the position for the next 10 frames. At a frame rate of 0.4, it means that we observe 4 s and predict the future for the next 4 s. Further more, We use linear interpolation to do data augmentation for our model.

For the second one, we test our approach on one publicly available human trajectory dataset New York Grand Central (GC) [27]. It consists of around 12600 trajectories. We train our model on randomly selected $\frac{3}{4}$ trajectories and test our model on the rest $\frac{1}{4}$ of the trajectories. In this experiment, we set the observation length of our model to be 8 and the model will predict the next 8 positions for a trajectory.

Let n be the number of trajectories in the testing set, $X_{i,t}^{pred}$ be the predicted position for the trajectory i at time t, and $X_{i,t}^{truth}$ be the respective observed positions, obs is the length of observation frames and prediction frames. $2obs - 1$ represents the final frame of one prediction period. Same with [1], we report the prediction error with two metrics:

* Average displacement error. The mean euclidean distance over all predicted points and the ground truth points.

$$ADE = \frac{\sum_{i=1}^{n} \sum_{t=obs}^{2obs-1} (X_{i,t}^{pred} - X_{i,t}^{truth})^2}{n \times obs} \tag{13}$$

* Final displacement error. The mean euclidean distance between the final predicted location and the ground truth location.

$$FDE = \frac{\sum_{i=1}^{n} \sqrt{(X_{i,2obs-1}^{pred} - X_{i,2obs-1}^{truth})^2}}{n} \tag{14}$$

We compare the performance of our model with LSTM based state-of-the-art methods: social LSTM [1], combined social [7], social attention [24], and also compared with traditional classic methods social force [10]. Since some of the method is not open-source, we set test 1 to compare our model with social force [10], native LSTM, social LSTM [1] and social attention [24]. Similarly, we set test 2 to compare our model performance with social force, social LSTM and CMB [7].

Table 1. Test 1. Quantitative results on ETH and UCY dataset.

Metric	Methods	Social Force	LSTM	Social_LSTM	Social_Attention	Ours
ADE	ETH-Univ	0.46	0.60	0.50	0.39	**0.29**
	ETH-Hotel	0.44	0.15	0.11	0.29	**0.10**
	UCY-Zara1	0.22	0.43	0.22	**0.20**	0.22
	UCY-Zara2	0.31	0.51	**0.25**	0.30	0.32
	UCY-Univ	0.32	0.52	0.27	0.33	**0.23**
	Average	0.36	0.44	0.27	0.30	**0.24**
FPE	ETH-Univ	4.12	1.31	1.07	3.74	**0.35**
	ETH-Hotel	3.43	0.33	**0.23**	2.64	0.34
	UCY-Zara1	0.63	0.93	0.48	0.52	**0.44**
	UCY-Zara2	3.11	1.09	0.50	2.13	**0.43**
	UCY-Univ	4.01	1.25	0.77	3.92	**0.75**
	Average	2.97	0.98	0.61	2.59	**0.53**

Quantitative Results. Quantitative results of test 1 can be seen in Table 1. The first six rows are the average displacement error, the final six rows are the final displacement error. All methods forecast trajectories for 10 frames with a fixed observation length 10. We didn't include the prediction errors of pedestrians for whom we observed fewer than observation period obs when testing our model. Since the naive independent LSTM can't capture the interaction between people, it performs poorly with high prediction errors, especially in the scenes where there are a lot of people in it. Social Force, social LSTM, social attention and our model are all taking social interactions into account. Apparently LSTM based approach can model trajectory better than social force. And it can be seen roughly that our architecture can model human-human interaction better than the methods mentioned in other two LSTM based algorithms.

In first 6 rows, our approach performs better than the other methods in 3 datasets, and get the highest accuracy in average ADE. Especially in the ETH-Univ crowd set, our method outperforms the others by a large margin. Since the dataset contains lots of trajectory scenarios, for instance, UCY-Univ contains more crowded regions and more non-linearities compared to other crowd sets, the results show that our model can predict trajectory more accurately in most scenarios because our social encoder and the attention mechanism which take the history of the current trajectory and human-human interaction into consideration can model the moving pattern better.

In the last 6 rows, the results in which our model outperforms others in almost every crowd sets demonstrate that our method can predict the future more accurately with a longer period compared to the other methods.

Table 2. Test 2. Quantitative results on GC dataset.

Metric	Social Force	Social_LSTM	CMB [7]	Ours$_{ie}$	Ours
ADE	3.36	1.99	1.09	2.08	**1.05**
FPE	5.81	4.52	3.01	4.32	**2.98**

Quantitative results of test 2 can be seen in Table 2. In order to evaluate the strengths of the proposed model, we compare our full model with variation on our proposed approach: the model with only individual encoder (Our$_{ie}$). In this test, All methods forecast trajectories for 8 frames with a fixed observation length 8. Comparing the results of Our$_{ie}$ against the our final model, it can be verified that our social encoder for current pedestrian trajectory is important for future prediction. And the results of our final method shows that both historical data of current trajectory and the interaction between human and human are important for this task.

What's more, we can see that in both ADE and FPE, our proposed model outperforms the native LSTM, social LSTM and CMB model. It can be verified that the social encoder and social decoder we proposed is more effective of learning how the neighbours influence the current trajectory and how this impact varies under different neighbourhood locations. The experiments show that our method can reach the leading level in the domain.

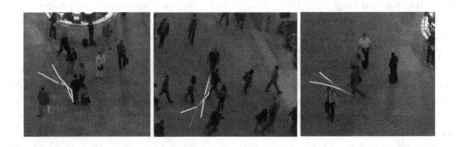

Fig. 5. Qualitative results on GC dataset. Two methods are compared: ours (red line) and social LSTM (blue line). Yellow line is the ground truth trajectories. (Color figure online)

Qualitative Results. Qualitative results on GC dataset [27] can be seen in Fig. 5. We illustrate the prediction results of our model and social LSTM. Yellow line is the ground truth trajectory, red line is the prediction of our model, and blue one is the prediction of Social LSTM [1]. Because the author of social LSTM haven't made their code opensource, we used the code implemented by [24]. We only show one trajectory in a scene to make sure we could describe the result clearly. When people walk in a group or as a couple like the third picture, our model is able to jointly predict their trajectories, and the prediction is more accuracy than social LSTM. And when people are crossing crowds like first and second picture, although there might be a gap between our prediction and the ground truth trajectory, our model can predict the trajectories plausible enough to avoid collision, and the prediction result are better than social LSTM. As can be seen, our model predict the trajectory with smaller error compared with social LSTM. The results demonstrate that our model can make more precision and reasonable prediction.

4   Conclusion

In this paper, we have presented a novel sequence to sequence model to predict human trajectory, which can model object trajectory and predict their future trajectory with the joint concern of their neighbor. We use one seq2seq model for each trajectory and encoding their motion into a vector by social encoder. We show that our model could outperforms the state-of-the-art method on public available datasets. Our model can predict trajectory effectively with a seq2seq model per object.

Currently, the model doesn't consider the image information which plays a very important role in modeling behavior. With the help of image, the model should be able to find out the information about the surrounding environments like static obstacles. Maybe it will help the model to predict more accurately by restricting the passable zone. As a part of our future work, we will try to change the architecture of the network to make it possible to consider the image information.

References

1. Alahi, A., Goel, K., Ramanathan, V., Robicquet, A., Fei-Fei, L., Savarese, S.: Social LSTM: human trajectory prediction in crowded spaces. In: Proceedings of the IEEE Conference on Computer Vision and Pattern Recognition, pp. 961–971 (2016)
2. Alahi, A., Ramanathan, V., Fei-Fei, L.: Socially-aware large-scale crowd forecasting. In: 2014 IEEE Conference on Computer Vision and Pattern Recognition, No. EPFL-CONF-230284, pp. 2211–2218. IEEE (2014)
3. Antonini, G., Bierlaire, M., Weber, M.: Discrete choice models of pedestrian walking behavior. Transp. Res. Part B Methodol. **40**(8), 667–687 (2006)
4. Bahdanau, D., Cho, K., Bengio, Y.: Neural machine translation by jointly learning to align and translate. arXiv preprint arXiv:1409.0473 (2014)

5. Chung, J., Kastner, K., Dinh, L., Goel, K., Courville, A.C., Bengio, Y.: A recurrent latent variable model for sequential data. In: Advances in Neural Information Processing Systems, pp. 2980–2988 (2015)
6. Dauphin, Y., de Vries, H., Bengio, Y.: Equilibrated adaptive learning rates for non-convex optimization. In: Advances in Neural Information Processing Systems, pp. 1504–1512 (2015)
7. Fernando, T., Denman, S., Sridharan, S., Fookes, C.: Soft+ hardwired attention: an LSTM framework for human trajectory prediction and abnormal event detection. arXiv preprint arXiv:1702.05552 (2017)
8. Fragkiadaki, K., Levine, S., Felsen, P., Malik, J.: Recurrent network models for human dynamics. In: 2015 IEEE International Conference on Computer Vision (ICCV), pp. 4346–4354. IEEE (2015)
9. Graves, A., Jaitly, N.: Towards end-to-end speech recognition with recurrent neural networks. In: International Conference on Machine Learning, pp. 1764–1772 (2014)
10. Helbing, D., Molnar, P.: Social force model for pedestrian dynamics. Phys. Rev. E **51**(5), 4282 (1995)
11. Hinton, G., et al.: Deep neural networks for acoustic modeling in speech recognition: the shared views of four research groups. IEEE Signal Process. Mag. **29**(6), 82–97 (2012)
12. Hochreiter, S., Schmidhuber, J.: Long short-term memory. Neural Comput. **9**(8), 1735–1780 (1997)
13. Jain, A., Zamir, A.R., Savarese, S., Saxena, A.: Structural-RNN: deep learning on spatio-temporal graphs. In: Proceedings of the IEEE Conference on Computer Vision and Pattern Recognition, pp. 5308–5317 (2016)
14. Karpathy, A., Joulin, A., Fei-Fei, L.F.: Deep fragment embeddings for bidirectional image sentence mapping. In: Advances in Neural Information Processing Systems, pp. 1889–1897 (2014)
15. Lerner, A., Chrysanthou, Y., Lischinski, D.: Crowds by example. In: Computer Graphics Forum, vol. 26, pp. 655–664. Wiley Online Library (2007)
16. Martinez, J., Black, M.J., Romero, J.: On human motion prediction using recurrent neural networks. In: 2017 IEEE Conference on Computer Vision and Pattern Recognition (CVPR), pp. 4674–4683. IEEE (2017)
17. Mnih, V., Heess, N., Graves, A., et al.: Recurrent models of visual attention. In: Advances in Neural Information Processing Systems, pp. 2204–2212 (2014)
18. Pellegrini, S., Ess, A., Schindler, K., Van Gool, L.: You'll never walk alone: modeling social behavior for multi-target tracking. In: 2009 IEEE 12th International Conference on Computer Vision, pp. 261–268. IEEE (2009)
19. Sutskever, I., Vinyals, O., Le, Q.V.: Sequence to sequence learning with neural networks. In: Advances in Neural Information Processing Systems, pp. 3104–3112 (2014)
20. Tang, D., Qin, B., Liu, T.: Document modeling with gated recurrent neural network for sentiment classification. In: Proceedings of the 2015 Conference on Empirical Methods in Natural Language Processing, pp. 1422–1432 (2015)
21. Tay, M.K.C., Laugier, C.: Modelling smooth paths using Gaussian processes. In: Laugier, C., Siegwart, R. (eds.) Field and Service Robotics, pp. 381–390. Springer, Heidelberg (2008). https://doi.org/10.1007/978-3-540-75404-6_36
22. Treuille, A., Cooper, S., Popović, Z.: Continuum crowds. In: ACM Transactions on Graphics (TOG), vol. 25, pp. 1160–1168. ACM (2006)
23. Tu, Z., Liu, Y., Shang, L., Liu, X., Li, H.: Neural machine translation with reconstruction. In: AAAI, pp. 3097–3103 (2017)

24. Vemula, A., Muelling, K., Oh, J.: Social attention: modeling attention in human crowds. arXiv preprint arXiv:1710.04689 (2017)
25. Vinyals, O., Toshev, A., Bengio, S., Erhan, D.: Show and tell: a neural image caption generator. In: 2015 IEEE Conference on Computer Vision and Pattern Recognition (CVPR), pp. 3156–3164. IEEE (2015)
26. Yao, D., Zhang, C., Zhu, Z., Huang, J., Bi, J.: Trajectory clustering via deep representation learning. In: 2017 International Joint Conference on Neural Networks (IJCNN), pp. 3880–3887. IEEE (2017)
27. Yi, S., Li, H., Wang, X.: Understanding pedestrian behaviors from stationary crowd groups. In: Proceedings of the IEEE Conference on Computer Vision and Pattern Recognition, pp. 3488–3496 (2015)

Pixel Saliency Based Encoding
for Fine-Grained Image Classification

Chao Yin, Lei Zhang$^{(\boxtimes)}$, and Ji Liu

College of Communication Engineering, Chongqing University,
No. 174 Shazheng Street, Shapingba district, Chongqing 400044, China
{chaoyin,leizhang,jiliu}@cqu.edu.cn

Abstract. Fine-grained image classification concerns categorization at
subordinate levels, where the distinction between inter-class objects is
very subtle and highly local. Recently, Convolutional Neural Networks
(CNNs) have almost yielded the best results on the basic image classification tasks. In CNN, the direct pooling operation is always used to
resize the last convolutional feature maps from $n \times n \times c$ to $1 \times 1 \times c$
for feature representation. However, such pooling operation may lead to
extreme saliency compression of feature map, especially in fine-grained
image classification. In this paper, to more deeply explore the representation ability of the feature map, we propose a *Pixel Saliency based
Encoding* method, which is called PS-CNN. First, in our PS-CNN, the
saliency matrix is obtained by evaluating the saliency of each pixel in
the feature map. Then, we segment the original feature maps into multiple ones with multiple generated binary masks via thresholding on the
obtained saliency matrix, and subsequently squeeze those masked feature
maps into the encoded ones. Finally, a fine-grained feature representation
is generated by concatenating the original feature maps with the encoded
ones. Experimental results show that our simple yet powerful PS-CNN
outperforms state-of-the-art classification approaches. Specially, we can
achieve 89.1% classification accuracy on the Aircraft, 92.3% on the Stanford Car, and 81.9% on the NABirds.

Keywords: Pixel saliency · Feature encoding · Fine-grained
Image classification

1 Introduction

Fine-grained image classification aims to recognize similar sub-categories in the
same basic-level category [1–3]. More specifically, it refers to the task of assigning
plenty of similar input images with specific labels from a fixed set of categories by
using computer vision algorithms. Till now, for such categorization in computer
vision area, Convolutional Neural Networks (CNNs) have played a vital role.
The impressive representation ability of CNNs, e.g., VGG [4], GoogleNet [5],
ResNet [1], and DenseNet [2], is also demonstrated in object detection [6], face

© Springer Nature Switzerland AG 2018
J.-H. Lai et al. (Eds.): PRCV 2018, LNCS 11256, pp. 274–285, 2018.
https://doi.org/10.1007/978-3-030-03398-9_24

recognition [7], and many other vision tasks. By using the CNN models pre-trained on the ImageNet, many image classification problems are well addressed and their classification accuracies almost approach to their extreme performance. However, fine-grained image classification, a sub-category of basic-level category, is still a challenging task in computer vision area due to high intra-class variances caused by deformation, view angle, illumination, and occlusion of images and low inter-class variances which are tiny differences occurred only in some local regions between inter-class object and these can only be recognized by certain experts. Moreover, we are faced with several under-solved problems in fine-grained image classification. One problem is that there are limited fine-grained images with labels due to the high cost of labeling and cleaning when collecting data [8]. Another is the difficulty of acquiring better annotations and bounding boxes which are helpful in the process of classifying fine-grained images.

For image classification, CNNs are always exceptionally powerful models. First, apart from some simple image pre-processing, CNN always uses the raw images with a pre-defined size as its input. Then, CNN progressively learns the low-level (detail), middle-level, and high-level (abstract) features from bottom, intermediate to top convolutional layers without any hand-craft feature extraction policy like SIFT and HOG [9,10]. Finally, the discriminating feature maps with a pre defined size from top-level layers are obtained. At the same time, if the size of input images, in some case, increases, the size of output convolutional layers also increases. In general way, we can directly perform an average or max pooling to produce the last feature representation which then will be sent to classifier of network. However, such coarse pooling operation will lead to extreme saliency compression of feature map especially for fine-grained image classification that concentrates on more fine-grained structure information. In fact, saliency compression is a bottleneck for information flow of CNN.

To solve aforementioned extreme saliency compression problem when classifying fine-grained images, we propose a *Pixel Saliency based Encoding* method for CNN. The motivations for our method are presented as follows.

(1) Considering the characteristic, tiny differences only occurred in some local regions, of fine-grained images, a simple solution for fine-grained image classification is magnifying images on both training and testing phases to 'look' into more details [11]. The magnified input images will result in an increasing size of the last convolutional feature map. If still using the straightforward coarse Avg/Max pooling operation as usual, it will lose a lot of detailed structural information which will be help for classification. Therefore, the method of re-encoding the feature map should be adopted to explore the crytic information for last convolutional feature map.

(2) In image segmentation area [6,12], it is expected that different pixels in a feature map with different range of saliency are explicitly segmented so that the interest of object is revealed and the background is hidden in a feature map, which is also ours goal here for fine-grained image classification. We argue this separation is necessary for recognizing the regions of interest and will be helpful for feature learning of the total CNN.

(3) After all of those 'parts' with different saliency are segmented and then squeezed in the next layer, to involve the global information of input image, the original feature map reflecting the overall characteristics should also be concatenated as the final feature representation.

Our PS-CNN is a saliency based encoding method within well-known Inception-V3 framework. By encoding, PS-CNN explores the better representation ability of the last convolutional feature maps rather than the average pooling used as usual. After encoding, more details of local regions are collected separately. Then, to involve global information of object, we concatenate encoded feature maps with the original one so that new feature maps carried with global image representations are generated. Our PS-CNN is a simple yet effective method. The details of our PS-CNN are shown as in Fig. 1. As can be seen from the encoded feature map in encoding part, the region of interest is successfully picked out from the original feature map extracted by convolutional part of CNN.

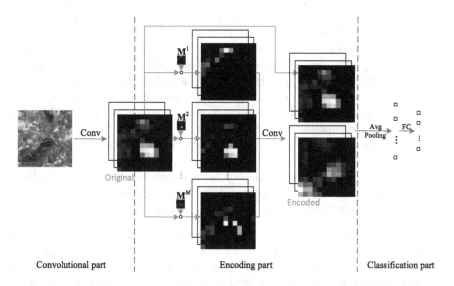

Fig. 1. Overview of the proposed encoding method. A input image passes through convolutional part of CNN to generate the (original) feature maps. First, we average those feature maps to get one saliency matrix. Then, M masks are generated based on this matrix and used to mask the original feature maps by using the *Hadamard product*. As a result, there will generate total M steamings. After that, we squeeze those M streamings into one feature representation map by using the 1×1 convolutional operation. At last, the original and encoded feature maps are concatenated to form the feature map for representation.

The main contributions of the paper are listed in the following.

(1) We firstly argue that pixels with different range of saliency in feature maps should be explicitly segmented. Then a simple saliency matrix calculation method is proposed to evaluate the saliency of each pixel in feature map.
(2) Multiple binary masks are calculated based on the selected thresholds along with the calculated saliency matrix to more explicitly segment the original feature maps. Then the information-richer feature representation is developed by concatenating the encoded feature maps with the original ones.
(3) Experimental results on accuracy with different number of masks are illustrated, showing that our encoding method is efficient. In addition, the pixel saliency based encoding method proposed in our paper, can be embedded into any CNNs.

The rest of this paper is organized as follows. Section 2 describes one CNN, i.e., Inception-V3. Then the existing part/object localization and feature encoding methods are summarized. In Sect. 3, a *Pixel Saliency based Encoding* method for CNN (PS-CNN) is proposed. In Sect. 4, we present experimental results to illustrate the classification accuracy improvement of the proposed PS-CNN and we also discuss the influence on classification accuracy with varying number of binary masks. Finally, Sect. 5 concludes this paper.

2 Related Work

Convolutional Neural Network defines an exceptionally powerful feature learning model. To better advance the image classification accuracy, one direct solution is to increase the depth and width of network. However, basic CNNs are still limited in some specific classification tasks, e.g., fine-grained image classification. The predominant approaches in fine-grained image classification domain can be categorized into two groups. One learns the critical parts of the objects, and the other one directly improves the basic CNN from the view of feature encoding.

2.1 Base Network: Inception-V3

Inception-V3 [13] is a CNN with a high performance in computer vision area and bears a relatively modest computation burden compared to those simpler and more monolithic architectures like VGG [4]. As reported in paper [13], Inception-V3 have achieved 21.2% top-1 and 5.6% top-5 error rates for single crop evaluation on the ILSVR 2012 classification task, which has set a new state of the art. Besides, it also has achieved relatively modest (2.5x) improvement in computational cost compared to the firstly proposed version, i.e., GoogleNet (Inception-V1) network described in [14].

2.2 Part and Object Localization

A common approach for fine-grained image classification is to localize various parts of the object and then model the appearance of part conditioned on their detected locations [8,15]. The method proposed in [8] can generate parts which can be detected in novel images and learn which of those parts are useful for recognition. This method is a big step towards the goal of training fine-grained classifiers without part annotations. Recently, many attentions [16,17] have been paid to the part and object localization method. The OPAM proposed in [17] is aimed for weakly supervised fine-grained image classification, which jointly integrates two level attention models: object-level one localizes objects of images and part-level one selects discriminative parts of objects. The paper proposed a novel part learning approach which is named Multi-Attention Convolutional Neural Network (MA-CNN) [16]. It is interesting that two functional parts, i.e., part generation and feature learning, can reinforce each other. The core of MA-CNN is that one channel grouping sub-network is firstly taken as input feature channels from convolutional layers and then generates multiple parts by clustering, weighting, and pooling from spatially-correlated channels.

2.3 Feature Encoding

The other kind of fine-grained image classification approach is to use a robust image representation from the view of feature encoding. Traditional images representation methods always include hand-craft descriptors like VLAD Fisher vector with SIFT features. Recently, rather than using SIFT extractor, the features extracted from convolutional layers in a deep network pre-trained on imageNet show better representation ability. Those CNN models have achieved state-of-the-art results on a number of basic-level recognition tasks.

There are many methods proposed to encode the feature maps extracted from the last convolutional layers. The representative methods include Bilinear Convolutional Neural Networks (B-CNN) [11] and Second-order CNN [10]. In B-CNN, the output feature maps extracted by the convolutional part are combined at each location, which refers to being encoded by using the matrix outer product. The representation ability after encoding is highly effective in various fine-grained image classification. The Second-order CNN [10] makes an adequate exploration of feature distributions and presents a Matrix Power Normalized Convariacne (MPN-COV) method that performs covariance pooling for the last convolutional features rather than the common pooling operation used in general (first-order) CNN. The Second-order CNN has achieved better performance than B-CNN, but needs a fully re-training on ImageNet ILSVRC2012 dataset.

3   The Proposed Approach

In this Section, we provide the description of our *Pixel Saliency based Encoding* method for CNN (PS-CNN). The details of our PS-CNN architecture and some mathematical presentation of the encoding method are presented as follows.

The convolutional part of Inception-V3 network (referring to [13]) is acted as feature extractor as in our PS-CNN. In general, given the input image $\mathbf{x}$ and the feature extractor $\Phi(\cdot)$, the output feature maps, can be written as

$$\mathbf{F}^0 = \Phi(\mathbf{x}). \tag{1}$$

Here, all the feature maps extracted by Inception-V3 are defined as $\mathbf{F}^{n,0}$, $n = 1, 2 \cdots, N$. Each feature map is with size of $s \times s$. As the default setting of Inception-V3, the s is set to 8. It is worth noting that the s is set to 1 in VGG model. In traditional way, an average pooling will be performed upon $\mathbf{F}^0$ to generate one feature vector. However, in our PS-CNN, we manage to encode those output information-richer feature maps $\mathbf{F}^0$.

3.1 Saliency Matrix Calculation

In order to evaluate the saliency of each pixel in the feature map with size $s \times s$, we perform an element-wise average operation across N feature maps, i.e.,

$$\mathbf{M}_{i,j}^0 = \frac{1}{N} \sum_{n=0}^{N} \mathbf{F}_{i,j}^{n,0}, \tag{2}$$

where $i, j = 1 \cdots s$. In this *saliency matrix* $\mathbf{M}^0$, the value $\mathbf{M}_{i,j}^0$ reflects the saliency of the each pixel. We then use this saliency matrix $\mathbf{M}^0$ to generate several binary masks $\mathbf{M}^m$ where $m = 1, 2 \cdots, M$,

$$\mathbf{M}_{i,j}^m = \begin{cases} 0, & t_m < \mathbf{M}_{i,j}^0 < t_{m+1} \\ 1, & Otherwise. \end{cases} \tag{3}$$

where t_m is threshold. The pair of (t_m, t_{m+1}) defines the range of saliency. If the saliency lays within the range of t_m and t_{m+1}, the corresponding pixels of feature map will be masked as zero. The other pixels of feature map will remain unchanged if saliency of those pixels is outside that range. Here the selection of value t_m is flexible. Notably, value t_m should be between the minimum and maximum values of $\mathbf{M}^0$. In this paper, four binary masks are utilized, i.e., $m = 1, 2, 3, 4$. Besides, the thresholds t_m and t_{m+1} shown in Eq. 3 are chosen as

$$t_m = \min(\mathbf{M}^0) + \text{percent}_m \times \left(\max(\mathbf{M}^0) - \min(\mathbf{M}^0)\right), \tag{4}$$

where the $\min(\cdot)$ and $\max(\cdot)$ find the minimum and maximum values of $\mathbf{M}^0$. The percent_m are chosen as $\text{percent}_1 = 0.1$, $\text{percent}_2 = 0.3$, $\text{percent}_3 = 0.5$, $\text{percent}_4 = 0.7$. When $m = 4$, the upper bound t_{m+1} in Eq. (3), i.e., $\text{percent}_5 = 1$.

3.2 Pixel Saliency Based Encoding

After obtaining the multiple binary masks, i.e., $\mathbf{M}^m$ for $m = 1 \cdots 4$, we encode the original feature maps $\mathbf{F}^{n,0}$ as follows,

$$\mathbf{F}^{n,m} = \mathbf{F}^{n,0} \circ \mathbf{M}^m, \tag{5}$$

where operation ∘ is *Hadamard product*. Thus, for masks $\mathbf{M}^m$, the $\mathbf{F}^{n,m}$ are the encoded feature maps of the original $\mathbf{F}^{n,0}$. Each feature map in $\mathbf{F}^{n,m}$ is encoded with all the information Implicitly carried by $\mathbf{M}^m$ of the original feature maps $\mathbf{F}^{n,0}$. In addition, N convolutional kernels [13], each of which is with size of 1×1, are used to squeeze the total $M \times N$ feature maps to a much smaller one, i.e., $\mathbf{G}$, that has only N feature maps. The feature maps encoding process and visualization are shown as in the encoding part of Fig. 1.

At last, to involve global information of image/object, the original feature maps are concatenated with the feature map $\mathbf{G}$ of subsequent layer by channel, which forms the last feature representation as

$$\mathbf{H} = \left[\mathbf{F}^{n,0}; \mathbf{G}\right]. \tag{6}$$

The classification part as shown in Fig. 1 is the same as the original Inception-V3. Our encoding method is transplantable and simple enough so that it can be embedded into any other CNN framework.

Remarks: Considering the number of feature maps of new representation, i.e., $\mathbf{H}$ in Eq. (6), is twice than the original one in Eq. (1) which is only with the number of N, we could reduce the size of representation by using $N/2$ convolutional kernel, each with the size of 1×1.

4   Experiments

We use AutoBD [18], B-CNN [11], M-CNN [19], and Inception-V3 [13] as compared methods. The model of Inception-V3 is fine-tuned by ourselves. We extend this baseline CNN to include our proposed pixel saliency encoding method and the parameters of our PS-CNN are directly adopted from the Inception-V3 without any sophisticated adjustment.

4.1   Fine-Grained Datasets

There are three datasets chosen in our experiments. The total number, total species, and default train/test split of Aircraft [20], Stanford Car [21], and NABirds [22] datasets are summarized as Table 1. All the image number of those three datasets are much smaller comparing to the basic image classification datasets, e.g., ImageNet, WebVision. The three datasets are also analyzed.

Aircraft [20] is a benchmark dataset for the fine-grained visual categorization of aircraft introduced in well-known FGComp 2013 challenge. It consists of 10,000 images of 100 aircraft variants. The airplanes tend to occupy a significantly large portion of the image and appear in relatively clear background. Airplanes also have a smaller representation in the ImageNet dataset on which the most CNN models are trained, compared to some other common objects.

Stanford Car [21] contains 16,185 images of 196 classes as part of the FGComp 2013 challenge as well. Categories are typically at the level of Year, Make, Model,

Table 1. Comparison about number, spices, and train/test split of Aircraft, Car, and NABirds datasets.

	Aircraft	Car	NABirds
Total number	10,000	16,185	48,562
Total spices	90	196	555
Train	6,667	8,144	23,929
Test	3,333	8,041	24,633

e.g., "2012 Tesla Model S" or "2012 BMW M3 coupe". It is special because cars are smaller and appear in a more cluttered background compared to Aircraft. Thus object and part localization may play a more significant role here.

NABirds [22] is a pretty large-scale dataset which consists of 48,562 birds images of North America. It has total 555 spices. This dataset provides not only label of each bird image, but also additional valuable parts and bounding-box annotations. However, we do not use those information in both of our training and testing. It means when training our models, only the raw birds images and corresponding category labels are used.

4.2 Implementation Details

We fine-tune the network with initial weight pre-trained on ImageNet ILSVRC2012 published by Google in TensorFlow model zone. Some implementation details in image pre-processing, training, and policy are as follows.

Image Pre-processing: We adopt almost the same way as Google Inception [13] for image pre-processing and augmentation, with several differences. Random crop rate is set to 0.2 rather than 0.1 in default. For network evaluation, the center crop is adopted and the corresponding crop rate is set as 0.8. To keep more details of the input image, following the experimental setup as [11], the inputs for both model training and testing are resized before sent to network to 448×448 rather than the default 229×229.

Training Policy: On the training phase, the batch size for Aircraft and Car are both set as 32 with single GPU. For NABirds, 4 GPUs are used to parallelly train the network where the batch size is also set as 32. Learning rate starts from 0.01 and exponentially decays with a decrease factor 0.9 every 2 epochs. RMSProp with momentum 0.9 is chosen as optimizer and decay 0.9, similar with Inception-V3. For Aircraft, two-stage fine-tune is adopted following from [11]. First, we train only the last fully connected layer for several epochs. After that, we train all the network until convergence. For all the networks training on all the datasets, dropout rates in network are set as 0.5.

Test Policy: On the testing phase, the image pre-processing and other hyperparameters are same as the training phase. Because forward calculation of CNN is more GPU-memory-efficient than gradient backward prorogation, the batch size setting is bigger than training phase and set as 100 so that the computation efficiency is more thoroughly advanced.

In addition, all experiments are performed on machine with 4 NVIDIA 1080Ti GPUs and Intel(R) Core(TM) i9-7900X CPU @ 3.30 GHz.

4.3   Experimental Results

As can be seen from the Table 2, our method is with the best performance in accuracy, compared with several state-of-the-art methods. Specially, for Aircraft classification problem, our PS-CNN is 1% higher than the best compared method Inception-V3. For Car classification, our proposed method achieves the best accuracy which is 2% higher compared to Inception-V3. For the larger NABirds dataset, our PS-CNN also achieves best classification rate. We choose 4 binary masks herein to perform a feature map segmentation. We find our proposed method works for all the three datasets. The influence on classification accuracy with varying number of masks thus multiple streams will be discussed then.

Table 2. Comparison of classification accuracy on the Aircraft [20], Cars [21] and NABirds [22] dataset with state-of-the-art methods. The Inception-V3 network is fine-tuned and evaluated by us. The PS-CNN is evaluated using the same hyper-parameters as Inception-V3. Dashed line means the absents of accuracy of the original paper.

	Aircraft	Car	NABirds
AutoBD	--	88.9%	68.0%
B-CNN	84.5%	91.3%	79.4%
M-CNN	--	--	80.2%
Inception-V3	88.2%	90.3%	80.8%
PS-CNN	**89.1%**	**92.8%**	**81.9%**

4.4   Discussion

Number of Masks: In some degree, the increase in the number of masks will also result in increase in the number of streamings, just like each Inception block in Google Inception family [5,13]. The classification accuracies of networks with 4 blocks are shown in Table 2. We will discuss the influence of different number of masks on image classification performance herein. We choose 2 (percent$_m$ setting as percent$_1$ = 0.1, percent$_2$ = 0.5, percent$_3$ = 1.0) and 3 (percent$_m$ setting as percent$_1$ = 0.1, percent$_2$ = 0.3, percent$_3$ = 0.5, percent$_4$ = 1) masks to evaluate the influence. The corresponding classification accuracies upon the three datasets are list in row 2 and 3 respectively in Table 3.

As can be seen from the Table 3, when we choose 4 masks, the classification accuracies are highest. In cases of 2 and 3 masks, the performance on both

Aircraft and NABirds will decrease because the feature maps are not explicitly enough separated. However, for Car dataset, the classification performance is still better than the basic network, i.e., Inception-V3.

Table 3. Influence of number of masks on the accuracy performance. The Inception-V3 is chosen as our base network.

	Aircraft	Car	NABirds
Inception-V3	88.2%	90.3%	80.8%
2 masks	88.0%	92.2%	80.5%
3 masks	87.8%	92.7%	79.3%
4 masks	**89.1%**	**92.8%**	**81.9%**

Fig. 2. Some images which are mis-classified in our experiments. The most of them are mis-classified because they bear a big view angle and 'strange' illumination. These problems should be addressed if we want to perform better in this fine-grained image classification problem. (Best viewed in color.)

Visualization: In the case of 4 masks, as can be seen from the Table 3, the error rate of Stanford Car dataset is about 7.2%, which means that 1165 cars images on Standard dataset are mis-classified. To explore the reason why those images are mis-classified, we pick out the mis-classified images in the test set. For simplicity, only 32 (forming as 4×8) of those total 1165 mis-classified images are selected as shown in Fig. 2.

We can see from this overall picture that all the mis-classified cars bear the same characteristics such as various view angle, strong illumination changing, and big occlusion. Those factors may have little influence on basic image classification. However, in this fine-grained tasks, there will be serious impact.

We have magnified the input images and then encode the enlarged feature maps exquisitely in order to make sure that more details of fine-grained image can be 'observed'. This is a solution to handle the small inter-class problem. But when big intra-class problem is encountered, e.g., view angle, the performance becomes embarrassing. Thus the solutions like pose normalization [23] or Spatial transformer [24] should be considered.

5   Conclusion

In this paper, to avoid the extreme information compression brought by the straightforward coarse Avg/Max pooling upon last convolutional feature maps in general CNN, one *Pixel Saliency based Encoding* method for CNN (PS-CNN) is proposed for fine-grained image classification. First, we provide a saliency matrix to evaluate the saliency of each pixel in feature map. Then, we segment the original feature maps into multiple ones with multiple thresholded saliency matrices, and subsequently squeeze those multiple feature maps into encoded one by using the 1×1 convolution kernel. At last, the encoded feature maps are concatenated with the original one as the last feature representation. By embedding such novel encoding method into the Inception-V3 framework, we achieve perfect performance on the three fine-grained datasets, i.e., Aircraft, Stanford Car, and NABirds. Especially, with this simple yet efficient method, we have achieved the best classification accuracy (81.9%) of large scale dataset NABirds, which demonstrates the efficiency of our PS-CNN. What's more, our pixel saliency based encoding method can be embedded into other convolutional neural networks frameworks as one simple net block.

References

1. He, K., Zhang, X., Ren, S., Sun, J.: Deep residual learning for image recognition. In: Proceedings of the IEEE Conference on Computer Vision and Pattern Recognition (CVPR), pp. 770–778 (2016)
2. Huang, G., Liu, Z., van der Maaten, L., Weinberger, K.Q.: Densely connected convolutional networks. In Proceedings of the the IEEE Conference on Computer Vision and Pattern Recognition (CVPR). IEEE (2017)
3. Schmidhuber, J.: Deep learning in neural networks: an overview. Neural Netw. **61**, 85–117 (2015)
4. Simonyan, K., Zisserman, A.: Very deep convolutional networks for large-scale image recognition. arXiv preprint arXiv:1409.1556 (2014)
5. Szegedy, C., et al.: Going deeper with convolutions. In: Proceedings of the IEEE Conference on Computer Vision and Pattern Recognition (CVPR), pp. 1–9 (2015)
6. Hariharan, B., Arbelez, P., Girshick, R., Malik, J.: Hypercolumns for object segmentation and fine-grained localization. In: Proceedings of the IEEE Conference on Computer Vision and Pattern Recognition (CVPR), pp. 447–456 (2015)

7. Duan, Q., Zhang, L., Zuo, W.: From face recognition to kinship verification: an adaptation approach. In: 2017 IEEE International Conference on Computer Vision Workshop (ICCVW), pp. 1590–1598. IEEE (2017)

8. Krause, J., Jin, H., Yang, J., Fei-Fei, L.: Fine-grained recognition without part annotations. In: Proceedings of the IEEE Conference on Computer Vision and Pattern Recognition (CVPR), pp. 5546–5555 (2015)

9. LeCun, Y., Bengio, Y., Hinton, G.: Deep learning. Nature **521**(7553), 436 (2015)

10. Li, P., Xie, J., Wang, Q., Zuo, W.: Is second-order information helpful for large-scale visual recognition? arXiv preprint arXiv:1703.08050 (2017)

11. Lin, T.-Y., RoyChowdhury, A., Maji, S.: Bilinear convolutional neural networks for fine-grained visual recognition. IEEE Trans. Pattern Anal. Mach. Intell. **40**(6), 1309–1322 (2017)

12. Chen, L.-C., Yang, Y., Wang, J., Xu, W., Yuille, A.L.: Attention to scale: scale-aware semantic image segmentation. In: Proceedings of the IEEE Conference on Computer Vision and Pattern Recognition (CVPR), pp. 3640–3649 (2016)

13. Szegedy, C., Vanhoucke, V., Ioffe, S., Shlens, J., Wojna, Z.: Rethinking the inception architecture for computer vision. In: Proceedings of the IEEE Conference on Computer Vision and Pattern Recognition (CVPR), pp. 2818–2826 (2016)

14. Ioffe, S., Szegedy, C.: Batch normalization: accelerating deep network training by reducing internal covariate shift. In: Proceedings of the International Conference on Machine Learning (ICML), pp. 448–456 (2015)

15. Zhang, X., Xiong, H., Zhou, W., Lin, W., Tian, Q.: Picking deep filter responses for fine-grained image recognition. In: Proceedings of the IEEE Conference on Computer Vision and Pattern Recognition (CVPR), pp. 1134–1142 (2016)

16. Zheng, H., Fu, J., Mei, T., Luo, J.: Learning multi-attention convolutional neural network for fine-grained image recognition. In: Proceedings of the IEEE Conference on Computer Vision and Pattern Recognition (CVPR), pp. 5209–5217 (2017)

17. Peng, Y., He, X., Zhao, J.: Object-part attention model for fine-grained image classification. IEEE Trans. Image Process. **PP**(99), 1 (2017)

18. Yao, H., Zhang, S., Yan, C., Zhang, Y., Li, J., Tian, Q.: AutoBD: automated bi-level description for scalable fine-grained visual categorization. IEEE Trans. Image Process. **27**(1), 10–23 (2018)

19. Wei, X.-S., Xie, C.-W., Wu, J., Shen, C.: Mask-CNN: localizing parts and selecting descriptors for fine-grained bird species categorization. Pattern Recognit. **76**, 704–714 (2017)

20. Mnih, V., Heess, N., Graves, A. et al.: Recurrent models of visual attention. In: Proceedings of the Advances in Neural Information Processing Systems (NIPS), pp. 2204–2212 (2014)

21. Krause, J., Stark, M., Deng, J., Fei-Fei, L.: 3D object representations for fine-grained categorization. In: Proceedings of the International Conference on Computer Vision Workshops (ICCVW), pp. 554–561. IEEE (2013)

22. Berg, T., Liu, J., Lee, S.W., Alexander, M.L., Jacobs, D.W., Belhumeur, P.N.: Birdsnap: large-scale fine-grained visual categorization of birds. In: Proceedings of the IEEE Conference on Computer Vision and Pattern Recognition (CVPR), pp. 2019–2026. IEEE (2014)

23. Branson, S., Van Horn, G., Belongie, S., Perona, P., Tech, C.: Bird species categorization using pose normalized deep convolutional nets. arXiv preprint arXiv:1406.2952 (2014)

24. Jaderberg, M., Simonyan, K., Zisserman, A.: Spatial transformer networks. In: Advances in Neural Information Processing Systems, pp. 2017–2025 (2015)

Boosting the Quality of Pansharpened Image by Adjusted Anchored Neighborhood Regression

Xiang Wang and Bin Yang[✉]

University of South China, Hengyang 421001, China
awoshi37@163.com, yangbin01420@16.com

Abstract. Pansharpening technology integrates low spatial resolution (LR) multi-spectral (MS) image and high spatial resolution panchromatic (PAN) image into a high spatial resolution multi-spectral (HRMS) image. Various pansharpening methods have been proposed, and each of them has its own improvements in different aspects. Meanwhile, there also exist specified shortages within each pansharpening method. For example, the methods based on component substitution (CS) always cause color distortion and multi-resolution analysis (MRA) based methods may loss some details in PAN image. In this paper, we proposed a quality boosting strategy for the pansharpened image obtained from a given method. The A+ regressors learned from the pansharpened results of a certain method and the ground-truth HRMS images are used to overcome the shortages of the given method. Firstly, the pan-sharpened images are produced by ATWT-based pansharpening method. Then, the projection from the pansharpened image to ideal ground truth image is learned with adjusted anchored neighborhood regression (A+) and the learned A + regressors are used to boost quality of pansharpened image. The experimental results demonstrate that the proposed algorithm provides superior performances in terms of both objective evaluation and subjective visual quality.

Keywords: Remote sensing · Pansharpening · Sparse representation
Anchored neighborhood regression

1 Introduction

Due to the trade-off of satellite sensors between spatial and spectral resolution, the earth observation satellites usually provide multi-spectral (MS) images and panchromatic (PAN) images [1]. The MS images have higher spectral diversity of bands. But they have lower spatial resolution than the corresponding monochrome PAN image [2]. HRMS images are widely used in many applications, such as land-use classification, change detection, map updating, disaster monitoring and so on [3]. In order to obtain the HRMS images, the pansharpening technique is used to effectively integrate the spatial details of the PAN image and the spectral information of the MS image to acquire the desired HRMS image.

The pansharpening algorithms based on component substitution (CS) strategy are the most classical methods which replace the structure component of low spatial

© Springer Nature Switzerland AG 2018
J.-H. Lai et al. (Eds.): PRCV 2018, LNCS 11256, pp. 286–296, 2018.
https://doi.org/10.1007/978-3-030-03398-9_25

resolution multi-spectral (LRMS) images with PAN images. The intensity-hue-saturation (IHS) [4], principal component analysis [5], the Gram–Schmidt (GS) [6] transform are usually used to extract the structure components of LRMS images. Most of CS-based methods are very efficient. Nevertheless, the pansharpened results may suffer from spectral distortion when the structure component of LRMS images not exactly equivalent to the corresponding PAN images. Differently, the MRA-based methods are developed with the ARSIS concept [7] that the missing spatial details of LRMS images can be obtained from the high frequencies of the PAN images. The stationary wavelet transform(SWT) [8], á trous wavelet transform (ATWT) [9] and high pass filter [10] are usually employed to extract the high frequencies of the PAN images. The MRA-based methods preserve color spatial details well. However, it is easy to produce spectral deformations when the algorithm parameters are set incorrectly. The pansharpening methods based on the spares representation [3, 11] and convolution neural network [12, 13] are becoming popular in the recent years. These methods have been proved to be effective and have achieved impressive pansharpened results.

All the presented pansharpening methods have various improvements in different aspects. Meanwhile, there also exist some shortages within each method and the specified shortages would be hard to overcome by optimizing itself parameters. We noticed that the shortages are always specific for a given method, which means that we can overcome the shortages by learning the projection from the pansharpened results of a certain method to the ground-truth HRMS images. Thus, we proposed a quality boosting strategy for the pansharpened images with adjusted anchored neighborhood regression in [14]. The pansharpened image are produced by the ATWT-based pansharpening method. The learned A+ regressors are used to obtain the residual image between the pansharpened result of a certain method and the ground-truth HRMS image. And the residual image is used to enhance the quality of the pansharpened image. QuickBird satellite images are used to perform the validation of the proposed method. The experimental results showed that the proposed algorithm outperformed the recent traditional pansharpening algorithms in terms of both subjective and objective measures.

The rest of this paper is organized into five sections. In Sect. 2, the A+ algorithm is briefly introduced. In Sect. 3, we give the general framework of the proposed algorithm. Experiment results and discussions are presented in Sect. 4. Finally, conclusions are given in Sect. 5.

2 Adjusted Anchored Neighborhood Regression (A+)

In our processing framework, the major task of A+ is to recover the HRMS images from the pansharpened version. In this section, we shortly review the A+ which combines the philosophy of neighbor embedding and spares representation [14]. The basic assumption of neighbor embedding is that low-dimensional nonlinear manifolds which formed from low-resolution image patches and it counterpart high-resolution image patches have similarity in local geometry. A+ use the sparse dictionary and the neighborhood of each atom in the dictionary to construct the manifold. We start the description of A+ from the stage of extracting pairs of observation.

Patch samples (or features obtained by feature extraction) and the corresponding original ground-truth patch samples are collected from training pool. A learned compact dictionary $D = \{d_1, d_2, \ldots, d_j\}$ is learned by dictionary training algorithms from the training samples. The atoms in the compact dictionary are served as anchored points (AP), each of which corresponding to a A+ regressor. For each atom d_j, K local neighbor samples (noticed by $S_{l,j}$), extracted from the training pool, that lie closest to d_j are densely sampling the manifold where the AP lie on. For any input observation x closest to d_j, the weight vectors δ are obtained from the local neighbor samples $S_{l,j}$ of d_j by solving the optimization problem as

$$\hat{\delta} = \min_{\delta} \|x - S_{l,j}\delta\|_2^2 + \beta\|\delta\|_2 \tag{1}$$

where β is balance term. The closed-form solution of (1) is

$$\hat{\delta} = \left(S_{l,j}^T S_{l,j} + \beta I\right)^{-1} S_{l,j}^T x \tag{2}$$

where I is a unit matrix. The A+ assumed that the image patches and its counterpart ground-truth patches lie on a low-dimensional nonlinear manifold with similar local geometry and the patches in the original feature domain can be reconstructed as a weighted average of local neighbors using the same weights as in the observation feature domain. Therefore, the corresponding restored sample can be recovered by

$$y = S_{h,j}\hat{\delta} \tag{3}$$

where $S_{h,j}$ is the high-resolution neighbors corresponding to $S_{l,j}$. From (2) and (3), we obtain

$$y = P_G^j x \tag{4}$$

where the projection matrix $P_G^j = S_{h,j}\left(S_{l,j}^T S_{l,j} + \beta I\right)^{-1} S_{l,j}^T$. We called P_G^j as the A+ regressor corresponding to the atom d_j. We can compute $\{P_G^1, P_G^2, \ldots, P_G^j\}$ for all the anchored points offline.

3   Boosting the Quality of Pansharpened Image

The general framework of our method is shown in Fig. 1. Just as the A+ used in single image super-resolution problem [14], the proposed method contains two main phases, namely offline training phase and online quality boosting phase. In order to better fit quality boosting task for pansharpened images slight change is made for A+. Instead of bicubic interpolation upsampling in [9], we need some pansharpening method to generate the input images as "starting points". In the training phase, the LRMS images and HR PAN images are firstly fused by ATWT-based pansharpening method which is very efficient. Noticed that our proposed method is capable of collaborating with other pansharpening methods. We regress from the pansharpened image patch features to the residual image to correct the pansharpened image so that to overcome the deficiency of ATWT-based pansharpening method. The pansharpened images as well as the residual difference images between the pansharpened and the ground-truth images are used as the training data to enhance the error structure between them. We treat both pansharpened images and the residual difference images patch-wise over a dense grid. For each pansharpened image patch, we compute vertical and horizontal gradient responses and use them concatenated lexicographically as gradient features. The PCA is utilized to reduce feature vector's dimension with 99.9% energy preservation (same as in A+ in [14]). Thus, we obtain extracted pairs of patch-wise features $\{v_i, i = 1, 2, \ldots, N\}$ from the pansharpened images and patch vectors (normalized by l_2 norm) of residual difference images.

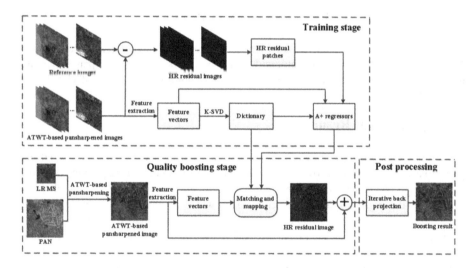

Fig. 1. The general framework of the proposed method

A compact dictionary is learned by KSVD dictionary learning method in [15] from the $\{v_i\}$. For each anchored atom d_j, K local neighbor samples (noticed by $N_{l,j}$) that lie closest to this atom is extracted from the $\{v_i\}$. The corresponding HR residual patches are construct the HR neighborhood $N_{h,j}$. A+ regressors for d_j are computed as:

$$F_j = N_{h,j} \left(N_{l,j}^T N_{l,j} + \beta I \right)^{-1} N_{l,j}^T \qquad (5)$$

We can get all the A+ regressors $\{F_1, F_2, \ldots, F_j\}$ using the same way as in (5).

During quality boosting phase, the features $\{u_i\}$ extract from the input ATWT-based pansharpened image using the same feature extraction method as in training phase. For each feature u_i, A+ search the nearest AP from D with highest correlation measured by Euclidean distance. The corresponding HR residual patch can be obtained by

$$r_i = F_k u_i \tag{6}$$

Then, HR residual image R is reconstructed by averaging assembly and the final HRMS image Y is recovered by

$$Y = P + R \tag{7}$$

where P is the input pansharpened image.

In addition, we used a post processing method called iterative back projection which is origin from computer tomography and applied to super-resolution in [16], to eliminate the inequality.

$$Y_{t+1} = Y_t + [(I_{MS} - MY_t) \uparrow s] * p \tag{8}$$

We set $Y_0 = Y$ and p is a Gaussian filter with the standard deviation and filter size are 1 and 5. M is a down-sample operator and I_{MS} is the input MS of a certain pansharpening method; t is the iteration number; $(.) \uparrow s$ means up-sampling by a factor of s.

4   Experimental Results

We adopt Quickbird remote sensing images to achieve the experiments [17]. And the performances are evaluated by the comparison with different pansharpening methods. According to Wald's protocol [18] that, any synthetic image should be as close as possible to the highest spatial resolution image which acquired by the corresponding sensor. Therefore, the experiments are implemented on original MS images using as reference images and degraded data sets which are down-sampling version of original MS and PAN images. In this paper, the objective measurement that reviewed in [20], the correlation coefficient(CC), the erreur relative global adimensionnelle de synthèse (ERGAS), the Q4 index and the spectral-angle mapper (SAM), are used to quantitative measure the quality of fused image and boosting image.

The QuickBird is a high-resolution remote sensing satellite and provides four band MS image with 2.88 m spatial resolution and PAN image with 0.7 m spatial resolution. In our experiment, we down-sample the 2.88 m four band MS images and 0.7 m PAN images by a factor of 4 to gain LRMS and PAN images which are used as input of pansharpening methods and the original 0.7 m MS images are used as reference image. In the experiments, the size of LRMS and PAN images is 125×125 and 500×500 and patch size is 3×3. The ATWT with three levels decomposition is employed to produce pansharpened images and ATWT results. The number of iteration and maximal sparsity of K-SVD algorithm is 20 and 8. The influence of dictionary size, balance term and neighborhood size are showed in Fig. 2. The standard settings are dictionary size of 1024, neighborhood size of 2048, and balance term of 0.1. In Fig. 2, we can see that the values of the index become better and stable with dictionary size, balance term and neighborhood size increased. Therefore, we set dictionary size, balance term and neighborhood size as 4096, 1 and 8192 respectively. We utilized our method on ATWT pansharpened image and the result is compared with six well-known pansharpening method as follow: SVT [19], SWT [8], ATWT [9], GS, generalized IHS(GIHS), Brovey transform(BT). The GS, GIHS and BT that used in our experiment are adopted from [20]. In the GS, the LR PAN image for processing is produced by pixel averaging of LRMS bands. In the SVT, the σ^2 in the Gaussian RBF kernel is set to 0.6, and the parameter γ of the mapped LSSVM is set to 1, which give the best results. In the SWT, we utilized three levels decomposition with Daubechies wavelet bases with six vanishing moments.

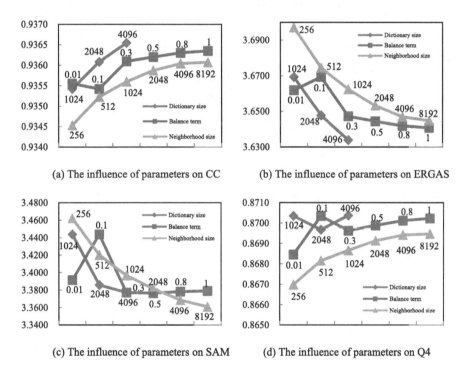

(a) The influence of parameters on CC   (b) The influence of parameters on ERGAS

(c) The influence of parameters on SAM   (d) The influence of parameters on Q4

Fig. 2. The influence of parameters (dictionary size, balance term and neighborhood size) on CC, ERGAS, SAM and Q4.

Figures 3 and 4 present two examples of the results of the proposed method and others methods. By comparing the results in Figs. 3 and 4 with corresponding reference image visually, we find that (1) the result of GIHS and BT suffer from spectral distortion while can improve spatial resolution in some extent; (2) It can be clearly observed that the SVT and GS result is blurring in some degree, but SVT result is clearer than GS result; (3) the SWT and ATWT can effectively improve the spatial resolution. However, the result of the SWT and ATWT looks unnatural, although preserve spectral information; (4) The proposed boosting method can improve the spectral quality of the ATWT result which make the image looks better as well as providing high spatial resolution. We showed two complete experiment results in Figs. 3 and 4. For other results, we only give the reference images, ATWT results and proposed method results in Fig. 5 due to the limitation of space.

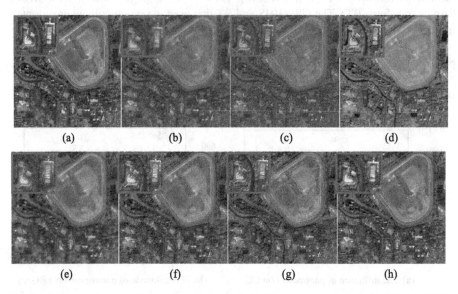

Fig. 3. Reference image and pansharpening result: (a) The reference image; (b) GS; (c) GIHS; (d) BT; (e) SVT; (f) SWT; (g) ATWT; (h) ATWT boosting result of the proposed method.

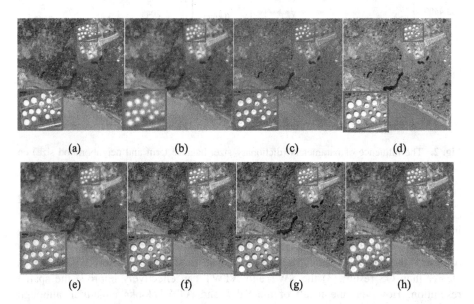

Fig. 4. Reference image and pansharpening result: (a) The reference image; (b) GS; (c) GIHS; (d) BT; (e) SVT; (f) SWT; (g) ATWT; (h) ATWT boosting result of the proposed method.

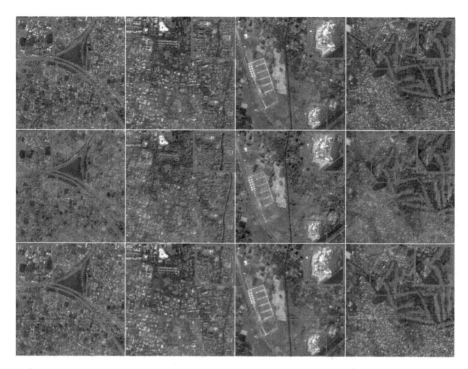

Fig. 5. Reference images, ATWT results and proposed results: The first row is the reference images; The second and third row are the corresponding ATWT results and proposed results respectively.

The quantitative evaluation results of Figs. 3, 4, and 5 are shown in Table 1. The best results for each index labeled in bold. The CC measures the correlation between reference image and pansharpened image, high value of CC means better performance. In Table 1, our method provides highest CC values for all experimental images. The SAM measures the spectral similarity of reference image and pansharpened image. The proposed method also provides the best SAM results except Fig. 4. The SAM value of proposed method demonstrates obviously improvements by comparing with ATWT result in Fig. 4. The ERGAS provides an overall spectral quality measure of the pansharpened image by measuring the difference with reference image and The Q4 index comprehensively measures the spectral and spatial quality of pansharpened image. The ERGAS and Q4 values of the proposed method are the best results for all experimental images as well. This is mainly due to the proposed method learn the difference between pansharpened image and reference image and generated a residual image to overcome the disadvantage of pansharpening method and enrich the information of pansharpened image. In our experiment, the proposed method can effectively improve the spectral and spatial quality of ATWT pansharpened image. By comparing with the ATWT result, all index value of our method has improved and the ATWT pansharpened image becomes the best result among these pan–sharpening approaches after processed by proposed method.

Table 1. Comparisons of our method with other method on Quickbird images.

Figures	Quality index	GS	GIHS	BT	SVT	SWT	ATWT	Ours
Figure 3	CC	0.9117	0.8481	0.7822	0.9223	0.8988	0.8487	**0.9367**
	SAM	3.6624	3.6741	3.7245	3.6381	3.8377	4.0938	**3.3559**
	ERGAS	4.7565	5.5766	7.7943	4.0625	4.5673	5.5413	**3.6271**
	Q4	0.7900	0.7479	0.7600	0.8035	0.7837	0.7085	**0.8707**
Figure 4	CC	0.9347	0.8636	0.6800	0.9372	0.9005	0.8694	**0.9416**
	SAM	2.5938	2.7268	**2.5737**	2.7633	3.077	3.3772	2.7124
	ERGAS	4.4729	5.4773	8.4521	3.5744	4.5721	5.2515	**3.5153**
	Q4	0.6726	0.6324	0.6408	0.6953	0.6364	0.5959	**0.7541**
Figure 5 first column	CC	0.8536	0.8117	0.7373	0.8663	0.8354	0.7787	**0.8974**
	SAM	3.4277	3.4845	3.5604	3.4835	3.7059	3.9806	**3.1386**
	ERGAS	5.6529	5.9881	8.2141	5.0192	5.3525	6.1069	**4.275**
	Q4	0.7228	0.6999	0.752	0.7698	0.7677	0.7097	**0.868**
Figure 5 second column	CC	0.9038	0.8511	0.8094	0.9101	0.8837	0.8397	**0.9282**
	SAM	3.7006	3.7594	3.8937	3.7433	3.9415	4.204	**3.3537**
	ERGAS	5.2043	5.8139	6.8049	4.4998	4.9733	5.7912	**3.9037**
	Q4	0.7728	0.7661	0.817	0.8241	0.8208	0.7694	**0.8994**
Figure 5 third column	CC	0.9168	0.8511	0.7054	0.9265	0.9021	0.8644	**0.9399**
	SAM	3.4945	3.5257	3.456	3.5908	3.969	4.2567	**3.3734**
	ERGAS	4.4093	5.3503	9.7689	3.8954	4.5613	5.3755	**3.5197**
	Q4	0.8095	0.7753	0.765	0.8168	0.799	0.743	**0.8804**
Figure 5 fourth column	CC	0.8925	0.8653	0.7085	0.9175	0.9033	0.8677	**0.9288**
	SAM	3.9124	4.0147	3.9581	3.9937	4.2159	4.5188	**3.6749**
	ERGAS	5.3595	5.8617	8.9643	4.2985	4.5318	5.2708	**3.8945**
	Q4	0.7698	0.7541	0.8033	0.8335	0.8373	0.795	**0.8879**

5   The Conclusion

In this paper, we present a novel pansharpening image quality boosting algorithm based on A+ which learns a set of A+ regressors mapping pansharpened MS image to HRMS residual images. The residual images are used to compensate the pansharpened image from any pansharpening method. The experiment which evaluated visually and quantitatively on Quickbird data compared with GS, GHIS, BT, ATWT, SVT and SWT show that the proposed method not only improve spatial resolution, but also can effectively enhance spectral quality. Noticed that the proposed method can be collaborating with any other existing pansharpening algorithms. Of course, the output results quality would be improved if the advanced pansharpening method is used as pre-processing steps.

Acknowledgements. This paper is supported by the National Natural Science Foundation of China (No. 61871210, 61102108), Scientific Research Fund of Hunan Provincial Education Department (Nos. 16B225, YB2013B039), the Natural Science Foundation of Hunan Province (No. 2016JJ3106), Young talents program of the University of South China, the construct program of key disciplines in USC (No. NHXK04), Scientific Research Fund of Hengyang Science and Technology Bureau(No. 2015KG51), the Postgraduate Research and Innovation Project of Hunan Province in 2018, and the Postgraduate Science Fund of USC.

References

1. Yuan, Q., Wei, Y., Meng, X., Shen, H., Zhang, L.: A multiscale and multidepth convolutional neural network for remote sensing imagery pan-sharpening. IEEE J. Sel. Top. Appl. Earth Observations Remote Sens. **PP**(99), 1–12 (2018)
2. Garzelli, A.: A review of image fusion algorithms based on the super-resolution paradigm. Remote Sens. **8**(10), 797 (2016)
3. Han, C., Zhang, H., Gao, C., Jiang, C., Sang, N., Zhang, L.: A remote sensing image fusion method based on the analysis sparse model. IEEE J. Sel. Top. Appl. Earth Observations Remote Sens. **9**(1), 439–453 (2016)
4. Choi, M.: A new intensity-hue-saturation fusion approach to image fusion with a tradeoff parameter. IEEE Trans. Geosci. Remote Sens. **44**(6), 1672–1682 (2006)
5. Shah, V.P., Younan, N.H., King, R.L.: An efficient pansharpening method via a combined adaptive PCA approach and contourlets. IEEE Trans. Geosci. Remote Sens. **46**(5), 1323–1335 (2008)
6. Laben, C.A., Brower, B.V., Company, E.K.: Process for enhancing the spatial resolution of multispectral imagery using pansharpening. Websterny Uspenfieldny, US (2000)
7. Ranchin, T., Wald, L.: Fusion of high spatial and spectral resolution images: the ARSIS concept and its implementation. Photogram. Eng. Remote Sens. **66**(1), 49–61 (2000)
8. Li, S.: Multisensor remote sensing image fusion using stationary wavelet transform: effects of basis and decomposition level. Int. J. Wavelets Multiresolut. Inf. Process. **6**(01), 37–50 (2008)
9. Vivone, G., Restaino, R., Mura, M.D., Licciardi, G., Chanussot, J.: Contrast and error-based fusion schemes for multispectral image pansharpening. IEEE Geosci. Remote Sens. Lett. **11**(5), 930–934 (2013)
10. Ghassemian, H.: A retina based multi-resolution image-fusion, In: Proceedings of IEEE International Geoscience and Remote Sensing Symposium, vol. 2, pp. 709–711 (2001)
11. Ghamchili, M., Ghassemian, H.: Panchromatic and multispectral images fusion using sparse representation. In: Artificial Intelligence and Signal Processing Conference, pp. 80–84 (2017)
12. Yang, J., Fu, X., Hu, Y., Huang, Y., Ding, X., Paisley, J.: PanNet: A deep network architecture for pansharpening. In: IEEE International Conference on Computer Vision, pp. 1753–1761. IEEE Computer Society (2017)
13. Wei, Y., Yuan, Q., Shen, H., Zhang, L.: Boosting the accuracy of multispectral image pansharpening by learning a deep residual network. IEEE Geosci. Remote Sens. Lett. **14**(10), 1795–1799 (2017)
14. Timofte, R., Smet, V.D., Gool, L.V.: A+: Adjusted anchored neighborhood regression for fast super-resolution. In: Asian Conference on Computer Vision, vol. 9006, pp. 111–126. Springer, Cham (2014)

15. Aharon, M., Elad, M., Bruckstein, A.: K-SVD: an algorithm for designing overcomplete dictionaries for sparse representation. IEEE Trans. Signal Process. **54**(11), 4311–4322 (2006)
16. Yang, J., Wright, J., Huang, T.S., Ma, Y.: Image super-resolution via sparse representation. IEEE Trans. Image Process. **19**(11), 2861–2873 (2010)
17. DigitalGlobe.: QuickBird scene 000000185940_01_P001, Level Standard 2A, DigitalGlobe, Longmont, Colorado, 1/20/2002 (2003)
18. Wald, L., Ranchin, T., Mangolini, M.: Fusion of satellite images of different spatial resolutions: assessing the quality of resulting images. Photogram. Eng. Remote Sens. **63**(6), 691–699 (1997)
19. Zheng, S., Shi, W.Z., Liu, J., Tian, J.: Remote sensing image fusion using multiscale mapped LS-SVM. IEEE Trans. Geosci. Remote Sens. **46**(5), 1313–1322 (2008)
20. Vivone, G., Alparone, L., Chanussot, J., Mura, M.D., Garzelli, A., Licciardi, G.A., et al.: A critical comparison among pansharpening algorithms. IEEE Trans. Geosci. Remote Sens. **53** (5), 2565–2586 (2015)

A Novel Adaptive Segmentation Method Based on Legendre Polynomials Approximation

Bo Chen[1,2(✉)], Mengyun Zhang[1], Wensheng Chen[1,2(✉)],
Binbin Pan[1,2], Lihong C. Li[3(✉)], and Xinzhou Wei[4(✉)]

[1] Shenzhen Key Laboratory of Advanced Machine Learning and Applications,
College of Mathematics and Statistics, Shenzhen University,
Shenzhen 518060, China
chenbo@szu.edu.cn
[2] Shenzhen Key Laboratory of Media Security, Shenzhen University,
Shenzhen 518060, China
[3] Department of Engineering Science and Physics, College of Staten Island,
City University of New York, Staten Island, NY 10314, USA
[4] Department of Electrical Engineering Tech,
New York City College of Technology, Brooklyn, NY 11201, USA

Abstract. Active contour models have been extensively applied to image processing and computer vision. In this paper, we present a novel adaptive method combines the advantages of the SBGFRLS model and GAC model. It can segment images in presence of low contrast, noise, weak edge and intensity inhomogeneity. Firstly, a region term is introduced. It can be seen as the global information part of our model and it is available for images with low gray values. Secondly, Legendre polynomials are employed in the local statistical information part to approximate region intensity and then our model can deal with images with intensity inhomogeneity or weak edges. Thirdly, a correction term is selected to improve the performance of curve evolution. Synthetic and real images are tested and Dice similarity coefficients of different models are compared in this paper. Experiments show that our model can obtain better segmental results.

Keywords: Image segmentation · Active contour model
Legendre polynomials

1 Introduction

Image segmentation is a basic technique in the field of computer vision and image processing. Many segmentation methods have been proposed during the past decades. Active contour model (ACM) is one of the most important segmentation methods. The existing ACM methods can be divided into two categories: edge-based models [1] and region-based models [2–5, 7–10].

The classical edge-based models is Geodesic active contour (GAC) model [1], which depends on the gradient of the given image to construct an edge stopping function (ESF). The main role of ESF is to stop the evolution contour on the true object boundaries. In addition, some other edge-based ACMs introduce a balloon force term

© Springer Nature Switzerland AG 2018
J.-H. Lai et al. (Eds.): PRCV 2018, LNCS 11256, pp. 297–308, 2018.
https://doi.org/10.1007/978-3-030-03398-9_26

to control the motion of the contour. However, the edge-based models often lead to local minimization, are sensitive to initial contour and cannot get good segmental result for noise image.

Region-based ACM has many advantages over edge-based ones. One of the most popular region-based ACMs is Chan-Vese (CV) [2] model, which proposed by Chan and Vese. The CV model is based on Mumford-Shah segmentation techniques and has been successfully applied to binary phase segmentation. However, this method usually fails to segment images with intensity inhomogeneity, because it is based on the assumption that the image domain contains a series of homogeneous region.

To solve the limitations of intensity inhomogeneity, various efficient methods have been developed. In 2005, Li et al. proposed a local binary fitting (LBF) [3–5] method to segment the image with intensity inhomogeneity and reduce the costly re-initialization. In 2012, Wang et al. proposed a local Chan-Vese (LCV) [6] model, by comparison with CV model and LBF model, LCV model can segment images with few iteration times and be less sensitive to initial contour. In 2014, Zhang et al. proposed a novel level set (LSACM) [7] method, which utilize a sliding window to map the original image into another domain where the intensity of each object is homogeneity, this method can achieve better segmentation results for images with severe intensity inhomogeneity. In 2015, Suvadip Mukherjee et al. [8] proposed a region-based method (L2S), which enables accommodate objects even in presence of intensity inhomogeneity or noise. However, this model may be slow, owing to computing Legendre basis functions. In 2016, Shi et al. [9] presented a local and global binary fitting active contour model (LGBF), which effectively overcomes shortcomings of the CV model and LBF model. LGBF model is superiority for the intensity inhomogeneous.

In this paper, we propose a novel adaptive segmentation method combines the advantages of the SBGFRLS model and GAC model. Our model is robust and efficient to deal with images in the presence of intensity inhomogeneity, noise and weak-edge object.

This paper is organized as follows. Section 2 reviews GAC, the L2S and SBGFRLS method briefly. Section 3 introduces the new model and corresponding algorithm. In Sect. 4, we carry out some experiments for synthetic and real images, and make a comparison with other active contour models. A summary of our work is drawn in Sect. 5.

2 The Related Works

2.1 The GAC Model

Let Ω be a bounded open subset of R^2 and $I : [0, a] \times [0, b] \to R^+$ be a given image. Let $C(q) : [0, 1] \to R^2$ be a parameterized planar curve. The GAC model is formulated by minimizing the following energy function:

$$E^{GAC}(C) = \int_0^1 g(|\nabla I(C(q))|)|C'(q)|dq \tag{1}$$

where ∇I is the gradient of image I, $C'(q)$ is the tangent vector of the curve C. g is an ESF, which can stop the contour evolution on the desired object boundaries. Generally speaking, ESF $g(|\nabla I|)$ is requested to be positive, decreasing and regular, such that $\lim_{t \to -\infty} g(t) = 0$. Such as

$$g(|\nabla I|) = \frac{1}{1 + |\nabla G_\sigma * I|^2} \tag{2}$$

where G_σ is a Gaussian kernel with standard deviation σ. According to calculation of variation, the corresponding Euler-Lagrange equation of Eq. (1) is as follows:

$$C_t = g(|\nabla I|)\kappa \vec{N} - (\nabla g \cdot \vec{N})\vec{N} \tag{3}$$

where κ is the curvature of the contour and $\vec{N}$ is the normal to the curve. The constant term α can be used for shrinking or expanding the curve. Then Eq. (3) can be rewritten as:

$$C_t = g(|\nabla I|)(\kappa + \alpha)\vec{N} - (\nabla g \cdot \vec{N})\vec{N} \tag{4}$$

The corresponding level set formulation is as follows:

$$\frac{\partial \phi}{\partial t} = g|\nabla \phi|(div(\frac{\nabla \phi}{|\nabla \phi|}) + \alpha) + \nabla g \cdot \nabla \phi \tag{5}$$

The GAC model is effective to extract the object when the initial contour surrounds its boundary and inefficient to detect the interior contour without setting the interior initial contour. In conclusion, the GAC model possesses local segmentation property, which can only segment the desired object with a more reasonable initial contour. However, this method cannot segment images with faint boundaries, ill-defined edges or low contrast.

2.2   The SBGFRLS Model

Zhang et al. proposed selective binary and Gaussian filtering regularized level set (SBGFRLS) [10] method in 2009. A new signed pressure force (SPF) function was proposed to substitute ESF function in Eq. (5). The corresponding gradient descent flow equation is obtained as follows:

$$\frac{\partial \phi}{\partial t} = spf(I(x)) \cdot (div(\frac{\nabla \phi}{|\nabla \phi|}) + \alpha)|\nabla \phi| + \nabla spf(I(x)) \cdot \nabla \phi, \, x \in \Omega \tag{6}$$

where the SPF function has values in the range $[-1, 1]$, that are smaller within the region(s)-of-interest. It modulates the signs of the pressure forces inside and outside the region of interest so that the contour shrinks when outside the object, or expands when inside the object. The SPF function as follows:

$$spf(I(x)) = \frac{I(x) - \frac{c_1 + c_2}{2}}{\max(|I(x) - \frac{c_1 + c_2}{2}|)}, x \in \Omega \tag{7}$$

where c_1 and c_2 are defined in Eqs. (8) and (9), respectively.

$$c_1(\phi) = \frac{\int_\Omega I(x) \cdot H(\phi)dx}{\int_\Omega H(\phi)dx} \tag{8}$$

$$c_2(\phi) = \frac{\int_\Omega I(x) \cdot (1 - H(\phi))dx}{\int_\Omega (1 - H(\phi))dx} \tag{9}$$

The regular term $div(\frac{\nabla\phi}{|\nabla\phi|})|\nabla\phi|$ is unnecessary since this model utilizes a Gaussian filter. In addition, the term $\nabla spf \cdot \nabla\phi$ can also be removed. Finally, the level set formulation of the proposed model can be written as follows:

$$\frac{\partial\phi}{\partial t} = spf(I(x)) \cdot \alpha|\nabla\phi|, x \in \Omega \tag{10}$$

The model utilizes the image statistical information to stop the curve evolution on the desired boundaries, which are less sensitive to noise, and is more efficient. However, for images with severe intensity inhomogeneity, this model and CV model have similar weaknesses, because the models utilize the global image intensities inside and outside the contour.

2.3   The L2S Model

Suvadip Mukherjee et al. [8] proposed a region-based segmentation by utilizing Legendre polynomials to approximate the foreground and background illumination. The traditional CV model can be reformulated and generalized by two smooth functions $c_1^m(x)$ and c_2^m instead of the scalars c_1 and c_2. To preserve the smoothness and flexibility of the functions, $c_1^m(x)$ and c_2^m can be represented as a liner combination of a set of Legendre basis functions. The two functions can be written as follow:

$$c_1^m(x) = \sum \alpha_k P_k(x), \quad c_2^m(x) = \sum \beta_k P_k(x) \tag{11}$$

where P_k is one dimensional Legendre polynomial of degree k, which can be seen as the outer product of the one dimensional counterparts. The 2-D polynomial is defined as

$$\rho_k(x, y) = P_k(x)P_k(y), X = (x, y) \in \Omega \subset [-1, 1]^2 \tag{12}$$

where P_k can be defined as

$$P_k(x) = \frac{1}{2^k}\sum_{i=0}^{k}\binom{k}{i}(x-1)^{k-i}(x+1)^i \tag{13}$$

$P(x) = (P_0(x), \cdots, P_N(x))^T$ is the vector of Legendre polynomials. $A = (\alpha_0, \cdots, \alpha_N)^T$, $B = (\beta_0, \cdots, \beta_N)^T$ are both the coefficient for the inside contour and outside contour, respectively. Then the energy functional of the L2S can be written as the following equation:

$$\begin{aligned}
E^{L2S}(\phi, A, B) &= \int_\Omega |f(x) - A^T P(x)|^2 H(\phi(x))dx + \lambda_1\|A\|_2^2 \\
&+ \int_\Omega |f(x) - B^T P(x)|^2 (1 - H(\phi(x)))dx + \lambda_1\|B\|_2^2 \\
&+ v\int_\Omega \delta_\varepsilon(\phi)\frac{\nabla\phi}{|\nabla\phi|}dx
\end{aligned} \tag{14}$$

where $\lambda_1 \geq 0, \lambda_2 \geq 0$ are fixed scalars. The last term in Eq. (14) is regulated by the positive parameter v, Let perform $\frac{\partial E^{L2S}}{\partial A} = 0$, $\frac{\partial E^{L2S}}{\partial B} = 0$, so $\hat{A}$ and $\hat{B}$ are respectively acquired as:

$$\begin{aligned}
\hat{A} &= [K + \lambda_1 I]^{-1}P, [K]_{i,j} = \langle\sqrt{H(\phi(x))}P_i(x), \sqrt{H(\phi(x))}P_j(x)\rangle \\
\hat{B} &= [L + \lambda_2 I]^{-1}Q, [L]_{i,j} = \langle\sqrt{1-H(\phi(x))}P_i(x), \sqrt{1-H(\phi(x))}P_j(x)\rangle
\end{aligned} \tag{15}$$

$\langle,\rangle$ denotes the inner product operator. The vector P and Q are obtained as $P = \int_\Omega P(x)f(x)H(\phi(x))dx$, $Q = \int_\Omega P(x)f(x)(1-H(\phi(x)))dx$. By minimizing Eq. (14), we obtain the corresponding variational level set formulation as follow:

$$\frac{\partial\phi}{\partial t} = \left[-|f(x) - \hat{A}^T P(x)|^2 + |f(x) - \hat{B}^T P(x)|^2\right]\delta_\varepsilon(\phi) + v\delta_\varepsilon(\phi)div(\frac{\nabla\phi}{|\nabla\phi|}) \tag{16}$$

$H(\phi(x))$ is the Heaviside function and $\delta(\phi)$ is the Dirac function. They are selected as follows:

$$\begin{cases} H(\phi) = \frac{1}{2}(1 + \frac{2}{\pi}\arctan(\frac{\phi}{\varepsilon})), \\ \delta_\varepsilon = \frac{1}{\pi}\cdot\frac{\varepsilon}{\varepsilon^2 + \phi^2}, \end{cases} \phi \in R \tag{17}$$

The model approximates foreground and background by computing $\hat{A}^T P(x)$, $\hat{B}^T P(x)$, respectively.

3   A Novel Adaptive Segmentation Model

3.1   Model Construction

Let Ω be an open subset of R^2, a given image $I : \Omega \to R$. Let us define the evolving curve C in Ω. For arbitrary point $x \in \Omega$, C can be represented by the zero level set of a Lipschitz function $\phi(x)$ such that $C=\{x \in \Omega : \phi(x)= 0\}$.

$$\begin{cases} inside(C) = \{x \in \Omega : \phi(x) > 0\}, \\ outside(C) = \{x \in \Omega : \phi(x) < 0\} \end{cases} \tag{18}$$

$inside(C)$, $outside(C)$ denote the foreground regions and background regions, respectively.

Similar as GAC model, in order to control the length of evolution curve, we introduce the area of the curve in this section. This can be more effective to avoid local minima and get desired result. The gradient descent flow equation is as follows:

$$\frac{\partial \phi}{\partial t} = g|\nabla \phi|(div(\frac{\nabla \phi}{|\nabla \phi|}) + \alpha) + \nabla g \cdot \nabla \phi - v \tag{19}$$

where $v \geq 0$ is fixed parameter. In our numerical calculations, we set $v \in [0, 1]$. Especially if the image background is white, we set $v= 0$.

Inspired by GAC model and SBGFRLS model, the balloon force α could control the contour shrinking or expanding, and then we can improve SPF function. The contour will expand when it is inside the object, and will shrink when it is outside the object. We substitute the SPF function in Eq. (7) for the ESP in Eq. (19), the level set formulation is defined as follows:

$$\frac{\partial \phi}{\partial t} = spf(I(x)) \cdot (div(\frac{\nabla \phi}{|\nabla \phi|}) + \alpha)|\nabla \phi| + \nabla spf(I(x)) \cdot \nabla \phi - v, x \in \Omega \tag{20}$$

In addition, SPF function employs statistical information of regions, which can well handle images with weak edges or without edges, so the term $\nabla spf(I(x)) \cdot \nabla \phi$ is not very important and can be removed. So the level set formulation can be simplified as:

$$\frac{\partial \phi}{\partial t} = spf(I(x))(div(\frac{\nabla \phi}{|\nabla \phi|}) + \alpha)|\nabla \phi| - v, x \in \Omega \tag{21}$$

Curvature $div(\frac{\nabla \phi}{|\nabla \phi|})$ [11] can smooth the contour, meanwhile the use of α has the effect of shrinking or expanding contour at a constant speed.

In order to overcome the shortcomings of SBGFRLS model, we substitute constants c_1, c_2 by $c_1^m(x)$, $c_2^m(x)$ in Eq. (7), and it is better to deal with images in presence of intensity inhomogeneity. The new SPF function is defined as follow:

$$spf(I(x)) = \frac{I(x) - \frac{\hat{A}^T P(x) + \hat{B}^T P(x)}{2}}{\max\left(\left|I(x) - \frac{\hat{A}^T P(x) + \hat{B}^T P(x)}{2}\right|\right)}, \quad x \in \Omega \tag{22}$$

We can replace $|\nabla\phi|$ by $\delta(\phi)$ in (21) to increase the speed of curve evolution, and the final proposed model is as follows:

$$\frac{\partial\phi}{\partial t} = \delta(\phi) \cdot spf(I(x))\left(div\left(\frac{\nabla\phi}{|\nabla\phi|}\right) + \alpha\right) - v, \quad x \in \Omega \tag{23}$$

where $\alpha \in R$ is a correction term, then we can ensure $div(\frac{\nabla\phi}{|\nabla\phi|}) + \alpha$ is a non-zero value. The constant α may be seen as a force to push the curve evolves towards object boundary and an adaptive constant to control direction of curve. In the case of gray level increasing (from black to grey), if the correction term is positive, the evolution curve will continuously evolve from outside to inside, it is more efficient to segment objects within initial contour. If the correction term is negative, the curve will evolve in an opposite direction, then it can sweep over objects outside the initial contour. Conversely, in the case of gray level decreasing (from grey to black), we will get the opposite result. Therefore, for each category of images, an appropriate correction term is necessary for achieving satisfying segmentation results.

The final energy function make full use of a region term (global information part) and Legendre polynomials (local information part). Our model has the flexibility to segment desired object and avoid edge leakage.

3.2 Algorithm Procedure

In the section, the main procedure of the proposed model is summarized as follows:

Input: I
Output: ϕ

---

a. Initialization: α, MaxIter, v, m, σ.
b. Initialize the level set function ϕ as

$$\phi(x, t = 0) = \begin{cases} -\rho & x \in outside(C) \\ 0 & x \in C \\ \rho & x \in inside(C) \end{cases} \quad \rho > 0$$

c. Compute A, B and $spf(I(x))$ by Eq. (15), Eq. (22), respectively.
d. Evolve the level set function according to Eq. (23).
e. Let $\phi = 1$ if $\phi > 0$; otherwise, $\phi = -1$.
f. Regularize the level set function ϕ with a Gaussian filter, i.e. $\phi = \phi * G_\sigma$.
g. Check whether the evolution of the level set has converged. If not, return to stage d.

The step (e) serves as an optional segmentation procedure.

4 Experimental Results

Synthetic and real images are tested in this section. In each experiment, parameters and initial contour are set manually. We choose $m = 1$, $\sigma = 1$ here. The correction term α and region term v are very important for image segmentation. The Dice Similarity Coefficients (DSC) is compared for results with different models. The Dice index $D \in [0, 1]$ represents the difference between the segmental result R_1 and the ground truth R_2. The DSC is defined as $D(R_1, R_2) = \frac{2Area(R_1 \cap R_2)}{Area(R_1) + Area(R_2)}$.

Figure 1 shows the performance of our model for noisy image segmentation. The image (two objects [12]) in the first, second and third row show the corresponding segmentation results by CV model, SBGFRLS model and our model. The first column, second column and third column are images with Gaussian noise of standard deviation 0.1, 0.2, and 0.3, respectively. As shown in Fig. 2, the Dice value of our model is more stable with the variance increasing.

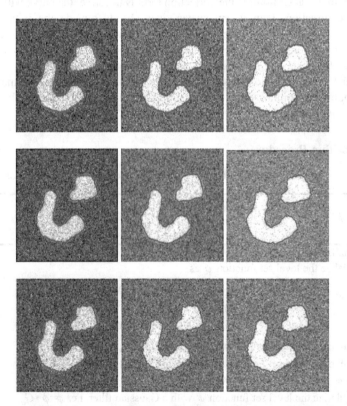

Fig. 1. Segmental results for images with Gaussian white noise of mean 0 and variance $\sigma = 0.1$, 0.2, 0.3 (From left to right) by CV, SBGFRLS and our model (from top to bottom).

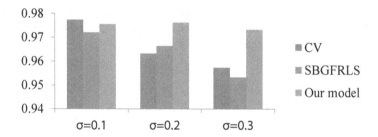

Fig. 2. The corresponding dice values of the segmental results in Fig. 1

Figure 3 shows comparison results for images (Yeast Fluorescence Micrograph, two X-ray images of vessels [12]) with intensity inhomogeneity. The edge around the blood vessels is blurred, which render it a challenging task for segmentation.

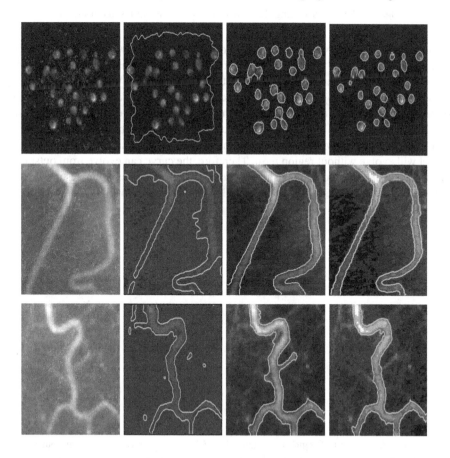

Fig. 3. Comparison result for various types of image, intensity inhomogeneity, low contrast, weak edge image. First column: results of GAC model. Second column: results of SBGFRLS model. Third column: results of L2S model. Fourth column: result of our proposed model.

Figures 3 and 4 show that our model is superior to GAC model, L2S model and SBGFRLS model. In conclusion, our model can obtain true boundaries and deal with images with intensity inhomogeneity.

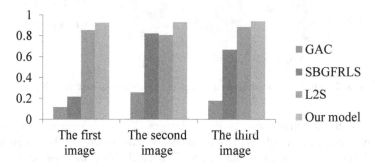

Fig. 4. The corresponding dice values of the segmental results in Fig. 3.

Figures 5 and 6 show the effectiveness of our model for low contrast images. The first column are original images. The second column, third column and fourth column show the contours of the regions-of-interest by LCV model, LSACM model and our model. As shown in Fig. 5, our model and LSACM model can successfully obtain segmentation objects, but our model gets more smoother curve and detects well the object's boundary. So our model has capability to segment images with weak boundary. For images with brighter background, we set $v = 0$ and $\alpha < 0$, then the new model will evolve without region term. Therefore, the curve can evolve from outside to inside quickly and effectively instead of $\alpha > 0$. Better segmentation results can be obtained, and the flexibility of our model also can be shown in Figs. 4 and 5.

Fig. 5. Detected contour of regions-of-interest by LCV model, LSACM model and our model. The corresponding figure shows from left to right. First column: the original image. Second column: results of LCV model. Third column: results of model. Fourth column: results of our model.

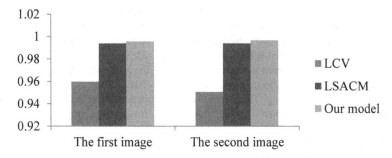

Fig. 6. The corresponding dice values of the segmental results in Fig. 5.

5 Conclusions

In this paper, a novel adaptive segmentation model for images in presence of low contrast, noise, weak edge and intensity inhomogeneity is proposed. The new model combines the advantages of GAC model and SBGFRLS model. The local and global information are all considered by our model. Legendre polynomials are employed to approximate region and then new model can deal with images with intensity inhomogeneity. The new model can choose the evolution direction adaptively and not very sensitive for initial contour. In addition our model can also handle images by selecting a rectangular or elliptical initial contour. Experimental results show that our model is more available and effective.

Acknowledgement. This paper is partially supported by the Natural Science Foundation of Guangdong Province (2018A030313364), the Science and Technology Planning Project of Shenzhen City (JCYJ20140828163633997), the Natural Science Foundation of Shenzhen (JCYJ20170818091621856) and the China Scholarship Council Project (201508440370).

References

1. Caselles, V., Kimmel, R., Sapiro, G.: Geodesic Active Contours. Int. J. Comput. Vis. **22**(1), 61–79 (1997)
2. Chan, T., Vese, L.: Active contours without edges. IEEE Trans. Image Process. **10**(2), 266–277 (2001)
3. Li, C., Kao, C., Gore, J., et al.: Minimization of region-scalable fitting energy for image segmentation. IEEE Trans. Image Process. **17**(10), 1940–1949 (2008)
4. Li, C., Xu, C., Gui, C., et al.: Level set evolution without re-initialization: a new variational formulation. In: IEEE Computer Society Conference on Computer Vision and Pattern Recognition 2005, vol. 1, pp. 430–436 (2005)
5. Li, C., Kao, C., Gore, J., et al.: Implicit active contours driven by local binary fitting energy. In: IEEE Conference on Computer Vision and Pattern Recognition 2007, vol. 2007, pp. 1–7 (2007)
6. Wang, X., Huang, D., Xu, H.: An efficient local Chan-Vese model for image segmentation. Pattern Recogn. **43**(3), 603–618 (2010)

7. Zhang, K., Zhang, L., Lam, K., et al.: A level set approach to image segmentation with intensity inhomogeneity. IEEE Trans. Cybern. **46**(2), 546–557 (2016)
8. Mukherjee, S., Acton, S.: Region based segmentation in presence of intensity inhomogeneity using Legendre polynomials. IEEE Sig. Process. Lett. **22**(3), 298–302 (2014)
9. Shi, N., Pan, J.: An improved active contours model for image segmentation by level set method. Opt. Int. J. Light Electron Opt. **127**(3), 1037–1042 (2016)
10. Zhang, K., Zhang, L., Song, H., et al.: Active contours with selective local or global segmentation: a new formulation and level set method. Image Vis. Comput. **28**(4), 668–676 (2010)
11. Xu, C., Yezzi, A., Prince, J., et al.: On the relationship between parametric and geometric active contours. In: IEEE Conference on Signals, Systems and Computers 2000, vol. 1, pp. 483–489 (2000)
12. Dietenbeck, T., Alessandrini, M., Friboulet, D., et al.: CREASEG: a free software for the evaluation of image segmentation algorithms based on level-set. In: IEEE International Conference on Image Processing 2010, vol. 119, pp. 665–668 (2010)

Spatiotemporal Masking for Objective Video Quality Assessment

Ran He$^{(\boxtimes)}$, Wen Lu, Yu Zhang, Xinbo Gao, and Lihuo He

School of Electronic Engineering, Xidian University, Xi'an 710071, China
{heran,zhangyu1993}@stu.xidian.edu.cn, {luwen,lhhe}@mail.xidian.edu.cn,
xbgao@ieee.org

Abstract. Random background and object motion may mask some distortions in video sequence, the masked distortions are ignored by humans and they aren't considered when humans assess video quality. The visual masking effect produces a gap between the subjective quality and predicted quality obtained by traditional video quality assessment (VQA) which measures all distortions to predict video quality. This paper proposed a novel spatiotemporal masking model (STMM) consists of spatial and temporal masking coefficients to narrow the gap. The spatial masking coefficient is computed by spatial randomness to count the error score between the subjective and objective score, and the temporal masking coefficient is combined by three parts that fused by eccentricity, magnitude of motion vectors and coherency of object motion to measure the degree of the masking effect. In addition, the proposed model is robust enough to integrate with several best known VQA metrics in the literature. The improvement achieved by utilizing the proposed model is evaluated in the LIVE database, MCL-V database and IVPL database. Experimental results show that the VQA metric based on STMM has a good consistency with the subjective perception and performs better than its original metric.

Keywords: Video quality assessment
Spatiotemporal masking effect · Visibility of distortions

1 Introduction

With the rapid development of video technology, video applications occupy a large part of our daily lives. However, the video may get degraded after acquisition, storage, compression and transmission, resulting in a decrease in video quality and affecting the viewers' visual experience. It's necessary to effectively control video quality and improve processing performance by accurately assessing the visual quality of videos. The most reliable quality assessment is subjective assessment because the final scores are the ultimate observers' judgements. However, it is limited by the cumbersome and laborious subjective experiments. Therefore, objective quality assessments become the replacement and have been widely researched in recent years [18].

© Springer Nature Switzerland AG 2018
J.-H. Lai et al. (Eds.): PRCV 2018, LNCS 11256, pp. 309–321, 2018.
https://doi.org/10.1007/978-3-030-03398-9_27

Objective video quality assessment can be classified into full-reference (FR), reduced-reference (RR), and no-reference (NR) assessment. FR VQA needs both references and the distorted video signals, RR VQA only needs partial information of the reference video, while NR VQA contains information only about the distorted video. A great number of successful VQA algorithms have been proposed. For example, SSIM [28], VIF [23], ST-MAD [27], ViS3 [26], VQM [20], STRRED [24]. The author in [21] analyzed the statistical characteristics of the local DCT coefficients of the frame differences, and combined the motion information to propose a NR assessment model. In [16], a NR assessment algorithm based on 3D shearlet transform and Convolutional Neural Network (CNN). Among these algorithms, the discrepancies between the reference videos and the distorted videos are regarded as the video distortions, and all discrepancies are measured to assess video quality based on the evaluation criterion that the amount of discrepancies is in negative proportion to the predicted quality. In fact, some of discrepancies can't be observed by humans, and these discrepancies can't reduce the perceptual quality with the result that a gap between the subjective quality and objective quality appears [7, 8].

Some local spatial or temporal distortions in video sequence may be masked, and the masked distortions aren't considered when humans assess video quality. The visual masking effect works on both spatial and temporal domains of video. The spatial masking effect is caused by the limited visual spatial resolution and the temporal masking effect is mapped by the "motion silencing" phenomenon. In [30] and [10], it's pointed out that the spatial masking effect depends on the degree of background randomness. When a single grating is flanked by other similar stimulate, its orientation become impossible to discern. The stimulus which contains some distorted signals is indistinguishable with neighborhood in the random background, and some distorted signals will be masked by the random background.

The temporal masking effect is mapped by the "motion silencing" phenomenon. Suchow *et al.* devised a series of experiments that one hundred dots arranged in a ring around a central fixation mark changed rapidly in hue, luminance, size, or shape. A "motion silencing" phenomenon was observed that the dots appeared to stop changing when the ring was briskly rotated [25]. The flickers are neglected or even invisible by the actual motion signals in the scene [4]. This motion silencing phenomenon can be mapped to the temporal masking effect that the local distortions of video can be masked by the motion signals in the video sequence, since the flickers represent spatial or temporal distortions in video and the amount of the non-neglected flickers is regarded as the visibility of distortions. Therefore, the temporal masking effect on VQA can be described by the visibility of video distortions. Recently, Choi *et al.* did a lot of subjective experiments to find out the factors which influence the flicker visibility on motion silencing [5, 6]. In [6], it is pointed out that the visibility of flicker distortions on naturalistic videos was silenced by the sufficiently fast, coherent motion. And then in [5], they focused on the effect of eccentricity. They found that the flicker distortions on naturalistic videos can be masked by highly eccentric and coherent object motion.

Some studies exploring the description of the visual masking effect include [2,10,11,30,31]. The author in [30] proposed entropy masking to measure the masking effect of the image background. In [10], the contrast masking and neighborhood masking were integrated to the contrast comparison measure to embed the visual perceptual masking into the quality assessment process. These methods measure the spatial masking effect effectively, but they are inadequate to be used in video sequence. In [31], the motion information content was used to measure the temporal activity, while the smooth motion was neglected. The author in [11] measured the masking effect of videos by utilizing the temporal and spatial randomness. However, this method only extends the spatial masking measurement to the temporal domain, and it doesn't describe the temporal masking effect caused by the physiological phenomena. In [2], locally shifted response deviations at each spatiotemporal subband was measured as the flicker sensitive quality. However, this method only takes account into the speed of object motion.

Inspired by these conclusions, spatial randomness is computed as the spatial masking feature, and the temporal masking features are extracted by eccentricity, magnitude of motion vectors and coherency of object motion. The spatial masking coefficient is computed by the spatial masking feature. This coefficient is regarded as the error score between the predicted score by utilizing all discrepancies and subjective score, and it should be subtracted from the predicted score. The temporal masking coefficient consists of three parts that fused by the temporal masking features, which aims to measure the degree of masking effect created by different video content adequately. After a non-linear combination, the spatial and temporal masking coefficient are fused into the proposed spatiotemporal masking model. Several best known VQA metrics integrate with the proposed model, and the experimental results show that the new combination achieves a better performance.

The rest of this paper is organized as follows. Section 2 details the proposed methodology. Section 3 presents the experimental results and analysis on the LIVE database, the MVL-V database and IVPL database.

2   Methodology

Understanding how human visual system works is important to design VQA algorithms, since humans are the ultimate adjudicator of videos. The local spatial and temporal distortions in video may be masked by the visual masking effect, with the results that the distortions can't be observed by human beings. Although the local distortions veritably exist in the distorted video, the quality of video doesn't decline obviously. In the proposed method, a spatiotemporal masking model includes spatial and temporal masking coefficients is built to measure the visual masking effect of video. Spatial randomness is computed as the spatial masking feature, and the temporal masking features are extracted by eccentricity and motion information which contains magnitude of motion vectors and coherency of object motion. The spatial masking feature is utilized to compute the spatial masking coefficient which represents the error score between the predicted score and subjective score. The temporal masking features are fused into three parts which are used to calculate the temporal masking coefficient. The temporal masking coefficient aims to measure the degree of masking effect created by different video content. Finally, the proposed model integrates with several best known VQA metrics to predict the video quality. The framework of the proposed algorithm is shown in Fig. 1, and each stage of the algorithm is described in the following subsections.

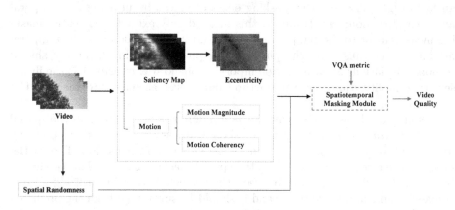

Fig. 1. Framework of the proposed model.

2.1 Spatial Masking Feature

The spatial masking effect highly depends on the degree of the background randomness in the video sequence. Therefore, the spatial randomness is computed as the spatial masking feature [11]. The variance of $n \times n$ block is calculated to indicate the local spatial randomness, and the spatial masking feature of each frame is computed as follows:

$$m_S = \frac{1}{N} \sum_{k=1}^{N} \sigma^2(k, i) \tag{1}$$

where $\sigma^2(k, i)$ is the variance of the kth block in the ith frame, N is the total number of blocks within a frame.

2.2 Temporal Masking Feature

Eccentricity. With the increase of the eccentricity, the visibility of distortions decreases [3]. It can be explained that when the eccentricity increases, the relevant signal that is masked by motion silences falls outside the response regions of the receptive fields, thus the visibility of distortions reduces. Therefore, the eccentricity can be calculated as the masking feature. The eccentricity e is related

Fig. 2. Eccentricity.

to viewing distance L and the Euclidean distance d from (x, y) to the fixation (k, l), the relationship is shown in Fig. 2.

The eccentricity is defined as:

$$\tan e = \frac{\sqrt{(k-x)^2 + (l-y)^2}}{L} \qquad (2)$$

In [17], the saliency value of each pixel is gaussian distributed, and the Euclidean distance is utilized to calculate the saliency map. In this method, we apply a more general distribution instead of gaussian distribution. The saliency map is calculated as follows:

$$S(x, y) = \exp\left[-\frac{\left(\sqrt{(k-x)^2 + (l-y)^2}\right)^\alpha}{\sigma^2}\right] \qquad (3)$$

where $S(x, y)$ is the saliency value of location (x, y), σ is the model parameter, and α is set to 4. Therefore, the eccentricity can be calculated by the saliency map of the video. Based on Eq. (2) and Eq. (3), the eccentricity can be calculated as follows:

$$e(x, y) = \arctan \frac{(-\sigma^2 \ln(S(x, y)))^{1/\alpha}}{L} \qquad (4)$$

In the proposed method, the saliency map $S(x, y)$ is obtained by RWR [14].

In order to simplify the calculation [11], the eccentricity can be approximated as:

$$e(x, y) = \frac{\sigma^{2/\alpha}}{L} \ln\left(\frac{1}{S(x, y) + c}\right)^{1/\alpha} \qquad (5)$$

where c is a constant that avoids zero appears in the denominator, and the value of c is extremely small to insure that it is far less than the value of $S(x, y)$. In addition, the values of $e(x, y)$ are normalized to [0,1].

Magnitude of Motion Vectors. The magnitude of motion vectors is calculated to measure the speed of the object motion. In [5], a phenomenon that flicker distortions were noticeable even at large eccentricity when the object was static was observed. The visibility of distortions is related to eccentricity and object motion simultaneously. Therefore, the speed of the object motion should also be computed to measure the temporal masking effect.

The motion vectors are estimated by a simple three-step search algorithm [15]. The magnitude map of motion vectors of each frame is calculated as follows:

$$M(x,y) = \sqrt{v_x(x,y)^2 + v_y(x,y)^2} \qquad (6)$$

where $v_x(x,y)$ and $v_y(x,y)$ are horizontal and vertical motion vectors at pixel (x,y) respectively.

Coherency of Object Motion. The temporal masking effect is related to the coherent object motion, thus, the coherency of the object motion should be computed to measure the visibility of distortions. A 2D structure tensor model is applied to characterize the coherency of object motion [21]. The motion coherence tensor is defined as:

$$C = \begin{bmatrix} f(v_x) & f(v_x \cdot v_y) \\ f(v_x \cdot v_y) & f(v_y) \end{bmatrix} \qquad (7)$$

where

$$f(v) = \sum_{l,k} w[x,y]v(x-l, y-k)^2 \qquad (8)$$

and w is a window of dimension $m \times m$. The eigenvalues of the motion coherence tensor are computed, and the discrepancy between the eigenvalues of each tensor is utilized to model the motion coherency as:

$$MC(x,y) = \left(\frac{\lambda_1 - \lambda_2}{\lambda_1 + \lambda_2} \right)^2 \qquad (9)$$

where λ_1 and λ_2 are the eigenvalues of the tensor at pixel (x,y).

2.3   Spatiotemporal Masking Model

The spatiotemporal masking model includes the temporal and spatial masking coefficients. The temporal masking coefficient consists of three parts. The first part contains both eccentricity and the magnitude of motion vectors aims to model the masking effect of the motion that appears in the peripheral vision. It avoids the situation that the distortions can be noticeable at large eccentricity when the object was static. Therefore, we multiply eccentricity map and motion magnitude to detect the region which contains both large eccentricity and object motion, the first part of the ith frame is defined as:

$$M_1^i = E_i \times M_i \qquad (10)$$

The second part only contains the magnitude of motion vectors, it aims to delineate the situation that motion silencing appears in foveal vision where the eccentricity is very small. The second part of the ith frame is defined as:

$$M_2^i = \frac{1}{N \times M} \sum_{x=1}^{N} \sum_{y=1}^{M} M(x,y) \tag{11}$$

where $N \times M$ is the size of each frame.

The third part is designed to characterize the coherent object motion. The fast and coherent object motion is considered in this part, and it in the ith frame is defined as:

$$M_3^i = \frac{1}{N \times M} \sum_{x=1}^{N} \sum_{y=1}^{M} M(x,y) \times MC(x,y) \tag{12}$$

The masking effect plays a negative role in predicting the final score, since it weakens the influence of distortions by decreasing the visibility of distortions. The masking coefficient which highly depends on video content measures the strength of masking effect. These three parts are integrated into the masking coefficient as follows:

$$M_T^i = 1 - \alpha(\beta_1 M_1^i + \beta_2 M_2^i) \times M_3^i \tag{13}$$

where α is a parameter weight that could be optimized based on different VQA metrics, $\beta_1 = 0.4$ and $\beta_1 = 0.6$, since the impact of the fast object motion is more obvious.

There is an "negative-peak and duration-neglect effect" when the quality of video changes as time goes by [19]. It implies that the relatively bad frames in the video sequence seem much more important to subjective perception. We use the lowest pooling strategy in the temporal pooling stage, $M_T^i(i = 1, 2, \ldots, K)$ are firstly placed in descending order, and then the worst p% M_T^i are chosen. The temporal masking feature of the whole video is defined as:

$$M_T = \frac{1}{P} \sum_{i=1}^{P} M_T^i \tag{14}$$

The spatial masking coefficient of the whole video is computed as follows:

$$M_S = \ln \left(\frac{1}{T} \sum_{i=1}^{T} m_S^i \right) \tag{15}$$

where T is the total number of frames in a video sequence.

In order to obtain the final score, the proposed spatiotemporal masking model is integrated with existing VQA metrics. The VQA metric based on the spatiotemporal masking module(STMM) is defined as follows:

$$STMM - VQA = (S_{VQA} - \gamma M_S) \times M_T \tag{16}$$

where S_{VQA} means the final score predicted by the applied VQA metric, γ is a parameter weight that could be optimized based on different VQA metrics.

3   Experimental Results

Three publicly available video databases are involved in our experiments to test the performance of the proposed module. The first one is the LIVE video quality database [22]. It contains 10 reference videos and 150 distorted videos with four common distortions, namely Wireless, IP, H.264 and MPEG distortion. The second one is MCL-V database [13]. It contains 12 reference videos and 96 distorted videos with two typical distortion types, namely H.264 compression and compression followed by scaling. The third database is the image & video processing laboratory(IVPL) video quality database [1]. It contains 10 reference videos and 128 distorted videos with four types of distortion, including MPEG-2 compression, Dirac wavelet compression, H.264 compression and packet loss on the H.264 streaming through IP networks.

In this paper, six widely recognized VQA metrics, namely SSIM, MS-SSIM [29], VIF, ST-MAD, ViS3, STRRED are applied in our evaluation. Pearsons correlation coefficient (PLCC) and Spearmans correlation coefficient (SROCC) [9] are used to evaluate the performance of the prosed module. PLCC measures the linear dependence between the objective prediction and subjective assessment, and SROCC measures the monotonic consistency between them. We compare the performance of original VQA metrics with STMM in terms of PLCC and SROCC. Tables 1 and 2 show the comparison of performance using PLCC and SROCC on LIVE database respectively. Here W refers to wireless transmitted distortion; I refers to IP transmitted distortion; H refers to H.264 compressed distortion; and M refers to MPEG-2 compressed distortion.

Table 1. Compression of performance by PLCC on LIVE database.

Metric	Mode	W	I	H	M	ALL
SSIM	Original	0.5459	0.5398	0.6750	0.5758	0.5423
	STMM	0.6720	0.5392	0.7993	0.6681	0.6186
MS-SSIM	Original	0.7395	0.7412	0.7414	0.7029	0.7602
	STMM	0.8033	0.7577	0.8128	0.8063	0.8377
VIF	Original	0.5640	0.5897	0.7187	0.5664	0.5520
	STMM	0.6850	0.5836	0.8278	0.6347	0.6249
ST-MAD	Original	0.8460	0.7963	0.9087	0.8555	0.8303
	STMM	0.8507	0.8144	0.9168	0.8521	0.8367
ViS3	Original	0.8574	0.8349	0.7993	0.7574	0.8336
	STMM	0.8675	0.8469	0.8161	0.7718	0.8436
STRRED	Original	0.7563	0.6479	0.8237	0.7474	0.8054
	STMM	0.8120	0.8029	0.8787	0.7351	0.8183

Table 2. Compression of performance by SROCC on LIVE database.

Metric	Mode	W	I	H	M	ALL
SSIM	Original	0.5221	0.4701	0.6561	0.5608	0.5251
	STMF	0.6377	0.5026	0.7674	0.6490	0.6095
MS-SSIM	Original	0.7405	0.6819	0.7332	0.6861	0.7534
	STMF	0.7848	0.7362	0.8486	0.7767	0.8345
VIF	Original	0.5561	0.4999	0.6987	0.5538	0.5511
	STMF	0.6771	0.5430	0.7953	0.6129	0.6256
ST-MAD	Original	0.8099	0.7758	0.9021	0.8460	0.8251
	STMF	0.8090	0.8073	0.9180	0.8341	0.8285
ViS3	Original	0.8394	0.7918	0.7685	0.7360	0.8168
	STMF	0.8433	0.8127	0.7867	0.7602	0.8271
STRRED	Original	0.7857	0.7722	0.8193	0.7191	0.8007
	STMF	0.7856	0.8007	0.8719	0.7034	0.8139

From Tables 1 and 2, it can be seen that the performance of a VQA metric based on STMM is higher than its original metric. It can be concluded that the proposed model employs a good performance with 4 different distortions of the LIVE database and characterizes the human visual perception effectively. And the model applied in VQA can improve the performance obviously. The Table 3 shows the performance gain of a VQA metric based on STMM over its original metric expressed by PLCC and SROCC on LIVE database.

Table 3 shows that the proposed model is robust enough to integrate with these widely recognized VQA metrics and gets a big performance gain. The comparison of performance and the performance gain between a VQA metric based on STMM and its original metric using PLCC and SROCC on MCL-V database is shown on Tables 4 and 5.

Table 3. Performance gain (Δ PLCC and Δ SROCC) between a VQA metric based on STMM and its original metric on LIVE database.

	SSIM	MS-SSIM	VIF	ST-MAD	ViS3	STRRED
Δ PLCC	+0.0763	+0.0775	+0.0729	+0.0064	+0.0100	+0.0129
Δ SROCC	+0.0844	+0.0811	+0.0745	+0.0034	+0.0103	+0.0132

From Tables 4 and 5, it can be concluded that STMM also has a good performance on the MCL-V database. Tables 6 and 7 shows the comparison of performance and the performance gain between a VQA metric based on STMM and its original metric using PLCC and SROCC on IVPL database.

Table 4. Compression of performance and performance gain (Δ PLCC) between a VQA metric based on STMM and its original metric by PLCC on MCL-V database.

Mode	Metric					
	SSIM	MS-SSIM	VIF	ST-MAD	ViS3	STRRED
Original	0.3829	0.6663	0.6540	0.6289	0.6342	0.7428
STMM	0.6263	0.7416	0.6720	0.6407	0.6625	0.8155
Δ PLCC	+0.2434	+0.0753	+0.0180	+0.0118	+0.0283	+0.0727

Table 5. Compression of performance and performance gain (Δ SROCC) between a VQA metric based on STMM and its original metric by SROCC on MCL-V database.

Mode	Metric					
	SSIM	MS-SSIM	VIF	ST-MAD	ViS3	STRRED
Original	0.4009	0.6585	0.6466	0.6163	0.6313	0.7385
STMM	0.6224	0.7191	0.6593	0.6301	0.6596	0.8001
Δ SROCC	+0.2215	+0.0606	+0.0127	+0.0138	+0.0283	+0.0616

From Tables 4, 5, 6 and 7, it can be seen that the performance gain in terms of PLCC and SROCC on MCLV database is more obvious than that on IVPL database. The reason can be explained that the Temporal Information(TI) defined in the ITU-T Recommendation [12] of videos on MCLV database is more than that on IVPL database. TI of all videos on IVPL database is below 30 [1]. However, the proportion of videos of which TI is below 30 on MCL-V database is 30% [13]. The proposed STMM aims to model the visual masking effect caused by both random background and object motion in the video sequence. Thus, STMM woks on the video which contains more TI better than the video of which less TI.

Table 6. Compression of performance and performance gain (Δ PLCC) between a VQA metric based on STMM and its original metric by PLCC on IVPL database.

Mode	Metric					
	SSIM	MS-SSIM	VIF	ST-MAD	ViS3	STRRED
Original	0.4474	0.6512	0.3	0.6652	0.7977	0.7329
STMM	0.4487	0.6978	0.3224	0.668	0.8026	0.7424
Δ PLCC	+0.0013	+0.0466	+0.0224	+0.0028	+0.0049	+0.0095

Table 7. Compression of performance and performance gain (Δ SROCC) between a VQA metric based on STMM and its original metric by SROCC on IVPL database.

Mode	Metric					
	SSIM	MS-SSIM	VIF	ST-MAD	ViS3	STRRED
Original	0.3560	0.6440	0.2681	0.6613	0.7955	0.7374
STMM	0.3657	0.7007	0.2725	0.6712	0.8014	0.7539
Δ PLCC	+0.0097	+0.0567	+0.0044	+0.0099	+0.0059	+0.0165

4   Conclusion

It's essential to take into account human visual properties in the design of VQA algorithms. Some of distortions are real existence in video, but these distortions can't be observed by humans by the visual masking effect. These distortions don't reduce the subjective score, thus, the visual masking effect is considered in this paper. This paper proposed a novel spatiotemporal masking model which contains two significant parts: spatial and temporal masking coefficients. The spatial masking coefficient is computed by the spatial randomness. The temporal masking coefficient is calculated by fusing the temporal masking features that include eccentricity, magnitude of motion vectors and coherency of object motion. Finally, the proposed model integrates with several best known VQA metrics. Experimental results on the LIVE database, MCL-V database and IVPL database demonstrate that the proposed model has good performance and has a good consistency with human perception.

Acknowledgments. This research was supported partially by the National Natural Science Foundation of China (No. 61372130, No. 61432014, No. 61871311), the Fundamental Research Funds for the Central Universities (No. CJT140201).

References

1. IVP subjective quality video database. http://ivp.ee.cuhk.edu.hk/research/database/subjective/index.shtml
2. Choi, L.K., Bovik, A.C.: Flicker sensitive motion tuned video quality assessment. In: Southwest Symposium on Image Analysis and Interpretation (SSIAI), pp. 29–32. IEEE, Santa Fe (2016)
3. Choi, L.K., Bovik, A.C., Cormack, L.K.: The effect of eccentricity and spatiotemporal energy on motion silencing. J. Vis. **16**(5), 19–31 (2016)
4. Choi, L.K., Bovik, A.C., Cormack, L.K.: A flicker detector model of the motion silencing illusion. J. Vis. **12**(9), 777 (2012)
5. Choi, L.K., Cormack, L.K., Bovik, A.C.: Eccentricity effect of motion silencing on naturalistic videos. In: IEEE Global Conference on Signal and Information Processing (GlobalSIP), pp. 1190–1194. IEEE, Orlando (2015)
6. Choi, L.K., Cormack, L.K., Bovik, A.C.: Motion silencing of flicker distortions on naturalistic videos. Sign. Process. Image Commun. **39**, 328–341 (2015)

7. Fan, D.P., Cheng, M.M., Liu, Y., Li, T., Borji, A.: Structure-measure: a new way to evaluate foreground maps. In: IEEE International Conference on Computer Vision (ICCV), pp. 4558–4567. IEEE, Venice (2017)

8. Fan, D.P., Gong, C., Cao, Y., Ren, B., Cheng, M.M., Borji, A.: Enhanced-alignment measure for binary foreground map evaluation. In: International Joint Conference on Artificial Intelligence (IJCAI) (2018)

9. Group, V.Q.E., et al.: Final report from the video quality experts group on the validation of objective models of video quality assessment (2000)

10. He, S., Cavanagh, P., Intriligator, J.: Attentional resolution and the locus of visual awareness. Nature **383**(6598), 334–337 (1996)

11. Hu, S., Jin, L., Wang, H., Zhang, Y., Kwong, S., Kuo, C.C.J.: Objective video quality assessment based on perceptually weighted mean squared error. IEEE Trans. Circ. Syst. Video Technol. **27**(9), 1844–1855 (2017)

12. ITU-T RECOMMENDATION, P.: Subjective video quality assessment methods for multimedia applications. International Telecommunication Union

13. Lin, J.Y., Song, R., Wu, C.H., Liu, T., Wang, H., Kuo, C.C.J.: MCL-V: a streaming video quality assessment database. J. Vis. Commun. Image Represent. **30**, 1–9 (2015)

14. Kim, H., Kim, Y., Sim, J.Y., Kim, C.S.: Spatiotemporal saliency detection for video sequences based on random walk with restart. IEEE Trans. Image Process. **24**(8), 2552–2564 (2015)

15. Li, R., Zeng, B., Liou, M.L.: A new three-step search algorithm for block motion estimation. IEEE Trans. Circuits Syst. Video Technol. **4**(4), 438–442 (1994)

16. Li, Y., et al.: No-reference video quality assessment with 3d shearlet transform and convolutional neural networks. IEEE Trans. Circuits Syst. Video Technol. **26**(6), 1044–1057 (2016)

17. Liu, H., Heynderickx, I.: Visual attention in objective image quality assessment: based on eye-tracking data. IEEE Trans. Circuits Syst. Video Technol. **21**(7), 971–982 (2011)

18. Aggarwal, N.: A review on video quality assessment. In: Recent Advances Engineering and Computational Sciences (RAECS), pp. 1–6. IEEE, Chandigarh (2014)

19. Pearson, D.E.: Viewer response to time-varying video quality. In: Electronic Imaging, vol. 3299, pp. 16–26. Human Vision and Electronic Imaging III, San Jose, CA, United States (1998)

20. Pinson, M.H., Wolf, S.: A new standardized method for objectively measuring video quality. IEEE Trans. Broadcast. **50**(3), 312–322 (2004)

21. Saad, M.A., Bovik, A.C., Charrier, C.: Blind prediction of natural video quality. IEEE Trans. Image Process. **23**(3), 1352–1365 (2014)

22. Seshadrinathan, K., Soundararajan, R., Bovik, A.C., Cormack, L.K.: Study of subjective and objective quality assessment of video. IEEE Trans. Image Process. **19**(6), 1427–1441 (2010)

23. Sheikh, H.R., Sabir, M.F., Bovik, A.C.: A statistical evaluation of recent full reference image quality assessment algorithms. IEEE Trans. Image Process. **15**(11), 3440–3451 (2006)

24. Soundararajan, R., Bovik, A.C.: Video quality assessment by reduced reference spatio-temporal entropic differencing. IEEE Trans. Circuits Syst. Video Technol. **23**(4), 684–694 (2013)

25. Suchow, J.W., Alvarez, G.A.: Motion silences awareness of visual change. Curr. Biol. **21**(2), 140–143 (2011)

26. Vu, P.V., Chandler, D.M.: ViS3: an algorithm for video quality assessment via analysis of spatial and spatiotemporal slices. J. Electron. Imaging **23**(1), 013016 (2014)
27. Vu, P.V., Vu, C.T., Chandler, D.M.: A spatiotemporal most-apparent-distortion model for video quality assessment. In: 18th IEEE International Conference on Image Processing (ICIP), pp. 2505–2508. IEEE, Brussels (2011)
28. Wang, Z., Bovik, A.C., Sheikh, H.R., Simoncelli, E.P.: Image quality assessment: from error visibility to structural similarity. IEEE Trans. Image Process. **13**(4), 600–612 (2004)
29. Wang, Z., Simoncelli, E.P., Bovik, A.C.: Multiscale structuralsimilarity for image quality assessment. In: Conference Record of the Thirty-Seventh Asilomar Conference on Signals, Systems andComputers, vol. 2, pp. 1398–1402. IEEE, Pacific Grove (2003)
30. Watson, A.B., Borthwick, R., Taylor, M.: Image quality and entropy masking. In: Electronic Imaging, pp. 2–13. Human Vision and Electronic Imaging II, San Jose (1997)
31. Xu, L., Li, S., Ngan, K.N., Ma, L.: Consistent visual quality control in video coding. IEEE Trans. Circuits Syst. Video Technol. **23**(6), 975–989 (2013)

A Detection Method of Online Public Opinion Based on Element Co-occurrence

Nanchang Cheng, Yu Zou[✉], Yonglin Teng, and Min Hou

National Broadcast Media Language Resources Monitoring and Research Center,
Communication University of China, Beijing 100024, China
{chengnanchang, zouiy, tengyonglin, houmin}@cuc.edu.cn

Abstract. Discovering and identifying public opinion timely and efficiently from web text are of great significance. The present methods of public opinion supervision suffer from being rough and less targeted. To overcome these shortcomings, this paper provides a public opinion detection method of network public opinion based on element co-occurrence for specific domain. This method, considering the nature of public opinion, represents three main factors (subject, object and semantic orientation) that constitute public opinion by employing their feature words, which can be dynamically combined according to their syntagmatic and associative relations. Thus, this method can not only generate topics related to public opinion in specific fields, but also identify public opinion information of these fields efficiently. The method has found its practical usage in "Language Public Opinion Monitoring System" and "Higher Education Public Opinion Monitoring System" with accuracies 92% and 93% respectively.

Keywords: Element co-occurrence · Online public opinion
Syntagmatic relations · Associative relations

1 Introduction

At present, public opinion recognition and monitoring is a popular research field. What is the public opinion? Reference [1] regarded public opinion as "the sum of many emotions, wills, attitudes and opinions, in certain historical stage and social space, held by individuals and various social groups, to the various kinds of public affairs which are closely related to their own interests".

In short, public opinion detection is to check whether the content of the text connects with the public opinion. According to the definition of text classification in Ref. [2], public opinion detection is a branch of text classification, which means that whether the text contains public opinion information can determine it is public opinion or not. Public opinion detection is at the predecessor position of public monitoring. Only if the public opinion information is gathered in time, the further analysis of public opinion is available, which involves classification, hotspot identification, orientation analysis etc. Because public opinion is characterized by its abruptness, it is hard to predict what and where to occur. Thus, it is critical to detect and identify public opinion information in time. However, at present, there is a scarcity of the literature related to

J.-H. Lai et al. (Eds.): PRCV 2018, LNCS 11256, pp. 322–334, 2018.
https://doi.org/10.1007/978-3-030-03398-9_28

the public opinion detection, and most publicized public opinion detection systems merely employ techniques such as text classification, information filtering and keyword retrieval [3]. To reduce redundancy, these systems graded the keywords. For example, we can input the word "housing removal" as the first-grade keyword, "Yun Nan Province" as the second-grade keyword (co-occurred word) and "Honghe Area" as the keyword to be excluded, which means that we want to find public opinions concerning the housing removal which happened in Yun Nan Province excluding "Hong He Area". The method of keyword grading and public opinion dictionary is of high speed when searching and identifying mass online information, and of high flexibility as well, for it permits the addition of batched keywords in a custom way according to user's needs. However, there are still two remaining problems: (I) the adding keywords must be the topics we have known, but yet the system lacks of ability in acquiring unknown public opinion information; (II) keywords only cover one point the text involves, which leads to the fact that it lacks enough tension to make sure that all the text extracted is concerned with public opinion information. These two drawbacks lead to high redundancy and high cost in processing texts.

Public opinion covers different fields in society, and in every field, public opinion shows unique characteristics. However, at present, public opinion detection method for a specific sub-field is still rare in literature, and the public opinion monitoring system mentioned above and other publicized systems are basically geared to all fields. Generally speaking, the more in detail the classification of sub-fields is, the deeper the research would go. Whole-field monitoring is one of the important reasons for the roughness in public opinion monitoring.

Therefore, in order to improve the roughness and the low specialization for sub-fields in the public opinion detection method, this paper, based on the nature of public opinion, and particularly imitating human's cognitive process of public opinion information, proposes the element co-occurrence method, a method that is specialized for online public opinion detection in subfields. This paper will take language public opinion detection as an example to illustrate this method and its detail implementation.

2   Relevant Studies

Studies related to public opinion detection mainly concentrates on the topic detection field. There used to be an international conference concerned with the evaluation of this field, whose name was Topic Detection and Tracing (TDT in short) [4]. In TDT, A topic refers to "a set of reports of a seed event or activity and its directly related events or activities" [5, 6]. Topic Detection (TD in short) task is to detect and organize topics that are unknown to the system [6]. Technically, statistical clustering algorithms are widely employed, such as K-Means [7], Centroid [8] and Hieratical Clustering [9], etc. Because of the mass calculation in clustering, when dealing with the massive online texts, it is rare to directly detect the public opinion related topics by clustering method.

Although TDT had stopped in 2004, related researches still go on. In recent years, Refs. [10, 11] proposed new event detection method based on topic classification and lemma re-evaluation respectively. But the TDT test corpus that they used have been carefully classified according to topics, however, in actual condition, online texts do not have related information as classification and sub-topics to use. Reference [12] used keyword-based search method to detect the emergency events in Sina blog, and, by restricting time period and domain names to narrow down the search results and reduce the redundancy. This is similar with the keyword search method mentioned above. Reference [13] recognize sentences which contain critical information through hot words. Then apply clustering to all the sentences recognized to implement hot topic recognition. The probability that the hot topic belongs to public opinion is relatively high, which is related with this research. Though Ref. [13] reduced the computation amount from paragraph level to sentence level, hot word and sentence recognition still consume a lot.

To sum up, deficiencies of the current public opinion detection can be generalized into following 3 points: (I) Low specification. Most of the publicized systems are whole-fielded, which perform ineffectively in specific field. (II) Most of the publicized systems based on batched keywords or public opinion dictionaries, whose deficiencies have thoroughly revealed in Sect. 1. (III) Most of the statistic-based clustering method and other new methods are still at the theoretical level, are still rare in real public opinion detection.

3   Main Idea of Element Co-occurrence

According to the definition in Ref. [1], the public opinion is the sum of many emotions, wills, attitudes and opinions, in certain historical stage and social space, held by individuals and various social groups, to the various kinds of public affairs which are closely related to their own interests. It is obvious that the public opinion is composed of three basic elements: subject (people), object (various public affairs) and semantic orientation (the sum of emotions, wills, attitudes and opinions). "Element co-occurrence" starts from the essence of public opinion, representing each element by a feature word. Three kinds of feature words can be combined with each other dynamically to generate a topic that is related to public opinion in the certain field. For example, in language field, there are public opinion events as "traditional characters or simplified characters", "protect the dialect" and "letter words tumult". The relation of three kinds of elements represented by feature words can be shown as Fig. 1.

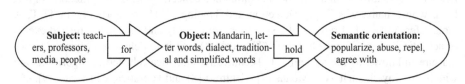

Fig. 1. Three kinds of feature words of public opinion on language and their relationship

The figure above expresses that: for language public opinion, subjects as professors and teachers hold opinions or attitudes as disagree, repel or agree for objects as letter words. In that, "for" and "hold" are the pre-set keyword in the pattern, and keywords in three elements as "subject", "object" and "semantic orientation" are automatically extracted from the text or summarized according to the experience. Three types of feature words can combine dynamically with strong tension. Such combination can cover all public opinion that may appear in language public opinion field and can exclude most of the non-public-opinion information. The theoretical basis is Combinatorial Polymerization theory of Saussure.

Sweden linguistic Saussure pointed out that in language status, all of them are based on relationships [14]. The core of it is the sentence segment relationship and association relationship, which, in another word, combination relationship and aggregation relationship. Combination relationship refers to the horizontal relationships among language units that appear in language and based on linear basis; aggregation relationship refers to the vertical relationships among language units that may appear at the same position with same functions. According to this theory of Saussure, the dynamic combination of three kinds of characteristic keywords that mentioned above can generate different topics. For example, according to combination relationship, the system can generate topics as "teachers popularize Mandarin", "experts repel dialects", "media abuse letter words" and "people agree with simplified words" etc.; according to aggregation relationship, the system can generate topics as "teachers popularize Mandarin", "experts popularize Mandarin", "media popularize Mandarin" and "people popularize Mandarin" etc. As one can discover, element co-occurrence method is the simulation of the corpus of certain field's knowledge in human brain (combination relationship) together with the comprehension and expression generation of objects (aggregation relationship), which has strong topic generation ability. Moreover, so long as the topic is able to generate by this method, the effective identification of the topic is almost indeed. If, for a specific field, according to the characteristics of its public opinion, a corpus containing three kinds of feature words can be build, it will be possible to detect the public opinion in that field effectively. The generative ability of element co-occurrence is potential, when keywords appeared in a piece of text, this method can automatically ignore other words that are not related with the feature words and dynamically generate matching topics. For instance, after ignoring other words, for text piece "some post-90s students very like traditional characters", topic "students like traditional characters" can be detected.

From the perspective of public opinion detection, the feature words of objects are most important. In the text, firstly, if only language-related words appeared, it is meaningful to discuss whether these belong to public opinion, and we can call them "topic words"; after that, the feature words with emotional inclination can be called "emotional words"; thirdly, the feature words associated with subjects, which are typically people as students, parents and teachers etc. Besides, the occurrence of public opinion requires certain time and space environment, and accordingly, their feature words are like "class, classroom, and school etc.", they also affect the public opinion detection, some even can replace the subjects, as "school popularizes Mandarin". In these condition, time and space feature words are similar to the feature words of subject, therefore, it is possible to combine these feature words into "people and environment" class, which, in short, "environment words". In three kinds of feature words, any of them alone cannot compose a public opinion topic directly, the co-occurrence of two or more feature words is a necessity to compose a public opinion topic. Based on that, this method is called "element co-occurrence method."

Element co-occurrence method detects the public opinion towards constructing a discourse knowledge system related to public opinion in some fields. This method, instead of concerning a single point, concerns the combination of three basic elements that relate to the public opinion, which shows strong tension. Thus, this method has an essential difference with traditional detecting methods as keyword method or public opinion dictionary method. By batched keywords or public opinion dictionary, one can only search a point of public opinion, which is one-dimensional. For example, as "demolition incident", "Zhao Yuan murder" and "terror incident". Element co-occurrence is three-dimensional and is formed by the combination of three kinds of feature words to form different topics. Keyword grading method or public opinion dictionary method also concerned co-occurrence, but the co-occurrence in these methods is associated with some certain words. However, all elements in element co-occurrence method can combine with each other dynamically and have powerful topic generation ability. Taking advantage of this dynamic combination, element co-occurrence method endows the public opinion monitoring system public opinion alert function by discovering the unknown topic in real time.

4   Implementation of Element Co-occurrence

4.1   Extracting the Feature Words of the Three Types

The prerequisite of element co-occurrence is to establish three feature words sets. Feature words can be collected manually or be obtained by automatic searching method. This paper has 9436 texts (referred as X set) with 12.5 million words, among which 1836 texts are related to public opinion (referred as Y set) with 2.5 million words, and the rest 7600 texts (referred as Z set) are non-public opinion articles which are over 10 million words. Then the word segmentation system, CUCBst, is used to extract words and calculate word frequency. The words extracted from X, Y and Z are then graded according to the frequency: Grade 1 (≥ 1000 times), Grade 2 (500–999 times), Grade 3 (100–499 times), Grade 4 (5–99 times), Grade 5 (1–4 times). To identify the feature words from tests related to public opinion on language issues, words extracted from Z set are compared with words from X set in their respective grades. Taking the word "language" as an example, its frequency in X set is 7161 times and thus is a Grade 1 word, but it only appears 62 times in Z set and is rated Grade 4. Without the process of comparing words' frequency according to their grade, it would be impossible to identify the feature words of public opinion on language issues.

The extracted words need to be further classified into topic words, emotion words and background words. An extracted word is identified as a topic word if it matches a term from Chines Term in Linguistic [15], and an emotion word is identified according to Emotion Term Dictionary [16]. Those that do not fall into these two categories are automatically classified as background words. Taking the Grade 1 words in X and Z sets as example, the extraction process of feature words is illustrated in Fig. 2.

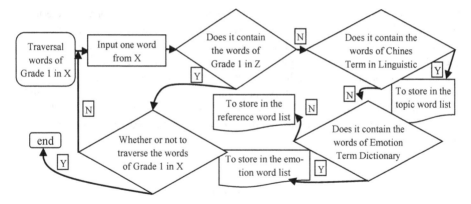

Fig. 2. Flow chart of three kinds of feature words extraction

The quality of feature set determines the accuracy and recall rate of public opinion detection. In order to guarantee the quality of feature word set, all of the feature words extracted automatically need to be manually confirmed.

4.2 Weighting Algorithm

Introduction to Weighted algorithm

The successful extraction of feature sets is the foundation of element co-occurrence method. Element co-occurrence is the main factor of public opinion judging, but it is not the only factor. In order to determine whether a given text is related to public opinion on language issues or not, the score of the text is affected by four factors: the normalized using rate of feature words, the co-occurrence of feature words, their location and the length of the text. When the score reaches a certain threshold, it can be determined that the text is related to public opinion on language issues.

Calculating the Weight of Feature Words

The importance of a word in a text set is usually indicated by its value of TF-IDF (term frequency-inverse document frequency). TF-IDF theory suggests that the importance of a word increases proportionally with the rising of its frequency in a certain text, but decreases with the increasing of the number of texts appearing in a corpus. That means the weight of special words appearing in only a few documents is higher than that of a word appearing in many documents [17]. However, the disadvantages of TF-IDF are obvious as it underestimates the importance of frequently occurring words in a certain domain. These words are usually highly representative and should be given a higher weight [18]. Therefore, this research chooses normalized using rate as an important quantification criterion. In fact, a text is more likely to be related to public opinion if the using rate of feature words in the text is high. For example, when feature words such as "Chinese" and "dialect" appear in the text, it is more likely to be related to the public opinion of language issues than a text with non-feature words such as "tone" and "syllable".

Therefore, this paper employs the normalized using rate of feature words to determine its weight. The analysis of the feature words' using rate demonstrates that the using rates of the most frequently appearing feature words are generally ≥ 0.01, mid using rate is between 0.01 and 0.001, and the using rate of rarely used feature words is lower than 0.001. According to this finding, the weight of a feature word is defined into three grades, and each grade is given different points (3, 2 or 1). For example, the weight value of the word "language" is 3 points, and the weight value of "silk book" is 1 point. Table 1 shows ten typical features words from each of the three categories and their normalized using rates.

Table 1. Feature words and its normalized using rate.

No	subject	normalized using rate	sentiment	normalized using rate	person / background	normalized using rate
1	语言	0.330874223	问题	0.42520583	学生	0.318084654
2	汉语	0.204262811	规范	0.266159498	教学	0.107089852
3	汉字	0.177317285	重要	0.205760296	孩子	0.096642725
4	文字	0.108518912	保护	0.026511905	大学	0.095541486
5	语文	0.071111208	反对	0.017997309	小学	0.088119925
6	普通话	0.035162926	正确	0.013631831	学校	0.074040796
7	方言	0.03020151	严重	0.012919792	历史	0.072185948
8	中文	0.024844734	错误	0.012746114	考试	0.055044716
9	母语	0.011750716	缺乏	0.010717178	教师	0.047914166
10	繁体字	0.00595579	质疑	0.008350154	老师	0.045335821

The formula for calculating normalized using rates is as follows:

$$U_i = \frac{F_i \times D_i}{\sum\limits_{j \in V} (F_j \times D_j)} \tag{1}$$

F denotes the frequency of the word and D denotes the distribution rate, and the denominator is the normalized term, V which denotes the set of all the homogenous survey objects (all word categories).

Calculate the Weights of Co-occurrence of Elements

Among the three kinds of feature words, topic words are the foundation: only when a topic word appears, an unknown segment of a text will be allowed to enter the next step of the analysis, otherwise, this segment will be abandoned directly. Thus the co-occurrence of the three types of feature words includes three cases: a. topic word + emotion word + background word; b. topic word + emotion word; c. topic word + background word. Case A, the co-occurrence of the three types of feature words, is most likely to be about public opinion. When there is only two types of feature words appearing in a text, case b is more likely to be public opinion related than case c. Therefore, co-occurrence of feature words of different types is a very important weighting factor. The possibility of being related to public opinion is: a > b > c. Table 2 shows the co-occurrence of three types of feature words in clauses.

Table 2. The co-occurrence condition of three feature words in clause.

No	Sentence	Subject	Sentiment	Person/background
1	The author did not respond to the question of why Lu Xun hated Chinese characters	Chinese character	Hate	Lu Xun
2	If it has a severe mistake in the usage of Chinese characters	Chinese character	Mistake	
3	About 1000 Chinese learners	Chinese		Learner

Table 2 shows that in example 1, the three types of feature words appear in one sentence, and thus can be determined as a public opinion related text; in example 2, with the co-occurrence of a topic word and an emotion word, it can be basically determined as a text about public opinion; and in example 3, only topic word and background word appear. This example might present some public opinion information of the international influence of Chinese or can be a part of the introduction of TCFL (Teaching Chinese as a Foreign Language) major of a school. Therefore, the sentence cannot be directly determined as containing public opinion information.

In most cases, the shorter the distance between different feature words is, the closer the syntactic and semantic relations of these words are, and thus the more likely they are public opinion related topics. In the examples above, the distances among feature words are short as they appear in clause. However, more than often, feature words are scattered over a sentence or even a passage. Therefore, to solve the problem of how to identify co-occurrence distance when feature words are scattered in different part of an article, this paper classifies the co-occurrence distance into four levels: article, paragraph, sentence and clause. Section 5 introduces the weighted algorithm used for the distance comparison in the four levels.

Apart from co-occurrence, the location of feature words in the text and the length of the text are also factors to be considered in the weighted algorithm. In terms of location, only the title and the text are considered in this paper. The weight of the feature words appearing in title is different from the words that appear in text. In the aspect of text length, since the score is higher when the text is simply longer than other texts, so it is necessary to constrain the factor. This paper uses the average length of texts of Y set to constrain it.

Additive Weighted Algorithm

Additive weighted algorithm needs to consider four factors: feature words weight, co-occurrence of three types of feature words, feature words position and text length. Algorithm needs to segment the text according to the co-occurrence distances among feature words. As stated above, this paper divides co-occurrence distances into four level: article level, paragraph level, sentence level and clause level. This section takes sentence level co-occurrence distance as example, illustrates the process of algorithm. The segmentation of sentences employs "。？！" as boundary of a sentence. The Score of a sentence is shown in Formula (2).

$$Sen_i = \sum_{a \in A}(F_a \times U_a + P_a) + \sum_{b \in B}(F_b \times U_b + P_b) + \sum_{c \in C}(F_c \times U_c + P_c) + G_i \quad (2)$$

In the formula, Seni represents the score of a sentence, a, b and c represents three types of feature words respectively, F represents word frequency, U represents weight and P represents position score. The score of one exact feature word in a sentence which is included in feature word list equals to: word frequency (F) first multiplies weight (U), then the result of multiplication adds position score (P). Gi is the co-occurrence score of three types of feature words, co-occurrence of all three types is highest, then is subject + sentiment, the lowest is subject + background.

At last, the total score of a text is represented in Formula (3).

$$Text_i = \sum_{k=1}^{n}(Sen_k) \times \frac{AL}{L_i} \quad (3)$$

Text$_i$ represent the score of text i, AL represents the average length of all texts in set Y, and L$_i$ represents the length of text i. the text score equals to all the sentence scores in the text, then multiplies the average length, at last divides the length of this text.

5   Experiment Result Analysis

5.1   Experiment Data

To test the performance of element co-occurrence method, 1200 texts whose length is around 1000–1500 words were picked. Among them, 160 texts were related to language public opinion.

5.2   Compute the Co-occurrence Distance and Threshold

At present, Precision (p), Recall (r) and F1-Measure (F1) are the factors to evaluate the effect of a classifier. Under different threshold, different precision and recall will get. To get the best recognition result, precision and recall under different threshold was computed. Also, F1-Measure was considered in computing the threshold.

In order to evaluate the system, precision-recall curve and F1 curve were drew, as in Figs. 3 and 4. Generally, the better performance a system can achieve, the greater prominence of precision-recall curve should be. Figure 3 illustrates that when the co-occurrence distances of three types of feature words are at sentence level and paragraph level, performance of system is better than the condition when the co-occurrence distances are at clause level and article level. Moreover, in that, sentence level performs better than paragraph level, and clause level performs a little better than article level. Figure 4 illustrates that when threshold is at 90, F1-Measure gets the highest (0.94).

For the phenomenon stated above, this research suggests that: in normal understanding, the smaller co-occurrence distance of these three types of words, the tighter connection these words will be; however, it is usually hard for people to express the topic clear in a clause, three elements of a topic usually distributed at a larger range than a clause. Experiments showed sentence level is the best co-occurrence distance. According to the Experiment, this research set the co-occurrence distance of three types of feature words at sentence level with threshold at 90.

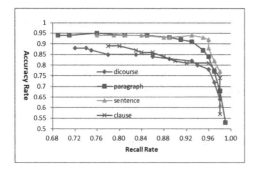

Fig. 3. Precision and recall curve of four lever

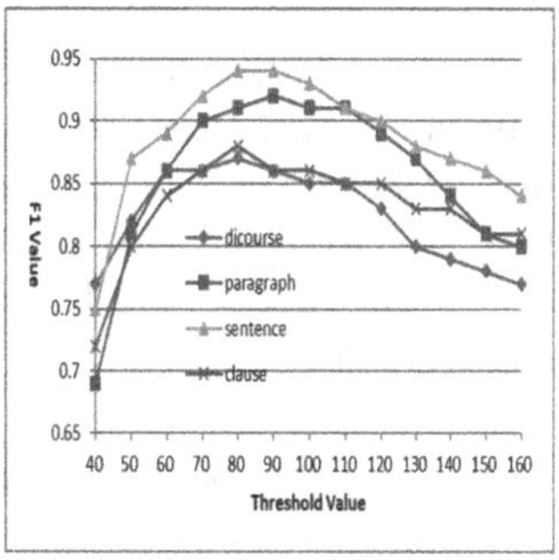

Fig. 4. Threshold and its corresponding F1 value of four level

5.3 Compute the Co-occurrence Distance and Threshold

The threshold was set to 90, and the result of the experiment is shown in Table 3.

Table 3. The experimental results when threshold is 90

Total texts	Identified texts	Relevant texts	Error texts	Precision	Recall	F1 value
161	165	153	12	0.93	0.95	0.94

Experiment Analysis

I. The language public opinion texts set adjusted from 160 texts to 161 texts. The reason is the detector found a not related text - China Daily: Beware of "Online Water Army" Kidnapping Online Public Opinion - from manually labeled as related texts; and found two language public opinion related texts - On the Revolution of "Country" and Nan Fangshuo: Chinese Shall Refind the Function of Talk - from manually labeled as not related texts. After careful analysis, the judgement of detector is right. Therefore, as one can see, the detector has a strong sense of objectivity.

II. The detector totally recognized 165 texts as relevance. In that, 153 are correctly judged, and 12 are misjudged. In the misjudged texts, 6 are education and culture category, 4 are music and dance category, and 2 are other categories. Through the analysis, the main reason of misjudgment is language public opinion also appears a lot in education and culture field, thus the feature word list of language public opinion shares some words with education and culture field. How to detect and classify such texts of high similarity with language public opinion text is the top topic of further researches.

III. For texts like People are Stupid, But They Seem Great, which have a sense of ridicule, detector can correctly classify them. This proves that the detector has strong analysis and recognition ability.

5.4   Detector in Actual Use

We calculated the result of the detection system on randomly picked language public opinion in one-week size. The statistic reveals that the average precision of detector is around 92%. This system has been adopted by Department of Language and Information Management Afflicted to Ministry of Education and National Language Resources Monitoring and Research Center. Runtime of the system is more than 6 continuous years.

5.5   Element Co-occurrence Method in Tertiary Education Public Opinion

To valid the universality of element co-occurrence, the same effect was achieved by implementing this method at tertiary education online public opinion detection. As the result of the detection system on randomly picked tertiary education public opinion in one-week size shown that the average precision of detector in tertiary education public opinion detection reached 93%. This system has been adopted by National Tertiary Education Quality Monitoring and Evaluation Center which affiliated to the Ministry of Education Evaluation of Tertiary Education Research Center for Communication and Public Opinion Monitoring. Runtime of this system is more than 4 continuous years.

5.6   Comparison of Other Similar Methods

Reference [19] proposed an improved single-pass text clustering algorithm called single-pass*. Their experimental results show that, compared to the single-pass algorithm, the improved algorithm achieved 86% average accuracy by the hot topic identification in Network. Furthermore, Ref. [20] used deep learning and OCC model to establish emotion rules to solve the problem of a lack of semantic understanding. Their work obtained 90.98% accuracy of emotion recognition in network public opinion. By comparing we found that the element co-occurrence method is significantly better than others.

6   Conclusion

This paper, based on the nature of public opinion, proposed an online public opinion detection method for specific field (element co-occurrence method), and gave the detailed implementation. Different with traditional methods, element co-occurrence method starts at people's recognition of public opinion. Through construct the language knowledge system of a specific field, this method can not only generate specific field related public opinion topics, but also retrieve the related public opinion information of that field. Based on these, this system can effectively detect the public opinion information. Experiments show that, this method is able to implement in real use, and have relatively good universality.

Acknowledgement. This paper is supported by the National Language Commission (No. ZDI135-4), National Social Science Foundation of China (No. 16BXW023 and AFA170005).

References

1. Liu, Y.: Introduction to Network Public Opinion Research. Tianjin Renmin Press (2007)
2. Zong, C.Q.: Statistical Natural Language Processing. Tsinghua University Press, Beijing (2013)
3. Luo, W.H., Liu, Q., Cheng, X.Q.: Development and analysis of technology of topic detection and tracing. In: Proceedings of JSCL-2003, pp. 560–566. Tsinghua University Press, Beijing (2003)
4. Carbonell, J., Yang, Y.M., Lafferty, J., Brown, R.D., Pierce, T., Liu, X.: CMU report on TDT-2. segmentation, detection and tracking. In: Proceedings of the DARPA Broadcast News Workshop, pp. 117–120 (1999)
5. Hong, Y., Zhang, Y., Liu, T., Li, S.: Topic detection and tracking review. J. Chin. Inf. Process. **21**(6), 71–87 (2007)
6. Li, B.L., Yu, S.W.: Research on topic detection and tracking. Comput. Eng. Appl. **39**(17), 7–10 (2003)
7. Allan, J. (ed.): Topic Detection and Tracking: Event-Based Information Organization. Kluwer Academic Publishers, Norwell (2002)
8. Forgy, E.W.: Cluster analysis of multivariate data: efficiency versus interpretability of classifications. Biometrics **21**(3), 768–769 (1965)
9. Allan, J.: Introduction to topic detection and tracking. In: Allan, J. (ed.) Topic Detection and Tracking. The Information Retrieval Series, vol. 12, pp. 1–16. Springer, Boston (2002). https://doi.org/10.1007/978-1-4615-0933-2_1
10. Hong, Y., Zhang, Y., Fan, J., Liu, T., Li, S.: New event detection based on division comparison of subtopic. Chin. J. Comput. **31**(4), 687–695 (2008)
11. Zhang, K., Li, J.Z., Wu, G., Wang, K.H.: A new event detection model based on term reweighting. J. Softw. **19**(4), 817–828 (2008)
12. Zhao, L., Yuan, R.X., Guan, X.H., Jia, Q.S.: Bursty propagation model for incidental events in blog networks. J. Softw. **05**, 1384–1392 (2009)
13. Chen, K.Y., Luesukprasert, L., Chou, S.C.T.: Hot topic extraction based on timeline analysis and multidimensional sentence modeling. IEEE Trans. Knowl. Data Eng. **19**(8), 1016–1025 (2007)
14. Switzerland, Saussure: General Linguistics. The Commercial Press, Beijing (1980)
15. Linguistic Terminology Committee: Linguistic Terms. The Commercial Press, Shanghai (2011)
16. Yang, J.: A research on basic methods and key techniques for monitoring public opinions on language. Ph.D. thesis, Communication University of China (2010)
17. Shi, C.Y., Xu, C.J., Yang, X.J.: Study of TFIDF algorithm. J. Comput. Appl. **29**(s1), 167–170 (2009)

18. Zhang, Y.F., Peng, S.M., Lü, J.: Improvement and application of TFIDF method based on text classification. Comput. Eng. **32**(19), 76–78 (2006)
19. Gesang, D.J., et al.: An internet public opinion hotspot detection algorithm based on single-pass. J. Univ. Electron. Sci. Technol. China **4**, 599–604 (2015)
20. Wu, P., Liu, H.W., Shen, S.: Sentiment analysis of network public opinion based on deep learning and OCC. J. China Soc. Sci. Tech. Inf. **36**(9), 972–980 (2017)

Efficient Retinex-Based Low-Light Image Enhancement Through Adaptive Reflectance Estimation and LIPS Postprocessing

Weiqiong Pan, Zongliang Gan$^{(\boxtimes)}$, Lina Qi, Changhong Chen,
and Feng Liu

Jiangsu Provincial Key Lab of Image Processing and Image Communication,
Nanjing University of Posts and Telecommunications, Nanjing 210003, China
{1016010508,ganzl,qiln,chenchh,liuf}@njupt.edu.cn

Abstract. In this paper, a novel Retinex-based low-light image enhancement method is proposed, in which it has two parts: reflectance component estimation and logarithmic image processing subtraction (LIPS) enhancement. The enhancement processing is performed in the V channel of the color HSV space. First, adaptive parameter bilateral filters are used to get more accurate illumination layer data, instead of Gaussian filter. Moreover, the weighting estimation method is used to calculate the adaptive parameter to adjust the removal of the illumination and obtain the reflectance by just-noticeable-distortion (JND) factor. In this way, it can effectively prevent the over-enhancement in high-brightness regions. Then, the logarithmic image processing subtraction (LIPS) method based on maximum standard deviation of the histogram is applied to enhance reflectance component part, where the interval of the parameter is according to the cumulative distribution function (CDF). Experimental results demonstrate that the proposed method outperforms other competitive methods in terms of subjective and objective assessment.

Keywords: Reflectance estimation · Logarithmic image processing subtraction
Just-noticeable-distortion · Maximum standard deviation

1 Introduction

Image enhancement is highly required for various application, such as video surveillance, medical image processing. However, images captured in low-light conditions often have low dynamic range and seriously degrade by noise. In this case, in order to obtain images with good contrast and details, various low-light image enhancement techniques are needed. In recent years, low-light image enhancement approaches have received stacks of studies, commonly used methods including histogram equalization [1], Retinex-based methods [2], dehaze-based methods [3], and logarithmic image processing (LIP) models [4]. In these approaches, the Retinex theory is first proposed

The work was supported by the National Nature Science Foundation P.R. China No. 61471201.

J.-H. Lai et al. (Eds.): PRCV 2018, LNCS 11256, pp. 335–346, 2018.
https://doi.org/10.1007/978-3-030-03398-9_29

by Land [5] to model the image process of human visual system. This theory assumes that the scene in human's eyes is the product of reflectance and illumination. In recent years, many Retinex-based image enhancement algorithms have been proposed as follows: Single Scale Retinex (SSR) [6], Multi-scale Retinex (MSR) [7], and MSR with color restoration (MSRCR) [8]. In few years later, Kimmel et al. [9] proposed an image enhancement method based on variational Retinex. The effects have greatly improved over the previous methods based on Retinex. He converted the previously estimated approximate illumination problem into a quadratic programming optimal solution problem, calculated the illumination through the gradient descent method, and enhanced the observation image with gamma correction. Ng et al. [10] used the idea of total variation to describe the nature of reflectance under the variational framework, and brought the reflection into the solution model to obtain an ideal reflectance image. Fu et al. [11] proposed a weighted variational model considering both illumination and reflection on the Kimmel and Ng's methods, in which the resulting reflection images can retain high-frequency details. What's more, the methods based on logarithmic image processing (LIP) models have been widely used in recent years. Jourlin et al. [12] developed a logarithmic image processing (LIP) model which is a mathematical framework based on abstract linear mathematics. The LIP models contains several specific algebraic and functional operations which can be used to manipulate image intensity values in a bounded range. HDR (high dynamic range) image generation is one of most important low light image enhancement method [13]. At present, the acquisition of high dynamic range image is mainly based on the software method. The most widely used software method is to obtain HDR image by multi-exposure, which is the mainstream HDR imaging technology. Multi-exposure HDR imaging technology includes two categories: one is the method based on the inverse camera response function recovery; the other is direct fusion method. The resulting HDR images exhibit fewer artifacts and encode a wider dynamic range, but the former one often cause color shift when used in RGB color space; the fusion method only can slightly expand the dynamic range, it's not enough for generating authentic image.

In this paper, we developed a weighted just-noticeable-distortion (JND) based MSR to adjust reflectance and utilize the logarithmic image processing model to enhance the contrast. Compare with existing techniques, the proposed method can't expand the dynamic range well than HDR methods, however, it can effectively prevent over enhancement in bright regions and adaptively select appropriate enhanced result. The main contribution of this work are as follows is include two part: Firstly, we obtain the illumination layer using adaptive bilateral filter instead of Gaussian filter. Secondly, we calculate the JND-based factor that is adjusted by adding a weighted factor based on illumination intensity to remove the illumination. Finally, we set the interval of the parameter according to the cumulative distribution function (CDF) of the reflectance and then we apply the logarithmic image processing subtraction (LIPS) based on maximum standard deviation of histogram to it. Experimental results demonstrate that the proposed method can effectively preserve the details in bright regions.

2 Related Works

2.1 Retinex Based Low Light Image Enhancement

The multi-scale Retinex (MSR) algorithm was raised by Jobson et al. [7]. This algorithm was developed to attain lightness and color constancy for machine vision. It is based on single scale Retinex (SSR) and could balance the dynamic compression and color constancy. The single scale Retinex is given by:

$$R_i(x, y) = log I_i(x, y) - \log[F(x, y) * I_i(x, y)] \tag{1}$$

where $R_i(x, y)$ is the Retinex output, $I_i(x, y)$ is the image distribution in the ith spectral band, "*" denotes the convolution operation, and $F(x, y)$ is a Gaussian kennel. The MSR output is simply a weighted sum of several different SSR outputs, and MSR is produced as follows:

$$R_{MSRi} = \sum_{n=1}^{N} w_n R_{ni} \tag{2}$$

where N is the number of scales, R_{ni} is the ith component of the MSR output, w_n is a collection of weights. In general, the weights w_n is a chosen to be equal.

2.2 Logarithmic Image Processing (LIP) Models

LIP model generally makes use of the logarithm, as transmitted images combine by logarithmic laws and the human visual system processes light logarithmically. The LIP model has been shown to satisfy Weber's Law and the saturation characteristics of the human visual system. From a physical point of the view, this LIP model is physically justified in a number of aspects. For example, the addition operation is consistent with the transmittance image formation model and the saturation characteristic of the human's eye, the contrast definition based on subtraction is consistent with Weber's law, and the zero gray-tone function corresponds to the highest intensity of an image, and the gray-tone function is the inverted images of the original images. The relative formula for the model [14] is:

$$f_1 \oplus f_2 = f_1 + f_2 - \frac{f_1 f_2}{M} \tag{3}$$

$$f_1 \ominus f_2 = M \frac{f_1 - f_2}{M - f_2} \tag{4}$$

where $\oplus(\ominus)$ is LIP addition(subtraction), $f_1 = 255 - f_1', f_2 = 255 - f_2'$, namely, f_1, f_2 are inverted images of the initial images f_1', f_2', and M is 256 by default. If we set f_2 as a constant C, the image f_1 will be darker or brighter when we use LIP addition or subtraction.

The LIP model has been adopted for various applications such as medical image enhancement [15] and edge detection [16]. In [15], an un-sharp masking framework for medical image enhancement is proposed, which combines a generalized un-sharp masking algorithm with operations of LIP and get the good effects.

3 Proposed Method

We propose a new approach to enhance the low-light images to prevent over enhancement in highlight region. The main contribution of proposed method is include two part: the first stage is to obtain the reflectance layer by weighted just-noticeable-distortion (JND) based MSR, In this part, a weighting factor is used to control the removal of the illuminance, in order to prevent the gloomy phenomenon in bright regions, we set a fixed range by normalized background brightness. The second part is applying adaptive logarithmic image processing subtraction (LIPS) on reflectance layer to enhance the contrast. The parameters is selected by maximum standard deviation of the enhanced images, in order to obtain best enhanced images, we adaptive fix the interval of the parameter by cumulative density function of the reflectance component in first part. As shown in Fig. 1, the framework of the proposed algorithm is presented.

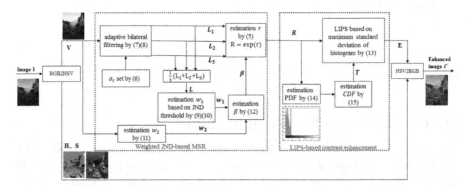

Fig. 1. Framework of the proposed algorithm: the first part is JND-based MSR process and the second part is LIPS-based contrast enhancement

3.1 Weighted JND-Based MSR

Unlike classical MSR methods, we perform the proposed methods in V channel of the color space HSV without considering color adjustment. As we all know, the most influential effect on the low light image is the luminance component. If we perform similar processing on the color channels, it will lead to color distortion. For the sake of preserving appropriate illumination and compressing the dynamic range of the image, we set a control factor to adaptively remove the illumination. According to the theory of MSR, we obtain the reflectance R as follows:

$$r(x, y) = \sum_{n=1}^{N} w_n \cdot \{ \lg[V(x, y)] - \beta \cdot \lg[L(x, y)] \} \tag{5}$$

where r is reflectance intensity after illumination adaptation, V is the channel of HSV color space, and β is the control factor based on JND thresholds.

Most classical MSR-based enhancement algorithms performs the convolution between Gaussian smoothing function and the original image to get the illumination layer and the halo artifacts and details loss appear frequently. In [17], adaptive filter was used to prevent halo artifacts by adapting the shape of filter to the high-contrast edges. In [17, 18], it used a canny edge detector to detect high-contrast edges. Then the factor σ of Gaussian smoothing function is defined as follows:

$$\sigma = \begin{cases} \sigma_1 & a\ high\ contrast\ edge\ was\ acrossed \\ \sigma_0 & no\ high\ contrast\ edge\ was\ acrossed \end{cases} \tag{6}$$

The bilateral filter is proposed in [19], and it has been proved to be good at edge-preserving. The bilateral filter performs better near the edge than the Gaussian filter by adding a coefficient defined by intensity value. In order to estimate approximate illumination accurately and prevent halo artifacts efficiency, we use an adaptive bilateral filtering instead of Gaussian filtering.

$$L_n(x, y) = \frac{\sum_{x,y} V(x, y) W_n(i, j, x, y)}{\sum_{x,y} W_n(k, l, x, y)} \tag{7}$$

$$W_n(i, j, x, y) = e^{-\frac{(i-x)^2 + (j-y)^2}{2\sigma_d^2} - \frac{\|V(i,j) - V(x,y)^2\|}{2\sigma_r^2}} \tag{8}$$

where $W_n(i, j, x, y)$ measures the geometric closeness between the neighborhood center (x, y) and a nearby point (i, j). If the difference between the two pixels is more than the threshold value, we set the range domain factor σ_r to σ_1; otherwise, we use σ_0. We set σ_1 to $0.6\sigma_0$ in this paper. Figure 2. has shown the differences between the Gaussian smoothing and adaptive bilateral smoothing. In Fig. 2(b), it causes halo artifacts along the strong edges, however, as shown in Fig. 2(c), the edges is preserved and artifacts is deduced.

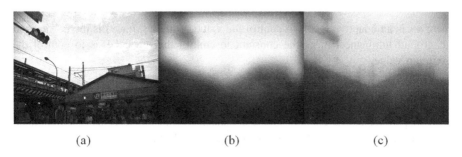

(a)   (b)   (c)

Fig. 2. Visual results for Gaussian filtering and adaptive bilateral filtering. (a) Initial image. (b) Mask with Gaussian smoothing. (c) Mask with adaptive bilateral smoothing.

According to the theory of MSR, we could compress the dynamic range by Eq. (5). The smaller β is, the more similar to the original images and the smaller dynamic range compression is. Also, the greater β is, the more obvious the details are and the more dynamic range compression is.

In [20], Barten et al. discovered the relationship between the actual luminance and the brightness by human eye perception through experiments. Then, Jayant et al. [21]

addressed a key concept of perceptual coding called just-noticeable-distortion (JND). Namely, if the difference between two luminance values in an image is below the JND value, the difference is imperceptible. In [19], it proposed the luminance adaptation Retinex-based contrast enhancement algorithms, which adopted the JND into the luminance adaptation and got the good effects.

According to the previous work [21], the relationship between the visibility and background luminance is obtained as follows:

$$T_l(x, y) = \begin{cases} 17(1 - \sqrt{\frac{L(x,y)}{127}}) + 3 & L(x, y) \leq 127 \\ \frac{3}{128}(L(x, y) - 127) + 3 & otherwise \end{cases} \quad (9)$$

where $L(x, y)$ is background luminance of the input low-light image, in this paper, $L(x, y)$ is the mean of $L_n(x, y)$, (n = 1, 2, 3); and T_l is the visibility threshold, namely JND value. The visibility thresholds are high in dark region while low in bright regions, thus, human's eyes are more sensitive to bright region than dark region, We proposed that human's eyes sensitively to background luminance is contrary to visibility threshold as follows:

$$w_1 = 1 - \frac{T_l(x, y) - min(T_l(x, y))}{max(T_l(x, y)) - min(T_l(x, y))} \quad (10)$$

Then we add a weighted factor based on illumination intensity to control w_1.

$$w_2 = k \cdot e^{\frac{l^2(x,y)}{\sigma_b^2}}$$

$$\beta = w_1 \cdot w_2 \quad (12)$$

where w_2 is an adaptive factor to control the value of the w_1, $l(x, y)$ is the normalized background luminance, σ_b is the constant to control the w_2 and k is to control the maximum value.

3.2   LIPS-Based Contrast Enhancement

In this paper, we utilize efficient image enhancement method to enhance its contrast. The algorithm is based on [14], in which an enhanced image is modeled as:

$$E' = R \ominus C = \frac{R' - C}{1 - \frac{C}{M}} \quad (13)$$

where C is a constant, M is constant as 256, R' and E' are inverted image by reflectance R and enhanced image E, $R' = 255 - R$, $E' = 255 - E$.

LIPS can enhance low light image effectively as we found the best parameter C, but it always causes over-enhancement if we choose a large one. Because in LIP subtraction models, there are some bright points existing in the initial low-light images. The bright region of R is expanded by subtraction of a constant $C \in [0, M]$, which can generate negative values by $R \ominus C$. In order to prevent the negative effects, we adaptively choose the constant number C.

Firstly, as the dynamic range of the low-light image is compressed, the probability density function (PDF) of reflectance image R can be used to adaptively choose the proper threshold value C. The PDF can be approximated by

$$\text{PDF}(l) = \frac{n_l}{M \cdot N} \tag{14}$$

where n_l is the number of pixels that have intensity l and $M \cdot N$ is the total number of pixels in the image. According to the PDF, we can calculate the cumulative distribution (CDF). The equation is formulated as:

$$CDF(l) = \sum\nolimits_{k=0}^{l} PDF(k) \tag{15}$$

Then, we set an error e. We do not take into account the pixels of CDF greater than $1 - e$, and we use the maximum pixel value that CDF value is equal to or approximately $1 - e$ as the threshold T, and the interval of parameter C is in $[0, 255 - T]$.

Finally, we adaptively selected the best parameter C_{op} in the interval by maximization of standard deviation of the histogram of $R \ominus C$ [16]. The specific steps is as follows:

(1) We compute the logarithmic subtraction on reflectance components by $R \ominus C$.
(2) Create the histogram $h(R \ominus C)$.
(3) Compute the standard deviation $\sigma[h(R \ominus C)]$.
(4) Compute the best parameter C such that:

$$\sigma[h(R \ominus C_{op})] = Max_{C \in [0, 255 - T]}\{\sigma[h(R \ominus C_{op})]\} \tag{16}$$

The proposed method is briefly described in Algorithm 1.

Algorithm 1. The proposed method.

Input: A low-light image I.
Output: An enhanced image I'.
1. $V \leftarrow HSV2RGB(I)$;
2. Apply adaptive bilateral filtering on V to obtain illumination layer L by (7)(8);
3. Calculate adaptation parameters β by (9)-(12);
4. Adaptively remove the illumination on V by (5) to obtain the reflectance layer r ;
5. $R \leftarrow exp(r)$;
6. Calculate the adaptation threshold T;
7. According to the T, perform logarithmic subtraction based on maximum standard deviation of histogram on reflectance layer R;
8. Generate the output E by (13);
9. Generate new HSV image;
10. $I' \leftarrow HSV2RGB(HSV)$;
11. **Return** I'.

---

4   Experimental Results

This section shows the qualitative comparison results of our method with five state-of-the-art methods, including classical multi-scale Retinex (MSR) [7], low-light image enhancement via Illumination Map Estimation (LIME) [22], joint intrinsic-extrinsic prior model for Retinex (JIEPMR) [23], and Retinex-based perceptual contrast enhancement (RPCE) [18], along with our proposed method.

All the methods were tested on 45 images with different degree of darkness. All the 45 low-light images and the enhanced results by the proposed method are briefly shown in Figs. 3 and 4 and the test images and results are compressed into 200 * 200 displays. Due to the space limitation, we just present four representative low-light images, as shown in Figs. 5, 6, 7 and 8.

Fig. 3. 45 tested images with various degree of darkness, most of image with high contrast

4.1   Subjective Assessment

Compared with these state-of-art methods, as show in Figs. 5, 6, 7 and 8, the proposed methods can adaptively control the contrast enhancement degree for different areas to prevent over-enhancement on high contrast image. Figures 5, 6, 7 and 8 show their zoomed results in highlight regions, As shown in Figs. 5(a)–(d), the region on the sky is over-enhancement, in Fig. 5(e), the clouds on the sky is close to the original image, but the wall of the house becomes darker. As shown in Fig. 5(f), our proposed method is outperform both in two regions. Compared with other four methods, details and edges in their zoomed result are enhanced best in our proposed method in Figs. 5, 6, 7 and 8.

Fig. 4. Enhanced results of 45 low light image

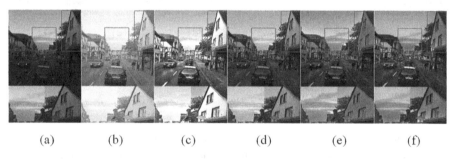

(a)   (b)   (c)   (d)   (e)   (f)

Fig. 5. Enhanced results for block (a) Original image (b) MSR [7] (c) LIME [22] (d) JIEPMR [23] (e) RPCE [18] (f) Ours

(a)   (b)   (c)   (d)   (e)   (f)

Fig. 6. Enhanced results for block (a) Original image (b) MSR [7] (c) LIME [22] (d) JIEPMR [23] (e) RPCE [18] (f) Ours

(a)   (b)   (c)   (d)   (e)   (f)

Fig. 7. Enhanced results for block (a) Original image (b) MSR [7] (c) LIME [22] (d) JIEPMR [23] (e) RPCE [18] (f) Ours

(a)   (b)   (c)   (d)   (e)   (f)

Fig. 8. Enhanced results for block (a) Original image (b) MSR [7] (c) LIME [22] (d) JIEPMR [23] (e) RPCE [18] (f) Ours

4.2   Objective Assessment

Objective assessment is always used to explain some important characteristics of an image. According to the [24], a blind image quality assessment called natural image quality evaluator (NIQE) is used to evaluate the enhanced results. The lower NIQE value represents the higher image quality. As shown is Table 1, it demonstrates the average NIQE of all the 45 images enhanced by the mentioned five methods. The results obviously shown our method has a lower value compared with other methods.

Table 1. Quantitation performance comparison on 45 images with NIQE

Algorithms	NIQE
MSR [7]	3.5332
LIME [22]	3.4099
JIEPMR [23]	3.3840
RPCE [19]	3.2473
Ours	**3.2372**

5 Conclusion

In this paper, an effective Retinex-based low-light image enhancement method was presented. By utilizing JND-based illumination adaptation, the over-enhancement in bright areas and the loss of details and textures are all eliminated. Additionally, we add the adaptive LIPS based on maximum standard deviation of histogram to the reflectance images, which can effective preserve the details in highlight regions. Experimental results show that the proposed algorithm can achieve better image quality and succeed in keeping textures in highlight regions. In future work, we will study an effective low light video enhancement methods, and improve the performance of the algorithm.

References

1. Kaur, M., Verma, K.: A novel hybrid technique for low exposure image enhancement using sub-image histogram equalization and artificial neural network. In: Proceedings of the IEEE Conference Inventive Computation Technologies, vol. 2, pp. 1–5 (2017)
2. Wang, S., Zheng, J., Hu, H.: Naturalness preserved enhancement algorithm for non-uniform illumination images. IEEE Trans. Image Process. **22**(9), 3538–3548 (2013)
3. Li, L., Wang, R., Wang, W.: A low-light image enhancement method for both denoising and contrast enlarging. In: Proceedings of the IEEE International Conference on Image Processing, pp. 3730–3734 (2015)
4. Panetta, K.A., Wharton, E.J., Agaian, S.S.: Human visual system-based image enhancement and logarithmic contrast measure. IEEE Trans. Syst. Man Cybern., Part B (Cybernetics) **38**(1), 174–188 (2008)
5. Land, E.H.: The retinex. Am. Sci. **52**(2), 247–264 (1964)
6. Jobson, D.J., Rahman, Z., Woodell, G.A.: Properties and performance of a center/surround retinex. IEEE Trans. Image Process. **6**(3), 451–462 (1997)
7. Rahman, Z., Jobson, D.J., Woodell, G.A.: Multi-scale retinex for color image enhancement. In: Proceedings of the International Conference on Image Processing, vol. 3, pp. 1003–1006 (1996)
8. Jobson, D.J., Rahman, Z., Woodell, G.A.: A multiscale retinex for bridging the gap between color images and the human observation of scenes. IEEE Trans. Image Process. **6**(7), 965–976 (1997)
9. Kimmel, R., Elad, M., Shaked, D.: A variational framework for retinex. Int. J. Comput. Vis. **52**(1), 7–23 (2003)
10. Ng, M.K., Wang, W.: A total variation model for retinex. SIAM J. Imaging Sci. **4**(1), 345–365 (2011)
11. Fu, X., Zeng, D.: A weighted variational model for simultaneous reflectance and illumination estimation. In: Proceedings of the IEEE Conference on Computer Vision and Pattern Recognition, pp. 2782–2790 (2016)
12. Jourlin, M., Pinoli, J.C.: A model for logarithmic image processing. J. Microsc. **149**, 21–35 (1988)
13. Sun, N., Mansour, H., Ward, R.: HDR image construction from multi-exposed stereo LDR images. In: IEEE International Conference on Image Processing, pp. 2973–2976 (2010)
14. Hawkes, P.W.: Logarithmic Image Processing: Theory and Applications, vol. 195. Academic Press, Cambridge (2016)

15. Zhao, Z., Zhou, Y.: Comparative study of logarithmic image processing models for medical image enhancement. In: Proceedings of the IEEE International Conference on Systems, Man, and Cybernetics, pp. 001046–001050 (2016)
16. Jourlin, M., Pinoli, J.C., Zeboudj, R.: Contrast definition and contour detection for logarithmic images. J. Microsc. **156**(1), 33–40 (1989)
17. Meylan, L., Susstrunk, S.: High dynamic range image rendering with a retinex-based adaptive filter. IEEE Trans. Image Process. **15**(9), 2820–2830 (2006)
18. Xu, K., Jung, C.: Retinex-based perceptual contrast enhancement in images using luminance adaptation. In: Proceedings of the IEEE International Conference on Acoustics, Speech and Signal Processing, pp. 1363–1367 (2017)
19. Tomasi, C., Manduchi, R.: Bilateral filtering for gray and color images. In: Proceedings of Sixth International Conference on Computer Vision, pp. 839–846 (1998)
20. Barten, P.G.J.: Contrast Sensitivity of the Human Eye and Its Effects on Image Quality, vol. 19. SPIE Optical Engineering Press, WA (1999)
21. Jayant, N.: Signal compression: technology targets and research directions. IEEE J. Sel. Areas Commun. **10**(5), 796–818 (1992)
22. Guo, X., Li, Y., Ling, H.: LIME: low-light image enhancement via illumination map estimation. IEEE Trans. Image Process. **26**(2), 982–993 (2017)
23. Cai, B., Xu, X., Guo, K.: A joint intrinsic-extrinsic prior model for retinex. In: Proceedings of the IEEE International Conference on Computer Vision, pp. 4020–4029 (2017)
24. Mittal, A., Soundararajan, R., Bovik, A.C.: Making a "completely blind" image quality analyzer. IEEE Sig. Process. Lett. **20**(3), 209–212 (2013)

Large-Scale Structure from Motion with Semantic Constraints of Aerial Images

Yu Chen[1], Yao Wang[1], Peng Lu[2], Yisong Chen[1], and Guoping Wang[1(✉)]

[1] GIL, Department of Computer Science and Technology,
Peking University, Beijing, China
{1701213988,yaowang95,yisongchen,wgp}@pku.edu.cn
[2] School of Computer Science,
Beijing University of Posts and Telecommunications, Beijing, China
lupeng@bupt.edu.cn

Abstract. Structure from Motion (SfM) and semantic segmentation are two branches of computer vision. However, few previous methods integrate the two branches together. SfM is limited by the precision of traditional feature detecting method, especially in complicated scenes. As the research field of semantic segmentation thrives, we could gain semantic information of high confidence in each specific task with little effort. By utilizing semantic segmentation information, our paper presents a new way to boost the accuracy of feature point matching. Besides, with the semantic constraints taken from the result of semantic segmentation, a new bundle adjustment method with equality constraint is proposed. By exploring the sparsity of equality constraint, it indicates that constrained bundle adjustment can be solved by Sequential Quadratic Programming (SQP) efficiently. The proposed approach achieves state of the art accuracy, and, by grouping the descriptors together by their semantic labels, the speed of putative matches is slightly boosted. Moreover, our approach demonstrates a potential of automatic labeling of semantic segmentation. In a nutshell, our work strongly verifies that SfM and semantic segmentation benefit from each other.

Keywords: Structure from Motion · Semantic segmentation
Equality bundle adjustment · Sequential Quadratic Programming

1 Introduction

Structure from Motion (SfM) has been a popular topic in 3D vision in recent two decades. Inspired by the success of Photo Tourism [1] in dealing with a myriad amount of unordered Internet images, respectable methods are proposed to improve the efficiency and robustness of SfM.

Incremental SfM approaches [1–7] start by selecting seed image pairs that satisfy two constraints: wide baseline and sufficient correspondences, then repeatedly register new cameras in an incremental manner until no any camera could

---

Y. Chen and Y. Wang—Contributed equally.

© Springer Nature Switzerland AG 2018
J.-H. Lai et al. (Eds.): PRCV 2018, LNCS 11256, pp. 347–359, 2018.
https://doi.org/10.1007/978-3-030-03398-9_30

be added in the existing scene structure. This kind of method achieves high accuracy and is robust to bad matches thanks to the using of RANSAC [9] in several steps to filter outliers, but suffers from drift in large-scale scene structures due to the accumulated errors. In addition, incremental SfM is not efficient for the repeated bundle adjustment [10].

Global SfM approaches [11,12] estimate poses of all cameras by rotation averaging and translation averaging and perform bundle adjustment just one time. However, Global SfM approaches are sensitive to outliers thus are not as accurate as incremental approaches.

Far more different from incremental SfM and global SfM approaches, hierarchical SfM methods [13–16] start from two-view reconstructions, and then merge into one by finding similarity transformation in a bottom-up manner.

While a vast of efforts are taken to improve the accuracy of SfM, most SfM approaches are affected greatly by the matching results. The success of incremental SfM is mainly due to the elimination of wrong matches in several steps, such as geometric verification, camera register and repeatedly bundle adjustment. Owing to executing only one bundle adjustment, global SfM is more easily affected by outliers. Thus how to filter outliers out still be a key problem in global SfM.

Recently, more and more works concentrate on semantic reconstruction [17, 18]. They cast semantic SfM as a maximum-likelihood problem, thus geometry and semantic information are simultaneously estimated. So far, semantic 3D reconstruction methods have been limited to small scenes and low resolution, because of their large memory and computational cost requirements. Different from that, our works aim at large scale 3D reconstruction from UAV images.

From our perspective, the state-of-the-art SfM methods still have insufficient geometric/physical constraints. Semantic information is considered as additional constraints for robust SfM process to enhance its accuracy and efficiency. Our contributions are mainly two folds: (1) we propose to fuse the semantic information into feature points by semantic segmentation (2) we formulate the problem of bundle adjustment with equality constraints and solve it efficiently by Sequential Quadratic Programming (SQP).

Our work expedite the cross field of Structure from Motion and semantic segmentation. Also, to the best of our knowledge, our work achieve state-of-the-art in both efficiency and accuracy.

2   Related Work

2.1   Structure from Motion

With the born of Photo Tourism [1], incremental SfM methods are proposed to deal with large scale scene structures. Though many efforts (Bundler [3], VisualSfM [5], OpenMVG [6], Colmap [7], Theia [8]) are taken, drift and efficiency are still the two main limitations of incremental SfM. Besides, the most 2 time consuming parts of reconstruction are feature matching and repeated bundle adjustment [10].

As mentioned in Multi-View Stereo [19], the integration of semantic information will be a future work for 3D reconstruction. Recently, it appears more and more works about semantic reconstruction. As the first work of semantic SfM is based on geometric constrains [17], the later work [18] takes advantage of both geometric and semantic information. Moreover, they [17,18] deem scene structure as not merely points, but also regions and objects. The camera poses can be estimated more robustly.

Haene et al. [20] propose a mathematical framework to solve the joint segmentation and dense reconstruction problem. In their work, image segmentation and 3D dense reconstruction benefit from each other. The semantic class of the geometry provides information about the likelihood of the surface direction, while the surface direction gives clue to the likelihood of the semantic class. Blaha et al. [21] raise an adaptive multi-resolution approach of dense semantic 3D reconstruction, which mainly focuses on the high requirement of memory and computation resource issue.

2.2 Outdoor Datasets

Street View Dataset. The street view datasets [22,23] are generally captured by cameras fixed on vehicles. The annotations of street views are ample, usually from 12 to 30 classes [22,24]. Since it provides detailed elevation information and lacks roof information, it is essential to fuse it with aerial or satellite datasets in the 3D reconstruction task.

Drone Dataset. The drone datasets [25,26] are mostly annotated for object tracking tasks. There are no public pixel-level annotated datasets.

Remote Sensing Dataset. The remote sensing datasets [27,28], like its name implies, is collected from a far distance, usually by aircraft or satellite. It is so far away from the earth that, the camera view is almost vertical to the ground. It is short of elevation information. In addition, the resolution of the remote sensing image is always unsatisfying.

In a nutshell, constructing a drone dataset with refined semantic annotation is critical to get semantic point cloud for large-scale outdoor scenes.

3 Semantic Structure from Motion

3.1 Semantic Feature Generation

In 3D reconstruction tasks, SIFT [29] is widely adopted to extract feature points. For each feature point, there is a 2-dimensional coordinate representation and a corresponding descriptor. After extracting the feature points and computing the descriptors, exhaustive feature matching is then performed to get putative matches. While the SIFT features are robust to the variation of scale, rotation, and illumination, more robust features are required to produce more accurate

models. The traditional hand-crafted geometric features are limited in complicated aerial scenes. Intuitively, we can take semantic information into consideration to get more robust feature points.

Semantic Label Extraction. Inspired by [30], which deals with the problem
of drift of monocular visual simultaneous localization and mapping, uses a CNN
to assign each pixel x to a probability vector P_x, and the $(i^t)^h$ components of
P_x is the probability that x belongs to class i. By taking the result of semantic
segmentation of original images, the process of scene labeling [30] is replaced
to avoid a time-consuming prediction. Since we already get its coordinate in
the raw image, the semantic label can be easily searched in the corresponding
semantic segmentation image. Then each feature point has two main information:
2 dimensional coordinate, and semantic label.

Grouped Feature Matching. Though wrong matches are filtered by geometric
verification, some still exist due to the complication of scenes. It suggests that
epipolar geometry is not strong enough to provide sufficient constraints. We
could apply the semantic label for additional constraints in feature matching.
The candidate matches of Brute-Force matching method may not have the same
semantic label (a feature point indicates road may match to a building, e.g.). As
we annotate the images into three categories, we can simply cluster the feature
points into three semantic groups. Performing matches only in each group could
eliminate the semantic ambiguity.

To reconstruct the semantic point clouds, 2D semantic labels should be transmitted to 3D points. After performing triangulation, the 2D semantic label is
assigned to the triangulated 3D point accordingly.

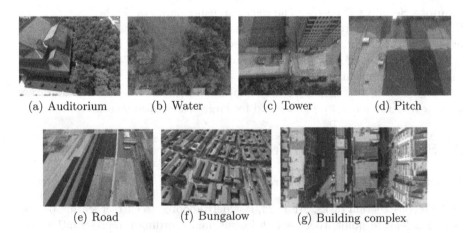

(a) Auditorium   (b) Water   (c) Tower   (d) Pitch

(e) Road   (f) Bungalow   (g) Building complex

Fig. 1. Example images from UDD. (a)–(g) are typical scenes in drone images. Best
viewed in color.

3.2 Equality Constrained Bundle Adjustment

As mentioned in Sect. 3.1, each 3D feature has a semantic label. Then we seek approaches to optimize the structures and camera poses further.

Review the unconstrained bundle adjustment equation below:

$$min \frac{1}{2} \sum_{i=1}^{n} \sum_{j=1}^{m} \|x_{ij} - P_i(X_j)\|^2 \tag{1}$$

where n is the number of cameras, m is the number of 3D points, and x_{ij} is the 2D feature points, X_j is the 3D points, P_i is the nonlinear transformations of 3D points.

While Eq. (1) minimizes the re-projection error of 3D points, due to the existence of some bad points, an additional weighting matrix W_e should be introduced. As a result, the selection of W_e affects the accuracy of the final 3D model, and the re-projected 2D points may be located at some wrong places (For example, a 3D building point corresponds to a 2D tree point). Intuitively, we can force the 3D points and the re-projected 2D points satisfy some constraints, that is *Semantic Consistency*, which means the 3D points and re-projected 2D points have the same semantic label.

Different with traditional bundle adjustment, with additional semantic constraints, we modify the bundle adjustment as an equality constrained nonlinear least square problem. Take semantic information from features, we can rewrite Eq. (1) as follows:

$$min \frac{1}{2} \sum_{i=1}^{n} \sum_{j=1}^{m} \|x_{ij} - P_i(X_j)\|^2, s.t. \ L(x_{ij}) = L(P_i(X_j)) \tag{2}$$

where L represents the semantic label of observations.

Then we show how to transform Eq. (2) into a Sequential Quadratic Programming problem. Let $f(x)$ be a nonlinear least square function that need to be optimized, $c(x) = L(x_{ij}) - L(P_i(X_j)) = 0$ be the equality constraints, A be the Jacobian matrix of the constraints, then the Lagrangian function for this problem is $F(x, \lambda) = f(x) - \lambda^T c(x)$. By the first order KKT condition, we can get:

$$\nabla F(x, \lambda) = \begin{bmatrix} \nabla f(x) - A^T \lambda \\ -c(x) \end{bmatrix} = 0 \tag{3}$$

Let W denotes the Hessian of $F(x, \lambda)$, we can get:

$$\begin{bmatrix} W & -A^T \\ -A & 0 \end{bmatrix} \begin{bmatrix} \delta x \\ \lambda_k \end{bmatrix} = \begin{bmatrix} -\nabla f + A^T \lambda_k \\ c \end{bmatrix} \tag{4}$$

By subtracting $A^T \lambda$ from both side of the first equation in Eq. (4), we then obtain:

$$\begin{bmatrix} W & -A^T \\ -A & 0 \end{bmatrix} \begin{bmatrix} \delta x \\ \lambda_{k+1} \end{bmatrix} = \begin{bmatrix} -\nabla f \\ c \end{bmatrix} \tag{5}$$

Equation (5) can be efficiently solved when both W and A are sparse. It is also easy to prove that W and A are all sparse in unconstrained bundle adjustment problem by the Levenburg-Marquart method.

Then the original constrained bundle adjustment problem is formulated to an unconstrained problem, and we seek approaches to solve the linear equation set $Ax = b$. Since A is symmetric indefinite, LDL^T factorization can be used. Besides, to avoid the computation of Hessian, we replace W with reduced Hessian of Lagrangian.

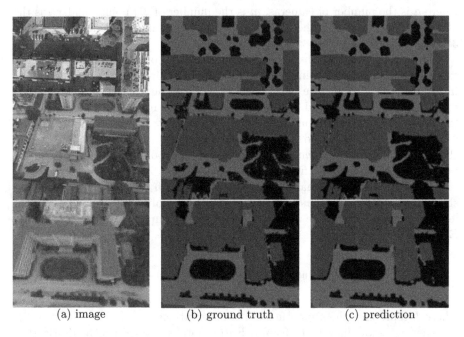

(a) image   (b) ground truth   (c) prediction

Fig. 2. Visualization of Urban Drone Dataset (UDD) validation set. **Blue**: Building, **Black**: Vegetation, **Green**: Free space. Best viewed in color. (Color figure online)

4   Experiments

4.1   Dataset Construction

Our dataset, Urban Drone Dataset (UDD)[1], is collected by a professional-grade UAV (DJI-Phantom 4) at altitudes between 60 and 100 m. It is extracted from 10 video sequences taken in 4 different cities in China. The resolution is either 4k (4096 * 2160) or 12M (4000 * 3000). It contains a variety of urban scenes (see Fig. 1). For most 3d reconstruction tasks, 3 semantic classes are roughly enough [31]: Vegetation, Building, and Free space [32]. The annotation sampling rate is between 1% to 2%. The train set consists of 160 frames, and the validation set consists of 45 images.

---

[1] https://github.com/MarcWong/UDD.

(a) H-n15

(b) e33

(c) e44

(d) hall

(e) m1

(f) n1

Fig. 3. Semantic reconstruction results with our constrained bundle adjustment. **Red**: Building, **Green**: Vegetation, **Blue**: Free space. Best viewed in color. (Color figure online)

Table 1. Statistics of reconstruction results of original and semantic SfM. **Black:** Original value/unchanged value compared to the original SfM, **Green:** Better than the original SfM, **Red:** Worse than the original SfM.

	Dataset	Images	Poses	Points	Tracks	RMSE	Time
Original SfM	cangzhou	400	400	1,287,539	2,541,961	0.819215	16 h 49 min 23 s
	e33	392	392	559,065	810,390	0.565699	3 h 28 min 43 s
	e44	337	337	468,978	641,171	0.546114	3 h 17 min 16 s
	hall	195	195	476,853	760,769	0.536045	2 h 10 min 39 s
	m1	288	288	422,158	650,072	0.564724	2 h 32 min 10 s
	n1	350	350	479,813	622,243	0.471467	4 h 7 min 21 s
	n15	248	244	484,229	667,029	0.529639	2 h 40 min 07 s
Semantic SfM	cangzhou	400	400	1,326,858	2,660,869	0.719897	14 h 28 min 51 s
	e33	392	392	554,449	803,395	0.561667	3 h 21 min 29 s
	e44	337	337	469,371	635,279	0.538501	3 h 07 min 13 s
	hall	195	195	473,056	745,969	0.531877	2 h 05 min 39 s
	m1	288	288	420,044	644,405	0.560242	2 h 30 min 49 s
	n1	350	350	481,983	617,487	0.466910	4 h 16 min 02 s
	n15	248	248	484,915	647,101	0.520202	2 h 37 min 10 s

4.2 Experiment Pipeline

For each picture, we predict the semantic labels first. Our backbone network ResNet-101 [33] is pre-trained on ImageNet [34]. We employ the main structure of deeplab v2 [35] and fine-tune it on UDD. The training is conducted on single GPU Titan X Pascal, with tensorflow 1.4. The fine-tuning is 10 epochs in total, with crop size of 513 * 513, and Adam optimizer (momentum 0.99, learning rate 2.5e−4, and weight decay 2e−4). The prediction result is depicted in Fig. 2.

Then, SfM with semantic constraints is performed. For reconstruction experiments that without semantic constraints, we just perform a common incremental pipeline as described in [6], and referred as *original SfM*. Our approach refers to *Semantic SfM* in this article. All the experiments statistics are given in Table 1, and the reconstruction results are depicted in Fig. 3.

4.3 Reconstruction Results

Implementation Details. We adopt SIFT [29] to extract feature points and compute descriptors. After extracting feature points, we predict their semantic label according to views and locations. For feature matching, we use cascade hashing [36] which is faster than FLANN [37]. After triangulation, each semantic label of a 2D feature is assigned to a computed 3D point, and every 3D point has a semantic label. Constrained bundle adjustment is realized by the algorithm given in Sect. 3.2. All of our experiments perform on a single computer and an Intel Core i7 CPU with 12 threads.

(a) semantic reconstruction result of dataset H-n15

(b) original reconstruction result of dataset H-n15

Fig. 4. Results of dataset H-n15. We can see from the left-up corner of (a) and (b), our semantic SfM can recover more camera poses than original SfM. Best viewed in color. (Color figure online)

Efficiency Evaluation. As shown in Table 1, our semantic SfM is slightly faster than original SfM. It's quite important, because as the additional constraints are added, the large-scale SQP problem may not always be solved efficiently in practice. In datasets of e44 and n1, however, the time spent by original SfM is much higher than expected, it may be caused by other usages of CPU resources when running the program, so we marked it out by red color.

Accuracy Evaluation. For most of the datasets, original SfM and our semantic SfM can recover the same number of camera poses. But in the n15 dataset, our method recovers all of the camera poses while the original SfM misses 4 camera poses. Detailed result is depicted in Fig. 4. As there are more than 200 hundred cameras, we just circled one part for demonstration. Besides, the number of 3D points reconstructed by our semantic SfM reduced slightly in m1, e33 and hall datasets, but in cangzhou, e44, n1 and n15 dataset, the number of points increased. Though the number of tracks decreased in most of our datasets. We use the Root Mean Square Error (RMSE) of reprojection as the evaluation. The RMSE of our semantic SfM is less than the original SfM in all of the datasets. Especially in cangzhou, a much more complicated dataset, the accuracy of RMSE has improved by almost 0.1, which suggests the accuracy of our semantic SfM surpasses original SfM, and our semantic SfM has advantages over the original one in complicated aerial image datasets.

5   Conclusion

As mentioned above, we propose a new approach for large-scale aerial images reconstruction by adding semantic constraints to Structure from Motion. By assigning each feature point a corresponded semantic label, matching is accelerated and some wrong matches are avoided. Besides, since each 3D point has a semantic constraint, nonlinear least square with equality constraints is used to model the bundle adjustment problem, and our result shows it could achieve the state-of-the-art precision while remaining the same efficiency.

Future Work. Not only should we consider the semantic segmentation as additional constraints in reconstruction, but to seek approaches taken the semantic label as variables to be optimized. What's more, with the rise of deep learning, and some representation works on learning feature [38], we would seek approaches to extract features with semantic information directly. With our approaches proposed in this article, we could further generate a dense reconstruction, which leads to automatic semantic segmentation training data generation.

Acknowledgements. This work is supported by The National Key Technology Research and Development Program of China under Grants 2017YFB1002705 and 2017YFB1002601, National Natural Science Foundation of China (NSFC) under Grants 61472010, 61632003, 61631001, and 61661146002, Equipment Development Project under Grant 315050501, and Science and Technology on Complex Electronic System Simulation Laboratory under Grant DXZT-JC-ZZ-2015-019.

References

1. Seitz, S.M., Szeliski, R., Snavely, N.: Photo tourism: exploring photo collections in 3D. ACM Trans. Graph. **25**(3), 835–846 (2006)
2. Agarwal, S., Snavely, N., Simon, I.: Building Rome in a day. Commun. ACM **54**(10), 105–112 (2011)
3. Snavely, K.N.: Scene Reconstruction and Visualization from Internet Photo Collections. University of Washington (2008)
4. Frahm, J.-M., et al.: Building Rome on a cloudless day. In: Daniilidis, K., Maragos, P., Paragios, N. (eds.) ECCV 2010. LNCS, vol. 6314, pp. 368–381. Springer, Heidelberg (2010). https://doi.org/10.1007/978-3-642-15561-1_27
5. Wu, C.: Towards linear-time incremental structure from motion. In: International Conference on 3DTV-Conference. IEEE, pp. 127–134 (2013)
6. Moulon, P., Monasse, P., Marlet, R.: Adaptive structure from motion with a *Contrario* model estimation. In: Lee, K.M., Matsushita, Y., Rehg, J.M., Hu, Z. (eds.) ACCV 2012. LNCS, vol. 7727, pp. 257–270. Springer, Heidelberg (2013). https://doi.org/10.1007/978-3-642-37447-0_20
7. Schönberger, J.L., Frahm, J.M.: Structure-from-motion revisited. In: Computer Vision and Pattern Recognition. IEEE (2016)
8. Sweeney, C., Hollerer, T., Turk, M.: Theia: a fast and scalable structure-from-motion library, pp. 693–696 (2015)
9. Fischler, M.A., Bolles, R.C.: Random sample consensus: a paradigm for model fitting with applications to image analysis and automated cartography. Read. Comput. Vis. **24**(6), 726–740 (1987)
10. Triggs, B., McLauchlan, P.F., Hartley, R.I., Fitzgibbon, A.W.: Bundle adjustment — a modern synthesis. In: Triggs, B., Zisserman, A., Szeliski, R. (eds.) IWVA 1999. LNCS, vol. 1883, pp. 298–372. Springer, Heidelberg (2000). https://doi.org/10.1007/3-540-44480-7_21
11. Wilson, K., Snavely, N.: Robust global translations with 1DSfM. In: Fleet, D., Pajdla, T., Schiele, B., Tuytelaars, T. (eds.) ECCV 2014. LNCS, vol. 8691, pp. 61–75. Springer, Cham (2014). https://doi.org/10.1007/978-3-319-10578-9_5
12. Crandall, D., Owens, A., Snavely, N., et al.: Discrete-continuous optimization for large-scale structure from motion. In: Computer Vision and Pattern Recognition, pp. 3001–3008. IEEE (2011)
13. Farenzena, M., Fusiello, A., Gherardi, R.: Structure-and-motion pipeline on a hierarchical cluster tree. In: IEEE International Conference on Computer Vision Workshops. IEEE, 1489–1496 (2009)
14. Gherardi, R., Farenzena, M., Fusiello, A.: Improving the efficiency of hierarchical structure-and-motion. In: Computer Vision and Pattern Recognition, pp. 1594–1600. IEEE (2010)
15. Toldo, R., Gherardi, R., Farenzena, M., et al.: Hierarchical structure-and-motion recovery from uncalibrated images. Comput. Vis. Image Underst. **140**(C), 27–143 (2015)
16. Chen, Y., Chan, A.B., Lin, Z., et al.: Efficient tree-structured SfM by RANSAC generalized Procrustes analysis. Comput. Vis. Image Underst. **157**(C), 179–189 (2017)
17. Bao, S.Y., Savarese, S.: Semantic structure from motion. In: Computer Vision and Pattern Recognition, pp. 2025–2032. IEEE (2011)
18. Bao, S.Y., Bagra, M., Chao, Y.W.: Semantic structure from motion with points, regions, and objects. IEEE **157**(10), 2703–2710 (2012)

19. Furukawa, Y.: Multi-View Stereo: A Tutorial. Now Publishers Inc., Hanover (2015)
20. Haene, C., Zach, C., Cohen, A.: Dense semantic 3D reconstruction. IEEE Trans. Pattern Anal. Mach. Intell. **39**(9), 1730–1743 (2016)
21. Blaha, M., Vogel, C., Richard, A., et al.: Large-scale semantic 3D reconstruction: an adaptive multi-resolution model for multi-class volumetric labeling. In: Computer Vision and Pattern Recognition, pp. 3176–3184. IEEE (2016)
22. Cordts, M., Omran, M., Ramos, S., et al.: The cityscapes dataset for semantic urban scene understanding. In: Proceedings of the IEEE Conference on Computer Vision and Pattern Recognition, pp. 3213–3223 (2016)
23. Sturm, J., Engelhard, N., Endres, F., et al.: A benchmark for the evaluation of RGB-D SLAM systems. In: 2012 IEEE/RSJ International Conference on Intelligent Robots and Systems (IROS), pp. 573–580. IEEE (2012)
24. Brostow, G.J., Shotton, J., Fauqueur, J., Cipolla, R.: Segmentation and recognition using structure from motion point clouds. In: Forsyth, D., Torr, P., Zisserman, A. (eds.) ECCV 2008. LNCS, vol. 5302, pp. 44–57. Springer, Heidelberg (2008). https://doi.org/10.1007/978-3-540-88682-2_5
25. Mueller, M., Smith, N., Ghanem, B.: A benchmark and simulator for UAV tracking. In: Leibe, B., Matas, J., Sebe, N., Welling, M. (eds.) ECCV 2016. LNCS, vol. 9905, pp. 445–461. Springer, Cham (2016). https://doi.org/10.1007/978-3-319-46448-0_27
26. Robicquet, A., Alahi, A., Sadeghian, A., et al.: Forecasting social navigation in crowded complex scenes. arXiv preprint arXiv:1601.00998 (2016)
27. Maggiori, E., Tarabalka, Y., Charpiat, G., et al.: Can semantic labeling methods generalize to any city? The inria aerial image labeling benchmark. IEEE International Symposium on Geoscience and Remote Sensing (IGARSS) (2017)
28. Xia, G.S., Bai, X., Ding, J., et al.: DOTA: a large-scale dataset for object detection in aerial images. In: Proceedings of CVPR (2018)
29. Lowe, D.G., Lowe, D.G.: Distinctive image features from scale-invariant keypoints. Int. J. Comput. Vis. **60**(2), 91–110 (2004)
30. Salehi, A., Gay-Bellile, V., Bourgeois, S., Chausse, F.: Improving constrained bundle adjustment through semantic scene labeling. In: Hua, G., Jégou, H. (eds.) ECCV 2016. LNCS, vol. 9915, pp. 133–142. Springer, Cham (2016). https://doi.org/10.1007/978-3-319-49409-8_13
31. Savinov, N., Ladicky, L., Hane, C., et al.: Discrete optimization of ray potentials for semantic 3d reconstruction. In: Proceedings of the IEEE Conference on Computer Vision and Pattern Recognition, pp. 5511–5518 (2015)
32. Hne, C., Zach, C., Cohen, A., et al.: Joint 3D scene reconstruction and class segmentation. In: 2013 IEEE Conference on Computer Vision and Pattern Recognition (CVPR), pp. 97–104. IEEE (2013)
33. He, K., Zhang, X., Ren, S., et al.: Deep residual learning for image recognition. In: Proceedings of the IEEE Conference on Computer Vision and Pattern Recognition, pp. 770–778 (2016)
34. Krizhevsky, A., Sutskever, I., Hinton, G.E.: ImageNet classification with deep convolutional neural networks. In: Advances in Neural Information Processing Systems, pp. 1097–1105 (2012)
35. Chen, L.C., Papandreou, G., Kokkinos, I.: DeepLab: semantic image segmentation with deep convolutional nets, atrous convolution, and fully connected CRFS. IEEE Trans. Pattern Anal. Mach. Intell. **40**(4), 834–848 (2018)
36. Cheng, J., Leng, C., Wu, J., et al.: Fast and accurate image matching with cascade hashing for 3D reconstruction. In: Computer Vision and Pattern Recognition, pp. 1–8. IEEE (2014)

37. Muja, M.: Fast approximate nearest neighbors with automatic algorithm configuration. In: International Conference on Computer Vision Theory and Application VISSAPP, pp. 331–340 (2009)
38. Yi, K.M., Trulls, E., Lepetit, V., Fua, P.: LIFT: Learned Invariant Feature Transform. In: Leibe, B., Matas, J., Sebe, N., Welling, M. (eds.) ECCV 2016. LNCS, vol. 9910, pp. 467–483. Springer, Cham (2016). https://doi.org/10.1007/978-3-319-46466-4_28

New Motion Estimation
with Angular-Distance Median Filter
for Frame Interpolation

Huangkai Cai, He Jiang, Xiaolin Huang, and Jie Yang[✉]

Institution of Image Processing and Pattern Recognition,
Shanghai Jiao Tong University, Shanghai, China
jieyang@sjtu.edu.cn

Abstract. A novel method of motion estimation based on block matching and motion refinement is proposed for frame interpolation. The new motion estimation is a two-stage method consisting of coarse searching and fine searching. Coarse searching aims to reduce the amount of calculation and the algorithm complexity, while fine searching is utilized to refine motion vectors for improving the final performance. In the stage of coarse searching, a new algorithm of motion refinement, that Angular-Distance Median Filter (ADMF), is proposed to correct wrong motion vectors, which can solve the blurry-problems resulted from overlapped situations. Overlapped situations mean that different blocks move towards similar position after the initial motion estimation. Experimental results show that the proposed approach outperforms the other compared approaches in subjective and objective evaluation.

Keywords: Frame interpolation · Frame Rate Up-Conversion
Motion estimation · Motion refinement
Angular-Distance Median Filter

1 Introduction

Frame interpolation, that is also called Frame Rate Up-Conversion (FRUC), is to generate new frames on the basis of the prior information, which increases the frame rate. For example, we can utilize the technique of FRUC to convert a video at 30 frames per second to 60 frames per second or more by interpolating new frames. Techniques of frame interpolation can be applied to improve the visual effect of videos in various electronic equipments such as the television, game consoles, computers and so on.

The conventional framework of frame interpolation is composed of block matching motion estimation and Motion-Compensated Interpolation. Block matching motion estimation is our main concern. Furthermore, there are various kinds of algorithms using block matching motion estimation. [8] paid more attention to reducing the computational complexity. [1,9,15] took use of multivariate

© Springer Nature Switzerland AG 2018
J.-H. Lai et al. (Eds.): PRCV 2018, LNCS 11256, pp. 360–371, 2018.
https://doi.org/10.1007/978-3-030-03398-9_31

information including multi-frame and multi-level. [4, 6, 7, 12, 14] concentrated on getting true motion vectors through motion estimation and motion refinement.

Motivated by the efficiency and the performance of block matching motion estimation and motion refinement, new motion estimation with coarse-to-fine searching and Angular-Distance Median Filter (ADMF) is proposed for frame interpolation as illustrated in Fig. 1. The reasons how we design the framework from coarse to fine and the algorithm of motion refinement called ADMF will be explained as follows.

In [4, 6, 12, 14], some researchers combined Unidirectional Motion Estimation (UME) and Bidirectional Motion Estimation (BME), while other some researchers combined Forward Motion Estimation and Backward Motion Estimation. The combinations of various kinds of motion estimation aim to obtain more accurate motion vectors. But, simply combining them together is not efficient and maintains much redundant calculation.

For the purpose of reducing the redundant computation, Bidirectional Motion Estimation is applied in both coarse and fine searching. Because, the computation of BME is much less than the motion estimation abovementioned. In addition, relatively accurate motion vectors generated by BME can be used to refine wrong motion vectors by the proposed algorithm ADMF. Based on BME, the framework from coarse to fine not only reduces the amount of calculation, but also improves the final performance.

After the initial motion estimation, a variety of methods of motion refinement can be applied to refine motion vectors. These algorithms include Spatio-Temporal Motion Vector Smoothing [12], Two-Dimensional Weighted Motion Vector Smoothing (2DW-MVS) [14] and Trilateral Filtering Motion Smoothing [4]. These methods are unable to correct all the wrong motion vectors generated by the initial motion estimation, which results in blurry-problems. Blurry-problems are resulted from overlapped situations that different estimative blocks move towards similar position.

In order to effectively correct wrong motion vectors, a new algorithm of motion refinement, that Angular-Distance Median Filter, is proposed to applied after the initial motion estimation. ADMF is based on the angular and the distance of motion vectors. Furthermore, wrong motion vectors can be refined according to neighbouring motion vectors of them and their neighbours. So, it is an excellent algorithm for refining most wrong motion vectors. More details of ADMF will be elaborated in Sect. 2.

The contributions of this paper are summarized as follows. Firstly, a new method of motion estimation, which is a two-stage method from coarse searching to fine searching, is proposed for frame interpolation. Secondly, a novel algorithm of motion refinement called Angular-Distance Median Filter is put forward to effectively correct wrong motion vectors. Thirdly, experimental results demonstrate that the proposed approach outperforms the other compared techniques for frame interpolation in both subjective and objective evaluation.

The rest of this paper is organized as follows. In Sect. 2, we will elaborate the proposed algorithm including coarse-to-fine searching and Angular-Distance Median Filter. In Sect. 3, the experimental results will be showed and analysed. In Sect. 4, conclusions will be discussed.

2   Methodology

As illustrated in Fig. 1, the framework of frame interpolation is composed of motion estimation and Motion-Compensated Interpolation. This article proposes a new method of motion estimation based on coarse-to-fine searching and Angular-Distance Median Filter (ADMF).

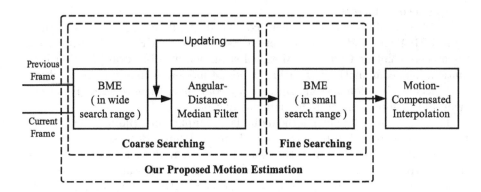

Fig. 1. The proposed motion estimation for frame interpolation

Firstly, from the previous frame and the current frame in test video sequences, the initial motion vectors are estimated by Bidirectional Motion Estimation (BME) in a wide search range. Secondly, ADMF will be applied to update motion vectors until it meets terminal conditions. Thirdly, on the basis of updated motion vectors generated by ADMF, BME is employed again to refine motion vectors in a small search range. Fourthly, the algorithm of Motion-Compensated Interpolation will utilize the final motion vectors to generate interpolated frames.

2.1   Coarse Searching

In coarse searching, BME [3] is applied to estimate the initial motion vectors. The reasons why BME is chosen will be explained as follows. Firstly, its computational complexity is much less than the combination of Forward Motion Estimation and Backward Motion Estimation [12]. Secondly, the hole-problems resulted from Unidirectional Motion Estimation (UME) will not exist in BME. The hole-problems exist where no estimative blocks move to. Thirdly, the initial motion vectors calculated by BME are sufficient for the following motion refinement, which can utilize true motion vectors to correct wrong motion vectors.

The schematic diagram of BME is as illustrated in Fig. 2. In the left half of Fig. 2, $F(n-1)$, $F(n-\frac{1}{2})$ and $F(n)$ denote the previous frame, the interpolated frame and the current frame, respectively. The motion of blocks is assumed to be linear. In addition, motion vectors v are estimated by comparing the similarity of different blocks. The discriminate criterion of the similarity is the sum of absolute

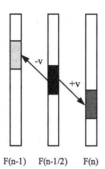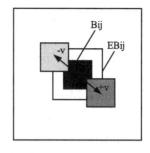

F(n-1)   F(n-1/2)   F(n)

Fig. 2. Bidirectional motion estimation

difference (SAD) between the pixel values in the previous frame $F(n-1)$ and that in the current frame $F(n)$.

As shown in the right half of Fig. 2, B_{ij} represents a block which is in the i th row and the j th column of the interpolated frame. It is defined as:

$$B_{ij} = \{(x,y)|1 + (j-1) \times BS \leq x \leq j \times BS,$$
$$1 + (i-1) \times BS \leq y \leq i \times BS\} \tag{1}$$

where (x,y) denotes the position of the pixel in the interpolated frame and BS means the block size of B_{ij}. In order to enhance the accuracy of motion estimation, a trick is applied here, which expands the block size of B_{ij}. EB_{ij} represents an expanding block of B_{ij} with expanded size ES:

$$EB_{ij} = \{(x,y)|1 + (j-1) \times BS - ES \leq x \leq j \times BS + ES,$$
$$1 + (i-1) \times BS - ES \leq y \leq i \times BS + ES\}. \tag{2}$$

After the definitions of block and block size, SAD is used to calculate motion vectors $\{v_{ij}\}$. $v_{ij} = (v_x, v_y)$, a motion vector, denotes the distance which the block EB_{ij} moves relative to the previous frame and the current frame. In order to differentiate SAD values in various stages, the SAD value in coarse searching is called $SADC$. The mathematical expressions of $SADC$ and motion vectors $\{v_{ij}\}$ are:

$$SADC(v_x, v_y) = \sum_{(x,y) \in EB_{ij}} |F_{n-1}(x - v_x, y - v_y) - F_n(x + v_x, y + v_y)| \tag{3}$$

and

$$v_{ij} = (v_x, v_y) = \arg\min_{(v_x, v_y) \in CSR} \{SADC(v_x, v_y)\} \tag{4}$$

where

$$CSR = \{(v_x, v_y)| - CWS \le v_x, v_y \le CWS\}. \tag{5}$$

In the above Eq. (5), CSR represents the search range in coarse searching, while CWS means the search window size in coarse searching.

2.2 Angular-Distance Median Filter

When the initial motion vectors $\{v_{ij}\}$ are generated by BME, Angular-Distance Median Filter is proposed to refine motion vectors as illustrated in Fig. 3. Red arrows mean wrong motion vectors, while black arrows mean true motion vectors. As the blue circle of Fig. 3 shows, motion vectors of adjacent blocks point to the similar position, which will result in blurry-problems in the final interpolated frame. It is observed that there exists a main direction in most frames of test video sequences, which means that wrong motion vectors can be improved or corrected by neighbouring motion vectors. Then, the mathematical theory about ADMF algorithm will be explained as follows.

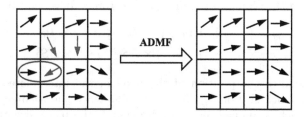

Fig. 3. Motion vectors refined by ADMF (Color figure online)

ADMF is an algorithm using the angular and the distance. The definitions of the angular A and the distance D are:

$$A(v, v_0) = \arccos\left(\frac{v \cdot v_0^T}{\|v\|\|v_0\|}\right) \tag{6}$$

and

$$D(v) = \|v\| \tag{7}$$

where v denotes the initial motion vector generated by BME, while $v_0 = (1, 0)$ and it is chosen as a reference direction.

On the basis of $A(v, v_0)$ and $D(v)$, Absolute Angular Difference (AAD) and Absolute Distance Difference (ADD) are calculated to judge the validity of motion vectors $\{v_{ij}\}$. $AAD(v_{ij})$ and $ADD(v_{ij})$ are defined as:

$$AAD(v_{ij}) = |A(v_{ij}, v_0) - \frac{1}{N}\sum_{k=0}^{N-1} A(v_k, v_0)| \tag{8}$$

and

$$ADD(\boldsymbol{v}_{ij}) = |D(\boldsymbol{v}_{ij}) - \frac{1}{N}\sum_{k=0}^{N-1} D(\boldsymbol{v}_k)| \qquad (9)$$

where $N = 8$ and $\{\boldsymbol{v}_k\}$ means 8 neighbour motion vectors of the center motion vector $\boldsymbol{v}_{ij}$.

After the calculation of $AAD(\boldsymbol{v}_{ij})$ and $ADD(\boldsymbol{v}_{ij})$, the reasonable threshold is set to judge the validity V_{ij} of the motion vector $\boldsymbol{v}_{ij}$:

$$V_{ij} = \begin{cases} 1, & AAD(\boldsymbol{v}_{ij}) \leq \dfrac{\pi}{6}, \ ADD(\boldsymbol{v}_{ij}) \leq \dfrac{BS}{16} \\[2mm] 0, & AAD(\boldsymbol{v}_{ij}) \geq \dfrac{\pi}{4}, \ ADD(\boldsymbol{v}_{ij}) \geq \dfrac{BS}{8}. \end{cases} \qquad (10)$$

If $V_{ij} = 0$, the motion vector $\boldsymbol{v}_{ij}$ will be updated through median filter:

$$\boldsymbol{v}_{ij} = median\{\boldsymbol{v}_1, \boldsymbol{v}_2, \ldots, \boldsymbol{v}_k\}, \quad if \ V_{ij} = 0. \qquad (11)$$

Terminal conditions include two parts that the number of times of filtering and the percentage of valid motion vectors. The upper limit of the number is set to be $num \leq 5$, because the visual effect of the interpolated frames will become blurry after so many times of median filtering. The lower limit of the percentage of valid motion vectors is set to be 95% that

$$\sum_{i=1}^{m}\sum_{j=1}^{n} V_{ij} \geq 95\% \times m \times n \qquad (12)$$

where m denotes the number of blocks in row direction, while n denotes the number of blocks in column direction.

The proposed ADMF is composed of three steps as shown in Table 1. Firstly, num and V are initialized to zero. Secondly, Validity V_{ij} and the motion vector $\boldsymbol{v}_{ij}$ are updated according to Eqs. (10) and (11). Thirdly, repeat step 2 until it meets terminal conditions.

Table 1. The proposed ADMF algorithm

---

step 1: Initialization: $num = 0$, $V = \begin{pmatrix} 0 & \cdots & 0 \\ \vdots & \ddots & \vdots \\ 0 & \cdots & 0 \end{pmatrix}_{m \times n}$.

step 2: Update V_{ij} and v_{ij} according to Eqn.(10) and Eqn.(11), and $num = num + 1$.

step 3: Repeat step 2 until $num = 5$ or $\sum_{i=1}^{m}\sum_{j=1}^{n} V_{ij} \geq 95\% \times m \times n$.

2.3 Fine Searching

After ADMF, not only wrong motion vectors will be corrected, but also true motion vectors will have a minor adjustment. Ensuring the accuracy of motion vectors refined with a fine adjustment is a major concern in fine searching. So, BME is utilized to refine motion vectors in a small search range. The main difference between coarse searching and fine searching is the search range because of their own purposes. Coarse searching aims to get the initial motion vectors in a wide search range, while fine searching aims to refine motion vectors in a small search range.

The SAD value in fine searching is called $SADF$. $\hat{\boldsymbol{v}}_{ij} = (\hat{v}_x, \hat{v}_y)$ generated by ADMF denotes the refined motion vector, while $\boldsymbol{v}_{ij} = (\hat{v}_x + v_x, \hat{v}_y + v_y)$ denotes the final motion vector for Motion-Compensated Interpolation. The mathematical expressions of $SADF$ and motion vectors $\{\boldsymbol{v}_{ij}\}$ are:

$$SADF(v_x, v_y) = \sum_{(x,y)\in EB_{ij}} |F_{n-1}(x - \hat{v}_x - v_x, y - \hat{v}_y - v_y) \\ -F_n(x + \hat{v}_x + v_x, y + \hat{v}_y + v_y)| \tag{13}$$

and

$$\boldsymbol{v}_{ij} = (\hat{v}_x + v_x, \hat{v}_y + v_y) = \underset{(v_x,v_y)\in FSR}{\arg\min} \{SADF(v_x, v_y)\} \tag{14}$$

where

$$FSR = \{(v_x, v_y)| - FWS \le v_x, v_y \le FWS\}. \tag{15}$$

In the above Eq. (15), FSR represents the search range in fine searching, while FWS means the search window size in fine searching.

3 Experiments

In our experiments, 10 test video sequences are applied to verify the validity of the proposed motion estimation for frame interpolation. These video sequences include Akiyo, Crew, Football, Foreman, Ice, Mobile, Paris, Silent, Soccer and Stefan. Especially in the sequences of Football and Soccer, there exists significant difference between adjacent video sequences because of high-speed moving objects, which means a great challenge for motion estimation. The resolution of 10 test video sequences is 352×288. Furthermore, experiments are conducted on the platform that Matlab R2015b.

In order to evaluate the performance of interpolated frames, even frames of video sequences are skipped and generated according to neighbouring odd frames by various methods of Frame Rate Up-Conversion. For example, the 2nd frame predicted can be calculated by the 1st frame and the 3rd frame. Peak signal-to-noise ratio (PSNR) and structural similarity (SSIM) [13] are utilized as the evaluative criteria for describing the difference between even frames predicted and true even frames.

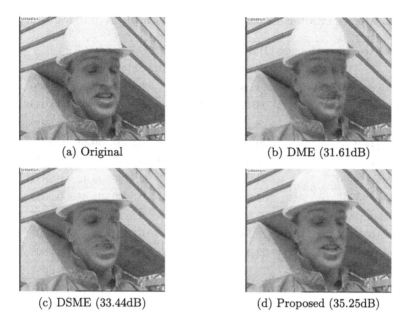

(a) Original

(b) DME (31.61dB)

(c) DSME (33.44dB)

(d) Proposed (35.25dB)

Fig. 4. As shown in (a), the original frame is the 78th frame in foreman sequences. As shown in (b), (c) and (d), there are the 78th interpolated frames with PSNR values generated by other methods and the proposed method.

A complete framework of frame interpolation can be divided into two modules including motion estimation and Motion-Compensated Interpolation. Motion estimation is a major focus, so our proposed motion estimation will be compared with five other methods. These algorithms in this paper are called Bidirectional Motion Estimation (BME) [3], Forward-Backward Jointing Motion Estimation (FBJME) [12], Dual Motion Estimation (DME) [6], Direction-Select Motion Estimation (DSME) [14] and Linear Quardratic Motion Estimation (LQME) [4]. In the procedure of Motion-Compensated Interpolation, Overlapped Block Motion Compensation (OBMC) described in [2,5] is applied to generate the final interpolated frames.

Experimental settings of the proposed approach will be detailed in the following. Block size is set to be $BS = 16$, while expanded size is set to be $ES = 8$. In coarse searching, coarse-searching window size is set to be $CWS = 12$, and step size is set to be 2. In fine searching, fine-searching window size is set to be $FWS = 4$, and step size is set to be 1. In addition, experimental settings of compared methods are according to those in [3,4,6,12,14].

Experimental results will be analysed in both subjective evaluation and objective evaluation. In subjective evaluation, interpolated frames generated by various methods will be displayed in the form of pictures. In objective evaluation, three numerical indexes including PSNR, SSIM [13] and running time will be considered.

Table 2. Average PSNR and SSIM values of various methods in 10 test sequences

Test sequences (frames)	BME [3]		FBJME [12]		DME [6]	
	PSNR	SSIM	PSNR	SSIM	PSNR	SSIM
Akiyo (300)	44.26	0.9926	45.75	0.9951	47.20	0.9960
Crew (300)	28.47	0.8328	31.16	0.8963	31.07	0.8939
Foreman (300)	28.65	0.8636	31.73	0.8992	32.64	0.8939
Ice (240)	26.26	0.9180	31.17	0.9561	30.88	0.9549
Mobile (300)	20.63	0.7095	27.60	0.9385	28.31	0.9543
Paris (1065)	34.25	0.9746	35.35	0.9795	36.42	0.9834
Silent (300)	34.54	0.9518	35.66	0.9606	35.88	0.9636
Stefan (90)	25.02	0.8465	27.47	0.9173	26.58	0.8557
Football (260)	22.58	0.6981	23.17	0.7123	22.49	0.6805
Soccer (300)	23.48	0.7552	25.30	0.8154	24.32	0.7808
Average	28.81	0.8543	31.44	0.9070	31.58	0.8957
Test sequences (frames)	DSME [14]		LQME [4]		Proposed	
	PSNR	SSIM	PSNR	SSIM	PSNR	SSIM
Akiyo (300)	47.39	0.9961	46.61	0.9960	47.15	0.9959
Crew (300)	31.59	0.9067	-	-	31.91	0.9074
Foreman (300)	33.13	0.9041	32.65	0.9050	33.72	0.9336
Ice (240)	32.00	0.9663	-	-	32.12	0.9633
Mobile (300)	28.64	0.9604	27.72	0.9440	29.15	0.9598
Paris (1065)	36.80	0.9847	36.14	0.9830	36.15	0.9822
Silent (300)	36.11	0.9656	-	-	36.13	0.9645
Stefan (90)	27.77	0.8943	28.03	0.9280	28.70	0.9338
Football (260)	22.87	0.7044	22.96	0.6690	23.92	0.7557
Soccer (300)	24.89	0.8073	-	-	26.70	0.8487
Average	32.12	0.9090	-	-	**32.57**	**0.9245**

3.1   Subjective Evaluation

In order to test the superiority of diverse methods of motion estimation subjectively, the original frame and interpolated frames generated by DME, DSME and the proposed are as shown in Fig. 4. The 78th frame in foreman sequences is utilized as a reference picture, so we can compare the visual effect of it with interpolated frames.

As (b) and (c) of the Fig. 4 show, there exist the blurry-problems on the face of the person. It means that DME and DSME are inaccurate especially in details such as eyes, the nose and the mouth. Compared to DME and DSME, the interpolated frame of the proposed, that the picture (d), is much more clear and similar to the original picture (a). Furthermore, PSNR values of various methods also indicate that the proposed motion estimation outperforms DME and DSME.

Table 3. Average running time of various methods in 10 test sequences

Average	FBJME [12]	DME [6]	DSME [14]	Proposed
PSNR	31.44	31.58	32.12	**32.57**
SSIM	0.9070	0.8957	0.9090	**0.9245**
Time (s/frame)	2.97	1.01	3.66	**0.89**

3.2 Objective Evaluation

In objective evaluation, a series of experiments are performed for testing the performance of 6 methods of motion estimation. The 6 types of motion estimation are BME, FBJME, DME, DSME, LQME and the proposed, and they are used together in 10 test video sequences. Three numerical indexes including PSNR, SSIM and running time will be considered.

As shown in Table 2, it is firmly convinced that the proposed motion estimation outperforms other compared methods in consideration of average PSNR and SSIM values. In addition, the proposed approach has outstanding performance especially in the sequences of Football and Soccer. It means that ADMF is an excellent algorithm of motion refinement, which can effectively refine wrong motion vectors in scenes that objects move fast.

For the purpose of comparing the efficiency of motion estimation, these methods that FBJME, DME, DSME and the proposed will be analysed in comprehensive consideration of average PSNR, average SSIM and average running time. The running time means the time of generating every interpolated frame. As shown in Table 3, the proposed motion estimation is the most efficient algorithm in contrast to the compared methods.

4   Conclusion

This paper has proposed a novel method of motion estimation based on block matching and motion refinement for frame interpolation. Firstly, the proposed framework consists of coarse searching and fine searching using Bidirectional Motion Estimation. The framework has been proven to be efficient due to requiring only low computation. Secondly, Angular-Distance Median Filter as an excellent algorithm of motion refinement has been verified that it can effectively correct wrong motion vectors. Thirdly, our proposed motion estimation has been analysed in overall consideration of PSNR, SSIM, running time and different scenes. Fourthly, experimental results have shown that the performance of the proposed method outperforms the other compared techniques for frame interpolation in both subjective and objective evaluation.

In the research of Frame Rate Up-Conversion, how to get true motion vectors in motion estimation is our main focus. In addition, how to generate interpolated frames in Motion-Compensated Interpolation still need to be studied. Furthermore, it is also interesting to implement frame interpolation in other frameworks, e.g., the phase-based method [10] and the method based on convolution neural network [11].

Acknowledgements. This research is partly supported by NSFC, China (No: 61572315, 6151101179) and 973 Plan, China (No. 2015CB856004).

References

1. Cho, Y.H., Lee, H.Y., Park, D.S.: Temporal frame interpolation based on multiframe feature trajectory. IEEE Trans. Circuits Syst. Video Technol. **23**(12), 2105–2115 (2013)
2. Choi, B.D., Han, J.W., Kim, C.S., Ko, S.J.: Motion-compensated frame interpolation using bilateral motion estimation and adaptive overlapped block motion compensation. IEEE Trans. Circuits Syst. Video Technol. **17**(4), 407–416 (2007)
3. Choi, B.T., Lee, S.H., Ko, S.J.: New frame rate up-conversion using bi-directional motion estimation. IEEE Trans. Consum. Electron. **46**(3), 603–609 (2002)
4. Guo, Y., Chen, L., Gao, Z., Zhang, X.: Frame rate up-conversion using linear quadratic motion estimation and trilateral filtering motion smoothing. J. Disp. Technol. **12**(1), 89–98 (2016)
5. Ha, T., Lee, S., Kim, J.: Motion compensated frame interpolation by new block-based motion estimation algorithm. IEEE Trans. Consum. Electron. **50**(2), 752–759 (2004)
6. Kang, S.J., Yoo, S., Kim, Y.H.: Dual motion estimation for frame rate up-conversion. IEEE Trans. Circuits Syst. Video Technol. **20**(12), 1909–1914 (2011)
7. Kim, D.Y., Lim, H., Park, H.W.: Iterative true motion estimation for motion-compensated frame interpolation. IEEE Trans. Circuits Syst. Video Technol. **23**(3), 445–454 (2013)
8. Kim, U.S., Sunwoo, M.H.: New frame rate up-conversion algorithms with low computational complexity. IEEE Trans. Circuits Syst. Video Technol. **24**(3), 384–393 (2014)
9. Lu, Q., Xu, N., Fang, X.: Motion-compensated frame interpolation with multiframe-based occlusion handling. J. Disp. Technol. **12**(1), 45–54 (2016)
10. Meyer, S., Wang, O., Zimmer, H., Grosse, M., Sorkinehornung, A.: Phase-based frame interpolation for video. In: IEEE Conference on Computer Vision and Pattern Recognition, pp. 1410–1418 (2015)
11. Niklaus, S., Mai, L., Liu, F.: Video frame interpolation via adaptive separable convolution. In: IEEE Conference on Computer Vision and Pattern Recognition, pp. 2270–2279 (2017)
12. Vinh, T.Q., Kim, Y.C., Hong, S.H.: Frame rate up-conversion using forward-backward jointing motion estimation and spatio-temporal motion vector smoothing. In: International Conference on Computer Engineering & Systems, pp. 605–609 (2010)

13. Wang, Z., Bovik, A.C., Sheikh, H.R., Simoncelli, E.P.: Image quality assessment: from error visibility to structural similarity. IEEE Trans. Image Process. **13**(4), 600–612 (2004)
14. Yoo, D.G., Kang, S.J., Kim, Y.H.: Direction-select motion estimation for motion-compensated frame rate up-conversion. J. Disp. Technol. **9**(10), 840–850 (2013)
15. Yu, Z., Li, H., Wang, Z., Hu, Z., Chen, C.W.: Multi-level video frame interpolation: exploiting the interaction among different levels. IEEE Trans. Circuits Syst. Video Technol. **23**(7), 1235–1248 (2013)

A Rotation Invariant Descriptor Using Multi-directional and High-Order Gradients

Hanlin Mo[1,2(✉)], Qi Li[1,2], You Hao[1,2], He Zhang[1,2], and Hua Li[1,2]

[1] Key Lab of Intelligent Information Processing, Institute of Computing Technology, Chinese Academy of Sciences, Beijing 100190, China
{mohanlin,liqi,haoyou,zhanghe,lihua}@ict.ac.cn
[2] University of Chinese Academy of Sciences, Beijing 100049, China

Abstract. In this paper, we propose a novel method to build a rotation invariant descriptor using multi-directional and high-order gradients (MDHOG). To this end, a new dense sampling strategy based on the local rotation invariant coordinate system is first introduced. This method gets more neighboring points of the sample point in the interest region so that the intensity distribution of the sample point neighborhood can be described better. Then, with this sampling strategy, we design the multi-directional strategy and use 1D Gaussian derivative filters to encode MDHOG for each sample point. The final descriptor is built using the histograms of MDHOG. We have carried out image matching and object recognition experiments based on some popular image databases. And the results demonstrate that the new descriptor has better performance than other commonly used local descriptors, such as SIFT, DAISY, MROGH, LIOP and so on.

Keywords: Local descriptor · Rotation invariant coordinate system
Multi-directional strategy · High-order gradients
1D Gaussian derivative · SIFT

1 Introduction

How to extract effective local descriptor for image interest points/regions is one of the fundamental problems in pattern recognition and computer vision, because many practical applications need to use this kind of feature, including object detection [1], wide baseline matching [2] and texture classification [3]. Researchers believe that a good local descriptor should be able to discriminate different image interest points/regions and be robust to diverse image transformations, such as rotation, viewpoint changes, illumination changes and so on.

In the past decades, a large number of methods have been presented to achieve this goal. Most are first to detect image interest points/regions and then extract their descriptors. Finally, we can match these points/regions according to the distances of their descriptors. There are many approaches to detect

© Springer Nature Switzerland AG 2018
J.-H. Lai et al. (Eds.): PRCV 2018, LNCS 11256, pp. 372–383, 2018.
https://doi.org/10.1007/978-3-030-03398-9_32

interest points/regions which have covariance for some geometric deformations. Among them, Harris corner [4] and DOG (Difference of Gaussian) [1] can obtain interest points which are covariant under the similarity transformations. Harris-affine [5], Hessian-affine [6], MSER (Maximally Stable Extremal Region) [7], IBR (Intensity-Based Region) and EBR (Edge-Based Region) [2] can detect interest regions which are covariant under the affine transformations. A comprehensive study of them can be found in [6,8].

Extracting good descriptors for detected interest points/regions is more important. The commonly used method is to construct the descriptor using gradient-based histograms, such as SIFT (Scale Invariant Feature Transform) [1], PCA-SIFT [9], GLOH (Gradient Location-Orientation Histogram) [10] and DAISY [11]. However, these descriptors usually need to estimate a dominant orientation to achieve their rotation invariance. Some researchers have found that the dominant orientation assignment based on local image statistics is an error-prone process, thus resulting in many mismatches [12]. To address this problem, Lazebnik et al. proposed constructing a local coordinate system to calculate rotation invariant gradient in [3]. They divided the interest region into several rings and accumulated the histograms of rotation invariant gradient in these subregions to construct the final descriptor, which is called RIFT (Rotation-Invariant Feature Transform). Although RIFT has rotation invariance without estimating the dominant orientation, it is less distinctive since the region division method causes the loss of spatial information [13].

Recently, Fan et al. proposed the interest regions can be divided using intensity orders of sample points [12]. With this division method and the rotation invariant gradient introduced in [3], they designed a novel local descriptor, MROGH (Multi-Support Region Order-Based Gradient Histogram), which showed better performance than traditional local descriptors in experiments. Along this way, many other descriptors, such as LIOP [14], OIOP [15], MIFH [16], have been proposed by using intensity order patterns of sample points rather than rotation invariant gradients. Compared to MROGH, they are constructed based on the single support region, thus greatly simplifying the construction process and reducing the computational time. However, most intensity order patterns only use a small number of neighboring points to describe the sample point in the interest region, which leads to a lot of useful information being lost.

In this paper, we propose a rotation invariant descriptor using multi-directional and high-order gradients (MDHOG). Our main contributions are summarized as follow:

– We design a new dense sampling strategy based on the local rotation invariant coordinate system. This method gets more neighboring points of the sample point in the interest region so that the intensity distribution of the sample point neighborhood can be described better.
– In order to enhance the discriminability of our descriptor, we propose a multi-directional strategy and use 1D Gaussian derivative filters to encode MDHOG for the sample point, whose histograms are used to build the final descriptor.

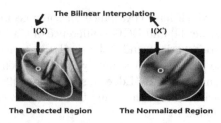

The Detected Region   The Normalized Region

Fig. 1. The detected elliptical region is normalized to the circular region. And $I(X')$, which denotes the intensity value of the point X', can be calculated by using the bilinear interpolation.

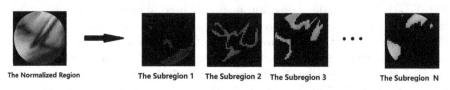

The Normalized Region   The Subregion 1   The Subregion 2   The Subregion 3   The Subregion N

Fig. 2. The normalized region is divided into N subregions based on intensity orders.

2   Related Works

In this section, we introduce some methods which can be used for constructing MDHOG.

2.1   Interest Region Detection and Normalization

As previously mentioned, most point detectors can get scale and location information of keypoints, which is covariant under the similarity transformations. So, they are not robust to complex viewpoint changes which can be approximated by the affine transformations. In this paper, we focus on some region detectors, such as Harris-affine, Hessian-affine and so on. They can get many elliptical regions which are covariant under the affine transformations. In fact, one affine transformation can be decomposed into three single-parameter transformations: rotation, scale and shear. In order to achieve scale and shear invariance, the detected elliptical regions are usually normalized to circular regions [3,10,12], as shown in Fig. 1.

2.2   Interest Region Division Based on Intensity Orders

In fact, when we use the histogram-based method to construct the local descriptor, the spatial information of the normalized region is discarded. A remedy is to divide the region. Then, the descriptor is generated by concatenating the histograms of all subregions. The traditional division methods are based on the spatial location. For example, SIFT adopts a 4×4 squared grid to divide the

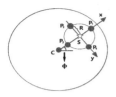 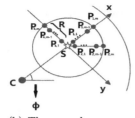 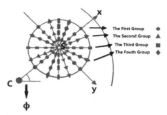

(a) The rotation invariant coordinate system.

(b) The new dense sampling strategy to get neighboring points not only along the circle but also along the radial direction.

(c) When $n = 16$ and $m = 4$, 64 neighboring points can be divided into 4 groups. Different shapes are used to indicate which group the neighboring point belongs to.

Fig. 3. The dense sampling strategy and the multi-directional strategy.

normalized region. It's obviously the order of 16 subregions will change after rotation. Therefore, this method needs to estimate a dominant orientation of the region to achieve rotation invariance. In [3], Lazebnik *et al.* proposed dividing the normalized region into several rings. Theoretically, the order of these rings won't change after rotation. However, the sample points with far distance are divided into the same ring, thus resulting in the loss of the spatial information.

Recently, more and more researchers pay attention to the division method based on intensity orders of sample points [12]. In this method, we need to sort all sample points in the normalized region according to their intensity values. Then, this non-descending sequence is equality divided into N groups. As shown in Fig. 2, a subregion consist of the points belonging to the same group.

2.3 Rotation Invariant Coordinate System and Gradient

In order to calculate rotation invariant gradient or intensity order pattern, a local coordinate system should be established [3]. As shown in Fig. 3(a), $\overrightarrow{CS}$ is defined as the positive x-axis of this coordinate system, where C is the central point of the normalized region and S is the sample point.

When we set the radius of the circle, which is denoted by R, n neighboring points $\{P_1, P_2, ..., P_n\}$ can be regularly sampled along the circle, whose coordinates in the global coordinate system can be calculated by

$$X_{P_i} = X_S + R \cdot cos(i \cdot \frac{2\pi}{n} + \phi) \qquad Y_{P_i} = Y_S + R \cdot sin(i \cdot \frac{2\pi}{n} + \phi) \quad (1)$$

where (X_S, Y_S) is the position of S in the global coordinate system and $\phi = arctan\left(\frac{Y_S - Y_C}{X_S - X_C}\right)$. Obviously, the local coordinates of these neighboring points won't change, when we rotate the normalized region at any angle. When $n = 4$, as shown in Fig. 3(a), we can define the rotation invariant gradient by

$$Dx(S) = I(P_1) - I(P_3) \qquad Dy(S) = I(P_4) - I(P_2) \quad (2)$$

Then, the gradient magnitude and orientation can be calculate by

$$m(S) = \sqrt{Dx(S)^2 + Dy(S)^2} \qquad \theta(S) = arctan\left(\frac{Dy(S)}{Dx(S)}\right) \qquad (3)$$

3 Our Method

In this section, we demonstrate in detail how MDHOG is constructed. First, we use the methods introduced in Sect. 2 to normalize and divide the interest region. Then, with the local rotation invariant coordinate system, a new dense sampling strategy is designed to get more neighboring points of the sample point in the normalized region. Finally, we propose a multi-directional strategy and use 1D Gaussian derivative filters to encode MDHOG for the sample point. This gradient-based feature can better describe the intensity distribution of the sample point neighborhood and has high discriminability.

3.1 A New Dense Sampling Strategy

As shown in Fig. 3(a), most previously works usually use a small number of neighboring points, which are regularly sampled along the circle, to describe the sample point in the normalized region [12–15]. Therefore, much useful information about the intensity distribution of the sample point neighborhood is lost, especially, when the radius of the circle is large.

To address this problem, we propose a new dense sampling strategy to get neighboring points not only along the circle but also along the radial direction. Suppose $n \times m$ neighboring points $(P_{1,1}, ..., P_{1.m-1}.P_{1,m}, ..., P_{k,1}, ..., P_{k,m-1}, P_{k,m}, ..., P_{n,1}, ..., P_{n,m-1}, P_{n,m})$ are regularly sampled around the sample point, shown in Fig. 3(b), their coordinates in the global coordinate system can be calculated by

$$X_{P_{i,j}} = X_S + j \cdot \left(\frac{R}{m}\right) \cdot cos(i \cdot \frac{2\pi}{n} + \phi) \qquad Y_{P_{i,j}} = Y_S + j \cdot \left(\frac{R}{m}\right) \cdot sin(i \cdot \frac{2\pi}{n} + \phi) \quad (4)$$

where n is the number of neighboring points along the circle, and m is the number of neighboring points along the radial direction. In our paper, in order to use the multi-directional strategy introduced in Sect. 3.2, we set $n = 4k$, $k \in \{1, 2, 3, ...\}$.

3.2 The Multi-directional and High-Order Gradients

In fact, when the number of neighboring points along the circle is n, $\frac{n}{4}$ directional gradients can be calculated. For example, when $n = 16$ and $m = 4$, Fig. 4(c) shows that we can divide 64 neighboring points into 4 groups and estimate the directional gradient for each group.

In order to obtain MDHOG, which means the high-order gradient based on this multi-directional strategy, we use the $(2k - 1)$-th Gaussian derivative filter,

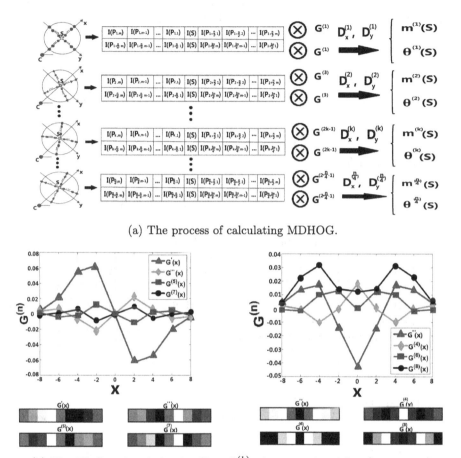

(a) The process of calculating MDHOG.

(b) The 1D Gaussian derivative filter $G^{(k)}$ when $m = 4$ and $k \in \{1, 2, ..., 7, 8\}$.

Fig. 4. The multi-directional and high-order gradients.

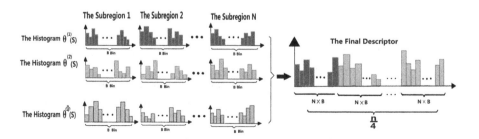

Fig. 5. The process of constructing the final descriptor.

which is denoted by $G^{(2k-1)}$, to convolute with the neighboring points in the k-th group. Specifically, we define MDHOG by

$$D_x^k(S) = G^{(2k-1)} \otimes I_k \qquad D_y^k(S) = G^{(2k-1)} \otimes I_{k+\frac{n}{4}} \qquad (5)$$

I_k is constructed by

$$I_k = (I(P_{k,m}), I(P_{k,m-1}), ..., I(P_{k,1}), I(S), I(P_{k+\frac{n}{2},1}), ..., I(P_{k+\frac{n}{2},m-1}), I(P_{k+\frac{n}{2},m})) \qquad (6)$$

where $k \in \{1, 2, ..., \frac{n}{4}\}$. Similar to Eq. 3, the magnitude and orientation of MDHOG can be defined by

$$m^k(S) = \sqrt{D_x^k(S)^2 + D_y^k(S)^2} \qquad \theta^k(S) = arctan\left(\frac{D_y^k(S)}{D_x^k(S)}\right) \qquad (7)$$

Figure 4(a) shows the process of calculating MDHOG more clearly. Obviously, the size of $G^{(2k-1)}$ should be $(2m+1)$. As shown in Fig. 4(b), we calculate the 1D Gaussian derivative filter $G^{(t)}$ when $m = 4$ and $t \in \{1, 2, ..., 7, 8\}$. In theory, all of them can be used to computer MDOGH. However, based on some experimental results, we observed that the orientation of MDHOG is distributed in a narrow interval when t is even. This problem will reduce the discriminability of the final descriptor. So, in this paper, we only use G', G''', G^5 and G^7.

3.3   The Construction of the Final Descriptor

As mentioned above, we divide the normalized region into N subregions based on intensity orders and sample n neighboring points around the sample point. Similar to [12], we first calculate the histogram of $\theta^k(S)$ for each subregion and use $m^k(S)$ as the weight function, $k \in \{1, 2, ..., \frac{n}{4}\}$. As shown in Fig. 5, $[0, 2\pi)$ is split into B equal bins, which determines the dimension of the histogram. Then, for each k, N histograms for all subregions are concatenated. Obviously, we get $\frac{n}{4}$ concatenated histograms which can be used to construct the final descriptor. Therefore, the dimension of the descriptor is $B \cdot N \cdot \frac{n}{4}$.

Table 1. The parameters of MDHOG.

Denotation	Values	Description
R	4,6,8	The radius of the circle
n	8,12,16	The number of neighboring points along the circle
m	2,3,4	The number of neighboring points along the radial direction
N	4	The number of subregions
B	16	The number of orientation bins

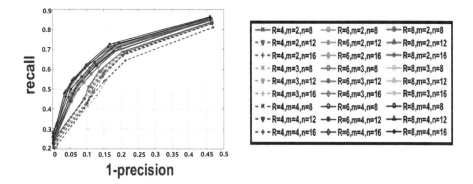

Fig. 6. The average performance of our descriptor with different parameter settings for the Hessian-affine.

4 Experiments

In this section, experiments using popular image databases were carried out to evaluate the performance of MDHOG. First, in order to get the optimal parameter setting, we tested the performance of our descriptors constructed by using different parameter settings. Then, image matching and object recognition experiment were conducted on the Oxford database and 53 objects database. Five commonly used local descriptors were chosen for comparison: SIFT, DAISY, MROGH, LIOP and OIOP. Our results show that MDHOG hold better performances for image transformations than other traditional local descriptors.

4.1 Parameters Evaluation

In Table 1, we list all parameters which are used to constructing MDHOG. In [12], Fan *et al.* have found that the performance of MROGH is improved with the increase of N and B. Therefore, we fix their values and focus on the influence of (R, n, m) on MDHOG. To this end, we downloaded 135 image pairs from Mikolajczyk's website [17]. They are mainly selected from three databases: Rotation, Zoom, Rotation & Zoom. Then, we calculated MDHOG for interest regions in each image which were detected by Hessian-affine. Finally, the evaluation codes [18] provided by Mikolajczyk and Schmid [10] were used to computer the *recall*-(*1-precision*) curves of MDHOG with different parameter settings. As shown in Fig. 6, we find the performance of MDHOG is improved with the increase of n. This is because n completely determines the dimension MDHOG when we fix the values of N and B. In addition, when R is large, MDHOG with larger m achieves better results. This proves that the dense sampling strategy can indeed get more information about the sample point neighborhood. Considering the computational efficiency, the max settings of m and n are 4 and 16. Also, we observe that MDHOG achieves the best performance, when $R = 8$, $n = 12$ and $m = 4$. Therefore, it will be used in the subsequent experiments.

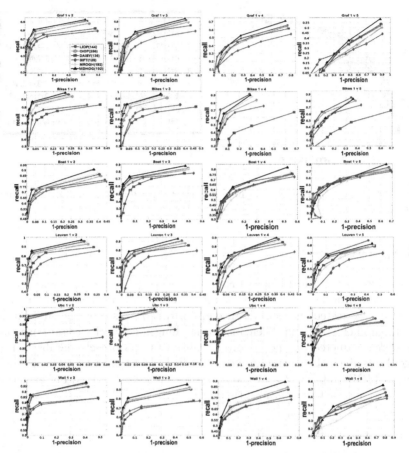

(a) Experimental results under viewpoint changes, image blur, rotation &zoom, illumination changes and JPEG compression. The interest region was detected by Hessian-affine.

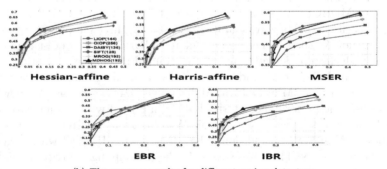

(b) The average results for different region detectors.

Fig. 7. The experimental results of image matching.

4.2   Image Matching

To test the stability and discriminability of MDHOG for diverse image transformations, we chose the Oxford database [19] which is widely used to evaluate the performance of local descriptors. SIFT (128D), DAISY (136D), MROGH (192D), LIOP (144D) and OIOP (256D, with standard quantization) were chosen for comparison, whose codes were provided by their authors. To be fair, all descriptors were calculated based on the single support region which was detected by using Hessian-affine. In fact, in order to increase the dimension of MROGH, we used the multi-directional strategy introduced in Sect. 3.2 by setting $n = 12$, $m = 1$, $R = 6$, $B = 16$, $N = 4$. The performance of these descriptors were evaluated by the same criterion as in Sect. 4.1. As shown in Fig. 7(a), MDOHG has outstanding performance over other descriptors in most cases, especially for viewpoint changes. MDOGH and MROGH have the same dimensions and both use the multi-directional strategy. Therefore, the performance difference between them indicates that high-order gradients calculated by using the dense sampling strategy and 1D Gaussian derivative filters do have better stability and discriminability.

For further comparison, we repeated the image matching experiment by using various region detectors, including Hessian-affine, Harris-affine, MSER, IBR and EBR. The average results of image matching are shown in Fig. 7(b). We can find MDHOG achieves better results than others on Hessian-affine, Harris-affine and IBR. Meanwhile, when EBR or MSER is used to detect interest regions, the image matching result obtained by using MDHOG are also comparable to the best one.

4.3   Object Recognition

We conducted object recognition experiment on the 53 objects database [20]. As shown in Fig. 8, this database contains 53 objects. For each object, five images are taken from different viewpoints. We followed the evaluation criterion used in [12,15,16]. Suppose that I_Q and I_P are two images, and $(f_1^Q, f_2^Q, ..., f_U^Q)$ and $(f_1^P, f_2^P, ..., f_V^P)$ are feature sets of them, respectively. The similarity between two images is defined by

$$Sim(I_Q, I_P) = \frac{\sum_{i,j} H(f_i^Q, f_j^P)}{U \times V} \tag{8}$$

where

$$H(f_i^Q, f_j^P) = \begin{cases} 1 & if \ \ Euclidean\_distance(f_i^Q, f_j^P) < T \\ 0 & Otherwise \end{cases} \tag{9}$$

For each image in the 53 object database, we computed its similarity to others and obtained four images which are most similar to it. (*The number of correctly returned images/The number of total returned images*) is recorded as the recognition accuracy. In order to achieve the best results, we set different T for different local descriptors.

Table 2. The accuracy of object recognition on the 53 objects database with different local descriptors.

Descriptor	Accuracy	Description	Accuracy	Description	Accuracy
SIFT	45.9%	DAISY	60.6%	LIOP	64.3%
OIOP	58.1%	MROGH	61.2%	MDHOG	**69.7%**

Fig. 8. Some images in the 53 objects database.

In Table 2, we can find that MDHOG performs better than other commonly used local descriptors, consistent with the image matching experiment in Sect. 4.2. Meanwhile, with the multi-directional strategy, MROGH constructed based on the single support region has also achieved good recognition accuracy.

5 Conclusion

In this paper, we propose a novel local descriptor using multi-directional and high-order gradients (MDHOG), which is invariant under the rotation transformations. First, with the local rotation invariant coordinate system, a dense sampling strategy is designed to get more neighboring points of the sample point in the interest region. This method can get richer information about the intensity distribution of the sample point neighborhood. Then, based on this sampling strategy, we design a multi-directional strategy and use 1D Gaussian derivative filters to encode MDHOG for the sample point. The histograms of MDHOG are used to build the final descriptor. Our experimental results show that the proposed descriptor holds better performances for image matching and object recognition than traditional local descriptors.

Acknowledgment. This work has partly been funded by the National Key R&D Program of China (No. 2017YFB1002703) and the National Natural Science Foundation of China (Grant No. 60873164, 61227802 and 61379082). We would like to thank the reviewers for their valuable comments.

References

1. Lowe, D.G.: Distinctive image features from scale-image keypoints. Int. J. Comput. Vis. **60**, 91–11 (2004)
2. Tuytelaars, T., Gool, L.V.: Matching widely separated views based on affine invariantfeatures. Int. J. Comput. Vis. **59**, 61–85 (2004)
3. Lazebnik, S., Schmid, C., Ponce, J.: A sparse texture representationusing local affine regions. IEEE Trans. Pattern Anal. Mach. Intell. **27**(8), 1265–1278 (2005)
4. Harris, C., Stephens, M.: A combined corner and edge detector. In: Proceedings Alvey Visualization Conference, pp. 147–151 (1988)
5. Mikolajczyk, K., Schmid, C.: Scale & affine invariant interest point detectors. Int. J. Comput. Vis. **60**(1), 63–86 (2004)
6. Mikolajczyk, K., et al.: A comparison of affine region detectors. Int. J. Comput. Vis. **65**(1–2), 43–72 (2004)
7. Matas, J., Chum, O., Martin, U., Pajdla, T.: Robust wide baseline stereo from maximally stable extremal regions. Proc. BMVC **1**, 384–393 (2002)
8. Gauglitz, S., Höllerer, T., Turk, M.: Evaluation of interest point detectors and feature descriptors for visual tracking. Int. J. Comput. Vis. **94**(3), 335–360 (2011)
9. Ke, Y., Sukthankar, R.: PCA-SIFT: a more distinctive representation for local image descriptors. In: Proceedings of CVPR, pp. 506–513 (2004)
10. Mikolajczyk, K., Schmid, C.: A performance evaluation of local descriptors. IEEE Trans. Pattern Anal. Mach. Intell. **27**(10), 1615–1630 (2005)
11. Tola, E., Lepetit, V., Fua, P.: DAISY: an effcient dense descriptor applied to wide-baseline stereo. IEEE Trans. Pattern Anal. Mach. Intell. **32**(5), 815–830 (2010)
12. Fan, B., Wu, F.C., Hu, Z.Y.: Aggregating gradient distributions into intensity orders: a novel local image descriptor. In: Proceedings of CVPR, pp. 2377–2384 (2011)
13. Fan, B., Wu, F.C., Hu, Z.Y.: Rotationally invariant descriptors using intensity order pooling. IEEE Trans. Pattern Anal. Mach. Intell. **34**(10), 2031–2045 (2012)
14. Wang, Z.H., Fan, B., Wu, F.C.: Local intensity order pattern for feature description. In: Proceedings of ICCV, pp. 603–610 (2011)
15. Wang, Z.H., Fan, B., Wu, F.C.: Exploring local and overall ordinal information for robust feature description. IEEE Trans. Pattern Anal. Mach. Intell. **38**(11), 2198–2211 (2016)
16. Yang, Y., Duan, F.J., Ma, L.: A rotationally invariant descriptor based on mixed intensity feature histograms. Pattern Recognit. **76**, 162–174 (2018)
17. Mikolajczyk's Website. http://lear.inrialpes.fr/people/mikolajczyk/. Accessed 30 Aug 2018
18. The Evaluation Codes. http://www.robots.ox.ac.uk/~vgg/research/affine/desc. Accessed 30 Aug 2018
19. The Oxford Database. http://www.robots.ox.ac.uk/~vgg/research/affine/. Accessed 30 Aug 2018
20. The 53 Objects Database. http://www.vision.ee.ethz.ch/datasets/. Accessed 30 Aug 2018

Quasi-Monte-Carlo Tree Search for 3D Bin Packing

Hailiang Li[1](✉), Yan Wang[1](✉), DanPeng Ma[2](✉), Yang Fang[2](✉),
and Zhibin Lei[1](✉)

[1] Hong Kong Applied Science and Technology Research Institute Company
Limited, Sha Tin, Hong Kong
{harleyli, yanwang, lei}@astri.org
[2] Anji Technology Company Limited, Shanghai, China
{madanpeng, fangyang}@anji-tec.com

Abstract. The three-dimensional bin packing problem (3D-BPP) is a classic NP-hard combinatorial optimization problem, which is difficult to be solved with an exact solution, so lots of heuristic approaches have been proposed to generate approximated solutions to this problem. In this paper, we present a novel heuristic search algorithm, named Quasi-Monte-Carlo Tree Search (QMCTS), where efficiency and effectiveness are balanced via clipping off the search space in both the breadth and depth range. Furthermore, the QMCTS scheme can be sped up in parallel processing mode, which can theoretically outperform the depth-first search (DFS) and breadth-first search (BFS) based algorithms. Experiments on the benchmark datasets show that the proposed QMCTS approach can consistently outperform state-of-the-art algorithms.

Keywords: 3D bin packing problem · Monte-Carlo tree search
Combinatorial optimization problem

1 Introduction

Bin packing problems are classical and popular optimization problems since 1970s, which have been extensively studied and widely applied in many applications [2], such as manufacturing, computer memory management [3], cloud resource assignment [4], logistics transportation, etc. As a set of combinatorial optimization problems [5], the bin packing problems have been derived into numerous variants based on different constraints for specific application scenarios, such as 1D/2D/3D packing, linear packing, packing with weight or cost constraint, etc. The objective of the single container 3D bin packing problem (3D-BPP) is to find a solution to pack a set of small boxes with possibly different sizes into a large bin, so that the volume utilization of the bin is maximized. A typical 3D bin packing solution is shown in Fig. 1. From decision making point of view, the 3D-BPP can be considered as a Markov Decision Process (MDP), where each step with an observed state $s_t \in S$ (in the state space: S), an action $a_t \in A$ (in the action space: A) is chosen to be taken based on a policy $\pi : S \to A$, and the target is to find an optimal policy π^* to fulfill the packing task. Since the 3D-BPP is strongly NP-hard, it is hard to find an exact solution; therefore, lots of research works

© Springer Nature Switzerland AG 2018
J.-H. Lai et al. (Eds.): PRCV 2018, LNCS 11256, pp. 384–396, 2018.
https://doi.org/10.1007/978-3-030-03398-9_33

that focus on approximation algorithms and heuristic algorithms have been proposed. The first approximation algorithm for the 3D-BPP was proposed in [7] and its performance bound was thoroughly investigated. Based on conventional heuristic algorithms for the 3D-BPP and the Monte-Carlo Tree Search (MCTS) [1, 10], a novel heuristic search algorithm with dynamically trimmed search space, namely, the Quasi-Monte-Carlo Tree Search (QMCTS), is proposed to achieve high efficiency and effectiveness.

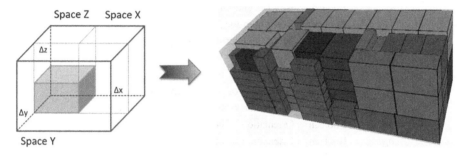

Fig. 1. A visualized 3D bin packing process of the first step (left), in which one box is packed into the left-bottom-back corner then cut the original space into 3 sub-spaces, and a final packing solution (right) generated by our system for the case BR7_0.

The remainder of this paper is organized as follows: the objective of the 3D-BPP is set and its related works are reviewed in Sect. 2. The proposed QMCTS scheme is detailed and discussed in Sect. 3. Its evaluation and performance comparison with state-of-the-art heuristic based approaches are shown in Sect. 4. Conclusions are drawn in Sect. 5, where future works will be envisioned as well.

2   Problem Definition and Related Work

2.1   The Objective of 3D Bin Packing Problem

Given a bin $\mathbb{B}$ with its dimensions: width (W), height (H) and depth (D), and a set of boxes with their respective dimensions: width (w_i), height (h_i) and depth (d_i), the objective of 3D Bin Packing Problem (3D-BPP) is to find a solution that maximizes the volume utilization by filling these boxes into the given bin $\mathbb{B}$. This objective is represented in the following Eq. (1) with the constraints specified from Eq. (2a) to Eq. (2p). The left-bottom-back of the bin is set as the $(0, 0, 0)$ coordinate, and (x_i, y_i, z_i) is the coordinate of box_i in the given bin $\mathbb{B}$. The details of variables used in the 3D-BPP definition are described in Table 1.

Table 1. The variables used for the 3D-BPP definition

Variable	Data type	Meaning
W	Integer	The width of the bin
H	Integer	The height of the bin
D	Integer	The depth of the bin
x_i	Integer	Box i coordinate in x axis
y_i	Integer	Box i coordinate in y axis
z_i	Integer	Box i coordinate in z axis
$\mathbb{I}_i$	Boolean	Box i is chosen or not
s_{ij}	Boolean	Box i is in the left side of box j or not
u_{ij}	Boolean	Box i is under the box j or not
b_{ij}	Boolean	Box i is at the back side of box j or not
δ_{i1}	Boolean	Orientation of box i is front-up or not
δ_{i2}	Boolean	Orientation of box i is front-down or not
δ_{i3}	Boolean	Orientation of box i is side-up or not
δ_{i4}	Boolean	Orientation of box i is side-down or not
δ_{i5}	Boolean	Orientation of box i is bottom-up or not
δ_{i6}	Boolean	Orientation of box i is bottom-down or not

Based on the descriptions of the 3D-BPP and notations in Table 1, given a bin $\mathbb{B}$, the mathematical formulation for obtaining maximum volume utilization $u(\mathbb{B})$ on the 3D-BPP is defined as follows.

$$\max_{\mathbb{I}_i} u(\mathbb{B}) = max_{\mathbb{I}_i} \sum_i \mathbb{I}_i \times (x_i \times y_i \times z_i) \tag{1}$$

$$s.t. \begin{cases} u(\mathbb{B}) \leq W \times H \times I & \text{(a)} \\ \mathbb{I}_i \in \{0,1\} & \text{(b)} \\ s_{ij}, \ u_{ij}, \ b_{ij} \in \{0,1\} & \text{(c)} \\ \delta_{i1} \ \delta_{i2} \ \delta_{i3} \ \delta_{i4} \ \delta_{i5} \ \delta_{i6} \in \{0,1\} & \text{(d)} \\ s_{ij} + u_{ij} + b_{ij} = 1 & \text{(e)} \\ \delta_{i1} + \delta_{i2} + \delta_{i3} + \delta_{i4} + \delta_{i5} + \delta_{i6} = 1 & \text{(f)} \\ x_i - x_j + W \times s_{ij} \leq W - w_i^* & \text{(h)} \\ y_i - y_j + H \times u_{ij} \leq H - h_i^* & \text{(i)} \\ z_i - z_j + D \times b_{ij} \leq D - d_i^* & \text{(j)} \\ 0 \leq x_i \leq W - w_i^* & \text{(k)} \\ 0 \leq y_j \leq H - h_i^* & \text{(l)} \\ 0 \leq z_j \leq D - d_i^* & \text{(m)} \\ w_i^* = \delta_{i1} w_i + \delta_{i2} w_i + \delta_{i3} h_i + \delta_{i4} h_i + \delta_{i5} d_i + \delta_{i6} d_i & \text{(n)} \\ h_i^* = \delta_{i1} h_i + \delta_{i2} d_i + \delta_{i3} w_i + \delta_{i4} d_i + \delta_{i5} w_i + \delta_{i6} h_i & \text{(o)} \\ d_i^* = \delta_{i1} d_i + \delta_{i2} h_i + \delta_{i3} d_i + \delta_{i4} w_i + \delta_{i5} h_i + \delta_{i6} w_i & \text{(p)} \end{cases} \tag{2}$$

where $s_{ij} = 1$ if box_i is in the left side of box_j, $u_{ij} = 1$ if box_i is under box_j, $b_{ij} = 1$ if box_i is in the back of box_j, $\delta_{i1} = 1$ if the orientation of box_i is front-up, $\delta_{i2} = 1$ if the orientation of box_i is front-down, $\delta_{i3} = 1$ if the orientation of box_i is side-up, $\delta_{i4} = 1$ if the orientation of box_i is side-down, $\delta_{i5} = 1$ if orientation of box_i is bottom-up, and $\delta_{i6} = 1$ if orientation of box_i is bottom-down. Constraints 2(n), (o), (p) denote the width, height and depth of box_i after orientating it. Constraints 2(e), (h), (i), (j) are used to make sure that there is no overlap between two packed boxes while constraints 2(k), (l), (m) are used to make sure that all boxes will not be put outside the bin, and constraint (2) guarantees that the total volume of all the packed boxes will not be greater than the volume of the given bin $\mathbb{B}$.

2.2   Related Works

Although there can be lots of constraints on a real application based the 3D-BPP, the volume utilization is the primary objective in most scenarios. Most research works focus on the Single Container Loading Problem (SCLP), which means there is only one given bin and a set of boxes. The SCLP problem is proved as an NP-hard problem in the strict sense [18], so an exact solution can only be attained for a problem with small number of boxes as an example shown in [17]. Lots of heuristics, metaheuristics and incomplete tree search based methods have been proposed to generate approximated solutions. These algorithms can be roughly classified into three categories: constructive methods, divide-and-conquer methods and local search methods. The constructive methods [15, 22] can yield loading plans when recursively packing boxes into a given bin until when there is no box left for packing or when there is no space to fill. The divide-and-conquer methods [20, 21] divide the space of the given bin into sub-spaces, then recursively solve all the sub packing problems in the divided sub-spaces, and finally combine all the sub-solutions into a complete solution. The local search methods [6, 22] start with an existing solution, then new solutions can be further produced by applying neighborhood operators repeatedly.

The approaches with the best performance in recent literature [15, 22] share similar algorithm structures with block building inside, and the block building based approaches are constructive methods. Compared to the approaches with original simple boxes, the basic elements in the block building based approaches are blocks, in which a block is compactly pre-packed with a subset of homogenous or approximately homogenous boxes. Each packing step of a block building based approach involves an additional step to search potential blocks for the left free space in the given bin, and this operation will be repeated until no block can be found or be packed into the bin. As block building based approaches are technically superior to their competitors, it is thus chosen as the underlying technique of this proposed scheme rather than approaches that are directly dealing with simple boxes.

3   Proposed Method

3.1   Monte-Carlo Tree Search for Game Playing

Monte Carlo Tree Search (MCTS) is a heuristic search algorithm for decision making and is most notably employed in game playing. A very famous example of using

MCTS on game playing is the computer Go programs [1]. Since its creation, a lot of improvements and variants have been published, and huge success has been achieved in board and card games such as chess, checkers, bridge, poker [27], and real-time video games.

The Workflow of Monte-Carlo Tree Search

Monte Carlo Tree Search (MCTS) is first employed in the Go game using the best-first search strategy, which is to find the best move (action) among all the potential moves. MCTS evaluates all the next move's expected long-term repay by simulation techniques (using stochastic playouts on game playing). Potential moves are generated unequally via Monte Carlo sampling based on the simulation performance, then the most promising move(s) will be analyzed and expanded. Conventional MCTS algorithm normally consists of the following four steps, as shown in Fig. 2:

- *Selection*: each round of the MCTS starts from the *root-node* and then select successive child-nodes down to a *leaf-node*. The *Selection* step tries to choose those child-nodes with exploration and exploitation strategy based on the biggest Upper Confidence Bound (UCB) value, the details of which will be discussed in the following section. With this strategy, the MCTS can expand the tree towards the most promising moves, which is the essence of MCTS.
- *Expansion*: unless *leaf-node* ends the game with a win/loss for either player, the *Expansion* process will create one child-node or several child-nodes and then choose one child-node as the *working-node* among them.
- *Simulation*: play with a random policy or with default policy to playout for the *working-node*.
- *Backpropagation*: based on the playout result (e.g., the played times and won times for game playing), the node information is updated on the path from *working-node* back up to the *root-node*.

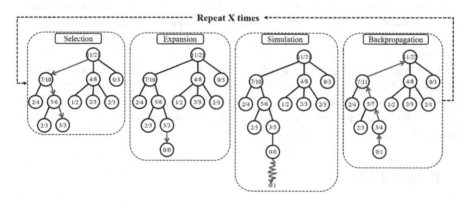

Fig. 2. The four regular steps of Monte Carlo Tree Search (MCTS) algorithm.

An example for the Go game playing is illustrated in Fig. 2, in which each tree node has the number of "won times/played times", which is obtained from previous working rounds. So, in the *Selection* diagram, the path of nodes from the *root-node* with statistics 11/21, to 7/10, and then 5/6, and finally ended up at 3/3 is chosen. Then the *leaf-node* with statistics 3/3 is chosen as the *working-node* and is expanded. After the *Simulation* operation, all nodes along the *Selection* path increase their simulation count (the denominator) and won times (the numerator). Rounds of MCTS will be repeated until time out or when other conditions are satisfied. Then the optimal plan for the game playing is chosen, which is the move path with child-nodes having the optimal values (high average win rate).

Exploration and Exploitation via Upper Confidence Bound
The main consideration on MCTS is how to choose child-nodes. On game playing, MCTS tries to exploit the nodes (states) with high average win rate after moves (actions), at the same time, explores the nodes with few simulations. This balance is also the essence of MCTS. The first formula for balancing exploitation and exploration in game playing is the UCT (Upper Confidence Bound (UCB) applied to Trees) strategy, which is the selection strategy of the standard MCTS. The UCT strategy can also work for move pruning, and its performance is comparable to other classical pruning algorithms, e.g., the α-β pruning [28], which is a powerful technique to prune suboptimal moves from the search tree.

Given a state (node) s and the set $A(s)$ of all potential actions (moves) in state s, MCTS selects the most promising action $a^* \in A(s)$ based on following UCB formula:

$$a^* = \mathrm{argmax}_{a \in A(s)} \left\{ Q(s,a) + c\sqrt{\frac{\ln N(s)}{N(s,a)}} \right\} \tag{3}$$

where $N(s)$ is the visiting count of the node (state) s, $N(s,a)$ is the count of move (action) a which is chosen based on node s visited and $Q(s,a)$ is the average score (performance) after all the simulations with move a acted based on node s. In this formula, the first component corresponds to exploitation, which is high for moves with high average win ratio, the second component corresponds to exploration, which is high for moves with few simulations, and the constant parameter c controls the balance. For the game playing, the UCB can be alternated with following formula:

$$UCB = \frac{w_i}{n_i} + c\sqrt{\frac{\ln N_i}{n_i}} \tag{4}$$

- w_i stands for the count of won for the node after the i_{th} move;
- n_i stands for the count of simulations for the node after the i_{th} move;
- N_i stands for the total number of simulations for the node's parent-node after the ith move;
- c is the balance coefficient to represent the trade-off between exploration and exploitation, which is equal to $\sqrt{2}$ theoretically and can also be set empirically.

3.2 Quasi-Monte-Carlo Tree Search for 3D Bin Packing

The Framework of Quasi-Monte-Carlo Tree Search

Based on the principle of the Monte-Carlo Tree Search (MCTS), a framework for solving the 3D Bin Packing problem (3D-BPP) is designed, in which conventional heuristic skills are incorporated into the MCTS based tree search scheme, and therefore, this new MCTS approximated scheme is named Quasi-Monte-Carlo Tree Search (QMCTS). As illustrated in Fig. 3, the proposed QMCTS algorithm also consists of four steps:

- *Selection*: start from *root-node* and select successive child-nodes down to a *leaf-node*. Different from MCTS for game playing, here each node stores an evaluation value of the volume utilization, rather than the win-rate. During the *Selection* step, a *leaf-node* is selected by traversing the tree from the *root-node* onwards until a *leaf-node* if all the child-nodes in the path are no smaller than their respective Top-K values.
- *Expansion*: Different from MCTS for game playing, that only one child-node is created for the *leaf-node*, for the 3D-BPP, several child-nodes are created as *working-nodes*.
- *Simulation*: Simulating playout(s) for *working-nodes* is a domain problem. For the 3D-BPP, as shown in Fig. 3, an evaluation module is designed to do the playout part. Firstly, the *working-nodes* are expanded with a certain number of layers (e.g., 2) and several *child-nodes* (e.g., 3) for each layer. Then calculate all the volume utilization values for all the leaf nodes in the last expanded layer via our defined Generalized Rapid Action Value Estimation (GRAVE) module, which means to pack a block for every step (start from a chosen leaf node) with default policy (i.e., packing with the max size block). Finally, the maximum volume utilization value achieved from all leaf nodes is set to the simulated *working-node*.
- *Backpropagation*: The volume utilization values for the *working-nodes* need to be updated after *Simulation* step. In the QMCTS scheme for the 3D-BPP, the volume utilization values are used to update a Top-K table, which will be described in the following section.

Exploration and Exploitation via Top-K Table

As discussed in previous section, conventional MCTS algorithms use the Upper Confidence Bound (UCB) to balance the exploitation of the estimated best move and the exploration of less visited moves for game playing. For the 3D-BPP, a Top-K table is designed to implement the same function as the UCB. As shown in Fig. 3, A Top-K table is designed, where each row works for each layer (except the top-layer: Layer0) for constructing the tree. To every tree node, only when its simulated volume utilization value is no less than the Top-K values in its layer (stored in the Top-K table), it can be expandable. Based on this idea, compared to conventional tree search based heuristic approaches, QMCTS can balance the search efficiency and effectiveness via clipping off the search space in both the breadth range and the depth range.

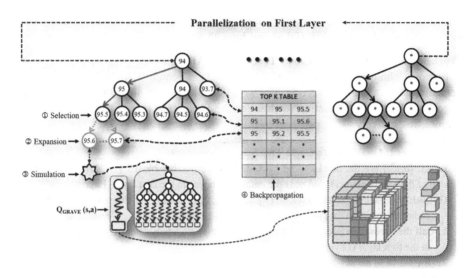

Fig. 3. The framework of Quasi-Monte-Carlo Tree Search (QMCTS) for 3D Bin Packing.

Generalized Rapid Action Value Estimation

The Rapid Action Value Estimation(RAVE) is a selection strategy proposed to speed up the move sampling inside the MCTS tree [23, 24], which can be considered as an enhancement to the All Moves As First (AMAF) [25, 26] strategy. RAVE recorded previous optimal moves as global optimal moves, which can be reused in future states. In this QMCTS scheme, a Generalized Rapid Action Value Estimation (GRAVE) strategy $Q_{GRAVE}(s, a)$ is proposed for the 3D-BPP, which is derived from the concept of RAVE in MCTS. Using the GRAVE strategy, starting from a chosen leaf node (state) s, an action a with default policy (i.e., packing the max size block) iterates until there is no block that can be packed or when other stop criterion is satisfied. After that, a packing plan can be generated and the its volume utilization will be compared with other rapid estimation values of the current node.

Parallelization of Quasi-Monte-Carlo Tree Search

The nature of MCTS, with its repeated and rapid playouts along with separable steps in the algorithm, enables parallel processing. There are generally three ways to parallelize search in an MCTS tree: at the leaves of the search tree, throughout the entire tree, and at its root. The parallelization scheme of QMCTS is to combine the merits from tree and root parallelization in MCTS. Firstly, in the *root-node*, multiple independent trees are built by separate threads, but different from the root parallelization in MCTS, all the threads can communicate among them via reading from and writing to the Top-K table, as illustrated in Fig. 3. Same to the tree parallelization in MCTS, multiple threads perform all four phases of the QMCTS scheme (descend through the search tree, add nodes, conduct playouts and propagate statistics with the Top-K table) at the same time. To prevent data corruption from simultaneous memory access, mutexes (locks) are placed on all the working threads for writing the shared Top-K table. The QMCTS scheme can be sped up in parallel process mode, which is able to theoretically out-perform the depth-first search (DFS) and breadth-first search (BFS) based algorithms.

Workflow of Quasi-Monte-Carlo Tree Search Algorithm

The main technique of the Quasi-Monte-Carlo Tree Search (QMCTS) algorithm has been discussed in previous section. The workflow of QMCTS algorithm is described in Algorithm 1 and the evaluation module for the *Simulation* step is described in Algorithm 2, respectively.

Algorithm 1: Quasi-Monte-Carlo Tree Search Procedure:

Input: $\{b_i\}_{i=1}^N$ are the blocks to be packed, N is the number blocks. $\{W \times H \times D\}$ is the size of the bin (container), and m is the number of nodes in the first layer (Layer0).

Output: the packing solution: $\wp^* = (P_1, ..., P_i, ..., P_N)$, where P_i is the placement, which means the position (x_i, y_i, z_i) of the block b_i to be placed.

1: Call the *evaluation procedure* to evaluate volume utilization values for all the m nodes in the first layer (Layer0).

2: **for** $t=1$ to m **do in parallelization mode**

   Do:

   Selection: From the *root-node* in Layer0 to all the *leaf-nodes*, select a *leaf-node* which is expandable, i.e., the volume utilization values of all the *tree-nodes* on the trace path are no less than their corresponding Top-K values in the Top-K table for their respective layers;

   Expansion: Expand current selected *leaf-node* with a certain number of *child-nodes*;

   Simulation: Call the *evaluation procedure* to evaluate all the volume utilization values for all the expanded *child-nodes*;

   Backpropagation: Check all the volume utilization values of the expanded *child-nodes*, set non-expandable if the value is less than the minimum of all the Top-K values in the same layer; Otherwise, set it expandable and put its value into the Top-K value list and update the list. Compute current packing solution and update the best packing solution: $\wp^*$.

   Until no *leaf-node* is expandable
   end for

3: Return the final best packing solution: $\wp^* = (P_1, ..., P_i, ..., P_N)$.

Algorithm 2: Evaluation Procedure:

Input: a *tree-node $node_i$* with current placement situation $P = (P_1, ..., P_i)$, and the remaining block list: $\{b_i\}_{i=j}^N$.

Output: the volume utilization.

1: Expand from the *working-node $node_i$* with a certain number of layers, and each layer contains a certain number of *child-nodes*;

2: Compute all the volume utilization values for all the *leaf-nodes* in the last expanded layer using the defined GRAVE module, which is to pack every remaining space with default policy (i.e., packing each space with maximum-sized block);

3: Return the maximum value from all the computed values.

---

4 Experiments

The proposed Quasi-Monte-Carlo Tree Search (QMCTS) algorithm is compared with a number of state-of-the-art algorithms with these practical benchmark datasets: BR1–BR7, including the Iterated Construction (IC) [11], the Simulated Annealing (SA) [12], the Variable Neighborhood Search (VNS) [13], the Fit Degree Algorithm (FDA) [14], the Container Loading by Tree Search (CLTRS) [15] and the Multi-Layer Heuristic Search (MLHS) [16]. The experimental results are listed in Table 2 (some statistics come from the published paper). As the data in the table shown, our proposed QMCTS method is obviously superior to most listed algorithms and even can achieve an average more 0.1% volume utilization gain when compared to the best algorithm.

Table 2. Comparison on BR instances (BR1–BR7)

Method ⇒	IC	SA	VNS	FDA	CLTRS	MLHS	QMCTS
BR1	91.60	93.40	94.93	92.92	95.05	94.91	**95.12**
BR2	91.99	93.49	95.19	93.93	95.43	95.48	**95.55**
BR3	92.30	93.24	94.99	93.71	95.47	95.69	**95.73**
BR4	92.36	93.00	94.71	93.68	95.18	95.54	**95.68**
BR5	91.90	92.63	94.33	93.73	95.00	95.42	**95.49**
BR6	91.51	92.68	94.04	93.63	94.79	95.39	**95.47**
BR7	91.01	92.03	93.53	93.14	94.24	95.00	**95.14**
Avg	91.81	92.92	94.53	93.53	95.02	95.35	**95.45**

Table 3 lists the properties of BR instances (BR1–BR7). The heterogeneity gets higher as the box type value gets larger, no matter how the number of type gets smaller.

Table 3. Properties of BR instances (BR1–BR7)

Dataset ⇒	BR1	BR2	BR3	BR4	BR5	BR6	BR7
Box type	3	5	8	10	12	15	20
Avg type number	50.15	27.33	16.79	13.28	11.07	8.76	6.52

From Fig. 4, it can be clearly seen that the QMCTS algorithm constantly outperforms other algorithms in all the test datasets. The computation time among different algorithms is difficult to compare, as they are written in different languages and some of them are tested in dated platforms. The QMCTS algorithm is implemented C++ and tested in Intel-i7 machine (8 cores). It can achieve an average speed of around 60 s for one case, which is acceptable for real applications.

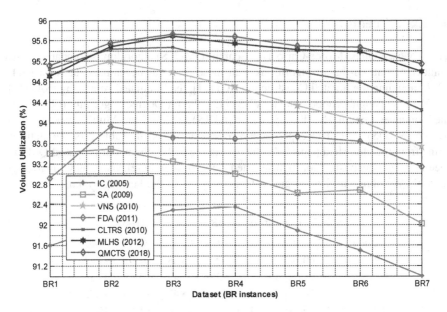

Fig. 4. Comparison on BR instances (BR1–BR7) between QMCTS and other methods

5   Conclusion and Future Works

During the past decades, classic three-dimensional bin packing problem (3D-BPP) has been tackled by lots of handcrafted heuristic algorithms, meanwhile the classic Monte-Carlo Tree Search (MCTS) algorithm has been widely employed in decision making applications, such as: computer games. In this paper, a Quasi-Monte-Carlo Tree Search (QMCTS) algorithm is proposed, which integrates conventional heuristic skills into the MCTS framework. The QMCTS scheme provides an efficient and effective tree search based heuristic technique to solve the 3D-BPP. Experiments have shown that QMCTS approach can consistently outperform recent state-of-the-art algorithms in terms of volume utilization. Furthermore, QMCTS can be sped up due to its parallel working mode.

In the future, firstly, intensive evaluation and optimization on dataset with higher heterogeneity, such as the BR8–BR15 datasets, is planned. Secondly, a more efficient Generalized Rapid Action Value Estimation (GRAVE) component is needed to further improve the QMCTS scheme. Finally, as the techniques on tasks with visual observations in Atari games [8], path-planning [9], and Google DeepMind's AlphaGo algorithm [10] have witnessed the recent achievements in deep reinforcement learning (DRL), the question whether the 3D-BPP can be solved by combing DRL technology and the QMCTS algorithm is worthy of future research. The recent attempt [19] has tried to use DRL to solve the 3D-BPP with a Long-Short Term Memory (LSTM) based Recurrent Neural Networks (RNN), though no performance comparison on the standard benchmark datasets has been shown. DRL based artificial intelligence (AI) algorithm remains to be a possible solution to solve the classical NP-hard 3D-BPP.

References

1. Gelly, S., Silver, D.: Monte-Carlo tree search and rapid action value estimation in computer Go. Artif. Intell. **175**(11), 1856–1875 (2011)
2. Coffman Jr., E.G., Csirik, J., Galambos, G., Martello, S., Vigo, D.: Bin packing approximation algorithms: survey and classification. In: Pardalos, P., Du, D.Z., Graham, R. (eds.) Handbook of Combinatorial Optimization, pp. 455–531. Springer, New York (2013). https://doi.org/10.1007/978-1-4419-7997-1_35
3. Bender, M.A., Bradley, B., Jagannathan, G., Pillaipakkamnatt, K.: Sum-of-squares heuristics for bin packing and memory allocation. J. Exp. Algorithmics **12**, 2.3:1–2.3:19 (2008)
4. Bansal, N., Elias, M., Khan, A.: Improved approximation for vector bin packing. In: Proceedings of the Twenty-Seventh Annual ACM-SIAM Symposium on Discrete Algorithms, SODA 2016, Philadelphia, PA, USA, pp. 1561–1579. Society for Industrial and Applied Mathematics (2016)
5. Korte, B., Vygen, J.: Combinatorial Optimization: Theory and Algorithms, 4th edn. Springer, Heidelberg (2007). https://doi.org/10.1007/978-3-540-71844-4
6. Gehring, H., Bortfeldt, A.: A parallel genetic algorithm for solving the container loading problem. Int. Trans. Oper. Res. **9**, 497–511 (2002)
7. Scheithauer, G.: A three dimensional bin packing algorithm. Elektronische Informationsverarbeitung und Kybernetik **27**(5/6), 263–271 (1991)
8. Mnih, V., et al.: Human-level control through deep reinforcement learning. Nature **518** (7540), 529–533 (2015)
9. Tamar, A., Wu, Y., Thomas, G., Levine, S., Abbeel, P.: Value iteration networks. In: Advances in Neural Information Processing Systems, pp. 2154–2162 (2016)
10. Silver, D., et al.: Mastering the game of Go with deep neural networks and tree search. Nature **529**(7587), 484–489 (2016)
11. Lim, A., Zhang, X.: The container loading problem. In: Proceedings of the 2005 ACM Symposium on Applied Computing. ACM (2005)
12. Zhang, D.F., Peng, Y., Zhu, W.X., et al.: A hybrid simulated annealing algorithm for the three-dimensional packing problem. Chin. J. Comput. **32**(11), 2147–2156 (2009)
13. Hansen, P., Mladenović, N., Moreno Pérez, J.A.: Variable neighborhood search: methods and applications. Ann. Oper. Res. **175**(1), 367–407 (2010)
14. He, K., Huang, W.: An efficient placement heuristic for three-dimensional rectangular packing. Comput. Oper. Res. **38**(1), 227–233 (2011)
15. Fanslau, T., Bortfeldt, A.: A tree search algorithm for solving the container loading problem. INFORMS J. Comput. **22**(2), 222–235 (2010)
16. Zhang, D., Peng, Y., Leung, S.C.H.: A heuristic block-loading algorithm based on multilayer search for the container loading problem. Comput. Oper. Res. **39**(10), 2267–2276 (2012)
17. Fekete, S.P., Schepers, J., van der Veen, J.C.: An exact algorithm for higher dimensional orthogonal packing. Oper. Res. **55**, 569–587 (2007)
18. Pisinger, D.: Heuristics for the container loading problem. Eur. J. Oper. Res. **141**, 382–392 (2002)
19. Hu, H., et al.: Solving a new 3D bin packing problem with deep reinforcement learning method. arXiv preprint arXiv:1708.05930 (2017). IJCAI-2017 Workshop
20. Lins, L., Lins, S., Morabito, R.: An n-tet graph approach for non-guillotine packings of n-dimensional boxes into an n-container. Eur. J. Oper. Res. **141**, 421–439 (2002)
21. Chien, C.F., Wu, W.T.: A recursive computational procedure for container loading. Comput. Ind. Eng. **35**, 319–322 (1998)

22. Parreño, F., Alvarez-Valdes, R., Oliveira, J.E., Tamarit, J.M.: Neighborhood structures for the container loading problem: a VNS implementation. J. Heuristics **16**, 1–22 (2010)

23. Gelly, S., Silver, D.: Combining online and offline knowledge in UCT. In: Proceedings of the 24th International Conference on Machine Learning, pp. 273–280. ACM (2007)

24. Finnsson, H., Bjornsson, Y.: Learning simulation control in general game-playing agents. In: AAAI, vol. 10, pp. 954–959 (2010)

25. Brugmann, B.: Monte Carlo Go. Max Planck Institute of Physics, Munchen, Germany, Technical report (1993)

26. Bouzy, B., Helmstetter, B.: Monte-Carlo Go developments. In: Van Den Herik, H.J., Iida, H., Heinz, E.A. (eds.) Advances in Computer Games. ITIFIP, vol. 135, pp. 159–174. Springer, Boston, MA (2004). https://doi.org/10.1007/978-0-387-35706-5_11

27. Van den Broeck, G., Driessens, K., Ramon, J.: Monte-Carlo tree search in poker using expected reward distributions. In: Zhou, Z.-H., Washio, T. (eds.) ACML 2009. LNCS (LNAI), vol. 5828, pp. 367–381. Springer, Heidelberg (2009). https://doi.org/10.1007/978-3-642-05224-8_28

28. Knuth, D.E., Moore, R.W.: An analysis of alpha-beta pruning. Artif. Intell. **6**(4), 293–326 (1975)

Gradient Center Tracking: A Novel Method for Edge Detection and Contour Detection

Yipei Su, Xiaojun Wu$^{(\boxtimes)}$, and Xiaoyou Zhou

Harbin Institute of Technology Shenzhen Graduate School, Shenzhen, China
`wuxj@hit.edu.cn`

Abstract. Detecting complete contours with less clutters is a very challenging task in edge detection. This paper presents a new lightweight edge detection method, Gradient Center Tracking (*GCT*), to detect the main contours including the boundary and the structural lines of the objects. This method tracks the center curve of contours in the gradient image and detects edges while tracking. It makes full use of the edge correlation and contour continuity to choose edge candidates, then computes the gradient intensities of the candidates to select the real edge. In this method, the intensity of the edge is redefined as the Directional Weighted Intensity (*DWI*) which helps to present the result with more complete contours and less clutters. The *GCT* method outperforms *Canny* detector and shows better results than several learning based methods. The comparison results are shown in our experiments and a typical scheme to apply the *GCT* method is also provided.

Keywords: Edge detection · Complete contours · Less clutters

1 Introduction

Edge detection, which aims to extract visually salient edges and object boundaries from natural images, is one of the most studied problems in computer vision. It is usually considered as a low-level technique, and varieties of high-level tasks have greatly benefited from the development of edge detection, such as object detection [7,23] and image segmentation [4,17,26]. Broadly speaking, edge detection methods can be generally grouped into two categories. (1) the classical edge detection methods based on brightness gradient and image filters represented by *Roberts* [20], *Prewitt* [18], *Sobel* [9], zero-crossing [15], and *Canny* [2]. (2) the modern methods, including methods based on the probability distributions and cluster [1,10,14], and methods based on learning [5,19,24]. Methods in the first category are usually lightweight and fast with good detection results in many cases. The *Canny* detector is nearly the most widely used edge detection method even now. However, these methods simply apply a highpass filter to detect edges, which lead to lots of redundancy. Furthermore, these

© Springer Nature Switzerland AG 2018
J.-H. Lai et al. (Eds.): PRCV 2018, LNCS 11256, pp. 397–407, 2018.
https://doi.org/10.1007/978-3-030-03398-9_34

methods show poor effect in a complex situation as their limited use of features. The proposed method in this paper, Gradient Center Tracking (GCT), is also based on brightness gradient and image filter, however, we redefine the gradient intensity of an edge by Directional Weighted Intensity (DWI) and set a tracking strategy Inherited Edge Detection (IED) with special starting points to effectively detect contours with less clutters. Directional structure elements help to complete our detected contours comparing to $Canny$ results. In the second category, the modern methods [6,13] show the state-of-the-art performance in some specific high-level applications such as object segmentation. However, there are still two main problems remained. (1) The modern edge detection methods are always much more complex in computation and demand higher-performance equipment. (2) They fail to meet the single response rule, which means that only one point should be detected for each given edge. This rule is declared by $Canny$ and widely accepted in this filed. On the contrary, our GCT method is lightweight and fully meet the single response rule. Furthermore, for the contour detection task, both these two categories are two-step methods that they first detect edges independently, then connect them into contours by post process, such as topology coding [21]. On the contrary, our GCT method gets contours and edges simultaneously, which means no post process is needed and the detection result can apply to some subsequent work directly, such as segmentation task.

In recent years, the research on edge detection has developed into different directions to serve different applications. For examples, most of the learning-based methods are used in the object segmentation task [3,6,13]. While classical edge detection methods like $Canny$ and lots of other improved method based on $Canny$ [8,11,12,16,22,25] are widely adopted in the situation with simpler scene and high real-time requirements, such as the detecting tasks in industrial application. This paper presents a new lightweight edge detection method, Gradient Center Tracking (GCT), to extract the main contours including the boundary and the structural lines of the objects in a gray image. This method tracks the center curve of a contour in the gradient image and detect edges while tracking. It presents the result with more complete contours and less clutters. It outperforms $Canny$ detector and shows better results than several learning based methods in some application, such as the industrial scene.

The main contributions of this paper are as follows. (1) Propose a novel method, GCT, to unite edge detection and contour detection. (2) Propose a new local searching scheme based on the edge correlation and contour continuity. (3) Redefine the gradient intensity of an edge as weighted intensity along a certain direction (DWI).

Before the detailed description, it is necessary to explain the relationship among an edge, contours and edges. In this paper, an edge is defined as a detected point in an image, and "edges" means the detection result which can be divided into several contours according to visual perception. The details of GCT method are stated in Sect. 2 and the results of our experiment are presented in the Sect. 3.

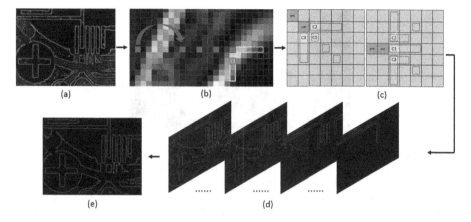

Fig. 1. Illustration of the *GCT* method. From (a) to (e): gradient image, searching new starting point, *IED* and *DWI*, tracking all the contours, detection result. Firstly, blur the source image to get a gradient image, then search a new starting point and apply the inherited edge detection method (*IED*) and a new defined edge intensity (*DWI*) to repeatedly find the "next edge" to complete the current contour. All the contours form the detection result.

2   Gradient Center Tracking Method

This paper proposes the Gradient Center Track method (*GCT*) to make full use of the edge correlation and contour continuity. Following this idea, the GCT method is designed as shown in Fig. 1. A given image will first be smoothed by *Sobel* or other detectors to compute the gradient image. Then *GCT* method begins by searching starting points in the gradient image and extend the contour by tracking the center of the high intensity band. While tracking, the Inherited Edge Detection (*IED*) strategy is applied to decide which point should be the next edge in current contour. A new definition of edge intensity marked as Directional Weighted Intensity (*DWI*) is used here. *GCT* method will repeatedly search a new starting point and track contours until all the contours are found.

2.1   Starting Point Selection

The first step of *GCT* method is to find a starting point. Figure 2 shows the strategy to select the starting points. It will first find a rough staring point and then modify it to be a real one. The *GCT* method sets a high enough threshold T_s in the gradient intensity and search the whole gradient image to choose the rough starting points. During this searching process, it skips the points that have been marked as edges already. Usually, a rough starting point is not a real edge, even though it is always close to the center of the gradient band.

In order to find a better starting point, the *GCT* method extends the rough starting point along the positive direction of the image coordinate axes, and then compute the weighted intensity to choose the best starting point. For example,

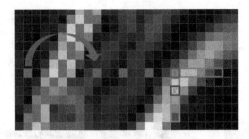

Fig. 2. Illustration of starting point searching in the gradient image. Every small square represents a pixel point, and there are two strong contours in this small picture. The searching will skip the first contour as it has already been detected (paint in green), then choose the point S (the single point with red box) and extend along the positive directions (the yellow boxes), next value each extended points by weighted intensity (the 3×3 region with red boxes), finally modify S into S' (the single point with green boxes). (Color figure online)

if the rough starting point is $P(x,y)$, then all the points $P(x+1,y)$, $P(x+2,y)$ ... $P(x+t,y)$ and $P(x,y+1)$, $P(x,y+2)$ ... $P(x,y+t)$ (t is set to be 5 in our experiment) will be valued by weighted intensity in a small region (a 3×3 region is used in the experiments), and the point with the highest intensity will be chosen to be the real starting point.

2.2 Define an Edge by Directional Weighted Intensity

For most of the exist edge detection methods, a prescribed gradient intensity threshold is required and the edges are the points with gradient intensity higher than the threshold. They use only the intensity of the point itself to compare with the threshold. However, this definition is based on a hypothesis that all the real edges have the local highest intensity. But it is difficult to make this assumption come true in many cases. For example, with noise in it, sometimes the intensity of the real edge may be a little lower than its neighbor points, although both the intensity of them are higher than the threshold. In this situation, the real edge will be abandoned for its non-maximum intensity according to the general edge definition.

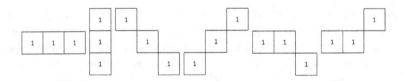

Fig. 3. Structural elements for direction expansion.

In this paper, the intensity of the edge is redefined as the weighted intensity along a directional, marked as DWI. The direction depends on the precious edge in the same contour. This definition contains the edge correlation and contour continuity, which can better represent the gradient intensity of a real edge to a certain extent. The advantage of this definition is showed in our experiment in Sect. 3. In our method, to match this definition, we set structural elements, such as rectangle kernel and diagonal kernel, to compute the DWI along a certain local direction, which helps to track the contours in our Inherited Edge Detection method (IED). Figure 3 shows the Directional kernels.

2.3   Inherited Edge Detection Method

Ignoring the edge correlation and contour continuity, most of the gradient-based edge detection methods detect edges individually. However, this paper takes full consideration of them by proposing the Inherited Edge Detection method (IED). Edge correlation and contour continuity is the fact that each edge in a contour is connected to its last edge and next edge along the contour. We find that edges in the same contour are most likely to distribute in a line segment along the contour curve, especially in a very small region. While tracking a contour, the position of the next edge is related to the positions of the current edge and the previous edge. This helps us to find the points with the higher probability which named candidate points in this paper, rather than searching 8-neighbor points or 4-neighbor points. After that, the remaining work is to find the real edge point among the candidate points.

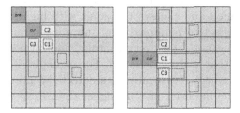

Fig. 4. Illustration of the inherited detection method (IED). The previous edge and current edge form a small line (the green points), which leads to the candidate points (the yellow points). Each kernel consists of three pixels and each candidate point uses one kernel to compute the DWI. For horizontal and vertical line, apply one more kernel to candidate point C_2 and C_3. (Color figure online)

$$P_{next} = \arg\max(DWI(C_1), DWI(C_2), DWI(C_3)) \qquad (1)$$

The Fig. 4 shows how the IED works. First of all, the starting point is set to be the first edge of the contour, also be the previous edge at this moment. Then it selects the second edge in 8-neighborhood to be the current edge at this moment. Next it will choose edge candidates based on the positions of the previous edge and the current edge. Focusing on a 3×3 region, the point, lying in the extended line formed by the previous edge and the current edge, is the first candidate point C_1. Then the two closest points to C_1 are the other two candidates C_2 and C_3. Afterward, the IED computes the DWI of each edge candidate and the next edge P_{next} which is defined in Eq. (1) should be the one with the highest DWI. Finally, the previous edge and current edge is moved forward to find new next edge.

Actually, this inherited method is not limited to a 3×3 kernel. We also tried other sizes such as 5×5, 7×7. However, the size of 3×3 always performs better. In practice, the GCT method uses the first edge and the second edge twice in a contour. For the latter, it exchanges the roles of them and start new tracking along the opposite direction of the contour.

2.4   Local Threshold

Canny method sets a high threshold and a low threshold to filter out the edges. Points connected to the determined edge with the intensity higher than the low threshold will be chosen to be the edge. The defect of this method is that the thresholds, especially the low threshold are difficult to set in different applications. Too low a threshold can lead to too much noise or other useless edges, and too high a threshold can make the contours incomplete. The essence of the problem is that the thresholds of *Canny* method are global thresholds, not local thresholds.

In this paper, for the edge detection, our tracking based method is natural equipped with the advantage of local thresholds. Firstly, while detecting, it focuses on a local region and chooses the point with highest DWI. This strategy shows a similar effect to non-maximum suppression but simpler. Secondly, it searches the starting point for every contour, and once a contour is chosen, the edges in this contour will be detected. For example, it is assumed that P and Q are two points where P is located in a detected contour while Q is not. In this situation, even the intensity of Q is higher than P, Q will not be detected as an edge. The advantage of this strategy is obviously that only the edges in strong contours will be detected, meanwhile, the very week contours and others like small spots in the image will be discarded. Deeply, for the detected contours, they tend to be more complete than the result using other detectors like *Canny*. Experiments in Sect. 3 show the advantage of this strategy.

2.5   Ending Conditions and Coding the Contour

The GCT method needs an ending threshold T_e which is always much lower than the starting point, even lower than the low threshold of *Canny* in the same situation. The first ending condition is set by T_e. The tracking will stop when:

- the intensities of the candidates are all lower than the ending threshold T_e;
- it reaches the boundary of the image;
- it hits the points that have been marked as the edges.

Each contour will be coded with a unique number from the very beginning. For the third ending condition, the GCT records the number of the hit contour. This record table will help to merge the contours and compute some statistics to get the feature of the contours, such as the length of the contour or the average intensity of the contour. It's useful if the user wants to do any subsequent work based on edge detection or contours detection.

3   Experiment

The experiment consists of two parts. It first compares the detection results of our GCT method to one classical method $Canny$ [2] and two learning-based methods SE [6], RCF [13]. Facing the fact in this field that there is not a standard and uniform evaluation method to compare different edge detection methods, especially for industrial application, we tried to make the comparative experiment in this paper more comprehensive. The remaining part of this section will show the experimental results when adjusting and improving the GCT method with smooth filters, thresholds and kernels. Finally, we provide a typical scheme of GCT method for general application.

3.1   Comparison Among Different Edge Detection Methods

As $Canny$ is the most typical gradient-based edge detection method and our GCT method is based on the brightness gradient as well, we compare these two methods in same situation. The starting and ending thresholds of our GCT method are set to be equal to the high and low thresholds of $Canny$ respectively. Meanwhile, both of these two methods use $Gaussian$ filter with the same kernel size 3×3. Another two edge detection methods SE and RCF are learning-based methods and RCF achieved state-of-the-art performance on the BSDS500 benchmark. However, in industrial scene they fail to perform as well as in natural scene. The original results of these learning-based methods are always coarse. Here, we add extra non-maximum suppression to their results to thin the contours before comparison. Note that the results of our GCT method are original detection results without any post process. Deeply, our GCT result is already merged into contours, but others are still independent edge points.

The test images in our experiments vary from simple structures to complex. As shown in Fig. 5, our GCT method detects much more clean contours of the objects than $Canny$ and outperforms the SE and RCF in most of the contours. To compare the details, we choose some regions of interest and enlarge them to watch the contours in pixel level. Notice that in the realization of GCT method, it is set to ignore the outermost 5 pixels of the source image which leads to losing some edges at the outer boundary. A better result can be achieved by using other boundary strategy such as adding another several columns and rows before detecting. Even though, the results show that the detected contours of our GCT method are more complete than others in most of the regions.

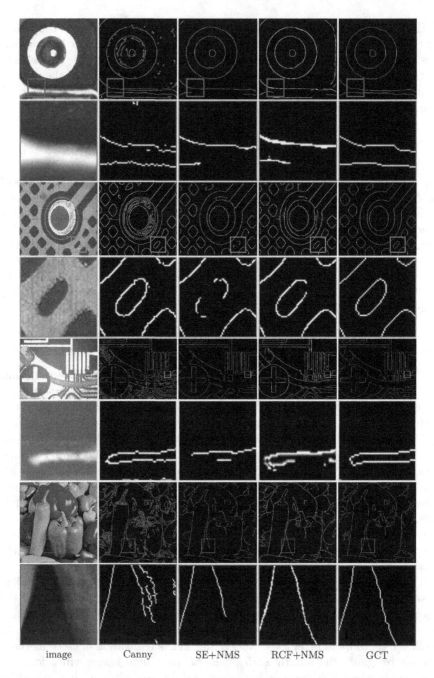

| | | | | |
| image | Canny | SE+NMS | RCF+NMS | GCT |

Fig. 5. Detection results of *Canny* [2], *SE* [6], *RCF* [13] and our *GCT* method in Industrial test images. *SE* and *RCF* are learning-based methods with coarse original results. We add extra non-maximum suppression (*NMS*) to *SE* and *RCF* to thin the contours, even though, our *GCT* contours are more clean with less clutters and more complete for the detected contours.

3.2 Different Scheme of GCT

In practice, we tried different schemes to meet different needs. In the comparison experiment with other detectors, the *Gaussian* filter is used to smooth the test images. However, there are some other choices, such as mean filter and bilateral filter. Figure 6 shows part of the detection results of *GCT* method with different smooth filters. The experiments show that all these three filters can help to detect the contours of the objects with a clean surroundings (the column 2 to column 4 in Fig. 6). In some situations, bilateral filter leads to less clutters, however, sometimes leads to the incompleteness of the edges. Bilateral filter takes much more running time which is more than three times as much as *Gaussian* filter takes under the experimental environment. The performance of *Gaussian* filter and mean filter with the same kernel size is almost the same. While using these two filters, the kernel size may affect the detection results. Which to choose is depends on the application scene and the size of the image. One useful suggestion is to use filters with larger size for larger images.

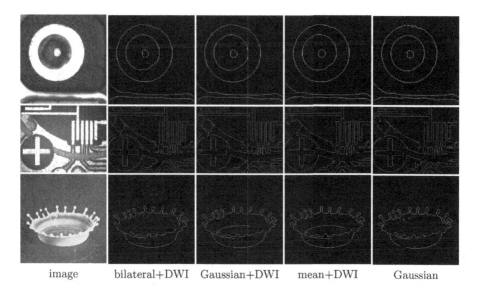

image   bilateral+DWI   Gaussian+DWI   mean+DWI   Gaussian

Fig. 6. In some situations, bilateral filter leads to less clutters, however, sometimes leads to the incompleteness of the edges. Using directional kernels to redefine the intensity of an edge (*DWI*) makes the contours more complete with less clutters.

While detecting the "next edge" in *IED*, we use the *DWI* to redefine the intensity of an edge. The last column in Fig. 6 presents the detecting results with the traditional strategy that only uses a single point value. On the contrary, other columns are the results with *DWI*. Experiments show the advantage that the results using *DWI* could better tracking the gradient center leading to more complete contours.

Ending threshold and starting threshold also affect the detection. One of the starting threshold and ending threshold is set to be constant, meanwhile the other one is adjusted to detect edges and compare the results of all images. The experiments show that the detection results are insensitive to the ending threshold. In practice, users can easily set the ending threshold as 20–40. On the contract, the detection result is sensitive to the starting threshold. Users can get detection results with different level by setting the starting threshold.

As a conclusion of this part, we could give a typical scheme of our *GCT* method:

- *Gaussian* filter with the size of 3×3 to smooth the given image
- *Sobel* detector with the kernel size of 3×3 to get the gradient image
  For a gray-scale image, the ending threshold could be 20–40, and the starting threshold could be 80–120
- Apply the inherited edge detection method with the kernel size of 3×3.

4   Conclusions

In this paper, we propose a novel pixel level edge detection method, *GCT*, by tracking the center curve of the edge band in the gradient image. This method is also a contour detection method for its detection result is presented by contours. We describe the edge correlation and contour continuity, and then put forward to the edge detection process, which is stated as the Inherited Edge Detection method (*IED*) in this paper. This paper also redefines the intensity of the edge by Directional Weighted Intensity (*DWI*), which helps to complete the contours. Comparing to the classical *Canny* method, our *GCT* method focus on the main structure of the object and achieves a much cleaner detection result without redundant clutters. Meanwhile, the detected contours are continuous and complete. Furthermore, our *GCT* method outperforms several learning-based methods in industrial scene. A typical scheme to apply the *GCT* method is also provided.

References

1. Arbeláez, P., Maire, M., Fowlkes, C., Malik, J.: Contour detection and hierarchical image segmentation. IEEE Trans. Pattern Anal. Mach. Intell. **33**(5), 898–916 (2011)
2. Canny, J.: A computational approach to edge detection. IEEE Trans. Pattern Anal. Mach. Intell. **6**, 679–698 (1986)
3. Chen, L.C., Barron, J.T., Papandreou, G., Murphy, K., Yuille, A.L.: Semantic image segmentation with task-specific edge detection using CNNS and a discriminatively trained domain transform. In: IEEE Conference on Computer Vision and Pattern Recognition, pp. 4545–4554 (2016)
4. Cheng, M.-M., et al.: HFS: hierarchical feature selection for efficient image segmentation. In: Leibe, B., Matas, J., Sebe, N., Welling, M. (eds.) ECCV 2016. LNCS, vol. 9907, pp. 867–882. Springer, Cham (2016). https://doi.org/10.1007/978-3-319-46487-9_53

5. Dollar, P., Tu, Z., Belongie, S.: Supervised learning of edges and object boundaries. In: IEEE Conference on Computer Vision and Pattern Recognition, pp. 1964–1971 (2006)
6. Dollar, P., Zitnick, C.L.: Fast edge detection using structured forests. IEEE Trans. Pattern Anal. Mach. Intell. **37**(8), 1558–1570 (2015)
7. Ferrari, V., Fevrier, L., Jurie, F., Schmid, C.: Groups of adjacent contour segments for object detection. IEEE Trans. Pattern Anal. Mach. Intell. **30**(1), 36 (2008)
8. Freeman, W.T., Adelson, E.H.: The design and use of steerable filters. IEEE Trans. Pattern Anal. Mach. Intell. **13**(9), 891–906 (1991)
9. Kittler, J.: On the accuracy of the sobel edge detector. Image Vis. Comput. **1**(1), 37–42 (1983)
10. Konishi, S., Yuille, A.L., Coughlan, J.M., Zhu, S.C.: Statistical edge detection: learning and evaluating edge cues. IEEE Trans. Pattern Anal. Mach. Intell. **25**(1), 57–74 (2003)
11. Lindeberg, T.: Edge detection and ridge detection with automatic scale selection. Int. J. Comput. Vis. **30**(2), 117–156 (1998)
12. Liu, H., Jezek, K.C.: Automated extraction of coastline from satellite imagery by integrating canny edge detection and locally adaptive thresholding methods. Int. J. Remote. Sens. **25**(5), 937–958 (2004)
13. Liu, Y., Cheng, M.M., Hu, X., Wang, K., Bai, X.: Richer convolutional features for edge detection, pp. 5872–5881 (2016)
14. Martin, D.R., Fowlkes, C.C., Malik, J.: Learning to detect natural image boundaries using local brightness, color, and texture cues. In: International Conference on Neural Information Processing Systems, pp. 1279–1286 (2002)
15. Mehrotra, R., Zhan, S.: A computational approach to zero-crossing-based two-dimensional edge detection. Graph. Model. Image Process. **58**(1), 1–17 (1996)
16. Moore, D.J.: Fast hysteresis thresholding in Canny edge detection (2011)
17. Pont-Tuset, J., Barron, J., Marques, F., Malik, J.: Multiscale combinatorial grouping. In: IEEE Conference on Computer Vision and Pattern Recognition, pp. 328–335 (2014)
18. Prewitt, J.M.S.: Object enhancement and extraction. Pict. Process. Psychopictorics **10**(1), 15–19 (1970)
19. Ren, X.: Multi-scale improves boundary detection in natural images. In: Forsyth, D., Torr, P., Zisserman, A. (eds.) ECCV 2008. LNCS, vol. 5304, pp. 533–545. Springer, Heidelberg (2008). https://doi.org/10.1007/978-3-540-88690-7_40
20. Roberts, L.G.: Machine perception of three-dimensional solids **20**, 31–39 (1963)
21. Suzuki, S., Be, K.: Topological structural analysis of digitized binary images by border following. Comput. Vis. Graph. Image Process. **30**(1), 32–46 (1985)
22. Tai, S.C., Yang, S.M.: A fast method for image noise estimation using Laplacian operator and adaptive edge detection. In: International Symposium on Communications, Control and Signal Processing, pp. 1077–1081 (2008)
23. Ullman, S., Basri, R.: Recognition by linear combinations of models. IEEE Trans. Pattern Anal. Mach. Intell. **13**(10), 992–1006 (1991)
24. Wang, R.: Edge detection using convolutional neural network. In: Cheng, L., Liu, Q., Ronzhin, A. (eds.) ISNN 2016. LNCS, vol. 9719, pp. 12–20. Springer, Cham (2016). https://doi.org/10.1007/978-3-319-40663-3_2
25. Wang, Z., Li, Q., Zhong, S., He, S.: Fast adaptive threshold for the canny edge detector. In: Proceedings of SPIE - The International Society for Optical Engineering, vol. 6044, pp. 501–508 (2005)
26. Wei, Y., et al.: STC: a simple to complex framework for weakly-supervised semantic segmentation. IEEE Trans. Pattern Anal. Mach. Intell. **39**(11), 2314–2320 (2017)

Image Saliency Detection with Low-Level Features Enhancement

Ting Zhao[(⊠)] and Xiangqian Wu

Harbin Institute of Technology, Harbin 150001, China
17S003073@stu.hit.edu.cn, xqwu@hit.edu.cn

Abstract. Image saliency detection has achieved great improvements in last several years as the development of convolutional neural networks (CNN). But it is still difficult and challenging to get clear boundaries of salient objects. The main reason is that current CNN based saliency detection approaches cannot learn the structural information of salient objects well. Thus, to address this problem, this paper proposes a deep convolutional network with low-level feature enhanced for image saliency detection. Several shallow sub-networks are adopted to capture various low-level information with heuristic guidance separately, and the guided features are fused and fed into the following network for final inference. This strategy can help to enhance the spatial information in low-level features and further improve the accuracy in boundary localization. Extensive evaluations on five benchmark datasets demonstrate that the proposed method outperforms the state-of-the-art approaches in both accuracy and efficiency.

Keywords: Saliency detection · Low-level features enhancement
Deep neural networks

1 Introduction

As a classic and challenging computer vision task, salient object detection aims to locate the most visually distinctive objects or regions which attract our attention in an image. Recently, salient detection has attracted much research attention. As an important basic work in many computer vision tasks, salient object detection has wide range of applications, such as content-aware image cropping [20] and resizing [3], image segmentation [11], visual tracking [7], video compression [5, 10], object recognition [21,25], etc.

In the past decade, a lot of salient object detection approaches have been proposed. The early approaches estimate the salient value based on hand-crafted local and global features which are extracted from pixels or regions. Those methods detect salient object with humanlike intuitive feelings and heuristic priors. These direct techniques are known to be helpful for keeping fine image structures. Nevertheless, such low-level features and priors can hardly capture high-level and global semantic knowledge about the objects.

J.-H. Lai et al. (Eds.): PRCV 2018, LNCS 11256, pp. 408–419, 2018.
https://doi.org/10.1007/978-3-030-03398-9_35

Because convolutional neural networks (CNNs) have powerful modeling complexity to learn from large number of supervised data, the methods used CNN got great success in many computer vision tasks. Recently, deep neural network architectures have shown excellent performance in saliency object detection. However, most of the methods mainly focus on the non-linear combination of high-level features extracted from the top layers of networks, ignoring the low-level information from shallow layers. Therefore, the predicted results of these methods are prone to have poorly detected object boundaries.

How to capture high-level semantic knowledge about the objects and keep the structural information of salient objects simultaneously becomes an urgent problem. Zhang et al. [29] and Hou et al. [8] try to address this issue by fusing multi-level features, and achieved great performance. However, experiments show that object boundaries of these methods are still less than satisfactory. It means that directly fusing low-level features is not as effective as predicted, and some significant information is ignored. We found that some multitask methods achieved great results [6,14] in other tasks, their methods learn more effective features and remedy the defect of single supervised signal methods with the help of extra labels. However, supplementary labels usually require a lot of manual annotations, which is laborious and time-consuming. If we use computers to finish the work, it is hard to achieve trade offs between accuracy and model complexity. Simple algorithms cannot get accurate labels. Relatively, complex methods require extensive computational modeling and huge amount of calculation. It is unacceptable for some basic tasks, such as image saliency detection.

In this paper, we propose a novel deep networks with low-level features enhancement (denoted LFE net) for effective image saliency detection. Our LFE net is designed as a variant multitask network. We adopt two assistant feature extraction tasks to optimize saliency detection. Different from the traditional multitask networks, the assistant tasks are learnt based on the low-level features, aiming to enhance the bottom features to reserve more diversified information. In order to get more details and structure features with no interference to each other, we design the bottom network with three shallow sub-networks in parallel to extract various features. In addition, the supplementary labels, which are supervised data of assistant feature extraction task, are just the guiders. They could not be very precise, we can get them by traditional algorithm.

Overall, this paper makes the following main contributions: (1) We propose a method to introduce heuristic guidance into low-level feature extraction via supervised multi-task learning. This strategy is proved to be beneficial for saliency object detection. (2) We propose a low-level feature enhancement network for saliency detection, which can effectively use the enhanced low-level features with deep supervision to detect and refine the saliency. (3) The proposed model achieves the state-of-the-art on several challenging datasets, which proves the effectiveness and superiority of the proposed method.

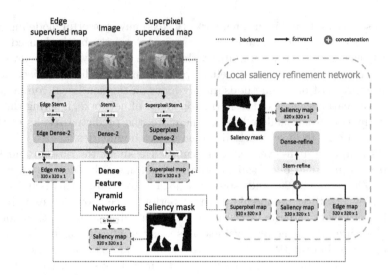

Fig. 1. The pipeline of the proposed low-level features enhancement deep network. The image input size is 320 × 320. The gray area shows the low-level features guided network, and the three low-level feature extraction has the same structure but don't share parameters. The dense feature pyramid networks follow architectures presented in previous works [9,15,19].

2 Proposed Method

The pipeline of the proposed LFE net is illustrated in Fig. 3. In this section, we will first introduce the main architecture of network. And then we'll present a strategy to refine the saliency maps.

2.1 Low-Level Features Guided Network

The low-level feature guided network (the gray area in Fig. 1) is supposed to extract richer features through multi-task supervised learning. This part is consisted of three branches, and two of them are supplied with heuristic labels (edge supervised map and superpixel supervised map in Fig. 3). With the same structure and none-shared parameters, the proposed branches extract features independently, then concatenating the low-level features fed into the following network for salient object detection (more detailed about the backbone network will be found in supplementary material).

Each branch of the low-level Feature guided network is constructed by two cascaded blocks: a stem block and a dense block. The stem block is consist of two 3 × 3 convolution layers and the dense block is consist by the similar structure introduced in DenseNets [9] where all preceding layers in the block are connected to the current layer. Transition pooling layers (2 × 2) is set between the two blocks and the final concatenation after the three branches.

There are three main advantages in this structure: (1) Different heuristic guidence for each branch can ensure the diversity of low-level features and bring cross complementation to some degree. (2) The desirable byproduct of the supplement tasks (edge or superpixel) can provide extra information for other applications. (3) It is beneficial to learn semantically meaningful high-level features with various low-level features, and it cannot bring unexpected interference to the final saliency map as no direct connection between heuristic guidence and the final result.

We select edge and superpixel as heuristic task. It is not necessary to get high-precise labels for each branch, as the supplementary task is designed to guide the process of feature learning rather than predict a accurate results. In this paper, we use canny detector [4] to get edge maps, and SLIC [1] algorithm to get superpixel maps.

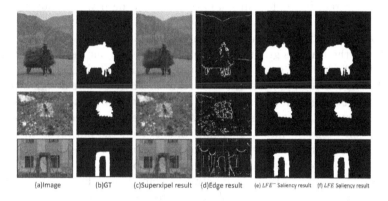

(a)Image   (b)GT   (c)Superxipel result   (d)Edge result   (e) *LFE*⁻ Saliency result   (f) *LFE* Saliency result

Fig. 2. The results of LFE net. (a) Input image. (b) Ground truth. (c) Superpixel map in low-level features guided network. (d) Edge map in low-level features guided network. (e) Saliency map without local saliency refinement. (f) Saliency map with local saliency refinement.

2.2 Dense Feature Pyramid Network

For generating high-quality saliency map, the most common strategy is fusing multi-level feature maps. The architecture of fusing multi-level feature network is optional. In this paper, we select a variant of the deeply supervised DenseNet [9] with feature pyramid [15] structure as backbone framework.

Our Dense feature pyramid network uses a top-down architecture with lateral connections to build an in-network feature pyramid similarity to FPN [15]. The network extracts multi-scale feature maps are extracted from different dense blocks. In order to utilize multi-scale features better and save parameters, we adopt the GCN [19]. GCN structure increases kernel size of the convolution layer to get more receptive field and uses less parameters, which is proved is effective in segment task [19]. In this work, we set GCN kernel size k = 7, and output channel c = 64 by experiments. Similar to [19], feature maps of lower resolution will be upsampled with a deconvolution layer, then add to the feature maps output from GCN of the same size. The final saliency map will be generated after the last upsampling layer. After gradually enlarging and refining the coarse saliency feature maps with multi-scale features, we will get a high-quality and clear-edged saliency map S_e.

2.3 Local Saliency Refinement Network

From the backbone network, we can get three maps: saliency map S_e, edge map E and superpixel map C. Although the salient objects have been highlighted, there still exist some local regions where the saliencies are poorly estimated. Therefore, we want to combine E and C with S_e to refine the results. We designing a small network to extract fusion features, and then generating new refinement saliency map.

For precisely extracting features from local regions, it is not a good idea to downsample the features gradually as done as the backbone network introduced in Sect. 2.1. And at the same time, the receptive field of the designed network should be large enough to cover the local regions. Therefore, we design a network without downsampling for local saliency refinement. The input of local saliency refinement network combines saliency map S_e, edge map E and superpixel map C, which concatenated into a 5-channel image. And the output is the refined salient map as the final result for performance evaluation. The base structure is similar to the low-level features guided network, containing a stem block and a dense block but no transition block between them. The architecture of the local saliency refinement network is displayed in green dotted box part on the right side of Fig. 1.

2.4 Loss Function

The loss functions need to be presented before model training, which are the target of network learning. In this paper, the loss functions are defined as follows:

$$L^S = -\alpha \sum_{y \in |Y_+|} \log(P(y = 1|Y'))$$
$$- (1 - \alpha) \sum_{y \in |Y_-|} \log(P(y = 0|Y')) \tag{1}$$

$$L^C = \| C - C' \|_2^2 \tag{2}$$

Formula 1 is the loss function of saliency map generation. As done as other works, the cross-entropy loss function defined in [26] is used to balance the loss between salient and non-salient pixels. Where $|Y_+|$ and $|Y_-|$ mean the number of salient pixels and non-salient pixels in ground truth respectively. Y' means the saliency map of network output. In order to distinguish between the saliency maps of backbone network result and local saliency refinement network result, we respectively mark them as L_e^S and L_r^S. The edge map generation L^E is the same as L^S. Formula 2 is the loss function of superpixel map generation. And the whole loss function is as follows:

$$L = \alpha_s L_e^S + \alpha_e L^E + \alpha_c L^C + \alpha_r L_r^S \tag{3}$$

where $\alpha_s = 1$, $\alpha_e = 1$, $\alpha_c = 0.01$ and $\alpha_r = 1$.

3   Experiments

3.1   Experimental Setup

MSRA10K dataset [26] and DUTS-TR [29] are used to train our LFE model, which contains 20,553 images with high quality pixel-wise annotations in total. The datasets are split into a training set containing 17,000 image and a validate set containing 3,553 images. We run our approach on a single PC machine with an Intel I7-7700K CPU (with 16G memory) and a NVIDIA Titan X GPU (with 12G memory). When testing, the work runs at about 24 fps with $320 \times 320 \times 3$ input.

3.2   Datasets and Evaluation Criteria

The performance evaluation is conducted on five standard benchmark datasets: SED [2], ECSSD [26], PASCAL-S [13], DUT-OMRON [28] and HKU-IS [27]. All datasets provide the corresponding ground truths in the form of accurate pixel-wise hand-annotated labels for salient objects.

Three main metrics are used to evaluate performance. The first one is precision and recall curve (denoted PR curve), which is drawn using the precision and recall under different threshold. The precision and recall are computed by comparing the binary map under different threshold the predicted saliency map with the ground truth, the thresholds form 0 to 255. F-measure (denoted F_β), which is the overall evaluation standard computed by the weighted combination of precision and recall:

$$F_\beta = \frac{(1 + \beta^2) \times Precision \times Recall}{\beta^2 \times Precision + Recall} \tag{4}$$

Where $\beta^2 = 0.3$ as used by other approaches. But in this paper, we will use a variation of the F_β, the weighted F-measure (wF_β) which is proposed recently in [18], which affected less from defects of curve interpolation, improper independence assumptions between pixels, and weighted importance assignment to all errors. The last one is MAE. Given salient map S, its mean absolute error (MAE) is computed by

$$MAE = \frac{1}{W \times H} \sum_{x=1}^{W} \sum_{y=1}^{H} |Y'(x,y) - Y(x,y)| \tag{5}$$

where Y is the ground truth (GT), and Y' is saliency map the network output.

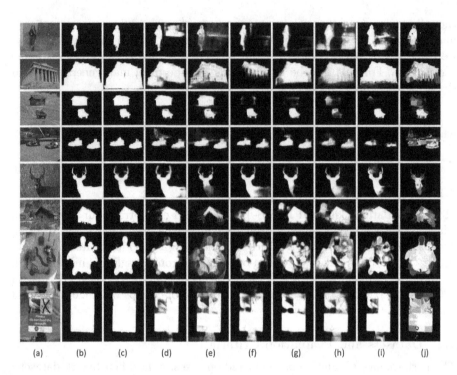

Fig. 3. Visual Comparisons of different saliency detection approaches vs. our method (LFE) in various challenging scenarios. (a) Image. (b) Ground truth. (c) Ours. (d) Amulet [29]. (e) UCF [30]. (f) SRM [24]. (g) DSS [8]. (h) DCL [12]. (i) DHS [16]. (j) MC [31]

Table 1. The wF_β and MAE of different salient object detection approaches on all test datasets. The best three results are shown in red, blue, and green.

Methods	ECSSD		SED		HKU-IS		PASCAL-S		DUT-OMRON	
	wF_β	MAE	wF_β	MAE	wF_β	MAE	wF_β	MAE	wF_β	MAE
Ours	0.8585	0.0532	0.8542	0.0626	0.8379	0.0431	0.7761	0.0636	0.7215	0.0674
Amulet [29]	0.8396	0.0607	0.8564	0.0631	0.8100	0.0531	0.7547	0.0997	0.6984	0.0976
UCF [30]	0.7879	0.0797	0.8320	0.0752	0.7476	0.0749	0.7129	0.1268	0.6991	0.1003
SRM [24]	0.8495	0.0564	0.8099	0.0852	0.8310	0.0469	0.7445	0.0835	0.7097	0.0698
DSS [8]	0.8318	0.0646	0.8003	0.0934	0.8194	0.0509	0.7108	0.1016	0.6913	0.1155
NLDF [17]	0.8354	0.0658	0.7815	0.0983	0.8353	0.0490	0.7267	0.0979	0.6182	0.1493
WSS [22]	0.7113	0.1059	0.7656	0.1006	0.7136	0.0796	0.6182	0.1395	0.5934	0.1307
RFCN [23]	0.7253	0.0972	0.7538	0.1088	0.7051	0.0804	0.6573	0.1176	0.6824	0.1629
DHS [16]	0.8368	0.0621	0.8683	0.0680	0.8158	0.0529	0.7123	0.0918	0.7487	0.0424
DCL [12]	0.7824	0.0800	0.7742	0.0938	0.7675	0.0637	0.7038	0.1147	0.6770	0.1564
MC [31]	0.7293	0.1019	0.8242	0.0972	0.6899	0.0914	0.6064	0.1422	0.6154	0.1692

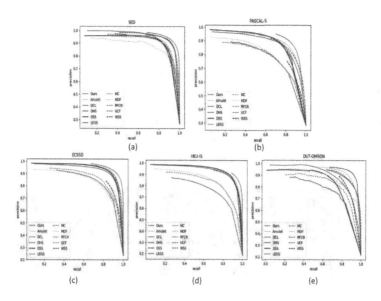

Fig. 4. The PR curves of the proposed algorithm and other state-of-the-art methods. (a) SED dataset [2]. (b) PASCAL-S dataset [13]. (c) ECSSD dataset [26]. (d) HKU IS dataset [27]. (e) DUT-OMRON dataset [28].

Table 2. Run times and parameters analysis of the compared methods

	Ours	Amulet	UCF	SRM	DSS	NLDF	WSS	RFCN	DHS	DCL	MC
Time	0.04 s	0.07 s	0.05 s	0.08 s	0.04 s	0.04 s	0.03 s	4.72 s	0.05 s	0.71 s	1.72 s
Parameters	45M	132.6M	117.9M	412M	237M	428M	56.2M	1047M	358M	252M	222M

3.3 Comparison with State-of-the-arts

The performance of the proposed method (LFE) is compared with ten state-of-the-art CNN based salient object detection approaches on five test datasets, including Amulet [29], UCF [30], SRM [24], DSS [8], NLDF [17], WSS [22], RFCN [23], DHS [16], DCL [12] and MC [31]. For fair comparison, we use the implementations with recommended parameter settings or the saliency maps provided by the authors.

Visual Comparison. Figure 3 provides a visual comparison of our approach and other methods. In Fig. 3, we selects some representative examples. The first and second lines show the single object in different sizes, the third and fourth lines display multiple disconnected salient objects, the fifth and sixth lines exhibit complex backgrounds, and the last two lines illustrate the complex structure objects. It can be seen that our method generates more accurate saliency maps which are much close to the ground truth in various challenging cases. The low-level features with a much wider variety of information can gradually refine the results. Therefore, compared with the blurred results obtained by other approaches which only use the explicit saliency supervised data, our proposed method is able to generate the salient maps with clear boundaries and consistent saliencies.

Figure 2 shows all results from LFE net. It can been seen that the edge maps and superpixel maps could be well generated, and with the power of the proposed local saliency refinement network, the poor estimations of saliency maps can be corrected.

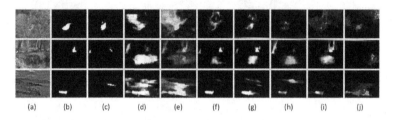

Fig. 5. Some failure examples of different approaches. (a) Image. (b) Ground truth. (c) Ours. (d) Amulet [29]. (e) UCF [30]. (f) DSS [8]. (g) NLDF [17]. (h) DCL [12]. (i) DHS [16]. (j) MC [31].

Quantitative Comparison. Figure 4 provides the quantitative evaluation results of the proposed method and other approaches on all test datasets in terms of PR curve. And Table 1 lists the results of all approaches in terms of wF_β and MAE over all test datasets. As shown in Fig. 6 and Table 1, the LFE model can be largely superior to other compared counterparts across most datasets in terms of near all evaluation metrics, which demonstrate the efficiency of the proposed method. Table 2 shows the run times and parameters analysis of the proposed method and other approaches. From the table, we can see that our method can be short running even adopt a deeper network. And we only need 45 MB parameters compared to other methods, which require hundreds MB of parameters. Proving that our method of feature extraction is more efficient.

We also find that performance of our method is not the best on DUT-OMRON (although our proposed LFE net ranks the second on the dataset). We found some typical examples shown in Fig. 5. When the salient objects are very small and have similar colors with backgrounds, it is hard to correctly detect them with our network.

3.4 Analysis of the Effectiveness of LFE

In this subsection we try to do some experiments to analyze the effectiveness of LFE. We adopt the same base backbone network among those structures to ensure fairness of the experiment. From Table 3, we could see that the results of

Table 3. The wF_β and MAE of different network structures on all test datasets. LFE^- means LFE net without refinement. $BaseModel$ means base net without extra input and supervised data. 3−Input means image, edge map and superpixel map encode as input. $Multitask$ means using edge map and superpixel map supervised data as top side supervised data. The best results are shown in red

Methods	ECSSD		SED		HKU-IS		PASCAL-S		DUT-OMRON	
	wF_β	MAE	wF_β	MAE	wF_β	MAE	wF_β	MAE	wF_β	MAE
LFE	0.859	0.053	0.854	0.061	0.838	0.043	0.776	0.064	0.722	0.067
LFE^-	0.850	0.056	0.859	0.060	0.831	0.047	0.764	0.068	0.727	0.066
$BaseModel$	0.799	0.081	0.807	0.097	0.759	0.074	0.703	0.115	0.617	0.122
$3-Input$	0.821	0.075	0.812	0.094	0.812	0.053	0.737	0.091	0.648	0.119
$Multitask$	0.800	0.084	0.791	0.102	0.823	0.061	0.733	0.100	0.661	0.118

base model without extra input and supervised data only generate rough salient object shape, which cannot have clear boundaries and the MAE increase 3%–6% compared with LFE net. The results of multi-input network structures are better than base model, but the MAEs are still high as the supplementary features cannot be extracted effectively. The results of multitask structure contain too much details, and weaken the saliency region. Under the condition of finding the objects, our proposed method keeps the clear boundaries of the objects, and achieves the best result.

4 Conclusions

In this paper, we propose a deep convolutional network with low-level feature enhanced for effective image saliency detection. We introduce heuristic guidance into low-level feature extraction to capture various low-level features. Then predict saliency maps with the integrated features from a top-bottom progressive multi-level fusion network. Experiments demonstrate that LFE net not only gets the state-of-the-art performance over five benchmark datasets, but also requires much less computation cost: 24 fps on GPU and 45 MB parameters. Given the effectiveness of pixel-level detection, we expect the structure of LFE net be an effective framework for other pixel-level tasks, such as semantic segmentation and instance segmentation. Our future work will consider the benefits of low-level features enhancement, and apply it to more visual tasks.

References

1. Achanta, R., Shaji, A., Smith, K., Lucchi, A., Fua, P., Süsstrunk, S.: Slic superpixels compared to state-of-the-art superpixel methods. IEEE Trans. Pattern Anal. Mach. Intell. **34**(11), 2274–2282 (2012)
2. Alpert, S., Galun, M., Brandt, A., Basri, R.: Image segmentation by probabilistic bottom-up aggregation and cue integration. IEEE Trans. Pattern Anal. Mach. Intell. **34**(2), 315–327 (2012)
3. Avidan, S., Shamir, A.: Seam carving for content-aware image resizing. ACM Trans. Graph. (TOG) **26**, 10 (2007)
4. Canny, J.: A computational approach to edge detection. In: Readings in Computer Vision, pp. 184–203. Elsevier (1987)
5. Guo, C., Zhang, L.: A novel multiresolution spatiotemporal saliency detection model and its applications in image and video compression. IEEE Trans Image Process. **19**(1), 185–198 (2010)
6. He, K., Gkioxari, G., Dollár, P., Girshick, R.: Mask R-CNN. In: 2017 IEEE International Conference on Computer Vision (ICCV), pp. 2980–2988. IEEE (2017)
7. Hong, S., You, T., Kwak, S., Han, B.: Online tracking by learning discriminative saliency map with convolutional neural network. In: International Conference on Machine Learning, pp. 597–606 (2015)
8. Hou, Q., Cheng, M.M., Hu, X., Borji, A., Tu, Z., Torr, P.: Deeply supervised salient object detection with short connections. In: 2017 IEEE Conference on Computer Vision and Pattern Recognition (CVPR), pp. 5300–5309. IEEE (2017)
9. Huang, G., Liu, Z., Weinberger, K.Q., van der Maaten, L.: Densely connected convolutional networks. In: Proceedings of the IEEE Conference on Computer Vision and Pattern Recognition, vol. 1, p. 3 (2017)
10. Itti, L.: Automatic foveation for video compression using a neurobiological model of visual attention. IEEE Trans. Image Process. **13**(10), 1304–1318 (2004)
11. Jung, C., Kim, C.: A unified spectral-domain approach for saliency detection and its application to automatic object segmentation. IEEE Trans. Image Process. **21**(3), 1272–1283 (2012)
12. Li, G., Yu, Y.: Deep contrast learning for salient object detection. In: Proceedings of the IEEE Conference on Computer Vision and Pattern Recognition, pp. 478–487 (2016)
13. Li, Y., Hou, X., Koch, C., Rehg, J.M., Yuille, A.L.: The secrets of salient object segmentation. In: 2014 IEEE Conference on Computer Vision and Pattern Recognition (CVPR), pp. 280–287. IEEE (2014)
14. Lin, D., Dai, J., Jia, J., He, K., Sun, J.: ScribbleSup: scribble-supervised convolutional networks for semantic segmentation. In: Proceedings of the IEEE Conference on Computer Vision and Pattern Recognition pp. 3159–3167 (2016)
15. Lin, T.Y., Dollár, P., Girshick, R., He, K., Hariharan, B., Belongie, S.: Feature pyramid networks for object detection. In: CVPR, vol. 1, p. 4 (2017)
16. Liu, N., Han, J.: DHSNet: deep hierarchical saliency network for salient object detection. In: 2016 IEEE Conference on Computer Vision and Pattern Recognition (CVPR), pp. 678–686. IEEE (2016)
17. Luo, Z., Mishra, A., Achkar, A., Eichel, J., Li, S., Jodoin, P.M.: Non-local deep features for salient object detection. In: IEEE CVPR (2017)
18. Margolin, R., Zelnik-Manor, L., Tal, A.: How to evaluate foreground maps? In: Proceedings of the IEEE Conference on Computer Vision and Pattern Recognition, pp. 248–255 (2014)

19. Peng, C., Zhang, X., Yu, G., Luo, G., Sun, J.: Large kernel matters-improve semantic segmentation by global convolutional network. In: Proceedings of the IEEE Conference on Computer Vision and Pattern Recognition, pp. 4353–4361 (2017)
20. Rother, C., Bordeaux, L., Hamadi, Y., Blake, A.: Autocollage. ACM Trans. Graph. (TOG) **25**, 847–852 (2006)
21. Rutishauser, U., Walther, D., Koch, C., Perona, P.: Is bottom-up attention useful for object recognition? In: Proceedings of the 2004 IEEE Computer Society Conference on Computer Vision and Pattern Recognition, CVPR 2004. vol. 2, p. II. IEEE (2004)
22. Wang, L., et al.: Learning to detect salient objects with image-level supervision. In: Proceedings of IEEE Conference on Computer Vision Pattern Recognition (CVPR), pp. 136–145 (2017)
23. Wang, L., Wang, L., Lu, H., Zhang, P., Ruan, X.: Saliency detection with recurrent fully convolutional networks. In: Leibe, B., Matas, J., Sebe, N., Welling, M. (eds.) ECCV 2016. LNCS, vol. 9908, pp. 825–841. Springer, Cham (2016). https://doi. org/10.1007/978-3-319-46493-0_50
24. Wang, T., Borji, A., Zhang, L., Zhang, P., Lu, H.: A stagewise refinement model for detecting salient objects in images. In: The IEEE International Conference on Computer Vision (ICCV), October 2017
25. Wei, Y., et al.: STC: a simple to complex framework for weakly-supervised semantic segmentation. IEEE Trans. Pattern Anal. Mach. Intell. **39**(11), 2314–2320 (2017)
26. Xie, S., Tu, Z.: Holistically-nested edge detection. In: Proceedings of the IEEE International Conference on Computer Vision, pp. 1395–1403 (2015)
27. Yan, Q., Xu, L., Shi, J., Jia, J.: Hierarchical saliency detection. In: 2013 IEEE Conference on Computer Vision and Pattern Recognition (CVPR), pp. 1155–1162. IEEE (2013)
28. Yang, C., Zhang, L., Lu, H., Ruan, X., Yang, M.H.: Saliency detection via graph-based manifold ranking. In: 2013 IEEE Conference on Computer Vision and Pattern Recognition (CVPR), pp. 3166–3173. IEEE (2013)
29. Zhang, P., Wang, D., Lu, H., Wang, H., Ruan, X.: Amulet: aggregating multi-level convolutional features for salient object detection. In: The IEEE International Conference on Computer Vision (ICCV), October 2017
30. Zhang, P., Wang, D., Lu, H., Wang, H., Yin, B.: Learning uncertain convolutional features for accurate saliency detection. In: The IEEE International Conference on Computer Vision (ICCV), October 2017
31. Zhao, R., Ouyang, W., Li, H., Wang, X.: Saliency detection by multi-context deep learning. In: Proceedings of the IEEE Conference on Computer Vision and Pattern Recognition, pp. 1265–1274 (2015)

A GAN-Based Image Generation Method for X-Ray Security Prohibited Items

Zihao Zhao, Haigang Zhang, and Jinfeng Yang[✉]

Tianjin Key Lab for Advanced Signal Processing,
Civil Aviation University of China, Tianjin, China
jfyang@cauc.edu.cn

Abstract. Recognizing prohibited items intelligently is significant for automatic X-ray baggage security screening. In this field, Convolutional Neural Network (CNN) based methods are more attractive in X-ray image contents analysis. Since training a reliable CNN model for prohibited item detection traditionally requires large amounts of data, we propose a method of X-ray prohibited item image generation using recently presented Generative Adversarial Networks (GANs). First, a novel pose-based classification method of items is presented to classify and label the training images. Then, the CT-GAN model is applied to generate many realistic images. To increase the diversity, we improve the CGAN model. Finally, a simple CNN model is employed to verify whether or not the generated images belong to the same item class as the training images.

Keywords: Generative Adversarial Network
X-ray prohibited item images · Image generation
Feature transformation

1 Introduction

X-ray security baggage screening is widely used to ensure transport security [1]. But the accuracy of manual detection have not been desirable for a long time. The prohibited items are very difficult to detect when they are placed closely in baggage and occluded by other objects [2]. Furthermore, operators are usually allowed only a limited working time to recognize the prohibited items in baggage. A reliable automatic detection system for X-ray baggage images can significantly speed the screening process up and improve the accuracy of detection [3]. Recently, the deep learning based approaches have drawn more and more attentions in image contents analysis. They probably perform well on prohibited item detection. Unfortunately, the dataset of X-ray prohibited item images used in training human inspectors could not meet the requirements of network training. In addition, it is also difficult to collect enough X-ray images containing prohibited items with pose and scale variety in practice.

It is traditional to address the problem via using data augmentation of collected images, such as translation, rotation, and scale. But little additional information can be gained by these ways [4]. Besides data augmentation, training

© Springer Nature Switzerland AG 2018
J.-H. Lai et al. (Eds.): PRCV 2018, LNCS 11256, pp. 420–430, 2018.
https://doi.org/10.1007/978-3-030-03398-9_36

the network on a pre-trained model slightly improve the performance of image processing algorithm. The Generative Adversarial Network [5] has enjoyed considerable success in data generation. It can be used to generate realistic images according to the recent development of GAN in network architecture and training process [6–9]. WGAN-GP [10] is a popular model for image generation, while PGGAN [11] and SNGAN [12] can generate images with high resolution and rich diversity.

But for the task of generating X-ray prohibited item images, existing GAN-based approaches are not trainable since the amount of training images is not enough. In addition, the items in baggage are placed randomly and packed tightly, so the X-ray prohibited items generally present various visual angles. Figure 1 shows some images of handguns. The guns in images have many poses, and the backgrounds are greatly varied. These factors are unfavorable for GAN to learn the common features of all guns.

Fig. 1. X-ray handgun images

In this paper, we propose an image generation method of X-ray security prohibited items using GAN-based approach. We take dealing with the handgun images as an instance since the detection of handgun is a classical subject. First, we introduce a pose-based classification method of handguns. Then, we facilitate the network training by adding pose labels for the collected images and extracting the object foreground with KNN-matting [13]. Next, CT-GAN [14] model is used for image generation. In order to increase the diversity of images, such as pose, scale and position, we improve the CGAN model [15]. Finally, a simple CNN model is used to verify whether or not the generated images and real images belong to the same item class. Only the images with a correct matching result given by CNN model can be used as new samples of dataset.

The rest of paper is organized as follows. In Sect. 2, we present an image preprocess method. Section 3 introduces the CT-GAN model and the improved CGAN model, Sect. 4 details the experiments and shows some generated images. In Sect. 5, we perform a verification experiment. Finally, Sect. 6 summarizes this paper.

2   Image Preprocessing

Most GAN models for image generation need a large training dataset, such as ImageNet and LSUN. The absence of training images and the pose variety of prohibited items increase the difficulty of network training. If these images are directly fed into GAN model for unsupervised learning, the network is hard to learn their common features. As shown in Fig. 2, the generated images have unreasonable shapes of handguns. To solve this problem, we remove the background and add labels for images before training the GAN model.

Fig. 2. Generated images without preprocessing

2.1   Image Classifying and Labeling

A space rectangular coordinate system is constructed as shown in Fig. 3, and its origin corresponds to the geometrical center of the handgun. Different poses of handguns can be regarded as how many angles the gun rotated around three axes in the coordinate system. And we can classify the handgun images according to the angles of rotation.

Fig. 3. Construction of space rectangular coordinate system

Rotation around z-axis changes the direction of guns, while rotation around x-axis and y-axis changes the angle. The result of classification is illustrated in Fig. 4. We set the standard position where the handgun turns the muzzle to left. The images can be divided into two classes according to the direction of muzzle. The rotations around z-axis can be roughly divided into 4 classes, include $0° \pm 45°$, $90° \pm 45°$, $-90° \pm 45°$ and $180° \pm 45°$. The rotations around x-axis and y-axis can be divided into two classes, $0° \sim 45°$ and $-45° \sim 0°$. The geometrical view of handguns in actual security screening that corresponding to the rotation more than $\pm 45°$ is unusual, so it is not considered. When the rotation angle is more than $\pm 90°$, it repeats with the mirror position. Therefore, the handgun images can be divided into $32(2 \times 4 \times 2 \times 2)$ point classes.

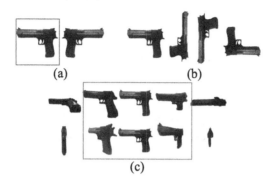

(a)   (b)

(c)

Fig. 4. The classification result of handgun images. (a) Standard and mirror position, and the red box is the standard position. (b) Classes of direction. (c) Classes of angle, the image in the green box is what this paper considers. (Color figure online)

2.2 Foreground Extracting

X-ray prohibited item images always have complex background. It is hard for network to extract common feature of background when the size of training data is not big enough. Furthermore, object foreground is much more important than background. So, matting method is here used to extract foreground of the X-ray prohibited item images, where original image, background image and trimap are required. The trimap only contains foreground, background and unknown pixel. The image foreground is extracted by Eq. (1),

$$I = \alpha F + (1 - \alpha)B, \tag{1}$$

where I is any pixel in the image, F is foreground pixel, B is background pixel, and α is fusion coefficient among 0 and 1. For certain background, $\alpha=0$, for certain foreground, $\alpha=1$. The α matrix can be obtained by KNN-matting [13]. The process for extracting foreground of handgun in X-ray images is shown in Fig. 5. Matting result shows that this method can remove the complex background and leave the foreground of interest in image.

3   Image Generative Model

The generated X-ray prohibited item images must be increased greatly in quantity and diversity. This can be achieved by two steps. First, many new images are

background   image   trimap   alpha   matting-result

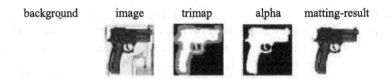

Fig. 5. Image foreground extraction process. From left to right are the background image, original image, trimap, α matrix, and X-ray image that only has object foreground.

generated based on CT-GAN. Then, the CGAN model is improved for effectively re-adjusting the poses and scales of the generated item images. The flowchart of image generation is shown in Fig. 6.

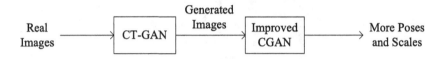

Fig. 6. Image generation flowchart

3.1 CT-GAN

CT-GAN is proposed based on the improvements of WGAN-GP. Compared with WGAN-GP, it performs better on small datasets and improves the stability of training. Here, CT-GAN is used to generate many images of X-ray prohibited items with high quality. It should be mentioned that we make some modifications to the loss function compared with Reference [14]. The loss function is defined as Eq. (2),

$$L = D(G(z)) - D(x) + \lambda_1 GP \mid_{x'} + \lambda_2 CT \mid_{x_1, x_2}, \tag{2}$$

the gradient penalty (GP) and consistency regularization (CT) are defined as Eqs. (3) and (4),

$$GP \mid_{x'} = E_{x'}[(\parallel \nabla_{x'} D(x') \parallel_2 - 1)^2], \tag{3}$$

$$CT \mid_{x_1, x_2} = E_{x \sim P_r}[max(0, d(D(x_1), D(x_2)) - M')], \tag{4}$$

where x' is uniformly sampled from the straight line between the generated data and real data. Both x_1, x_2 are real data. M' is a constant. The basic architecture of generator G is a deconvolutional neural network. The input is random Gaussian noise vector while the output is a generated image. The basic architecture of discriminator D is a convolutional neural network. Selecting suitable values of λ_1 and λ_2 can optimize the quality of generated images.

3.2   Improved CGAN

Many new images could be generated by CT-GAN, but they vary little compared with the real images. We improve the CGAN model [15] to increase the diversity of the generated images, including poses, position and scales. This model is different from the traditional GAN models, where the input of generator G is random noise. It uses an original image A and a target image B (there are different prohibited item poses in A and B) as the real data. The aim of G is to transform image A to image B'. So, image A and image B' are the fake data. Several training image pairs, $A - B$, are used to train the network. Finally, G can generate a new image based on image A without corresponding image B.

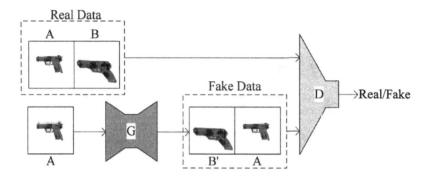

Fig. 7. The architecture of improved CGAN

The architecture of improved CGAN is shown in Fig. 7. The handguns in image A and image B are different in pose and scale. The architecture of D is still a convolution neural network, and the architecture of G adopts the structure of encoder-decoder. The images can be generated better by adding the gradient penalty. The loss function is defined as Eq. (5),

$$L = D(x, G(x)) - D(x, y) + \lambda GP, \tag{5}$$

4   Experiments and Results

In this section, the experimental details are discussed. Most X-ray prohibited item images used here are collected from Google, and a part of images is taken by a X-ray machine. This Section shows the results of various handgun images generated by CT-GAN and improved CGAN. In addition, some images of other prohibited items are also generated using the proposed method.

4.1 Generating Many Images Based on CT-GAN

CT-GAN is used to generated many new images. The dataset consists of more than 500 X-ray handgun images. All the images are resized to 96×64 pixels. The batch size is set to 64. Our model is trained for 1500 epochs with a learning rate 0.0001. The best generated image samples can be obtained when the training frequency of D is same with that of G.

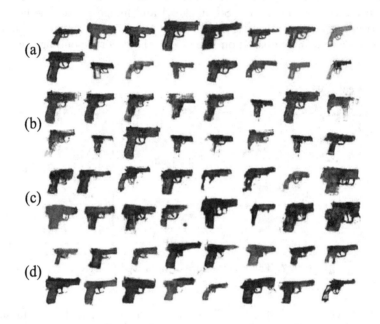

Fig. 8. Some generated image samples. (a) Some real X-ray images. (b) Images generated by DCGAN. (c) Images generated by WGAN-GP. (d) Images generated by CT-GAN.

Images with different visual quality are generated based on CT-GAN and several other GAN models (shown in Fig. 8). The images that generated by DCGAN model are poor in quality. As for WGAN-GP, the resolution of most images have been improved, but some images still have ghost shapes of handguns. Compared with these models, the quality of images generated by CT-GAN have been improved obviously. Many handgun images with different poses are generated by CT-GAN, here some image samples are shown in Fig. 9.

4.2 Generating Images to Increase the Diversity by Improved CGAN

Firstly, we build 50 pairs of training image samples $A - B$. The handgun of B is different to that of A in pose, position and scale. Then, the improved

Fig. 9. Image samples generated by CT-GAN

CGAN model is trained for 500 epochs based on this dataset with a learning rate 0.0001. The new images generated (shown in Fig. 10) by the proposed method are different from rotating the images directly. There are more changes between the generated images and real images.

4.3   More Prohibited Item Image Generation

In order to test the generalization ability of the proposed method, we also generate some images of other prohibited items respectively, such as wrench, pliers, blade, lighter, kitchen knife, screwdriver, fruit knife and hammer. All the experiments performed on a dataset of 100–200 images. Some generated images are shown in Fig. 11.

The images generated here using our method only contain foreground. The complete X-ray images can be obtained by fusing the generated item images with existing background images through some rules. Here we have more interests on the foreground of images.

5   Verification

Most images generated by CT-GAN and the improved GAN are realistic. However, a part of images have poor quality because of the instability of training. Before using the generated images as new samples of dataset, it is necessary to verify whether or not the generated images belong to the same item class as the original images.

It can be verified by a simple CNN model that include three convolutional layers and three full connected layers. Both the training images and testing images are real X-ray security images, and they account for 75% and 25% respectively. The dataset has ten classes, include handgun, wrench, pliers, blade, lighter, kitchen knife, screwdriver, fruit knife, hammer and other items. Each class has

(a)

(b)

(c)

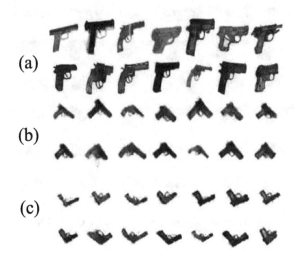

Fig. 10. The generated images based on improved CGAN. (a) Original handgun images. (b), (c) Two different generated image samples that have different handgun pose, position and scale.

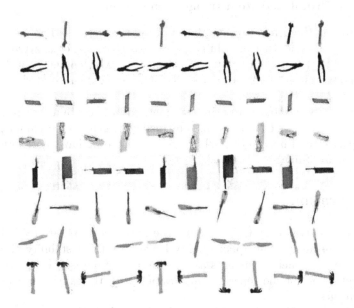

Fig. 11. Generated images of eight prohibited items. From top to bottom, the generated images are respectively wrench, pliers, blade, lighter, kitchen knife, screwdriver, fruit knife and hammer.

200 images, and different images have different item poses. Batch size is set to 64. After 25 epochs of training, the accuracy of classification on training dataset is 99.84% while the accuracy on testing dataset is 99.22%.

One hundred generated images are select randomly from each prohibited item class. Table 1 reports the count of images with correct matching labels. We can find that most images are classified correctly by CNN model.

Table 1. Matching results of CNN model

Prohibited item	Number
Handgun	100
Wrench	100
Pliers	100
Blade	87
Lighter	100
Kitchen knife	92
Screwdriver	91
Fruit knife	95
Hammer	100

6 Conclusions

In this paper, a GAN-based method was proposed to generate images of X-ray prohibited items. After image classifying and foreground extracting, many new images with various poses were generated by the CT-GAN model and the improved CGAN model. We also verified that most generated images belong to the same class with real images. Our work can increase the X-ray prohibited item image dataset effectively in both quantity and diversity.

Acknowledgments. This work was supported by the National Natural Science Foundation of China Nos. 61379102, 61806208.

References

1. Akcay, S., Kundegorski, M.E., Devereux, M., et al.: Transfer learning using convolutional neural networks for object classification within x-ray baggage security imagery. In: International Conference on Image Processing, pp. 1057–1061 (2016)
2. Mery, D., Svec, E., Arias, M.: Modern computer vision techniques for x-ray testing in baggage inspection. IEEE Trans. Syst. Man Cybern. **47**(4), 682–692 (2017)
3. Turcsany, D., Mouton, A., Breckon, T.P.: Improving feature-based object recognition for x-ray baggage security screening using primed visual words. In: International Conference on Industrial Technology, pp. 1140–1145 (2013)

4. Frid-Adar, M., Diamant, I., Klang, E., et al.: GAN-Based Synthetic Medical Image Augmentation for Increased CNN Performance in Liver Lesion Classification. arXiv preprint arXiv:1803.01229 (2018)

5. Goodfellow, I.J., Pouget-Abadie, J., Mirza, M., et al.: Generative adversarial nets. In: International Conference on Neural Information Processing Systems, pp. 2672–2680 (2014)

6. Mirza, M., Osindero, S.: Conditional Generative Adversarial Nets. Computer Science (2014)

7. Radford, A., Metz, L., Chintala, S.: Unsupervised Representation Learning with Deep Convolutional Generative Adversarial Networks. Computer Science (2015)

8. Salimans, T., Goodfellow, I.J., Zaremba, W., et al.: Improved techniques for training GANs. In: International Conference on Neural Information Processing Systems, pp. 2226–2234 (2016)

9. Gurumurthy, S., Sarvadevabhatla, R.K., Babu, R.V.: DeLiGAN: generative adversarial networks for diverse and limited data. In: IEEE Conference on Computer Vision and Pattern Recognition, pp. 4941–4949 (2017)

10. Gulrajani, I., Ahmed, F., Arjovsky, M., et al.: Improved training of Wasserstein GANs. In: International Conference on Neural Information Processing Systems, pp. 5769–5779 (2017)

11. Karras, T., Aila, T., Laine, S., et al.: Progressive Growing of GANs for Improved Quality, Stability, and Variation. arXiv preprint arXiv:1710.10196 (2017)

12. Miyato, T., Kataoka, T., Koyama, M., et al.: Spectral Normalization for Generative Adversarial Networks. arXiv preprint arXiv:1802.05957 (2018)

13. Chen, Q., Li, D., Tang, C.: KNN matting. IEEE Trans. Pattern Anal. Mach. Intell. **35**(9), 2175–2188 (2013)

14. Wei, X., Gong, B., Liu, Z., et al.: Improving the Improved Training of Wasserstein GANs: A Consistency Term and Its Dual Effect. arXiv preprint arXiv:1803.01541 (2018)

15. Isola, P., Zhu, J., Zhou, T., et al.: Image-to-image translation with conditional adversarial networks. In: IEEE Conference on Computer Vision and Pattern Recognition, pp. 5967–5976 (2017)

Incremental Feature Forest for Real-Time SLAM on Mobile Devices

Yuke Guo[1] and Yuru Pei[2(✉)]

[1] Luoyang Institute of Science and Technology, Luoyang, China
[2] Key Laboratory of Machine Perception (MOE),
Department of Machine Intelligence, Peking University, Beijing, China
Peiyuru@cis.pku.edu.cn

Abstract. Real-time SLAM is a prerequisite for online virtual and augmented reality (VR and AR) applications on mobile devices. Under the observation that the efficient feature matching is crucial for both 3D mappings and camera locations in the feature-based SLAM, we propose a clustering forest-based metric for feature matching. Instead of a predefined cluster number in the k-means-based feature hierarchy, the proposed forest self-learn the underlying feature distribution, where the affinity estimation is based on efficient forest traversals. Considering the spatial consistency, the matching feature pair is assigned a confident score by virtue of contextual leaf assignments to reduce the RANSAC iterations. Furthermore, an incremental forest growth scheme is presented for a robust exploration in new scenes. This framework facilitates fast SLAMs for VR and AR applications on mobile devices.

1 Introduction

The simultaneous localization and mapping (SLAM) play an important role in the VR and AR applications on mobile devices (Fig. 1). The SLAM has undergone rapid developments in recent years with an inception of several SLAM systems, such as PTAM [8], LSD-SLAM [6], and ORB-SLAM [10]. The feature-based SLAM is known to be effective for the 3D global mapping and camera locations, especially invariant to viewpoints and illuminations compared with the direct SLAM methods. A group of image features, including SIFT [9], SURF [1], BRIEF [4], ORB [14], and bag of words [7] have been used in feature-based SLAMs. The ORB feature has obvious advantages over others in fast extractions for the real-time SLAM. However, without the GPU and PC support, the ORB-SLAM has limited processing frame rates on mobile devices [15], which is not enough for online applications.

Considering the time-consuming feature matching for map generations as well as the camera locations in feature-based SLAMs, we investigate an adaptation of the ORB-SLAM by proposing a clustering forest for the fast feature correspondence establishment (see Fig. 2). Compared with the hierarchical vocabulary tree [10], there is no need to predefine the clustering number in the training phase

© Springer Nature Switzerland AG 2018
J.-H. Lai et al. (Eds.): PRCV 2018, LNCS 11256, pp. 431–438, 2018.
https://doi.org/10.1007/978-3-030-03398-9_37

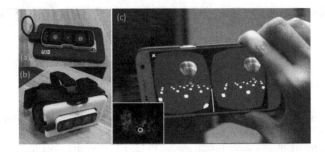

Fig. 1. Real-time feature-based SLAM on mobile devices. (a) A mobile phone mounted with a stereo camera Fingo. (b) A mobile phone on an HMD. (c) One sampled view of the hand-held mobile phone in the exploration of the virtual scene with a colored balloon. The 3D maps (red dots) are shown at the lower left corner along with the viewpoints of keyframes (green pyramids). The corresponding viewpoints are yellow circled in the 3D maps. (Color figure online)

Fig. 2. Flowchart of the proposed forest-based feature matching for the SLAM on mobile devices.

of the feature forest. Moreover, there is just a limited number of binary comparisons in forest traversals for feature affinity estimation. Taking into account the spatial consistency, we propose a confident score for the feature matching by virtue of feature contexts. The matching pairs with similar contextual leaf assignments are assumed to be reliable. Furthermore, we present an incremental adaptation of the forest to accommodate newly-explored keyframes compared with the fixed vocabulary tree. The main point of this paper is to propose a forest-based method for efficient feature matching, and further the fast SLAM on mobile devices.

2   Feature Forest

The clustering forest works in an unsupervised manner without prior labeling, which is known for its self-learning underlying data distributions. The optimal node splitting parameters are learned by maximizing the information gain I as in the density forest [5]. We use the trace operator [12] to avoid the rank deficiency of the covariance matrix $\sigma(F)$ of the high dimensional ORB feature set F. Here we measure the information gain by the Hamming metric.

$$I = - \sum_{k=l,r} \frac{|F_k|}{|F|} \ln tr(\sigma(F_k)), \tag{1}$$

where $|\cdot|$ returns the cardinality of feature set F_k in left and right children nodes. The ORB feature is a 256-dimensional binary vector with each 8-bit byte serving as a feature channel. The binary function $\phi(s, \rho, \tau) = [\|f_{(s)} - \rho\|_h < \tau]$, where $[\cdot]$ is an indicator function. The features bearing channel $f_{(s)}, s \in [1, 32]$ with the Hamming distance to byte ρ lower than threshold τ is assigned to the left child node.

The forest is composed of five independent decision trees learned from randomly-selected feature subsets. The tree growths terminate when the number of instances inside the leaf node is below a predefined threshold γ, and $\gamma = 50$. Each tree has approx. 10 layers. Of course, the binary decision tree in the feature forest is deeper than the vocabulary tree. Fortunately, the forest traversals are extremely fast considering binary tests in branch nodes. Since the parameters of the hierarchical forest model are composed of binary tests in branch nodes, as well as the mean representor f_ℓ and instance number n_ℓ of the leaf nodes, it is easy to load the forest model into the memory of the mobile devices.

2.1 Affinity Estimation

When given the feature forest, it's straightforward to estimate pairwise affinities of ORB features. The ORB feature pair reaching the same leaf node is assumed to be similar with a distance set at 0, and 1 otherwise. The distance matrix $D = \frac{1}{n_T} \sum_{k=1}^{n_T} D_k$ by the forest with n_T trees, where $D_k(f_i, f_j) = 1$ if $\ell(f_i) = \ell(f_j)$. $\ell(f)$ denotes the leaf node of feature f. Given the distance matrix D between ORB feature set F_n of the newly-explored frame and F_o of the already stored keyframes, the feature matching

$$C = \{(f_i^n, f_j^o) | f_i^n \in F_n, f_j^o \in F_o\}, D(f_i^n, f_j^o) = \arg \min_{j' \in [1, |F_o|]} D_{ij'}. \qquad (2)$$

The feature pair with the smallest pairwise distance is assumed to be the matching pair.

Note that, the pairwise distance entry is set according to binary functions ϕ stored in branch nodes. The balanced tree depth ν depends on the cardinality of the training data F, and $\nu = \log_2 |F|$. The time cost for the pairwise distance matrix between ORB feature set F_i and F_j is $O((|F_i| + |F_j|) \cdot \nu \cdot n_T)$. In our experiments, $\nu \in [9, 12]$ and $n_T = 5$. The time cost is lower than the common pairwise distance computation of ORB features with a complexity of $O(|F_i| \cdot |F_j|)$.

Similar to the vocabulary tree [10], the feature forest stores the direct and inverse indices between leaf nodes and features on keyframes. There are approx. $|F|/\gamma$ leaf nodes. The leaf index can be denoted by $\log_2(|F|/\gamma)$ bits. On the keyframes of already explored scenes, there is a direct index from the ORB feature to leaf nodes of the feature forest as shown in Fig. 3. On the other hand, the inverse index stores all the ORB features of keyframes that reach the leaf node. For the correspondence estimation between the newly-explored frame F_n and stored keyframes, just the forest traversals of F_n are needed with a complexity of $O(|F_n| \cdot \nu \cdot n_T)$ on byte-based binary comparisons. As we can see, the online distance matrix update cost for the newly-explored frame is extremely lower than the common pairwise distance computation with a complexity of $O(|F_n| \cdot |F_o|)$. The time cost is also lower than the vocabulary tree with $O(|F_n| \cdot k \cdot \nu)$ of Hamming distance computations for the 256-dimensional features with k clusters for each splitting.

2.2 Matching Confidence

Considering the spatial consistency and perspective geometry, the correspondences of neighboring ORB features of one frame tend to be close in other frames or 3D maps. We no longer treat the matching pairs equally as in traditional features-based SLAMs. Instead, we present a confident score of the matching feature pair (f_i, f_j).

$$\alpha(f_i, f_j) = \frac{1}{Z} \sum_{k=1}^{n_T} \theta_k \left(\mathcal{N}(f_i) \right) \wedge \theta_k(\mathcal{N}(f_j)), \tag{3}$$

where function $\theta_k(\mathcal{N}(f))$ returns leaf indices of surrounding context $\mathcal{N}(f)$ of feature f with respect to the k-th decision tree. The direct index of ORB feature as described in Sect. 2.1 is utilized to get the leaf index set of feature context $\mathcal{N}(f)$. The confident score is computed by the intersection $\wedge$ of the contextual leaf assignments of corresponding features f_i and f_j. Since decision trees in the feature forest are constructed almost independently, we consider all decision trees in the forest to measure the consistency of contextual leaf assignments. Z is a normalization constant. In our experiments, the size of the context patch is set at 1% of the image size. The matching pair is denoted as a triplet $\langle f_i, f_j, \alpha(f_i, f_j) \rangle$.

The feature pairs bearing large confident scores are likely to be correct matchings. The feature matchings are sorted according to the confident scores. The 3D mapping and camera location are prone to use the feature pairs with high confident scores. For instance, the RANSAC process for camera locations prefers the matching pairs with large confident scores. We observe that the weighted RANSAC using the confident scores is likely to terminate after a small number of iterations.

2.3 Online Forest Refinement

The feature forest is trained offline. When the scene exploration goes on, more and more keyframes and ORB features are located and stored. In this work, we present an online forest refinement scheme with incremental tree growths to accommodate the newly-added features on the keyframes, which facilitates the adaptation to the new scene. Similar to [13], we incrementally split the leaf nodes with available online data. There are two criteria to split the candidate leaf node in online forest refinements: (1) The number of newly-added features in the leaf node is larger than a predefined threshold, i.e. γ, the same as the predefined leaf size; (2) The deviation from the mean of the newly-added features $F_{n,\ell}$ to the offline learned leaf node representor f_ℓ is large enough.

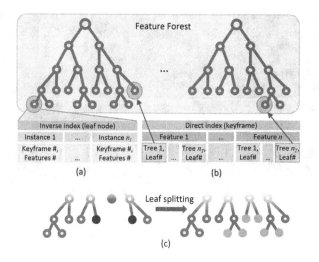

Fig. 3. (a) Inverse and (b) direct index of leaf nodes and keyframes. (c) The online forest refinement with incremental tree growths of leaf splitting. The nodes to be split are purple colored, and the newly-added nodes are orange-colored. (Color figure online)

We measure the deviation between f_ℓ and the representor f'_ℓ of its brother node. When $\|f_\ell - \bar{F}_{n,\ell}\| > \beta \|f_\ell - f'_\ell\|$, the second criterion is met. The constant coefficient β is set at 0.5. The leaf nodes of the feature forest is incrementally split and the tree grows when the above two criteria are met as shown in Fig. 3(c). The optimal splitting parameters are determined by maximizing the information gain as described in Sect. 2. Taking into account the features assigned to the leaf node in the training phase, we employ the weighted covariance matrix to estimate the information gain. The following weights are assigned to newly-added features $F_{n,\ell}$ and offline learned leaf node representor f_ℓ.

$$u_i = \begin{cases} \frac{1}{n_\ell + |F_n|}, \text{for} f_i \in F_{n,\ell} \\ \frac{n_\ell}{n_\ell + |F_n|}, \text{for} f_\ell \end{cases} \tag{4}$$

Different from the unweighted information gain estimation in the training phase (Sect. 2), the trace of the covariance matrix $\sigma(F_k)$ of the child node is defined as

$$tr(\sigma) = \sum_{i=1}^{|F_k|} \frac{u_i^2 \|f_i - \bar{F}_k\|_h^2}{\sum_{i',j}^{|F_k|} u_{i'} u_j}. \tag{5}$$

The center of the leaf node is computed as a weighted mean, and $\bar{F} = \sum_{i=1}^{|F|} u_i f_i$. Note that, the incremental tree growth changes the tree configurations, and the direct and inverse indices update accordingly. We keep a dynamic leaf node index list. The features in the already explored keyframes can be assigned to the online-split leaf nodes. Considering that the leaf node splitting just handles a limited number of instances, the leaf-splitting-based forest refinement is efficient enough for the online adaptation to new scenes.

Fig. 4. (a) 3D map (red dots) with the connection of keyframes (blue lines) and viewpoints (green pyramids). (b)–(f) Sampled views with the hand-held mobile phone in the exploration of the virtual scene of a colored balloon with viewpoints (1–5) annotated in the 3D maps. (Color figure online)

3   Experimental Results

We perform experiments on the mobile device to evaluate the proposed method. We use Samsung Galaxy S7 with Snapdragon 820 processor 1.6 GHz and 4 GB RAM. The stereo gray images are captured by uSens Fingo camera as shown in Fig. 1(a, b). The proposed method establishes the feature correspondences in both 3D mapping and tracking processes by the feature forest. The proposed system works real-time and achieves up to 60 FPS without the common GPU and PC support.

Given the feature correspondence, the 3D maps and continuous camera locations are obtained as shown in Figs. 1 and 4. We test one virtual scene with a colored balloon and several white blocks. With the hand-held mobile phone, we can freely explore the virtual environments as shown in the supplemental video. We illustrate the feature matching between keyframes in Fig. 5. The proposed method is robust to obtain the ORB feature matching regardless of the viewpoint and illumination variations.

We report the precision and recall rates of the proposed feature forest (FF) and the incremental feature forest (IFF) with online refinement on public SLAM datasets, including New College [16], Bicocca25b [3], Ford2 [11], and Malaga6L [2] as listed in Table 1. The proposed IFF method achieves an improvement over the comparable bag of word (BoW) [7] and the FF methods.

We also report the precision and recall of the proposed FF and the IFF methods of different types indoor scenes, including the table/chair, the plant, and the poster as shown in Table 2. We observe that the posters with abundant textures have higher precision and recall rates than other types of objects. The IFF approach with online refinement produces an improvement over the original feature forest. We believe the reason is that the adaptation to the new scene enables the accurate affinity estimation and feature matching.

Fig. 5. Feature matching between keyframes. (Color figure online)

Table 1. Precision and recall.

Dataset	Precision (%)	Recall (%)		
		BoW [7]	FF	IFF
New College	100	55.9	63.2	**66.4**
Bicocca25b	100	81.2	81.5	**82.4**
Ford2	100	79.4	80.1	**81.1**
Malaga6L	100	74.7	73.2	**75.1**

Table 2. Precision and recall of indoor objects.

Dataset	Precision (%)		Recall (%)	
	FF	IFF	FF	IFF
Table/Chair	80.1	**82.6**	29.9	**30.5**
Plant	87.8	**90.5**	**40.1**	**40.1**
Poster	93.5	**95.9**	59.7	**60.7**

4 Conclusion

This paper presents a random-forest-based fast feature matching technique for the mobile device mounted SLAM. The proposed method takes advantage of the offline feature forest together with the online incremental forest adaptation for the feature affinity and matching confidences. The matching confident scores reduce the candidate searching space and facilitate the real-time SLAM for VR and AR applications on mobile devices.

References

1. Bay, H., Tuytelaars, T., Van Gool, L.: SURF: speeded up robust features. In: Leonardis, A., Bischof, H., Pinz, A. (eds.) ECCV 2006, Part I. LNCS, vol. 3951, pp. 404–417. Springer, Heidelberg (2006). https://doi.org/10.1007/11744023_32
2. Blanco, J.L., Moreno, F.A., Gonzalez, J.: A collection of outdoor robotic datasets with centimeter-accuracy ground truth. Auton. Robots **27**(4), 327 (2009)
3. Bonarini, A., Burgard, W., Fontana, G., Matteucci, M., Sorrenti, D.G., Tardos, J.D.: Rawseeds: robotics advancement through web-publishing of sensorial and elaborated extensive data sets. In: Proceedings of IROS, vol. 6 (2006)
4. Calonder, M., Lepetit, V., Strecha, C., Fua, P.: BRIEF: binary robust independent elementary features. In: Daniilidis, K., Maragos, P., Paragios, N. (eds.) ECCV 2010, Part IV. LNCS, vol. 6314, pp. 778–792. Springer, Heidelberg (2010). https://doi.org/10.1007/978-3-642-15561-1_56
5. Criminisi, A., Shotton, J., Konukoglu, E.: Decision forests for classification, regression, density estimation, manifold learning and semi-supervised learning. Microsoft Research Cambridge, Technical report MSRTR-2011-114 **5**(6), 12 (2011)
6. Engel, J., Schöps, T., Cremers, D.: LSD-SLAM: large-scale direct monocular SLAM. In: Fleet, D., Pajdla, T., Schiele, B., Tuytelaars, T. (eds.) ECCV 2014, Part II. LNCS, vol. 8690, pp. 834–849. Springer, Cham (2014). https://doi.org/10.1007/978-3-319-10605-2_54
7. Gálvez-López, D., Tardos, J.D.: Bags of binary words for fast place recognition in image sequences. IEEE Trans. Robot. **28**(5), 1188–1197 (2012)
8. Klein, G., Murray, D.: Parallel tracking and mapping for small AR workspaces. In: IEEE and ACM International Symposium on Mixed and Augmented Reality, pp. 225–234. IEEE (2007)
9. Lowe, D.G.: Distinctive image features from scale-invariant keypoints. Int. J. Comput. Vis. **60**(2), 91–110 (2004)
10. Mur-Artal, R., Montiel, J.M.M., Tardos, J.D.: ORB-SLAM: a versatile and accurate monocular SLAM system. IEEE Trans. Robot. **31**(5), 1147–1163 (2015)
11. Pandey, G., McBride, J.R., Eustice, R.M.: Ford campus vision and lidar data set. Int. J. Robot. Res. **30**(13), 1543–1552 (2011)
12. Pei, Y., Kim, T.K., Zha, H.: Unsupervised random forest manifold alignment for lipreading. In: IEEE International Conference on Computer Vision, pp. 129–136 (2013)
13. Ristin, M., Guillaumin, M., Gall, J., Van Gool, L.: Incremental learning of random forests for large-scale image classification. IEEE Trans. Pattern Anal. Mach. Intell. **38**(3), 490–503 (2016)
14. Rublee, E., Rabaud, V., Konolige, K., Bradski, G.: ORB: an efficient alternative to SIFT or SURF. In: IEEE International Conference on Computer Vision, pp. 2564–2571. IEEE (2011)
15. Shridhar, M., Neo, K.Y.: Monocular slam for real-time applications on mobile platforms (2015)
16. Smith, M., Baldwin, I., Churchill, W., Paul, R., Newman, P.: The new college vision and laser data set. Int. J. Robot. Res. **28**(5), 595–599 (2009)

Augmented Coarse-to-Fine Video Frame Synthesis with Semantic Loss

Xin Jin[✉], Zhibo Chen[iD], Sen Liu, and Wei Zhou

CAS Key Laboratory of Technology in Geo-spatial Information Processing
and Application System, University of Science and Technology of China,
Hefei 230027, China
{jinxustc,weichou}@mail.ustc.edu.cn, chenzhibo@ustc.edu.cn,
elsen@iat.ustc.edu.cn

Abstract. Existing video frame synthesis works suffer from improving perceptual quality and preserving semantic representation ability. In this paper, we propose a Progressive Motion-texture Synthesis Network (PMSN) to address this problem. Instead of learning synthesis from scratch, we introduce augmented inputs to compensate texture details and motion information. Specifically, a coarse-to-fine guidance scheme with a well-designed semantic loss is presented to improve the capability of video frame synthesis. As shown in the experiments, our proposed PMSN promises excellent quantitative results, visual effects, and generalization ability compared with traditional solutions.

Keywords: Video frame synthesis · Augmented input
Coarse-to-fine guidance scheme · Semantic loss

1 Introduction

Video frame synthesis plays an important role in numerous applications of different fields, including video compression [2], video frame rate up-sampling [12], and pilot-less automobile [9]. Given a video sequence, video frame synthesis aims to interpolate frames between the existing video frames or extrapolate future video frames as shown in Fig. 1. However, constructing a generalized model to synthesize video frames is still challenging, especially for those videos with large motion and complex texture.

A lot of efforts have been dedicated towards video frame synthesis. Traditional approaches focused on synthesizing video frames from estimated motion information, such as optical flow [10,16,22]. Recent approaches have proposed deep generative models to directly hallucinate the pixel values of video frames [4,13,15,17,19,21,26,27]. However, these models always generate significant artifacts since the accuracy of motion estimation cannot be guaranteed. Meanwhile, due to the straightforward non-linear convolution operations, the results of deep generative models are suffered from blur artifacts.

J.-H. Lai et al. (Eds.): PRCV 2018, LNCS 11256, pp. 439–452, 2018.
https://doi.org/10.1007/978-3-030-03398-9_38

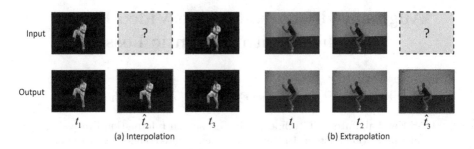

Input

Output

t_1 $\hat{t}_2$ t_3 t_1 t_2 $\hat{t}_3$

(a) Interpolation   (b) Extrapolation

Fig. 1. Interpolation and extrapolation tasks in the video frame synthesis problem.

In order to tackle the above problems, we propose a deep model called Progressive Motion-texture Synthesis Network (PMSN), which is a global encoder-decoder architecture with coarse-to-fine guidance under a brain-inspired semantic objective. Overview of the whole process of PMSN is illustrated in Fig. 2. Specifically, we first introduce an augmented frames generation process to produce Motion-texture Augmented Frames (MAFs) containing coarse-grained motion prediction and high texture details. Second, in order to reduce the loss of detailed information in the feed-forward process and assist the network to learn motion tendency, MAFs are fed into the decoder stage with different scales in a coarse-to-fine manner, rather than the scheme of directly fusion into a single layer as described in [12]. Finally, we also adopt a brain-inspired semantic loss to further enhance the subjective quality and preserve the semantic representation ability of synthesized frames in the learning stage. The contributions of this paper are summarized as follows:

1. Instead of learning synthesis from scratch, we introduce a novel Progressive Motion-texture Synthesis Network (PMSN) to learn frame synthesis with triple-frame input under the assistant of augmented frames. These augmented frames provide effective prior information including motion tendency and texture details to compensate the video synthesis.
2. A coarse-to-fine guidance scheme is adopted in the decoder stage of the network to increase its sensitivity to informative features. Through this scheme, we can maximally exploit the informative features and suppress less useful ones at the same time, which acts as a bridge which combines conventional motion estimation methods and deep learning-based methods.
3. We develop a brain-inspired semantic loss for sharpening the synthetic results and strengthening object texture as well as motion information. The final results demonstrate better perceptual quality and semantic representation preserving ability.

2   Related Work

Traditional Methods. Early attempts at video frame synthesis focused on motion estimation based approaches. For example, Revaud *et al.* [22] proposed

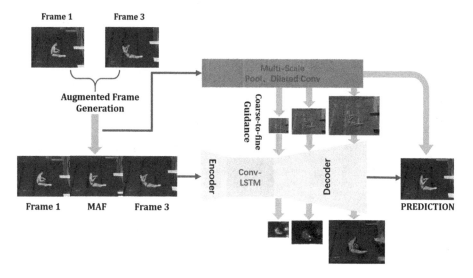

Fig. 2. Overview of our Progressive Motion-texture Synthesis Network (PMSN).

the EpicFlow to estimate optical flow by edge-aware distance. Li *et al.* [10] adopted a Laplacian Cotangent Mesh constraint to enhance the local smoothness for results generated by optical flow. Meyer *et al.* [16] leveraged the phase shift information for image interpolation. The results of these methods are highly relied on the precise estimation of motion information. Significant artifacts can be generated when unsatisfactory estimation happens for videos with large or complex motion.

Learning-Based Methods. The renaissance of deep neural network (DNN) remarkably accelerates the progress of video frame synthesis. Numbers of methods were proposed to interpolate or extrapolate video frames [13–15,17,19,26, 27]. [17] focused on representing series transformation to predict small patches based on recurrent neural network (RNN). Xue *et al.* [27] proposed a model which generates videos with an assumption that the background is uniform. Lotter *et al.* [13] proposed a network called PredNet, which contains a series of stacked modules that forward the deviations in video sequences. Mathieu *et al.* [15] proposed a multi-scale architecture with adversarial training, which is referred as BeyondMSE. Niklaus *et al.* [19] tried to estimate a convolution kernel from the input frames. Then, the kernel was used to convolve patches from the input frames for synthesizing the interpolated ones. However, it is still hard to hallucinate realistic details for videos with complex spatiotemporal information only by the non-linear convolution operation.

Recently, Liu *et al.* [12] utilized the pixel-wise 3D voxel flow to synthesize video frames. Lu *et al.* [14] presented a Flexible Spatio-Temporal Network (FSTN) to capture complex spatio-temporal dependencies and motion patterns with diverse training strategies. [19] just focused on video frame interpolation

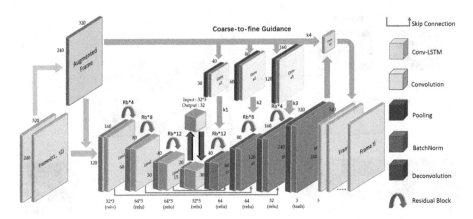

Fig. 3. The whole architecture of our Progressive Motion-texture Synthesis Network (PMSN).

task via adaptive convolution. Liang *et al.* [11] developed a dual motion Generative Adversarial Network (GAN) for video prediction. Villegas *et al.* [25] proposed a deep generative model named MCNet to extract the features of the last frame as content information and then encode the temporal differences between previous consecutive frames as motion information. Unfortunately, these methods usually only have the ability to deal with videos with tiny object motion and simple background which often cause blur artifacts in video scenes with large and complex motion. On the contrary, our proposed PMSN is able to achieve much better results, especially in complex scenes. In the experiment section Sect. 4, we will show adequate evaluations between our method and above methods.

3   Progressive Motion-Texture Synthesis Network

The whole architecture of our Progressive Motion-texture Synthesis Network (PMSN) is shown in Fig. 3, which takes advantage of the spatial invariance and temporal correlation for image representations. Instead of learning from scratch, the model receives original video frames combined with the produced augmented frames as the whole inputs. These triple-frame inputs provide more reference information for motion trajectory and texture residue, which leads to more reasonable high-level image representations. In the following sub-sections, we will first describe the augmented frames generation process. Then, the coarse-to-fine guidance scheme and semantic loss are presented.

Encoder Stage: Each convolutional block is shown in Fig. 4(a). The size of the receptive field for all convolution filters is $(4, 4)$ along with stride $(2, 2)$. A group of *Residual Blocks* [5] (number of blocks in the group is shown in Fig. 3) is used to strengthen the non-linear representation and preserve more spatial-temporal details. To overcome the overfitting and internal covariant shift problems, we add a batch normalization layer before each Rectified Liner Unit (ReLU) layer [18].

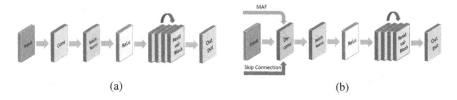

(a)   (b)

Fig. 4. Two sub-components in PMSN. (a) Convolutional block in PMSN. (b) Deconvolutional block in PMSN.

Decoder Stage: The deconvolutional block is used to upsample the feature maps, as demonstrated in Fig. 4(b), which has a receptive field of $(5,5)$ with stride $(2,2)$. The block also contains BatchNorm, ReLU layer and Residual Block, their parameters are shown in Fig. 3. To maintain the image details from low-level to high-level, we build skip connections, which are illustrated as the thin blue arrows in Fig. 3.

3.1   Augmented Frames Generation

Intrinsically, our PMSN utilizes augmented frames rather than learning from scratch. Then it is important for the augmented frame to preserve coarse motion trajectory and less-blurred texture, for PMSN to further improve the quality under the assistance of coarse-to-fine guidance and semantic loss. Therefore, any frame augmentation scheme satisfying above-mentioned two factors can be adopted in the PMSN framework, we introduce a simple augmented frames generation process in this paper to produce Motion-texture Augmented Frames (MAFs) containing coarse-grained motion prediction and high texture details. Similar to motion-estimation based frame synthesis methods, the original input frames are first decomposed into block-level matrixes. Then, we directly copy the matching blocks to MAFs according to the estimated motion vectors of these blocks. As shown in Fig. 5(a), to calculate the motion vector for generating MAF f_i', we first partition the frame $\hat{f}_{i-1}$ into regular 4×4 blocks, then search backward in the frame $\hat{f}_{i-2}$. When building each 4×4 block of MAF, the motion vectors of corresponding 4×4 block in frame $\hat{f}_{i-1}$ are utilized to locate and copy the data from frame $\hat{f}_{i-1}$. This block-sized thresholding 4×4 is sufficient for our purpose of generating the MAFs.

Note that this frame augmentation scheme can be replaced by any other frame synthesis solution, we verified this in the experiment section Sect. 4.3 by replacing MAFs with augmented frames generated from [19] and then demonstrate the effectiveness of our proposed PMSN.

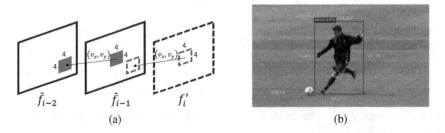

(a)   (b)

Fig. 5. (a) The generation precess of MAFs where the direction of motion vectors is backward. (b) Attention object bounding box extracted by faster R-CNN.

3.2   Coarse-to-Fine Guidance

In order to make use of the information aggregated in the MAFs as well as triple-frame input groups for selectively emphasizing informative features and suppressing less useful ones, we propose a coarse-to-fine guidance scheme to guide our network in an end-to-end manner, which is illustrated as orange arrows in Figs. 2, 3 and 4(b). Specifically, given the double-frame input X and single augmented frame $\tilde{Y}$, our goal is to obtain the synthesized interpolated/extrapolated frames Y', which can be formulated as:

$$Y' = f(G(X + \tilde{Y}), \tilde{Y}), \tag{1}$$

where G denotes a generator which learns motion trajectory and texture residue from triple-frame input group $X + \tilde{Y}$. Function f represents the fusion process to fully capture channel-wise dependencies through a concatenation operation.

In order to progressively improve the quality of synthesized frames in a coarse-to-fine way, we make a series of synthesis from MAFs with gradual increase resolutions, which is depicted as below:

$$
\begin{aligned}
Y_1' &= f(G_1(X + \tilde{Y}_1), e_1(\tilde{Y}_1)), \\
Y_2' &= f(G_2(Y_1' + \tilde{Y}_2), e_2(\tilde{Y}_2)), \\
&\cdots \\
Y_k' &= f(G_k(Y_{k-1}' + \tilde{Y}_k), e_k(\tilde{Y}_k)),
\end{aligned}
\tag{2}
$$

where k represents each level of the coarse-to-fine synthesis process. In our PMSN, we set the size of each level to 40×30 ($k = 1$), 80×60 ($k = 2$), 160×120 ($k = 3$), 320×240 ($k = 4$). G_k is the middle layer of G, and $G_1, G_2, ..., G_k$ compose an integrated network. And e_k is the feature extractor of $\tilde{Y}_k$, we employ two dilated convolutional layers [28] instead of simple downsample operations to preserve the texture details of original images. Since the output Y_k' is produced by a summation through all channels (X and Y), the channel dependencies are implicitly embedded in them. In order to ensure that the network is able to increase its sensitivity to informative features and suppress less useful ones, the final output of each level is obtained by assigning each channel a corresponding weighting factor W. Then we design a Guidance Loss ℓ_{guid} containing four sub-loss functions for each level $\hat{Y}'_k$. Let Y denotes the Ground Truth and δ refers to the activation function ReLu [18]:

$$\hat{Y}'_k = F(Y'_k, W) = \delta(W * Y'_k), \qquad \ell_{guid} = \sum_{k=1}^{4} \|\hat{Y}'_k - Y\|_2. \tag{3}$$

3.3 Semantic Loss

In the visual cortex, neurons are mapped to the visible or salient parts of an image and activated first, then followed by a later spread to neurons that are mapped to the missing parts [3,6]. Inspired by this visual cortex representation process, we design a hybrid semantic loss ℓ_{sem} to further sharpen the texture details of synthesized results and strengthen informative motion information, which consists of four sub-parts: Guidance Loss ℓ_{guid} mentioned above, Lateral Dependency Loss ℓ_{ld}, Attention Emphasis Loss ℓ_{emph}, and Gradient Loss ℓ_{grad}. First, to imitate the cortical neuron filling-in process and capture lateral dependency between neighbors in the visual cortex, ℓ_{ld} is proposed:

$$\ell_{ld} = \frac{1}{N} \sum_{i,j=1}^{N} |\|\hat{Y}_{i,j} - \hat{Y}_{i-1,j}\|_2 - \|Y_{i,j} - Y_{i-1,j}\|_2| +$$
$$|\|\hat{Y}_{i,j} - \hat{Y}_{i,j-1}\|_2 - \|Y_{i,j} - Y_{i,j-1}\|_2|. \tag{4}$$

Second, ℓ_{emph} is employed to strengthen the texture and motion information of attention objects in the scene, namely, to emphasize the gradients for attention objects through feedback values during the back-propagation. As shown in Fig. 5(b), we take advantage of the excellent Faster R-CNN [20] to extract the foreground attention objects through a priori bounding box where (W_{box}, H_{box}) is the pair of width and height. Then we define the Attention Emphasis Loss ℓ_{emph} as follows:

$$\ell_{emph} = \frac{1}{W_{box} \times H_{box}} \sum_{i,j}^{(i,j)\in box} |\|\hat{Y}_{i,j} - \hat{Y}_{i-1,j}\|_2 - \|Y_{i,j} - Y_{i-1,j}\|_2| +$$
$$|\|\hat{Y}_{i,j} - \hat{Y}_{i,j-1}\|_2 - \|Y_{i,j} - Y_{i,j-1}\|_2|. \tag{5}$$

Finally, ℓ_{grad} is also used to sharpen the texture details by incorporating with image gradients as shown in Eq. 6, and similar operation is also described in [15]. In summary, the semantic loss ℓ_{sem} is a weighted sum of all the losses in our experiment where $\alpha = 1, \beta = 0.3, \gamma = 0.7, \lambda = 1$ are the weights for Guidance Loss, Lateral Dependency Loss, Attention Emphasis Loss and Gradient Loss, respectively:

$$\ell_{grad} = |\nabla\hat{Y} - \nabla Y|^2. \tag{6}$$

$$\ell_{sem} = \alpha\ell_{guid} + \beta\ell_{ld} + \gamma\ell_{emph} + \lambda\ell_{grad}. \tag{7}$$

4   Experiments

In this section, we present comprehensive experiments to analyze and understand the behavior of our model. We first evaluate our model in terms of qualitative and quantitative performance for video interpolation and extrapolation. Then we show more capacities of our PMSN on various datasets. In the end, we analyze the effectiveness of different components in the PMSN separately. **Datasets:** We train our network on 153,971 triplet video sequences sampled from UCF-101 [24] dataset, and test the performance on UCF-101 (validation), HMDB51 [8], and YouTube-8m [1] datasets. **Training Details:** We adopt an Adam [7] solver to learn the model parameters by optimizing the semantic loss. The batch size is set as 32, and our initial learning rate is 0.005 that decays every 50K steps. We train the model for 100K iterations. The source code will be released in the future. **Baselines:** Here, we divide existing video synthesis methods into three categories for comparison: **(1) Interpolation-Only,** Phase-based frame interpolation [16] is a traditional and well-performed method just for video interpolation. Ada-Conv [19] also only focuses on video frame interpolation task via adaptive convolution operations. **(2) Extrapolation-Only,** PredNet [13] is a predictive coding inspired CNN architecture. MCNet [25] predicts frames by decomposing motion and content. FSTN [14] and Dual-Motion GAN [11] both only focus on video extrapolation task, and the authors do not release their pre-trained weights or training details. Hence, we only compare the PSNR and SSIM presented in their paper. **(3) Interpolation-Plus-Extrapolation,** EpicFlow [22] is a state-of-the-art approach for optical flow estimation, the synthesized frames are constructed by pixel compensation. For CNN-based methods, BeyondMSE [15] is a multi-scale architecture. The official model is trained by using 4 and 8 input frames. Since our method uses 2 input frames, BeyondMSE with 2 input frames is implemented for comparison. U-Net [23], which has a well-received structure for pixel-level generation, is also implemented for comparison. Deep Voxel Flow (DVF) [12] trains a deep network that learns to synthesize video frames by flowing pixel values from existing frames.

4.1   Quantitative and Qualitative Comparison

For quantitative comparison, we use both Peak Signal-to-Noise Ratio (PSNR) and Structural SIMilarity (SSIM) index to evaluate the image quality of interpolated/extrapolated frames, higher values of PSNR and SSIM indicate better results. In terms of qualitative quality, our approach is compared with several latest state-of-the-art methods in Figs. 6 and 7.

Single-Frame Synthesis. As shown in Table 1, it is obvious that our solution outperforms all existing solutions. Compared with the existing best interpolation-only solution Ada-Conv and best extrapolation-only solution Dual-Motion GAN, over 0.5 dB and 0.8 dB PSNR improvement can be achieved respectively. Compared with the existing best interpolation-plus-extrapolation scheme Deep Voxel Flow, over 2.2 dB and 1.7 dB PSNR improvement can be achieved

Table 1. Performance of frame synthesis on UCF-101 validation dataset.

Methods	Interpolation		Extrapolation	
	PSNR	SSIM	PSNR	SSIM
Pred Net [13]	—	—	22.6	0.74
Phase-based [16]	28.4	0.84	—	—
Beyond-MSE [15]	28.8	0.90	28.2	0.89
Epic-Flow [22]	30.2	0.93	29.1	0.91
U-Net [23]	30.2	0.92	29.2	0.92
FSTN [14]	—	—	27.6	0.91
MCNet [25]	—	—	28.8	0.92
Deep Voxel Flow [12]	30.9	0.94	29.6	0.92
Dual-Motion GAN [11]	—	—	30.5	0.94
Ada-Conv [19]	32.6	0.95	—	—
Ours	**33.1**	**0.96**	**31.3**	**0.94**

for interpolation and extrapolation operation respectively. We also show some subjective results for perceptual comparison. As illustrated in Figs. 6 and 7, our PMSN demonstrates better perceptual quality with clearer integrated objects, non-blurred background scene and more accurate motion prediction, compared with existing solutions. For example, Ada-Conv generates strong distortion and losses partial object in the bottom-right "leg" area due to failed motion prediction. On the contrary, our PMSN demonstrates much better perceptual quality without obvious artifacts.

Multi-Frame Synthesis. We further explore the multi-frame synthesis ability of our PMSN on various datasets, which can be used for up-sampling video frame rate and generating videos with slow-motion effect. We can see that the qualitative results in Fig. 8(a) have reasonable motion and realistic texture. And as demonstrated in Fig. 8(b), the PMSN can provide outstanding performance compared with other state-of-the-art methods.

4.2 Generalization Ability

Furthermore, we show the generalization ability of our PMSN by evaluating the model on YouTube-8m and HMDB-51 validation datasets without re-training. Table 2 demonstrates that our model outperforms all previous state-of-the-art models by a even larger gain (over 1.2 dB PSNR improvement on both datasets for interpolation and extrapolation) compared with results in Table 1, which means our PMNS has a much better generalization ability.

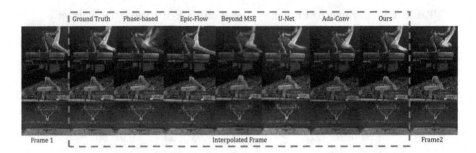

Fig. 6. Qualitative comparisons of video interpolation.

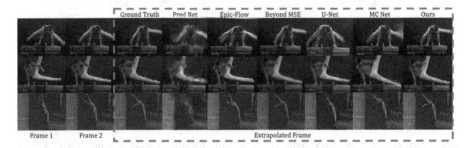

Fig. 7. Qualitative comparisons of video extrapolation.

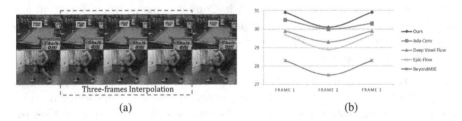

Fig. 8. (a) Three-frame interpolation. (b) Performance comparisons on three-frame interpolation.

4.3 Ablation Study

Effectiveness of Coarse-to-Fine Guidance Scheme: We first visualize the output of each deconvolutional block in the decoder stage, which indicates these gradually improved results using MAFs with different resolutions through a coarse-to-fine guidance scheme. As shown in the gray-images of Fig. 9(a), the texture details of the image are enhanced progressively, and the texture of the object becomes increasingly realistic.

In addition, as we mentioned in Sect. 3.1 that frame augmentation scheme can be replaced by any other frame synthesis solution, we adopt more complex adaptive convolution [19] to replace our basic generation of augmented frames

Table 2. Performance of frame synthesis on YouTube-8M and HMDB-51 validation datasets.

Methods	Interpolation		Extrapolation	
	PSNR	SSIM	PSNR	SSIM
Pred Net	—	—	19.7/18.4	0.65/0.59
Phase-based	21.0 /21.7	0.66/0.68	—	—
U-Net	24.2/23.8	0.73/0.72	22.7/22.4	0.70/0.70
BeyondMSE	26.6/26.8	0.78/0.80	25.7/26.1	0.74/0.76
MCNet	—	—	26.9/27.9	0.79/0.81
Epic-Flow	29.5/29.5	0.92/0.92	29.2/29.3	0.90/0.92
Ada-Conv	29.5/29.6	0.93/0.92	—	—
Ours	**31.1/31.4**	**0.94/0.92**	**30.4/30.7**	**0.94/0.93**

(MAFs) in video frame interpolation experiment, then we find that our PMSN obtains extra 0.5 dB gain in PSNR. In general, above ablation studies demonstrate that the proposed coarse-to-fine guidance scheme is really effective in further improving synthesis quality.

Effectiveness of MAFs: As shown in Fig. 9(b), the pure results of MAFs are unsatisfactory with a certain degree of blocking artifacts and uneven motions, the results without MAFs also have significant blur artifacts, which demonstrates that MAFs can provide informative motion tendency and texture details for synthesis.

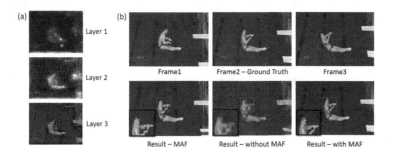

Fig. 9. (a) Output of each layer in the decoder stage. (b) Interpolation example.

Effectiveness of Semantic Loss: The Semantic Loss ℓ_{sem} is comprised of Guidance Loss ℓ_{guid}, Lateral Dependency Loss ℓ_{ld}, Attention Emphasis Loss ℓ_{emph}, and Gradient Loss ℓ_{grad}. To evaluate the contribution of each loss, we implement four related baselines for comparison. As shown in Table 3, we find that $\ell_{ld}+\ell_{guid}$, $\ell_{ld}+\ell_{emph}$ and $\ell_{ld}+\ell_{grad}$ are all higher than basic ℓ_{ld}, which

Table 3. Performance of hybrid losses.

Methods	Interpolation		Extrapolation	
	PSNR	SSIM	PSNR	SSIM
ℓ_{ld}	31.9	0.92	30.5	0.90
$\ell_{ld} + \ell_{guid}$	32.4	0.93	30.6	0.90
$\ell_{ld} + \ell_{grad}$	32.8	0.95	30.9	0.91
$\ell_{ld} + \ell_{emph}$	32.9	0.95	31.0	0.93
ℓ_{sem}	**33.1**	**0.96**	**31.3**	**0.94**

means that Guidance, Attention Emphasis and Gradient Loss lead to better performance. The combination of them further improves the overall performance.

5   Conclusions

In order to solve the problems existing in the traditional synthesis framework based on pixel motion estimation or learning based solutions, we try to effectively combine the advantages of the two solutions by establishing the proposed Progressive Motion-texture Synthesis Network (PMSN) framework. Based on the augmented input, the network can obtain informative motion tendency and enhance the texture details of synthesized video frames through the well-designed coarse-to-fine guidance scheme. In the learning stage, a brain-inspired semantic loss is introduced for further refining the motion and texture of objects. We perform comprehensive experiment to verify the effectiveness of PMSN. In the future, we expect to extend PMSN to other types of tasks such as video tracking, video question answering, etc.

Acknowledgement. This work was supported in part by the National Key Research and Development Program of China under Grant No. 2016YFC0801001, the National Program on Key Basic Research Projects (973 Program) under Grant 2015CB351803, NSFC under Grant 61571413, 61632001, 61390514.

References

1. Abu-El-Haija, S., et al.: Youtube-8m: a large-scale video classification benchmark (2016). arXiv preprint: arXiv:1609.08675
2. Choudhary, S., Varshney, P.: A study of digital video compression techniques. PARIPEX-Indian J. Res. **5**(4), 39–41 (2016)
3. De Weerd, P., Gattass, R., Desimone, R., Ungerleider, L.G.: Responses of cells in monkey visual cortex during perceptual filling-in of an artificial scotoma. Nature **377**, 731–734 (1995)
4. Finn, C., Goodfellow, I., Levine, S.: Unsupervised learning for physical interaction through video prediction. In: NIPS, pp. 64–72 (2016)

5. He, K., Zhang, X., Ren, S., Sun, J.: Deep residual learning for image recognition. In: CVPR, pp. 770–778 (2016)
6. Huang, X., Paradiso, M.A.: V1 response timing and surface filling-in. J. Neurophysiol. **100**(1), 539–547 (2008)
7. Kingma, D., Ba, J.: Adam: a method for stochastic optimization (2014). arXiv preprint: arXiv:1412.6980
8. Kuehne, H., Jhuang, H., Stiefelhagen, R., Serre, T.: HMDB51: a large video database for human motion recognition. In: Nagel, W., Kröner, D., Resch, M. (eds.) High Performance Computing in Science and Engineering 2012, pp. 571–582. Springer, Heidelberg (2013). https://doi.org/10.1007/978-3-642-33374-3_41
9. Li, S., Yeung, D.Y.: Visual object tracking for unmanned aerial vehicles: a benchmark and new motion models. In: AAAI, pp. 4140–4146 (2017)
10. Li, W., Cosker, D.: Video interpolation using optical flow and laplacian smoothness. Neurocomputing **220**, 236–243 (2017)
11. Liang, X., Lee, L., Dai, W., Xing, E.P.: Dual motion GAN for future-flow embedded video prediction. In: ICCV (2017)
12. Liu, Z., Yeh, R., Tang, X., Liu, Y., Agarwala, A.: Video frame synthesis using deep voxel flow. In: ICCV, vol. 2 (2017)
13. Lotter, W., Kreiman, G., Cox, D.: Deep predictive coding networks for video prediction and unsupervised learning. In: ICLR (2017)
14. Lu, C., Hirsch, M., Schölkopf, B.: Flexible spatio-temporal networks for video prediction. In: CVPR, pp. 6523–6531 (2017)
15. Mathieu, M., Couprie, C., LeCun, Y.: Deep multi-scale video prediction beyond mean square error. In: ICLR (2016)
16. Meyer, S., Wang, O., Zimmer, H., Grosse, M., Sorkine-Hornung, A.: Phase-based frame interpolation for video. In: CVPR, pp. 1410–1418 (2015)
17. Michalski, V., Memisevic, R., Konda, K.: Modeling deep temporal dependencies with recurrent grammar cells. In: NIPS, pp. 1925–1933 (2014)
18. Nair, V., Hinton, G.E.: Rectified linear units improve restricted Boltzmann machines. In: Proceedings of the 27th International Conference on Machine Learning (ICML 2010) (2010)
19. Niklaus, S., Mai, L., Liu, F.: Video frame interpolation via adaptive convolution. In: CVPR, vol. 2, p. 6 (2017)
20. Ren, S., He, K., Girshick, R., Sun, J.: Faster R-CNN: towards real-time object detection with region proposal networks. In: NIPS, pp. 91–99 (2015)
21. Ren, Z., Yan, J., Ni, B., Liu, B., Yang, X., Zha, H.: Unsupervised deep learning for optical flow estimation. In: AAAI, pp. 1495–1501 (2017)
22. Revaud, J., Weinzaepfel, P., Harchaoui, Z., Schmid, C.: Epicflow: edge-preserving interpolation of correspondences for optical flow. In: CVPR, pp. 1164–1172 (2015)
23. Ronneberger, O., Fischer, P., Brox, T.: U-Net: convolutional networks for biomedical image segmentation. In: Navab, N., Hornegger, J., Wells, W.M., Frangi, A.F. (eds.) MICCAI 2015, Part III. LNCS, vol. 9351, pp. 234–241. Springer, Cham (2015). https://doi.org/10.1007/978-3-319-24574-4_28
24. Soomro, K., Zamir, A.R., Shah, M.: Ucf101: a dataset of 101 human actions classes from videos in the wild (2012). arXiv preprint: arXiv:1212.0402
25. Villegas, R., Yang, J., Hong, S., Lin, X., Lee, H.: Decomposing motion and content for natural video sequence prediction. In: ICLR, vol. 1(2), p. 7 (2017)
26. Wang, Y., Long, M., Wang, J., Gao, Z., Philip, S.Y.: PredRNN: recurrent neural networks for predictive learning using spatiotemporal LSTMs. In: NIPS, pp. 879–888 (2017)

27. Xue, T., Wu, J., Bouman, K., Freeman, B.: Visual dynamics: probabilistic future frame synthesis via cross convolutional networks. In: NIPS, pp. 91–99 (2016)
28. Yu, F., Koltun, V.: Multi-scale context aggregation by dilated convolutions (2015). arXiv preprint: arXiv:1511.07122

Automatic Measurement of Cup-to-Disc Ratio for Retinal Images

Xin Zhao[1,2], Fan Guo[1,2(✉)], Beiji Zou[1,2], Xiyao Liu[1,2],
and Rongchang Zhao[1,2]

[1] School of Information Science and Engineering, Central South University,
Changsha 410083, China
guofancsu@163.com
[2] Hunan Province Machine Vision and Intelligence Medical Engineering
Technology Research Center, Changsha 410083, China

Abstract. Glaucoma is a chronic eye disease which results in irreversible vision loss, and the optic cup-to-disc ratio (CDR) is an essential clinical indicator in diagnosing glaucoma, which means precise optic disc (OD) and optic cup (OC) segmentation become an important task. In this paper, we propose an automatic CDR measurement method. The method includes three stages: OD localization and ROI extraction, simultaneous segmentation of OD and OC, and CDR calculation. In the first stage, the morphological operation and the sliding window are combined to find the OD location and extract the ROI region. In the second stage, an improved deep neural network, named U-Net+CP+FL, which consists of U-shape convolutional architecture, a novel concatenating path and a multi-label fusion loss function, is adopted to simultaneously segment the OD and OC. Based on the segmentation results, the CDR value can be calculated in the last stage. Experimental results on the retinal images from public databases demonstrate that the proposed method can achieve comparable performance with ophthalmologist and superior performance when compared with other existing methods. Thus, our method can be a suitable tool for automated glaucoma analysis.

Keywords: Glaucoma diagnosis · Cup-to-disc ratio (CDR) · OD localization OD&OC segmentation · Deep neural network

1 Introduction

Glaucoma is the second leading cause of blindness worldwide, as well as the foremost cause of irreversible blindness [1]. Although there is no cure, early detection and treatment can decrease the ratio of blindly. Digital retinal image is widely used for screening of glaucoma as it consumes less time, has higher accuracy. However, manual assessments by trained clinicians are not suitable for large-scale screening. Hence it is essential to design a reliable early detection system for glaucoma screening.

Generally, besides the increasing pressure in the eye [2], the risk factors for diagnosing glaucoma in retinal images include rim to disk area ratio, the optic disk diameter, and the vertical cup-to-disc ratio (CDR) [3]. Among these factors, CDR is

© Springer Nature Switzerland AG 2018
J.-H. Lai et al. (Eds.): PRCV 2018, LNCS 11256, pp. 453–465, 2018.
https://doi.org/10.1007/978-3-030-03398-9_39

considered as the essential measurement and is widely accepted by clinicians as well. According to clinical experience, a larger CDR indicates a higher risk of glaucoma. In order to obtain accurate CDR, precise segmentation of OD and OC [see Fig. 1] are essential. In our work, we propose an effective optic disc localization method, and with the OD location results, an end-to-end deep neural network called U-Net+CP+FL is proposed to segment the OD and OC simultaneously. The main contributions of our work are as follows:

(1) A new optic disc localization algorithm based on sliding window is proposed in this paper. The algorithm adopts intensity information and blood vessels to locate optic disc. Experimental results show that the optic disc can be effectively localized in various condition.

(2) A modification of U-Net neural network named U-Net+CP+FL which introduces concatenating path in the encoder path is proposed to segment the optic disc and cup simultaneously. The concatenating path introduces feature maps sharing and multi-scale inputs from all the previous layers to help to segment the OD and OC simultaneously.

(3) To segment OD and OC simultaneously and independently, we proposed a multi-label fusion loss function which consists of weighted binary cross-entropy loss and dice coefficient. The proposed loss function can deal with data imbalance problem, which is essential for the segmentation of OC.

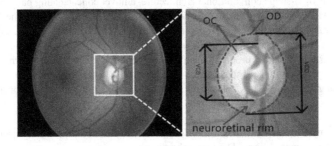

Fig. 1. Retinal fundus image and cropped ROI region. The region enclosed by the blue dotted ellipse is optic disc (OD), the green one is optic cup (OC). The region between OD and OC is neuroretinal rim. The cup-to-disc ratio (CDR) is defined as the ratio of vertical diameter of OC (VCD) to the vertical diameter of OD (VDD). (Color figure online)

The structure of the paper is as follows. We review the existing methods related to OD/OC localization and segmentation in Sect. 2. In Sect. 3, we describe the proposed algorithm in detail. Specifically, the framework of our method is first given. Then, the proposed OD localization method is described in Subsect. 3.2. Next, the proposed network architecture to OD and OC segmentation is presented in Subsect. 3.3, and post-processing after segmentation and CDR calculation are described in Subsect. 3.4. In Sect. 4, subjective and quantitative evaluations are performed to verify the effectiveness of our proposed method. Finally, we conclude the paper in Sect. 5.

2   Related Works

Accurate CDR calculation depends on precise segmentation of OD and OC. In this section we mainly introduce the related works on OD segmentation and OC segmentation. In [4], image gradient was applied to extract the optic disc contour. The spuerpixel method was also applied to OD and OC segmentation [5]. In [6], morphological operations were used to segment the optic cup. After removing the blood vessels, Babu et al. [7] employed fuzzy C-means clustering and wavelet transformed to extract OC. Common limitation of these algorithms is highly dependent on hand-crafted features, which are susceptible to different imaging conditions.

Few researchers Segment OD and OC simultaneously. For example, Yin et al. [8] employed a statistical model-based method for both OD and OC segmentation. In [9], a general energy function and structure constraint together with optimization of graph cut enables precise OD and OC segmentation. However, these algorithms segment them sequentially not simultaneously.

Aim at the above problems, an effective and robust OD localization method is first proposed to crop the OD region as ROI. Then the method segments the OD and OC from the ROI with the proposed U-Net+CP+FL which improves the U-Net with concatenating path and multi-labels fusion fundus loss function.

3   Our CDR Measurement Algorithm

3.1   Algorithm Framework

The proposed CDR measurement algorithm consists of three main phases: (i) OD localization and ROI extraction, (ii) Simultaneous segmentation of OD and OC, and (iii) CDR calculation, as shown in Fig. 2. These phases are further divided into several steps as follows:

i. OD localization and ROI extraction: OD localization consists of brightest region extraction, blood vessel extraction and confidence calculation of the sliding window. Firstly, Morphological processing is applied for both brightest region and blood vessel extraction. Secondly, sliding window is employed to find the OD location based on the retinal fusion image. Finally, ROI region is cropped for OD and OC segmentation.

ii. Simultaneous segmentation of OD and OC: U-Net+CP+FL is proposed for simultaneously segmenting OD and OC. Specifically, a U-shape network is adopted as our main architecture, and multi labels with fusion loss function are employed for better segmentation results. Besides, a novel concatenating path is also proposed and introduced along encoder path, which means multi-scale inputs and feature map reuse, resulting better segmentation results especially in OC.

iii. CDR calculation: Once OD and OC are segmented, post processing like erosion and dilation operations can eliminate the isolated points which mostly are noise. Besides, ellipse fitting is employed to smooth the boundary of the segmented results. Finally, CDR is calculated by the ratio of the vertical OC diameter to the vertical OD diameter.

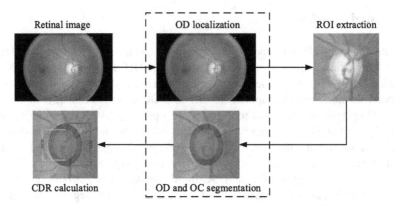

Fig. 2. Framework of our work

3.2   OD Localization and ROI Extraction

In the retinal image, the OD and OC occupy small portions, which are hard to segment. To handle this problem, we propose a novel OD localization algorithm that combines the intensity information with the blood vessels to localize the center of OD through the sliding window. The sub-image cropped from the center of the OD is considered as the ROI region. Thus, the segmentation of OD and OC will be operated on the cropped ROI. Figure 3 depicts the flowchart of the OD localization algorithm. It can be seen that there are three key steps for localizing the optic disc: Image enhancement and brightest region extraction, blood vessel extraction, and confidence calculation of the sliding window. Following we will discuss the three steps in details.

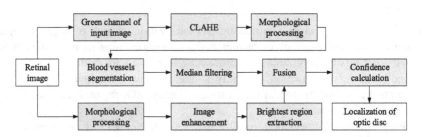

Fig. 3. Our OD localization algorithm flowchart. The intermediate steps are shown as red blocks and the key steps are shown as blue blocks. (Color figure online)

Step 1: Image Enhancement and Brightest Region Extraction. Due to the various imaging conditions, morphological processing is applied on the input retinal image (see Fig. 4(a)) to enhance the retinal image and to extract brightest pixels from the fundus. Top-hat transformation (G_T) is used to enhance bright objects of interest in a dark background (see Fig. 4(b)), and bottom-hat (G_B) enhances the dark objects of interest in a bright background (see Fig. 4(c)). Thus, the enhanced gray-level retinal image (F') can be defined as:

$$F' = F + G_T - G_B \tag{1}$$

As can be seen in Fig. 4(d), the region of OD is obviously enhanced, and the contrast of the gray-level retinal image is enhanced too. Thus, the pixels larger than 6.5% of the maximum pixel value are considered to be the candidate pixels of OD, since the OD accounts for brightest region of the retinal image, as shown in Fig. 4(e).

Step 2: Blood Vessel Extraction. For the blood vessel extraction, Contrast Limited Adaptive Histogram Equalization (CLAHE) is applied to enhance the blood vessel in the green channel of the input retinal image. Then, bottom-top hat transformation is employed to extract blood vessels. Since the intensity of the blood vessels is generally smaller than that of background, the vessels of blood can be extracted by the difference between bottom-hat transformation and top-hat transformation. Besides, to eliminate the salt and pepper noise from the blood vessel segmentation result, median filtering is performed. Thus, the vessel extraction result F_{vessel} can be obtained as shown in Fig. 4(f). This process can be written as:

$$F_{vessel} = G_B - G_T \tag{2}$$

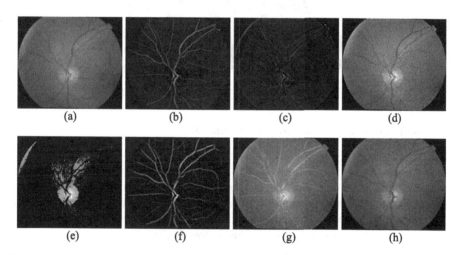

Fig. 4. Key steps for OD localization. (a) Input retinal image. (b) Bottom-hat transformation result. (c) Top-hat transformation result. (d) Enhanced retinal image by bottom-top-hat transformation. (e) Brightest region of retinal image. (f) Extracted blood vessels. (g) Fusion image which combined enhanced retinal image with the blood vessels. (h) Our OD localization result.

Step 3: Confidence Calculation of the Sliding Window. To locate the OD fast and effectively, sliding window is employed to scan three different feature maps including brightest region of gray-level retinal image, blood vessels and the fusion image which combines brightest region and blood vessels, as shown in Fig. 4(g). Let $f(i)$, $f(bv)$ and $f(ibv)$ represent score of each sliding window which is scanned through the three feature maps: intensity map I, blood vessel map bv, and intensity & blood vessel map ibv. In addition, min-max normalization is also applied to the scores of sliding windows in each feature map to normalize the data between 0 and 1. Thus, the final score of each window S is the mean value of $f(i)$, $f(bv)$ and $f(ibv)$.

Finally, the localization of the sliding window with the maximum score will be considered to be the location of OD, as shown in Fig. 4(h).

Once the OD is located, the square region containing OD can be extracted from the retinal image as ROI region. In our work, all the ROI regions have the same size and the size is equal to 1.5 times of the maximum diameter of OD, where the maximum diameter of OD is calculated by the OD mask of retinal images from existing dataset before OD localization. Experiment on test images show that our method can effectively extract the OD inside the ROI region. An illustrative example is shown in Fig. 5.

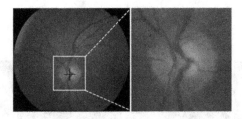

Fig. 5. OD localization result and cropped ROI region

3.3 Simultaneous Segmentation of OD and OC

Inspired by U-Net [10] and DenseNet [11] architecture, we propose a novel architecture called U-Net+CP+FL which consists of U-shape convolutional architecture, concatenating path and fusion loss function, as shown in Fig. 6. As can be seen in the figure, the network includes three components: (i) U-shape deep convolutional neural network architecture, (ii) concatenating path—an additional connection design between encoder layers (iii) multi-label output layer with fusion loss function.

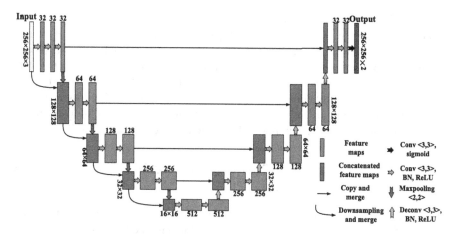

Fig. 6. Our proposed network architecture

3.3.1 U-Shape Network Architecture

U-shape network is an effective and powerful fully convolutional neural network for biomedical image segmentation even for small dataset. The network mainly consists of two parts: encoder path and decoder path, and skip connections.

Encoder path is responsible for feature extraction, which consists of convolutional block including batch normalization (BN), ReLU activation and convolutions successively. Maxpooling is employed to reduce the resolution of the feature maps. Decoder path is a reverse process of the encoder path, which is trained to reconstruct the input image resolution. To recover the resolution of the feature maps, deconvolution is employed in the decoder layer which matches pooling layer in the encoder path. Finally, the output at the final decoder layer is fed to a multi-label classifier.

Skip connection is a crucial design in encoder-decoder networks. The skip architecture relays the intermittent feature maps from encoder layer to the matched decoder layer, which not only helps reconstructing the input image resolution but also overcome the vanishing gradient problem.

3.3.2 Concatenating Path

Inspired by Densenet, we introduce new connections between encoder layers called concatenating path, which contributes to the feature maps sharing and multi-scale inputs for the encoder path. Along the concatenating path, the input of current layer is consisted of last pooling output and last resized input. Thus, the encoder path receives feature maps not only from the last layer, but also from the input layer and the semantic information from all the previous layers, which equals multi-scale inputs and feature maps sharing. Experimental results show that our proposed network improves the segmentation accuracy.

3.3.3 Multi-label Loss Function

OD and OC occupy small parts of retinal image (see Fig. 1), thus overfitting is prone to happen even trained on the cropped ROI region. In U-NET+CP+FL, we propose combining the weighted binary cross-entropy loss with the dice coefficient as the object function to optimize, where the introduction of dice coefficient relives the data imbalance problem effectively. For the proposed network, multi-label loss means that the pixel belongs to OD or/and OC independently, and this helps to mitigate the data imbalance problem too. The multi-label loss function is described as:

$$L(p,g) = -\sum_{i=1}^{N}\sum_{c=1}^{K} w^c \left(g_i^c \cdot \log(p_i^c) + \frac{2 \cdot p_i^c \cdot g_i^c}{(p_i^c)^2 + (g_i^c)^2} \right) \tag{3}$$

where p_i^c denotes the probability of pixel i belong to class c, and g_i^c denotes the ground truth label for pixel i. In our experiments, pixels belonging to OD or OC independently, thus k is set to be 2. w^c in Eq. (3) is a trade-off weight to decide the contribution of OD and OC. For glaucoma diagnosis, both OD and OC are important, so we set w^c to 0.5.

3.4 CDR Calculation

To achieve accurate CDR measurement, postprocessing on the segmentation result can mitigate the effects of noise and uneven boundaries. Most isolated points can be eliminated by erosion and dilation operations. Since another distinct feature of OD is its elliptical shape, we then use the least-squares optimization to fit the segmented OD contour with an ellipse, where the contour pixels are extracted by means of a Canny edge detector. Finally, the centroid and the long/short-axis length of the OD, which are obtained by ellipse fitting, are used to overlay ellipse on the input image to segment OD of the input retinal image. The same operations are conducted on the OC. At Last, CDR is calculated by the ratio of the vertical OC diameter (VCD) to the vertical OD diameter (VDD), as shown in Fig. 1.

4 Experimental Results

In this section, we present our experiment results. First, we evaluate our OD localization, simultaneous segmentation of OD and OC, and CDR calculation in terms of subjective evaluation. Next, the quantitative evaluation is carried out for CDR measurement to verify the effectiveness of the proposed method. The proposed method is implemented in python3.5. The experiments are performed on a PC with 3.40 GHz Intel CPU and Nvidia Titan XP.

4.1   Subjective Evaluation

4.1.1   OD Locating Performance

Both ORIGA [12] and DRISHTI-GS1 [13] are famous retinal datasets which contain 650 and 101 fundus images, respectively. We evaluate our OD localization method on both ORIGA and DRISHTI-GS1. Besides, we treat the OD as localized accurately when the predicted location of OD is inside the practical optic disc. The statistic results for OD location are shown in Table 1.

Table 1. Performance validation of OD localization on different retinal datasets

Dataset	Image size	Total number	Localization correctly	Accuracy	Runtime (s)
DRISHTI-GS1	1755 × 2048	101	101	100%	0.3 s
ORIGA	2048 × 3072	650	644	99.1%	0.6 s

From Table 1, one can clearly see that the proposed OD location method achieve high accuracy (100% and 99.1%, respectively) for the two public databases, and the running speed is relatively fast since the proposed method only takes 0.3 s on average to process a retinal image with a size of 1755 × 2048. This speed can be further improved by using a GPU-based parallel algorithm.

4.1.2   Segmentation Performance

For subjective evaluation, different methods are compared with our proposed U-Net +CP+FL, including U-Net [10] and M-Net with Polar Transformation (M-Net+PT) [14]. The reason why we choose these methods to compare with the proposed U-Net +CP+FL is that U-Net, M-Net+PT and our proposed U-Net+CP+FL are all deep neural network based method, and the M-Net+PT method is regarded as one of the best OD and OC segmentation methods at present. Figure 7 shows the results of OD and OC segmentation for different methods. We can clearly see that our proposed U-Net+CP +FL achieves best segmented boundaries.

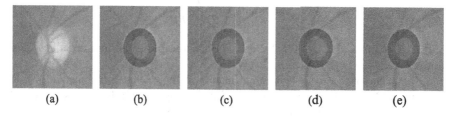

| (a) | (b) | (c) | (d) | (e) |

Fig. 7. Performance comparison of OD and OC Segmentation with different methods. (a) Cropped ROI region. (b) Ground truth. (c) Segmentation result obtained by U-Net. (d) M-Net+PT segmentation result. (e) Proposed method.

Note that all the OD boundaries obtained by different methods are similar. However, the OC segmentation is more a difficult task, and the OC boundary obtained by M-Net+PT is rough and irregular, which will mislead the calculation of CDR. The U-Net achieves a smooth but larger OC. For our results, the boundary of OC is not only smooth but also relatively accurate, thus CDR measurement and glaucoma diagnosis can benefit much from the results.

4.2 Quantitative Evaluation

For only 50 retinal images with segmentation ground truth are available in DRISHTI-GS1 database, this leads to few data for training, let alone testing. Thus, quantitative evaluation on OD and OC segmentation are only conducted on ORIGA dataset, and the CDR measurement obtained by proposed method is compared with the ophthalmologist. In our experiments, 500 retinal images are randomly selected for training and 150 for testing.

4.2.1 Segmentation Performance Evaluation

We use the overlap score S and average accuracy AVG_ACC respectively to evaluate the segmentation performance. The two indexes are defined as

$$S = \frac{\text{Area}(g \cap p)}{\text{Area}(g \cup p)} \tag{4}$$

$$AVG\_ACC = \frac{\text{sensitivity} + \text{specificity}}{2} \tag{5}$$

In Eq. (4), g and p denote the ground truth and segmented mask, respectively. Area (.) denotes the region areas. Apart from S, we also adopt the index AVG_ACC which consists of sensitivity (true positive rate) and specificity (false positive rate) described as follows:

$$\text{sensitivity} = \frac{TP}{TP + FN} \tag{6}$$

$$\text{specificity} = \frac{TN}{TN + FP} \tag{7}$$

In Eqs. (6) and (7), TP, TN, FP and FN are true positives, true negatives, false positives and false negatives respectively.

Several state-of-the-art OD/OC segmentation methods: Superpixel method [5], U-Net [10], and M-Net+PT [14] are also adopted to compare with the proposed method. Besides, two improved networks proposed in our work are also included: U-Net +Fusion Loss (U-Net+FL) and U-Net+Concatenating Path (U-Net+CP). Among these methods, Superpixel, U-Net+FL, U-Net+CP and U-Net+CP+FL are employed with ellipse fitting while U-Net and M-Net+PT are not.

Table 2 shows the segmentation comparison results of different methods on ORIGA dataset. Results shows that compared with U-Net, Superpixel method achieve better segmentation results both in OD and OC. M-Net+PT which introduced side-output layers and polar transformation makes huge strides in segmentation compared with the original U-Net. However, polar transformation strongly depends on the precise localization of OD, failure of localization would cause the irregular reconstructed segmentation results. Besides, our network is directly trained on ROI region with image augmentation (i.e. image translation and image rotation), which is not sensitive to the result of OD localization. And our proposed U-Net+CP+FL can achieve best results for most measurements, such as S_{disc}, AVG_ACC_{disc}, S_{cup}, and δ_{CDR}. Besides, both U-Net +FL and U-Net+CP, the two modified version of U-Net proposed in our work, can achieve comparable or even better results (e.g. AVG_ACC_{cup}), which demonstrates that the concatenating path and the fusion loss introduced by our work contribute to the OD and OC segmentation.

Table 2. Performance comparison of different methods on ORIGA dataset

Method	S_{disc}	AVG_ACC_{disc}	S_{cup}	AVG_ACC_{cup}	δ_{CDR}
Superpixel [5]	0.090	0.964	0.736	0.918	0.077
U-Net [10]	0.885	0.959	0.713	0.901	0.102
M-Net+PT [14]	0.929	0.983	0.770	0.930	0.071
U-Net+FL	0.932	0.982	0.801	**0.950**	0.057
U-Net+CP	0.934	0.983	0.800	0.945	0.058
U-Net+CP+FL	**0.939**	**0.984**	**0.805**	0.942	**0.054**

4.2.2 CDR Measurement Evaluation

We evaluate our CDR performance with absolute CDR error, which is defined as $\delta_{CDR} = |CDR_g - CDR_P|$. Here, CDR_g denotes the ground truth from trained clinician, and CDR_P is the CDR calculated by our proposed method. From Table 2, we can conclude that our proposed method can achieve smallest CDR error compared with other methods. Smaller error of the calculated CDR shows the boundaries obtained by the proposed U-Net+CP+FL network are much finer.

Furthermore, the distribution of glaucoma and non-glaucoma measured by CDR is illustrated in Fig. 8. We can clearly see that the overall distribution of calculated CDR is close to ophthalmologist especially in the inter-quartile range. Besides, the inter-quartile range is separated completely, which means that CDR can be an important clinical measurement for glaucoma diagnosis. In summary, we can conclude that the CDR performance of our proposed method is close to expert level. Observations on other test images also confirm this conclusion.

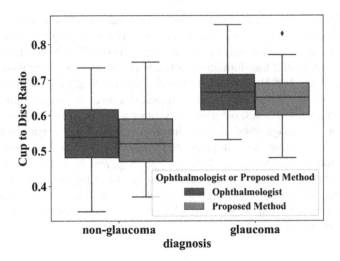

Fig. 8. Box plots for CDR of ophthalmologist and proposed method in test cases.

5 Conclusion

A novel CDR measurement method is proposed in this paper. The proposed method first uses morphological operation and sliding window to locate OD and further extract ROI. Then, an end-to-end deep neutral network called U-Net+CP+FL, which consists of U-shape convolutional architecture, a novel concatenating path and a multi-label fusion loss function, is proposed to simultaneously segment OD and OC. Based on the segmentation results, the CDR value can be effectively calculated. There are several advantages in the proposed method compared with the other existing algorithms. First, the OC segmentation is more accurate than other existing methods. Second, the proposed method can automatically and simultaneously segment OD and OC in an end-to-end way without any user-interaction. Finally, our work combines traditional image processing technologies with deep learning to achieve better results.

However, the proposed algorithm also has some limitations and it may lead to invalid result in some situations. For example, when OD is surrounded by parapapillary atrophy (PPA), the PPA blurs the boundary of the OD, which may result in the over segmentation problem for both OD and OC regions. Nevertheless, we provide a new way to solve the CDR calculation problem and the result appears to be quite successful in most cases. Therefore, the proposed method could be suitable for automatic glaucoma analysis in a variety of clinical settings. In the future, we will try to build our own fundus image dataset to validate the effectiveness of the proposed method.

Acknowledgments. This work was supported by the National Natural Science Foundation of China (61502537, 61573380, 61702558, 61602527), Hunan Provincial Natural Science Foundation of China (2018JJ3681, 2017JJ3416), and the Fundamental Research Funds for the Central Universities of Central South University (2018zzts576).

References

1. Tham, Y.C., Li, X., Wong, T.Y., Quigley, H.A., Aung, T., Cheng, C.Y.: Global prevalence of glaucoma and projections of glaucoma burden through 2040: a systematic review and meta-analysis. Ophthalmology 121(11), 2081–2090 (2014)
2. Hollows, F.C., Graham, P.A.: Intra-ocular pressure, glaucoma, and glaucoma suspects in a defined population. Br. J. ophthalmol. 50(10), 570 (1966)
3. Foster, P.J., Buhrmann, R., Quigley, H.A., et al.: The definition and classification of glaucoma in prevalence surveys. Br. J. Ophthalmol. 86(2), 238–242 (2002)
4. Lowell, J., Hunter, A., Steel, D., et al.: Optic nerve head segmentation. IEEE Trans. Med. Imaging 23(2), 256–264 (2004)
5. Cheng, J., Liu, J., Xu, Y., et al.: Superpixel classification based optic disc and optic cup segmentation for glaucoma screening. IEEE Trans. Med. Imaging 32(6), 1019–1032 (2013)
6. Nayak, J., Acharya, R., Bhat, P.S., et al.: Automated diagnosis of glaucoma using digital fundus images. J. Med. Syst. 33(5), 337 (2009)
7. Babu, T.G., Shenbagadevi, S.: Automatic detection of glaucoma using fundus image. Eur. J. Sci. Res. 59(1), 22–32 (2011)
8. Yin, F., et al.: Automated segmentation of optic disc and optic cup in fundus images for glaucoma diagnosis. In: Proceedings of the 25th IEEE International Symposium on Computer-Based Medical Systems (CBMS), pp. 1–6. IEEE, Rome (2012)
9. Zheng, Y., Stambolian, D., O'Brien, J., Gee, J.C.: Optic disc and cup segmentation from color fundus photograph using graph cut with priors. In: Mori, K., Sakuma, I., Sato, Y., Barillot, C., Navab, N. (eds.) MICCAI 2013. LNCS, vol. 8150, pp. 75–82. Springer, Heidelberg (2013). https://doi.org/10.1007/978-3-642-40763-5_10
10. Ronneberger, O., Fischer, P., Brox, T.: U-Net: convolutional networks for biomedical image segmentation. In: Navab, N., Hornegger, J., Wells, W.M., Frangi, A.F. (eds.) MICCAI 2015. LNCS, vol. 9351, pp. 234–241. Springer, Cham (2015). https://doi.org/10.1007/978-3-319-24574-4_28
11. Huang, G., et al.: Densely connected convolutional networks. In: Proceedings of the IEEE Conference on Computer Vision and Pattern Recognition, vol. 1, no. 2, p. 3. IEEE, Honolulu (2017)
12. Zhang, Z., et al.: ORIGA(-light): an online retinal fundus image database for glaucoma analysis and research. In: 2010 Annual International Conference of the IEEE Engineering in Medicine and Biology Society (EMBC), pp. 3065–3068. IEEE, Buenos Aires (2010)
13. Sivaswamy, J., Krishnadas, S., Chakravarty, A., et al.: A comprehensive retinal image dataset for the assessment of glaucoma from the optic nerve head analysis. JSM Biomed. Imaging Data Pap. 2(1), 1004 (2015)
14. Fu, H., Cheng, J., Xu, Y., et al.: Joint optic disc and cup segmentation based on multi-label deep network and polar transformation. IEEE Trans. Med. Imaging (2018)

Image Segmentation Based on Local Chan Vese Model by Employing Cosine Fitting Energy

Le Zou[1,2,3], Liang-Tu Song[1,2], Xiao-Feng Wang[3(✉)],
Yan-Ping Chen[3], Qiong Zhou[1,2,4], Chao Tang[3], and Chen Zhang[3]

[1] Hefei Institute of Intelligent Machines, Hefei Institutes of Physical Science,
Chinese Academy of Sciences, P.O. Box 1130, Hefei 230031, Anhui, China
[2] University of Science and Technology of China, Hefei 230027, Anhui, China
[3] Key Lab of Network and Intelligent Information Processing, Department
of Computer Science and Technology, Hefei University, Hefei 230601, China
xfwang@hfuu.edu.cn
[4] School of Information and Computer, Anhui Agricultural University,
Hefei 230036, China

Abstract. Image segmentation plays a critical role in computer vision and image processing. In this paper, we propose a new Local Chan–Vese (LCV) model by using the cosine function to express the data fitting term in traditional level set image segment models and present a new distance regularized based on a polynomial. We discuss two algorithms of the new model. The first algorithm is a traditional algorithm based on finite difference, which is slow. The second algorithm is a sweeping algorithm, which didn't need to solve the Euler-Lagrange equation. The second algorithm only needs to calculate the energy change when a pixel was moved from the outside region to the inside region of evolving curves and vice versa. The second algorithm is high speed and can avoid solving the partial differential equation. There is no need for the reinitialization step, and stability conditions, and the distance regularization term. The experiments have shown the effectiveness of the two algorithms.

Keywords: Image segmentation · Region-based model · Level set
Cosine fitting energy · Sweeping

1 Introduction

Image segmentation plays a very fundamental role in image processing and computer vision. Over the past decades, many scholars studied a significant amount of image segmentation methods. The level set method (LSM) is a famous one of them. Although the level set image segmentation has been widely studied and utilized for decades, it is still a hot research problem. The LSM can be classified into edge-based methods [1], global region-based methods [2] and hybrid methods [3]. Global region-based methods have a better result when the segmented images which have weak boundaries and are less sensitive to initial placement. Among them, the Chan-Vese (CV) model [2] is the most famous one. It has better performance for images containing homogeneous

© Springer Nature Switzerland AG 2018
J.-H. Lai et al. (Eds.): PRCV 2018, LNCS 11256, pp. 466–478, 2018.
https://doi.org/10.1007/978-3-030-03398-9_40

regions with distinct intensity means. However, CV model cannot segment the image with intensity inhomogeneity, and the method is sensitive to the placement of the initial contour and set of initial parameters, and the convergence is slow and apt to plunge into local minimal value. To improve the performance of global region-based methods, some local region-based methods were proposed. The classical ones include, the local Chan-Vese (LCV) model [4], the region-scalable fitting (LBF) model [5] the local intensity clustering (LIC) model [6], etc. Recently, some hybrid methods [3] had been studied, which combined global and local image information to stabilize and accelerate process of the evolution convergence. Wang [7] discussed global and local region-based active contours with cosine fitting energy, but the parameters of the model are challenging to set.

Most of the region based image segmentation methods mentioned above are based on energy minimization which is performed by different techniques. The most widely used method of energy minimization is the gradient descent (GD) method. One must solve the partial differential equation (PDE) until it reach the minimum and can meet local minimal value in this process. To ensure the steady evolution, it must be satisfied with Courant Friedrichs Lew (CFL) condition. The evolution is time-consuming. After the PDE was obtained, some scholars present many methods to solve the PDE, such as implicit difference [1], Hermite differential operator [8], additional operator splitting [9], operator splitting [10] and so on. Recently, many scholars constructed many new algorithms to get better image segmentation results. The authors [11] use the max-flow algorithm to optimize local Chan-Vese model. The authors [12–14] use the sweeping principle algorithm of Chan Vese model to get the optimization of the energy functional of the region based level set model. In this paper, we present a new image segment method named local Chan Vese model by employing cosine fitting energy and give two algorithms. The model can segment image with severe intensity inhomogeneity or edge blurred.

The remaining of this paper is structured as follows: In Sect. 2, the Local Chan Vese model based on cosine fitting energy model is constructed, and finite difference algorithm of Local Chan Vese by employing cosine fitting energy (LCVCF) is given. In Sect. 3, the sweeping optimization principle algorithm (SLCVCF) of the model is presented. In Sect. 4, some examples are given to show the effectiveness of the proposed method. Finally, some conclusions are provided in Sect. 5.

2 Local Chan Vese Model by Employing Cosine Fitting Energy

In this section, we present the Local Chan Vese by employing cosine fitting energy model and then propose its numerical algorithm based on the gradient descent method.

2.1 Data Fitting Energy Functional Term

Let $\Omega \subset \Re^2$ be the two-dimensional image domain and $I : \Omega \to \Re$ be the intensity image. For a given grayscale image on the interval [0, 1], the cosine power error preserves smaller error and more gentle than L2 norm on the interval [0, 1], so we think the cosine fitting energy is less sensitive to the interference of the noise and robust to low contrast than the fitting energy in the LCV model. The fitting data energy of the Local Chan Vese by employing cosine fitting energy model is defined by

$$
\begin{aligned}
E_{data}^{LCVCF}(c_1, c_2, d_1, d_2, \phi) = {}& \alpha \int_\Omega (-\cos(I - c_1))H(\phi(x)) + \beta \int_\Omega (-\cos(g_k * I - I - d_1))H(\phi(x))dx \\
& + \alpha \int_\Omega (-\cos(I - c_2))(1 - H(\phi(x))) + \beta \int_\Omega (-\cos(g_k * I - I - d_2))H(\phi(x))dx
\end{aligned}
\tag{1}
$$

Where and β are two nonnegative constants. The meaning of c_1 and c_2 are the intensity means of the evolving contour as the same as that of global cosine fitting (GCF) model [7]. d_1 and d_2 are the intensity means of $(g_k * I(x) - I(x))$ inside and outside of the evolving contour. Here $H(z)$ and $\delta(z)$ denote Heaviside function and Dirac delta function respectively, g_k computes the averaging convolution in a $k \times k$ size window.

For a fixed level set function ϕ, we minimize the energy functional in (1) concerning two pairs of constants: c_1 and c_2, d_1 and d_2. By calculus of variations, it can be shown that the constant functions c_1, c_2, d_1 and d_2 that minimize $E_{data}^{LCVCF}(c_1, c_2, d_1, d_2, \phi)$ for a fixed function ϕ are given by

$$
c_1(\phi) = \arctan\frac{\int_\Omega \sin(I(x))H(\phi(x))dx}{\int_\Omega \cos(I(x))H(\phi(x))dx}, c_2(\phi) = \arctan\frac{\int_\Omega \sin(I(x))(1 - H(\phi(x)))dx}{\int_\Omega \cos(I(x))(1 - H(\phi(x)))dx}
\tag{2}
$$

$$
d_1(\phi) = \arctan\frac{\int_\Omega \sin(g_k * I(x) - I(x))H(\phi(x))dx}{\int_\Omega \cos(g_k * I(x) - I(x))H(\phi(x))dx}
\tag{3}
$$

$$
d_2(\phi) = \arctan\frac{\int_\Omega \sin(g_k * I(x) - I(x)) \cdot (1 - H(\phi(x)))dx}{\int_\Omega \cos(g_k * I(x) - I(x))(1 - H(\phi(x)))dx}
\tag{4}
$$

2.2   Regularization Energy Term

To prevent small and isolated curves happening in the final segmentation result, we use energy term as Eq. (5).

$$
L(\phi) = \int_\Omega \delta(\phi(x))|\nabla\phi(x)|dx
\tag{5}
$$

We use the following function as distance penalty energy term to naturally maintain level set function being a signed distance function (SDF) during the contour evolution

$$R(\phi) = \int_\Omega P(|\nabla\phi(x)|)dx \quad where \, P(s) = \begin{cases} \frac{1}{2}s^2(s-1)^2, & if \quad s \leq 1 \\ \frac{1}{2}(s-1)^2, & if \quad s \geq 1 \end{cases} \quad (6)$$

Where is a double-well potential function based on interpolant polynomial. In paper [3], $P(s)$ is a sixth times polynomial. In this paper, we only use the fourth times to avoid high order instability of polynomial. By utilizing distance regularization penalty energy term in (6), the level set function can be maintained as an SDF [3].

Thus, the final regularization energy term E^R of our method was given in Eq. (7)

$$E^R(\phi) = \mu \cdot L(\phi) + v \cdot R(\phi) = \mu \cdot \int_\Omega \delta(\phi(x))|\nabla\phi(x)|dx + v \cdot \int_\Omega P(|\nabla\phi(x)|)dx \quad (7)$$

where μ and v are constants to control the length penalization effect and signed distance function maintaining effect separately.

2.3   Level Set Formulation for the Proposed Model

Due to the introduction of distance regularization energy term in (6), a binary step function can be used to the initial level set function. Thus, the total energy functional is reformulated as follows:

$$\begin{aligned} E^{LCVCF}(c_1,c_2,d_1,d_2,\phi) = & \alpha \int_\Omega (-\cos(I-c_1))H(\phi(x)) + \beta \int_\Omega (-\cos(g_k * I - I - d_1))H(\phi(x))dx \\ & + \alpha \int_\Omega (-\cos(I-c_2))(1 - H(\phi(x))) + \beta \int_\Omega (-\cos(g_k * I - I - d_2))H(\phi(x))dx \\ & + \mu \cdot \int \delta_\epsilon(\phi)|\nabla\phi|dxdy + v \cdot \int_\Omega P(|\nabla\phi(x)|)dx, \end{aligned}$$

$$(8)$$

Like other methods, the level set function $\phi(x)$ can be updated according to the Eq. (9):

$$\begin{aligned} \frac{\partial\phi}{\partial t} = & \delta(\phi)[-(\alpha \cdot (-\cos(I-c_1)) + \beta \cdot (-\cos(g_k * I - I - d_1))) + (\alpha \cdot (-\cos(I-c_2)) \\ & + \beta \cdot (-\cos(g_k * I - I - d_2)))] + [\mu \cdot \delta(\phi)div(\frac{\nabla\phi}{|\nabla\phi|}) + v \cdot div(d(|\nabla\phi|)\nabla\phi)], \end{aligned} \quad (9)$$

Where $H(x)$ is Heaviside function, $\delta_\epsilon(x)$ is the regularized approximation of Dirac delta function, $d(s) = P'(s)/s$. We use the finite difference scheme to solve the above equation. We call the finite difference scheme algorithm of the proposed model LCVCF.

3 Fast Algorithm to Minimize the Local Chan Vese Model by Employing Cosine Fitting Energy

In the last section, we give a finite difference scheme of the model. However, finite difference scheme in level set method has some drawbacks, such as lager approximation error and time-cost consuming and so on. Inspired from work published by Song [12] and Boutiche [13, 14], we propose a sweeping optimization principle algorithm to minimize the local Chan Vese model by employing cosine fitting energy. The algorithm doesn't need to solve any PDE and have numerical stability conditions. We only sweep all the pixels of the given image and then test each pixel to check the energy change when we change a pixel from the outside of the curve to inside and vice versa.

In the local Chan Vese model by employing cosine fitting energy functional (1), the curve evolution is dominated by the fidelity to data term which is written as follows:

$$
F = [\alpha(-\cos(I(x) - c_1)) + \beta \cdot (-\cos(g_k * I - I - d_1)))] - \\
[\alpha(-\cos(I(x) - c_2)) + \beta \cdot (-\cos(g_k * I - I - d_2)))]
\tag{10}
$$

Remind that the first and the third terms indicate the global region fitting energy and the second and the fourth terms present the local statistical information fitting energy. However, the outside and inside energy are deducted as follows:

$$
\begin{cases}
\alpha(-\cos(I(x) - c_1)) + \beta \cdot (-\cos(g_k * I - I - d_1)) & \text{if} \quad \phi(x) > 0 \\
\alpha(-\cos(I(x) - c_2)) + \beta \cdot (-\cos(g_k * I - I - d_2)) & \text{if} \quad \phi(x) < 0
\end{cases}
\tag{11}
$$

From Eq. (11), we define the old and the new energy change according to the energy inside and outside of the evolving curve:

$$
\Delta F_{12} = [\alpha(-\cos(I(x) - c_1)) + \beta \cdot (-\cos(g_k * I - I - d_1)))]\frac{m}{m+1} - \\
[\alpha(-\cos(I(x) - c_2)) + \beta \cdot (-\cos(g_k * I - I - d_2)))]\frac{n}{n-1} + vP
\tag{12}
$$

$$
\Delta F_{21} = [\alpha(-\cos(I(x) - c_2)) + \beta \cdot (-\cos(g_k * I - I - d_2)))]\frac{n}{n+1} \\
- [\alpha(-\cos(I(x) - c_1)) + \beta \cdot (-\cos(g_k * I - I - d_1)))]\frac{m}{m-1} + vP
\tag{13}
$$

Where m and n are the areas (number of pixels) inside and outside the initial level set curve ϕ respectively, v is a nonnegative small constant. We have added a length term P to increase the capability of segmentation with noisy images. For intensity image, we don't need this term.

The length term P is approximated by Eq. (14).

$$P = \sum_{i,j} \sqrt{(H(\phi(i+1,j)) - H(\phi(i,j)))^2 + (H(\phi(i,j+1)) - H(\phi(i,j)))^2} \qquad (14)$$

We call the sweeping optimization principle algorithm of the model SLCVCF.

The steps of the sweeping optimization principle algorithm are given as follows.

Step 1: Change the given grayscale image to the interval [0, 1].

Step 2: Place the initial level set on the given image on the interval [0, 1]. Initialize the level set function $\phi = 1$ for one part and $\phi = -1$ for another one.

Step 3: Initialize the parameters ε (for computing $H(z)$ and $\delta(z)$) and k, v, α, β Set F is a matrice of the size ϕ set to 1.

Step 4: Compute c_1, c_2, d_1, d_2 by Eqs. (2–4),

Compute m, n which are the area (number of pixels) inside and outside of the evolving curves for $\phi = 1$ and $\phi = -1$ For each pixel of ϕ do

If $\phi = 1$ then compute ΔF_{12} as shows in Eq. (12),

If $\Delta F_{12} < 0$ then change ϕ from +1 to −1.

If $\phi = -1$ then compute ΔF_{12} as shows in Eq. (13),

If $\Delta F_{21} < 0$ then change ϕ from −1 to +1.

$F = \Delta F_{21} + \Delta F_{12}$

Step 5: Repeat the step 4 until the total energy F remains unchanged

As it is shown, the algorithm scan all the pixels of image and then check the energy change for every pixel when the pixel is moved from the inside to the outside of the evolving curve and vice versa. The algorithm needn't derivative calculations and does not require any numerical stability condition. There is no need for F to be differentiable, the re-initialization step and the distance regularization term. Furthermore, sweeping principle algorithm allows using a binary level set function during the minimization process, avoiding its negative effects and speeding up the optimization process. So we have greatly saved the time of calculation.

4   Experimental Results

In this section, we shall present the experiments of the proposed algorithm on several synthetic and real images. The proposed algorithm was implemented by Matlab R2016a on a computer with Intel Core (TM) i7-6700 2.6 GHz CPU, 16G RAM, and 64 bit Windows 10 operating system. Here, for algorithm LCVCF, we used the same parameters $\varepsilon = 1, \lambda_1 = \lambda_2 = 255, r = 35, \sigma = 25, \Delta t = 0.4, \mu = 15, v = 0.4$ for all experiments unless mentioned otherwise. For algorithm SLCVCF, we used the same parameters $\varepsilon = 1, \alpha = 4, \beta = 1, r = 35, \sigma = 35$ for all experiments unless mentioned otherwise, the initial level set is a binary level set function, the outside of the evolving curve is set to -1, and the inside is set to 1. We use the green line to represent the initial contour and the red line for final evolution results.

Firstly, we present an example to show the effectiveness of our model on the images with intensity inhomogeneity. The first two images are severe intensity inhomogeneity. The initial contours were all placed as shown in the upper row of Fig. 1. The parameters of SLCVCF are chosen as follows: $r = 35$, $\sigma = 35$, for the image (a) $\alpha = 22, \beta = 3$ or image (b), $\alpha = 22, \beta = 5$ for the image (c), (d) and (e) $\alpha = 5, \beta = 1$. The final evolving contours of our algorithm LCVCF and SLCVCF are presented in the lower row of Fig. 1. All five images have good segmented performance as expected with algorithm SLCVCF, but for algorithm LCVCF, it extract only last two object's boundaries successfully. It can be seen that our algorithm SLCVCF can achieve good performance on the synthetic image with severe intensity inhomogeneity.

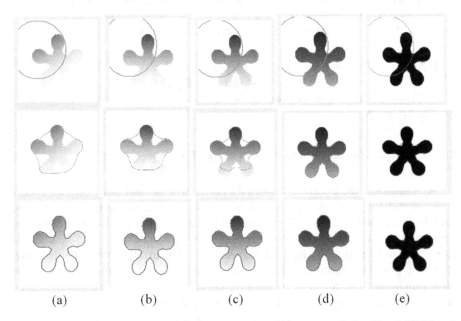

Fig. 1. Segmentation comparisons of the computation of the proposed algorithm LCVCF and SLCVCF on synthetic images. The first row: Different intensity inhomogeneity image. The second row: Final segmentation results of the proposed algorithm LCVCF. The third row: Final segmentation results of the proposed algorithm SLCVCF. Image size: 100×100. (Color figure online)

In the second experiment, we give some real image segmentation results based on the LCVCF and SLCVCF algorithms. The parameters of SLCVCF are chosen as follows: $r = 25$, $\sigma = 45$, $\alpha = 4, \beta = 1$ for the image (a); $r = 35$, $\sigma = 35$, $\alpha = 4, \beta = 1$, for the image (b), (c) and (e); $r = 25$, $\sigma = 35$, $\alpha = 4, \beta = 1$, for the image (d). The final evolving contours of our algorithm LCVCF and SLCVCF are presented in the lower row of Fig. 2. All five images were well segmented as expected with algorithm

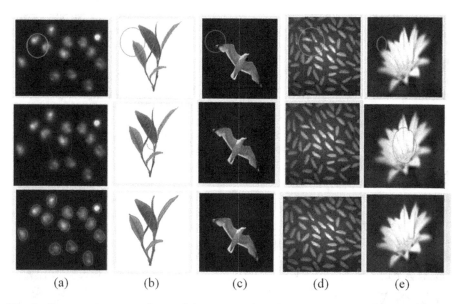

(a)   (b)   (c)   (d)   (e)

Fig. 2. Segmentation comparisons of the computation of the proposed algorithm LCVCF and SLCVCF on real images. The first row: given images. The second row: Final segmentation results of SLCVCF. The third row: Final segmentation results of SLCVCF. Image size: 217×161, 209×193, 256×256, 400×266, 141×139.

SLCVCF, but for algorithm LCVCF, it cannot extract object's boundaries successfully. It can be seen that algorithm SLCVCF can achieve good performance on the real image with intensity inhomogeneity by using very few iterations and time.

To show the segment performance of the proposed algorithm SLCVCF, we compare the proposed two algorithms with the LCV [4] model and LBF [5] model. Segmentation results are presented for different types of images in Fig. 3 (the same initial evolving curve). For LCV model, we choose the parameters as follows, $\Delta t = 0.1$, $\alpha = 0.1$, $\beta = 1$, $h = 1$, $\varepsilon = 1$, $r = 35$, $k = 20$, $\mu = 0.01 \times 255^2$ and $v = 0$. For LBF model, the parameters are set as follows: $\lambda_1 = 1$, $\lambda_2 = 2$, $\varepsilon = 1$, $\sigma = 3$, $r = 25$, $\Delta t = 0.1$, $\mu = 1$ and $v = 0.04 \times 255^2$. All the above methods used the same initialization. The parameters of SLCVCF are chosen as follows: $r = 35$, $\sigma = 45$, $\alpha = 4$, $\beta = 1$ for the image (a), $r = 25$, $\sigma = 45$, $\alpha = 4$, $\beta = 1$, for the image (b), (c), (d) and (e). The second row shows that segmentation results for the SLCVCF algorithm. It has the best performance and can completely segment all the images and use the least time even though the images with serious intensity inhomogeneity. The third to the fifth rows show that the LCVCF, LCV, LBF models cannot obtain a satisfactory segmentation model for images in some cases. Compared with the above algorithms or models from Table 1, we can get our algorithm SLCVCF obtaining satisfactory segmentation results at a faster convergence speed than the LCVCF, LCV and LBF model.

In the fourth example, we shall show the performance of the proposed algorithm LCVCF and SLCVCF of the local Chan Vese model by employing cosine fitting energy, when comparing the proposed algorithms with the LCV model, the LBF model

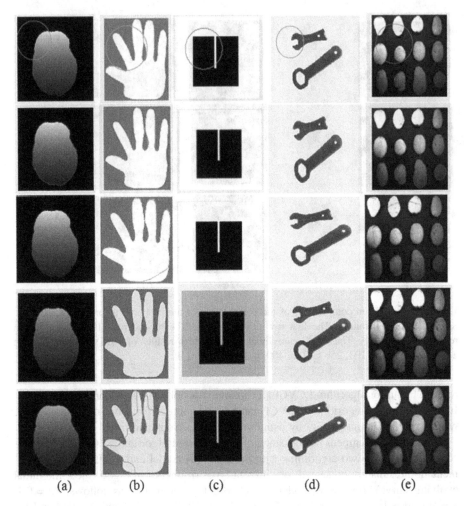

(a)   (b)   (c)   (d)   (e)

Fig. 3. Segmentation comparisons of the computation of the proposed algorithm SLCVCF and LCVCF, LCV, LBF on synthetic images. The first row: given images. The second to the seventh row: Final segmentation results of SLCVCF, LCVCF, LCV, LBF. Image size: 154×152, 108×130, 114×101, 200×200, 143×145.

Table 1. Comparison of the computation cost (times (s))/iteration numbers of the proposed algorithm SLCVCF and LCVCF, LCV, LBF on synthetic images in Fig. 3

	1	2	3	4	5
SLCVCF	**0.0482/1**	**0.0602/1**	**0.0560/1**	**0.1208/2**	**0.1062/2**
LCVCF	16.114/400	42.7831/900	17.1104/600	14.4784/600	39.0716/900
LCV	18.4156/100	18.5619/150	10.1106/60	28.9602/140	29.116067/200
LBF	6.8695/600	4.2097/400	7.6606/800	8.2455/600	10.9447/1000

on medical images. The parameters of SLCVCF, LCV model and the LBF model are chosen as the third example. Segmentation results are obtained for medical images as shown in Fig. 4. The second column shows that segmentation results for the SLCVCF. The SLCVCF model can get better performance for the medical images with weak boundaries. The LCVCF model in the third column cannot extract target. In addition, the LCVCF model is more sensitive to initial contour, and the contour can quickly fall into the local minimum. The fourth and the fifth columns show the segment results of LCV and LBF models. Compared with the LCVCF, LCV and LBF models, our algorithms SLCVCF can drive satisfactory segmentation results at a faster convergence speed.

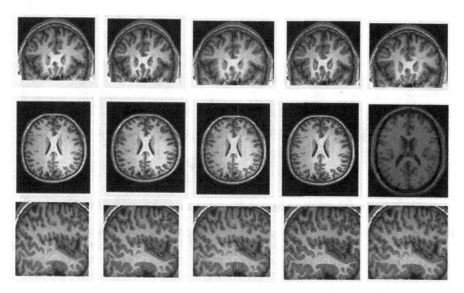

Fig. 4. Segmentation comparisons of the computation of the proposed algorithm SLCVCF and LCVCF, LCV, LBF model on medical images. The first column: given images. The second column: Final segmentation results of the proposed algorithm SLCVCF. The third column: Final segmentation results of the proposed algorithm LCVCF. The fourth column: Final segmentation results of LCV model. The fifth column: Final segmentation results of LBF model. Image size: 147×99, 128×128, 122×91.

In the fifth example, we shall show the performance of the proposed algorithm LCVCF and SLCVCF, when comparing the proposed method with the LCV model, the LBF model on complex images. The parameters of SLCVCF are chosen as the fourth example. The parameters of LCVCF are chosen as, $\lambda_1 = \lambda_2 = 255$, $\varepsilon = 1$, $\mu = 15$, $v = 0.4$, for image (a) and (c) $r = 15$, $\sigma = 45$, $\Delta t = 1.6$, image (b) $r = 15$, $\sigma = 45$, $\Delta t = 118.6$, image (d) $r = 25$, $\sigma = 45$, $\Delta t = 16.4$, image (e) $r = 35$, $\sigma = 45$, $\Delta t = 1.6$. Segmentation results are presented for diffcrent types of complex images in Fig. 5 (the same initial evolving curve). The second column shows the segmentation results for the LCVCF. The LCVCF model can completely segment images with weak boundaries. The SLCVCF

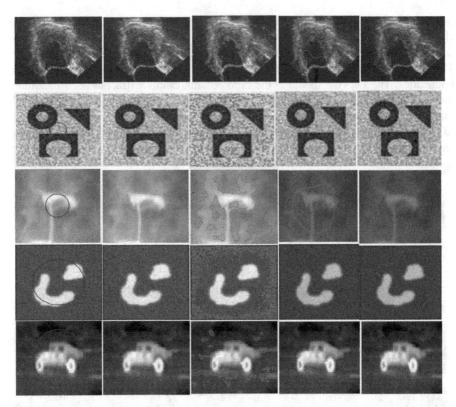

Fig. 5. Segmentation comparisons of the computation of the proposed algorithm SLCVCF and LCVCF, LCV, LBF model. The first column: given images. The second column: Final segmentation results of the proposed algorithm LCVCF. The third column: Final segmentation results of the proposed algorithm SLCVCF. The fourth column: Final segmentation results of LCV model. The fifth column: Final segmentation results of LBF model. Image size: 100×87, 152×152, 111×94, 84×84, 118×93.

Table 2. Comparison of the computation cost (times (s)) and iteration numbers of the proposed algorithm SLCVCF and LCVCF, LCV, LBF on images in Fig. 5

	1	2	3	4	5
SLCVCF	**0.2353/2**	**0.3299/2**	**0.2019/2**	**0.2266/2**	**0.2721/2**
LCVCF	5.5479/200	3.1038/120	43.3077/900	2.1084/100	12.6084/450
LCV	10.0734/80	19.8453/100	18.3114/100	15.5644/150	11.6560/80
LBF	8.2617/600	10.0133/900	8.4823/900	7.9044/900	4.9697/500

model in the third column can't extract target. The fourth and fifth columns show that the LCV and LBF models can't get a satisfactory segmentation model for images in some cases. Compared with the SLCVCF, LCV and LBF models, our algorithm LCVCF can achieve satisfactory segmentation results. Just as shown in Table 2, the SLCVCF algorithm use least time and iteration numbers, it couldn't get satisfy results. The LCVCF algorithm use less time and iteration numbers for most cases, it can get better segment results than the LCV and LBF model.

5 Conclusion

In this paper, we present a new model to segment image based on LCV model with the cosine fitting energy and give two algorithms of the new model. The LCVCF is an algorithm based on gradient decent method which can segment the image with the complex background. The SLCVCF is a fast algorithm based on a sweeping algorithm. For the SLCVCF, there is neither need to CFL condition nor re-initialize level set. It can avoid solving any partial differential equation. When the segment ends, the program terminates automatically. Furthermore, the distance regularization term doesn't needed, which speeds up the energy functional optimization process, and makes the algorithm convergence very fast by using only some sweeping steps, which is very suitable to real-time applications. Successful and accurate segmentation results are obtained on synthetic and real images, and the speed is very fast when compared with the LCVCF algorithm. The results demonstrate the performance of the proposed algorithm SLCVCF and LCVCF in weak boundaries and serve intensity inhomogeneity, edge blurred and simple background image.

SLCVCF and LCVCF are the two algorithms of the local Chan Vese model by employing cosine fitting energy. The algorithm SLCVCF is very fast with some advantages, but it still has some shortcomings. For example, it can't segment image with strong noise, complex images or texture images. Although the algorithm LCVCF is slow, it can segment the image with complex background. We will combine the proposed two algorithms with some new methods and image features to deal with those complex images. We will extend our algorithm to the multiphase segmentation model and segment the White Matter, Gray Matter and cerebrospinal fluid for MRI of brain image in future.

Acknowledgements. The authors would like to express their thanks to the referees for their valuable suggestions. This work was supported by the grant of the National Natural Science Foundation of China, Nos. 61672204, 61806068, the grant of Major Science and Technology Project of Anhui Province, No. 17030901026, the Project of National Science and Technology Support Plan of China, No. 2015BAD18B05, the grant of the key Scientific Research Foundation of Education Department of Anhui Province, Nos. KJ2018A0555, KJ2017A152, KJ2017A542, KJ2016A603, Excellent Talents Training Funded Project of Universities of Anhui Province No. gxfx2017099. The grant of Key Constructive Discipline Project of Hefei University, No. 2016xk05.

References

1. Malladi, R., Sethian, J.A., Vemuri, B.C.: Shape modeling with front propagation: a level set approach. IEEE Trans. Pattern Anal. Mach. Intell. **17**(2), 158–175 (1995)
2. Chan, T.F., Vese, L.A.: Active contours without edges. IEEE Trans. Image Process. **10**(2), 266–277 (2001)
3. Wang, X.F., Min, H., Zou, L., Zhang, Y.G.: A novel level set method for image segmentation by incorporating local statistical analysis and global similarity measurement. Pattern Recognit. **48**(1), 189–204 (2015)
4. Wang, X.F., Huang, D.S., Xu, H.: An efficient local Chan-Vese model for image segmentation. Pattern Recogn. **43**(3), 603–618 (2010)
5. Li, C.M., Kao, C.Y., Gore, J.C., Ding, Z.H.: Minimization of region-scalable fitting energy for image segmentation. IEEE Trans. Image Process. **17**, 1940–1949 (2008)
6. Li, C.M., et al.: A level set method for image segmentation in the presence of intensity inhomogeneities with application to MRI. IEEE Trans. Image Process. **20**(7), 2007–2016 (2011)
7. Wang, Y., Huang, T., Wang, H.: Region-based active contours with cosine fitting energy for image segmentation. J. Opt. Soc. Am. A Opt. Image Sci. Vis. **32**(11), 2237–2246 (2015)
8. Wang, X.F., et al.: An efficient level set method based on multi-scale image segmentation and hermite differential operator. Neurocomputing **188**, 90–101 (2016)
9. Weicert, J., Kühne, G.: Fast methods for implicit active contour models. In: Geomeric Level Set Methods in Imaging, Vision, and Graphics, pp. 43–57 (2003)
10. Li, Y., Kim, J.: An unconditionally stable hybrid method for image segmentation. Appl. Numer. Math. **82**, 32–43 (2014)
11. Li, Z., Zeng, L., Wang, T.: Image segmentation based on local Chan-Vese model optimized by max-flow algorithm. In: IEEE/ACIS International Conference on Software Engineering, Artificial Intelligence, Networking and Parallel/distributed Computing. IEEE, pp. 213–218 (2016)
12. Song, B., Chan, T.: A fast algorithm for level set based optimization, CAM-UCLA 68, pp. 2–68 (2002)
13. Boutiche, Y.: Fast algorithm to minimize model combining dynamically local and global fitting energy for image segmentation. In: International Conference on Control, Engineering & Information Technology, pp. 1–6. IEEE (2015)
14. Boutiche, Y., Abdesselam, A.: Fast algorithm for hybrid region-based active contours optimisation. IET Image Proc. **11**(3), 200–209 (2017)

A Visibility-Guided Fusion Framework for Fast Nighttime Image Dehazing

Xiongbiao Luo[1][✉], Yingying Guo[1], Henry Chidozie Ewurum[1], Zhao Feng[1], and Jie Yang[2]

[1] Xiamen University, Xiamen 361005, FJ, China
lurowan@aliyun.com
[2] Shanghai Jiao Tong University, Minhang, Shanghai 200240, China

Abstract. Defogging is an important image enhancement and restoration technique that is widely used for various computer vision and computational photography applications. While the vast majority of currently available defogging methods work well for daytime foggy images, they generally remain challenging to dehaze nighttime hazy images. This work proposes a new visibility-guided fusion framework to defog nighttime images. We first use fast visibility recovery to restore the hazy image. On the other hand, we enhance the foggy image to improve its contrast. Finally, an illumination fusion step is performed to precisely remove fog. The experimental results demonstrate that our proposed method is effective to remove fog or haze on nighttime images. In particular, it provides an efficient strategy to defog nighttime foggy images.

Keywords: Defogging · Nighttime dehazing · Image fusion
Visibility restoration · Illumination estimation
Computational photography

1 Introduction

Haze, fog, and smoke weather commonly degenerates the visual quality of images or videos acquired at outdoor environments during daytime and nighttime. In particular, haze, fog, and smoke deteriorate image details such as contrast, colorfulness, texture, structures or sharpness, which lead to difficulty in various computer vision and computational photography tasks, e.g., object detection and tracking, video surveillance, intelligent transportation, and stereo reconstruction. Defogging is a topic of computer photography, for which various algorithms are developed to enhance or restore images degraded by haze, fog, and smoke.

Most currently available defogging methods have been focused on process foggy images at daytime. These methods are generally classified into two categories: (1) enhancement and (2) restoration techniques. Enhancement algorithms directly process pixel intensity of foggy images to improve their contrast. Typical enhancement methods include intensity transform or histogram analysis. While enhancement techniques are generally efficient and easy implementation,

J.-H. Lai et al. (Eds.): PRCV 2018, LNCS 11256, pp. 479–489, 2018.
https://doi.org/10.1007/978-3-030-03398-9_41

they are generally inaccurate and poor robustness. Most researchers have been worked on restoration approaches. These approaches usually define dehazing as an inverse and ill-posed issue on the basis of a physical imaging model. This model formulates a haze-free image (also called scene radiance) by its corresponding foggy image, atmospheric light, and scene transmission map. Based on this model, various restoration methods have been discussed to estimate the unknown atmospheric light and scene transmission map on daytime foggy images in the literature. He et al. [3] calculated the atmospheric light and transmission map using dark channel prior plus soft editing to defog single image under a heavy computational load. By skipping soft editing, Meng et al. [5] introduced the boundary constraint and contextual regularization to improve the dark channel-based dehazing method. Tarel et al. [11] employed a median of median filtering framework that can efficiently restore hazy image at daytime but it usually results in color distortion. Nishino et al. [6] recovered foggy visibility by a Bayesian defogging method that computes two statistically independent components of the scene albedo and depth. More recently, Sulami et al. [8] established a reduced formation model to analyze image pixels in small patches as lines that are used to estimate the atmospheric light orientation. Tang et al. [10] proposed a learning-based strategy to calculate the scene transmission, while Galdran et al. [2] introduced an improved variational defogging framework using inter-channel contrast. Generally speaking, the restoration-based defogging methods work better than the enhancement-based defogging algorithms.

(a) Image 07   (b) Tarel et al. [11]   (c) Li et al. [4]   (d) Ours

Fig. 1. An example of compared defogged results from different methods. The (*signal-to-noise ratio, peak signal-to-noise ratio, structural similarity index*) for measuring defogged image quality of Tarel et al. [11], Li et al. [4], and ours were (8.67, 19.8, 0.7992), (5.69, 16.9, 0.5479), and (13.0, 24.2, 0.8775), respectively.

Although most current dehazing approaches work well on daytime foggy images, few of them can defog nighttime foggy images. A recently published paper has been proposed a nighttime dehazing method that uses glow and multiple light colors [4]. Our work also aims to defog nighttime foggy images. The contribution of our paper is clarified as follows. We propose a new visibility-guided fusion strategy for single nighttime image defogging. Compare to the previous methods [4,11], our method provides better quality (Fig. 1). In addition, our proposed method is much faster than the nighttime defogging approach [4].

The remainder of this paper is organized as follows. Section 2 describes the technical details of our proposed defogging method that fuses fast visibility and lighting enhancement for nighttime images. We show the experimental results and discuss them in Sect. 3, followed by concluding this work in Sect. 4.

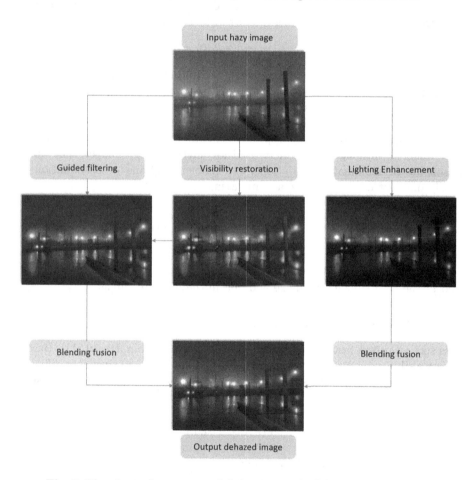

Fig. 2. Flowchart of our proposed defogging method for nighttime images

2 Visibility-Guided Fusion

This section details our visibility-guided fusion framework for defogging night-time. Such a framework consists of three main steps: (1) visibility restoration, (2) lighting enhancement, and (3) blending fusion (Fig. 2). Each step will be explained after we define the nighttime haze model in the following.

2.1   Nighttime Haze Model

In the literature, a widely used physical imaging model is established for hazy images in accordance with the Koschmieder's law [3]:

$$\mathbf{I}(u,v) = \mathbf{J}(u,v)\mathbf{T}(u,v) + \mathbf{A}_\infty(1 - \mathbf{T}(u,v)), \tag{1}$$

where $\mathbf{I}(u,v)$ denotes an observed (foggy) image, $\mathbf{J}(u,v)$ refers to as a haze-free image (also called scene radiance), and $\mathbf{A}_\infty$ indicates the atmospheric light or the sky luminance. The transmission map $\mathbf{T}(u,v)$ describes the amount of the unscattered light entering a camera, and can be computed by

$$\mathbf{T}(u,v) = \exp(-kd(u,v)) \tag{2}$$

where k and $d(u,v)$ are the atmosphere's scattering factor and the depth or distance between the camera and any objects in a scene, respectively.

Based on Eq. 1, we aims to solve hazy-free image $\mathbf{J}(u,v)$ under the unknown variables $\mathbf{A}_\infty$ and $\mathbf{T}(u,v)$. In this respect, defogging is an ill-posed problem. Theoretically, the model is inappropriate to be directly introduced for nighttime hazy imaging, although it is widely used for daytime foggy images. The main reason lies in illumination variations, i.e., ambient lighting or illumination is totally different during daytime and nighttime.

Similar to the recent work [4], we modify Eq. 1 by adding a new term $\mathbf{L}(u,v)$:

$$\mathbf{I}(u,v) = \mathbf{J}(u,v)\mathbf{T}(u,v) + \mathbf{A}_\infty(1 - \mathbf{T}(u,v)) + \mathbf{L}(u,v), \tag{3}$$

where $\mathbf{L}(u,v)$ characterizes the luminance change between daytime and nighttime on foggy images. We estimate $\mathbf{J}(u,v)$ and $\mathbf{L}(u,v)$ and combine them to recover the nighttime foggy image and obtain the hazy-free image.

2.2   Visibility Restoration

This section uses a fast visibility recovery method to obtain $\mathbf{J}(u,v)$ [11]. Based on fast visibility recovery, we did not directly estimate $\mathbf{T}(u,v)$ since it is difficult to precisely predict the transmission map related to depth information. To skip $\mathbf{T}(u,v)$, the atmospheric veil $\mathbf{X}(u,v)$ was introduced [1]:

$$\mathbf{X}(u,v) = \mathbf{A}_\infty(1 - \mathbf{T}(u,v)), \mathbf{T}(u,v) = 1 - \frac{\mathbf{X}(u,v)}{\mathbf{A}_\infty}. \tag{4}$$

Then, Eq. 1 can be rewritten to calculate $\mathbf{J}(u,v)$:

$$\mathbf{J}(u,v) = \frac{\mathbf{A}_\infty(\mathbf{I}(u,v) - \mathbf{X}(u,v))}{\mathbf{A}_\infty - \mathbf{X}(u,v)}. \tag{5}$$

This requires the atmospheric light $\mathbf{A}_\infty$ and veil $\mathbf{X}(u,v)$ for which robust estimates can be obtained much more easily than the depth and transmission maps in the original formulation (Eq. 1). The methods that are used to determine $\mathbf{A}_\infty$ and veil $\mathbf{X}(u,v)$ have been discussed in the previous work [11]. Here we skip the technical details of how to estimate light $\mathbf{A}_\infty$ and veil $\mathbf{X}(u,v)$.

2.3   Lighting Enhancement

Nighttime foggy images are low-contrast and limited illumination, especially in hazy regions. The purpose of lighting enhancement is to increase the contrast of hazy-less regions on the foggy image and obtain the luminance $\mathbf{L}(u, v)$, and to improve the illumination of the final defogged nighttime image.

The contrast enhancement step usually takes into consideration two rules (1) most regions on the foggy image are hazy pixels that critically affect the mean of the foggy image and (2) the level of haze in these regions depends on the distance between the atmospheric light and the scene, as discussed in a previous work [1]. Based on these rules, we calculate the enhanced luminance $\mathbf{L}(u, v)$ by magnifying difference between nighttime hazy image $\mathbf{I}(u, v)$ and its average luminance value λ in the three channels $c \in \{r, g, b\}$:

$$\mathbf{L}_c(u, v) = \beta(\mathbf{I}_c(u, v) - \lambda), \lambda = \frac{\sum_U \sum_V \mathbf{H}(u, v)}{UV}, \qquad (6)$$

where β is the magnification factor to control the luminance of the augmented foggy regions and $U \times V$ are the width and height of the nighttime hazy image. The original luminance $\mathbf{H}(u, v)$ at each pixel is computed by [9]

$$\mathbf{H}(u, v) = 0.299 \times \mathbf{I}_r(u, v) + 0.587 \times \mathbf{I}_g(u, v) + 0.114 \times \mathbf{I}_b(u, v). \qquad (7)$$

2.4   Blending Fusion

This step is to estimate illumination on image $\mathbf{J}(u, v)$ and $\mathbf{L}(u, v)$ and blend their illumination to improve the illumination of the defogged image.

We transfer the images $\mathbf{J}(u, v)$ and $\mathbf{L}(u, v)$ from the RGB to $YCbCr$ color space. For the Y-component of them, we used recursive filtering [7] to estimate the illumination of $\mathbf{J}(u, v)$ and $\mathbf{L}(u, v)$ and obtain $\mathbf{G}_J(u, v)$ and $\mathbf{G}_L(u, v)$. By using image illumination $\mathbf{G}_J(u, v)$ and $\mathbf{G}_L(u, v)$, we seek to recognize pixels in hazy regions. So, a weight function $W_K(\mathbf{G}_K(u, v)), K \in \{J, L\}$ is empirically introduced, and output $\mathbf{O}_q(u, v)$ of the blending fusion can be formulated:

$$\mathbf{O}_q(u, v) = \frac{\sum_{K \in \{J,L\}} W_K(\mathbf{G}_K(u, v))\mathbf{O}_q(u, v)}{\sum_{K \in \{J,L\}} W_K(\mathbf{G}_K(u, v))}, \quad q \in \{Y, Cb, Cr\}. \qquad (8)$$

The Y-component output $\mathbf{O}_Y(u, v)$ may not be distributed into the full range of pixel intensity, resulting in a low-contrast image. We implement the following linear transformation to stretch its histogram to a specific intensity range $[P, Q]$:

$$\hat{\mathbf{O}}_Y(u, v) = P + \frac{\mathbf{O}_Y(u, v) - \mathbf{O}_{Min}(u, v)}{\mathbf{O}_{Max}(u, v) - \mathbf{O}_{Min}(u, v)}(Q - P), \qquad (9)$$

where $\hat{\mathbf{O}}_Y(u, v)$ denotes the final Y-component result, $\mathbf{O}_{Min}(u, v)$ and $\mathbf{O}_{Max}(u, v)$ are the minimum and maximum intensity of the blending output $\mathbf{O}_Y(u, v)$, respectively. We empirically set $P = 15$ and $Q = 236$ in our work.

Eventually, we combine the Y-component $\hat{\mathbf{O}}_Y(u, v)$ and the chromatic components $\mathbf{O}_{Cb}(u, v)$ and $\mathbf{O}_{Cr}(u, v)$ and transform them into the RGB color space, obtaining the final defogged nighttime image.

3   Results and Discussion

All the nighttime foggy images with various visual quality were collected through
the Internet. We validated our proposed method on these images, and compared
it to two methods: (1) M1, a daytime single image defogging approach by Tarel
et al. [11], (2) M2, a nighttime single image defogging strategy on the basis of
glow and multiple light colors [4], and (3) M3, our proposed method as discussed
in Sect. 2. On the other hand, we used three measures to evaluate the defogged
results from the compared three approaches: (1) SNR: signal-to-noise ratio, (2)
PSNR: peak signal-to-noise ratio, and (3) SSIM: structural similarity index [12].
Note that all the experiments were tested on a laptop installed with Windows 8.1
Professional 64-Bit System, 16.0-GB Memory, and Processor Intel(R) Core(TM)
i7 CPU × 8 and were implemented on the platform of Matlab 2017a.

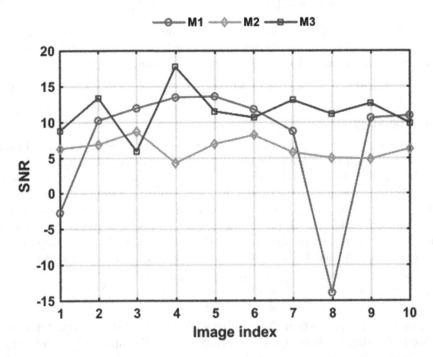

Fig. 3. Comparison of SNR of using the three nighttime defogging methods

Figures 3, 4 and 5 compare the SNR, PSNR, and SSIM of the defogged night-
time images of using the three different approaches. The average SNR of M1,
M2, and M3 was 9.46, 6.25, and 11.4, respectively, while the average PSNR of
the three methods were 17.2, 16.0, and 21.2. Moreover, the average SSIM of M1,
M2, and M3 was 0.72, 0.42, and 0.85. General speaking, the SNR, PSNR, and
SSIM of our proposed method were much better than the other two.

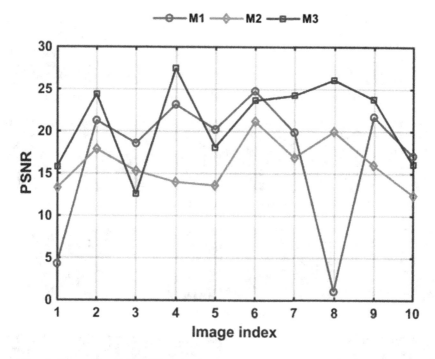

Fig. 4. Comparison of PSNR of using the three nighttime defogging methods

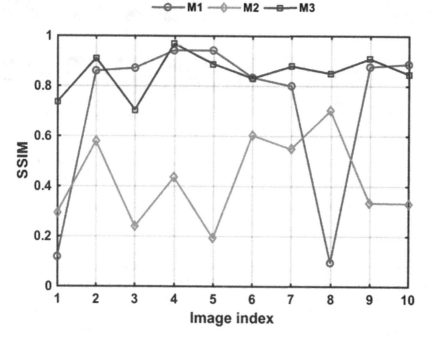

Fig. 5. Comparison of SSIM of using the three nighttime defogging methods

(a) Image 01, results of using M1, M2, and M3 (from *left* to *right*), respectively

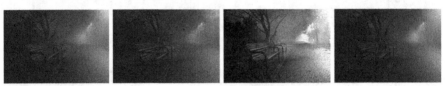

(b) Image 02, results of using M1, M2, and M3 (from *left* to *right*), respectively

(c) Image 04, results of using M1, M2, and M3 (from *left* to *right*), respectively

(d) Image 08, results of using M1, M2, and M3 (from *left* to *right*), respectively

(e) Image 09, results of using M1, M2, and M3 (from *left* to *right*), respectively

Fig. 6. Visual comparison of several defogged images of using the methods: The first column shows the input nighttime foggy images 01, 02, 04, 08, and 09, and the other columns correspond to their defogged results of using M1 [11], M2 [4], and M3 (ours), respectively. The forth column displays better or comparable results of using our proposed visibility-guided fusion approach.

Figure 6 displays several examples of nighttime foggy images that were defogged by the three compared approaches. Our visibility-guided fusion framework outperforms the other two methods. In particular, the visual naturalness was much better than that of M2 [4], while our proposed visibility-guided fusion framework provides much better colorfulness than the other two methods. In addition, note that M1 does not work for images 01 and 08 and introduces

(a) Image 03, results of using M1, M2, and M3 (from *left* to *right*), respectively

(b) Image 05, results of using M1, M2, and M3 (from *left* to *right*), respectively

(c) Image 06, results of using M1, M2, and M3 (from *left* to *right*), respectively

(d) Image 10, results of using M1, M2, and M3 (from *left* to *right*), respectively

Fig. 7. Our proposed approach processed images 03, 05, 06, and 10 with comparable or worse SNR, PSNR, and SSIM values, compared to the method M1.

sometimes introduces *white* images without any information. The essential step of median filtering used in the method M1 commonly brings some Null pixels to the output or filtered image. These Null pixels on the filtered image failed the local white-balance procedure in the method of Tarel et al. [11].

Figure 7 illustrates some night foggy images that our proposed approach does not work well. Compared to the method M1, our method provides worse or comparable quantitative results of SNR, PSNR, and SSIM (Figs. 3, 4, and 5). This is because of nonuniform fog. However, the visual quality of our approach defogged images was much better than that of the method M2.

Table 1 investigates the computational time on each nighttime foggy image that was defogged by the three methods of M1, M2, and M3. The average com-

Table 1. Computational time of using different nighttime defogging methods

Images	Width × Height	M1	M2	M3
01	1024 × 679	44.429	42.975	1.1781
02	576 × 382	5.0037	11.455	0.2819
03	538 × 328	2.8603	15.011	0.2064
04	500 × 333	3.4019	14.596	0.1937
05	648 × 432	6.8581	24.008	0.3482
06	686 × 475	7.9103	27.320	0.3786
07	360 × 540	3.5129	12.619	0.2133
08	612 × 384	5.1262	13.372	0.2832
09	653 × 384	6.3085	13.017	0.2932
10	1292 × 1444	151.26	102.67	2.3347
Average time (second)		23.667	27.704	0.5711

putational time of these approaches was 23.667, 27.704, and 0.5711 seconds, respectively. Our method significantly improved the computational efficiency.

The objective of this work is to remove haze or fog on nighttime images. Currently, most of single dehazing algorithms work well for daytime foggy images but they are difficult to process nighttime foggy images. This work developed a visibility-guided fusion strategy to deal with nighttime hazy images. Our strategy generally outperforms the two compared defogging methods. In particular, our proposed method combines the advantages of the enhancement- and restoration-based dehazing algorithms to address illumination variations during nighttime imaging, while it also provides an efficient nighttime defogging framework.

Unfortunately, our method remains challenging to deal with nighttime images with nonuniform fog or haze (Fig. 7). Illumination on these nighttime images were not estimated precisely. On the other hand, it is still difficult to establish a precise nighttime hazy imaging model. The model proposed by Li et al. [4] is difficult to precisely characterize the procedure of nighttime imaging since it usually over-defogs the image, results in loss of image naturalness, and introduces big color shift or distortion. Our future work is to address these issues.

4   Conclusions

This paper proposes a visibility-guided fusion approach for single nighttime image defogging. We combine fast visibility recovery and lighting enhancement to address illumination variations during nighttime imaging. The experimental results demonstrate the effectiveness and efficiency of the proposed method. Compared to a recent nighttime defogging method, our approach provides much better performance in image naturalness and colorfulness. Particularly, our method can significantly improve the SNR, PSNR, and SSIM of the defogged images.

References

1. Ancuti, C.O., Ancuti, C.: Single image dehazing by multi-scale fusion. IEEE Trans. Image Process. **22**(8), 3271–3282 (2013)
2. Galdran, A., Vazquez-Corral, J., Pardo, D., Bertalmio, M.: Enhanced variational image dehazing. SIAM J. Imaging Sci. **8**(3), 1519–1546 (2015)
3. He, K., Sun, J., Tang, X.: Single image haze removal using dark channel prior. IEEE Trans. Pattern Anal. Mach. Intell. **33**(12), 2341–2353 (2011)
4. Li, Y., Tan, R.T., Brown, M.S.: Nighttime haze removal with glow and multiple light colors. In: IEEE International Conference on Computer Vision (ICCV), pp. 226–234 (2015)
5. Meng, G., Wang, Y., Duan, J., Xiang, S., Pan, C.: Efficient image dehazing with boundary constraint and contextual regularization. In: IEEE International Conference on Computer Vision (ICCV), pp. 617–624 (2013)
6. Nishino, K., Kratz, L., Lombardi, S.: Bayesian defogging. Int. J. Comput. Vis. **98**(3), 263–278 (2012)
7. Ramirez, J.M., Paredes, J.L.: Recursive weighted myriad based filters and their optimizations. IEEE Trans. Signal Process. **64**(15), 4027–4039 (2016)
8. Sulami, M., Glatzer, I., Fattal, R., Werman, M.: Automatic recovery of the atmospheric light in hazy images. In: IEEE International Conference on Computational Photography (ICCP), pp. 1–11 (2014)
9. Szeliski, R.: Computer Vision: Algorithms and Applications. Springer, London (2011). https://doi.org/10.1007/978-1-84882-935-0
10. Tang, K., Yang, J., Wang, J.: Investigating haze-relevant features in a learning framework for image dehazing. In: IEEE Conference on Computer Vision and Pattern Recognition (CVPR), pp. 2995–3002 (2014)
11. Tarel, J.P., Hautiere, N.: Fast visibility restoration from a single color or gray level image. In: IEEE International Conference on Computer Vision (ICCV), pp. 2201–2208 (2009)
12. Wang, Z., Bovik, A.C., Sheikh, H.R., Simoncelli, E.P.: Image quality assessment: from error visibility to structural similarity. IEEE Trans. Image Process. **13**(4), 600–612 (2004)

Blind Deblurring Using Discriminative Image Smoothing

Wenze Shao[1(⊠)], Yunzhi Lin[2], Bingkun Bao[1], Liqian Wang[1], Qi Ge[1], and Haibo Li[1,3]

[1] Nanjing University of Posts and Telecommunication, Nanjing 210003, China
shaowenze@njupt.edu.cn
[2] Southeast University, Nanjing 211189, China
[3] KTH Royal Institute of Technology, 10044 Stockholm, Sweden

Abstract. This paper aims to exploit the full potential of gradient-based methods, attempting to explore a simple, robust yet discriminative image prior for blind deblurring. The specific contributions are three-fold: Above all, a pure gradient-based heavy-tailed model is proposed as a generalized integration of the normalized sparsity and the relative total variation. On the second, a plug-and-play algorithm is deduced to alternatively estimate the intermediate sharp image and the nonparametric blur kernel. With the numerical scheme, image estimation is simplified to an image smoothing problem. Lastly, a great many experiments are performed accompanied with comparisons with state-of-the-art approaches on synthetic benchmark datasets and real blurry images in various scenarios. The experimental results show well the effectiveness and robustness of the proposed method.

Keywords: Blind deblurring · Discriminative prior · Low-illumination

1 Introduction

Undergone a few years of exploration since the daring work of Fergus et al. [1] for blind image deblurring, unnatural image models have been predominating the blind deblurring literature until now. On this line, the first inspiring try is harnessing the normalized sparsity measure in [4] with the idea that the image prior should favor a sharp image to its blurry one. Nevertheless, the method cannot produce state-of-the-art performance on this or that benchmark dataset, let alone blurry images in the wild [2]. The normalized sparsity is mathematically an approximation of the L0-norm in essence, indicating that the salient edges matter a bit more than the faint textures to the final success of blind deconvolution for natural images. In fact, unnatural image priors are not only requested in the MAP framework but also advocated in the VB case in spite of its more robustness in posterior inference. For example, another work by the authors of the present paper has proposed to determine priors for blind image deblurring as a self-learning problem [6] in the VB framework. The results show that the learned model resembles in a sense the non-informative Jeffreys prior, whose negative-logarithm is of course a new approximation to the L0-based model. Instead of approximating the L0-norm with diverse strategies, a pure L0-based image prior was

© Springer Nature Switzerland AG 2018
J.-H. Lai et al. (Eds.): PRCV 2018, LNCS 11256, pp. 490–500, 2018.
https://doi.org/10.1007/978-3-030-03398-9_42

firstly proposed in [7] for blind deblurring. However, they are found not generalized well to the large blur especially in specific imaging scenarios, e.g., face, text, or low-illumination images. In [8] a new L0-norm-based intensity and gradient prior is presented for deblurring of the specific text images. Furthermore, an exemplar-driven method with L0-norm-based regularization on image gradients is proposed in [9] for face image deblurring.

In the blind deblurring field, the comforting thing is that numerous algorithms have been put forward in the past decade, which achieve better and better performance on one or another synthetic dataset. However, as claimed in [2] the performance of early methods on the benchmark datasets is generally found inferior to that on those real blurred images. In other words, those methods are far from being practical in terms of the restoration quality. Actually a real breakthrough for blind deblurring is just made very recently in [3] which combines the L0-regularized sparsity of both the image gradient and dark channel. The experimental results prove its superior performance to all the representative methods in the past decade as studied in [2]. Note that, although the L0-based dark channel prior is discriminative as desired, the whole composite sparse model of [3] is not necessarily so. Besides, it can be actually thought of as a smart generalization over [8] and therefore is not a pure gradient-based method.

In spite of the recent great progress in this field, this paper aims to formulate the blind problem with a simper modeling perspective. What is more important, the newly proposed approach is expected to achieve comparative or even better performance towards the real blurred images. Specifically, the core innovation idea is the proposal of a pure gradient-based discriminative prior for accurate and robust blur kernel estimation. Experimental results on both benchmark datasets and real-world images in various imaging scenarios, e.g., natural, manmade, low-illumination, text, or people, demonstrate well the effectiveness and robustness of the proposed method.

2 A Plug-and-Play Approach to Gradient-Based Discriminative Blind Deconvolution

2.1 Gradient-Based Discriminative Prior

Our discussion begins with the first daring attempt towards discriminative image modeling for blind image deconvolution, i.e., the normalized sparsity [4]. As indicated in [2, 3], its discriminativeness and effectiveness is, however, questionable in both synthetic and practical experiments. Discriminativeness generally guarantees that the optimum should be not the pair of blurred image and delta kernel. While, the effectiveness means that image details such as the textures should be removed from the intermediate sharp image for accurate kernel estimation, as being validated in existing methods [7, 10, 11].

Taking above two factors into consideration, a new candidate prior for blind image deconvolution is presented as

$$\mathcal{R}(u) = \sum_p \varpi_{x,p}(u) \cdot \left| \partial_x u_p \right|^\alpha + \sum_p \varpi_{y,p}(u) \cdot \left| \partial_y u_p \right|^\alpha, \qquad (1)$$

where u is a sharp image, $p \in \Omega(u)$ a pixel index, and α a positive value far less than 1, ∂ a derivative operator, $\varpi_{x,p}(u)$ a positive value related to pixel index and derivative direction. It is not hard to deduce that the core novelty of the prior $\mathcal{R}(u)$ should be in the definition of ϖ which embodies the demanded discriminativeness and effectiveness for plausible intermediate image update.

We find that the requested discriminativeness can be naively achieved by adapting the simple normalized sparsity [4], while the effectiveness of accurate intermediate image update can be further ensured by adapting the relative total variation [5]. Then, we could simply express $\mathcal{R}(u)$ as a gradient-based composite image prior. Specifically, $\varpi_{o,p}(u)$, $o \in \{x, y\}$ is defined as

$$\varpi_{o,p}(u) = \frac{1-t}{(\mathcal{D}_o(u))^\beta + \varepsilon} + \frac{t}{(\mathcal{S} \ominus_o (p))^\beta + \varepsilon}, \ominus \tag{2}$$

where β is a positive power, t is a value between 0 and 1, ε is a small positive number to avoid division by zero, and $\mathcal{D}_o(u)$ and $\mathcal{S}_o(p)$ are expressed respectively as

$$\mathcal{D}_o(u) = \left(\sum\nolimits_{p \in \Omega(u)} |\partial_o u_p|^2 \right)^{1/2} = \|\partial_o u\|_2, \tag{3}$$

$$\mathcal{S}_o(p) = \left| \sum\nolimits_{q \in \Omega(p)} \phi_{p,q} \cdot \partial_o u_q \right|, \tag{4}$$

where $\Omega(p)$ is the rectangular field centered at pixel p, and $\phi_{p,q}$ is defined according to the spatial affinity as a distance function of Gaussianity, i.e.,

$$\phi_{p,q} \propto \exp\left(-\frac{(x_p - x_q)^2 + (y_p - y_q)^2}{2\sigma^2} \right),$$

where σ is a spatial scale to be specified in implementation. We should claim that $\mathcal{S}_o(p)$ was originally proposed in [5] for image filtering and manipulation, whose value in a window just with textures is found statistically smaller than that in a window also containing structural edges.

Let's dive into (1) and (2) for more details. One finding is that, $\sum_p |\partial_x u_p|^\alpha / (\mathcal{D}_x(u))^\beta + \sum_p |\partial_y u_p|^\alpha / (\mathcal{D}_y(u))^\beta$ rises a primary function on discriminating sharp images from blurred ones as proper settings are provided to α, β. It is apparent that the above regularization term will degenerate to the normalized sparsity [4] as α, β are equal to 1. Another finding is that, the performance of above regularization term can be further boosted via $\sum_p |\partial_x u_p|^\alpha / (\mathcal{S}_x(p))^\beta + \sum_p |\partial_y u_p|^\alpha / (\mathcal{S}_y(p))^\beta$. The reason is that it is able to remove the interfering textures while making the salient structures stand out more accurately in the intermediate sharp image. Such additional amending is proved very critical to the high quality blind deconvolution in spite that the amending strength governed by the parameter t is relatively less. A large amount of experiments demonstrate that t set as 0.05 satisfactorily serves the plug-and-play algorithm deduced in the following subsection.

2.2 A Plug-and-Play Numerical Scheme to Blind Deconvolution

As the blur is assumed spatially-invariant, the blurred image observation process can be described as

$$g = k * u + n, \tag{5}$$

where u denotes the latent sharp image, g the captured blurry image, k the blur kernel corresponding to the camera shake or out-of-focus, and n the possible random noise. It is known that blind image deconvolution is mathematically ill-posed because there are infinite solution pairs (u, k) satisfying the formulation (5). Therefore, appropriate regularization should be imposed on both the image u and the kernel k.

Harnessing the proposed model (1), a MAP-based objective function for blind deblurring can be expressed as

$$\mathcal{J}(u, k) \triangleq \|g - k * u\|_2^2 + \lambda \mathcal{R}(u) + \eta \|k\|_2^2, \tag{6}$$

where λ and η are the two positive adjusting parameters. The first quadratic term is for the image fidelity, while the third term is a Tikhonov regularization on the blur kernel k. Note that, the formulation (6) works free of any ad-hoc modeling tricks, e.g., continuation, or additional image processing operations such as bilateral smoothing or shock filtering. In consequence, the blind deconvolution performance of the proposed algorithm will be overwhelmingly determined by the discriminative image prior (1), considering that the Tikhonov penalty on the blur kernel is a standard configuration in a large majority of existing methods. This paper sets the tuning parameter η as 2.

Now, the image and the kernel can be obtained by solving the joint minimization problem $(\hat{u}, \hat{k}) - \arg\min_{u,k} \mathcal{J}(u, k)$ in an alternatingly iterative manner. Provided the $(i - 1)$th iterative solution of $k^{(i-1)}$, $u^{(i)}$ and $k^{(i)}$ are then respectively solved by $u^{(i)} = \arg\min_u \mathcal{J}(u, k^{(i-1)})$ and $k^{(i)} = \arg\min_k \mathcal{J}(u^{(i)}, k)$.

In this paper, the half-quadratic regularization strategy is used to estimate $u^{(i)}$ via decomposing the original minimization problem into two simper sub-problems. An auxiliary variable is firstly introduced corresponding to u, i.e., let $u = z$, and then a new objective function can be obtained as

$$\mathcal{J}(u, z, k^{(i-1)}) \triangleq \left\|g - k^{(i-1)} * u\right\|_2^2 + \lambda \mathcal{R}(z) + \rho \|u - z\|_2^2,$$

whose minimizing solution, i.e., the intermediate sharp image, approaches that of $\mathcal{J}(u, k^{(i-1)})$ as ρ is close to infinity. In each alternative minimization over u and z, it is obvious that u can be efficiently gained via use of fast Fourier transform (FFT) in a closed form solution. That is,

$$u = \mathcal{F}^{-1}\left(\frac{\overline{\mathcal{F}(k^{(i-1)})}\mathcal{F}(g) + \rho\mathcal{F}(z)}{\overline{\mathcal{F}(k^{(i-1)})}\mathcal{F}(k^{(i-1)}) + \rho}\right), \tag{7}$$

where $\mathcal{F}$ and $\bar{\mathcal{F}}$ represent the FFT and its complex conjugate, respectively, and $\mathcal{F}^{-1}$ represent the operation of inverse FFT. Besides, as usual z is initialized to be a zero image. Given u, z is numerically computed by minimizing the sub-problem

$$\|u - z\|_2^2 + \frac{\lambda}{\rho}\mathcal{R}(z). \tag{8}$$

Apparently, solving (8) actually amounts to an amendatory step of image smoothing regularized by (1) and is implemented via the reweighted least squares approximation [5]. In this perspective, the intermediate sharp image estimation falls into a plug-and-play framework seminally proposed in [12, 13]. To the very best of our knowledge, this paper is the first to apply the plug-and-play idea for blind image deconvolution via use of a specifically customized discriminative prior.

With an estimated intermediate image $u^{(i)}$, blur kernel $k^{(i)}$ can be produced by solving the Tikhonov-based energy functional $k^{(i)} = \arg\min_k \mathcal{J}(u^{(i)}, k)$. In spite of that, a slightly modified functional defined in the gradient domain as commonly practiced in blind deblurring [3, 19] is used for better estimation. That is,

$$k^{(i)} = \arg\min_k \left\|\nabla g - k * \nabla u^{(i)}\right\|_2^2 + \eta\|k\|_2^2, \tag{9}$$

wherein $k^{(i)}$ can be solved very efficiently in a closed-form via FFT in exactly the same way as updating the image u in (7). One more point to be noted is that, blur kernel $k^{(i)}$ should be projected onto the set $\mathcal{C} = \{\, k \geq 0,\ \sum_i \sum_j |k_{i,j}| = 1 \,\}$ considering the physical property of blur kernels.

3   Experimental Results

This section validates the proposed approach on the datasets proposed by Lai et al. [2] with comparisons against the current representative blind deblurring algorithms: [1, 7, 10, 11, 14–19]. Besides the PSNR, the SSIM in [20] and the no-reference metric in [21] are also harnessed for quantitative assessment of different methods in this part. Note that, [21] is specifically proposed to evaluate the motion deblurring quality which is consistent with human feelings and ratings to a certain degree.

The datasets in Lai et al. [2] include a synthetic one consist of 100 blurred images generated by 4 blur kernels shown in Fig. 1 and 25 true clear images divided into 5 categories, i.e., natural (**N**), manmade (**M**), text (**T**), people (**P**), and saturated (**S**), as well as a real one containing 100 blurred color images collected from either previous deblurring works, or Flicker and Google Search, or those captured by the authors themselves, which also fall into the above five categories.

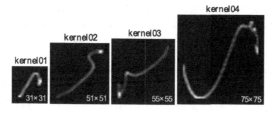

Fig. 1. Blur kernels with different sizes used for generating the 100 synthetic blurry images in Lai et al. [2].

3.1   Synthetic Experiment Results

Tables 1, 2, 3, and 4 list the average statistics of the three metrics for the deblurred images corresponding to each of the blur kernels in Fig. 1. In every table, each row represents the average evaluation across the five image categories, i.e., **N, M, T, P, S**. It is seen that the overall performance of our approach ranks the first in almost all scenarios in terms of either PSNR, or SSIM, or no-reference metric, proving its effectiveness and robustness in dealing with various kinds of blurred images with different kernel sizes.

Table 1. Average statistics of PSNR (dB), SSIM [20], and no-reference (no-ref.) metric [21] of the final deblurred images corresponding to each blind deblurring approach on the 25 blurred images generated by **kernel01 (31 × 31)** in the dataset of Lai et al. [2]. Red denotes the best, blue the second, and green the third.

Metric	[1]	[10]	[11]	[14]	[15]	[16]	[7]	[17]	[18]	[19]	Ours
PSNR	16.66	19.07	22.64	19.45	18.95	22.26	22.11	21.25	21.44	21.28	23.47
SSIM	0.5429	0.6846	0.8346	0.7287	0.6576	0.8181	0.8102	0.7826	0.7774	0.8191	0.8880
No-ref.	-18.05	-11.94	-10.43	-11.23	-13.91	-10.53	-10.82	-11.30	-10.81	-10.87	-10.28

Table 2. Average statistics of PSNR (dB), SSIM, and no-reference (no-ref.) metric of the final deblurred images corresponding to each blind deblurring approach on the 25 blurred images generated by **kernel02 (51 × 51)** in the dataset of Lai et al. [2]. Red denotes the best, blue the second, and green the third.

Metric	[1]	[10]	[11]	[14]	[15]	[16]	[7]	[17]	[18]	[19]	Ours
PSNR	15.67	17.65	21.65	18.77	17.59	21.05	20.96	18.58	19.33	18.13	21.92
SSIM	0.4606	0.5892	0.8096	0.6812	0.5183	0.7658	0.7765	0.6172	0.6547	0.6460	0.8322
No-ref.	-18.02	-13.00	-11.64	-12.29	-14.75	-11.38	-12.10	-12.21	-11.73	-12.86	-11.27

Table 3. Average statistics of PSNR (dB), SSIM [20], and no-reference (no-ref.) metric [21] of the final deblurred images corresponding to each blind deblurring approach on the 25 blurred images generated by **kernel03 (55 × 55)** in the dataset of Lai et al. [2]. Red denotes the best, blue the second, and green the third.

Metric	[1]	[25]	[26]	[19]	[17]	[41]	[27]	[65]	[40]	[23]	Ours
PSNR	15.25	18.06	20.95	18.95	17.39	21.20	19.96	19.21	18.90	19.15	21.87
SSIM	0.4571	0.6251	0.7739	0.6923	0.5402	0.7948	0.7185	0.6802	0.6470	0.7295	0.8419
No-ref.	-17.96	-12.61	-11.05	-11.73	-14.24	-11.22	-12.07	-12.21	-11.31	-12.30	-10.91

Table 4. Average statistics of PSNR (dB), SSIM [20], and no-reference (no-ref.) metric [21] of the final deblurred images corresponding to each blind deblurring approach on the 25 blurred images generated by **kernel04 (75 × 75)** in the dataset of Lai et al. [2]. Red denotes the best, blue the second, and green the third.

Metric	[1]	[10]	[11]	[14]	[15]	[16]	[7]	[17]	[18]	[19]	Ours
PSNR	14.31	15.19	17.71	16.78	15.56	17.81	16.64	16.59	16.00	18.27	19.13
SSIM	0.3346	0.4383	0.6128	0.5614	0.3988	0.5844	0.5736	0.4994	0.4473	0.6474	0.6969
No-ref.	-20.57	-16.32	-16.07	-14.23	-14.04	-13.34	-18.22	-14.36	-11.70	-14.49	-13.82

We note an exception that in terms of the no-reference metric [21], our approach seems perform slightly inferior to [18] and [16] as dealing with images convolved by kernel04, as shown in Table 4. However this objective evaluation does not comply with the practical visual perception and the comparison should be more based on the PSNR and SSIM in this situation. A notable instance can be observed from Fig. 2, where our approach has produced a blur kernel of very high precision and therefore a reasonably good deblurred image. It is found that, however, it only ranks the last among the eight compared methods in terms of no-reference metric. In fact, all the other approaches completely fail in this example. Thus, the visual comparisons show that, to some extent [21] is not applicable for fairly measuring the saturated image deblurring quality. Therefore, in this case PSNR and SSIM should be more relied on for fair assessment of various algorithms. In brief, the comprehensive evaluation shows that our approach performs comparatively or better in all the five blur scenarios.

3.2 Realistic Experiment Results

Since there is not a reliable quantitative metric of measuring the deblurring quality for the real, comparisons are made merely based on our visual perception. In this part, the practical performance of the recent breakthrough work [3] is also tested.

The comprehensive assessment validates that the proposed method is more robust than most of the compared approaches in Subsect. 3.1, which achieves comparative (**N, M, P**) or better (**T, S**) performance on the whole set of 100 real images. In the meanwhile, it is found that our approach performs much comparatively to [3] and [38] on the five categories of blurred images, particularly on those text and saturated ones.

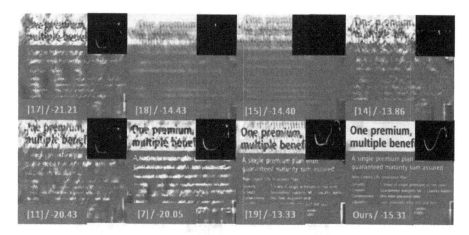

Fig. 2. Deblurring results of the blurred image text04-kernel04 in the dataset Lai et al. [2] corresponding to the top eight approaches in terms of PSNR/SSIM. The value of no-reference metric [67] is shown in each image for visual perception assessment. Their PSNR/SSIM values are respectively [17] (13.63 dB/0.5611), [18] (13.72 dB/0.5634), [15] (13.74 dB/0.5605), [14] (13.83 dB/0.5903), [11] (13.91 dB/0.5724), [7] ((14.03dB / 0.6386)), [19] ((16.30dB / 0.7166)), Ours ((21.43dB / 0.8437)).

Considering the restricted paper space, we just take three challenging images for example. Figures 3, 4, and 5 provide the deblurred results for three blurred images for visual perception. It is seen that the proposed method, [3, 8] can produce plausible kernels in most cases. Most of the kernels are with tiny differences, which naturally lead to visually similar and acceptable deblur images. Nevertheless, other approaches just get occasional success on those challenging experiments.

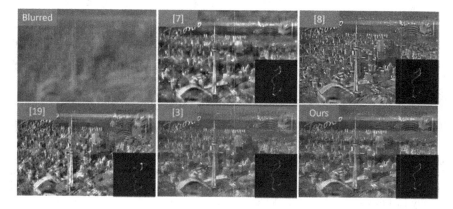

Fig. 3. Results for the manmade (M) image 'postcard' corresponding to the methods [3, 7, 8, 19] and ours with reasonable kernels produced.

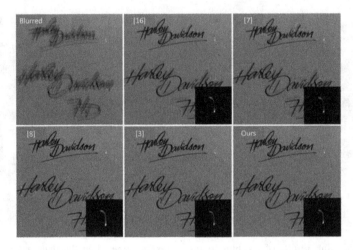

Fig. 4. Results for the text (**T**) image 'text2' corresponding to the methods [3, 7, 8, 16] and Ours with reasonable kernels produced.

Fig. 5. Results for the saturated (**S**) image 'car5' corresponding to the methods [3, 8] and ours with reasonable kernels produced.

Fig. 6. Visual comparison among [3, 8], and the proposed approach on the two saturated (**S**) images 'garden' and 'sydney_opera' where both [3, 8] have completely failed to a great degree while the proposed approach succeeds in producing very reasonable kernels which naturally lead to visually acceptable deblurred images.

In spite of similar deblurring performance among [3, 8] and our approach on the above blurred images, as for two saturated images 'garden' and 'sydney_opera', both [3, 8] have completely failed to a great degree. However, our method succeeds to recover a very plausible blur kernel for each image. Figure 6 provides the deblurring results for the three methods. Meanwhile, we observe several examples including: 'car4', 'night1', 'night4', 'notredame', 'text1', and 'text12', where either [8] or [3] or occasionally both generate much less accurate kernels than those of our approach.

4   Conclusion

Blind image deblurring, as a fundamental low-level vision problem, is far from being solved due to the challenging blur process in practical imaging, e.g., Gaussian-shaped kernels of varying sizes, ellipse-shaped kernels of varying orientations, curvilinear kernels of varying trajectories. In distinction to the previous methods, this paper is inspired by a rule of work from Albert Einstein: Out of clutter find simplicity, aiming to exploit the full potential of gradient-based approaches with the new proposal of a simple, robust yet discriminative prior for nonparametric blur kernel estimation. Our new discriminative approach achieves decent performance on both synthetic and realistic blurry images, and could be served as a new start point to develop more reliable, robust, effective and efficient blind image deblurring approaches.

Acknowledgements. The work was supported in part by the Natural Science Foundation of China under Grant 61771250, Grant 61402239, Grant 61502244, Grant 61602257. Wen-Ze Shao is also grateful to Prof. Zhi-Hui Wei, Prof. Michael Elad, Prof. Yi-Zhong Ma, Dr. Min Wu, and Mr. Ya-Tao Zhang for their kind support in the past years.

References

1. Fergus, R., Singh, B., Hertzmann, A., Roweis, S.T., Freeman, W.T.: Removing camera shake from a single photograph. ACM Trans. Graph. **25**(3), 787–794 (2006)
2. Lai, W.S., Huang, J.B., Hu, Z., Ahuja, N., Yang, M.H.: A comparative study for single image blind deblurring. In: IEEE Conference on Computer Vision and Pattern Recognition (CVPR), pp. 1701–1709 (2016)
3. Pan, J., Sun, D., Pfister, H., Yang, M.H.: Blind image deblurring using dark channel prior. In: CVPR, pp. 1628–1636 (2016)
4. Krishnan, D., Tay, T., Fergus, R.: Blind deconvolution using a normalized sparsity measure. In: CVPR, pp. 233–240 (2011)
5. Xu, L., Yan, Q., Xia, Y., Jia, J.: Structure extraction from texture via relative total variation. ACM Trans. Graph. **31**(6), 139 (2012)
6. Shao, W., Deng, H., Ge, Q., Li, H., Wei, Z.: Regularized motion blur-kernel estimation with adaptive sparse image prior learning. Pattern Recogn. **51**, 402–424 (2016)
7. Xu, L., Zheng, S., Jia, J.: Unnatural L0 sparse representation for natural image deblurring. In: IEEE Conference on Computer Vision and Pattern Recognition, pp. 1107–1114 (2013)
8. Pan, J., Hu, Z., Su, Z., Yang, M.H.: Deblurring text images via L0-regularized intensity and gradient prior. In: CVPR, pp. 1628–1636 (2014)

9. Pan, J., Hu, Z., Su, Z., Yang, M.-H.: Deblurring Face Images with Exemplars. In: Fleet, D., Pajdla, T., Schiele, B., Tuytelaars, T. (eds.) ECCV 2014, Part VII. LNCS, vol. 8695, pp. 47–62. Springer, Cham (2014). https://doi.org/10.1007/978-3-319-10584-0_4

10. Cho, S., Lee, S.: Fast motion deblurring. ACM Trans. Graph. **28**(5), 145 (2009)

11. Xu, L., Jia, J.: Two-phase kernel estimation for robust motion deblurring. In: Daniilidis, K., Maragos, P., Paragios, N. (eds.) ECCV 2010, Part I. LNCS, vol. 6311, pp. 157–170. Springer, Heidelberg (2010). https://doi.org/10.1007/978-3-642-15549-9_12

12. Zoran, D., Weiss, Y.: From learning models of natural image patches to whole image restoration. In: ICCV, pp. 479–486 (2011)

13. Venkatakrishnan, S.V., Bouman, C.A., Wohlberg, B.: Plug-and-play priors for model based reconstruction. In: IEEE Global Conference on Signal and Information Processing, pp. 945–948 (2013)

14. Levin, A., Weiss, Y., Durand, F., Freeman, W.T.: Efficient marginal likelihood optimization in blind deconvolution. In: CVPR, pp. 2657–2664 (2011)

15. Whyte, O., Sivic, J., Zisserman, A., Ponce, J.: Non-uniform deblurring for shaken images. Int. J. Comput. Vision **98**(2), 168–186 (2012)

16. Sun, L., Cho, S., Wang, J., Hays, J.: Edge-based blur kernel estimation using patch priors. In: International Conference on Computational Photography (2013)

17. Zhang, H., Wipf, D., Zhang, Y.: Multi-image blind deblurring using a coupled adaptive sparse prior. In: CVPR, pp. 1051–1058 (2013)

18. Michaeli, T., Irani, M.: Blind deblurring using internal patch recurrence. In: Fleet, D., Pajdla, T., Schiele, B., Tuytelaars, T. (eds.) ECCV 2014, Part III. LNCS, vol. 8691, pp. 783–798. Springer, Cham (2014). https://doi.org/10.1007/978-3-319-10578-9_51

19. Perrone, D., Favaro, P.: A clearer picture of total variation blind deconvolution. IEEE Trans. Pattern Anal. Mach. Intell. **38**(6), 1041–1055 (2016)

20. Wang, Z., Bovik, A.C., Sheikh, H.R., Simoncelli, E.P.: Image quality assessment: from error visibility to structural similarity. IEEE Trans. Image Process. **13**(4), 600–612 (2004)

21. Liu, Y., Wang, J., Cho, S., Finkelstein, A., Rusinkiewicz, S.: A no-reference metric for evaluating the quality of motion deblurring. ACM Trans. Graph. **32**(6), 175 (2013)

End-to-End Bloody Video Recognition
by Audio-Visual Feature Fusion

Congcong Hou[1], Xiaoyu Wu[1(✉)], and Ge Wang[2]

[1] Communication University of China, Beijing, China
`770258506@qq.com, wuxiaoyu@cuc.edu.cn`
[2] Columbia School of Engineering and Applied Science, Computer Science,
Columbia University, New York, USA
`gw2372@columbia.edu`

Abstract. With the rapid development of Internet technology, the spread of bloody video has become increasingly serious, causing huge harm to society. In this paper, a bloody video recognition method based on audio-visual feature fusion is proposed to complement the limitation of the single vision-modality methods. In the absence of open bloody video data, this paper first constructed a database of bloody videos through web crawlers and data augmentation methods; then it used CNN and LSTM methods to extract the spatiotemporal features of visual channels. Meanwhile, the audio channel features were extracted directly from the original waveforms using the 1D convolutional network. Finally, the neural network based on the audio-visual feature fusion layer was constructed to achieve the early fusion of multimodal cues. The accuracy of the proposed method on the bloody video test data is 95%. The experimental results on self-built bloody video databases demonstrate that the extracted audio-visual feature representations are effective and the proposed multimodal fusion model can obtain the better and discriminative recognition performance than the single-channel model.

Keywords: Bloody video recognition · Feature extraction · Multimodal fusion

1 Introduction

With the development of smart phones and mobile Internet technologies, the volume of online video data has experienced explosive growth, and the number of users viewing videos on major video sites has also increased significantly. Faced with such a huge amount of video data, manual review of video content is no longer possible. This will expose some violent and bloody videos directly to the users watching the video and bring a negative impact on the visual and mind of people, especially for the healthy growth of young people. So this paper focuses on the classification of bloody videos to decrease these adverse effects.

Due to the discomfort caused by bloody content and absence of public related dataset, fewer scholars pay attention to this problem. Violent video recognition technology develops slowly and still faces a lot of open and difficult problems. Even the definition of the bloody class with complex scenes is still vague. European MediaEval

© Springer Nature Switzerland AG 2018
J.-H. Lai et al. (Eds.): PRCV 2018, LNCS 11256, pp. 501–510, 2018.
https://doi.org/10.1007/978-3-030-03398-9_43

proposes the VSD-Violent Scene Detection game task, which defines the definition of violence video in its competition [1]: 'Videos containing physical violence that children under 8 years of age watch are not permitted'. This paper uses this concept to define bloody videos. There are currently more than a dozen battle scenes in the MediaEval 2015 database violence videos that have been publicly published. However, there are only a dozen bloody scene videos with more psychological harm, and the total duration of a bloody screen video is only about one minute. In view of the lack of current bloody video data and the low intelligence of blood-stained video detection algorithms, this paper constructed a bloody video database and proposed an end-to-end bloody video recognition system based on audio-visual feature fusion to purify the network environment and improve users experience and more.

This article is divided into five parts: Sect. 2 introduces the related research, Sect. 3 puts forward the end-to-end bloody video recognition system based on audio-visual feature fusion, Sect. 4 compares and analyzes the experimental results. The conclusion and future research ideas are given in Sect. 5.

2 Related Work

Related research work mainly focuses on feature extraction and multimodal fusion. In visual feature extraction, convolutional neural networks are often used to extract image features of static frames [2]. For example, violence frames are used as input in [3], and the model is fine-tuned by a model pre-trained on ImageNet. The experimental results show that compared with the classification effect of traditional features, the advanced and sematic features can help improve the performance of violent video system recognition. The literature [4] draws on the two-stream CNN network structure, uses static video frames and optical flow streams as two-way CNN input to extract violent video features, and uses the output of CNN network as the input of LSTM network to analyze long-time video sequences. A variety of hand-craft features are also extracted, and then several different SVM classifiers are trained based on the features of the manual design and the features learned from deep learning to obtain the final decision result. In [5], the adjacent video frames are used as the input of the neural network, and only the convolved LSTM network is used to extract the inter-frame change information and scene semantic information of the violent video. In summary, the above methods are only the use of visual information to recognize violent videos. We know that in addition to bloody videos on the screen, bloody audios like screams and explosions can provide complementary information. It is unreasonable to classify videos only from visual or audio information.

Compared with the single vision model classification method, the audio and video multimodal fusion model can capture the complementary information that is not obtained by the single mode and perform a more robust prediction. In [6], the CNN network is used as both a deep audio feature extractor and a violent video classifier, and the audio is windowed at intervals of 25 ms and 10 ms to get the MFB feature and sent to the CNN network to extract high-level audio features. Finally, the decision scores of audio and visual modalities were merged. However, this method used the MFB feature obtained after processing the original waveform into the CNN network instead of sending the original waveform information directly to the CNN network to extract the audio feature. This undoubtedly causes the loss of the original audio information to affect the audio feature extraction the CNN network. In [7], deep learning features and manual design features are used to extract visual channel features, MFCC methods are used to extract audio features, and a SVM-based late fusion method is used to classify violent videos. These above methods adopt the late fusion method in using the audio and video information. The disadvantage of late fusion is that it fails to utilize the feature level correlation among modalities because the feature information of each mode has been lost. Due to the limited fused information, the improvement of the recognition performance is also limited for the late fusion method. In contrast, the audio-visual feature fusion can simultaneously 'see' more information of each mode, and can better capture the connection of each mode, and can significantly improve the video classification performance. However, it is still scientific research issues how to effectively extract and integrate audio-visual features, and recognize bloody videos. This paper will focus on this problem.

The main contribution of this paper is to propose an end-to-end bloody video recognition system by audio-visual feature fusion using deep learning: Based on the self-built bloody video database, firstly use the CNN and LSTM methods to extract the temporal and spatial characteristics of the visual channel. The network directly extracts the time domain features from the original audio waveform through 1D convolutional neural network. Finally, the feature fusion layer of neural network is constructed to achieve the audio-visual feature fusion, and the proposed method for end-to-end bloody video recognition is implemented. The accuracy of classification on bloody video test dataset reaches 95%, which provide a valuable theoretical reference for violent video recognition problems.

3   End-to-End Bloody Video Recognition Algorithm

The block diagram of the end-to-end bloody video recognition system proposed in this paper is shown in Fig. 1. In terms of visual feature extraction, we get the static frame features extracted from the ResNet network into the LSTM network to obtain visual features with temporal and spatial information; In the feature extraction of audio modals, in order to not destroy the original information of the signal as much as possible, we take the original waveform input directly into the CNN network. After the audio and visual features are obtained in the above two steps, a feature fusion layer is trained using the neural network method to fully capture the correlations between the features while preserving their respective characteristics. Through this feature fusion layer, the shared feature subspace of the bloody audio and video is built, and then two modal features transformed into the same space are concatenated together and fed into the classifier to obtain a decision score for the video.

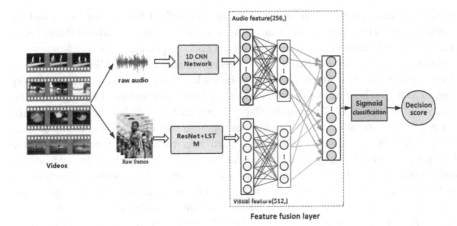

Fig. 1. Overall network structure of our method

3.1   Visual Feature Extraction Based on CNN and LSTM

At present, the ResNet network is used to extract the static image features. However, for the feature extraction in the visual modality of bloody videos, it is not enough to perform static features extraction and analysis for each frame because there is a temporal relationship between frames. A frame has a content relationship with its adjacent frames. However, the spatial convolutional neural networks like ResNet cannot simulate the temporal continuity characteristics of video frames. So we introduce the LSTM structure, which allows the information to be persistent and changes memory with adding a 'process to determine whether the information is useful or not in the algorithm' remember, update, and focus on information. In order to make full use of the context information between video frames, we use bidirectional LSTM [8] to extract video sequence information.

We first use the ResNet-50 model to extract the static frame characteristics of bloody videos. The ResNet-50 model trained on bloody video static frames is considered as a bloody static feature extractor, removing the last layer of the full ResNet connection layer. Take the 2048-dimensional vector after average pooling as the extracted blood feature maps and input them to the two-layer LSTM network for training instead of sending the original video directly to the LSTM network. The model diagram is shown in Fig. 2.

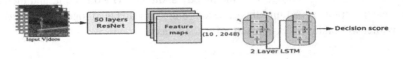

Fig. 2. ResNet+ bidirectional LSTM network model

The detailed implementation process: First, the video takes a frame every half second, and the obtained frame is firstly input to the 50-layer residual network so as to extract 2048-D feature vector for each frame. And then, the 2048-D feature vector will be fed into the LSTM network and the decision result can be obtain from the output of LSTM network. Because each of video is different lengths, we first find an average of 10 frames in all the videos in the training set to ensure that the length of the sequence entered into the LSTM remains the same. After that, the truncation method is used for any number of frames greater than 10, and the feature dimension size of all video outputs is the same.

3.2   Audio Feature Extraction Based on Raw Waveform and 1D CNN Model

The traditional audio models are divided into two steps: designing audio features and building a suitable model based on this type of feature. However, we often find that the features designed using prior knowledge cannot be guaranteed to be suitable for some specific statistical classification models. Therefore, we try to send the original waveform as input to the CNN network in order to keep the original signal information as much as possible.

This article designed a shallower full convolutional network without any fully connected network and dropout layer applied. According to [9], in the network we have designed, we introduce a separate global average pooling layer that can average the activation values in the time dimension and convert each feature map into a float type value. The network structure designed in this paper is as follows (Fig. 3):

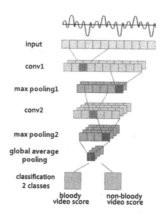

Fig. 3. The schematic of the raw waveform CNN network structure.

The specific implementation process is as follows: First, read the audio data according to the sampling rate of 8000 Hz, and then truncate or fill all audios to equal length. In this part, according to the length of the audio in the database, we take 32000 sampling points, so the input audio sequence is (32000, 1). The receptive field of our first convolutional layer is set to 80, and the convolution step is taken as 4, so the output eigenvector dimension of the first layer convolution is (8000, 256). After that, the eigenvectors output by 256 filters are passed through a time-domain pooling layer. The length of the pooling layer is 4, the maximum pooling method is used, and the output length is 2000 feature vectors. Then a convolution layer using a (3, 1, 256) convolution kernel also performs a one-dimensional convolution with a step size of 1, so the output feature vector is (2000, 256) dimensions. After this is the second max pooling layer, the pooling length is 4, and the output vector dimension is (500, 256). We use a global average pooling layer to average 256 feature maps and finally get a (256,) dimensional vector. The blood/non-blood labels of audio data are regarded as the supervised signal to guide the training of audio network. The weight of this network will be used to initialize the parameters of the following fusion network. After learning of neural network to autonomous learning to the most suitable for this paper research the bloody audio characteristics of the classification task.

3.3   Bloody Video Detection Based on Audio-Visual Feature Fusion

Early fusion, also called feature fusion, refers to fusing the extracted features of each modality. The simplest fusion method is to directly concatenate the visual and audio features. However, the visual channel features and the audio channel features have different meanings and are located in different feature spaces. Directly merging two types of features with different meanings and ambiguities sometimes leads to recognition performance decline. Therefore, how to eliminate the multimodal 'semantic gap', consider the inter-modal relationships, and established a shared feature fusion space is still a technical problem that needs to be solved.

In order to make full use of the correlation and complementarity between features, we introduced a shared feature fusion layer on the basis of the previous single-channel network, and transformed each modal feature into the same feature expression space through the newly created feature fusion layer. The multimodal network structure of the audio-visual feature fusion layer are shown in Fig. 1. We will use data as a driver, utilized deep neural network methods to train the whole network, and obtain shared feature subspaces for bloody audio and video. And then, the merged features are sent to network classifiers to get the recognition result.

The detailed implementation process is as follows: During the training phase, we firstly train the visual and audio networks separately that are introduced in Sects. 3.1 and 3.2. The fully connected layers are discarded and only the extracted features are considered. The audio network gets a 256-dimensional feature vector, the visual network gets a 512-dimensional feature vector; After that, the two feature vectors are input to a fully connected feature-fusion layer, and then a ReLU activation function is applied after each fully connected layer to make a nonlinear transformation. Two modal features transformed into the same space are put together and fed into the sigmoid classification layer to get the decision score for this video. We note that the multimodal network is initialized utilizing the weights of the unimodal models and trained end-to-end. The hyper-parameters of the network training are set as follows: in the feature fusion layer, the number of full-connected neurons in the visual channel is 256, the number of fully-connected neurons in the audio channel is 125, batch size is 32, the maximum training epoch number is 10, and the optimizer adopts the Adam method. The initial learning rate is set to 0.0001.

4 Experimental Results and Analysis

4.1 Database Description

The current bloody video public database is very few. The internationally published MediaEval 2015 violence database contains a total of 10,900 video clips with different resolutions. Most of them are 640 * 360, 1280 * 720, the average length is about 10 s, and the total length is about 10 s. For 30 h, only 4.6% of violent videos were recorded. The number of bloody videos in these violent videos was even smaller. So we collected about 50 bloody movies and more than 20 short videos on YouTube, all of which were 80% of the clips. All of them were clipped to cut out the entire bloody shot. It constitutes a positive sample of a bloody video database, and negative samples mostly use non-bloody video clips from MediaEval 2015. In the data set, most video resolutions are 1024 * 576, and the lengths are from 2 s to 4 s. The number of positive and negative samples in each category is 1:1. The total data collection time is 67 min. The data set distribution is shown in Table 1.

Table 1. Bloody video database composition

Name	Quantity
Train	680
Validation	160
Test	160
Total length of time	67 min

The database size and data quality play a key role in the deep learning algorithm. On the one hand, the data with a large enough amount can make the deep learning network more fully fit the complex function. On the other hand, it can accurately extract high-level semantic features of the data sample. Therefore, in order to overcome the problem of insufficient data, we use the data augmentation methods like rotation transform, flip transform, shear transform, scale transform, translation transform, scale transform, color shake, noise perturbation and other methods to expand the static frame data of bloody video, thereby training the Resnet50 network. The model obtains semantic features with better description of bloody video static frame information.

4.2 Evaluation Metric

The recall rate, precision rate, and accuracy rate are commonly used indicators to measure the predictive performance of the two-class model. In contrast, the accuracy rate is a single-number evaluation metric. This paper chooses the accuracy rate as the evaluation index of this algorithm. The accuracy rate is the proportion of the correct sample to all samples, as shown in formula (1).

$$Accuracy = (TP + TN)/(TP + TN + FN + FP) \qquad (1)$$

The TP (True Positive) indicates the number of the blood videos that are correctly classified as the number of blood class, TN (True Negative) indicates that the number of the normal samples that are correctly classified as the normal class, and FP (False Positive) indicates the number of the normal samples mistakenly predicted as blood class, FN (False Negative) is the number of samples in which blood samples are incorrectly predicted to be normal.

4.3 Experimental Results Using End-to-End Audio and Video Feature Fusion Method

All of the tests in this article were conducted on our own bloody video dataset. Table 2 shows the bloody video classification results based on the visual channel alone, the bloody video classification results based on the audio channel alone, and the bloody video classification results based on the audio and video feature fusion.

Table 2. Comparison of the test results of each model in the bloody video test library

Network model		Accuracy
Only visual channel	ResNet	89.37%
	ResNet+LSTM	93.75%
Only Audio channel	Spectral map as input	68.13%
	Raw waveform as input	71.25%
Fusion model	Pre-fusion: direct stitching	94.37%
	Pre-fusion: build a fusion layer	95%

In the visual channel-only bloody video recognition, the ResNet+LSTM-based method has a larger improvement than the simple residual network results. The main reason lies in the fact that we have introduced a bidirectional LSTM network and the temporal characteristics of the video frame. Modeling is performed and the time information in both directions is considered. The prediction result also confirms the effectiveness of the bidirectional LSTM network in bloody video detection tasks.

In the bloody video recognition based on the audio channel alone, the recognition result of inputting the original waveform diagram as a 1D convolutional network is better than the recognition result of processing the spectral map as a 2D convolutional network input. This is because the original waveform diagram is directly used as the information input of the network to reduce the loss of audio channel information. The features obtained after the 1D convolutional network can better describe the semantic information of the audio data. Here, we perform the same processing for each piece of test audio to the training phase, fill or truncate to 32,000 sampling points and send it to the trained one. The network gets its prediction score. However, as can be seen from Table 2 the indicators for detecting blood-stained video with audio channels are significantly lower than those with only visual channels. We believe that the main reason is that in the task of recognizing the bloody videos, audio information is just complementary and auxiliary to visual channel information. Not all audio channels of the video profiles contain obvious bloody features. For example, few videos may display bloody content without including screams and other sounds. On this condition, the cue from the sound cannot judge whether the video is bloody or not.

In the aspect of bloody video recognition based on audio-visual feature fusion, we implemented two bloody video recognition methods: one is based on the direct concatenation and fusion of audio-visual features, the other is based on the construction of feature fusion layer. By comparing the above experimental results, we can clearly see that the recognition accuracy of bloody video based on the multimodal fusion model is higher than that of the single-channel detection compared to the visual channel and the audio channel, which verifies the effectiveness of audio-visual feature fusion. However, due to the difficulty in collecting bloody video data, the number of our datasets is not large enough, making the difference in the recognition results of the two feature fusion methods not obvious. It is believed that the bloody video recognition method based on the feature fusion layer will exhibit better robustness as the amount of data increases.

5 Conclusion

5.1 Conclusion

This paper focuses on the use of multimodal fusion technology to achieve bloody video recognition. First of all, the related research is summarized in the aspects of feature extraction and multi-channel fusion technology; And then, the visual features of the frame is extracted from the residual network are sent to the two-layer LSTM to represent the spatial-temporal visual cues of bloody video. The raw audio waveform is input into the 1D convolution in the neural network to get the audio signal features in the time domain. Finally, we achieve bloody video recognition based on early-fusion multimodal fusion and implement end-to-end training using video label as a supervision signal. We aim to make full use of the correlation and complementarity of visual and audio channels to make joint decisions on bloody video. Using a effective fusion layer, the visual and audio features are projected into the same feature expression space and finally get 95% accuracy.

Due to less open bloody video data, we constructed bloody pictures and bloody video database using web crawlers and data augmented methods. The proposed multi-channel fusion model over the single-channel model is verified, and it can have a better discriminative effect on the videos in our self-built bloody video database. This research is also beneficial for the development of intelligent monitoring technology for bloody Internet content.

5.2   The Future Work

In this paper, CNN+LSTM is used to let the network automatically extract visual feature descriptors. However, bloody videos often contain some fighting scenarios. Therefore, the motion cues like optical flow information will be considered in order to obtain a higher-performance bloody violent video recognition system in the future.

References

1. He, K., Zhang, X., Ren, S., Sun, J.: Deep residual learning for image recognition. In: CVPR, pp. 1–6 (2016)
2. Sjberg, M., et al.: The mediaeval 2015 affective impact of movies task. In: MediaEval 2015 Workshop (2015)
3. Yi, Y., Wang, H., Zhang, B., Yu, J.: MIC-TJU. Affective impact of movies task. In: MediaEval Workshop (2015)
4. Dai, Q., et al.: Fudan-Huawei at MediaEval 2015: detecting violent scenes and affective impact in movies with deep learning. In: MediaEval Workshop (2015)
5. Sudhakaran, S., Lanz, O.: Learning to detect violent videos using convolutional long short-term memory. In: 14th IEEE International Conference on Advanced Video and Signal Based Surveillance (AVSS) (2017)
6. Mu, G., Cao, H., Jin, Q.: Violent scene detection using convolutional neural networks and deep audio features. In: Tan, T., Li, X., Chen, X., Zhou, J., Yang, J., Cheng, H. (eds.) CCPR 2016. CCIS, vol. 663, pp. 451–463. Springer, Singapore (2016). https://doi.org/10.1007/978-981-10-3005-5_37
7. Lam, V., Phan, S., Le, D.-D., Duong, D.A., Satoh, S.: Evaluation of multiple features for violent scenes detection. Multimed. Tools Appl. **76**(5), 1–25 (2016)
8. Schuster, M., Paliwal, K.K.: Bidirectional recurrent neural networks. IEEE Trans. Signal Process. **45**(11), 2673–2681 (1997)
9. Dai, W., Dai, C., Qu, S., et al.: Very deep convolutional neural networks for raw waveforms. In: 2017 IEEE International Conference on Acoustics, Speech and Signal Processing (ICASSP), pp. 421–425 (2016)

Robust Crack Defect Detection in Inhomogeneously Textured Surface of Near Infrared Images

Haiyong Chen[✉], Huifang Zhao, Da Han, Haowei Yan,
Xiaofang Zhang, and Kun Liu

School of Artificial Intelligence, Hebei University of Technology,
Tianjin 300130, China
{haiyong.chen,liukun}@hebut.edu.cn,
15731130631@163.com, han02315@gmail.com,
unlimitly@163.com, 13512890516@163.com

Abstract. Robust crack defect detection in solar cells has been challenging because of the inhomogeneously textured surface, low contrast between crack defect and background, the diversity of crack types, and so on. To overcome these challenges, this paper presents a new robust crack defect detection scheme for multicrystalline solar cells. Firstly, a steerable evidence filter is designed to process EL image to obtain the response map, which enhances the contrast between crack and background and provides evidence for the presence of crack defect. Secondly, complete crack extraction from the response map is employed. Finally, the complete crack can be located in the inspection image by the crack skeleton extraction. Experimental results on defective and defect-free EL images show that the proposed scheme is robust, and various cracks can be effectively detected, which outperforms the previous methods.

Keywords: Crack defect · Inhomogeneous texture · Steerable evidence filter

1 Introduction

Solar cells are the critical component of solar power system, which can convert solar energy into electricity. However, the crystal structure of multicrystalline solar cells is fragile, so crack defects are inevitably generated in many fabrication and installation links such as wire sawing, pick and place, transmission, collision, etc. [1]. The presence of crack defect will greatly reduce the power generation efficiency of solar cells and usable lifetime of photovoltaic modules [2]. Thus, the quality control of solar cells is a crucial aspect for solar power system. In the past, crack defects inspection relied on experienced technicians to identify the presence of crack from collected solar cells images. However, human inspection fails to meet the requirement of rapidity, reliability, and robustness for mass production of solar cells in industrial scenes. Hence, the requirement of automatic crack detection of solar cells is demanding.

© Springer Nature Switzerland AG 2018
J.-H. Lai et al. (Eds.): PRCV 2018, LNCS 11256, pp. 511–523, 2018.
https://doi.org/10.1007/978-3-030-03398-9_44

To capture efficacious crack information inside the wafer surface, we obtain the near infrared images of solar cells with a wavelength of 950 nm–1250 nm using the electroluminescence (EL) imaging technique [3, 4]. Compared with the defect-free regions, crack defects appear as dark characteristic with curvilinear and complicated geometry structures in the EL images. The difficulties of crack detection in EL images mainly are (1) the inhomogeneously textured surface of near infrared images; (2) low contrast between crack defect and surrounding background including random crystal grains; and (3) the diversity of crack types.

Figure 1(a) is a defect-free EL image and there are crystal grains with random shapes, sizes, positions and orientations forming the inhomogeneously textured surface. Specially, as shown in the red label frames of Fig. 1(b)–(c), the cracks are submerged by the randomly distributed crystal grains. Moreover, the crystal grains appearing as curvilinear shapes in the green dotted label frames are easy to be mistaken as crack. Therefore, robust crack defect detection has always been a challenging task in the field of defect detection.

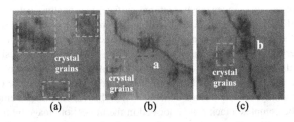

Fig. 1. Challenges of crack defect detection in solar cells. (a) Defect-free EL image. (b)–(c) Crack defective EL images with randomly distributed crystal grains.

Many computer vision-based methods have focused on the crack defect detection in road, bridge, and solar cells surfaces. Most of spatial methods were used by comparing the pixel intensities difference between crack defect and background. [5, 6] used intensity information for pavement crack detection, but the illumination and texture would affect the crack segmentation performance. For crack detection in solar cells, Tsai et al. [7] applied an anisotropic diffusion scheme and took the gray level and gradient features to adjust the diffusion coefficient. Chiou et al. [8] proposed a local thresholding-based crack extraction method. However, for these methods, the intensity information is the major consideration, but the intensity of crystal grains is very similar to crack. So, the crack defects cannot be correctly detected.

Spectral methods mainly use a set of filters to process the images and obtain the features that can distinguish the defect from background based the filter response. [9–11] used the Gabor filter to detect pavement cracks. Tsai [12] described crack defects as line-shaped and removed them by setting the corresponding frequency components to zero. However, these methods are applied to detect longitudinal or transverse cracks and the cracks with complicated geometry do not get involved.

Although the current research methods have achieved certain results, robust crack defect detection in solar cells is still challenging for the following reasons. (1) current methods fail to extract crack defect from the inhomogeneously textured surface, leading to the misdetection of some crystal grains as crack defect; and (2) most of current methods are proposed to detect line-shape cracks, so dendritic cracks with bends and bifurcations are not well solved. In this paper, we try to propose a robust crack detection scheme that can solve the above challenging problems.

The remaining part of this paper is organized as follows. In Sect. 2, a novel robust crack defect detection scheme in solar cells is described concretely. Section 3 presents the experimental results on defective and defect-free EL images. Finally, Sect. 4 gives the conclusion.

2   Crack Defect Detection Scheme

The overall scheme of the proposed crack defect detection method is shown in Fig. 2. The steerable evidence filter is designed, which contains a basic steerable filter and two additional oriented filters including a certain offset in angle and space distance. Firstly, a steerable evidence filter is used to process EL image to obtain the response map, which enhances the contrast between crack and background and provides evidence for the presence of crack defect. Secondly, complete crack extraction from the response map is employed. In this procedure, a local threshold based on sliding sub-image is applied to segment crack defect. Then, the morphology operation is used to remove some isolated non-crack pixels and minimum spanning tree is used to connect crack fragments. Finally, the complete crack can be located in the inspection image by using the skeleton extraction.

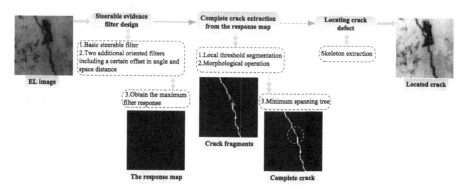

Fig. 2. Overall scheme of the proposed method.

2.1 Steerable Evidence Filter Design and Its Response Map

The steerable filters derived from a linear combination of basic filter with arbitrary orientations [13]. In this study, the basic filter generates from the Hessian matrix represents as $H(p)$, which is a square matrix and describes the local curvature of the function. For a 2-D image $f(p)$, at a position $p_0 = (x,y)$, the hessian function can be obtained by Eq. (1).

$$H(p_0) = \begin{pmatrix} g_{xx}(p_0) & g_{xy}(p_0) \\ g_{xy}(p_0) & g_{yy}(p_0) \end{pmatrix} * f(p_0) \tag{1}$$

Equation (2) gives the Gaussian kernel with variance σ and its corresponding second derivatives form part of the hessian function.

$$g(p_0; \sigma) = \frac{1}{\sqrt{2\pi}\sigma} e^{-\frac{x^2+y^2}{2\sigma^2}} \tag{2}$$

Considering the orientation $u_\theta = (\cos\theta, \sin\theta)^T$, the basic steerable filter with $\theta \in [-\pi/2, \pi/2]$ can be obtained by Eq. (3). To put it in another way, its detailed expression is shown in Eq. (4).

$$e(p_0, \theta; \sigma) = u_\theta^T H(p_0) u_\theta \tag{3}$$

$$e(p_0, \theta; \sigma) = g_{xx}\cos^2\theta + g_{yy}\sin^2\theta + g_{xy}\sin 2\theta \tag{4}$$

After the basic steerable filter e convolutes an image $f(p)$, the filter response E at a position p_0 can be calculated by Eq. (5). In addition, the parameter σ in the steerable basic filter can be fixed to adapt different widths. As shown in Fig. 3(a), the first row shows three basic steerable filters with $\theta = 0, -\pi/4, \pi/3$, respectively.

$$E(p_0, \theta; \sigma) = e(p_0, \theta; \sigma) * f(p_0) \tag{5}$$

However, the single basic steerable filter is incapable of detecting sharp bends, intensity variations, and completed crack morphology. Thus, inspired by the local directional evidence filtering [14], we design two additional oriented filters that include a certain offset in the angle and space distance of the detection point. Equations (6)–(7) are the corresponding two offset point p_1 and p_2.

Figure 3(b) is the demonstration of the local search region around the detection point $p_0(x, y) = (1, 1)$, and the parameter settings are $d = 1$, $\theta \in [-\pi/2, \pi/2]$ and $\varphi \in [-\pi/6, \pi/6]$ with step of $\pi/18$. The yellow point represents the detection point p_0, and the red points represent the p_1, and p_2 are displayed with green points, all of which appear as a circular search region with the center of detection point p_0 and the radius of d. Specially, the partial overlap of the red points and green points, which ensures the detection of crack defect at the entire circular region of the detection point, is caused by the offset angle φ and the offset distance d.

$$p_1 = [x - d\cos(\theta + \varphi), y + \sin(\theta + \varphi)] \tag{6}$$

$$p_2 = [x + d\cos(\theta + \varphi), y - \sin(\theta + \varphi)] \tag{7}$$

$$e^*(p; \sigma, \theta, \varphi) = e(p_0; \sigma, \theta) + e(p_1; \sigma, \theta + \varphi) + e(p_1; \sigma, \theta + \varphi) \tag{8}$$

Thus, a linear superposition of the basic steerable filter and two additional oriented filters form the steerable evidence filter e^* in Eq. (8), which provide evidence for the presence of crack defect. As shown in Fig. 3(a), the second row shows three sets steerable evidence filter with different orientations. It shows the steerable evidence filter is consistent with the geometric characteristics of the crack defect fragments including line and curve, so the problem of crack defect bending, bifurcation and complicated geometry can be addressed.

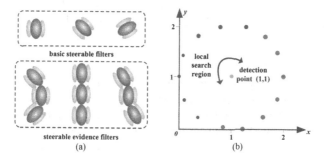

(a)

Fig. 3. (a) Examples of the basic steerable filters in the first row and steerable evidence filters in the second row. (b) The local search region of steerable evidence filter.

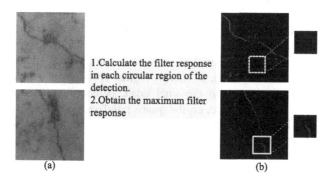

Fig. 4. Example of the response maps. (a) Defective images. (b) The response maps obtained by the steerable evidence filter.

In our application, we aim at finding the crack that lies in some uncertain position and orientation in an EL image. When convoluting an image with the steerable evidence filter in Eq. (9), a higher magnitude will be obtained if there is a crack in the EL image. To better highlight the crack information, the maximum response magnitudes

R^* are calculated by Eq. (10). Figure 4(a) presents two defective images and Fig. 4(b) shows the response maps obtained by the steerable evidence filter. The response maps show the response magnitudes can be approximately treated as zero in the defect-free region. In contrast, the crack region has higher response magnitudes, which contributes to the further crack defect acquirement.

$$R(p; \sigma, \theta, \varphi) = e^*(p; \sigma, \theta, \varphi) * f(p) \tag{9}$$

$$R^*(p; \sigma) = \max_{\theta, \varphi} R(p; \sigma, \theta, \varphi) \tag{10}$$

2.2   Complete Crack Extraction from the Response Map

In this section, we mainly extract the complete crack defect from the response map, which is implemented by local threshold segmentation, connecting crack fragments by minimum spanning tree and locating complete crack defect by crack skeleton extraction.

2.2.1   Local Threshold Segmentation

Owing to the random crystal grains, the defect-free region also represents certain response magnitudes in the response map. In order to obtain the crack defect structure, we first apply a local threshold by sliding sub-image to segment crack from the response map. Then, the threshold for the response map is given by

$$T(x, y) = u_R(x, y) + k\sigma_R(x, y) \tag{11}$$

where $u_R(x, y)$ and $\sigma_R(x, y)$ are the mean and standard deviation of each sliding sub-image of size $N \times N$ in the response map, and the size of mask is set 9×9 in our application. k is a predetermined constant.

We still select this EL images with crystal grains around the crack, and the corresponding segmentation results are given by Eq. (12). Although some background pixels are removed after the threshold, there are still some crystal grains structures in the threshold segmentation results, so morphological operation is adopted to remove some small non-crack pixels and the final crack defect fragments are shown in Fig. 5(a). For these EL images with crystal grains interference, the segmented crack is disconnected near the crystal grains, which makes crack defect incomplete and is unfavorable to detection performance.

$$B(x, y) = \begin{cases} 1, & if\ R(x, y) > T(x, y) \\ 0, & otherwise \end{cases} \tag{12}$$

2.2.2 Connecting Crack Fragments and Locating Complete Crack Defect

To get the complete crack defect, minimum spanning tree (MST) based on Kruskal's algorithm is applied. Minimum spanning tree is an important model in graph theory and it is used to solve the problem of minimum path cost. In this procedure, minimum spanning tree can minimize the sum of the weights of corresponding edges and connect these nodes. According to this function, we use minimum spanning tree to connect crack fragments. Figure 5(a) shows the nodes of a1 and b1, c1 and d1 belonging to the vertexes of crack fragments to be connected, and Fig. 5(b) shows the complete crack. In order to mark the crack defects, we compute the crack skeleton and locate them in the inspection images. As shown in Fig. 5(c), the complete crack defects are correctly located as red points.

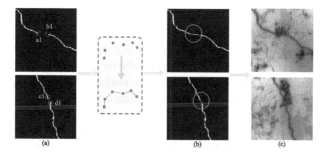

Fig. 5. Complete crack extraction by minimum spanning tree. (a) Crack fragments. (b) Complete crack. (c) Located crack. (Color figure online)

3   Experimental Results and Analysis

3.1   Data Set and Parameter Setting

In order to verify the performance of the proposed method, we collect the defective and defect-free EL images from the actual production line in. The defect-free EL images have no crack defect but crystal grains randomly distributed in the background. The defective EL images can be divided into five types according to the texture background and geometric property of crack defect. Some representative defective and defect-free EL images are shown in Fig. 6. Here, 300 defective EL images including different types of cracks and 200 defect-free EL images of size 125×125 are used to verify the proposed method.

Although there are several parameters in the proposed method, not all of them play important roles in crack detection performance. Three parameter are essential: scale size σ, offset d of the steerable evidence filter and threshold coefficient k. So, we select a certain number of defective and defect-free EL images to determine the optimal parameter values. The detailed characterizations of the data set used in the experiment are presented in Table 1.

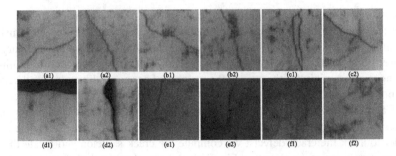

Fig. 6. Representative defective images and defect-free images. (a1)–(a2) Pure-type cracks. (b1)–(b2) Submerged-type cracks. (c1)–(c2) Dendritic-type cracks. (d1)–(d2) Break. (e1)–(e2) Dark-type cracks. (f1)–(f2) Defect-free.

In the designed steerable evidence filtering procedure, we have to determine two parameter for better performance: the scale size σ and the offset d. The parameter σ fits different widths of crack defects. If σ is set too small, the crack cannot be well highlight and it is easy to be missed. Conversely, if σ is set too large, the crystal grains near the crack will be treated as crack, and affect the detection performance. As shown in Fig. 7(a), for different types of defective and defect-free images, a better detection results can be obtained when the scale size σ is 1. Similarly, the offset d controls the locality of the steerable evidence filter. While a small value of d does not contribute enough, a large value will introduce false pixels that do not belong to the same crack structure. According to Fig. 7(b), the optimal performance is achieved when d is 1.

Table 1. Details of data set used in the experiment

Types	Number	Number of test images for optical parameters
Pure	90	20
Submerged	150	20
Dendritic	10	10
Break	30	10
Dark	20	10
Defect-free	200	20

Besides, the threshold coefficient k will affect the detection results in the segmentation procedure. Too small a control value of k gives a tight threshold and may identify the background pixels as crack defects.

However, too large a control value gives a loose threshold and may miss some true crack defect pixels. As shown in Fig. 7(c), although the same detection results can be obtained for dendritic crack images and defect-free images when k is 1 or 1.5, the threshold coefficient k is set to 1 for all the whole types of EL images. The detection results show the optimal parameters are adapted for defective and defect-free images.

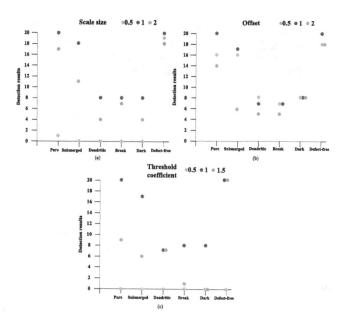

Fig. 7. Optimal parameter selection. (a) Effect of scale size. (b) Effect of offset. (c) Effect of threshold coefficient.

3.2 Robustness Analysis in Brightness Levels

In this study, we also test some dim defective images that present much low contrast between crack and background and dim defect-free images, and the proposed method still achieve satisfactory performance. As shown in Fig. 8(a), there is a horizontal line labeled as red, which passes through both crack defect and background. The corresponding gray level intensity is shown in Fig. 8(b). It shows the low contrast between crack defect and background, which greatly increases the difficulty of crack defect detection in the dim EL images. Figure 8(c1)–(d1) are two typical low-efficiency solar cells that show weak differences between crack and background, and Fig. 8(e1) is a dim defect-free EL image. The detection result of Fig. 8(e2) shows that no crack defect is detected in the defect-free EL image. At the same time, the crack defects can be completely located in the dim defective EL images. Thus, the conclusion is that the proposed method is robust to the inhomogeneously textured background and different brightness levels.

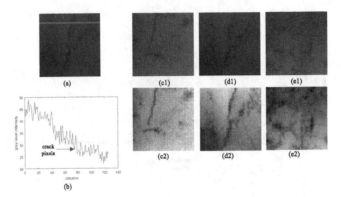

Fig. 8. Robustness to brightness levels of the proposed method. (a) A dim defective image. (b) Gray level intensity of red horizontal line in (a). (c1)–(e1) Two dim defective images and one defect-free image, respectively. (c2)–(e2) The corresponding response maps. (c3)–(e3) The detection results. (Color figure online)

3.3   Performance Evaluation

In this paper, our method is compared with some representative crack defect detection methods to prove the effectiveness of the proposed method. Specifically, the Aniso-tropic diffusion (AD) [7], the Local thresholding (LT) [8] and the basic steerable filter (BSF) [13] methods are used on the given image data set. As an illustration, Fig. 9 shows representative five types of defective EL images and a defect-free EL image and the corresponding detection results. Figure 9(a6)–(f6) show the crack defect ground truth by human labeled.

The AD method assumes that crack defect presents low level and high gradient, and applies anisotropic diffusion model to smooth crack defect and preserve background, simultaneously. The detection results in Fig. 9(a2)–(f2) show that some crystal grains are mistaken as crack defect because random crystal grains also exhibit the features of low gray level and high gradient. Moreover, the crack detection results are intermittent and this method is less adept at detecting crack defect in dim EL images, such as in Fig. 9(a2) and (e2). As shown in Fig. 9(f2), for defect-free image, this method easily generates false detections.

The LT method uses a local thresholding-based method to segment crack defect by calculating each sub-image's gray level mean and standard deviation. The detection results in Fig. 9(a3)–(f3) show the crystal grains are detected as crack defect due to taking gray level information into account only, and crack defect in dim EL image cannot be detected, such as in Fig. 9(e3). For Fig. 9(f3), this method is similar to the AD method and it is not robust to defect-free image.

The BSF method uses the single basic steerable filter to process the EL images. Figure 9(a4) shows that the BSF is less adept at solving intensity variations, making crack defect incomplete. Moreover, as shown in Fig. 9(c4), this method cannot well address the bifurcations due to the lack of consideration of local neighborhood infor-mation. In particular, the vertical dark region is not crack defect but finger interruption defect. Fortunately, the BSF method is robust to the dim and defect-free images, as shown in Fig. 9(e4)–(f4).

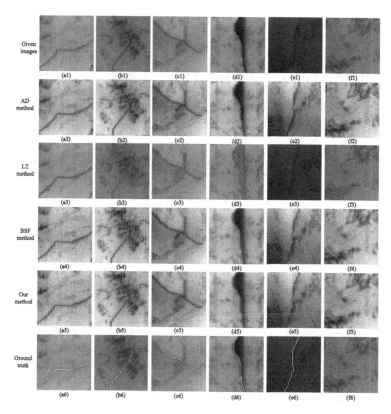

Fig. 9. Comparison of the proposed method with previous method. The first row is five different types of defective images and one defect-free image. The second to fifth row are the detection results of AD method [7], LT method [8], BSF method [13] and our method, respectively. The defective regions are labeled as red. The sixth shows crack defect ground truth.

The detection results based on our method are shown in Fig. 9(a5)–(f5). Although the inhomogeneously textured background caused by random crystal grains, even crystal grains distributed around the crack, the proposed method can detect various type crack defects and completely locate them on the inspection images. Moreover, all the false detections of crystal grains by the AD and LT methods are well addressed. Furthermore, the proposed method can well detect crack defect in dim EL image and it is robust to defect-free image. Overall, it preforms better than other three methods.

Furthermore, a quantitative evaluation is also given to compare our method with the above three representative methods. In this study, three performance indices including Precision (Pr), Recall (Re), and F-measure (Fm) are defined as follows:

$$Pr = \frac{TP}{TP + FP} \tag{13}$$

$$Re = \frac{TP}{TP + FN} \tag{14}$$

$$Fm = 2 \times \frac{Pr \times Re}{Pr + Re} \qquad (15)$$

where TP, FP, and FN represent true positives, false positives, and false negatives, respectively. The Fm can evaluate the overall performance of crack defect detection methods. The quantitative evaluation results are shown in Table 2. It shows the proposed method outperforms other methods.

Table 2. Comparison of quantitative evaluation using different methods

Method	Pr	Re	Fm
AD method	63.0	85.7	72.6
LT method	64.1	90.6	75.1
BSF method	88.2	91.1	89.6
Our method	93.6	95.1	94.3

4 Conclusion

In this paper, we proposed a robust crack defect detection scheme in inhomogeneously textured surface of near infrared images for multicrystalline solar cells. A steerable evidence filter is designed to provide evidence for the presence of crack defect. Moreover, the performance was evaluated on the challenging data set collected from solar cells production line. The experimental results show the proposed scheme is robust to the inhomogeneously textured background, crack defect types and brightness levels change, which can achieve satisfactory detection results.

Acknowledgement. This work was supported in part by National Natural Science Foundation (NNSF) of China under Grant 61403119, 61873315 Natural Science Foundation of Hebei Province under Grant F2018202078, Young Talents Project in Hebei province under Grant 210003 and technology Project of Hebei Province under Grant 17211804D.

References

1. Abdelhamid, M., Singh, R., Omar, M.: Review of microcrack detection techniques for silicon solar cells. IEEE J. Photovoltaics **4**(1), 514–524 (2014)
2. Dhimish, M., Holmes, V., Mehrddadi, B., et al.: The impact of cracks on photovoltaic power performance. J. Sci. Adv. Mater. Devices **2**(2), 199–209 (2017)
3. Israil, M., Anwar, S.A., Abdullah, M.Z.: Automatic detection of micro-crack in solar wafers and cells: a review. Trans. Inst. Measur. Control **35**(5), 606–618 (2013)
4. Frazao, M., Silva, J.A., Lobato, K., et al.: Electroluminescence of silicon solar cells using a consumer grade digital camera. Measurement **99**, 7–12 (2017)
5. Kamaliardakani, M., Sun, L., Ardakani, M.K.: Sealed-crack detection algorithm using heuristic thresholding approach. J. Comput. Civ. Eng. **30**(1), 04014110 (2014)

6. Sun, L., Kamaliardakani, M., Zhang, Y.: Weighted neighborhood pixels segmentation method for automated detection of cracks on pavement surface images. J. Comput. Civ. Eng. **30**(1), 04015021 (2015)

7. Tsai, D.M., Chang, C.C., Chao, S.M.: Micro-crack inspection in heterogeneously textured solar wafers using anisotropic diffusion. Image Vis. Comput. **28**(3), 491–501 (2010)

8. Chiou, Y.C., Liu, J.Z., Liang, Y.T.: Micro crack detection of multi-crystalline silicon solar wafer using machine vision techniques. Sens. Rev. **31**(2), 154–165 (2011)

9. Khan, H.A., Salman, M., Hussain, S., et al.: Automation of optimized gabor filter parameter selection for road cracks detection. Int. J. Adv. Comput. Sci. Appl. (IJACSA) **7**(3), 269–275 (2016)

10. Zalama, E., Gómez-García-Bermejo, J., Medina, R., et al.: Road crack detection using visual features extracted by Gabor filters. Comput. Aided Civ. Infrastruct. Eng. **29**(5), 342–358 (2014)

11. Medina, R., Llamas, J., Gómez-García-Bermejo, J., et al.: Crack detection in concrete tunnels using a gabor filter invariant to rotation. Sensors **17**(7), 1670 (2017)

12. Tsai, D.M., Wu, S.C., Li, W.C.: Defect detection of solar cells in electroluminescence images using Fourier image reconstruction. Sol. Energy Mater. Sol. Cells **99**, 250–262 (2012)

13. Freeman, W.T., Adelson, E.H.: The design and use of steerable filters. IEEE Trans. Pattern Anal. Mach. Intell. **13**(9), 891–906 (1991)

14. Mukherjee, S., Acton, S.T.: Oriented filters for vessel contrast enhancement with local directional evidence. In: ISBI, pp. 503–506 (2015)

Image Stitching Using Smoothly Planar Homography

Tian-Zhu Xiang, Gui-Song Xia$^{(\boxtimes)}$, and Liangpei Zhang

State Key Laboratory LIESMARS, Wuhan University, Wuhan, China
{tzxiang,guisong.xia,zlp62}@whu.edu.cn

Abstract. It is an important but challenging issue to construct a reasonable seamless image mosaic from images with non-ignorable different viewpoints or multiple distinct planes. The main limitations of existing image-stitching approaches lie in two facts: (a) the multiple plane nature of scenes has not been well considered in the image alignment step, which usually results in obvious misalignments; (b) the ignored alignment errors often lead to broken structures in the seam composition step. To overcome these problems, this paper proposed a *smoothly planar homography* model for image stitching, by considering the multi-plane geometry of natural scene. First, we integrate local warps estimated in each plane to achieve smoothly plane stitching. Then, we introduce a novel alignment-guided seam composition to handle parallax. Experimental results on a series of challenging data demonstrate that our model achieves the state-of-the-art stitching performance.

Keywords: Image stitching · Image alignment · Homography

1 Introduction

Image stitching has been extensively studied recently and applied in many fields, such as scene understanding [31], virtue reality [12], photogrammetry and remote sensing [10]. However, they often perform under the assumptions [22] that the imaging scene is approximately planar, or that images are taken under simple camera rotations. Obviously, these conditions are not always conformed with the real case, especially for photos taking by smart phones or cameras, as demonstrated in Fig. 1. The main challenges are:

– Global warps [2] or even local warps [28] are difficult to handle the complex scene with different dominant planes. The former adopts only one transformation, which lacks the flexibility for complex scenes. The latter often ignores the different planes in the scene and causes large alignment errors.

G.-S. Xia—This work was supported by the NSFC Grants under the contract No. 41501462 and No. 61771350, and the Outstanding Youth Project of Hubei Province under the contract No. 2017CFA037.

© Springer Nature Switzerland AG 2018
J.-H. Lai et al. (Eds.): PRCV 2018, LNCS 11256, pp. 524–536, 2018.
https://doi.org/10.1007/978-3-030-03398-9_45

- The existing methods cannot work well on images with large parallax, caused by random shooting positions and viewing angles [30]. Thus, they will inevitably bring noticeable artifacts or objectionable distortions.

Fig. 1. An illustration of our method. The top row display two input images taken casually and the scene contains multiple distinct planes. The bottom row shows the detected planes and transition regions (left) and the final stitching result (right). Planar regions are warped by planar homography $\mathbf{H}_i$, and the transition regions are transformed by the local weighted homography $\sum_{i=1}^{5} \alpha_i \mathbf{H}_i$.

Many approaches have been proposed to solve these problems. The main solution is spatially varying warps, *e.g.* multiple local warps [7] or the global warp with mesh optimization [29,30], which provide flexible warps to handle images with moderate parallax. However, these methods greatly depend on the number and distribution of point correspondences. In addition, distortions, resulted by non-linear transformations [9], are commonly obvious, *e.g.* projective and structure deformations. Many methods are developed to mitigate distortions, such as constraint of similarity transformation [4,5,14,25], or geometric structure cues [24,26,30], however, the reduction is limited under the scene with rich contents and structures. Besides, large parallax is a challenging task for these methods [15].

Another solution is seam-assist image stitching, which holds the advantages of dealing with large parallax. The common way is to perform the seam cutting after image alignment to hide the inevitable ghosting or artifacts [7,30]. The seam line is often selected by the color or gradient difference, image edges, etc., while they little consider the influence of alignment [15,30]. The seam cutting can be also closely integrated with alignment for interaction [8,15,29]. The main idea of these methods is that images are aligned well only in local area, where the seam line across. Seam quality assessment are proposed to guide the selection of homography estimated from a set of point correspondences. In fact, they rely on the selection of local homography/correspondence set. In some complex scene, the optimal selection is difficult to find if the local alignment region contains multiple planes, due to these methods only take one homography to tackle the whole scene.

To the best of our knowledge, few works consider how to deal with the scene with strong structural regularities, in the form of multiple distinct planes. Because one global or local homography cannot fit for the complex scene, dual-homography warping [7] clustered the match points into two groups to estimate the dual homographies for the scene containing two predominate planes: a distant plane and a ground plane. However, the difference between the rough plane partition and the true plane scene may cause misalignment and structure deformations. It may degrade the performance in the complex scene with more than two distinct planes.

Therefore, this paper proposes a smoothly planar homography model for image stitching. To obtain the plane warps, we propose to automatically detect plane points and segment the scene into piecewise planar regions. Then adaptive plane-based warps are estimated and integrated to perform local alignment. Once the images are geometrically aligned, a misalignment-guided seam is calculated to perform seamless stitching. This model can handle more than two distinct planes with large parallax. Figure 1 gives an example of the proposed method. Thus, the contribution of this paper is twofold:

- We propose a multi-plane homography estimation and integration strategy to handle the complex scene with multiple dominant planes and achieve plausible stitching.
- We propose a novel seam estimation method guided by alignment error to deal with parallax, which provides seamless image stitching.

2   Related Works

Numerous works have been devoted to image stitching. A exhaustive review was proposed in [22]. Here, we give a briefly survey of related works.

Global Parametric Models. Early methods adopt global parametric warps (e.g. affine, projective warps) to align images. The performance is degraded when images are taken with different viewpoints or scenes are not roughly planar. To remedy deficiency of single warp, Gao et al. [7] proposed a dual-homography warp to stitch images. However, it only fits for simple scene with two planes, ground and distant planes.

Spatially Varying Warps. Spatially varying warps are proposed to handle complex scene. Followed by composition techniques, these methods work well for images with moderate parallax. They can be roughly classified into two categories: local warps and mesh optimization-based warps. The former estimates multiple local transformations to align images locally, such as smoothly varying affine warps [17], *shape-preserving half-projective* (SPHP) [4], *as-projective-as-possible* (APAP) warps [28] and its variants [5,14,18]. The latter applies mesh optimization model with a series of feature constraints after general warps, such as feature alignment [23,27,30] and photometric alignment [16]. These methods cannot consider the particularity of multi-plane scenes [19], that is the difference of transformation of different plane regions, thus they may fail to produce satisfactory stitching results.

Seam-Assist Stitching Methods. To stitch images with large parallax, some seam-assist methods are proposed. Unlike the method that performs seam cutting after image alignment [13], Gao et al. [8] proposed a seam-driven image stitching method. The method evaluates the seam-cut quality to guide the selection of optimal transformation. Based on it, parallax-tolerant stitching model [29] and seam-guided local alignment model [15] are proposed to improve the stitching performance. However, these methods may only align one local regions at a time, and the applied seam may accidentally pass through the other regions with large misalignments.

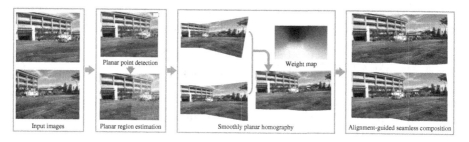

Fig. 2. The workflow of our smoothly planar stitching algorithm.

3   Smoothly Planar Stitching

The proposed stitching algorithm is illustrated in Fig. 2. The planar regions are estimated based on the detection of planar points, then the multiple planar homography are integrated by the designed weight strategy for smoothly stitching. To handle parallax, alignment errors are used to guide the seamline estimation for seamless composition.

3.1   Planar Region Estimation

For real scenes with multiple planes, we use a robust multi-structure geometric fitting method, called random cluster models sampler (RCMSA) [20], to detect planes from the point correspondences. RCMSA adopts random cluster models to perform hypothesis generation using subsets larger than minimal. Compared with random hypothesis generation, RCMSA provides good hypotheses, which are less affected by the vagaries of fitting on minimal subsets.

For two views of multiple-plane scene, given N point matches $P = \{p_i\}_{i=1}^{N}$ across two images, where each $p_i = (\mathbf{x}_i, \mathbf{x}_i')$ denotes a pair of match points in homogeneous coordinates. The RCMSA is to partition the match points into different planes (structures) as well as to remove the false matches. The number of structures is unknown and must also be estimated.

Basically, RCMSA works in the following way. Random cluster models is first used as hypothesis sampler to generate clusters for hypotheses $\Theta = \{\theta_c\}_{c=1}^{K}$. Next, an annealing method based on graph cuts is employed to optimize the fitting of structures. The graph $\mathcal{G} = (\mathcal{V}, \mathcal{N})$ is builded on the match points, where each vertice $\mathcal{V} = P$, and the edge $\mathcal{N}$ is constructed from the Delaunay triangulation of P. The goal is to assign each pair of match points p_i to one of the structures in Θ, denoted by labels $L = \{l_i\}_{i=1}^{N}$. That is, $l_i = k, k = \{1, 2, ..., K\}$ if p_i belongs to the k-th structures, otherwise $l_i = 0$ if p_i is an outlier. The energy function is defined as

$$E(\Theta, l) = \sum_{i=1}^{N} D(p_i, l_i) + \sum_{\langle i,j \rangle \in \mathcal{N}} V(l_i, l_j), \qquad (1)$$

where $D(p_i, l_i)$ is the data cost and constructed as

$$D(p_i, l_i) = \begin{cases} r(p_i, \theta_{l_i})^2, & \text{if } l_i \in \{1, 2, ..., k\} \\ \eta, & \text{if } l_i = 0 \end{cases}, \qquad (2)$$

where $r(p_i, \theta_{l_i})$ is the absolute residual of p_i to structure θ_{l_i}, and η is the penalty if p_i is an outlier. The smoothness cost V is defined as

$$V(l_i, l_j) = \begin{cases} 0, & \text{if } l_i = l_j \\ 1, & \text{if } l_i \neq l_j \end{cases}, \qquad (3)$$

The solution of $L = \{l_i\}$ can be obtained based on α-expansion [1].

In our implementation, RCMSA is iteratively adopted on outliers, until outliers are small enough or the new detected plane points are small. To refine the detection of plane points, the projective distance is employed to adjust the plane labels of points. If the projective distance of one point by k-th planar homography $\mathbf{H}_k$ is less than δ, the point is reassigned to this plane label $l_i = k$, where $\mathbf{H}_k$ is estimated by the correspondences in plane θ_k. Thus, the points are labeled to each plane.

One simple way is to warp each plane by its corresponding transformation, however, there may be gaps between the plane regions, or plane regions may overlap. In our idea, the images are partitioned into two regions: plane and transition regions. For plane regions, we adopt the homography estimated by the point correspondences belong to current plane. For transition regions, they are transformed by the local weighted homography, detailed below, so that to keep the continuity along the boundary of neighboring plane regions. Here, the neighborhood of each plane points, *e.g.* less than ε, is regarded as the plane regions, and the rest is transition region. Figure 3 shows the detection of plane points by applying RCMSA and the partition of plane regions.

Fig. 3. Plane region estimation. (a) Detection of multiple planar points based on RCMSA; (b) Estimation of planar and transition regions. Planar regions are highlighted red. (Color figure online)

3.2   Smoothly Planar Homography

For transition regions, the local weighted homography is employed to maintain the continuity and smoothness between neighboring plane regions. Given a pixel p in transition regions, the warps is estimated as

$$\mathbf{H}_p = \sum_{i=1}^{K} \alpha_i \mathbf{H}_i, \tag{4}$$

where $\mathbf{H}_i$ represent the each plane homography, K is the number of plane regions, and α_i denotes weight that adjusts the contribution of each plane homography. The weight is computed based on spatial proximity with Gaussian kernel,

$$\alpha_i = \exp(-d_i/\sigma^2), \tag{5}$$

where d_i denotes the distance to the closest pixel in i–th planar regions, and σ is set to $4-8$. To mitigate the projective distortions, the global similarity constraint proposed in [24] is employed by integration with local homography. The procedure of smoothly planar homography is given in Algorithm 1.

3.3   Alignment-Guided Seamless Composition

After alignment, seam cutting plays an important role in seamless stitching mosaic, especially for large parallax cases. To search for optimal seam line

---

Algorithm 1. Smoothly planar homography

Input: The plane homography $\{\mathbf{H}_i\}_{i=1}^K$ of each plane regions
Output: The stitching images by smoothly planar homography
1: **for** each pixel p_j **do**
2:   **if** p_j in planar regions **then**
3:     Estimate its homography $\mathbf{H}_{p_j}$ by point correspondences belong to this plane
4:   **else**
5:     Compute the weight factor α_i (5)
6:     Compute the local homography of this pixel $\mathbf{H}_{p_j}$ (4)
7:   **end if**
8: **end for**
9: **for** each local homography $\mathbf{H}_p$ **do**
10:   Integrate $\mathbf{H}_p$ with global similarity in [24]
11: **end for**
12: Warp the images by local homography to produce the stitching image.

---

between two images, the difference of image color, gradient and edge map [15,29] in the overlapping region are often adopted to construct smoothness terms in graph cut seam algorithm [11].

In fact, alignment error has a great influence on the seam finding [30]. The large misalignment pixels with similar colors will confusion seam cutting and produce bad seams. A plausible seam should traverse low-texture and inconspicuous regions, and avoid passing pixels with large alignment errors or distinct structures such as edges. Therefore, we propose to integrate alignment error and edge difference to generate good seams.

For match point, the alignment error is calculated as

$$e_x = \|\mathbf{x}_i - \mathbf{H}\mathbf{x}_i'\|, \tag{6}$$

where $(\mathbf{x}_i, \mathbf{x}_i')$ is a pair of match points. $\mathbf{H}$ is the corresponding plane homography.

According to point alignment error, we can generate a per-pixel error map by interpolation,

$$e_p = \sum_x w_{p,x} e_x / \sum_x w_{p,x}$$
$$w_{p,x} = exp(-\|p - x\|/\rho^2), \tag{7}$$

where $w_{p,x}$ is the weight factor calculated by the distance of the pixel p in overlapping region to match point x. ρ is scale parameter and set to 8. The interpolation is conducted by the M match points closet to the pixel p. To reduce the influence of large alignment errors, we define the alignment term as

$$E_a = 1 - exp(-e_p^2/(\tau)^2), \tag{8}$$

where τ is set to $0.003D$, where D denotes the length of image diagonal. The smoothness cost function is

$$E_{i,j}(p) = E_a(E_c + E_e), \tag{9}$$

where E_c is the color difference, E_e denotes the image edge probability difference computed by structured edge detector [6]. The smoothness cost is combined into graph cut seam finding algorithm [11] to search for a good seam. Then multiband blending [3] is applied.

4   Experiments

To verify the effectiveness of the proposed method, we test our algorithm on a series of challenging data and compared with other stitching methods. The parameters of the compared methods are set as recommendation in the respective papers. Given a pair of images, the keypoints are detected and matched by deep matching algorithm [21] in our implementation.

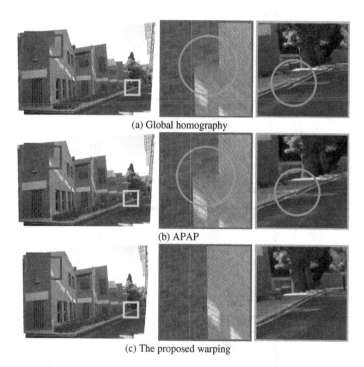

(a) Global homography

(b) APAP

(c) The proposed warping

Fig. 4. Warp comparison. The image are warped by (a) global homography [2], (b) APAP [28], and (c) the proposed warping. Then, the alignment-guided seam composition is applied on these three results. For comparison, we highlight some details in the blue and green boxes. Errors are shown in red circles. (Color figure online)

4.1   Warping Performance

Figure 4 compares the warp performance with other two common warp model, that is, global warping and local warping. Here, global homography [2] and APAP warps [28] are selected for comparison. After warping, the proposed alignment-guided seam composition is employed on these stitching results for seamless composition. Figure 4(a) shows the result by global method, which applies a global homography to warp images. On one hand, scene with multiple distinct planes cannot be represented by only one transformation, result in severe misalignments. On the other hand, even though seam-cutting is applied, the seam-cutting cannot find well-aligned regions across in some areas. Thus, the seam passes misalignment regions and produces broken structures. APAP adopts multiple local homographies to align as many point matches as possible, and improves the stitching performance, e.g. green region in Fig. 4(b). However, due to the adverse influence of point matches in different planes (blue region) or uneven and insufficient points (green region), it is hard to provide accurate warping model for well alignment, result in stitching errors. Our smoothly planar homography adopts two different warping model to align planar and transition regions, which provides satisfactory alignment locally. Together with our novel alignment-guided seam composition, the estimated seam finds locally well-aligned regions, which can avoid regions with large parallax.

(a) Enblend

(b) Without alignment guidance

(c) The proposed seam composition

Fig. 5. Seam composition. (a) Enblend, (b) The proposed seam composition without alignment guidance, (c) The proposed seam composition. For comparison, we highlight some details in the blue and green boxes. Seam errors are shown in red circles. (Color figure online)

4.2   Composition Performance

Figure 5 shows the seam composition performance of *Enblend*[1], our method without guidance of alignment, and our method with guidance of alignment. From the enlarged views, Enblend produces severe seam errors, e.g. the disappeared buoy and the distortions of construction. In fact, Enblend only considers the color difference and gradient difference, which may suffer from ghosts or errors. By adding edge or boundary constraints, our method without alignment guidance provides a relatively better result, but the seam error is still obvious, mainly because of the large mis-match on red concrete columns. With the constraint of alignment error, the proposed seam composition avoids the regions with big alignment errors and provide satisfactory seam composition.

(a) ICE   (b) APAP

(c) SPHP   (d) The proposed method

Fig. 6. Comparison with spatially varying methods, *i.e.* (a) ICE, (b) APAP [28], (c) SPHP [4] and (d) the proposed method. For comparison, we highlight some details in the green boxes. Errors are shown in red circles. (Color figure online)

4.3   Comparison with Other Methods

Figure 6 gives the comparison with some spatially varying methods, including image composition editor (ICE[2]), APAP [28], SPHP [4] and ours method. Some details are provided in enlarged views for comparison. Although ICE takes global transformation, it provides good stitching result because of the advanced image composition. However, the alignment errors remain obvious shown in red circle. APAP adopts local homographies to align as many correspondences as possible in the overlapping region. Due to rich correspondences, it provides satisfactory alignment performance, but it suffers from local distortions (shown in red circle) caused by feature matches in multiple planes. SPHP produces obvious stitching errors, because the applied warps cannot well represent the multiplane image transformation. The estimated seam may accidentally pass through

---

[1] http://enblend.sourceforge.net/.

[2] http://research.microsoft.com/en-us/um/redmond/projects/ice/.

(a) ICE

(b) Parallax-tolerant stitching

(c) The proposed method

Fig. 7. Comparison with seam-assist stitching methods, *i.e.* (a) ICE, (b) parallax-tolerant stitching [29] and (c) the proposed method. For comparison, we highlight some details in the green boxes. Errors are highlighted in red circles. (Color figure online)

regions with misalignments and thus generate broken structures. Our smoothly planar homography method uses different model to process planar regions and transition regions and thus aligns different planar regions well. Together with the alignment-guided seam composition, which finds local well-aligned regions for composition, our method provides visually appealing stitching results.

Figure 7 provides the comparison with seam-assist stitching methods, including ICE and parallax-tolerant stitching [29] method. In ICE results, the seam cutting does not consider alignment errors and thus causes obvious broken structures. In parallax-tolerant stitching, the best homography is choosed for good local alignment. However, the applied seam may still be stumbled by large misalignment. In comparison, the proposed method provides satisfactory stitching results.

5   Conclusion

In this paper, we present a smoothly planar homography model for stitching images with multiple planes and large parallax. The plane and transition regions are detected based on the multiple plane correspondences, and warped with respective transformations. The multiple plane homographies are integrated to perform the smoothly stitching on transition regions. In addition, the alignment-guided seam composition is adopted to perform seamless stitching. Experiments prove the effectiveness and robustness of the proposed method and confirm the state-of-the-art stitching performance. In the future, the advanced plane detection methods may be beneficial for accurate detection of plane regions.

References

1. Boykov, Y., Veksler, O., Zabih, R.: Fast approximate energy minimization via graph cuts. IEEE Trans. Pattern Anal. Mach. Intell. **23**(11), 1222–1239 (2001)
2. Brown, M., Lowe, D.G.: Automatic panoramic image stitching using invariant features. Int. J. Comput. Vis. **74**(1), 59–73 (2007)
3. Burt, P.J., Adelson, E.H.: A multiresolution spline with application to image mosaics. ACM Trans. Graph. **2**(4), 217–236 (1983)
4. Chang, C.H., Sato, Y., Chuang, Y.Y.: Shape-preserving half-projective warps for image stitching. In: CVPR, Columbus, USA, pp. 3254–3261 (2014)
5. Chen, Y.-S., Chuang, Y.-Y.: Natural image stitching with the global similarity prior. In: Leibe, B., Matas, J., Sebe, N., Welling, M. (eds.) ECCV 2016. LNCS, vol. 9909, pp. 186–201. Springer, Cham (2016). https://doi.org/10.1007/978-3-319-46454-1_12
6. Dollár, P., Zitnick, C.L.: Fast edge detection using structured forests. IEEE Trans. Pattern Anal. Mach. Intell. **37**(8), 1558–1570 (2015)
7. Gao, J., Kim, S.J., Brown, M.S.: Constructing image panoramas using dual-homography warping. In: CVPR, Colorado Springs, CO, USA, pp. 49–56 (2011)
8. Gao, J., Li, Y., Chin, T.J., Brown, M.S.: Seam-driven image stitching. In: Eurographics, Girona, Spain, pp. 45–48 (2013)
9. Hu, J., Zhang, D.Q., Yu, H., Chen, C.W.: Multi-objective content preserving warping for image stitching. In: ICME, Turin, Italy, pp. 1–6 (2015)
10. Kang, Z., Zhang, L., Zlatanova, S., Li, J.: An automatic mosaicking method for building facade texture mapping using a monocular close-range image sequence. ISPRS J. Photogramm. **65**(7), 282–293 (2010)
11. Kwatra, V., Schödl, A., Essa, I.A., Turk, G., Bobick, A.F.: Graphcut textures: image and video synthesis using graph cuts. ACM Trans. Graph. **22**(3), 277–286 (2003)
12. Lee, J., Kim, B., Kim, Y., Kim, Y., Noh, J.: Rich360: optimized spherical representation from structured panoramic camera arrays. ACM Trans. Graph. **35**(4), 63 (2016)
13. Li, L., Yao, J., Lu, X., Tu, J., Shan, J.: Optimal seamline detection for multiple image mosaicking via graph cuts. ISPRS J. Photogramm. **113**, 1–16 (2016)
14. Lin, C.C., Pankanti, S., Ramamurthy, K.N., Aravkin, A.Y.: Adaptive as-natural-as-possible image stitching. In: CVPR, Boston, MA, USA, pp. 1155–1163 (2015)

15. Lin, K., Jiang, N., Cheong, L.-F., Do, M., Lu, J.: SEAGULL: seam-guided local alignment for parallax-tolerant image stitching. In: Leibe, B., Matas, J., Sebe, N., Welling, M. (eds.) ECCV 2016. LNCS, vol. 9907, pp. 370–385. Springer, Cham (2016). https://doi.org/10.1007/978-3-319-46487-9_23

16. Lin, K., Jiang, N., Liu, S., Cheong, L.F., Do, M., Lu, J.: Direct photometric alignment by mesh deformation. In: CVPR, pp. 2405–2413 (2017)

17. Lin, W.Y., Liu, S., Matsushita, Y., Ng, T.T., Cheong, L.F.: Smoothly varying affine stitching. In: CVPR, Colorado Springs, CO, USA, pp. 345–352 (2011)

18. Liu, W.X., Chin, T.: Correspondence insertion for as-projective-as-possible image stitching. CoRR, arXiv: 1608.07997 (2016)

19. Lou, Z., Gevers, T.: Image alignment by piecewise planar region matching. IEEE Trans. Multimedia 16(7), 2052–2061 (2014)

20. Pham, T., Chin, T., Yu, J., Suter, D.: The random cluster model for robust geometric fitting. IEEE Trans. Pattern Anal. Mach. Intell. 36(8), 1658–1671 (2014)

21. Revaud, J., Weinzaepfel, P., Harchaoui, Z., Schmid, C.: Deepmatching: hierarchical deformable dense matching. Int. J. Comput. Vis. 120(3), 300–323 (2016)

22. Szeliski, R.: Image alignment and stitching: a tutorial. Found. Trends Comput. Graph. Vis. 2(1), 1–104 (2006)

23. Xia, G., Delon, J., Gousseau, Y.: Accurate junction detection and characterization in natural images. Int. J. Comput. Vis. 106(1), 31–56 (2014)

24. Xiang, T.Z., Xia, G.S., Bai, X., Zhang, L.: Image stitching by line-guided local warping with global similarity constraint. Pattern Recognit. 83, 481–497 (2018)

25. Xiang, T., Xia, G.S., Zhang, L.: Image stitching with perspective-preserving warping. In: XXIII ISPRS Congress, Prague, Czech Republic, pp. 287–294 (2016)

26. Xiang, T., Xia, G.S., Zhang, L., Huang, N.: Locally warping-based image stitching by imposing line constraints. In: ICPR, Cancun, Mexico, pp. 4178–4183 (2016)

27. Xue, N., Xia, G.S., Bai, X., Zhang, L., Shen, W.: Anisotropic-scale junction detection and matching for indoor images. IEEE Trans. Image Process. 27(1), 78–91 (2018)

28. Zaragoza, J., Chin, T.J., Tran, Q.H., Brown, M.S., Suter, D.: As-projective-as-possible image stitching with moving DLT. IEEE Trans. Pattern Anal. Mach. Intell. 36(7), 1285–1298 (2014)

29. Zhang, F., Liu, F.: Parallax-tolerant image stitching. In: CVPR, Columbus, OH, USA, pp. 3262–3269 (2014)

30. Zhang, G., He, Y., Chen, W., Jia, J., Bao, H.: Multi-viewpoint panorama construction with wide-baseline images. IEEE Trans. Image Process. 25(7), 3099–3111 (2016)

31. Zhang, Y., Song, S., Tan, P., Xiao, J.: PanoContext: a whole-room 3D context model for panoramic scene understanding. In: Fleet, D., Pajdla, T., Schiele, B., Tuytelaars, T. (eds.) ECCV 2014. LNCS, vol. 8694, pp. 668–686. Springer, Cham (2014). https://doi.org/10.1007/978-3-319-10599-4_43

Multilevel Residual Learning for Single Image Super Resolution

Xiaole Zhao[1(✉)], Hangfei Liu[1], Tao Zhang[1,2], Wei Bian[1,2], and Xueming Zou[1,2]

[1] School of Life Science and Technology, University of Electronic Science and
Technology of China (UESTC), Chengdu, Sichuan, China
`zxlation@foxmail.com`
[2] Alltech medical system co. LTD, Chengdu, Sichuan, China
{`tao.zhang,mark.zou`}`@alltechmed.com`

Abstract. Single image super-resolution (SISR) methods based on deep
learning techniques, especially convolutional neural networks (CNNs)
and residual learning, have made great achievements compared with traditional methods. Most of the current work focuses on the structural
design to increase the depth of the entire network and thus improve the
performance of the models. However, it is also important to improve the
efficiency of model parameters, especially in the case of limited resources.
To improve the performance of the models when the number of model
parameters keeps relatively small and fixed, we propose a novel multilevel
residual learning pattern for SISR in this work. The proposed method
shows a stable performance improvement over the compared structures
on several benchmark datasets with equal model parameters. Besides, we
empirically show that simply increasing the number of building blocks
(e.g. various residual blocks) to increase the depth of the networks will
not obtain the expected improvements of performance, which may imply
that the optimal performance of different network depths corresponds to
different structures of building blocks.

Keywords: Convolutional Neural Networks · Residual learning
Image Super Resolution · Skip connection

1 Introduction

Single image super resolution (SISR) is a classic ill-posed problem in computer
vision community which aims at recovering a high resolution (HR) image from
only one low resolution (LR) image. High resolution means that pixel density
within an image is higher than its LR counterparts and therefore an HR image
can offer more details that may be critical in various applications such as medical
imaging [1,2], aerial spectral imaging [3] and remote sensing imaging [4,5], face
recognition [6], security and surveillance [7] et al., where high-frequency details
are usually critical and greatly desired.

J.-H. Lai et al. (Eds.): PRCV 2018, LNCS 11256, pp. 537–549, 2018.
https://doi.org/10.1007/978-3-030-03398-9_46

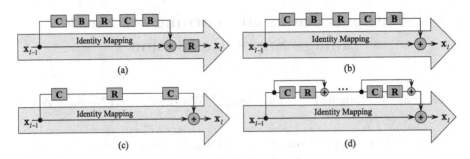

Fig. 1. The structure of several residual blocks. **C**, **B**, **R** and **+** represent conv, batch normalization, ReLU and element-wise addition respectively. (a) the original residual block [18]. (b) SRResNet [14]. (c) EDSR/MDSR [16]. (d) the proposed residual block.

In recent years, many image super resolution (SR) methods based on deep learning techniques [8], especially convolutional neural networks (CNNs) and residual learning, have emerged and greatly promoted the best state of SR. Some of the most representative are SRCNN [9], DRCN [10], DRRN [11], VDSR [12], ESPCNN [13], SRResNet [14], LapSRN [15], EDSR/MDSR [16] and RDN [17] etc. Residual learning [18,19] is a trick to increase the depth of the networks and thus improve the model performance. It was first proposed for image recognition and has been widely proved to be helpful for gradients propagation and model convergence, thus making it possible to build extremely deep networks. With the increased depth of networks, the expressive power and generalization ability of the models have also been improved. Though many methods based on residual learning (e.g. SRResNet [14], EDSR/MDSR [16] and RDN [17]) have achieved much better results than previous methods, the cost for getting further improvement of model performance becomes more and more expensive as the depth of the network increases. Therefore, it is useful to improve the efficiency of model parameters in the case of limited resources.

A key factor of residual learning that affects model training and performance is *residual connection* (or *skip connection, shortcut* [18]). The previous methods have a common feature in network structure design: residual learning is usually applied to the overall structure of the networks or building blocks, but not deep into the information paths of a residual block. Normally, a residual block is composed of a *residual path* (a identity mapping) and a *main path* (Fig. 1). In this work, we present a novel multilevel residual learning pattern for SISR, which we term ML-ResNet. In our model, residual connection is applied not only to the outermost layers and the internal residual blocks, but also to the main path within a residual block (Fig. 1(d)). Thus, the whole structure of the network exhibits the characteristic of multilevel residual learning.

We evaluate the proposed model on several benchmark datasets and compare it with some common block structures. The experimental results show that the multilevel residual structure has a stable performance improvement over the compared methods with equal model parameters. Moreover, we also empirically illustrate that simply increasing the number of building blocks does not achieve the expected performance gain, which implies that the optimal performance of the networks with different depth may correspond to different structures of building blocks. This observation might shed some light on the structural design of deep networks or building blocks.

2 Related Work

2.1 Super Resolution with Deep Learning

Dong et al. proposed the first SR model [9] based on CNNs in the modern sense and built an end-to-end mapping between the (bicubic) interpolated LR images and their HR counterparts. The further improvement based on this pioneering work mainly aimed at increasing network depth or sharing network weights at the beginning [10–12]. These methods use the interpolated version of the LR image as the input of their model, which is convenient for keeping the size of the output image consistent with the target HR image and works well for the fractional scaling factors. However, it hinders establishing end-to-end mappings from the original LR image to the corresponding HR image and suffers the computational and memory constraints as they operate feature maps in the HR image space. This problem can be solved by placing nonlinear mapping in the LR image space. There are two options for the purpose currently, i.e., transpose convolution (or deconvolution [20]) and efficient sub-pixel convolutional neural network (ESPCNN) [13]. As the amount of computation and memory occupancy are greatly reduced, Lim et al. [16] increased the depth and the width (the number of the feature maps' channel) of their networks aggressively (32 residual blocks for EDSR and 80 residual blocks for MDSR).

Although these networks have made great breakthroughs in improving SR results, their performance gains are mainly achieved by increasing network depth and adjusting the structure of the entire network. Changes in the structure of residual blocks also aim at increasing the network depth to a certain extent. On the contrary, the target of this work is to promote the information flow through the entire network and improve the efficiency of the model parameters.

2.2 Residual Learning for Super Resolution

Residual Network (ResNet) [18] is initially proposed for image recognition, which is further applied to a wide range of computer vision problems such as image classification, object detection, image segmentation and image generation. Most of the methods mentioned in Sect. 2.1 apply residual learning, e.g., DRRN [11], VDSR [12], SRResNet [14], EDSR [16] and RDN [17] etc. An impressive work was presented in [21], named HelloSR. Inspired by the effectiveness of learning high frequency residuals for SR, HelloSR presented a novel stacked residual refined network which generated HR image by explicitly learning the multilevel residuals in the HR image space.

These methods employ residual learning in different ways. However, most of them adopt residual connections only between the outermost layers or the middle modules of their network, but not within the information paths of a building block. In this work, the outermost layers, the intermediate building blocks and the information pathes within a block are viewed as different levels of a network and residual learning is applied to all of these levels. Experiments show that this multilevel residual structure is helpful to improve the performance of the model when the network structure is relatively shallow.

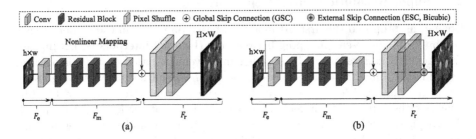

Fig. 2. The overall structure of two networks used in this work. (a) the same structure as EDSR [16] but the number of residual blocks is limited to 4. (b) Extension of (a) with an external skip connection.

3   Multilevel Residual Networks

3.1   Overall Network Structure

The overall structure of ML-ResNet is outlined in Fig. 2. The networks consist of three typical parts: feature extraction network (FEN), nonlinear mapping network (NMN) and HR image reconstruction network (HRN). The FEN is applied to represent the input image as shallow features. These shallow features are then fed into a set of cascaded building blocks, i.e., NMN that produces deep features. Next, a pixel shuffle layer is concatenated to upsample deep features to match the expected size (e.g. SR×2 or SR×4). Finally, the upsampled features are delivered to HRN to generate the HR outputs.

Denote $\mathbf{x}$ and $\mathbf{y}$ as the input and the output of the entire network, $\mathbf{x}_i$ and $\mathbf{y}_i$ as the input and output of the sub networks or building blocks. Formally, the operation for shallow features extraction could be expressed as:

$$\mathbf{y}_0 = F_e(\mathbf{x}) \tag{1}$$

where $F_e(\cdot)$ denotes the first feature extraction network FEN. It extracts the shallow features and expands the dimension along with channel direction. The output of FEN is directly fed into NMN ($\mathbf{x}_0 = \mathbf{y}_0$). Similarly, the operation for the whole nonlinear feature mapping network could be denoted as:

$$\mathbf{y}_n = F_m(\mathbf{x}_0) \tag{2}$$

where n denotes the number of the building blocks, and $\mathbf{y}_n$ indicates the output of the nonlinear feature mapping function $F_m(\cdot)$. Here, $F_m(\cdot)$ includes all the building blocks within nonlinear feature mapping network and the subsequent conv layer, as shown in Fig. 2.

After the global skip connection (GSC), the input of HR image reconstruction network is $\mathbf{x}_{n+1} = \mathbf{y}_n + \mathbf{x}_0$. In EDSR/MDSR [16], the final output of the entire network is as follow (Fig. 2(a)):

$$\mathbf{y} = F_r(\mathbf{x}_{n+1}) = F_r(\mathbf{y}_n + \mathbf{x}_0) \tag{3}$$

where $F_r(\cdot)$ denote HR reconstruction function that consists of a pixel shuffle followed by a conv layer. However, there is an external skip connection (ESC) before the final output of the proposed ML-ResNet, as shown in Fig. 2(b):

$$\mathbf{y} = \mathbf{x} + F_r(\mathbf{x}_{n+1}) = \mathbf{x} + F_r(\mathbf{y}_n + \mathbf{x}_0) \tag{4}$$

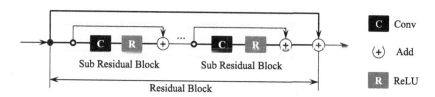

Fig. 3. Detailed illustration of the proposed residual block. Each residual block consists of many sub residual blocks, which are composed of the basic Conv + ReLU operations.

3.2   Building Residual Blocks

ResNet is usually modularized and consists of a series of stacked blocks. In a residual block, the main path augments the expressive ability of the model, while the residual path promotes the information propagation through the entire network. Denote the input and the output of a residual block $\mathcal{B}_l$ as $\mathbf{x}_l$ and $\mathbf{y}_l$ respectively. Then $\mathcal{B}_l$ can be expressed in a general form [18]:

$$\begin{aligned} \mathbf{y}_l &= h(\mathbf{x}_l) + \mathcal{F}_B(\mathbf{x}_l, \mathcal{W}_l) \\ \mathbf{x}_{l+1} &= f(\mathbf{y}_l) \end{aligned} \tag{5}$$

where $h(\cdot)$ and $\mathcal{F}_B(\cdot)$ are the mapping function of residual path and the main path respectively. $f(\cdot)$ is a function that converts the output of $\mathcal{B}_l$ to the input of $\mathcal{B}_{l+1}$. He et al. [19] theoretically explained that a compact information path (the identity mapping in Fig. 1) is helpful for easing optimization, i.e., $h(\mathbf{x}_l) = \mathbf{x}_l$ and $f(\mathbf{y}_l) = \mathbf{y}_l$. This is viewed as a contiguous memory mechanism [17] and most of the current SR models follow this principle.

However, most of the previous methods adopted direct nonlinear mapping in the main path $\mathcal{F}_B(\cdot)$. In this work, residual learning is also applied deep into the main path $\mathcal{F}_B(\cdot)$ of a residual block, as shown in Fig. 3 and Fig. 1(d). We call this ResNet-in-ResNet structure *fine-grained residual learning*, which is expected to promote data flow in the main path of a residual block. One can adjust the number of sub residual blocks (SRB) in a residual block (RB) and thus change the density of residual learning. If the NMN includes x residual blocks and each residual block contains y sub residual blocks, we call it ML-ResNet (BxSy).

3.3   Multilevel Residual Pattern

In addition to the fine-grained residual learning within residual blocks, we also introduce an external skip connection (ESC) between the outermost layers of the entire network, which we call *coarse-grained residual learning*. Thus, the residual pattern is applied to multiple abstract levels of the model and the whole network structure displays the characteristic of multilevel residual learning from fine to coarse grain. This multilevel residual structure is proved to be effective in our experiments, which is probably because it is related to the (multilevel) manifold simplification [22] although there is still no strict theoretical argument.

Interestingly, the experiments show that the external skip connection seems to have no obvious effect on the performance of the network with EDSR residual blocks (Fig. 1(c)), but it can slightly improve the performance of the model built with the proposed residual blocks (Fig. 1(d)). This also shows the validity of the multilevel residual structure to some extent.

4   Experiments

In this section, we first introduce some experiment settings. Next, we study the impact of residual density and the external skip connection on the performance of the model. The overall structure of the network is Fig. 2(b) and the reference structure is Fig. 2(a). The residual blocks shown in Fig. 1(b)−(d) are used for comparison. Finally, we compare the proposed model with several previous methods quantitatively and qualitatively. The performance is evaluated with PSNR and SSIM [23]. They are calculated with the built-in functions of Python skimage module during quick validation, but in the testing phase, we use different calculations for fair comparison.

4.1   Training Settings

DIV2K dataset [21,24] is used to train and quickly validate the models (only the first 10 validation images of DIV2K are used). Several standard benchmark datasets are used for testing, including Set5 [25], Set14 [26], B100 [27], Urban100 [28] and DIV2K validation set. For training, the HR images are randomly split into 96 × 96 RGB image patches and the size of LR patches are dynamically adjusted according to SR scales. Data augmentation and mean removal are the same as EDSR/MDSR [16].

Given a training dataset $\mathcal{D} = \{\mathbf{x}^i, \mathbf{y}^i\}_{i=1}^{|\mathcal{D}|}$, where $|\mathcal{D}|$ is the number of training samples, l_1 loss function is used for model training:

$$L(\boldsymbol{\theta}) = \frac{1}{|\mathcal{D}|} \sum_{i=1}^{|\mathcal{D}|} ||\mathbf{y}^i - \hat{\mathbf{y}}^i||_1 \qquad (6)$$

where $\hat{\mathbf{y}}$ is the estimate of the model and $\mathbf{y}$ is the corresponding target. $\boldsymbol{\theta}$ denotes the set of model parameters. It is worth noting that the number of parameters is the same for the compared architectures.

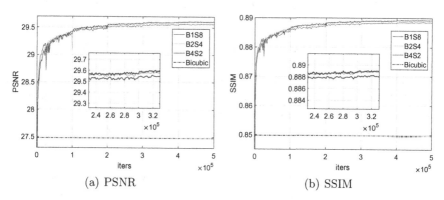

(a) PSNR   (b) SSIM

Fig. 4. The validation performance of the models with different residual density on the first 10 validation images of DIV2K (SR×4).

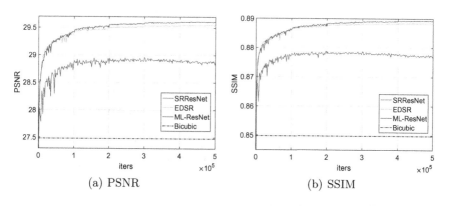

(a) PSNR   (b) SSIM

Fig. 5. The validation performance of the models with different residual blocks shown in Fig. 1(b)−(d). Only the first 10 validation images of DIV2K are used for comparison (SR×4).

The size of minibatch is 32 and that of filters is 5×5. The number of residual blocks and feature maps is 4 and 256 respectively. We trained the models with ADAM optimizer [30] by setting $\beta_1 = 0.9$, $\beta_2 = 0.999$ and $\epsilon = 10^{-8}$. The piecewise constant decay is used for learning rate, i.e., it is initialized as 10^{-4} and halved at every 10^5 iterations. All models are trained for 5×10^5 iterations.

4.2 Residual Density

In our settings, there are multiple combinations of residual blocks and their sub residual blocks when the total number of conv layers is fixed, which forms different residual density of the NMN. For comparison, we used the structure in Fig. 2(a) and set the total number of conv layers in NMN to 8. Thus, we have 4 combinations: B1S8, B2S4, B4S2 and B8S1, where B and S represent the number of residual blocks and sub residual blocks respectively. However, B8S1 is invalid due to the degradation of model structure, as shown in Fig. 3.

From Fig. 4, it can be seen that B2S4 and B4S2 perform almost the same, but obviously better than B1S8. The result is stable in our repeated experiments. It is probably because that a residual network can be viewed as a collection of many paths of differing length [29] and different residual densities lead the actual depth of the entire network to be different. This implies that the optimal performance of different network depths may correspond to different structures of building blocks, and simply increasing the number of building blocks to increase the depth of the network may not achieve expected performance improvements.

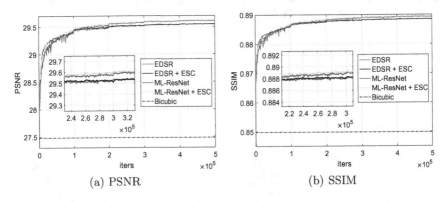

(a) PSNR   (b) SSIM

Fig. 6. The validation performance of the models with and without ESC. Only the first 10 validation images of DIV2K dataset are used for comparison (SR×4).

4.3 Different Residual Blocks

Because Fig. 1(a) is mainly used for classification, detection and other high-level computer vision problems, we exclude this structure in our experiments. For all of the compared structures, we set 4 residual blocks in the entire network with two convolutional layers in each block for fair comparison.

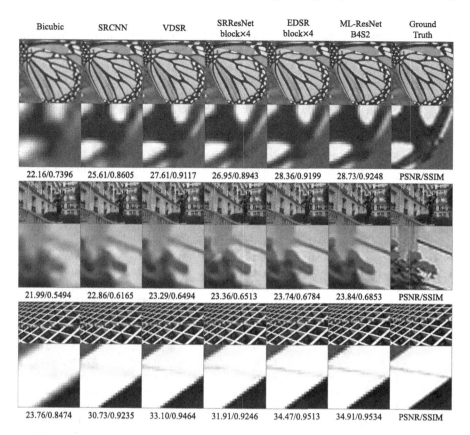

Fig. 7. Visual comparison with some previous SISR methods. (1) The first row shows image "butterfly" in Set5 with scale ×4. (2) The second and the third rows show image "img003" and "img043" in Urban100 with scale ×3.

As shown in Fig. 5 and Table 1, the proposed residual structure achieved the best SR performance. The residual block used in SRResNet [14] is obviously inferior than others. This is probably because the batch norm layer is not suitable for low-level computer vision problems. Although [16,17] removed the batch norm layer and stated its shortcomings (e.g., requires more computational and memory resources), they did not verify it experimentally.

4.4   External Skip Connection

The impact of ESC on the performance of the models is studied in this subsection. EDSR and ML-ResNet residual blocks are used for comparison. The validation performance of different architectures on the first 10 validation images of DIV2K is shown in Fig. 6.

Figure 6 exhibits an interesting phenomenon, i.e., ESC seems to have no obvious effect on the performance of the network with EDSR residual blocks but

Table 1. Quantitative comparison between some previous methods and the proposed ML-ResNet. SRResNet (block×4) and EDSR (block×4) are also included here. The maximal values are bold, and the second ones are underlined (PSNR/SSIM).

Datasets	Scale	Bicubic	SRCNN [9]	DRCN [10]	VDSR [12]
Set5	×2	33.66/0.9299	36.66/0.9542	37.63/0.9588	37.53/0.9587
	×3	30.39/0.8682	32.75/0.9090	33.82/0.9226	33.66/0.9213
	×4	28.42/0.8104	30.48/0.8628	31.53/0.8854	31.35/0.8838
Set14	×2	30.24/0.8688	32.42/0.9063	33.04/0.9118	33.03/0.9124
	×3	27.55/0.7742	29.28/0.8209	29.76/0.8311	29.77/0.8314
	×4	26.00/0.7027	27.49/0.7503	28.02/0.7670	28.01/0.7674
B100	×2	29.56/0.8431	31.36/0.8879	31.85/0.8942	31.90/0.8960
	×3	27.21/0.7385	28.41/0.7863	28.80/0.7963	28.82/0.7976
	×4	25.96/0.6675	26.90/0.7101	27.23/0.7233	27.29/0.7251
Urban 100	×2	26.88/0.8403	29.50/0.8946	30.75/0.9133	30.76/0.9140
	×3	24.46/0.7349	26.24/0.7989	27.15/0.8276	27.14/0.8279
	×4	23.14/0.6577	24.52/0.7221	25.14/0.7510	25.18/0.7524
DIV2K val	×2	31.01/0.9393	33.05/0.9581	33.70/0.9619	33.66/0.9625
	×3	28.22/0.8906	29.64/0.9138	30.15/0.9204	30.09/0.9208
	×4	26.66/0.8521	27.78/0.8753	28.23/0.8835	28.17/0.8841
		DRRN [11] B1U25	SRResNet [14] block×4	EDSR [16] block×4	ML-ResNet B4S2
Set5	×2	<u>37.74</u>/**0.9591**	36.94/0.9537	37.64/0.9586	**37.78**/<u>0.9589</u>
	×3	34.03/<u>0.9244</u>	33.08/0.9080	<u>34.05</u>/0.9234	**34.13**/**0.9248**
	×4	31.68/0.8888	31.01/0.8733	<u>31.90</u>/<u>0.8903</u>	**32.07**/**0.8921**
Set14	×2	33.23/0.9136	32.74/0.9087	<u>33.29</u>/<u>0.9148</u>	**33.32**/**0.9153**
	×3	29.96/0.8349	29.43/0.8232	<u>30.00</u>/<u>0.8367</u>	**30.04**/**0.8371**
	×4	28.21/0.7720	27.90/0.7620	<u>28.37</u>/<u>0.7772</u>	**28.45**/**0.7786**
B100	×2	<u>32.05</u>/0.8973	31.58/0.8900	32.01/<u>0.8975</u>	**32.11**/**0.8980**
	×3	**28.95**/0.8004	28.42/0.7853	28.91/<u>0.8012</u>	**28.95**/**0.8021**
	×4	27.38/0.7284	27.11/0.7185	<u>27.48</u>/<u>0.7329</u>	**27.54**/**0.7346**
Urban 100	×2	**31.23**/0.9188	29.84/0.9106	30.94/<u>0.9262</u>	<u>31.17</u>/**0.9278**
	×3	27.53/0.8378	26.69/0.8141	<u>27.59</u>/<u>0.8409</u>	**27.70**/**0.8440**
	×4	25.44/0.7638	25.01/0.7450	<u>25.77</u>/<u>0.7755</u>	**25.94**/**0.7808**
DIV2K val	×2	-/-	33.17/0.9582	<u>34.36</u>/<u>0.9665</u>	**34.42**/**0.9667**
	×3	-/-	29.47/0.9120	<u>30.66</u>/<u>0.9276</u>	**30.71**/**0.9283**
	×4	-/-	28.08/0.8818	<u>28.84</u>/<u>0.8948</u>	**28.93**/**0.8962**

it can slightly improve the performance of the model built with the proposed residual blocks. This shows the validity of the multilevel residual structure to some extent.

4.5   Comparison with Other Methods

In this section, we compare the proposed method with several typical methods quantitatively and qualitatively. When evaluating on DIV2K-val, we followed the way of EDSR/MDSR [16] to compute PSNR and SSIM; when testing on other datasets, i.e., Set5, Set14, B100 and Urban100, we followed the calculation of

DRCN [10]. Table 1 collects the quantitative results of the compared methods on the benchmark datasets, where SRResNet (block×4) and EDSR (block×4) are built with the structure shown in Fig. 2(a) and residual blocks shown in Fig. 1(b) and (c) respectively, but the number of residual blocks is limited to 4. The visual comparison is shown in Fig. 7. As we can see, ML-ResNet shows its superiority to the compared methods. It is worth noting that we only used B4S2 structure without ESC for comparison. Actually, the B2S4 structure perform better than B4S2 and ESC can further improve the performance of the model.

However, when we increase the network depth and make it have the same model parameters as the original EDSR, the performance of the proposed method is slightly worse than the original EDSR. This indicates that directly increasing the number of residual blocks to deepen the network will not get the desired performance improvement, and the multilevel residual structure promotes the propagation and the equilibrium of information flow through the network just when the network is relatively shallow.

5 Conclusion

In this paper, we studied several commonly used residual blocks for single image super resolution. Based on this, we proposed a new residual block structure and a multilevel residual learning pattern (ML-ResNet). The proposed ML-ResNet introduced fine-grained residual learning into the main path of a residual block and coarse-grained residual learning (ESC) between the outermost layers of the entire network. This multilevel residual structure seems to be helpful to simplify the structure of feature maps at multiple abstract levels of the deep model and promote the propagation and the equilibrium of information flow throughout the entire network. It shows superior performance over several compared structures when the entire network is relatively shallow. However, directly increasing residual blocks can not achieve the desired performance improvement, which may imply that the depth and internal structure of a network are related.

References

1. Hu, J., Wu, X., Zhou, J.: Single image super resolution of 3D MRI using local regression and intermodality priors. In: 8th International Conference on Digital Image Processing, vol. 10033, p. 100334C (2016)
2. Shi, W., et al.: Cardiac image super-resolution with global correspondence using multi-atlas patchmatch. In: Mori, K., Sakuma, I., Sato, Y., Barillot, C., Navab, N. (eds.) MICCAI 2013. LNCS, vol. 8151, pp. 9–16. Springer, Heidelberg (2013). https://doi.org/10.1007/978-3-642-40760-4_2
3. Rangnekar, A., Mokashi, N., Ientilucci, E., Kanan, C., Hoffman, M.: Aerial spectral super-resolution using conditional adversarial networks. arXiv:1712.08690 (2017)
4. Thornton, M.W., Atkinson, P.M., et al.: Sub-pixel mapping of rural land cover objects from fine spatial resolution satellite sensor imagery using super resolution pixel-swapping. Int. J. Remote Sens. **27**(3), 473–491 (2006)

548   X. Zhao et al.

5. Pan, Z., Yu, J., Huang, H., Zhang, A., Ma, H., Hu, S., et al.: Super-resolution based on compressive sensing and structural self-similarity for remote sensing images. IEEE Trans. Geosci. Remote Sens. **51**(9), 4864–4876 (2013)
6. Juefei-Xu, F., Savvides, M.: Single face image super-resolution via solo dictionary learning. In: IEEE International Conference on Image Processing, vol. 2, pp. 2239–2243 (2015)
7. Ahmad, T., Li, X.M.: An integrated interpolation-based super resolution reconstruction algorithm for video surveillance. J. Commun. **7**(6), 464–472 (2012)
8. Lecun, Y., Bengio, Y., Hinton, G.: Deep learning. Nature **521**, 436–444 (2015)
9. Dong, C., Loy, C.C., He, K., Tang, X.: Image super-resolution using deep convolutional networks. IEEE Trans. Pattern Anal. Mach. Intell. **38**(2), 295–307 (2016)
10. Kim, J., Lee, J.K., Lee, K.M.: Deeply-recursive convolutional network for image super resolution. In: IEEE Conference on Computer Vision and Pattern Recognition, pp. 1637–1645 (2016)
11. Tai, Y., Yang, J., Liu, X.: Image super-resolution via deep recursive residual network. In: IEEE Conference on Computer Vision and Pattern Recognition, pp. 2790–2798 (2017)
12. Kim, J., Lee, J.K., Lee, K.M.: Accurate image super-resolution using very deep convolutional networks. In: IEEE Conference on Computer Vision and Pattern Recognition, pp. 1646–1654 (2016)
13. Shi, W., Caballero, J., Huszar, F., Totz, J., et al.: Real-time single image and video super-resolution using an efficient sub-pixel convolutional neural network. In: IEEE Conference on Computer Vision and Pattern Recognition, pp. 1874–1883 (2016)
14. Ledig, C., Wang, Z., Shi, W., Theis, L., Huszar, F., Caballero, J., et al.: Photo-realistic single image super-resolution using a generative adversarial network. In: IEEE Conference on Computer Vision and Pattern Recognition, pp. 105–114 (2017)
15. Lai, W.S., Huang, J.B., Ahuja, N., Yang, M.H.: Deep laplacian pyramid networks for fast and accurate super-resolution. In: IEEE conference on Computer Vision and Pattern Recognition, pp. 5835–5843 (2017)
16. Lim, B., Son, S., Kim, H., Nah, S., Lee, K.M.: Enhanced deep residual networks for single image super-resolution. In: IEEE Conference on Computer Vision and Pattern Recognition Workshops, pp. 1132–1140 (2017)
17. Zhang, Y., Tian, Y., Kong, Y., Zhong, B., Fu, Y.: Residual dense network for image super-resolution. arXiv: 1802.08797 (2018)
18. He, K., Zhang, X., Ren, S., Sun, J.: Deep residual learning for image recognition. In: IEEE Conference on Computer Vision and Pattern Recognition, pp. 770–778 (2016)
19. He, K., Zhang, X., Ren, S., Sun, J.: Identity mappings in deep residual networks. In: Leibe, B., Matas, J., Sebe, N., Welling, M. (eds.) ECCV 2016. LNCS, vol. 9908, pp. 630–645. Springer, Cham (2016). https://doi.org/10.1007/978-3-319-46493-0_38
20. Dong, C., Loy, C.C., Tang, X.: Accelerating the super-resolution convolutional neural network. In: Leibe, B., Matas, J., Sebe, N., Welling, M. (eds.) ECCV 2016. LNCS, vol. 9906, pp. 391–407. Springer, Cham (2016). https://doi.org/10.1007/978-3-319-46475-6_25
21. Timofte, R., Lee, K.M., Wang, X., Tian, Y., et al.: NTIRE 2017 challenge on single image super-resolution: methods and results. In: Computer Vision and Pattern Recognition Workshops, pp. 1110–1121 (2017)
22. Bae, W., Yoo, J., Ye, J.C.: Beyond deep residual learning for image restoration: persistent homology-guided manifold simplification. In: Computer Vision and Pattern Recognition Workshops, pp. 1141–1149 (2017)

23. Wang, Z., Bovik, A.C., Sheikh, H.R., Simoncelli, E.P.: Image quality assessment: from error visibility to structural similarity. IEEE Trans. Image Process. **13**(4), 600–612 (2004)

24. Agustsson, E., Timofte, R.: NITRE2017 challenge on single image super-resolution: dataset and study. In: the IEEE Conference on Computer Vision and Pattern Recognition Workshops, pp. 1122–1131 (2017)

25. Bevilacqua, M., Roumy, A., Guillemot, C., Morel, A.: Low-complexity single image super-resolution based on nonnegative neighbor embedding. In: BMVC (2012)

26. Zeyde, R., Elad, M., Protter, M.: On single image scale-up using sparse-representations. In: Boissonnat, J.-D., Chenin, P., Cohen, A., Gout, C., Lyche, T., Mazure, M.-L., Schumaker, L. (eds.) Curves and Surfaces 2010. LNCS, vol. 6920, pp. 711–730. Springer, Heidelberg (2012). https://doi.org/10.1007/978-3-642-27413-8_47

27. Martin, D.R., Fowlkes, C., Tal, D., Malik, J.: A database of human segmented natural images and its application to evaluating segmentation algorithms and measuring ecological statistics. In: The 8th IEEE International Conference on Computer Vision (ICCV), pp. 416–423 (2001)

28. Huang, J.B., Singh, A., Ahuja, N.: Single image super-resolution from transformed self-exemplars. In: Computer Vision and Pattern Recognition, pp. 5197–5206 (2015)

29. Veit, A., Wilber, M., Belongie, S.: Residual networks behave like ensembles of relatively shallow networks (2016). arXiv:1605.06431 [cs.CV]

30. Kingma, D.P., Ba, J.L.: Adam: a method for stochastic optimization (2014). arXiv: 1412.6980v9 [cs.LG]

Attention Forest for Semantic Segmentation

Jingbo Wang⬚, Yajie Xing⬚, and Gang Zeng$^{(\boxtimes)}$⬚

Key Laboratory of Machine Perception, Peking University, Beijing 100871, China
{wangjingbo1219,yajie_xing}@pku.edu.cn,
zeng@cis.pku.edu.cn

Abstract. Semantic segmentation is a classical task in computer vision. In this paper, we target to address the *low confidence regions* which traditional CNN can not solve very well in semantic segmentation task. Depending on different characteristics of *low confidence regions*, an adaptive and robust attention mechanism is important to focus on the informative regions but ignore the noisy parts in the image. Intuitively, one attention map only is not sufficient to model the interaction between the *low confidence regions* and its surrounding patches. Thus, in this paper, we propose an Attention Forest structure, a novel and robust attention mechanism, to handle the *low confidence regions*. Each Attention Tree structure can capture more interactions between current patches with its adjacent regions. Experiments on PASCAL VOC 2012 Dataset validate the effectiveness of our proposed algorithm.

Keywords: Semantic segmentation · Deep learning
Attention mechanism

1 Introduction

Recently, fully convolutional networks (FCN) [16] is widely adopted as the general framework for semantic segmentation. FCN usually depends on the advanced deep network architectures, such as the ResNet, and classify every pixel in an image by shared convolution. It is difficult to predict all pixel correctly with high confidence in these structures. As shown in Fig. 1, the areas with different RGB surface are very easy to be mis-classified. According to the further experiments, their scores on probability map are also low. Thus, we define *low confidence regions* with prediction probability lower than ρ and *high confidence regions* on the counterpart. The FCN has a outstanding performance in the *high confidence regions*, but meet some trouble in *low confidence regions*, as shown in Table 1.

As shown in [4,6,10,24,26], the neural network only select some most representative regions but ignore other regions. However, in semantic segmentation task, the network should have the ability to adapt the different significations of all objects in the image. It is a challenge for the classification network architectures only based on the origin FCN network's presentation. This defect of FCN

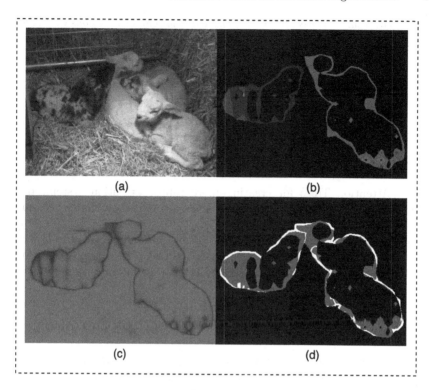

Fig. 1. This figure show the *low confidence regions* problem of semantic segmentation task we observed on PASCAL VOC 2012 [5] dataset. (b) is the prediction of FCN base network in *low confidence regions* and (d) is the ground truth in same region. (c) is the probability map of the FCN predicted categories. Shadow regions shown in (c) are the low confidence regions. In (a), boundary and complex regions always confuse the FCN.

network causes some *low confidence regions* could not be "focused on" and result in the *low confidence regions* having a terrible performance.

To adapt more object's significations and to solve the *low confidence regions* problem, we propose our Attention Forest network. Unlike others' attention mechanism, we not only generate the attention enhanced by the origin network layer by layer, but also generate the reverse attention of origin attention. Reverse attention can capture the objects or the parts which have the different significance of origin FCN network. By employing the reverse attention, the FCN network can focus on more objects. The interaction between *low confidence regions* on different objects and surroundings patches can modeled better with our sufficient attention maps and reverse attention maps. The Attention Module also can obtain large context information. So the network structure can pay close attention to all *low confidence regions* and classify these regions better. We embed this attention module into a binary tree structure and each node of the tree can generate an attention and a reverse attention. Furthermore, the Attention Forest is the combination of

Table 1. The result of *low confidence regions* and *high confidence regions* with different threshold ρ based on ResNet-101 [9]. The metric is the standard *mIOU* on PASCAL VOC 2012 [5] validation dataset.

ρ	Low confidence regions(%)	High confidence regions(%)
0.90	39.79	80.46
0.95	43.62	81.82
0.985	49.35	83.61

different Attention Trees for creating more robust attention system. In our *"search-classify"* modeling approach, we make a progress on the *low confidence regions* problem.

Our contributions are summarized as follows: (1) we propose the *low confidence regions* problem in semantic segmentation task. (2) we propose an Attention Module that has origin attention and reverse attention with large context information.

2   Related Work

Semantic Segmentation: In recently years, studies of the semantic segmentation always employ deep convolution neural networks [2,12,16] instead of the hand-crafts features [11]. In this task the most common method is enlarge the receptive field and embedding different receptive context information. In [2,3,12,24], convolution layer with dilation can capture larger receptive field information than the ordinary convolution layer. Driven by the image pyramid, mutli-scale feature ensemble is always employed in semantic segmentation to capture different scope context information. In [2], an "ASPP" module is applied for ensemble multi-scale feature and in [3] improved the"ASPP" module. [25] applied different scales average pooling in their pyramid pooling module instead of dilation convolution layers.

In [1,7,16,17] also use different level feature of the base network.They refine the outputs of the base network by using before level layer's context information. In [14] has a multi-path refine structure using different level features. In [18], a large kernel method is employed in CNN with encoder-decoder structure.

Attention in CNN: Attention mechanism is a import process in CNN to use top information guiding the feed-forward network [6,26]. In semantic segmentation task, attention mechanism is always used like a signification detection of the image. In [13], attention of CNN depends on the scale of input image. And in [19], the attention is used like a sign to let the network learn what not belong to the signification of the origin network.

3   Approach

In this section, we propose a novel network structure called Attention Forest to solve the *low confidence regions* problem in semantic segmentation task. We introduce the Attention Tree structure and its sub-module Attention Module in Sect. 3.1. In Sect. 3.2, we propose the Attention Forest structure. At last, we define our whole framework of Attention Tree and Attention Forest in Sect. 3.3.

3.1   Attention Tree

After getting the feature of the base network, the Attention Tree consists of two modules: the Binary Tree module and the Attention module. In the Binary Tree module, each branch of the tree creates refine features of the upper level features. In the Attention module, we create the attention which the network should focus on and the attention which the feature of the upper level doesn't focus on.

Definition. Let $I \in I$ donate the input image and F be the base FCN network. Feature f is created by the network as function $f = F(I)$. Let Att donate the attention map generated by attention network from feature f. The network structure of creating attention map can be written as F_{Att}.

$$Att = F_{Att}(f) \tag{1}$$

In Attention Tree module, we create reverse attention through the attention map Att from the network F_{Rev}.

$$Rev = F_{Rev}(Att) \tag{2}$$

We define the module which creates the attention feature map Att and reverse attention feature map Rev as Attention module. In attention tree ,the structure is defined like a binary tree. The ith layer jth father node of the binary tree is FC_{ij}. Based on FC_{ij}, we create attention Att_{ij} and reverse attention Rev_{ij}. LC_{ij} donates the left child node feature of FC_{ij} and RC_{ij} is the right child node feature. As shown in Fig. 3(b), we multiply LC_{ij} by Att_{ij} and multiply the RC_{ij} by Rev_{ij} to create the feature map pay attention to different regions of input image I. Each node of the binary tree structure can be a father node to create a sub-tree network like above method and then we can get a multi-layer binary tree network. We define this module as our Attention Tree module.

Attention Module: To capture the signification of different objects or parts in the image, we propose our Attention module with reverse attention in this paragraph. In Attention module, we use stack of convolution layers to estimate the function F_{Att}. As shown in Fig. 2, we use three convolution layers to create a spatial wise and channel wise attention map. Each convolution layer has a $3 \times 3 \times C$ kernel. We set BN [21] layer after each convolution layer and ReLU [8] layer only behind first two convolution layers. At the end of these layer we use a no-linear normalization function to normalize the output. Mathematically , the value of the ith layer jth attention can be wrote as

$$Att_{ij} = F_{Norm}(F_{Conv}(FC_{ij})) \tag{3}$$

In our experiment, we set the $C = 512$ and the F_{Norm} as *Sigmoid* function. So Att_{ij} can be wrote as

$$Att_{ij} = \frac{1}{1 + e^{-F_{Conv}(FC_{ij})}} \tag{4}$$

At the same time, we generate the reverse attention in this module. Reverse attention is the reverse signal of the origin attention. By using reverse attention, the network can capture semantic information or meaningful parts that the origin attention doesn't pay attention to. So we can solve the low confidence regions problem by finding the low confidence regions the network doesn't focus on firstly. To create the reverse attention, we F_{Rev} can be wrote as a simple function.

$$F_{rev}(x) = 1 - x \tag{5}$$

We suppose that the network only cares about the value of each pixel larger than 0.5. This function can create the reverse attention that care about different region from the origin attention. In our approach, we create the attention can cover all low confidence regions for semantic segmentation.

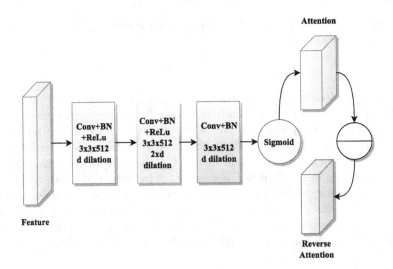

Fig. 2. Overview of our proposed attention module.We employ three *'atrous convolution'* layers to capture the attention of the given input feature. Different dilation rate can get different significations of objects or object parts. We create the reverse attention in this module.

Multi-Grid Dilation: To classify the *low confidence regions* correctly, we should use larger scale context information besides "focusing on" it. In [2], they develop the *'atrous convolution'* to capture larger context information. In our approach, we also use this attention module to capture larger scale context of the image. So as [3,23], the convolution layers in Attention module have *Multi-Grid* dilation rate and set a dilation multiplier d_i for *ith* layer' Attention module. For example, we can set the dilation grid *(1,2,1)* and the $d_i = 2$. In this setting, the three convolution layers in Attention module has dilation rate *(2,4,2)*. We can set different dilation multipliers to Attention Module in different layers. With the network going deeper, the network can capture larger extent context. The reverse attention generates different attention with the receptive field changing. In our attention tree, we set $d_{i+1} = 2 \times d_i$.

Binary Tree Module: In binary tree module, each branch of the binary tree is a Bottleneck block in ResNet-50 [9]. We set this branch to refine the feature map of the binary tree module's father node. In our model, we create a three layers binary tree for semantic segmentation task. The father node of the binary tree is the output of the base FCN model and the output of each branch is the father node of next sub binary tree module.In the third layer, we set the half of the before two layer's channel number in attention module to reduce the calculating.

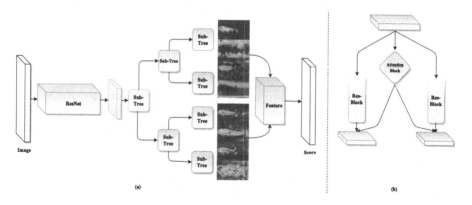

(a)   (b)

Fig. 3. (a) shows the whole pipeline of our Attention Tree Module. Given an input image, we first employ the CNN to get the output feature by the last convolution layer. Then we use a multi-layer Attention Tree module to capture part information of the input feature. The attention can pay attention to more parts of the objects than the base CNN and each branch can emphatically **solved a part region segmentation by our reverse attention mechanism.** In the Attention Tree Module, each sub-tree is shown in (b) and the Attention Block is shown in Fig. 2. The Res-Block is created same as the bottleneck module in [9].

3.2   Attention Forest

The Sect. 3.1, we particularly describe how to create an attention tree. Influenced by the random forest algorithm, we build an Attention Forest to improve the performance. The key of creating different attention trees is designing different attention module. We use different *multi-grid* rate, different base dilation rate and Global pooling attention module for designing attention forest to capture different receptive fields context information.

Atrous Convolution Attention Tree: As shown in Sect. 3.1, we employ three *atrous convolution*[2] in our attention module. Different dilation grid can capture different receptive filed and create different attention. In our attention forest, we create another two different attention trees with *atrous convolution* attention from the attention tree we proposed in Sect. 3.1 which we named $Tree_1$. Firstly, we can change the number of convolution in attention module. In $Tree_2$, We reduce one convolution layer and set the dilation grid $(1, 1)$ in $Tree_2$'s attention module. In $Tree_3$, we employ the same dilation gird but set a base dilation rate half of $Tree_1$.

Pooling Attention Tree: To make differences from the other trees, we create $Tree_4$ without *atrous convolution*. We replace the *atrous convolutions* in attention module by a global pooling and a 1×1 kernel convolution layer to capture global context but different from *atrous convolution*. This global context will enhance all point in the feature map by the same signal.

3.3   Framework

Our Attention Tree model is shown in Fig. 3. We use the pre-trained ResNet [9] as our feature network. After the feature network, we obtain the coarse segmentation feature map. We send this feature map to our Attention Tree. The outputs of our Attention Tree are 8 feature maps which have 128 channel. We concatenate these feature maps and use a $1 \times 1 \times 512$ convolution layer, a BN [21] layer and a ReLU [8] layer(*conv-bn-relu*) to ensemble different feature. Then we use a $1 \times 1 \times 21$ convolution layer and the Softmax function to obtain the prediction score map.

In our Attention Forest, as same as the Attention Tree, we send the output feature map of ResNet to each Attention tree and use the same *conv-bn-relu* block to capture different context information. We concatenate the coarse segmentation feature map and each Attention Tree's output feature map to obtion the prediction score map.

4   Experiment

In this section, we will introduce our experiment with Attention Tree and Attention Forest. We evaluate our approach on standard benchmark PASCAL VOC 2012 [5]. We choose the ResNet-101 (pre-trained on ImageNet [20]) as our base model for fine tuning.We use SGD optimization algorithm with batch size 16, momentum 0.9 and weight decay 1×10^{-5}, in our training process. We also set the a $'poly'$ learning rate (as in [12]) with initial learning 1×10^{-2} and 0.9 $power$. The performance is measured by standard mean intersection-over-union(IoU). Our baseline is the ResNet with 16× downsample by setting the last block a 2 dilation in 3×3 convolution layers.

In next subsection, we will enumerate a series of ablation experiments to evaluation the performance of our approach and show the function of the Attention Forest and Attention Tree. Then we will report the full results of our approach on PASCAL VOC 2012 test dataset.

4.1   Ablation Studies

In this subsection, we will firstly compare the results of different layer Tree structure model. Then, we will examine the effort of the attention and the reverse attention on our baseline network. Besides these, different Attention Trees and different combinations of Attention Forest will be compared.

$Layer\ matters:$ In Sect. 3.1 ,we propose that an attention tree has multi-layer structure rather than single-layer structure.The key of creating multi-layer Attention Tree is creating the different receptive field of attention in different layer. Like [3], we set gradually larger dilation rate with the Attention Tree going deeper. For example, if the attention module has three convolution layers, we can apply the multi-grid method to this module. $Mulit\text{-}Grid = (r_1, r_2, r_3)$ are applied for each attention module and the dilation rate(d_i) is multiplied by 2 with the attention adding one layer.

Table 2. The result of our model base on resnet101. The first column is the mean IOU with the whole Attention tree and the second is the tree structure without attention module in Table 2. The mean IOU is improved with the Attention tree going deeper. Compare with the tree structure has attention module or not, the attention module improve the performance in each layer.

Method	With Attention(%)	W/O Attention(%)
Baseline	73.02	73.02
Layer One	75.60	74.23
Layer Two	76.51	74.26
Layer Three	77.62	74.00

From Table 2, we can find that employing in ResNet-101, the performance of our model become better with the layer going deeper. We also compare the tree structure which has the Attention Module or not in each layer.

Reverse Attention matters: In our attention tree, the attention module is the key module of capture different region and enlarge the receptive. In our proposed model, we compare our attention module with the attention module doesn't have the reverse attention. As shown in 3, employing ResNet-101, our Attention Module achieve a better performance both in mIOU or the *low confidence regions* mIOU. So from Table 3, our reverse attention supplement the origin attention and both of them solve the low confidence regions jointly, better than only use the origin attention.

Table 3. Compare the mIOU and the *low confidence regions* mIOU based on ResNet-101,The first line is the baseline of ResNet-101 in mIOU and hard IOU, the second line is the result of the Attention Tree module without the reverse attention. The third line is the result of our Attention Tree.

Method	mIOU(%)	*LCR* mIOU(%)
Baseline	73.02	39.79
W/O Reverse	76.50	50.31
With Reverse	77.62	54.08

Further more, in Sect. 3.2, we create an Attention Forest model for segmentation task. The forest based on different tree with different Attention Module. Different Attention Module can capture different size receptive field context information and different type context information. As shown in Sect. 3.2, we compare different combination of these Attention Trees in Table 4.

In Table ??, we find that our Attention Tree which defines in Sect. 3.1 achieve the best performance of the four Attention Tree. But in our Attention forest, we just want to use some weak feature extractor and make a strong feature extractor. We compare the different combination of these trees.From the Table 4, we find that the performance in mIOU and Hard mIOU is improved by combining more

Table 4. Compare the mIOU and the *low confidence regions* mIOU of different attention tree combination based on ResNet-101.

Method	mIOU(%)	LCR mIOU(%)
Baseline	73.02	39.79
Tree-1	77.62	54.08
Tree-1,2	78.15	55.53
Tree-1,2,3,4	78.52	56.94

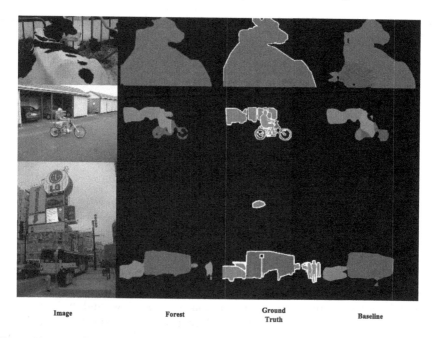

| Image | Forest | Ground Truth | Baseline |

Fig. 4. Examples of our prediction on Pascal VOC 2012 validation dataset.We can find that the low confidence regions can be solved and more objects can be found in our method.

Attention Trees. The whole Attention Forest can achieve 78.52% in mIOU and 56.94% in hard mIOU, which has a 0.9% and 2.86% improvement in mIOU and hard mIOU than the single Attention Tree.

4.2   Experiment

In this subsection, we will discuss our experiment on PASCAL VOC 2012 dataset. We use flip both in training and evaluation for our network.

PASCAL VOC 2012: We split our experiment into three stages. (1) *stage-1*,we mix up PASCAL VOC 2012 images and SBD for training, like ablation study. (2) *stage-1*,we only employ PASCAL VOC 2012 dataset and fine-tune the pre-train model in *stage-2*. We achieve a 80.52% mIOU on validation dataset and 79.97% on test dataset. (3) We fine-tune our model on MS-COCO [22] dataset and finally achieve 84.60% mIoU. We choose some prediction on PASCAL VOC 2012 validation dataset and show in Fig. 4 (Table 5).

Table 5. Results on PASCAL VOC 2012 testing set. [*] means pre-trained on MS-COCO dataset.

Method	mIOU(%)
FCN [16]	62.2
Deep [12]	71.6
CRF-RNN [27]	72.0
Piecewise [15]	75.3
Ours	79.97
Ours[*]	84.60

5 Conclusions

Our proposed Attention Forest is the combination of different types of Attention Tree. Each Attention Tree can capture large receptive context information and it's reverse information.This structure can find all objects in the image and solve the *low confidence regions* problem. In our ablation experiment, we find the large receptive attention and our reverse attention in Attention Forest structure can enhance the performance in *"low confidence regions"*. We do experiments on PASCAL VOC 2012 and achieve a comparable result against the *state-of-the-art* methods.

Acknowledgements. This work is supported by the National Key Research and Development Program of China (2017YFB1002601) and National Natural Science Foundation of China (61375022,61403005,61632003).

References

1. Badrinarayanan, V., Handa, A., Cipolla, R.: Segnet: A deep convolutional encoder-decoder architecture for robust semantic pixel-wise labelling. IEEE Trans. Pattern Anal. Mach. Intell. (2017)
2. Chen, L.C., Papandreou, G., Kokkinos, I., Murphy, K., Yuille, A.L.: DeepLab: semantic image segmentation with deep convolutional nets, atrous convolution, and fully connected CRFs. IEEE Trans. Pattern Anal. Mach. Intell. **40**, 834–848 (2018)
3. Chen, L.C., Papandreou, G., Schroff, F., Adam, H.: Rethinking atrous convolution for semantic image segmentation. arXiv preprint arXiv:1706.05587 (2017)
4. Walther, D., Itti, L., Riesenhuber, M., Poggio, T., Koch, C.: Attentional selection for object recognition — a gentle way. In: Bülthoff, H.H., Wallraven, C., Lee, S.-W., Poggio, T.A. (eds.) BMCV 2002. LNCS, vol. 2525, pp. 472–479. Springer, Heidelberg (2002). https://doi.org/10.1007/3-540-36181-2_47
5. Everingham, M., Van Gool, L., Williams, C.K.I., Winn, J., Zisserman, A.: The PASCAL Visual Object Classes Challenge 2012 (VOC2012) Results. http://www.pascal-network.org/challenges/VOC/voc2012/workshop/index.html
6. Wang, F., et al.: Residual attention network for image classification. In: Proceedings of the IEEE Conference on Computer Vision and Pattern Recognition, pp. 3156–3164 (2017)

7. Ghiasi, G., Fowlkes, C.C.: Laplacian pyramid reconstruction and refinement for semantic segmentation. In: Leibe, B., Matas, J., Sebe, N., Welling, M. (eds.) ECCV 2016. LNCS, vol. 9907, pp. 519–534. Springer, Cham (2016). https://doi.org/10.1007/978-3-319-46487-9_32

8. Glorot, X., Bordes, A., Bengio, Y.: Deep sparse rectifier neural networks. In: Proceedings of the Fourteenth International Conference on Artificial Intelligence and Statistics (2011)

9. He, K., Zhang, X., Ren, S., Sun, J.: Deep residual learning for image recognition. In: Proceedings of the IEEE Conference on Computer Vision and Pattern Recognition, pp. 770–778 (2016)

10. Gregor, K., Danihelka, I., Graves, A., Rezende, D.J., Wierstra, D.: Draw: a recurrent neural network for image generation (2015)

11. Kae A, Sohn K, Lee, H.: Augmenting CRFs with Boltzmann machine shape priors for image labeling, pp. 2019–2026 (2013)

12. Chen, L.-C., Papandreou, G., Kokkinos, I., Murphy, K., Yuille, A.L.: Semantic image segmentation with deep convolutional nets and fully connected CRFs (2015)

13. Chen, L.-C., Yang, Y., Wang, J., Xu, W., Yuille, A.L.: Attention to scale: scale-aware semantic image segmentation. In: Proceedings of the IEEE Conference on Computer Vision and Pattern Recognition, pp. 3641–3649 (2016)

14. Lin, G., Milan, A., Shen, C., Reid, I.: RefineNet: Multi-path refinement networks with identity mappings for high-resolution semantic segmentation (2017)

15. Lin, G., Shen, C., van den Hengel, A., Reid, I.: Efficient piecewise training of deep structured models for semantic segmentation. In: Proceedings of the IEEE Conference on Computer Vision and Pattern Recognition, pp. 3194–3203 (2016)

16. Long, J., Shelhamer, E., Darrell, T.: Fully convolutional networks for semantic segmentation. In: Proceedings of the IEEE Conference on Computer Vision and Pattern Recognition, pp. 3431–3440 (2015)

17. Noh, H., Hong, S., Han, B.: Learning deconvolution network for semantic segmentation. In: Proceedings of the IEEE International Conference on Computer Vision, pp. 1520–1528 (2015)

18. Peng, C., Zhang, X., Yu, G., Luo, G., Sun, J.: Large kernel matters-improve semantic segmentation by global convolutional network (2017)

19. Huang, Q., et al.: Semantic segmentation with reverse attention (2017)

20. Russakovsky, O., et al.: ImageNet large scale visual recognition challenge. Int. J. Comput. Vis. (IJCV) 115(3), 211–252 (2015). https://doi.org/10.1007/s11263-015-0816-y

21. Ioffe, S., Szegedy, C.: Batch normalization: Accelerating deep network training by reducing internal covariate shift, pp. 448–456 (2015)

22. Lin, T.-Y., et al.: Microsoft COCO: common objects in context. In: Fleet, D., Pajdla, T., Schiele, B., Tuytelaars, T. (eds.) ECCV 2014. LNCS, vol. 8693, pp. 740–755. Springer, Cham (2014). https://doi.org/10.1007/978-3-319-10602-1_48

23. Wang, P., et al.: Understanding convolution for semantic segmentation. arXiv preprint arXiv:1702.08502 (2017)

24. Yu, F., Koltun, V.: Multi-scale context aggregation by dilated convolutions. arXiv preprint arXiv:1511.07122 (2015)

25. Zhao, H., Shi, J., Qi, X., Wang, X., Jia, J.: Pyramid scene parsing network (2017)

26. Zhao B, Wu X, F.J.: Diversified visual attention networks for fine-grained object classification. arXiv:1606.08572 (2016)

27. Zheng, S., et al.: Conditional random fields as recurrent neural networks. In: Proceedings of the IEEE International Conference on Computer Vision, pp. 1529–1537 (2015)

Episode-Experience Replay Based Tree-Backup Method for Off-Policy Actor-Critic Algorithm

Haobo Jiang, Jianjun Qian[✉], Jin Xie, and Jian Yang

Key Laboratory Intelligent Perception and Systems for High Dimensional Information of Ministry of Education, School of Computer Science and Engineering, Nanjing University of Science and Technology, Nanjing 210094, China
{jiang.hao.bo,csjqian,csjxie,csjyang}@njust.edu.cn

Abstract. Off-policy algorithms have played important roles in deep reinforcement learning. Since the off-policy based policy gradient is a biased estimation, the previous works employed importance sampling to achieve the unbiased estimation, where the behavior policy is known in advance. However, it is difficult to choose the reasonable behavior policy for complex agents. Moreover, importance sampling usually produces the large variance. To address these problems, this paper presents a novel actor-critic policy gradient algorithm. Specifically, we employ the tree-backup method in off-policy setting to achieve the unbiased estimation of target policy gradient without using importance sampling. Meanwhile, we combine the naive episode-experience replay and the experience replay to obtain the trajectory samples and reduce the strong correlations between these samples. The experimental results demonstrate the advantages of the proposed method over the competed methods.

Keywords: Off-policy actor-critic policy gradient
Tree-backup algorithm · All-action method · Episode-experience replay

1 Introduction

In reinforcement learning, off-policy methods have been receiving much more attention. It breaks the dilemma of on-policy methods that the agent only can learn the policy it is executing. In off-policy setting, the agent is able to learn its target policy while executing another behavior policy. There are mainly two forms of off-policy algorithms, one based on the value function and the other based on the policy gradient.

The value-function approach has worked well in many applications. Q-learning, the prototype of DQN [9], is a classical value function based off-policy algorithm [16]. Different from the on-policy value function methods such as SARSA, Q-learning directly learns its optimal action-value function by executing an exploratory policy. However, Q-learning is just guaranteed to converge

© Springer Nature Switzerland AG 2018
J.-H. Lai et al. (Eds.): PRCV 2018, LNCS 11256, pp. 562–573, 2018.
https://doi.org/10.1007/978-3-030-03398-9_48

to optimal policy for the tabular case and may diverge when using function approximation [2]. The large overestimations of the action values also may lead it to perform poorly in many stochastic environments [1,3,5]. Using off-policy per-decision importance sampling Monte-Carlo method [11] is also a choice. However, using importance sampling to correct bias may produce large variance and therefore makes the learning unstable. In recent years, the work of Harutyunyan et al. [4] shows that if the behavior policy μ and target policy π are not too far away, off-policy policy evaluation, without correcting for the "off-policyness" of a trajectory, still converges to the desired Q^π. Using this conclusion, when μ is similar to π, we can directly think of the off-policy methods as the on-policy methods and don't need to use importance sampling technique as before. However, the similarity between policies are difficult to control which makes their method is restrictive and not practical. Thus, using importance sampling seems to be still inevitable. Remi Munos et al. [10] proposed a new off-policy algorithm, Retrace(λ), which uses an importance sampling ratio truncated at 1. and can safely use samples collected from any behavior policy μ regardless of the μ's degree of "off-policyness". However, one of its inherent disadvantages is that the existence of importance sampling ratio makes it have to select a explicit behavior policy μ in training and as we all know, the training performance is directly affected by behavior policy, but choosing a reasonable behavior policy, especially for a complex agent, is often a difficult task.

From the perspective of policy gradient, Degris et al. [5] proposes the off-policy policy-gradient theorem and introduces the first off-policy actor-critic method, called off-PAC. This method uses the actor-critic framework in which critic learns an off-policy estimator of the action value function by GTD(λ) algorithm and this estimator is then used by the actor to update the policy which uses incremental update algorithm with eligibility traces. However, facing the problem of biased estimation caused by different sample distribution, the gradient of objective function in off-PAC also chooses to use the importance sampling technique. Following the off-policy policy gradient theorem, Ziyu Wang et al. proposes a new off-policy actor critic algorithm with experience replay, called ACER [15]. To make it stable, sample efficient, and perform remarkably well on challenging environments, it introduces many innovations, such as truncated importance sampling technique, stochastic dueling network architectures, and a new trust region policy optimization method. However, like the problem in Retrace(λ), it also need to choose a reasonable behavior policy which sometimes is a hard work.

In summary, using importance sampling technique to correct the sample distribution difference is a popular method. Simultaneously, in order to avoid variance explosion problem of ordinary importance sampling, many variants of importance sampling are proposed, such as weighted importance sampling [8] or truncated importance sampling etc. However, it should be noted that these variants often come at the cost of increasing bias of the estimator. In addition, the most key drawback of importance sampling is that its behavior policy should be known, Markov(purely a function of the current state), and represented as explicit action probabilities. However, for complex agents, none of these may be true [11].

Based on the discussion above, we try to improve the estimator from the perspective of actor and critic to make our off-policy policy gradient estimator unbiased theoretically without using importance sampling technique. In detail, we use all-action method [14] in actor and exploit tree-backup method to achieve unbiased n-step return to estimate the action value function in critic. Meanwhile, inspired by the experience replay technique, in order to provide tree-backup algorithm with enough low correlation trajectory samples in learning process, we propose the episode-experience replay, which combines the naive episode-experience replay and experience replay. The experimental results demonstrate the advantages of the proposed method over the competed methods.

2 Preliminaries and Notation

In this paper, we consider the episodic framework, in which the agent interacts with its environment in a sequence of episodes, numbered $m = 1, 2, \ldots$, each of which consists of a finite number of time steps, $t = 0, 1, 2, \ldots, T_{end}^m$. The first state of each episode, $s_0 \in S$ is chosen according to a fixed initial distribution $p_0(s_0)$. We model the problem as a Markov decision processes which comprises: a state space S, an discrete action space A, a distribution $P : S \times S \times A \to [0, 1]$, where $p(s'|s, a)$ is the probability of transitioning into state s' from state s after taking action a, and an expected reward function $R : S \times A \to \mathbb{R}$ that provided an expected reward $r(s, a)$ for taking action a in state s and transitioning into s'. We assume here that A is finite and the environment is completely characterized by one-step state-transition probabilities, $p(s'|s, a)$, and expected rewards, $r(s, a)$, for all $s, s' \in S$ and $a \in A$.

The target policy of an agent is noted as π_θ which maps states to a probability distribution over the actions $\pi_\theta : S \to P(A)$, where $\theta \in \mathbb{R}^n$ is a vector of n parameters. The return from a state is defined as the sum of discounted future reward $R_t = \sum_{i=t}^{T_{end}} \gamma^{i-t} r(s_i, a_i)$ with a discounted factor $\gamma \in [0, 1]$. Note that the return depends on the actions chosen, and therefore on the policy, and may be stochastic. We defined the state-value function for π_θ to be: $V^{\pi_\theta}(s) = E_{\pi_\theta}(R_0|s_0 = s)$ and action-value function: $Q^{\pi_\theta}(s, a) = E_{\pi_\theta}(R_0|s_0 = s, a_0 = a)$, both of which are the expected total discounted reward.

The behavior policy is noted as $b_\mu : S \to P(A)$, where $\mu \in \mathbb{R}^m$ is a vector of m parameters. We observe a stream of data, which includes state $s_t \in S$, action $a_t \in A$, and reward $r_t \in \mathbb{R}$ for $t = 1, 2, \ldots$ with actions selected from a distinct behavior policy, $b_\mu(a|s) \in (0, 1)$. Our aim is to choose θ so as to maximize the following scalar objective function:

$$J(\theta) = \sum_{s \in S} d^b(s) V^{\pi_\theta}(s) \tag{1}$$

where $d^b(s) = lim_{t \to \infty} P(s_t = s|s_0, b)$ is the limiting distribution of states under b and $P(s_t = s|s_0, b)$ is the probability that $s_t = s$ when starting in s_0 and executing b. The objective function is weighted by d^b for the reason that in the off-policy setting, data is obtained according to the behavior distribution. For simplicity of notation, we will write π and implicitly mean π_θ.

3   Off-Policy Actor-Critic Combined with Tree-Backup

In off-policy setting, for the reason that using samples from behavior policy's distribution different from the sample distribution of target policy to calculate the naive policy gradient estimator may introduce the bias and therefore changes the solution that the estimator will converge to [12], many off-policy methods choose to use importance sampling technique, one general technique for correcting this bias of estimator. However, as discussed above, taking into account the shortcomings of this technology such as acquiring behavior policy to explicitly be represented as action probabilities and may leading the estimator to cause large variance, we choose to use all-action method and tree-backup algorithm to allow the estimator can estimate the policy gradient without using importance sampling.

3.1   Off-Policy Actor-Critic

The off-policy policy-gradient theorem proposed by Degris et al. [5] is:

$$g(\theta) = E_{s_t,a_t \sim b}[\rho(s_t, a_t)\psi(s_t, a_t)Q^\pi(s_t, a_t)] \tag{2}$$

where $\rho(s, a) = \frac{\pi(a|s)}{b(a|s)}$ is the ordinary importance sampling ratio, $\psi(s, a) = \frac{\nabla_\theta \pi(a|s)}{\pi(a|s)}$ is the eligibility vector. Using ordinary importance sampling radio $\rho(s, a)$ in equation above can achieve the unbiased estimator of the actor-critic policy gradient under target policy π given samples from the behavior policy b's sample distribution. However, in the case that an unlikely event occurs, $\rho(s, a)$ can be very large and thus leads the estimator to cause a high variance and instability. There are also many techniques to reduce the variance of the estimator, at the cost of introducing the bias, such as weighted importance sampling technique which performs a weighted average of the samples and therefore smooth the variance [8] or importance weight truncation technique which directly uses constant value c to truncate the importance sampling ratio, i.e. $\overline{\rho_t} = min\{c, \rho_t\}$ [15], etc. However, the most key inherent drawback of importance sampling technique is that its behavior policy should be known, Markov(purely a function of the current state), and represented as explicit action probabilities. But for complex agents, none of these may be true [6].

3.2   Off-Policy Actor-Critic Combined with All-Action and Tree-Backup

Based on the disadvantages of the importance sampling discussed above, we try to find another way to eliminate the bias without using importance sampling.

Here, firstly, we start from the Eq. (2) and do some changes on it. This process is shown as below:

$$
\begin{aligned}
g(\theta) &= E_{s_t,a_t \sim b}[\rho(s_t,a_t)\psi(s_t,a_t)Q^\pi(s_t,a_t)] \\
&= E_{s_t,a_t \sim b}[\rho(s_t,a_t)\psi(s_t,a_t)Q^\pi(s_t,a_t))] \\
&= E_{s_t \sim d^b}[\sum_{a \in A} b(a|s_t)\frac{\pi(a|s_t)}{b(a|s_t)}\frac{\nabla_\theta \pi(a|s_t)}{\pi(a|s_t)}Q^\pi(s_t,a)] \\
&= E_{s_t \sim d^b}[\sum_{a \in A} \nabla_\theta \pi(a|s_t)Q^\pi(s_t,a))] \\
&= E_{s_t \sim d^b}[\nabla_\theta \pi(a_t|s_t)Q^\pi(s_t,a_t) + \sum_{a \in A, a \neq a_t} \nabla_\theta \pi(a|s_t)Q^\pi(s_t,a)]
\end{aligned} \tag{3}
$$

where we extract the series over actions to remove random variable a_t. Such operation can avoid introducing importance sampling in the actor. Algorithms of this form are called all-action methods because an update is made for all actions possible in each state encountered irrespective of which action was actually taken [14].

Since the exact value of action value function $Q^\pi(s,a)$ is unknown, the next step is to replace $Q^\pi(s,a)$ with some estimator. Here, limited by the lack of trajectory samples starting with the s_t, $a(a \neq a_t)$, we can only use action-value function approximation $Q^\omega(s_t,a)$ to estimate $Q^\pi(s_t,a)$ directly. But for $Q^\pi(s_t,a_t)$, considering the error reduction property of n-step return [13] and that we can obtain the trajectory samples beginning with s_t, a_t, we choose to use n-step return to estimate it.

However, due to the difference of sample distribution, directly using naive n-step return to estimate will produce bias. Thus, we need some techniques to remove this bias. In order to avoid the disadvantages of importance sampling, we choose to use tree-backup algorithm to estimate the $Q^\pi(s_t,a_t)$. Tree-backup algorithm itself is designed to estimate the action-value function in off-policy setting. At each step along a trajectory, there are several possible choices according to the target policy. The one-step target combines the value estimations for these actions according to their probabilities of being taken under the target policy. At each step, the behavior policy chooses one of the actions, and for that action, one time step later, there is a new estimation of its value, based on the reward received and the estimated value of the next state. The tree-backup algorithm then forms a new target, using the old value estimations for the actions that were not taken, and the new estimated value for the action that was taken [11]. If the process above is iterated over n steps, we can get the n-step tree-backup estimator $G_{t:t+n}$ of $Q^\pi(s_t,a_t)$:

$$
G_{t:t+n} = \gamma^n Q(s_{t+n},a_{t+n})\prod_{i=t+1}^{t+n}\pi_i + \sum_{k=t+1}^{t+n}\gamma^{k-t+1}\prod_{i=t+1}^{k-1}\pi_i[r_k + \gamma\sum_{a \neq a_k}\pi(a|s_k)Q(s_k,a)] \tag{4}
$$

where π_i is short for $\pi(a_i|s_i)$. In order to improve the computational efficiency, we can use the iterative form as below:

$$G_{t:t+n} = r_{t+1} + \gamma \sum_{a \neq a_{t+1}} \pi(a|s_{t+1})Q(s_{t+1}, a) + \gamma\pi(a_{t+1}|s_{t+1})G_{t+1:t+n} \quad (5)$$

In general, we replace the $Q^\pi(s_t, a)$ with differentiable action-value function $Q^\omega(s_t, a)$ directly, and use n-step tree-backup estimator $G_{t:t+n}$ to replace the $Q^\pi(s_t, a_t)$. So, we can get the estimator $g(\hat\theta)$ as below to estimate the off-policy actor-critic policy gradient $g(\theta)$:

$$g(\hat\theta) = \frac{1}{N}\sum_{i=1}^{N}[\nabla_\theta\pi(a_i|s_i;\theta)G_{i:i+n} + \sum_{a \in A, a \neq a_i} \nabla_\theta\pi(a|s_i;\theta)Q^\omega(s_i, a))] \quad (6)$$

where $G_{i:i+n} = r_{i+1} + \gamma\sum_{a \neq a_{i+1}}\pi(a|s_{i+1};\theta)Q^\omega(s_{i+1}, a) + \gamma\pi(a_{i+1}|s_{i+1})G_{i+1:i+n}$.

One key advantage of tree-backup algorithm is that we won't need to determine the behavior policy any more. As we all know, the selection of behavior policy directly affects the algorithm's performance and choosing a reasonable behavior policy, especially for a complex agent, is always a difficult task.

It should be noted that the selection of n reflects the trade-off of bias and variance [15]. Typically the only-actor policy gradient estimators using Monte-Carlo return R_t as its critic, such as REINFORCE [17], will have higher variance and lower bias whereas the actor-critic estimators using function approximation as critic will have higher bias and lower variance. The greater the value of n is selected, the more information the $G_{t:t+n}$ will get and therefore the smaller bias the $G_{t:t+n}$ will produce, however, the larger the variance of $G_{t:t+n}$ will be. Extremely when $n = 0$, then $G_{t:t+n}$ degenerates the normal $Q^\omega(s_t, a_t)$. In the experimental part of this paper, we will explain this problem through one simple experiment.

3.3 Episode-Experience Replay

In practice, the experiences obtained by trial-and-error usually take an expensive price, such as the loss of the equipment or the consumption of the time, etc. If these experiences are just utilized to adjust the networks only once and then thrown away, it may be very wasteful [7]. Experience replay technique is a straight and effective way to reuse the experience. DQN [9] uses the experience replay which store the experiences from the Atari games to gain the excellent performance.

There is no doubt that experience replay technique is very useful for one-step TD algorithms. However, tree-backup algorithm or other n-step TD algorithms all need trajectory samples rather than single experience samples. In previous papers, people usually execute one behavior policy and exploit the eligibility trace with importance sampling to learn along off-policy trajectory in the on-line way or use one behavior policy to produce an off-policy episode, and then use this episode to achieve trajectory samples to learn in the off-line way, et. There are some inherent drawbacks in those sampling methods. Firstly, because these trajectory samples stems from a same episode, there is strong correlations between samples. Secondly, it is difficult to provide the training with sufficient samples productively like the experience replay. Last but not least, these sampling methods also need a behavior policy explicitly represented as action probabilities, which, as we discussed above, is not an easy work.

In order to overcome all these shortcomings above, we propose episode-experience replay technique which combines the naive episode-experience replay technique and experience replay technique. Unlike the experience replay which just stores the single experience $(s_t, a_t, r_t, s_{t+1}) \sim b$, episode-experience replay works on episodes by storing the complete episode $s_0, a_0, r_1, s_1, a_1, r_2, s_2 \ldots \sim b$ in the episode-experience pool and selecting episodes from the pool randomly. For the reason that the policy parameters are updated all the time, therefore the episodes stored in pool which are originated from policy with old parameters can be viewed as off-policy episodes. In off-policy setting, this way is able to provide enough off-policy episodes productively for agent to learn and can greatly improve the data efficiency and the speed that we achieve the off-policy samples. However, directly using consecutive samples $\{(s_t, a_t, r_{t+1}, s_{t+1})_{t=0:T^i_{end}-1}\}_{i=1\ldots M}$ from those selected episodes, which we called naive episode-experience replay, as a training batch to learn is ineffective, due to the strong correlations between samples. So we combine the experience replay and episode-experience replay to get off-policy episode samples effectively while reducing correlations between samples. The process is shown as below in Fig. 1:

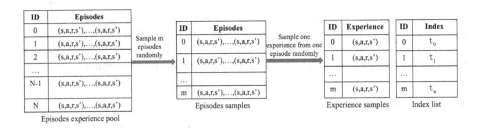

Fig. 1. The process of sampling in episode experience replay.

In this process, we first select m episode samples randomly from episode-experience pool. Then from each episode, we just produce only one trajectory sample. In detail, we also randomly choose one experience in each episode and use it as the starting point of the trajectory sample. The terminal point of trajectory point is the last experience of each episode. It should be noted that when we choose a starting experience in each episode, we should use one list to record the place in the corresponding episode for that experience which can help us go back to the trajectory's concrete position in episode quickly. At the same time, the m experience samples just can be used as the training samples to train critic.

3.4   Algorithm

Pseudocode for our method is shown in Algorithm 1. Here, in order not to introduce the importance sampling, we use deep q-learning algorithm to train the critic network and the training samples for critic come from the starting experiences sampled in the process of episode-experience replay. For the reason that the network Q^ω being updated is also used in calculating the target value and it will make the target value drastically change with the change of the Q^ω's parameters which may cause instability, inspired by [6], we use target network $Q^{\omega'}$ to calculate the target value and use the "soft" target update, rather than directly copying the weights.

Algorithm 1. Off-policy Actor-Critic With Tree-Backup Based On Episode Experience Replay

---

1: Initialize action-value function Q^ω and target policy π_θ with random weights.
2: Initialize target action-value function $Q^{\omega'}$ with weights $\omega' \leftarrow \omega$.
3: Initialize episode-experience memory D.
4: **for** $episodeIdx = 1 \rightarrow L$ **do**
5:      Initial episodeBuff=[ ], t=0.
6:      Receive initial observation state s_0.
7:      **while** $s_t \neq s_{end}$ **do**
8:          Select action a_t and execute a_t and observe r_{t+1}, s_{t+1}.
9:          Store transition $(s_t, a_t, r_{t+1}, s_{t+1})$ in episodeBuff.
10:          Sample M episodes from D and using episode-experience replay technique
11:          to choose a random trajectory from each episode:

$$\{(s_t, a_t, r_{t+1}, s_{t+1})_{t=l^i:T^i_{end}-1}\}_{i=1...M}$$

12:          Using experience samples $\{s_{l^i}, a_{l^i}, r_{l^i+1}, s_{l^i+1}\}_{i=1...M}$ to update Q^ω by
13:          minimizing the loss: $L_Q = \frac{1}{M}\sum_{i=1}^{M}(y_i - Q^\omega(s_i, a_i))^2$ where
14:

$$y_i = r_{i+1} + \gamma\mathbb{1}\{s_{i+1} \neq s_{end}\}max_a Q^{\omega'}(s_{i+1}, a)$$

15:          Using trajectory samples to update π_θ by policy gradient $g(\hat{\theta})$.
16:          Update the target networks: $\omega' \leftarrow \tau\omega + (1 - \tau)\omega'$.
17:      **end while**
18:      Store episodeBuff in D and t=t+1
19: **end for**

---

4   Experiment

In this section, we will check the rationality and effectiveness of our algorithm by learning under several simulation environments from OpenAI gym. We designed our experiment to investigative the following questions:

1. What are the effect that different choices of n make on the algorithm performance?
2. Compared to the original sampling method, using episode-experience Replay will bring much improvement in performance?
3. Compared to some commonly used reinforcement learning methods, how much improvement will out algorithm bring?

4.1 Performance Comparison on Difference Choices of n

As we propose in Sect. 3, the choice of n reflects the trade-off of variance and bias. Here, we use the CartPole-v0 simulation environment and choose $n = 1, 3, 6, 9, 15$ for training. Figure 2 shows performance comparison on different n. We can find that different choices of n have a direct effect on the algorithm' s performance and in this simulation environment, in terms of stability, convergence speed and performance, $n = 9$ is the best choice relatively (Here, we use naive episode-experience replay to highlight the effect).

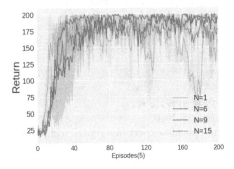

Fig. 2. Compare on different choice of n.

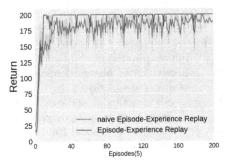

Fig. 3. Compare on different sampling methods.

4.2 Performance Comparison on Difference Sampling Methods

In this subsection, we mainly compare the algorithm's performance when using two kind different trajectory sampling methods, naive episode-experience replay and episode-experience replay during training. Due to the strong correlations between samples from naive episode-experience replay, as Fig. 3 shows, it has great fluctuations in performance during training. We can Obviously find that regardless of convergence speed and algorithm stability, episode-experience replay is more advantageous than naive episode-experience replay.

4.3 Performance Comparison with Other Conventional Algorithms

We compare the algorithm's performance with DQN and Actor-Critic algorithm under three simulation environments from OpenAI Gym: CartPole-v0, MountainCar-v0, Acrobot-v0. As Fig. 4 shows, compared to DQN, Actor-Critic policy gradient algorithm performs more stable during training. DQN seems to have a great volatility which may stems from the inherent drawback of value function method, discontinuous change of policy based on value function. However, although Actor-Critic algorithm is more stable than DQN, the final performance it converges to is worser than DQN. Table 1 lists the average return of each algorithm, our method achieve the highest average return under these three simulation environments. In general, from the perspective of convergence speed and performance stability, our method performs better.

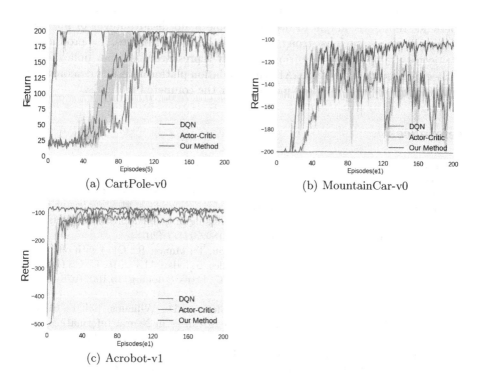

(a) CartPole-v0   (b) MountainCar-v0

(c) Acrobot-v1

Fig. 4. Compare with other methods.

Table 1. Compare average return

Environment	DQN	Actor-critic	Our method
CartPole-v0	135.24	105.5	**193.0**
MountainCar-v0	−154.5	−200.0	**−122.0**
Acrobot-v1	−115.0	−137.0	**−87.45**

5 Conclusion

In this paper, we mainly study the Actor-Critic policy gradient problems in off-policy setting. Considering sample distribution difference between behavior policy and target policy will cause the estimator to produce bias and the the limitations of using the importance sampling technique, we use all-action method and tree-backup algorithm to allow the estimator to use samples from behavior policy directly to unbiasedly estimate the target policy gradient. Here, the all-action method helps remove the random variable a_t, thus we can avoid importance sampling in the actor. The tree-backup method can help avoid importance sampling in the critic when using n-step return as the estimator of action value function.

In addition, in order to improve efficiency, we propose episode-experience replay technique which combines naive episode-experience replay technique and experience replay technique to overcome some main disadvantages of previous sampling methods, such as strong correlations between samples, low production of trajectory samples and requiring explicitly represented behavior policy, etc.

By experiments on the OpenAI gym simulation platform, results demonstrate the advantages of the proposed method over the competed methods.

References

1. Anschel, O., Baram, N., Shimkin, N.: Averaged-DQN: Variance reduction and stabilization for deep reinforcement learning. arXiv preprint arXiv:1611.01929 (2016)
2. Degris, T., White, M., Sutton, R.S.: Off-policy actor-critic. CoRR abs/1205.4839 (2012). http://arxiv.org/abs/1205.4839
3. Fujimoto, S., van Hoof, H., Meger, D.: Addressing function approximation error in actor-critic methods. arXiv preprint arXiv:1802.09477 (2018)
4. Harutyunyan, A., Bellemare, M.G., Stepleton, T., Munos, R.: Q(λ) with off-policy corrections. In: Ortner, R., Simon, H.U., Zilles, S. (eds.) ALT 2016. LNCS (LNAI), vol. 9925, pp. 305–320. Springer, Cham (2016). https://doi.org/10.1007/978-3-319-46379-7_21
5. Hasselt, H.V.: Double Q-learning. In: Lafferty, J.D., Williams, C.K.I., Shawe-Taylor, J., Zemel, R.S., Culotta, A. (eds.) Advances in Neural Information Processing Systems 23, pp. 2613–2621. Curran Associates Inc. (2010). http://papers.nips.cc/paper/3964-double-q-learning.pdf
6. Lillicrap, T.P., et al.: Continuous control with deep reinforcement learning. arXiv preprint arXiv:1509.02971 (2015)
7. Lin, L.J.: Reinforcement learning for robots using neural networks. Technical report. School of Computer Science, Carnegie-Mellon University, Pittsburgh, PA (1993)
8. Mahmood, A.R., van Hasselt, H.P., Sutton, R.S.: Weighted importance sampling for off-policy learning with linear function approximation. In: Advances in Neural Information Processing Systems, pp. 3014–3022 (2014)
9. Mnih, V., et al.: Playing Atari with deep reinforcement learning. arXiv preprint arXiv:1312.5602 (2013)

10. Munos, R., Stepleton, T., Harutyunyan, A., Bellemare, M.: Safe and efficient off-policy reinforcement learning. In: Advances in Neural Information Processing Systems, pp. 1054–1062 (2016)
11. Precup, D., Sutton, R.S., Singh, S.P.: Eligibility traces for off-policy policy evaluation. In: ICML, pp. 759–766. Citeseer (2000)
12. Schaul, T., Quan, J., Antonoglou, I., Silver, D.: Prioritized experience replay. arXiv preprint arXiv:1511.05952 (2015)
13. Sutton, R.S., Barto, A.G.: Reinforcement Learning: An introduction, vol. 1. MIT Press, Cambridge (1998)
14. Sutton, R.S., Singh, S., McAllester, D.: Comparing policy-gradient algorithms (2000). http://citeseerx.ist.psu.edu/viewdoc/download
15. Wang, Z., et al.: Sample efficient actor-critic with experience replay. arXiv preprint arXiv:1611.01224 (2016)
16. Watkins, C.J., Dayan, P.: Q-learning. Mach. Learn. **8**(3–4), 279–292 (1992)
17. Williams, R.J.: Simple statistical gradient-following algorithms for connectionist reinforcement learning. In: Sutton, R.S. (ed.) Reinforcement Learning. SECS, vol. 173, pp. 5–32. Springer, Boston (1992). https://doi.org/10.1007/978-1-4615-3618-5_2

Multi-scale Cooperative Ranking for Saliency Detection

Bo Jiang, Xingyue Jiang, Aihua Zheng, Yun Xiao, and Jin Tang[✉]

School of Computer Science and Technology, Anhui University,
No.111 Jiulong Road, Hefei, China
{jiangbo,ahzheng214,xiaoyun,tj}@ahu.edu.cn,
jxyahu@foxmail.com

Abstract. Saliency detection is an active research problem in computer vision and has been widely used in many applications. In this paper, we propose a new effective multi-scale cooperative ranking (MSR) model for image saliency detection. Our method begins with partitioning the input image into a set of super-pixels and constructing a neighborhood graph with super-pixels as nodes, both of which are performed at multiple scales of the input image, respectively. Then, we perform our MSR for super-pixels of different scales simultaneously and consistently with foreground cues or background cues as queries. MSR has a closed-form solution and thus can be computed efficiently. Experimental results on several benchmark databases show the effectiveness of the proposed MSR method.

1 Introduction

Visual saliency detection is an important problem in computer vision area. In past two decades, many bottom-up methods have been proposed for saliency detection problem, [4,9,12,13,17,20,27,31].

As a kind of popular bottom-up methods, graph based learning approaches have been widely studied for saliency detection [10,29]. For example, Gopalakrishnan et al. [8] exploit a random walk model for salient object location in an image. Jiang et al. [14] propose to use absorbing Markov chain for saliency detection problem in which the saliency value is measured by the absorbing time of transilient nodes in Markov chain. Yang et al. [33] use graph manifold ranking method to compute an optimal ranking function for image super-pixels and then measure the saliency of region using the corresponding ranking value. Zhu et al. [35] provide a general energy optimization framework to obtain a uniform saliency map by combining background and foreground cues together. Li et al. [16] propose to use a regularized random walks ranking model to achieve object saliency estimation. Wang et al. [28] present a saliency detection approach by exploiting both local graph structure and background priors.

Our aim in this paper is to propose a new effective multi-scale cooperative ranking (MSR) model for image saliency detection problem. Our method begins

J.-H. Lai et al. (Eds.): PRCV 2018, LNCS 11256, pp. 574–585, 2018.
https://doi.org/10.1007/978-3-030-03398-9_49

with generating multi-scale images for an input image and partitioning each scale image into a set of super-pixels, followed by constructing a graph in each scale with super-pixels as nodes. Then, we perform MSR for super-pixels across different scales with foreground cues or background cues as queries. At last, we obtain the saliency measurement of super-pixels based on MSR ranking results. One main aspect of MSR is that the ranking results at different scales are solved simultaneously and consistently, with an inter-scale consistent constraint ensuring communication and consistency between them. Also, MSR has a closed-form solution and thus can be computed efficiently. Comparing experimental results on four benchmark databases demonstrate the effectiveness and benefit of the proposed MSR method.

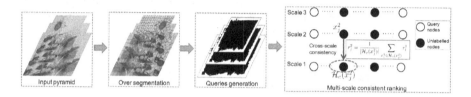

Fig. 1. An overview of our multi-scale ranking framework

2   Brief Review of Manifold Ranking

Graph based manifold ranking (GMR) has been widely used in image saliency detection task [16,28,33]. Given an input image $\mathcal{I}$, it is first segmented into n non-overlapping super-pixels via the simple linear iterative clustering (SLIC) approach [1]. Then, some super-pixels (e.g., super-pixels on the image boundary) are selected as labelled queries and the rest super-pixels are needing to be ranked according to their relevances to the queries. Formally, let $X = \{x_1, \cdots x_q, x_{q+1}, \cdots x_n\}$ be the set of super-pixels, where $X_q = \{x_1, \cdots x_q\}$ are labelled queries and the rest $X_u = \{x_{q+1}, \cdots x_n\}$ are unlabelled super-pixels. The aim of GMR is to assign a ranking value r_i for each unlabelled region $x_i \in X_u$ according to its relevance to the labelled queries X_q. In order to do so, a graph $G = (V, E)$ is first constructed, where nodes V represent the super-pixels X and edges E denote the affinities $\mathbf{W}$ between pairs of super-pixels. Let $\mathbf{y} = (\mathbf{y}_1, \mathbf{y}_2, \cdots \mathbf{y}_n)$ be the indication vector of queries, where $\mathbf{y}_i = 1$ if $x_i \in X_q$, and $\mathbf{y}_i = 0$ otherwise. Then, GMR computes the optimal ranking $\mathbf{r}$ by solving [33,34],

$$\min_{\mathbf{r}} \frac{1}{2} \sum_{i,j=1}^{n} \mathbf{W}_{ij} \left(\frac{\mathbf{r}_i}{\sqrt{\mathbf{d}_i}} - \frac{\mathbf{r}_j}{\sqrt{\mathbf{d}_j}} \right)^2 + \lambda \sum_{i=1}^{n} (\mathbf{r}_i - \mathbf{y}_i)^2 \qquad (1)$$

where $\mathbf{d}_i = \sum_{j=1}^{n} \mathbf{W}_{ij}$. It is known that the above GMR model has a closed-from solution and the optimal solution $\mathbf{r}^*$ is given by [34],

$$\mathbf{r}^* = \left(\mathbf{I} - \frac{\mathbf{S}}{\lambda + 1} \right)^{-1} \mathbf{y} \qquad (2)$$

where $\mathbf{I}$ is an identity matrix and $\mathbf{S} = \mathbf{D}^{-\frac{1}{2}}\mathbf{W}\mathbf{D}^{-\frac{1}{2}}, \mathbf{D} = \mathrm{diag}(\mathbf{d}_1, \mathbf{d}_2, \cdots \mathbf{d}_n)$.

3   Multi-scale Cooperative Ranking

Given an input image $\mathcal{I}$, we first build an image pyramid to generate multi-scale representations $\mathcal{I}^s, s = 1 \cdots K$, and segment each scaled image $\mathcal{I}^s$ into a set of non-overlapping super-pixels. Let $X^s = \{x_1^s \cdots x_q^s, x_{q+1}^s \cdots x_{N_s}^s\}$ be the set of super-pixels for $\mathcal{I}^s$, where $X_q^s = \{x_1^s \cdots x_q^s\}$ are queries and the rest $X_u^s = \{x_{q+1}^s \cdots x_{N_s}^s\}$ are unlabelled super-pixels needing to be ranked. Let $\mathbf{y}^s = (\mathbf{y}_1^s, \mathbf{y}_2^s \cdots \mathbf{y}_{N_s}^s)$ be the corresponding indication vector, where $\mathbf{y}_i^s = 1$ if $x_i^s \in X_q^s$, and $\mathbf{y}_i^s = 0$ otherwise. Also, we construct a graph $G^s = (V^s, E^s)$ where nodes V^s represent the super-pixels X^s and edges E^s encode the affinities/similarities $\mathbf{W}^s$ between pairs of super-pixels. Then, one can use GMR (Eq. (1)) to determine the ranking value $\mathbf{r}_i^s$ for each super-pixel x_i^s as

$$\min_{\mathbf{r}^s} \frac{1}{2} \sum_{i,j=1}^{N_s} \mathbf{W}_{ij}^s \left(\frac{\mathbf{r}_i^s}{\sqrt{\mathbf{d}_i^s}} - \frac{\mathbf{r}_j^s}{\sqrt{\mathbf{d}_j^s}} \right)^2 + \lambda \sum_{i=1}^{N_s} (\mathbf{r}_i^s - \mathbf{y}_i^s)^2 \tag{3}$$

where $\mathbf{d}_i^s = \sum_{j=1}^{N_s} \mathbf{W}_{ij}^s$.

3.1   Cross-Scale Consistency

The above optimization (Eq. (3)) computes the optimal ranking for each scale $\mathcal{I}^s$ separately. For multi-scale ranking, it is desired to propagate knowledge from one scale to another scale, i.e., we need to seek one consistent ranking across all scales. This multi-scale consistency point has been used and justified in previous multi-scale image methods [5,18]. Motivated by previous works, we achieve this consistency by projecting the super-pixels at the fine-scale to the coarse-level and introducing a cross-scale consistency constraint as follows.

Formally, let $f_{s,s+1}$ be the projection from fine-scale s to the coarse-scale $s + 1$. First, we define the **parent** of x_i^s at the coarse-scale $s + 1$ as follows. For any super-pixel x_j^{s+1}, if the overlap between it and the projected region $f_{s,s+1}(x_i^s)$ is more than half the area of x_j^{s+1}, then x_j^{s+1} is defined as the parent of x_i^s and x_i^s is the children of x_j^{s+1}. Then, we propose a cross-scale consistent ranking constraint as follows. For any super-pixel x_j^{s+1} at the coarse-scale $s + 1$, its ranking value $\mathbf{r}_j^{s+1}$ should be average of the ranking values of its **children** at the fine-scale s, i.e.,

$$\mathbf{r}_j^{s+1} = \frac{1}{|\mathcal{H}_c(x_j^{s+1})|} \sum_{x_i^s \in \mathcal{H}_c(x_j^{s+1})} \mathbf{r}_i^s, \tag{4}$$

where $\mathcal{H}_c(x_j^{s+1})$ denotes the children of x_j^{s+1}. Moreover, we define matrix $\mathbf{C}^{s+1,s} \in \mathbb{R}^{N_{s+1} \times N_s}$ as

$$\mathbf{C}^{s+1,s}(j,i) = \begin{cases} \dfrac{1}{|\mathcal{H}_c(x_j^{s+1})|} & \text{if } x_i^s \in \mathcal{H}_c(x_j^{s+1}) \\ 0 & \text{elsewise} \end{cases} \tag{5}$$

Then, the consistency constraint Eq. (4) between the coarse-scale $s + 1$ and the fine-scale s can be represented by

$$\mathbf{r}^{s+1} = \mathbf{C}^{s+1,s}\mathbf{r}^s, \quad s = 1 \cdots K - 1. \tag{6}$$

Furthermore, let $N = \sum_s N_s$, $\mathbf{r} = (\mathbf{r}^1 \cdots \mathbf{r}^s \cdots \mathbf{r}^K) \in \mathbb{R}^N$ be the concatenation of multi-scale ranking vectors, and matrix $\mathbf{C}$ be cross-scale constraint matrix defined as,

$$\mathbf{C} = \begin{pmatrix} \mathbf{C}^{2,1} -\mathbf{I}^2 & & \mathbf{0} \\ & \ddots & \ddots \\ \mathbf{0} & & \mathbf{C}^{K,K-1} -\mathbf{I}^K \end{pmatrix} \tag{7}$$

where $\mathbf{I}^2 \cdots \mathbf{I}^K$ denote identity matrices. Using matrix $\mathbf{C}$, we can reformulate Eq. (6) and obtain a compact form of the cross-scale consistency constraint as follows,

$$\mathbf{Cr} = \mathbf{0}, \tag{8}$$

where $\mathbf{0}$ is a zero vector with size $(\sum_{s=2}^K N_s) \times 1$.

3.2 Multi-scale Cooperative Ranking Model

By adding the cross-scale consistent constraint into ranking process, our multi-scale cooperative ranking (MSR) model is formulated as,

$$\min_{\mathbf{r}} \sum_{s=1}^K \left(\frac{1}{2} \sum_{i,j=1}^{N_s} \mathbf{W}_{ij}^s \left(\frac{r_i^s}{\sqrt{\mathbf{d}_i^s}} - \frac{r_j^s}{\sqrt{\mathbf{d}_j^s}} \right)^2 + \lambda \sum_{i=1}^{N_s} (r_i^s - y_i^s)^2 \right)$$

$$\text{s.t. } \mathbf{Cr} = \mathbf{0} \tag{9}$$

where $\mathbf{r} = (\mathbf{r}^1 \cdots \mathbf{r}^s \cdots \mathbf{r}^K) \in \mathbb{R}^N (N = \sum_s N_s)$ is the concatenation of multi-scale ranking vectors. The linear constraint $\mathbf{Cr} = \mathbf{0}$ encodes the consistency and communication across different scales, as discussed before. By imposing this constraint, the ranking results at different scales are simultaneously and consistently optimized. Figure 1 shows an overview of MSR process.

3.3 Closed-Form Solution

Let $\mathbf{y} = (\mathbf{y}^1 \cdots \mathbf{y}^s \cdots \mathbf{y}^K) \in \mathbb{R}^N$ be the concatenation of multi-scale query indication vectors and $\mathbf{W} \in \mathbb{R}^{N \times N}$ be block diagonal multi-scale affinity matrix $\mathbf{W}$

as follows

$$W = \begin{pmatrix} W^1 & & 0 \\ & \ddots & \\ 0 & & W^s \end{pmatrix}. \tag{10}$$

Then, the above objective (Eq. (9)) can be rewritten as,

$$\min_{r} \frac{1}{2} \sum_{i,j=1}^{N} W_{ij} \left(\frac{r_i}{\sqrt{d_i}} - \frac{r_j}{\sqrt{d_j}} \right)^2 + \lambda \sum_{i=1}^{N} (r_i - y_i)^2$$

$$s.t. \quad Cr = 0 \tag{11}$$

where $N = \sum_s N_s$, $d_i = \sum_j W_{ij}$. Equation (11) is equivalent to

$$\min_{r} \quad r^T (I - D^{-\frac{1}{2}} W D^{-\frac{1}{2}}) r + \lambda \|r - y\|^2$$

$$s.t. \quad Cr = 0 \tag{12}$$

where $D = \text{diag}(d_1 \cdots d_n)$. The above problem is a constrained optimization problem. In the following, we develop a subspace projection method to find the optimal solution.

It is known that, for any vector v, its projection onto the hyperplane $Cv = 0$ is Pv, where $P = I - C^T(CC^T)^{-1}C$ is a projection matrix. For projection P, one can prove that $P = P^T = PP^T$. Let $r = Pv$, then we have $Cr = CPv = 0$. Therefore, Eq. (12) can be reformulated as the following unconstrained optimization problem,

$$\min_{v} \quad v^T P^T (I - D^{-\frac{1}{2}} W D^{-\frac{1}{2}}) Pv + \lambda \|Pv - y\|^2 \tag{13}$$

The optimal solution v^* of the problem is given by

$$v^* = \left(P^T L P + \lambda P^T P \right)^{-1} P^T y$$

$$= \left(P L P + \lambda P \right)^{-1} Py \tag{14}$$

where $L = I - D^{-\frac{1}{2}} W D^{-\frac{1}{2}}$ is the normalized Laplacian matrix and $P = P^T = PP^T$. Therefore, the optimal r^* for our MSR problem Eq. (12) is given by

$$r^* = Pv^* = P \left(PLP + \lambda P \right)^{-1} Py. \tag{15}$$

4   Saliency Detection

In this section, we summarize our saliency detection algorithm based on MSR model. Our saliency detection algorithm consists of three main steps.

Step 1: Graph construction. For an input image, we first build an image pyramid to generate multi-scale images and use SLIC algorithm [1] to segment each scaled image into a set of non-overlapping super-pixels. Then, for each scale s, we construct k-regular graph $G^s = (V^s, E^s)$ whose nodes V^s represent super-pixels and edges E^s exploit the spatial relationships between super-pixels [33]. We compute the weight of edges as,

$$\mathbf{W}^s_{ij} = e^{\frac{\|\mathbf{c}_i - \mathbf{c}_j\|}{\sigma^2}}, \tag{16}$$

where $\mathbf{c}_i$ and $\mathbf{c}_j$ denote the mean of the super-pixels in the CIE LAB color space [33], and σ is a constant.

Step 2: Ranking with background queries. It is commonly observed that objects of interest in an image are rarely occur on the boundaries of the image. Thus, the image boundary regions are usually regarded as query regions in traditional ranking based saliency detection methods [28,33]. In our work, for each scale s, we use image boundary super-pixels as background queries. Also, we choose the super-pixels that are heavily connected to the image boundary as background queries. We use the boundary connectivity [35] as the measurement and select the super-pixels with high boundary connectivity as background queries. Based on these background queries, we then rank the super-pixels using MSR method and obtain the initial saliency map $\mathcal{S}_b$.

Step 3: Ranking with foreground queries. As observed in work [33], the above boundary background regions may be imprecise and thus leads to bad saliency result. In order to overcome this drawback, we further use the foreground queries obtained from the above first stage and use the proposed MSR ranking method to compute a more accurate saliency result. Similar to [33], we select the super-pixels as the foreground queries that have high ranking values $\mathcal{S}_b$ (higher than mean value) of the first stage. Based on foreground queries, we then rank the super-pixels using MSR method and obtain the final saliency map $\mathcal{S}_f$.

5 Experiments

In this section, we evaluate our MSR method on four public datasets and compare our method with seventeen state-of-the-art saliency detection algorithms including MST [27], RR [16], SO [35], MS [26], SS [11], MR [33], MC [14], HS [31], GCHC [32], BS [30], PCA [22], COV [7], FES [25], SIM [19], SWD [6], SEG [21], SeR [23], SUN [15], SR [12]. Note that, in these comparison methods, MS [26] and HS [31] also use multi-scale techniques.

5.1 Data Sets

The experiments are conducted on four public widely used datasets including ASD, SED, ECSSD and DUT-OMRON. They are summarized as follows.

- **ASD** [2][1] contains 1000 images with a binary pixel-wise object mask for each image. Images in this dataset usually have one main salient object.

---

[1] http://ivrgwww.epfl.ch/supplementarymaterial/RKCVPR09/.

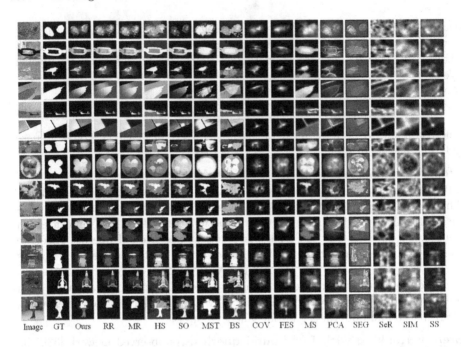

Image GT Ours RR MR HS SO MST BS COV FES MS PCA SEG SeR SIM SS

Fig. 2. Saliency detection results of different methods. Our method can generate saliency maps close to the ground truth

- **DUT-OMRON** [33][2] contains 5168 high-quality images manually selected from more than 140,000 natural images. These images have one or more salient objects with complex backgrounds. The pixel-wise object masks are provided for images.
- **SED** [3][3] consists of two parts. The first part consists of 100 images with only one salient object in each image. The second part contains another 100 images with two salient objects in each image.
- **ECSSD** [24][4] contains 1000 images, which is an extension of CSSD dataset. The binary masks for each salient object are labelled by five subjects.

5.2   Experimental Setup

Parameter Setting: Given an input image $\mathcal{I}$, we use a 3 level pyramid to generate three different scaled images $\mathcal{I}^s, s = 1, 2, 3$. For each scaled image, we set the number of super-pixels $N_s = 250$ in all the experiments. The parameter σ^2 in graph weight W^s is set to 0.1 and the balance weight λ in Eq. (9) is empirically set to 0.175 for all the experiments.

---

[2] http://ice.dlut.edu.cn/lu/dut-omron/homepage.htm.

[3] http://www.wisdom.weizmann.ac.il/~vision/SegEvaluationDB/.

[4] http://www.cse.cuhk.edu.hk/leojia/projects/hsaliency/.

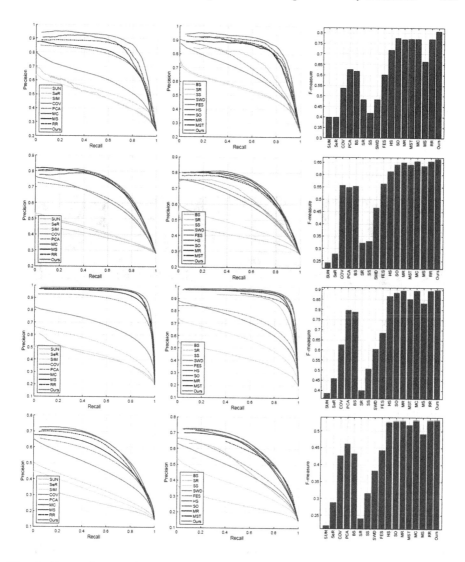

Fig. 3. Comparison results of PR curves and F-measure for different methods on different datasets

Evaluation Metrics: We evaluate the performance of our method by measuring its precision, recall and F-measure. Precision is defined as the ratio of real saliency pixels assigned to all predicting saliency pixels, and recall is computed as the ratio of the total saliency detected pixels to the ground-truth number. Similar as previous works [2,33], we obtain precision-recall curves by binarizing the saliency map using the thresholds from 0 to 255. In additional to precision-recall curves, we also evaluate our method using the overall performance measurement F-measure. F-measure is computed as follows. First, the saliency map

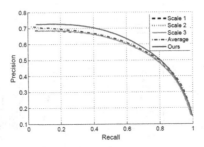

Fig. 4. Single scale ranking vs. our multi-scale ranking

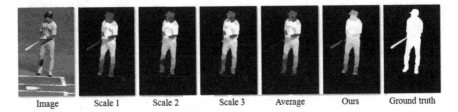

| Image | Scale 1 | Scale 2 | Scale 3 | Average | Ours | Ground truth |

Fig. 5. Saliency cue maps in different scales and our final saliency map. MSR highlights the salient object more clearly than the naive average of different scale rankings

is binarized using the adaptive threshold as suggested in many previous works [2,16,33,35]. Then, the precision and recall values are computed respectively based on the binarization results. At last, the F-measure value is defined as the harmonic mean of precision and recall values, i.e.,

$$F = \frac{(1 + \alpha)\text{Precision} \times \text{Recall}}{\alpha \text{Precision} + \text{Recall}}, \tag{17}$$

We set $\alpha = 0.3$ to give more weight to precision than recall [2,16,33].

5.3   Experimental Results

Figure 2 shows some visual comparison of the different saliency methods. Intuitively, we can note that, the proposed MSR method generally highlights the salient object and preserves the finer object boundaries more clearly than other compared methods. Figure 3 shows the precision-recall curves and F-measure of all methods on different datasets, respectively. Overall, the results demonstrate that the proposed MSR method outperforms the state-of-the-art methods on all the four public benchmark datasets. More detailly, we can note that: (1) Comparing with the traditional manifold ranking (MR) [33] method, our MSR can obtain obviously better results, which clearly demonstrates the effectiveness of the proposed MSR method by finding the global optimal consistent ranking across different scales. (2) MSR performs better than other multi-scale methods including HS [31] and MS [26], which indicates the more effectiveness of our MSR on conducting saliency object detection task. (3) Our method generally obtains better performance when compared to some recent saliency methods such as SO [35], MST [27] and RR [16].

To validate the special benefit of the cross-scale consistency in our MSR ranking process, we also conduct manifold ranking on different scales independently, as well as the average of them as the saliency values and evaluate how they work respectively on DUT-OMRON dataset. Figure 5 shows some examples of saliency maps. Figure 4 shows the comparison of precision-recall curves. We can note that, the result of our MSR method is obviously better than the result obtained by naively averaging the three different scale saliency maps.

6   Conclusions

This paper proposes a new multi-scale cooperative ranking (MSR) model for image saliency detection problem. MSR aims to conduct ranking for super-pixels at different scales of the input image simultaneously and cooperatively by imposing the cross-scale constraint to the ranking process. MSR has a closed-form optimal solution and thus can be implemented efficiently and simply. Experimental results show the effectiveness and benefits of the proposed MSR method.

Acknowledgement. This study was funded by the National Nature Science Foundation of China (61602001, 61502006); Natural Science Foundation of Anhui Province (1708085QF139); Natural Science Foundation of Anhui Higher Education Institutions of China (KJ2016A020)

References

1. Achanta, R., Shaji, A., Smith, K., Lucchi, A., Fua, P., Süsstrunk, S.: SLIC superpixels compared to state-of-the-art superpixel methods. PAMI **34**(11), 2274–2282 (2012)
2. Achanta, R., Hemami, S., Estrada, F., Susstrunk, S.: Frequency-tuned salient region detection. In: CVPR, pp. 1597–1604 (2009)
3. Alpert, S., Galun, M., Basri, R., Brandt, A.: Image segmentation by probabilistic bottom-up aggregation and cue integration. In: CVPR, pp. 1–8 (2007)
4. Cheng, M.M., Zhang, G.X., Mitra, N.J., Huang, X., Hu, S.M.: Global contrast based salient region detection. In: CVPR, pp. 409–416 (2011)
5. Cour, T., Benezit, F., Shi, J.: Spectral segmentation with multiscale graph decomposition. In: CVPR, pp. 1931–1938 (2005)
6. Duan, L., Wu, C., Miao, J., Qing, L.: Visual saliency detection by spatially weighted dissimilarity. In: CVPR, pp. 473–480 (2011)
7. Erdem, E., Erdem, A.: Visual saliency estimation by nonlinearly integrating features using region covariances. J. Vis. **13**(4), 103–104 (2013)
8. Gopalakrishnan, V., Hu, Y., Rajan, D.: Random walks on graphs for salient object detection in images. TIP **19**(12), 3232–3242 (2010)
9. Han, B., Zhu, H., Ding, Y.: Bottom-up saliency based on weighted sparse coding residual. In: International Conference on Multimedea 2011, Scottsdale, AZ, USA, 28 November–01 December, pp. 1117–1120 (2011)

10. He, Z., Jiang, B., Xiao, Y., Ding, C., Luo, B.: Saliency detection via a graph based diffusion model. In: Foggia, P., Liu, C.-L., Vento, M. (eds.) GbRPR 2017. LNCS, vol. 10310, pp. 3–12. Springer, Cham (2017). https://doi.org/10.1007/978-3-319-58961-9_1

11. Hou, X., Harel, J., Koch, C.: Image signature: highlighting sparse salient regions. PAMI **34**(1), 194–201 (2012)

12. Hou, X., Zhang, L.: Saliency detection: a spectral residual approach. In: CVPR, pp. 1–8 (2007)

13. Itti, L., Koch, C., Niebur, E., et al.: A model of saliency-based visual attention for rapid scene analysis. PAMI **20**(11), 1254–1259 (1998)

14. Jiang, B., Zhang, L., Lu, H., Yang, C., Yang, M.H.: Saliency detection via absorbing Markov chain. In: ICCV, pp. 1665–1672 (2013)

15. Kanan, C., Tong, M.H.: SUN: top-down saliency using natural statistics. Vis. Cogn. **17**(6–7), 979–1003 (2009)

16. Li, C., Yuan, Y., Cai, W., Xia, Y., Feng, D.D.: Robust saliency detection via regularized random walks ranking. In: CVPR, pp. 2710–2717 (2015)

17. Li, X., Lu, H., Zhang, L., Ruan, X., Yang, M.H.: Saliency detection via dense and sparse reconstruction. In: ICCV, pp. 2976–2983 (2013)

18. Liu, X., Lin, L., Yuille, A.L.: Robust region grouping via internal patch statistics. In: CVPR, pp. 1931–1938 (2013)

19. Murray, N., Vanrell, M., Otazu, X., Parraga, C.A.: Saliency estimation using a non-parametric low-level vision model. In: CVPR, pp. 433–440 (2011)

20. Perazzi, F., Krähenbühl, P., Pritch, Y., Hornung, A.: Saliency filters: contrast based filtering for salient region detection. In: CVPR, pp. 733–740 (2012)

21. Rahtu, E., Kannala, J., Salo, M., Heikkilä, J.: Segmenting salient objects from images and videos. In: Daniilidis, K., Maragos, P., Paragios, N. (eds.) ECCV 2010. LNCS, vol. 6315, pp. 366–379. Springer, Heidelberg (2010). https://doi.org/10.1007/978-3-642-15555-0_27

22. Ran, M., Tal, A., Zelnikmanor, L.: What makes a patch distinct? In: CVPR, pp. 1139–1146 (2013)

23. Seo, H.J., Milanfar, P.: Static and simspace-time visual saliency detection by self-resemblance. J. Vis. **9**(12), 1–27 (2009)

24. Shi, J., Yan, Q., Li, X., Jia, J.: Hierarchical image saliency detection on extended CSSD. PAMI **38**(4), 1 (2015)

25. Rezazadegan Tavakoli, H., Rahtu, E., Heikkilä, J.: Fast and efficient saliency detection using sparse sampling and kernel density estimation. In: Heyden, A., Kahl, F. (eds.) SCIA 2011. LNCS, vol. 6688, pp. 666–675. Springer, Heidelberg (2011). https://doi.org/10.1007/978-3-642-21227-7_62

26. Tong, N., Lu, H., Zhang, L., Ruan, X.: Saliency detection with multi-scale super-pixels. IEEE Signal Process. Lett. **21**(9), 1035–1039 (2014)

27. Tu, W.C., He, S., Yang, Q., Chien, S.Y.: Real-time salient object detection with a minimum spanning tree. In: CVPR, pp. 2334–2342, June 2016

28. Wang, Q., Zheng, W., Piramuthu, R.: GraB: visual saliency via novel graph model and background priors. In: CVPR, pp. 535–543, June 2016

29. Xiao, Y., Wang, L., Jiang, B., Tu, Z., Tang, J.: A global and local consistent ranking model for image saliency computation. J. Vis. Commun. Image Represent. **46**, 199–207 (2017)

30. Xie, Y., Lu, H., Yang, M.H.: Bayesian saliency via low and mid level cues. TIP **22**(5), 1689–1698 (2013)

31. Yan, Q., Xu, L., Shi, J., Jia, J.: Hierarchical saliency detection. In: CVPR, pp. 1155–1162 (2013)

32. Yang, C., Zhang, L., Lu, H.: Graph-regularized saliency detection with convex-hull-based center prior. IEEE Signal Process. Lett. **20**(7), 637–640 (2013)
33. Yang, C., Zhang, L., Lu, H., Ruan, X., Yang, M.H.: Saliency detection via graph-based manifold ranking. In: CVPR, pp. 3166–3173 (2013)
34. Zhou, D., Bousquet, O., Lal, T., Weston, J., Scholkopf, B.: Learning with local and global consistency. In: NIPS (2003)
35. Zhu, W., Liang, S., Wei, Y., Sun, J.: Saliency optimization from robust background detection. In: CVPR, pp. 2814–2821 (2014)

Author Index

Printed in the United States
By Bookmasters